SEVENTEENTH – CENTURY
English Poetry
THE ANNOTATED ANTHOLOGY

SEVENTEENTH – CENTURY
— *English Poetry* —
THE ANNOTATED ANTHOLOGY

edited by
TERENCE DAWSON
and
ROBERT SCOTT DUPREE

New York London Toronto Sydney Tokyo Singapore

First published 1994 by
Harvester Wheatsheaf
Campus 400, Maylands Avenue
Hemel Hempstead
Hertfordshire, HP2 7EZ

A division of
Simon & Schuster International Group

Typeset in 10/12pt Palacio
by Mathematical Composition Setters, Salisbury

Printed and bound in Great Britain by
Biddles Ltd, Guildford and King's Lynn

British Library Cataloguing in Publication Data

A catalogue record for this book is available from the British Library

ISBN 0-7450-1504-2 (pbk)

---

1 2 3 4 5 98 97 96 95 94

CONTENTS

◇

JOURNAL TITLES AND ABBREVIATIONS

◇

The following journal titles have been abbreviated:

ANQ	*ANQ: A Quarterly Journal of Short Articles, Notes, and Reviews*
BUSE	*Boston University Studies in English*
CE	*College English*
C&L	*Christianity and Literature*
CL	*Comparative Literature*
CP	*Concerning Poetry*
EIC	*Essays in Criticism*
ELH	*ELH: English Literary History*
ELR	*English Literary Renaissance*
ES	*English Studies*
JEGP	*Journal of English and Germanic Philology*
JWCI	*Journal of the Warburg and Courtauld Institutes*
L&P	*Literature and Psychology*
MLN	*Modern Language Notes*
MLR	*The Modern Language Review*
MQR	*Michigan Quarterly Review*
MP	*Modern Philology: A Journal Devoted to Research in Medieval and Modern Literature*
PMLA	*PMLA: Publications of the Modern Language Association*
PQ	*Philological Quarterly*
RES	*Review of English Studies: A Quarterly Journal of English Literature and the English Language*
RMS	*Renaissance and Modern Studies*
RN	*Renaissance News*
SAQ	*South Atlantic Quarterly*
SCN	*Seventeenth Century News*

SEL	*SEL: Studies in English Literature, 1500–1900*
SP	*Studies in Philology*
TSLL	*Texas Studies in Literature and Language*
WS	*Women's Studies*

PREFACE

◇

This fully annotated anthology is designed to provide, in a single volume, a sound introduction to the great English lyric tradition of the seventeenth century. It begins with John Donne, whose early works date from the 1590s, and ends with Thomas Traherne, whose works belong to about 1670.

The selection of poems is designed to be as consensual as it is possible to be. Some readers may well look for a favourite text in vain: this is – sadly – inevitable in a work of this kind. The editors' purpose has not been to reformulate the canon, but to offer substantial help with reading those poems which have most consistently excited admiration and commentary, including many by women poets.

This is *not* a critical edition in any usually accepted sense. Its aim is altogether more modest – to provide brief explanations for all words or phrases which might not be *immediately* understood by the general reader today, whether because the word or phrase is archaic, or because the word or phrase is being used in an unfamiliar way, or because it has lost its resonance, or because it makes reference to an unfamiliar social or cultural practice, or because it comments on historical events that may have been forgotten. Many of the annotations seek to draw attention to ambivalence. Very often they consist only of 'thinking an image through' so as to underline its implications.

The editors have been acutely conscious of the fine line that divides reading and interpretation. Their objective has been to provide as much help as possible, but only the better to enable readers to come to their *own* opinions about the poem as a whole. For this reason, they have steered as neutral a course as was possible in terms of current ideological debate.

The texts of the poems included in this anthology, together with most passages quoted from other seventeeth-century texts, have been modernised so that they are immediately accessible to a reader today. Readers who have enjoyed their first experience of the lyric poetry of this period are much more likely to want to read more of it, and there will be plenty of time in their lives for them to pursue the pleasures offered by an 'authentic' text.

References to the Bible have proved more problematic. Whilst the editors acknowledge that the cadences of the various sixteenth-century translations that culminated in the celebrated King James or 'Authorised Version' of 1611 are an integral part of a biblical allusion, they came to the conclusion that there was little point in citing phrases that might mean little or nothing to a reader who is not already familiar with the passage in question. Thus biblical references have also been modernised, except where doing so would confuse the point being made.

The editors would like their annotations to help deepen the reader's appreciation of the intrinsic merits of the finest poems of the time. Their aim has been not only to make the study of the seventeenth-century lyric a stimulating and rewarding experience, but also to provide an incentive to read further in the poetry of this extraordinary period. It will have been frustrated if readers think that having 'read' the notes, they understand the poem. Students are strongly encouraged to read a poem through several times not only before but also – and especially – *after* consulting the explanatory notes. The annotations are not intended to provide an interpretation of the text, let alone a comprehensive assessment of the poem's worth. They serve only to explicate the lexical difficulties a present-day reader might have, for the business of personal appreciation can begin only once all these difficulties have been resolved.

An anthology such as this rests upon the scholarship of many generations. Although we hope, of course, that some of the notes will cast new light on even the best-known poems (e.g. Herbert's 'Man', Crashaw's 'Hymn to Saint Teresa', or the witty ending to Donne's 'The Good-Morrow'), relatively few of the annotations are original. The editors are deeply conscious of their debt to all the previous scholars who have wrestled with these texts, and very much regret the impossibility of acknowledging all their borrowings. The suggested 'further readings' and other bibliographical references indicate only some of the past and recent publications that might be consulted for in-depth analyses of either a poet's work or the period. But the editors would like to record here their debt to the authors and editors of countless other publications, from innumerable reference books to note-length articles, which space alone forbade a mention of in the following pages.

Terence Dawson
Robert Scott Dupree

INTRODUCTION

◇

The seventeenth-century English lyric grew out of a period of colossal upheaval that was to transform not only the social and political fabric of England, but also the situation and function of the poet and writer. The eighty or so years with which this anthology is concerned were to see unprecedented changes in every domain of private and public life. In 1590, society was still essentially feudal. Elizabeth I ruled through her own chosen ministers, and 'degree' ensured that the hierarchical pyramid of power remained firm. By 1670, the rise of capitalism and a Puritan but none the less tolerant middle-class culture had radically transformed England. The steady increase in trade during the Elizabethan period meant that people began to enjoy a greater prosperity than they had ever known. The English began to adopt customs from other parts of the world: potatoes were introduced from the New World; spices, china and tea came from the Far East; and coffee from Yemen. But most importantly, Parliament established itself as the decisive legislative body. Feudalism had been replaced by a constitutional monarchy. At the outset of our period, the Church was an inseparable arm of the state, and employed as such. It was obligatory for everyone to attend Church of England services on Sunday, including Catholics and Presbyterians (Presbyterianism was a variant of Calvinism, a rigorous form of Protestantism established in Scotland by John Knox). By 1670 the Church had lost its political power, and minorities were tolerated and allowed to worship in their own churches. In 1590, the authority of the Church held sway over all branches of learning, and science meant only developing an established tradition.

The period covered by this anthology spans an 'English Renaissance' that saw the birth of empirical – that is, 'modern'

– science, beginning with Francis Bacon's *The Advancement of Learning* (1605), proceeding via William Harvey, who published his observations on the circulation of the blood in 1628, and culminating with the great works of the 1680s and 1690s. Isaac Newton revolutionised the understanding of physics, lifting science from its adherence to a belief in divinely established 'hierarchies' and replacing this with a view of a mechanistic universe that operated according to scientific laws that could be discovered and ascertained by study (*Philosophiae naturalis*, 1687). John Locke gave philosophical expression to such developments in a series of studies that revolutionised analytic philosophy: *Essay Concerning Human Understanding* and *Treatises of Government* (both 1690).

Strong opinions often led to extremes. Every advance was met with vehement reaction. But gradually the new cult of individual conscience in religion fostered by the Puritans promoted a new self-confidence that led people to search beyond the known horizons of the day. The spirit that prompted the development of English trade was largely Puritan. The irony of the age, however, is that the Puritans began by calling for the abolition of frills in worship, but ended the century defending the material frills they had won by what has been called 'the Protestant work ethic'. It would be difficult to overestimate the importance of the early-seventeenth-century ideological debate, for the remainder of English history was rooted in its outcome.

For a full appreciation of the poetry written between 1593 and the early 1670s, it is necessary to know something about these violent changes. During the second half of Elizabeth I's reign, Parliament became more and more insistent that it be given a greater say in government. Instead of meeting their demands, however, the queen appealed to the Members' personal loyalty and more or less coerced them into accepting her right to rule as she wanted. The problem was shelved, but not resolved.

When Elizabeth died she was succeeded by her cousin, James I of England (reigned 1603–25), who was already James VI of Scotland in his own right. He had been brought up as a Presbyterian, but he was an intellectual who believed in the 'divine right of kings', an attitude that came into ever-greater conflict both with the religious convictions of Members of Parliament, and with the prevalent mood of the country. He was still on his way to London when he was presented with the Millenary Petition (1603), so called because it was said to have been signed by a thousand Puritan clergymen. The Petition itself was a moderate document, and the king agreed to meet the Puritans at Hampton Court (1604). The ensuing conference was a failure. The bishops called for the suppression of both Catholicism and Puritanism; the Puritans responded by calling for the abolition of bishops. Whilst James was sympathetic to Puritan feeling, he shrewdly realised that he needed episcopal support, so he dismissed the conference. As one bishop later remarked: 'No bishop, no king, no nobility' – the practice of government rested on these three pillars. In the event, the only result achieved was the agreement to promote a new translation of the Bible. The King James Bible or 'Authorised Version' duly appeared in 1611; it has been recognised ever since as one of the finest examples of English prose.

But Catholic irritation over the bishops' demands led to the best-known event of the period: the Gunpowder Plot (1605). A group of Catholics, famously including Guy Fawkes, planned to blow up Parliament while the king was present. The plot was revealed; the guilty were punished. Parliament, packed by Puritans, decreed that Catholics be made to swear that the Pope had no authority to instruct them to resist the authority either of the Church of England or of the state. The king, however, was more lenient, neither punishing them for not attending Church of England services (as they were obliged to do by law) nor insisting on the oath – thereby earning the dissatisfaction of both Catholics (who felt outraged by the laws) and Puritans for his failure to take action. His inability to solve this problem lay behind the mounting constitutional crisis.

From Divine Right to Constitutional Monarchy

The way one reads seventeenth-century English poetry will very much depend on the way one reacts to the central historical event of the age. At two o'clock on the 30 January 1649, King Charles I was executed and, for a few years, England became a republic. The event was noted with shock by many observers, and has been much romanticised since. Indeed, it is only relatively recently that historians have tried to penetrate beneath the 'myth'.

The half-century that preceded the most dramatic change in modern English history was centrally concerned with two issues: one religious, the other political. In religious affairs, the authority of the Church of England had been coming under constant pressure from both extremes of the Christian spectrum: from those who remained faithful to Catholic orthodoxy and from those who advocated a more severe Protestantism – that is, the Puritans. In political affairs, the power of the monarchy was also coming under increasing threat from the rising power of the middle classes and their growing demand for a more effective voice in government. From the time of the Hampton Court Conference Parliament itself became increasingly recalcitrant, and it is significant that many of the leading voices in Parliament belonged either to Puritans or to Puritan sympathisers.

The king needed Parliament to vote him the money for his projects. The Commons refused to grant it until their grievances were addressed. The first Parliament of James I's reign lasted for six years and achieved little except to establish the pattern for the next forty years. There were to be three further short-lived Parliaments, in which the Commons fought for a say in decision-making at every turn until gradually they won the initiative. The king, offered no help from Parliament, resorted to the unpopular practice of selling peerages, titles and monopolies (tax-farming) as a means of supplementing his income, thereby increasing the tension between him and his legislative assembly.

Charles I (reigned 1625–49) was not temperamentally suited to resolving such issues. A small, proud man, he was a great patron of the arts – he laid the foundation of the present Royal Collection – and was also inquisitive about new developments in science. But, like his father, he thought he could govern the country by selecting his own ministers, referred to as 'favourites', notably George Villiers, Duke of Buckingham. He seems not to have understood the determination of Parliament.

The Commons were angered both by the concessions given to Catholics in the treaty related to the king's marriage with Henrietta Maria of France and by the privileges accorded to the Duke of Buckingham. The third Parliament in Charles's reign presented him with the Petition of Right (1628) which, in effect, demanded that henceforth the country be governed by rule of law established by Parliament. It is one of the great landmarks in English history, fully as significant as Magna Carta and arguably much more so. The King felt compelled to sign, but within a year he dissolved Parliament with little having been achieved. The scene was set for the coming conflict.

From 1629, the king endeavoured to rule without Parliament: the so-called 'Eleven Years' Tyranny'. After initial setbacks the economy stabilised, and for about five years (1632–7) the country seemed to prosper. This was the age of John Milton's early works ('On the Morning of Christ's Nativity', 1629; and 'Lycidas', 1637) and of George Herbert's *Temple* (1633). It was the age of the so-called 'Cavalier Poets' (Robert Herrick, Sir John Suckling, Richard Lovelace), and of the high Anglican William Laud as Archbishop of Canterbury (1633–45) who once again tried to move the Church of England back towards Catholicism. While Charles I posed for portraits, the country grew more and more embittered at his disdain of popular opinion, so well suggested by Van Dyck.

In April 1640 the king, badly needing money, called Parliament for the first time since 1629. The House of Commons demanded that its various grievances be addressed before discussing finance. The king refused and dissolved it: hence the name by which it is known, 'The Short Parliament'. Thereupon the Scots invaded the North of England and demanded £850 a day until peace was signed. The king was forced to recall Parliament. It met again in November 1640 and, because the same Parliament lasted on and off until 1649, it has become known as 'The Long Parliament'.

They were angry fights. Parliament impeached another of the king's favourite ministers, Sir Thomas Wentworth, abolished the judicial courts over which the king still held sway, and decreed that it could not be dissolved without its own consent. It refused to be browbeaten. There was renewed talk of abolishing bishops. The king tried to arrest the leading voices of protest, including John Pym and John Hampden. He failed, and the country, divided right down the middle, prepared for civil war. A great many of the nobility were Royalist, but support for Parliament came from all quarters, especially the City merchants.

The first phase of the Civil War lasted from 1642 to 1646. From 1644, the year of the Battle of Marston Moor, the tide turned in favour of Parliament: General Fairfax and Oliver Cromwell won the Battle of Naseby in 1645, and the following year Charles I surrendered to the Scots, who handed him back to the English army.

Three uneasy years followed, during which each side was prepared to allow the king's return, but in exchange for something different. Parliament was prepared to tolerate the continuation of Anglicanism in exchange for its right to rule for twenty years. One faction of the army called for electoral reform. The Scots wanted Presbyterianism to be guaranteed for three years.

While Cromwell drew up the 'Heads of Proposals' to reconcile the different views, the king engaged in secret negotiations with all factions, hoping to get them to fight one another. Fearing discovery, he fled to the Isle of Wight, but to no avail. In 1648 the Scots army again invaded the North of England and Cromwell was sent to defeat it; this he did, at Preston. The army seized control of the country. Moderate Members of Parliament were excluded from debates, and the so-called 'Rump Parliament' declared itself the legitimate legislative body. It decided to try Charles I for treason. He was found guilty, and executed in January 1649.

England was a republic, a 'Commonwealth'. In 1649 Cromwell was sent to Ireland; the following year he defeated the Scots at the Battle of Dunbar. Peace reigned, even if it was bitterly resented by both the Irish and the Scots. When the latter again invaded England in 1651, Cromwell once again quelled them brutally. After some twenty years of economic confusion and decline the nation began to flourish again, and the four years during which the republic lasted were a period of growth in trade, and of rising prosperity. In 1650 and the following year, two Navigation Acts were passed to encourage English merchants to replace the Dutch as leaders of the carrying trade (transporting goods for other countries). But not everyone thought highly of the achievement. In 1651 Thomas Hobbes, in self-imposed exile in Paris, published *Leviathan,* in which he argued that man is not a naturally social being, but a solitary individual aggressively seeking to pursue and defend his own self-interest.

Ironically, the one failure of the Commonwealth was its government. Cromwell had gradually risen to power since 1649. As Commander-in-Chief of the army, he decided to abolish the useless 'Rump'. He replaced it with an even less representative body, which has become known as 'The Barebones Parliament' (1653). Six months later, it dissolved itself. A body of Cromwell's officers drew up 'The Instrument of Government' in which government was invested in a Protector, who presided over a Council, who were further backed by a single House of Parliament. Cromwell, of course, was made Lord Protector.

The Protectorate of Oliver Cromwell (1653–8) was, on the whole, a period of peace and tolerance. The Jews were once again allowed to live in England. The carrying trade flourished, and prosperity increased. When Cromwell died, his son assumed his office. But Richard Cromwell was not a natural leader, and partly owing to his mismanagement, and partly owing to a widespread feeling of political uncertainty, the country was thrown into confusion. It was during this troubled and disillusioned period that Milton began his masterpiece, *Paradise Lost* (*c.*1658). Richard Cromwell resigned from office in 1659, and five forms of republican government were established in one year before the decision was taken to invite Charles II back to the throne.

Charles II (reigned 1660–85) had been brought up in exile at the court of Louis XIV of France, the 'sun-king'. He enjoyed life and pleasures, and reopened the theatres that had been closed by the Puritans. Many people wanted to forget the excessive severity of what has been called the Puritan Revolution.

The reign of Charles II was not an easy one. The battle between the crown and Parliament continued. An economic slide followed the disbanding of the army. Unemployment was a problem. The economy recovered slowly. Foreign affairs were often mismanaged, and there were two major tragedies: the Plague (1665) and the Great Fire of London (1666). But effective power had passed from the monarchy to Parliament. Gone were the various 'prerogatives' by which the monarch was able to raise money without consulting Parliament. Monopolies virtually disappeared; so too did the hated practice of farming out taxes. A new body of professional administrators arose, responsible for all aspects of government, including taxation. It could even be said that the period saw the first signs of a 'two-party' system. Although both Charles II and his brother James II (reigned 1685–8) tried to resist all these moves, they had little success.

The major reason for the permanence of the changes brought about by the Interregnum lay, of course, with the middle classes that had grown up during the Commonwealth. Many of the most successful merchants, financiers and tradesmen of the previous seventy years had come from Puritan backgrounds. It was because of them that England's economy survived the incompetence of government in the early seventeenth century; they continued to lay the foundations of further prosperity during the Interregnum. Cromwell's Navigation Acts were re-endorsed by the Restoration Parliament. Their object was to 'protect' English shipping, to ensure that the nation's interests did not fall into the hands of the powerful Dutch navy. So successful were they that England rapidly became the world's most powerful trading nation. The 'commercial revolution' brought about by the Puritans prepared the way for the 'Industrial Revolution' of the next century.

Moderate Puritan voices helped to ensure that extremist elements were no longer allowed a voice in Parliament. The reason, of course, was Hobbesian self-interest. By 1660, many had built up their 'empires' and were loath to lose them. The Puritans who composed the Cavalier Parliament (1661–79) were a quite different set from those who had made up the Parliaments of James I and Charles I. During the Interregnum, they had either increased their estates or become landowners. As an anonymous pamphlet of 1660 claimed:

> This island . . . is . . . governed by the influence of a sort of people that live plentifully and at ease upon their rents, extracted from the toil of their tenants and servants, each . . . of whom within the bounds of his own estate acts the prince. *(A Discourse for a King and Parliament)*

The new Members of Parliament, keen to defend their gains, quickly set about building the country houses from which effective political power was to flow for the next two hundred years.

Bishops did not recover the political power they had enjoyed before the Interregnum, and the various petitions and cries for fundamentalism were gradually replaced by the tolerant episcopalianism which continues to define the Anglican Church. There were many for whom the Restoration signified the end of the dream of establishing God's kingdom here on earth. Milton was not alone in regretting the republic, and he was imprisoned for his views. So too was John Bunyan. The two great masterpieces of Puritan verse and prose – Milton's *Paradise Lost* (1667) and Bunyan's *Pilgrim's Progress* (1678) – could not have been conceived had it not been for the Commonwealth. Ironically, they were actually written after its demise, during a period of frivolous 'Restoration comedies', for example, Sir George Etherege's *Love in a Tub* (1664) or William Wycherley's *The Country Wife* (1675). Never again was religion to be a major political issue. As the diarist Samuel Pepys noted in 1667, 'We do not think religion will so soon cause another war'.

In short, between 1590 and 1670 England changed from a minor nation on the fringe of Europe to an international trading power. Within forty years it was to emerge as one of the greatest European powers. Whilst it is obvious that the Puritans were by no means the only factor in this achievement, there can be little doubt that the part they played was the dominant one.

The Literary Currents

Literary historians have tended to refer to our period as the 'early seventeenth century'. This designation may seem odd for an era that is said to reach well into the second half of the century. The explanation for it is literary rather than chronological. There has long been an assumption by historians of literature that major literary activity was over by the mid 1640s. The usual supposition – not altogether inaccurate – was that civil disorder kept writers too preoccupied with political concerns to pursue bellettrist activities; thus the major thrust of the movement that had begun in 1580 was over by then. But this conclusion is tenable only if one envisages certain kinds of writing as central to the whole age. The Puritans forced the closing of the theatres, bringing about an end to the astonishingly rich period of English drama that had begun fifty years earlier; nevertheless, some theatrical activity – in particular the writing and staging of operas – continued. The court masque, however, was defunct. John Donne, Ben Jonson and George Herbert all died in the 1630s. Of the principal 'Cavalier' poets, Thomas Carew and Sir John Suckling were both dead by 1642, and Robert Herrick must have written much of his poetry by then, since he had planned to publish a volume in 1640 (*Hesperides* appeared eight years later). Richard Lovelace, a younger poet, wrote his most famous poems in the 1640s, partly in response to the political dilemma. A host of minor poets who wrote in the same or similar modes ceased their activities or died in the same decade. Richard Crashaw, likewise, was a victim of the times, at least as far as his residence in England was concerned. Nevertheless, Henry Vaughan, who wrote in the Cavalier vein until about 1647, switched to poems on religious themes shortly afterwards; is it mere coincidence that so many of them are concerned with retirement, retreat, and return to innocence? Of the remaining poets represented in this volume, it may be said that they survived the years of the Civil War and Commonwealth by changing sides (Edmund Waller and Andrew Marvell), by residing in isolation from the centres of power (Henry Vaughan and Katherine Philips), or simply by being born too late to be seriously affected (Thomas Traherne).

As a consequence of these historical circumstances, much criticism and scholarship on seventeenth-century poetry has inevitably focused on the first four decades of the century as the formative years during which the predominant themes, styles and poetic forms of the period were defined. Twentieth-century scholars have seen Donne and Jonson as the bellwethers of two new movements, 'Metaphysical' and 'Cavalier', which divided lyric poetry into separate kingdoms, each with its own monarch and succession. For some time, however, critics have disputed this interpretation of the history and development of seventeenth-century lyric. Nevertheless, there is some validity in the distinction, and one cannot hope to understand the revisionists without a knowledge of what they claim to be revising. Perhaps a shift of perspective can clarify the relationship between these two tendencies.

By the late 1590s, when Donne and Jonson had begun to write, Elizabethan society was well defined. It centred on the court, that small, select community of persons which constituted the social milieu of the monarch. However artificial this environment might have been, it provided a coherent audience for poets and, consequently, an elaborate code whose vocabulary, structures, genres and subjects were meaningful to a small, elite group. The sonnet is the most typical of these codified lyric forms; it usually speaks of love, utilises highly formulaic vocabulary, imagery and metaphors, and possesses a flexible structure capable of a surprising range of variation within a mere fourteen lines. Likewise, the notion of beauty, masculine or feminine, was highly conventionalised; the changes rung on the courtly code were subtle and sophisticated, perceptible only to someone who was well informed of their social meaning.

Against the background of this seeming stability, which masked the power struggles and uncertainties of the political and social realms, John Donne appeared as a brash challenger with his witty language, clever use of traditional themes, and wary scepticism towards the established courtly ideals. In his 1921 essay 'The Metaphysical Poets', T.S. Eliot chose to see in Donne's poetry the mark of a 'unified sensibility'; the impression one has in reading it, however, is that of a man confronting the rapid erosion of familiar values and beliefs by subjecting them to a continual irony that never completely masks his anxiety. This situation sounds so much like what we know now to have been that of Eliot himself that it is small wonder Donne was so attractive to him and other modern readers.

Looking at Donne from a formal or generic perspective, one senses that he was concerned less with creating new forms than with doing unusual things with those that already existed. If he wrote sonnets, they were about love of God rather than love of woman; he never attempted that conspicuous display of Elizabethan lyric architecture typified by the sonnet cycle. The songs and 'sonets' he did write display an impressive metrical and stanzaic variety, a formal sophistication, and a command of every other popular style, but mainly they show their poet's determination to turn the conventions on their heads. Though verse satire and the epigram in English were hardly his invention, Donne did achieve a measure of originality in his satires that was not fully appreciated until Alexander Pope revived them in the eighteenth century. He was as much a poet inspired by classical Antiquity as many another Elizabethan writer; he wrote his own variety of 'elegies', inspired by the love lyrics of such Roman poets as Catullus, Ovid and Propertius, and he practised the popular epistolary form as assiduously as any of his contemporaries. He could even write an eclogue or an epithalamion if the occasion called for it. Nevertheless, his two 'anniversaries' for Elizabeth Drury, while not lacking in poetic precedents, are certainly formally unique.

Ben Jonson was an exact contemporary and friend of John Donne, but the two poets are often presented as rivals and founders of opposing poetic movements, usually described under the rubrics of a 'school of Donne' and a 'tribe of Ben'. Yet though they were profoundly different in temperament and personality, both men had a great deal in common, beginning with the large number of intellectual and artistic acquaintances they shared and the fact that both, though members of the Church of England, had also been Roman Catholics at one time. Indeed, even their poetic styles sometimes overlap. Both poets marked a departure from certain practices of sixteenth-century poetry, and opened the way to new techniques. Despite the fact that he may appear less original than Donne to modern readers, Jonson was as least as much of a formal innovator as his friend, if not more. He began the tradition of the country-house poem, wrote the first important Pindaric ode in English, and created a style and manner that were to have a long future ahead of them. Like Donne, he broke with the mode prevalent in the Elizabethan court and created one to take its place. With the shift from the Elizabethan to the Jacobean court, Jonson found himself poised to redefine the role of the poet.

As A. Alvarez (1961), Earl Miner (1969), and Joseph Summers (1971) have been at pains to point out, Donne wrote for a private, limited audience of educated readers who could savour his ironies and emotional detachment; he writes as a poet who is confident of his tone, not afraid that it will be misinterpreted or misunderstood. Jonson had a different audience. Having worked his way up through society from obscure middle-class origins, he was concerned above all to make himself heard by a larger public – a public which, in fact, his poems strive to create. He provided a model that remained influential for two centuries.

Jonson subscribed to the classical notion of the poet as responsible for giving glory to contemporary men of worth – much as Homer, for instance, celebrated the heroes of the Grecian past. Most eulogy during this period had little of the ring of sincerity; Jonson wished to make poetic praise more convincing and more interesting than it usually was. His was a conscious effort to imitate the Greeks and Romans and make them seem closer to the experience of the contemporary Englishman; at the same time, he wished to gain for English poetry some of the prestige previously reserved for Greek and Latin writings. Unlike Milton, who attempted to write an English that embodied some of the stylistic effects of Latin or Greek, Jonson created a 'classical' language in English terms – mostly native in both manner and vocabulary, plain and devoid of the elaborate effects cultivated by other poets of the period. His preference for what he called 'pure and neat language . . . , yet plain and customary' and his dislike of metaphors that were far-fetched and hard to understand were emulated by the poets of the Restoration and the eighteenth century. Jonson became known to contemporaries and to subsequent generations as a special kind of classicist, a man who imitated the ancient writers not as though they belonged to an irretrievable past but as exemplars whose descriptions of human nature and character still had validity.

Though both poets had their direct imitators, it is true that for the most part their influence was not manifest in exclusive fashion, distributed discretely to two sets of distinct disciples. Carew and Lovelace were certainly indebted to Donne for part of their tone and metaphorical language, if less so metrically. Herbert often seems as close to Jonson in style as to Donne; in 'Jordan (1)', for instance, he follows Jonson in rejecting complicated or unnecessary ornament. Vaughan, also, could be considered a follower of both; he wrote secular verse that consorts easily with the style of the Cavalier poets and religious poetry which – while it is quite unlike that of Herbert, whom he admired – clearly owes its ultimate inspiration to Donne's example. Herbert was deliberately evoked by Crashaw in *Steps to the Temple* (though, once again, Crashaw's style is quite distinct); and Marvell could manage either mode, Donnean or Jonsonian, with exquisite grace. No one doubts that both Donne and Jonson were powerful influences on most of the poets who came after – at least until mid-century, when Donne's impact began to wane – but their impact was certainly not felt as two separate forces, one of which excluded the other.

Though Donne and Jonson do seem to bestride the early-seventeenth-century literary world like two colossi, they did not and could not altogether overcome the continuing influence of the Elizabethan conventions they challenged, ignored or modified. The presence of Edmund Spenser, the most experimental of the sixteenth-century poets, was evident well into the seventeenth. One reason why it is not more readily recognisable is the simple fact that the Spenserian manner was confined to poets – like Giles and Phineas Fletcher – who are now considered to be of lower stature than those most frequently anthologised. Yet it might be said that Milton, who in many ways seems unique, was that Elizabethan poet's very greatest disciple. Certainly, considering the important role Puritanism played during the period, Spenser was a key model for anyone who felt uncomfortable with the High Church devotional writings of Donne and Herbert or the unfriendly wit directed against the Puritans by Jonson and his 'tribe'. Furthermore, one should not overlook the continuing influence of Shakespeare, who had avid readers in as diverse a pair of admirers as King Charles I and John Milton. Finally, though the vogue of the sonnet sequence did not last long into the century, the poetry of Sir Philip Sidney also continued to have an impact – somewhat attenuated, to be sure – upon these writers.

Milton is usually ranked alongside Chaucer and Shakespeare as one of the three greatest poets in the English language. Indeed, as an influence on later poets he is second only to Shakespeare. Furthermore, Milton seems to have been aware of his literary destiny at an early stage in his career. In his early poetry he shows himself to be conscious not only of his vocation as a poet but of his extraordinary gifts; and though he questions his actual achievements from time to time, he never appears to doubt his native abilities. He was a man of great learning; his contributions to English literature embody the full range of his scholarship, yet they were addressed to a wide audience. 'Our wives read Milton . . .' wrote Alexander Pope, indicating the penetration of his works into the very centre of the household, where they shared some of the spiritual prestige accorded normally only to the Bible. Milton enjoys, like the Shakespeare he admired, a sort of dual relationship to his audience as a poet whose intellectual depth has not prevented him from being a popular writer century after century.

The Milton represented here – the lyric rather than the dramatic or epic poet – would have been an important figure even if he had not survived into the Restoration. Nevertheless, one must not overlook the larger context that gives weight to his achievement. Milton's accomplishment is best understood as the climax of a centuries-long effort to reconcile the two major strains of European culture: Judaeo-Christian and Graeco-Roman. In the early days of Christianity, when the new religion was still seeking a foothold in a world hostile to its vision, the conflict between these two strains was very real. In order to survive in the highly urbanised environment of the Roman Empire, a person needed to be well educated, or at least literate – but literacy had to be attained through the study of books whose moral values seemed diametrically opposed to the teachings of Christianity. The conflict between pagan learning and Christian beliefs troubled many early Christian intellectuals, such as St Jerome or St Augustine. This tension between the two was still being felt as late as the fourteenth century when Petrarch, the great Italian poet, intellectual and man of letters, had qualms about his irresistible attraction to the literature of the pagan past. Yet throughout the Middle Ages, pagan Roman authors such as Virgil, Horace and Ovid had continued to be read and appreciated. By the time of the High Renaissance in the sixteenth century, few were troubled by the apparent contradiction between the two traditions of learning. It remained for a great poet like Milton to demonstrate not only that they could be reconciled but that the tension between them was fruitful and had, indeed, been responsible for the peculiar character of European culture and civilisation. In his masterpiece,

Paradise Lost, Milton achieved this goal by creating the last great classical epic poem in European literature. He transcended national boundaries and redefined the scope of English letters by devising a new elevated style for poetry – one which could recall simultaneously the grandeur of Virgilian heroic language, the magnificent phrasing of the King James Bible, and the dramatic power of Shakespearean blank verse. At the same time he managed to provide, in an authoritative, imaginative vision, the last great mythic articulation of Europe's dual heritage. Yet even in the early poetry – the Nativity Ode and 'Lycidas' are excellent examples – this synthesis is everywhere evident.

Ode, Elegy and Sonnet: Seventeenth-Century Lyric Forms and Themes

In the later years of the eighteenth century, Samuel Johnson ridiculed the revival of 'antique ruff and bonnet' among the younger poets who were attempting to return to early-seventeenth-century poetic forms. However, the ode and the elegy, at least, along with verse satire, were perceived as innovative revivals of classical types when they began to appear in Jonson's and Donne's poetry. The sense of form was strong during this period, and because the forms and themes of the classical past offered a point of stability in a world conscious of the psychological perils of melancholy (the first edition of Robert Burton's encyclopaedic *Anatomy of Melancholy* was published in 1621), the doubts induced by 'new philosophy', and the 'anxious and dangerous times' (Cicero) of contemporary politics and religion, the models of order that Greece and Rome stood for possessed great prestige. Jonson wished to offer moral images of the times, so he lauded those whom he considered worthy exemplars of proper moral behaviour and made fun of would-be courtiers and greedy Puritans whom he saw as unethical because they were incapable of unselfish action.

For the Cavaliers, support of the king was a pledge of loyalty to an institution greater than any individual; when that institution was lost, they turned inward for consolation and order. Jonson's praise of the country estate, though it was written in a more tranquil period than the civil disturbances that followed not long after his death, already suggests a withdrawal from the court and its hypocrisy. His epistle inviting a new member to join the 'tribe of Ben' is taken up, to a great extent, with his disappointment over his treatment by the court; it suggests consolation in the same kind of society and fellowship that Lovelace describes two decades later in 'The Grasshopper'. Throughout the poetry of Jonson and those who came after him is this image, usually nostalgic, of the Good Society or the Good Life. One need not look to the biographies of the poets themselves for evidence that they did not enjoy this for long. Their notion of order was an ideal created in a time of perceived tension; in their lives they lived out that tension in ways that are not always evident in their poetry. The Pindaric ode, which evoked images of greatness from the classical past, and the Hellenic elegy, which offered a ritualised language for containing grief, were forms that reflected an ideal, not an actual, way of life.

Poems of praise eulogising those worthy of emulation and poems of regret – whether for a dead infant or for a dying way of life – present one side of this new attempt to define society, beginning with Jonson. Lady Mary Wroth's sonnets also reveal a parallel sense of withdrawal and retreat from the intrigues and even from the characteristic activities, both pleasant and unpleasant, of the court. But the uncertainties that were evident at every turn gave birth to a different attitude towards language as well. These are embodied in the celebrated 'metaphysical conceit', defined by Samuel Johnson in his life of Abraham Cowley as a 'combination of dissimilar images or discovery of occult resemblances in things apparently unlike', in which the 'most heterogeneous ideas are yoked by violence together, nature and art are ransacked for illustrations, comparisons, and allusions'. Johnson's language is unfriendly, but it reveals something of importance about the kind of metaphor Donne and his followers found attractive. The world they saw was not open and self-evident; it required interpretation and translation. Resemblances had to be sought and discovered; they were no longer as direct and unproblematic as the charming Elizabethan pastoral lyrics of *England's Helicon* and other sixteenth-century anthologies of high celebratory verse. As the 'sons' of Ben learned increasingly to retreat into a realm kept warm by fellowship, so the Metaphysical poets turned to meditation and study of the world and the self. But then this tendency was everywhere: the Puritans looked to the 'inner light' for inspiration in reading the Bible; emblem-books, containing allegorical figures consisting of motto, image and descriptive verses, invited their readers to interpret, not simply to read, a text.

As Louis Martz pointed out in 1957, the influence of the continental meditative tradition, shared (surprisingly enough) by Catholic and Protestant, High Churchman and Puritan alike, invited the contemplation and decipherment of such pictures. Herbert's and Herrick's 'shaped' poems are also a part of this movement, which is still in evidence at mid-century on the cover page of Vaughan's *Silex Scintillans*. The Puritan preacher interpreted scriptural passages in minute detail according to this same method – pushed, it is true, to extremes on occasion – and thus demonstrated that the 'hieroglyphic' nature of the word was not the exclusive notion of any one party or sect. One of the most interesting aspects of the entire seventeenth century is its proclivity to insist on the necessity of *interpreting,* not simply passively experiencing, the world.

Even the exiled Royalists participated in this focus on images, though they tended to see in the 'royal ikon' the centre of their loyalties and attention. Lovelace apologises only faintly to the ladies he addresses when he assures them that love itself depends on loyalty to a cause greater than either of them. The seventeenth century was an era of great love poetry, but it was equally one of the poetry of fellowship and social solidarity. Constantly aware of the fragility of those ties that bind one human being to another, the poets turned inward to find strength, that 'paradise within happier far' which Milton's Adam and Eve were promised as solace after their exile. Love of man and woman could, for Donne, make a 'little room an everywhere', and 'Orinda', anxious to gather a group of worthy friends about her, could bestow fanciful names on them; but in the end the poets of the period recognised – as would William Butler Yeats almost two centuries later – that words and images, too, can break hearts. The men and women who wrote the poems assembled in this anthology were respectful yet distrustful of language and imagery. We still have much to learn from them.

Further Reading

Students seeking to pursue seventeenth-century lyric poetry beyond the limits of this anthology will find many additional texts and poets in *The New Oxford Book of Seventeenth-Century Verse,* ed. Alastair Fowler (Oxford, 1991), which includes selections from many of the minor poets of the period. One of the most revealing anthologies, however, is Norman Ault's *Seventeenth-Century Lyrics from the Original Texts* (London, 1928; revised 1950), which not only prints previously unpublished pieces but presents all the poems in chronological order, so that it is possible to see at a glance what styles and forms were current in a given year. Two volumes in the Norton Critical Editions series, *Ben Jonson and the Cavalier Poets,* ed. Hugh Maclean (New York, 1974) and *George Herbert and the Seventeenth-Century Religious Poets,* ed. Mario A. Di Cesare (New York, 1978), include a generous selection of texts, lightly annotated, and critical essays on various poets. Two collections in the Everyman's Library are also convenient sources for a number of minor poets: R.G. Howarth, ed., *Minor Poets of the Seventeenth Century* (London, 1931; frequently reprinted) and George Parfitt, *Silver Poets of the Seventeenth Century* (London, 1974). Thomas Clayton has grouped Herrick, Lovelace, Suckling and Carew in a volume of *Cavalier Poets: Selected poems* (Oxford, 1978) which contains notes on many of the poems. The older three-volume set edited by George Saintsbury, *Minor Poets of the Caroline Period* (Oxford, 1905–21) is the only convenient source for a number of lesser-known writers.

Still perhaps the best historical introduction to the period as a whole is Christopher Hill, *A Century of Revolution: 1603–1714* (Edinburgh, 1961); see also his *Change and Continuity in Seventeenth-Century England* (London, 1974). Indispensable for its essays, bibliographies and other helpful features is C.A. Patrides and Raymond B. Waddington, eds, *The Age of Milton: Backgrounds to seventeenth-century literature* (Manchester and Totowa, NJ, 1980). Its comprehensive surveys and lists should be consulted for guidance in studying historical and other background.

Out of date in many respects but still a standard source for much information, especially in its bibliographies, is Douglas

Bush, *English Literature in the Earlier Seventeenth Century* (Oxford, 1945; revised 1962). Recent histories of poetry in the period include George A. Parfitt, *English Poetry of the Seventeenth Century* (London and New York, 1985); Graham Parry, *Seventeenth-Century Poetry: The social context* (London, 1985) and Lauro Martines, *Society and History in English Renaissance Verse* (Oxford and New York, 1985). The last two offer a sociohistorical approach.

The period of the Civil War and the Commonwealth, doubtless in compensation for earlier neglect by literary scholars, has begun to receive a great deal of attention in the last few years. The university presses of Oxford and Cambridge, for instance, have published numerous titles directly concerned with it. Examples of this new focus are Michael Wilding, *Dragon's Teeth: Literature in the English Revolution* (Oxford, 1987); Lois Potter, *Secret Rites and Secret Writing: Royalist literature, 1641–1660* (Cambridge, 1989); Nigel Smith, *Perfection Proclaimed: Language and literature in English radical religion, 1640–1660* (Oxford, 1989); Thomas Healey and Jonathan Sawday, eds, *Literature and the English Civil War* (Cambridge, 1990); Thomas N. Corns, *Uncloistered Virtue: English political literature, 1640–1660* (Oxford, 1992).

On the influence of Donne and Jonson, see Joseph Summers, *The Heirs of Donne and Jonson* (New York and London, 1970); Earl Miner, *The Metaphysical Mode from Donne to Cowley* (Princeton, NJ, 1969) and *The Cavalier Mode from Jonson to Cotton* (Princeton, NJ, 1971). A. Alvarez, *The School of Donne* (London, 1961) is still important. George A. Parfitt, 'Donne, Herbert, and the matter of schools', *EIC*, **22** (1972), 381–95 offers another perspective. A recent look at the Cavaliers is Lawrence Venuti, 'Cavalier love poetry and Caroline court culture', in *Our Halcyon Days: English prerevolutionary texts and postmodern culture* (Madison, WI, 1989), pp. 212–60. For the influence of Spenser, see Joan Grundy, *The Spenserian Poets* (London, 1969). For a collection of older essays, some of them fundamental, consult W.R. Keast, ed., *Seventeenth-Century English Poetry: Modern essays in criticism*, rev. edn (Oxford, 1971). Contemporary continental poetry, particularly of the 'Baroque' variety, is covered in two useful anthologies: Frank J. Warnke, ed., *European Metaphysical Poetry* (New York, 1961) [and his critical study

Versions of Baroque: European literature in the seventeenth century (New Haven, CT, 1972)]; J.P. Hill and E. Caracciola-Trejo, eds, *Baroque Poetry* (London, 1975).

The character of the religious poetry is analysed in Louis Martz's well-known and influential account *The Poetry of Meditation* (New Haven, CT, 1954; rev. edn 1962) and *The Paradise Within* (New Haven, CT, 1964); and in Anthony Low, *Love's Architecture: Devotional modes in seventeenth-century English poetry* (New York, 1978); Barbara K. Lewalski, *Protestant Poetics and the Seventeenth-Century Lyric* (Princeton, NJ, 1979); Claude J. Summers and Ted-Larry Pebworth, *'Bright Shootes of Everlastingness': The seventeenth-century religious lyric* (Columbia, MO, 1987) is a recent collection of essays by various critics.

Bridge Gellert Lyons, *Voices of Melancholy: Studies in literary treatments of melancholy in Renaissance England* (New York, 1971) provides useful background for the psychology of the period and, especially, for Milton's 'Il Penseroso'. Rosalie Osmond, *Mutual Accusation: Seventeenth-century body and soul dialogues in their literary and theological context* (Toronto, ON, 1990) gives background for Marvell's 'Dialogue' and much more. For a comprehensive account of the conventions of love poetry, see A.J. Smith, *The Metaphysics of Love: Studies in Renaissance love poetry from Dante to Milton* (Cambridge, 1985). For a more restricted account, Anne Ferry, *All in War with Time: Love poetry of Shakespeare, Donne, Jonson, Marvell* (Cambridge, MA, 1975).

For background on the country-house tradition, besides entries listed under Jonson, see G.R. Hibbard, 'The country house poem of the seventeenth century', *JWCI*, **19** (1956), 159–74; William Alexander McClung, *The Country House in English Renaissance Poetry* (Berkeley, CA, 1977); Mary Ann C. McGuire, 'The Cavalier country-house poem: mutations on a Jonsonian tradition', *SEL*, **19** (1979), 93–108; Malcolm Kelsall, *The Great Good Place: The country house and English literature* (Hemel Hempstead, 1992); Marc Girouard, *Life in the English Country House* (New Haven, CT, 1978) gives the architectural and social background. Harold Toliver, *Lyric Provinces in the English Renaissance* (Columbus, OH, 1985) is more generally concerned with the poetry of place. Michael Brennan, *Literary Patronage in the English Renaissance: The Pembroke family* (London and New York, 1988) studies one family as a case history of the patronage system.

Rosemond Tuve, *Elizabethan and Metaphysical Imagery* (Chicago, 1947) is still a valuable introduction to the subject, as is Mario Praz, *Studies in Seventeenth-Century Imagery*, 2nd rev. edn (Rome, 1964). Earl Miner has edited a collection of essays on the subject: *Seventeenth-Century Imagery* (Berkeley, CA, 1971); Gerald Hammond, *Fleeting Things: English poets and poems: 1616–1660* (Cambridge, MA and London, 1990) is a study of themes and images in numerous poets. Jonathan Goldberg, *Voice Terminal Echo: Postmodernism and English Renaissance texts* (New York and London, 1986) offers a recent perspective on Herbert's 'temple' and Marvell's 'nymph'. A.J. Smith, *Metaphysical Wit* (Cambridge, 1991) is a thorough and up-to-date account of this central topic. On shaped poems, anagrams and acrostics, see Elizabeth Cook, *Seeing Through Words: The scope of Late Renaissance poetry* (New Haven, CT and London, 1986).

JOHN DONNE

(1572–1631)

1633 *Poems* (posthumous)
'Songs and Son[n]ets' is the subtitle of the first section in the 1635 edition; 'Divine Poems' is the subtitle of the last.

◇

Few poets have had such an intriguing personality as John Donne. One cannot read his poems and not wonder about the man, and it is a great pity that we still know so little about him that is certain. He himself, in the last fifteen years of his life, helped to foster the notion that his early amatory poems were written by 'Jack Donne', a wit and a rake, while the later ones were written by 'Doctor John Donne', a sincere 'divine' or churchman. The division is a useful but flawed generalisation. Knowing even a little about the poet's unusual life should warn against any simplification.

John Donne was born in London into a prosperous family: his father, also called John, was a member of the Ironmongers' Company. His mother, Elizabeth, came from a family known as much for its interest in literature as for its strong adherence to Catholicism: her father was John Heywood, a well-known poet at the time; her mother was the daughter of John Rastell (author of at least one 'interlude' – a short play or masque performed between two courses of a banquet or two acts of a longer entertainment) and Elizabeth More (sister of Thomas More, author of *Utopia*). The poet's father died when he was four. His mother then married a physician, Dr John Syminges, who died in 1588. In 1590 she married Richard Rainsford, with whom she went to live in Antwerp five years later so that she could practise Catholicism more freely.

As Catholics, Donne and his younger brother Henry were privately schooled and were sent to study at Oxford when John was still only eleven. This may have been because they were unusually gifted; it was more probably because at sixteen they would have been obliged to subscribe to the 'Thirty-Nine Articles of Faith' contained in the Church of England's *Book of Common Prayer* (1559). By attending lectures before they reached sixteen, they could ensure their education without compromising their family's religious convictions. The brothers then spent three years at Cambridge, but could not join any college because of their religion. They may have spent some time travelling in Europe in about 1590–91. In 1592 they were at Lincoln's Inn, either to study law or to complete their education. The following year Henry Donne was arrested for harbouring a Catholic priest in his rooms. The priest was executed; Henry died of plague in Newgate prison awaiting trial.

Very few of John Donne's lyrics can be precisely dated, but most of the amorous poems that were eventually published as 'Songs and Sonets' and 'Elegies' in the posthumous *Poems* were probably composed sometime between 1590 and 1600 – that is, before his marriage. From about 1594 he was also writing satires modelled on those of Horace, Juvenal and Martial.

It is probable that Donne converted to the Church of England soon after his brother's death, as his prospects would have been severely limited if he had remained a Catholic. But when this happened, and for what precise reason, is not known. At any rate, in about 1596 he volunteered to serve in the expedition sent to fight the Spaniards in Cadiz; the following year he was part of an expedition sent to the Azores. He became a friend of the son of Sir Thomas Egerton, Lord Keeper of the Great Seal, who agreed to employ him as secretary. At the end of 1597, his future looked assured.

Lady Egerton had a niece called Ann More. In 1601, when she was about eighteen, Donne secretly married her: a friend, Samuel Brooke, performed the ceremony; Christopher Brooke was witness. When Donne broke the news to her father, Sir George More, the latter had him and the two Brookes arrested. More eventually decided not to press charges, and even asked Egerton to take Donne back into his services, but to no avail. Donne's prospects were suddenly thrown into question.

By this time James I was king; he was to reign from 1603 to 1625. At the time it was obligatory to attend the Anglican Church; Catholics and others who did not want to do so were forced to pay heavy fines. Although James lifted these penalties shortly after his accession, he reimposed them under pressure – a decision which led directly to the Gunpowder Plot, in which a small group of Catholics tried to blow up the Houses of Parliament while the king was there (November 1605). As a result, Catholics were made to swear an oath repudiating any adherence to the Pope's dictate encouraging them to rebel against their sovereign. The king himself, a learned man, wrote a defence of this policy in 1607. The Jesuits began circulating an attack on the policy in which they encouraged rebellion even if it led to martyrdom. In 1610, clearly with his sights set on royal favour, Donne wrote a treatise called *Pseudo-Martyr*, in which he argued that a Catholic need have no fear of taking the oath, as it would be a false martyrdom to seek death by refusing to do so. The king was impressed, and tried to persuade Donne to go into the Church. Donne, however, was more interested in state office.

From his dismissal by Egerton in 1601 to his eventual entry into the Church in 1615 Donne was constantly looking for work, and frequently having to move house. He and his wife had twelve children in all, seven of whom survived their mother, Ann (who died in 1617). These were difficult years, but the couple seem to have been happy. Somehow – it is not known quite how – the growing family survived, and many of Donne's greatest poems appear to date from this time. Donne had many friends, including Sir James Hay and Sir Robert Carr, both of whom were close to the king, and Lady Bedford, who also patronised Jonson. Sir Robert Drury eventually gave him a home and some kind of position: it was for his fifteen-year-old daughter Elizabeth, who died in December 1610, that Donne wrote *The First Anniversary: An Anatomy of the World*, a witty yet philosophic meditation in which he asserts that Elizabeth, a paragon of excellence, was all that held the fallen world together. He made at least two lengthy journeys during these years: one with Sir Walter Chute, in 1605–06; the other with Sir Robert Drury, in 1611–12.

In 1608 he wrote an extraordinary treatise on suicide, *Biathanatos*. Most of his verse epistles and obsequies also belong to these years. In 1613 he wrote two 'epithalamia', poems celebrating a marriage: the first for Princess Elizabeth, the other for the Earl of Somerset. It is also probable that he began writing his so-called 'divine poems' from about 1609.

In 1615 he was finally ordained into the Church of England and, at James's command, was awarded an honorary doctorate of divinity by Cambridge University. He was also made royal chaplain. He preached both at court and at Lincoln's Inn. In 1619 he accompanied Sir James Hay, now Viscount Doncaster, on a journey abroad. In 1621 he was made Dean of St Paul's – not, of course, the present St Paul's (designed by Sir Christopher Wren), but the previous cathedral which was burnt down in the Great Fire of London in 1666. He preached there regularly for the remainder of his life. His sermons are amongst the finest in the English language: for example, his last sermon, called 'Death's Duel'. He suffered a serious illness in 1623, and his famous prose *Devotions*, short meditations, were probably written during his convalescence: the celebrated phrases 'No man is an island' and 'never send to know for whom the bell tolls; it tolls for thee' come from 'Devotion: 17'. He died in 1631 after another protracted illness, anxious that his early works should be destroyed: he wanted to be remembered only by his sermons.

Context

The suspicion with which Catholics were regarded must be set in its historical context. Henry VIII (reigned 1509–47) established himself as head of a Church of England that differed little from the Catholic Church. It was only during his son's reign (Edward VI, 1547–53) that the Church of England began to assume a more Protestant character. Edward's premature death brought Mary to the throne, and she, as the daughter of Catherine of Aragon (Henry's first wife), was a Catholic. In the course of her five-year reign (1553–8), some three hundred Protestants were burnt at the stake. Subsequent English suspicion of Catholicism has owed much more to fear of such reprisals than to a dislike of Catholic ritual. Elizabeth I, daughter of Anne Boleyn (Henry's second wife), sought to give people freedom to worship as they liked. In 1570, bowing to pressure from Spain, the Pope officially excommunicated Elizabeth. He not only declared that the primary allegiance of Catholics in a non-Catholic country was to the Roman Church (*not* to their state), but he also encouraged them to depose or murder their non-Catholic sovereign. This inevitably put English Catholics under some suspicion: they were debarred from holding public office and even attending universities. The fact that Donne was a Catholic was thus bound to be an obstacle to his professional advancement.

We know that Donne was well liked by the relatively small circle of aristocrats who had a marked interest in literature. He attended numerous social gatherings where he would read his amorous lyrics, which were then copied and shown to others: they certainly came to be known far beyond their original audience. All who knew him spoke of him with great admiration. Indeed, as a Catholic he would not have received hospitality or been given either employment or support by so many people unless he had been unusually gifted.

His verse belongs to a golden age in English literature: it is almost exactly contemporary with Shakespeare's plays. It can be seen either as the culmination of the first phase of the English Renaissance, or as an entirely new beginning. Only recently, however, has it been emphasised how many parallels exist between what Donne was doing in England and what other poets were doing on the Continent. Warnke (1987) argues that Montaigne's endeavour to capture thought 'in the process of being formed' marks a new tendency in European writing, and that Donne's poems reveal very much the same kind of self-consciousness. He appears never to have sought to publish the lyrics that are still the basis of his reputation.

Donne's poems were published in 1633, soon after his death: the first section (of the 1635 edition) has the subtitle 'Songs and Son[n]ets'; the second, 'Elegies'; the seventh, 'Letters to Several Personages'; the eleventh (and last), 'Divine Poems'. Although this anthology includes only works from these sections, it must be stressed that Donne also wrote a great many epigrams, satires, verse epistles, and celebratory poems – including two long 'Anniversaries' (the first was originally entitled 'An Anatomy of the World'; the second, 'The Progress of the Soul'), as well as 'Epithalamions' and another long poem called 'Metempsychosis'. These works reflect a great many other aspects of Donne's poetry, but the most useful introduction to his work is by way of the 'Songs and Sonnets' and the 'Divine

Poems'. One of his verse letters has also been included, to give a flavour of Donne's 'celebratory' style and his satirical vein.

The amorous poems included in this anthology are all from the 'Songs and Sonnets' with the exception of 'Elegy 19', which, as will be seen, is not really an elegy at all. There are significant discrepancies between the first and second editions (1635) of the *Poems*, and there is no way of knowing in what order Donne would have liked the poems published. Consequently, the order of the poems in the first section is the editors' own.

Genre

Renaissance poetry is mostly concerned with the exploration of a conceit borrowed from the legacy of Petrarch (love for an idealised mistress, life as a storm-tossed sea-journey, the end of which the poet seeks in the 'haven' of his mistress's arms, etc.). Even when it pretends to be most personal – for example, the famous last line of the opening sonnet of Sidney's *Astrophil and Stella* (1591): '"Fool!" said my muse to me, "look in thy heart and write"!' – it never convinces the reader that the poet is exploring a personal experience. The love the poet feels for his idealised mistress is merely the subject of an art form that has still not become conscious of the possibilities art offers for the exploration of personal experience. Donne's poetry takes up many of the themes found in earlier Renaissance verse (love, devotion, the exploration of paradox, etc.), but transforms them by the much broader range of his metaphors, his greater daring in juxtaposing one metaphor with another, the toughness of his argumentation and, perhaps most strikingly, by the greater insistence on the immediacy of the experience described. It is not autobiographical, in the sense that a great deal of Romantic poetry is autobiographical, but its emotional charge is always so central to its argument that one cannot doubt the poet's personal involvement with what he writes.

Donne owes much to the Petrarchan lyric of earlier Tudor poets (e.g. Sir Thomas Wyatt [1503–42], Henry Howard, Earl of Surrey [1517–47], Sir Philip Sidney [1554–86] and Edmund Spenser [1552–99]), but his works also show a new beginning.

He is the first and possibly the greatest of the so-called 'Metaphysical poets', a term applied to a relatively small number of poets writing in the first half of the seventeenth century. The word 'Metaphysics' was first used by Dryden in a pejorative remark about Donne, but it was left to Samuel Johnson to label these poets for all time: 'about the beginning of the seventeenth century', he wrote in his *Life of Cowley* (1781), 'appeared a race of writers that may be termed the metaphysical poets.' Clearly, he too was no great admirer of the style, which he considered lacking in the properties of true poetry which, he thought – following Aristotle – should imitate either life or nature, and the 'Metaphysical poets' do neither. He also strongly objected to what he saw as their endeavour to display their learning in 'metaphysical' abstractions. Johnson may not, in fact, have been as critical of their writing as he is usually reputed to have been (see A.J. Smith, ed. [1975], pp. 214–31), but his very label highlights aspects of their style which may not be essential to their works; thus it may not be the most useful label for either the poets or their poetry. The kind of poetry that has variously been labelled 'metaphysical', 'devotional' and 'meditative' is perhaps better characterised by the degree to which it reflects a conscious attempt to wrestle with a paradox so as to explore its effect than by any other single feature. In this sense, it is essentially explorative and highly self-reflexive.

Broadly speaking, the characteristics of Donne's work are also the characteristics of so-called Metaphysical poetry. It is remarkable for its formal variety. Earlier Renaissance poets had tended to exploit well-known forms (e.g. the sonnet): Donne creates a new form for almost every poem. Even on the few occasions when he writes in an established metre (e.g. 'A Valediction: Forbidding Mourning'), he handles the material in such a startling fashion that one forgets the conservative form.

His works are also strikingly immediate – a trait he has in common with Sir Thomas Wyatt, but which he develops much further. Earlier Renaissance poetry tends to description ('One day I wrote her name upon the strand': Spenser, *Amoretti*, 75). Donne's poetry has the immediacy of conversation designed to startle, if not to outrage. Long before Wordsworth, he was writing in 'the language of men' (see Wordsworth's famous 'Preface' to *Lyrical Ballads*, 1805) – not of the 'common man', perhaps, but of the well-educated and sophisticated upper classes whose wealth and leisure had given them a taste for novelty.

Thirdly, his works employ imagery and juxtapose ideas in a way that is both startling and extraordinarily clever (that is, showing great 'wit', in the seventeenth-century sense of this word). Both the fundamental conceits and the ways in which they are elaborated are as arresting as the very best images employed by Shakespeare. Many of these images are not themselves original to Donne (e.g. the image of a flea in the poem of this name, or a pair of compasses in the 'Valediction: Forbidding Mourning'), but the outrageous use he makes of them, both in his amorous and in his equally daring divine poems, is highly personal. Whereas earlier Elizabethan poets had tended to rely on the resources of the Petrarchan legacy, Donne borrowed many of his most striking images from contemporary issues: from science, medicine, travel to the New World, and so on. Just as the Futurists (Marinetti, Boccioni, Balla, etc.) sang the praises of the motorcar in the second decade of the twentieth century, so Donne devised his imagery from topical subjects and events.

Many of these images are not only strikingly visual, but also conceptual: in other words, Donne's poetry requires readers to turn over an idea in their minds, to play with it, to see it from an unexpected angle. He is not a 'philosophical' poet in any accepted sense of this phrase; but he takes a delight in playing with ideas, even in his divine poems, and invites the reader to share this pleasure.

Critical Reception

Although they were known only to a restricted audience of mostly aristocratic friends who admired them, copied them and sent them to their friends and relatives, Donne's writings were highly regarded during his lifetime. So they circulated remarkably widely, albeit only within a very limited social group, and continued to be influential throughout the first half of the century. He was especially praised for his wit and learning, and his style was imitated by successors, including George Herbert, Henry Carey, Henry King, Abraham Cowley, John Cleveland

and Andrew Marvell. An important early account is the *Life of Donne* by Sir Izaak Walton, first published in 1640 and in repeatedly revised editions in 1658, 1670 and 1675. The *Poems* themselves went through seven editions during the century, the last of which is dated 1669. During the Restoration period there was a reaction to the intellectuality of earlier poetry, and this signalled a decline in Donne's influence. John Dryden wrote: 'He affects the metaphysics, not only in his satires, but in his amorous verses, where nature only should reign; and perplexes the minds of the fair sex with nice [i.e. fanciful] speculations of philosophy, when he should engage their hearts, and entertain them with the softnesses of love' (1693). There was only one edition (in 1719) of his works before they were reprinted in John Bell's *Poets of Great Britain* (1779). Samuel Johnson was as disapproving of him as Dryden had been. Early in the following century, however, Samuel Taylor Coleridge wrote a short appreciation of him in the form of an epigram, and Edmund Gosse published an error-ridden *Life and Letters* in 1899. However, Palgrave did not include any of his works in his celebrated and influential anthology *The Golden Treasury* (1861, rev. 1897).

Donne's present reputation stems from the edition of his works prepared by H.J.C. Grierson in 1912. Poets as different as W.B. Yeats, Ezra Pound and T.S. Eliot all praised Donne for his brilliant paradoxes and daring metaphors, and his influence is apparent in their work. Eliot's essay on 'The Metaphysical Poets' (1921) established the criteria for admiring Donne, who has held a central position in both the recognised 'canon' and critical debate ever since, largely because the key terms of 'New Criticism' (paradox, ambiguity, tension, etc.) were so appropriate to a discussion of his work. Both Ernest Hemingway and Vita Sackville-West borrowed from him for the titles of very different works: *For Whom the Bell Tolls* (1940), a novel about the Spanish Civil War; and *The Eagle and the Dove* (1943), a contrast between St Teresa of Avila and St Thérèse of Lisieux.

Donne's position is currently being re-examined from a number of different perspectives: by critics attempting to reassert the Romantic tradition which his poetry served partly to displace; by critics who argue that literature is an expression of sociopolitical and ideological debate; and by critics interested in literature in its relation to a biographical or historical context. But Donne's formal variety and intellectual daring continue to fascinate each new generation of readers, and guarantee his place in the canon. He continues to be recognised as one of the two most influential poets of the late sixteenth and early seventeenth centuries – the other, of course, being his contemporary, Ben Jonson.

Further Reading

Editions

Although the standard edition is still *Poetical Works*, ed. Sir Herbert Grierson, 2 vols (Oxford, 1912/1971), *The Complete English Poems of John Donne*, ed. C.A. Patrides, 'Everyman Classics' (London, 1985) provides a more readily accessible text and an invaluable bibliography. *Donne*, ed. John Carey, 'Oxford Authors' (Oxford, 1990) offers a chronological ordering of the poems. The standard edition of the lyric poems is *John Donne: The Elegies and the Songs and Sonnets*, ed. Helen Gardner (Oxford, 1965), although both *The 'Songs and Sonnets' of John Donne*, ed. Theodore Redpath, 2nd edn (London, 1983), and *John Donne: Selected poetry and prose*, ed. T.W. and R.J. Craik, 'Methuen English Texts' (London, 1986) are more reader-friendly. The standard editions of the other poetical works are *Satires, Epigrams and Verse Letters*, ed. W. Milgate (Oxford, 1967), *The Epithalamions, Anniversaries and Epicedes*, ed. W. Milgate (Oxford, 1979), *The Anniversaries*, ed. Frank Manley (Baltimore, MD, 1963) and *The Divine Poems*, ed. Helen Gardner (Oxford, 1959). Gary A. Stringer is currently preparing a 'Variorum Edition'.

Critical Studies

For good introductions to this fascinating but enigmatic poet, see J. Winny, *Preface to Donne* (London, 1981); Frank J. Warnke's recent 'Twayne' edition, *John Donne* (Boston, MA, 1987), which is particularly useful for situating Donne in a more European context than is usual; and George Parfitt, *John Donne: A literary life* (London, 1989), which examines selected aspects of Donne's life and work in the context of his time.

Amongst the various collections of critical essays, Peter A. Fiore, ed., *Just so much Honor* (University Park, PA, 1972); Julian Lovelock, ed., *John Donne: 'Songs and Sonnets': A casebook* (London, 1973); and John R. Roberts, ed., *Essential Articles for the Study of John Donne's Poetry* (Hamden, CT, 1975) are all very useful. More recent collections include Harold Bloom, ed., *John Donne and the Seventeenth-Century Metaphysical Poets* (New York, 1986) and Claude Summers and T.-L. Pebworth, eds, *The Eagle and the Dove: Reassessing John Donne* (Columbia, MO, 1985). A.J. Smith (ed.) surveys critical reception of Donne's works from the early seventeenth to the end of the nineteenth century in *John Donne: The critical heritage* (London, 1975).

J.B. Leishman, *The Monarch of Wit: An analytical and comparative study of the poetry of John Donne* (London, 1953) was one of the first full-length studies to do justice to the poems. Clay Hunt, *Donne's Poetry: Essays in literary analysis* (New Haven, CT, 1954) is especially useful for his analyses of 'The Good-Morrow' and 'The Canonisation'. Often more provocative, if only because it goes into interesting detail, is Arnold Stein, *John Donne's Lyrics: The eloquence of action* (Minneapolis, MN, 1962). In *The Breaking of the Circle*, rev. edn (New York, 1960), Marjorie Hope Nicolson explores the effect of the scientific revolution on the English poetic imagination, with frequent reference to Donne. A.C. Partridge, *John Donne: Language and style* (London, 1979) draws attention to a necessary issue. Terry G. Sherwood examines Donne as an intellectual in *Fulfilling the Circle: A study of John Donne's thought* (Toronto, ON, 1984); while Dennis McKevlin, *A Lecture in Love's Philosophy: Donne's vision of the world of human love in the 'Songs and Sonets'* (Lanham, MD, 1984) offers a study of the amorous verse. Frank J. Warnke, *Versions of Baroque: European literature in the seventeenth century* (New Haven, CT, 1972) provides a survey of European Baroque poetry with frequent reference to and comparison with Donne.

Amongst more recent historicist studies are A. Marotti, 'John Donne and patronage', in G. Lytle and S. Orgel, eds, *Patronage in the Renaissance* (Princeton, NJ, 1981); Dayton Haskin, 'New historical contexts for appraising the Donne revival from A.B. Grosart to Charles Eliot Norton', *ELH*, **56** (1989), 869–95, which explores criticism of the Victorian period; and Anthony Low's review article 'Donne and the new historicism', *John Donne*

Journal, **7** (1988), 125–31. Janet E. Halley provides a feminist perspective in 'Textual intercourse: Anne Donne, John Donne, and the sexual politic of textual exchange', in Sheila Fisher and J.E. Halley, eds, *Seeking the Woman in Late Medieval and Renaissance Writings: Essays in feminist contextual criticism* (Knoxville, TN, 1989), pp. 187–206. For a recent overview of critical reaction to the poet, see Deborah Aldrich Larson, *John Donne and Twentieth-Century Criticism* (London, 1989), which explores the question of why Donne's poetry provokes such a wide range of critical and emotional reaction.

Further essays on individual poems include H. David Brumble III, 'John Donne's "The Flea": some implications of the encyclopedic and poetic flea traditions', *Critical Quarterly*, **15** (1973), 147–54; J.D. Jahn, 'The eschatological scene of Donne's "A Valediction: Forbidding Mourning"', *College Literature*, **5** (1978), 34–47; Jack F. Stewart, 'Image and idea in Donne's "The Good Morrow"', *Discourse*, **12** (1969), 465–76. Two articles on one of the more controversial amorous poems may also be recommended: Albert C. Labriola, 'Donne's "The Canonization": its theological context and its religious imagery', *Huntington Library Quarterly*, **36** (1973), 327–39, and A.P. Riemer, 'A pattern for love: the structure of Donne's "The Canonization"', *Sydney Studies in English*, **3** (1977), 19–31, which discusses the poem's use of numerology. For a recent analysis of one of the 'Divine Poems', see Sibyl Lutz Severance, 'Soul, sphere, and structure in "Goodfriday, 1613: Riding Westward"', *SP*, **84** (1987), 24–43.

The standard biography is still R.C. Bald, *John Donne: A life*, ed. W. Milgate (New York and Oxford, 1970), although John Carey's *John Donne: Life, mind and art* (London and New York, 1981) provides an interesting focus on the issues of Catholicism and the poet's fascination with death.

Robert H. Day, *A John Donne Companion* (New York, 1990) is a useful introductory reference work. Although it is now in need of updating, John R. Roberts, *John Donne: An annotated bibliography of modern criticism: 1912–67* (Columbia, MO, 1973), and its sequel, John R. Roberts, *John Donne: An annotated bibliography of modern criticism: 1968–1978* (Columbia, MO, 1979) provide an indispensable annotated bibliography of secondary material. Also in need of revision is Homer C. Combs and Zay R. Sullens,

A Concordance to the English Poems of John Donne (Chicago, 1940). The *John Donne Journal: Studies in the Age of Donne*, ed. M. Thomas Hester and R.V. Young, founded in 1982, provides a useful starting point for enquiring into the most recent developments in critical thinking.

1/ *The Flea*

Mark but this flea, and mark in this,
How little that which thou deny'st me is.
It sucked me first and now sucks thee,
And in this flea our two bloods mingled be:
Thou know'st that this cannot be said
A sin, nor shame, nor loss of maidenhead.
Yet this enjoys before it woo
And, pampered, swells with one blood made of two:
And this, alas, is more than we would do.

Oh, stay! Three lives in one flea spare,
Where we almost – nay! *more* than married are.
This flea is you and I, and this
Our marriage bed and marriage temple is:
Though parents grudge, and you, we're met
And cloistered in these living walls of jet.
Though use make you apt to kill me,
Let not to *this* self-murder added be,
And sacrilege, three sins in killing three.

Cruel and sudden! Hast thou since
Purpled thy nail in blood of innocence?
Wherein could this flea guilty be
Except in that drop which it sucked from thee?
Yet thou triumph'st, and say'st that thou
Find'st not thyself nor me the weaker now.
'Tis true: then learn how false fears be:
Just so much honour, when thou yield'st to me,
Will waste as this flea's death took life from thee.

Throughout Europe during the Renaissance there appeared a great many poems about fleas, in many of which the poet wishes he were a flea so that he could lie on his mistress's breast and either so enjoy her, or else 'die' (sixteenth–seventeenth-century slang for 'experience sexual orgasm': cf. Shakespeare, *Much Ado About Nothing*, III, ii, 61–3), when she pinched – i.e. 'embraced' – him. Donne's treatment of the subject is both more interesting and original; this is why his poem continues to amuse long after most other flea poems have been forgotten. It consists of three stanzas, each of nine lines of alternating iambic tetrameters and pentameters, rhyming *a a / b b c c / d d d*. The last two lines of each stanza are pentameters.

'The Flea' has been called a seduction poem. The poet is shown trying to convince his reluctant mistress to allow him to make love to her: in the first stanza, he argues that what he asks will do her no more harm than the bite of a flea; in the second, he asks her not to kill the flea because they are united in the blood it has taken from them both; in the third, he neatly reverses her triumph. It is unusual amongst Donne's works in that it explores a single conceit; note also how well constructed it is: how each stanza begins with an arresting rhetorical address to the mistress, and how the first two lines of each stanza *present* an argument which is then *elaborated* in lines 3–6; the last three lines consist of its *application*.

The tradition of flea poems seems to begin with 'Carmen de Pulice' (Song of the Flea), attributed during the Renaissance to Ovid, but more probably written by Ofilius Sergianus during the late medieval period. A poem called 'Encomium Pulicis' (In Praise of Fleas) appears to have sparked off a further fashion for writing such works. The French poet Ronsard wrote a flea poem in 1553 ('Ha, seigneur Dieu, que de graces encloses'), although he removed the offending phrases when he revised the poem in 1578. In 1579 another Frenchman, Etienne Pasquier, noticed while talking with Catherine des Roches that a flea had settled on her bosom. He celebrated the occasion by assembling a collection of some fifty 'flea poems' in French, Spanish, Italian, Latin and Greek, and published it as *La Puce de Madame des Roches* (The Flea of Madame des Roches, 1582). Donne would not need to have known any of these works to be aware of the tradition.

[1] **this . . . this**
humorously emphasises the opposites: the flea and the conceit (argument) used by the poet; the frequent use of 'this' also heightens the poem's immediacy.

[2] **How little that . . . is**
half the humour in this line arises from the image of the flea, which is, of course, very 'little', and thereby suggests that the issue of his mistress's virtue is of no greater consequence; the other half comes from the energy with which he argues his case: the poet is making a great deal of the flea, which suggests that his mistress has good reason to make much of her virtue.

[4] **our two bloods mingled be**
much of the poem depends on the notion that each partner's 'blood' mixes in the act of love; blood clearly means vital fluid (i.e. also 'semen').

[6] **maidenhead**
virginity; the word involves a pun translated from the French: *puce* (flea), *pucelle* (virgin), *pucelage* (virginity).

[7] **Yet this . . . woo**
woo to court or ask for in marriage; refers to the flea, which takes its pleasure without committing itself to marriage.

[8] **And, pampered . . . made of two**
pampered spoiled, overindulged, crammed; the flea has taken more than its fill of blood from both the poet and his mistress – blood which is now mixed into 'one' inside it.

[10] **stay**
stay (stop) your hand, i.e. 'Don't kill the flea'.

[11] **married**
At a time when making love with someone of the opposite sex was often accepted in lieu of marriage (i.e. a 'common-law' bond), the union of the poet's blood with that of his mistress in the flea could indeed signal '*more* than' a marriage.

[12–13] **and this . . . marriage temple is**
this is ambiguous: (a) the flea, in whom the marriage of the poet and his mistress has been sanctified; (b) the bed on which they are lying (for the image of a bed as a temple, cf. 'Elegy 19', lines 17–18, p. 38).

[14] **Though parents grudge, and you**
grudge reluctant to allow; thus: 'Although your parents do not want us to become lovers, and neither, it seems, do you . . .'

[14] **we're met**
(a) we have come face to face with one another, like two antagonists (anticipating line 16); (b) we have joined together; (c) we have satisfied one another's wishes.

[15] **cloistered . . . walls of jet**
cloistered enclosed within cloisters, the covered and secluded courtyard attached to a monastery or cathedral where monks walk and meditate – note the religious implications; *jet* hard black lignite (a stone), usually with a brilliant polish: here (a) the hard shell of a flea and (b) the marble walls of a 'marriage temple', described as 'living' because it refers to a bed that moves.

[16] **Though use . . . kill me**
use custom, habit; *apt* having a tendency; kill involves the familiar Renaissance pun on sexual orgasm: thus (a) 'Although your customary or habitual rejection of my advances has made it likely that you will kill me'; (b) 'Although our previous lovemaking has given you a constant desire for me to achieve orgasm'.

[17] **this**
i.e. his mistress's desire to kill him, in both senses.

[18] **sacrilege, three sins . . .**
sacrilege destroying a holy place (e.g. a temple); the three sins are thus murder, self-murder, and sacrilege.

[19] **Cruel and sudden**
not only tells the reader that the poet's mistress has killed the flea, but also provides a succinct indication of her impulsive character.

[19–20] **since**
just now, a moment ago, in spite of my warnings; ***Purpled . . . innocence purple*** a royal colour, suggesting the degree of her crime; ***innocence*** (a) free from moral guilt; (b) free from hurt (***nocere*** = to hurt) – i.e. the flea was neither guilty in its action, nor guilty of hurting us.

[22] **Except in that drop . . .**
note the poet's tongue-in-cheek gallantry in conceding that his mistress had not consented to being bitten.

[23–4] **thou triumphst . . . weaker now**
i.e. she is laughing in triumph, thinking she has won the argument, as she has not suffered for having killed the flea.

[25]
Note how the poet neatly turns his mistress's 'triumph' against her by 'demonstrating', as in a logical or algebraic problem, the truth of the claim he made in the first stanza.

[26–7] **Just so . . . from thee**
his mistress will lose only as much honour in yielding to his persuasion as she lost life by killing the flea which had bitten her – i.e. none.

2 / *Elegy 19: To His Mistress Going to Bed*

Come, Madam, come! All rest my powers defy:
Until I labour, I in labour lie.
The foe oft-times, having the foe in sight,
Is tired with standing, though he never fight.
Off with that girdle, like heaven's zone glistering,
But a far fairer world encompassing.
Unpin that spangled breastplate which you wear
That th'eyes of busy fools may be stopped there.
Unlace yourself, for that harmonious chime
Tells me from you that now 'tis your bed time.
Off with that happy busk, which I envy,
That still can be, and still can stand so nigh.
Your gown going off, such beauteous state reveals
As when from flowery meads th'hills shadow steals.
Off with that wiry coronet and show
The hairy diadem which on you doth grow.
Now off with those shoes, and then safely tread
In this Love's hallowed temple, this soft bed.
In such white robes heaven's angels used to be
Received by men. Thou, angel, bring'st with thee
A heaven like Mahomet's paradise – and though
Ill spirits walk in white, we easily know
By this, these angels from an evil sprite:
Those set our hairs, but these our flesh upright.
  Licence my roving hands, and let them go
Before, behind, between, above, below.
O, my America! my New-found-land!
My kingdom, safeliest when with one man manned!
My mine of precious stones! my empery!
How blessed am I in this discovering thee.
To enter in these bonds is to be free:
Then where my hand is set, my seal shall be.
  Full nakedness, all joys are due to thee!
As souls unbodied, bodies unclothed must be,
To taste whole joys. Gems which you women use
Are, like At'lanta's balls, cast in men's views
That when a fool's eye lighteth on a gem,
His earthly soul may covet theirs, not them.
Like pictures, or like books' gay coverings made
For laymen, are all women thus arrayed.

Themselves are mystic books, which only we,
Whom their imputed grace will dignify,
Must see revealed. Then, since that I may know,
As liberally as to a midwife show
Thyself: cast all, yea, this white linen hence!
There is no penance due to innocence.
   To teach thee, I am naked first – why, then,
What need'st thou have more covering than a man?

An elegy was originally a lament for someone who has died. It was Ovid, a Roman poet who lived about the time of Christ, who first used the word to describe some of his amatory poems written in metre: by the end of the sixteenth century, his *Amores* were widely referred to as elegies. Donne's twenty or so elegies were amongst his most highly admired works in his time. 'Elegy 19' (the number accorded it by Grierson), which probably belongs to the mid 1590s, is his best-known work in the genre. Bearing in mind its original meaning, the title is amusing, as it suggests that the mistress is going to bed to 'die', with obvious innuendo.

'Elegy 19' is in forty-eight iambic pentameters rhyming in heroic couplets. The poet is trying to persuade his mistress to join him in bed. The first four lines present the argument. In lines 5 to 18, he persuades her to remove her items of clothing one by one until she is standing only in her slip. The second half of the poem is concerned with various rhetorical strategies designed to achieve his aim.

Although this poem was first published in the 1669 edition of Donne's works, there is little or no reason to doubt his authorship. Note how the poem exploits the tradition of the poetic *blason* or catalogue of a woman's most attractive attributes.

[1] **Come, ... my powers defy**
come (a) approach; (b) be reasonable; ***powers*** the poet's ability to act, his masculine identity – i.e. his lust is so heated that he cannot rest. Note the paradox of ***passive*** 'rest' defying ***active*** 'powers'.

[2] **Until I labour ... lie**
labour (a) work i.e. engage in the act of love; (b) an ordeal of expectation; note how this second meaning of 'labour' belongs to the language of childbearing: consider the implications.

[3–4] **The foe ... never fight**
foe (a) enemy: the image is of two hostile armies eager for action after a period of facing one another on the alert; (b) the male and female sexual organs – the image is of the man's erection subsiding because the penis has not engaged in its proper activity.

[5] **girdle, like heaven's zone glistering**
girdle belt or corset used to encircle the waist and hips; the metaphor likens the mistress's girdle to the canopy of stars, the outermost 'layer' of the earth-centred universe.

[6] **encompassing**
a military term meaning to surround, as when soldiers form a circle of defence; as ***heaven's zone*** is traditionally seen as 'fairer' than the earth, the girdle covering/surrounding a ***far fairer world*** is, of course, a paradox.

[7] **breastplate**
(a) an outer garment, worn under the bodice of a gown, which covered the woman's chest – this one is covered with spangles, small pieces of shiny material sewn on to it as decoration;

(b) a piece of armour covering the chest.

[8] **stopped**
the breastplate serves to 'protect' the woman from the lascivious glances of 'fools' who are so captivated by the beauty of the ornamented breastplate that they have no thoughts for the greater beauty beneath; ***busy*** overcurious.

[9] **Unlace yourself**
the lacing belongs to the busk, mentioned two lines later; ***that harmonious chime*** the sound produced by the spangles as the breastplate is removed is likened to the chiming of a small clock or watch, hence the following line.

[11] **that happy busk**
a closely fitting and stiffened bodice or corset worn as an undergarment, laced at the back.

[12] **That still . . . so nigh**
still (a) unmoved, unperturbed; (b) yet; ***nigh*** near. The poet is marvelling at the busk because it can lie so close to his mistress *without* being thrown into amorous confusion; the poet 'envies' the busk because it embraces his mistress more closely than he is allowed to.

[13] **gown**
a full and loose skirt worn as an elegant outer garment.

[14] **As when from flowery meads th'hills shadow steals**
'As when, in the morning, the shadow of a range of hills diminishes as the sun rises to reveal the full beauty of the flower-filled meadows' – a deliberately self-conscious (i.e. ironic or parodic) 'poetic' analogy.

[15] **wiry coronet**
not a small crown (coronet) but an elegant headpiece, probably made of gold or silver wire.

[16] **hairy diadem**
diadem (a) a headband worn as a badge of sovereignty; (b) a crowning distinction or glory – here, paradoxically, it refers to the mistress's own hair: cf. the paradox of girdle/heaven's zone in line 5.

[17–18] **safely tread/ . . . hallowed temple**
the removal of the shoes recalls God's instructions to Moses: 'Take off your shoes, for the place where you are standing is holy ground' (Exodus 3: 5); having removed her shoes, the mistress can safely proceed into the 'Temple' of Love – i.e., in Donne's poem the carnal and profane *is* sacred.

[19–24]
The poet likens his mistress to an angel: these lines are not essential to the development of the poem, but they contain two comic conceits which set the tone for the explicit sensuality of lines 25–32.

[20] **Received by men**
the phrase is deliberately ambivalent. In Christian tradition, angels were either male or sexless; they may have walked on earth with people, but they did not sleep with them. Because the image is shocking, Donne diminishes possible offence to Christian readers by suggesting that he is referring to a Muslim tradition (line 21). ***Received*** (a) seen (i.e. in former times people had visions of angels dressed in white); (b) taken into possession (i.e. in former times people would welcome angels dressed in white into their rooms, for obvious purposes).

[21] **like Mahomet's paradise**
Refers to the Mahommedan 'garden of delights' (i.e. heaven of sensual pleasure): see The Koran, sura 56: 'That Which is Coming'. The passage was often misinterpreted in the sense meant by Donne.

[21–2] **though/Ill spirits walk in white**
having likened his mistress to an angel, the poet clearly has to rescue her from the charge that she is an 'ill spirit' (evil angel): thus he jokingly concedes that ill spirits also walk in white, but only in order to be able to make the following distinction.

[23] **By this**
i.e. the distinction made in the following line.

[24] **Those set our hairs, but these our flesh upright**
evil angels frighten a man – i.e. make his hair stand on end – whereas 'good angels' give him an erection. Bawdy (humorously indecent) these lines certainly are, but they also serve to remind us to read the sexual content of the poem in a light-hearted spirit.
[25–32]
The poet asks his mistress for permission to fondle her.
[27] **my America**
note the emphatic possessive, used here to heighten the comic effect; ***America*** discovered by Christopher Columbus in 1492 but named after Amerigo Vespucci, who sailed on Columbus's second and third voyages and was responsible for drawing a map of the land; in 1507 the humanist Martin Waldseemüller reprinted some of Vespucci's letters, suggesting that the new land should be called America; it was on one of Waldseemüller's planispheres that the name America first appeared; expeditions to America continued throughout the sixteenth century, as successive leaders discovered its different riches; ***New-found-land*** (a) Newfoundland, an island off the south-east coast of Canada, formally annexed to England in 1583 by Sir Humphrey Gilbert; it was one of England's few American 'colonies' in the 1590s; also (b) the American continent as a land newly discovered and requiring exploration.
[28] **My kingdom . . . one man manned**
safeliest safest; ***with one man manned*** (a) garrisoned (i.e. guarded) by only one man – a deliberately paradoxical military conceit; (b) in happiest state when sexually possessed by a man (cf. 'The Sun Rising', line 21).
[29] **My mine of precious stones**
likening a mistress's attributes to jewels was a commonplace; likening *her* to a mine from which precious stones are extracted is much more original, and anticipates the metaphor in lines 37–38; ***my empery*** dominion – cf. the word 'empire'.
[30] **in this discovering thee**
(a) for being able to see you uncovered (i.e. naked); (b) for being able to explore you in this way (i.e. with 'roving hands').
[31] **these bonds**
(a) contractual obligations – the legal term anticipates line 32; (b) his mistress's arms.
[32] **where . . . seal shall be**
seal a piece of wax or lead, impressed with a monarch's or nobleman's personal device, attached to a document to validate it; thus (a) a legal phrase implying the poet's readiness to fulfil his obligations in the 'contract' which he wants to make with his mistress; (b) the phrase has a self-evident sexual innuendo.
[33–46]
A hymn to nakedness, combining sacred and profane imagery.
[33] **Full nakedness**
The poet's mistress is still wearing a linen slip; the ensuing lines are therefore designed to persuade her (or him?) that she should unclothe herself completely.
[34] **As souls unbodied . . . To taste whole joys**
in Christian teaching, just as the soul which aspires to heaven must first divest itself of the body in which it is enclosed, so the body, if it is to experience complete fulfilment, must divest itself of its covering – i.e. cast aside all clothes.
[35] **use**
wear.
[36] **like At'lanta's balls, cast in men's views**
Atalanta is a minor figure of Greek myth. The Delphic oracle warned her against marriage. Thus when her father insisted that she prepare herself to choose a husband, she consented only on the condition that any suitor for her hand 'must either beat her in a foot race or else allow her to kill him'. Many princes lost the race and their lives, until Melanion invoked

Aphrodite's assistance. The Greek goddess of love gave him three golden apples and told him to drop them in Atalanta's path as they ran. He did so. Atalanta, stooping to pick each apple up, lost time, thereby allowing Melanion to win. Donne adapts the myth to his own use, suggesting that Atalanta drops the 'balls' ahead of the men in order to distract them from their proper goal.

[38] **His earthly soul . . . not them**
theirs the balls; ***them*** the women. Thus, the fool's dull, spiritless soul lusts after what he sees, not for what lies behind – i.e. the jewel's 'essence', the woman herself (cf. line 8 and note).

[39–40] **Like pictures . . . for laymen**
The fact that women always ensure that their portraits show them wearing their most expensive jewels illustrates his point; ***like books' gay coverings made for laymen*** the fact that publishers provide a brightly coloured cover for any book they hope to sell to a wide readership also illustrates his point. Laymen are equivalent to the 'fool/s' in lines 8 and 37. Both are unable to understand 'mystic books'.

[41–3] **Themselves are . . . revealed**
mystic books (a) spiritual works; (b) works with hidden, secret meanings – i.e. designed only for those with a special understanding of spiritual secrets; ***imputed grace*** according to Calvinist theology, man cannot save himself: grace can be imputed (i.e. accorded) to him only by God, who chooses those whom he will save. Thus, only men who are attributed with grace by a woman, and are thereby dignified, are allowed to see women 'revealed' – i.e. naked. The equation of woman with God is even more risqué than the point in line 20.

[43–4] **since that I may know**
(a) as I *am* allowed to know these 'mystic' secrets; (b) in order that I can experience, with clearly sexual implications: to know = to lie with – cf. 'And Adam *knew* Eve his wife; and she conceived . . . ' (Genesis 4: 1); ***As liberally . . . show thyself liberally*** freely, completely and unashamedly. The poet tells his mistress to remove her final piece of clothing with as little shame as she would have were he a midwife; the sudden shift from sacred and pseudo-sacred imagery to the roughness of the midwife is deliberately shocking.

[46] **penance**
(a) sacrament including contrition (repentance) and confession; (b) an act of self-mortification as an expression of penitence, especially one imposed by a priest; it was usual for a penitent to wear a white sheet to signal his or her repentance, often for sexual offences; ***innocence*** freedom from moral wrong – the phrase 'There is no penance due to innocence' thus means there is no need for his mistress to repent, since she is still innocent of any wrong, with the implication that nakedness is innocence (cf. Adam and Eve, before their Fall: Genesis); none the less a paradox, as he is inviting her to commit a sin.

[47] **To teach**
an ironic underlying of the paradox referred to in the previous line.

[48] **than a man**
(a) than a man ***has*** (i.e. if he is naked, why should she need clothes?); (b) than a man (i.e. the only covering she needs is a man).

3 / *The Good-Morrow*

I wonder, by my troth, what thou and I
   Did till we loved? Were we not weaned till then,
But sucked on country pleasures, childishly?
   Or snorted we in the seven sleepers' den?
'Twas so. But this, all pleasures fancies be.
If ever any beauty I did see
Which I desired and got, 'twas but a dream of thee.

And now good-morrow to our waking souls
   Which watch not one another out of fear,
For love all love of other sights controls
   And makes one little room an everywhere.
Let sea-discoverers to new worlds have gone,
Let maps to others, worlds on worlds have shown,
Let us possess one world: each hath one, and is one.

My face in thine eye, thine in mine appears,
   And true plain hearts do in the faces rest.
Where can we find two better hemispheres
   Without sharp north, without declining west?
Whatever dies was not mixed equally:
If our two loves be one, or thou and I
Love so alike that none do slacken, none can die.

An aubade in three stanzas, each of seven lines and rhyming *a b a b / c c c*. The first six lines are iambic pentameters; the last is a hexameter. The poet is reflecting on the nature of the special love which exists between him and another: note that we only *assume* this is a woman (cf. Marvell, 'The Definition of Love' (p. 459); and for a similar problem in a different kind of poem, Donne, 'Holy Sonnet 10' p. 77).

Like 'The Flea', 'The Good-Morrow' elaborates a single conceit. In the first stanza, the poet imagines the inadequacy of his state before he fell in love with his mistress; in the second, he meditates on their present love; in the third, drawing on an alchemical notion that equally mixed substances cannot die, he concludes that he and his mistress are enjoying a perpetual orgasm.

An aubade is a poem whose action takes place in the early morning (*aube* = dawn). The most common kind of aubade is one in which the poet pleads with the sun to delay its rising so that he can enjoy lovemaking for a little longer. Note how Donne, although not exactly reversing this, offers a highly original approach to the theme.

[1] **by my troth**
truly, upon my word.

[2–3] **weaned**
(literally) accustomed to food other

than milk; here, to pass from childhood to maturity – note the irony implicit in the choice of word as used in this sense.

[3] **country pleasures**
merely sexual love (cf. 'Do you mean country matters?': *Hamlet*, III, ii, 109); ***childishly*** like infants, innocently, irresponsibly (like children) – i.e. merely physical pleasures are equivalent to the period when an infant 'sucks' milk from its mother's breast.

[4] **snorted we in the seven sleepers' den**
a reference to a popular legend about seven young Christians who, fleeing from persecution in AD 249, took refuge in a cave just outside Ephesus (a city on the west coast of present-day Turkey. A group of Christians worshipped there from very early times; it was visited by St Paul about AD 57: see Acts 19). The young men were discovered and walled up, but miraculously slept (***snorted*** snored like animals) for nearly 200 years before waking and being set free.

[5] **but this**
(a) but this is certain; (b) apart from our love (i.e. our pleasure is qualitatively different from that of others); ***all pleasures fancies be*** refers back to country pleasures; i.e. merely physical gratification is not, properly speaking, love, but fancy (a delusion, unfounded belief, only a mental image, not real).

[6–7] **If ever . . . a dream of thee**
'If the poet was ever infatuated by a beautiful girl, desired her, and slept with her, these (real) actions were but illusions, mental anticipations of his present mistress' – note how 'dream' develops the idea of sleep (line 4) from bestial snorting to dreaming of true beauty.

[8] **good-morrow to our waking souls**
the first indication of the difference between merely physical pleasures and love (mentioned in line 2) – love engages the *soul*; note how 'waking' refers back to 'weaned'.

[9–10] **Which watch not . . . controls**
a further distinction: whereas physical 'pleasures' always involve fears and jealousy, love proper is free from any such thoughts, because it keeps any inclination (love) towards other pleasures (other sights) in check (controls).

[11] **And makes one little room an everywhere**
a paradox; ***little room*** a bedroom: this wittily undermines the poet's distinctions between country pleasures and love.

[12–13] **Let sea-discoverers**
what difference does it make to us if explorers (e.g. Columbus); ***Let maps . . . have shown*** 'What difference does it make to us if maps have shown worlds on worlds to others?' The 'worlds on worlds' may be countries after countries, or refer to maps of the heavens and the different planets.

[14] **Let us . . . and is one**
our world (a) 'one little room', i.e. the bedroom; (2) the world made up of the union of their souls – each partner has a private world, and a joint world; a deliberate paradox playing on the (Christian) theological concept of trinitarian unity: three in one.

[15] **My face in thine eye, thine in mine appears**
refers to the reflection of his face in the pupils of his mistress's eyes, and vice versa (cf. 'The Canonisation', lines 40–43, p. 49).

[16] **true plain hearts do in the faces rest**
their faces reveal that their hearts are free from all disguises and defences. There was much wider belief in physiognomy (the art of judging character from features of face or form of body) than there is today.

[17] **hemispheres**
(a) the faces of the lovers (see previous line); (b) the eyes of each partner (see line 15): the conceit develops the notion of 'world' from the previous stanza.

[18] **Without . . . declining west**
sharp north extreme cold; ***declining***

west where the sun sets, thus representing a falling away of their present love – i.e. their love is free of extremes and any possibility of decay.

[19] **Whatever dies, was not mixed equally**
cf. the medieval-Renaissance-Hermetic belief that perfectly constituted matter is imperishable – thus, if anything dies, it is because it was imperfectly balanced or mixed. This notion was central to alchemy.

[20–21] **If our two loves be one . . . none can die**
'If our love really is one [cf. stanza 2, esp. line 14], and is so perfectly "mixed" that neither of us ever slackens in our lovemaking, then neither of us will die'; ***die*** (a) literally die – i.e. they will become immortal; (b) figuratively, in the seventeenth century, it usually means 'to experience orgasm', and most commentators assume that this is its meaning here; but even a brief consideration of the context suggests that here it must mean '(neither of us will) fall away from exhaustion after sexual orgasm', which implies that the poet is likening the love between him and his mistress to a *perpetual* orgasm.

4/ *The Sun Rising*

Busy old fool! Unruly sun!
Why dost thou thus
Through windows and through curtains call on us?
Must to thy motions lovers' seasons run?
Saucy pedantic wretch, go chide
Late schoolboys and sour 'prentices!
Go tell court-huntsmen that the king will ride;
Call country ants to harvest offices:
Love, all alike, no season knows nor clime,
Nor hours, days, months, which are the rags of time.

Thy beams so reverend and strong
Why shouldst thou think?
I could eclipse and cloud them with a wink
But that I would not lose her sight so long.
If her eyes have not blinded thine,
Look, and tomorrow late, tell me
Whether both th'Indias, of spice and mine,
Be where thou left'st them, or lie here with me.
Ask for those kings whom thou saw'st yesterday
And thou shalt hear, all here in one bed lay.

She's all states, and all princes, I:
Nothing else is.
Princes do but play us; compared to this,
All honour's mimic, all wealth alchemy.
Thou, sun, art half as happy as we,
In that the world's contracted thus;
Thine age asks ease, and since thy duties be
To warm the world, that's done in warming us.
Shine here to us, and thou art everywhere:
This bed thy centre is, these walls thy sphere.

Surely one of Donne's wittiest poems. This too is an aubade in three stanzas, each of ten lines of iambic tetrameters, dimeters and pentameters, rhyming *a b b a / c d c d / e e*. The opening is particularly arresting, beginning with the poet angrily chiding the sun for having disturbed him and his mistress while they are still in bed; in the second and third stanzas, he develops a series of startling conceits which culminates in the assertion that not only is their bed the whole world, but it is also the sun. Note how the poet exploits variations in his tone.

[1] **Busy . . . unruly**
busy meddlesome, over-inquisitive; ***unruly*** (a) disorderly (a joke, as the sun's apparent movement, being regular, does obey a heavenly 'order' or 'rule'); (b) a pun on 'un-rule' (i.e. not, or no longer, in command).

[3] **curtains**
the curtains of a four-poster bed.

[4] **Must to thy motions lovers' seasons run?**
(lit.) 'Do you think that lovers' desires are subject to your cyclical movement?'; note, however, the implicit inversion: ***motion*** moving, working, with a suggestion of doing so only superficially (as in the phrase 'going through the motions'); ***season*** (a) time of year when a plant flourishes; although the word stems from Latin *serere* (to sow), it was always applied to seed-time; thus 'season' combines notions of fertilisation, growth *and* harvest; also (b) 'favourable opportunity' or 'proper time', the implication being that lovers' seasons are a far more powerful factor than the sun's motions.

[5] **Saucy pedantic wretch**
saucy impertinent (because the sun has disturbed the poet and his mistress); ***pedantic*** someone who insists on adherence to formal rules; ***wretch*** (a) despicable person – the use indicates contempt; (b) someone without conscience or shame – may be used in playful depreciation.

[6] **sour 'prentices**
sour-faced apprentices – sour-faced because it was their duty to get to work early, before their master, to clean up the shop or business before opening.

[7] **the king**
possibly an oblique reference to James I, who succeeded Elizabeth I in 1603 and had a passion for hunting.

[8] **Call . . . offices**
country ants farm workers. The phrase does not necessarily indicate any contempt for rural labour; it is used humorously; ***harvest offices*** rural duties; thus, 'chase farm workers to their rural duties'. Note that 'office' was usually applied to court office; thus the poet is also indirectly laughing at

the courtiers whose duty it was to accompany the king when he went hunting.

[9] **all alike . . . nor clime**
all alike always the same; ***knows*** recognises, obeys; ***clime*** climate, in the sense of prevailing trend of opinion or feeling; thus, 'love, always the same, is subservient neither to season nor to prevailing opinions'.

[10] **the rags of time**
a phrase probably coined by Donne (cf. his sermon on Isaiah 7: 14, preached at St Paul's Cathedral on Christmas Day 1624).

[11–12] **Thy beams . . . think**
the unusual syntax is more apparent than real: in normal speech, line 12 would be read before line 11; ***reverend*** deserving high regard or reverence, a word which stems from Latin *vereri* (to fear) and is usually applied to religious objects or persons; the poet is thus challenging the sun to justify the traditional view that its beams or rays are holy, fearful, or even powerful.

[12] **eclipse and cloud**
eclipse (a) the sun is in eclipse when the moon comes between it and the earth; (b) deprivation of light or lustre by something coming between the source of light and the eye; ***cloud*** cause to become darkened as if by cloud; ***wink*** i.e. merely by 'blinking', the poet can eclipse the sun.

[13] **But . . . so long**
so long the time of a blink; thus, 'Except that I would not want to stop enjoying the sight of my mistress for even the time of a blink'.

[14] **If her eyes . . . thine**
although the mistress does not emit light of her own (in this she is like the moon), her eyes can none the less dazzle even the sun.

[15] **and tomorrow late**
i.e. take your time about it.

[16] **th'Indias, of spice and mine**
the East and West Indies respectively: the East Indies (the Malay archipelago) were famous for their spices – indeed, the Celebes were called the Spice Islands; the West Indies were Central and South America, known for their mines of gold, silver and precious stones – i.e. the poet's mistress is conceived as a source of untold riches (cf. 'Elegy 19', line 27); note also the pun on ***mine*** possessive pronoun.

[18] **where thou left'st them**
where the sun last saw them (i.e. in their geographical location), with a play on 'leave' in the sense of 'to forget inadvertently' – i.e. what the sun misplaced has been discovered by the poet in the person of his mistress.

[19–20] **Ask for those kings . . . all here in one bed lay**
This unexpected conceit is suggested by reference to the riches of the world implied by the two Indies, for if there are riches, there must be people who own them – i.e. kings; thus, 'Just as all the world's riches are embodied in the poet's mistress, so all the world's kings lie with her – i.e. are embodied in the poet.' The image is a reference to a stage in the alchemical process in which the figures of a 'king' and 'queen' (representing masculine and feminine principles respectively) lie together in a bed; their union was conceived as crucial to the success of the process: cf. J.D. Mylius, *Philosophia reformata* (1622).

[21–2] **She's all states . . . Nothing else is**
the movement of solipsistic 'contraction' (begun in the previous stanza), in which the cosmos is reduced to the world of the lovers, is further developed.

[23] **Princes do but play us**
the phrase implies that the poet and his mistress are a Platonic or archetypal 'ideal', of which the real kings and queens of the world are only imitations (i.e. they 'play' at being kings and queens); ***to this*** i.e. to the ideal union of the poet and his mistress.

[24] **All honour's mimic, all wealth alchemy**
honour princely office, distinction, reputation or glory; ***mimic*** a fraudulent imitation; ***wealth*** the riches of the

world, especially of the Indias; ***alchemy*** here it means dross, the valueless or base matter which alchemists sought to transform into gold. Note how lines 23–4 ironically invert not only the relationship between the ideal (alchemical, symbolic) and the real – the ideal is seen as the real and the real as fraudulent imitation – but also the value of the poet's own alchemical image: their tone is thus very much tongue-in-cheek.

[25–6] **Thou, sun . . . contracted thus**
happy fortunate in possessing riches; ***half as happy*** only half as fortunate, (a) because possessing less riches than the poet and his mistress; and (b) because the world has been ***contracted*** – i.e. its duties have been considerably lightened, since the world has been 'made smaller or shrunk': the poet and his mistress *are* the world.

[27] **Thine age asks ease**
i.e. because the sun is 'old', it is appropriate that it should not have to work so hard, that it should enjoy more 'ease' (rest) – note the tongue-in-cheek condescension and impertinence.

[30] **This bed . . . thy sphere**
centre (a) centre of attention; (b) centre of the sun; ***sphere*** (a) sphere of activity; (b) circumference. This final line underlines the alchemical imagery – the poet's bedroom has become the sun; the bed is its centre: the sun, chided at the outset for intruding into the room, has become the room, in alchemy, Sol (i.e. sun) was a virtue whose function it was to promote the union of opposites (i.e. of Rex and Regina).

5 / *The Canonisation*

For God's sake! Hold your tongue, and let me love!
Or chide my palsy, or my gout;
My five grey hairs, or ruined fortune, flout!
With wealth your state, your mind with arts improve;
Take you a course, get you a place;
Observe his Honour or his Grace,
Or the King's real, or his stamped face
Contemplate – what you will, approve,
So you will let me love.

Alas, alas! Who's injured by my love?
What merchant's ships have my sighs drowned?
Who says my tears have overflowed his ground?
When did my colds a forward spring remove?
When did the heats which my veins fill
Add one more to the plaguy bill?
Soldiers find wars, and lawyers find out still
Litigious men which quarrels move,
Though she and I do love.

Call us what you will, we are made such by love.
  Call her one, me another fly.
We're tapers too, and at our own cost die,
And we in us find the eagle and the dove.
  The phoenix riddle hath more wit
  By us: we two, being one, are it.
So to one neutral thing both sexes fit.
  We die and rise the same, and prove
    Mysterious by this love.

We can die by it, if not live by love.
  And if unfit for tombs and hearse
Our legend be, it will be fit for verse!
And if no piece of chronicle we prove,
  We'll build in sonnets pretty rooms.
  As well a well-wrought urn becomes
The greatest ashes as half-acre tombs.
  And by these hymns, all shall approve
    Us canonised for love

And thus invoke us: 'You whom reverend love
  Made one another's hermitage;
You to whom love was peace, that now is rage;
Who did the whole world's soul contract, and drove
  Into the glasses of your eyes
  (So made such mirrors and such spies
That they did all to you epitomise)
  Countries, towns, courts – beg from above
    A pattern of your love!'

This dramatic monologue is one of Donne's most amusing works, drawing on analogies ranging from mythical animals to Roman Catholic religious practices. The poet's increasingly hyperbolic defence of his relationship with his new mistress ironically suggests that the unnamed friend had good reason to be concerned about the interest the poet was taking in her.

It is in five stanzas, each of nine iambic lines rhyming *A b b a / c c c / a A*: the first, third, fourth and seventh lines in each stanza are pentameters; the remainder are tetrameters, except for the last line, which is a trimeter.

In the first stanza, the poet impatiently interrupts some unnamed addressee who has been criticising his behaviour, requesting him to speak on any other subject except his love; in the second, he reflects that no one is injured by his love; in the third and fourth stanzas, he meditates on the nature of their love; and in the last stanza, having arrived at a hyperbolic conclusion, he imagines other lovers seeking to model themselves on their love.

[1] **Hold your tongue**
stop your idle chatter: a phrase which becomes increasingly ironic as the poem unfolds, for it is the poet who will not hold his tongue.

[2–3] **chide my palsy . . . flout**
chide scold or rebuke (the poet for . . .); ***palsy*** paralysis, especially with involuntary tremors; ***gout*** very uncomfortable swelling of the smaller joints, especially the toes; ***flout*** mock, scoff, insult or express scorn for. The sense of these lines is that whilst the poet might be criticised for other failings, he can scarcely be reproached for being in love with someone.

[4] **With wealth . . . improve**
this and the following lines indicate the nature of the friend's concerns: he is worrying about how the poet is threatening his chances of social advancement because of his relationship with his mistress. The poet's offhand peremptoriness indicates his scorn for people who are more interested in social position than in the quality of human love, and so he tells his friend: 'Find ways to increase your own wealth and social position, and to improve your own mind' – i.e. 'Let me work out my own priorities for myself'.

[5] **Take you a course**
plan a strategy to attain your objective; ***get you a place*** i.e. a place at court, the society immediately surrounding the king.

[6] **Observe . . . his Grace**
observe watch, in the sense of attend upon; ***Honour*** a lord; ***Grace*** an archbishop or duke.

[7–8] **Or . . . Contemplate**
the King's real (face) his person, at court; his ***stamped face*** the impression of the king stamped on a coin; ***Contemplate*** gaze upon, with implication of expecting a favour from the king. The word 'contemplate' belongs to the language of spiritual meditation, and thus implies that the listener's ideal is to gaze upon the king – in this sense, it is clearly ironic.

[8] **What you will, approve**
commend whatever pleases you.

[9] **So**
so long as, provided that.

[10] **Alas, alas! Who's injured by my love?**
a peevish outburst, but note the irony: the poet asks to be allowed to love his mistress neither in order to please her nor even to please himself, but because it will not harm anyone. The next five lines, which are intended to demonstrate that no one is injured by the poet's love, are parodies of some typical Petrarchan conceits (sighs, tears, colds, heats).

[11] **drowned**
i.e. by sighs as strong as tempests which have caused the ships to founder and sink.

[12] **overflowed his ground**
caused a flood on his estate – the 'his' is general and does not necessarily refer back to the merchant.

[13] **a forward spring remove**
cause a spell of warm weather ('early spring') in the late winter months, only to revert again to cold 'winter' weather.

[14] **the heats . . . the plaguy bill?**
heats passionate desires; ***plaguy*** of the Plague – a specific disease, carried by rats, which struck London periodically throughout the sixteenth and seventeenth centuries; ***bill*** the list, issued weekly during times of plague, of all those who had died in London parishes, with causes of their deaths; thus, 'add another person to the list of those who have died'.

[16–18] **Soldiers find wars . . . she and I do love**
litigious men men who are quick to take their grievances to court; thus, 'Soldiers can still go to wars, and lawyers are still free to discover men keen to take their case to court, notwithstanding the fact that she and I are in love.' Thus people interested in 'injuring' one another can still go about their business, even though he and his mistress are in love; but note the irony that soldiers are not the

cause of wars, any more than lawyers are the cause of law cases.

[19] **what you will**
whatever you like.

[20] **fly**
the image is deliberately shocking, more so to a seventeenth-century audience, for whom flies were associated with copulation and shortness of life.

[21] **tapers . . . own cost die**
tapers small, slender candles, such as one might have beside a bed; a lighted candle is self-consuming; ***die*** (a) die down, like a candle which has been burned out; (b) experience sexual orgasm, which was believed to reduce life expectancy.

[22] **And we . . . the eagle and the dove**
'Each of us sees in the other both the eagle and the dove' – the eagle, associated with Zeus, king of the gods, is a symbol of the power of male love; the dove, associated with Aphrodite (Venus), goddess of love, is a symbol of the power of female love.

[23] **The phoenix . . . are it**
phoenix riddle hath more wit 'The riddle of the phoenix, which was said to die in flames and be born again from its own ashes, is finally explained by our love, for we two are one [as explained in the previous line], and so sexless' (hence 'it').

[25] **So to one neutral thing both sexes fit**
'In the same way, we who were male and female have become one single hermaphroditic being.'

[26] **We die and rise the same**
die as in line 21; ***rise*** (a) wake and get up, as if from a bed; (b) ascend, mount upwards as if from our grave, resurrect.

[26–7] **and prove . . . by this love**
prove demonstrate that we are; ***Mysterious*** (a) beyond ordinary comprehension, like the mysteries of religion; (b) initiates into a secret religious sect such as the 'mystery religions' of classical Antiquity (e.g. the rites celebrating the grain goddess Demeter and her daughter, Kore, which were practised at Eleusis in Greece from about 1000 BC to about the fourth century AD, often called the Eleusinian Mysteries).

[29] **unfit . . . legend be**
Many seventeenth-century tombs had a panel bearing a 'legend' (i.e. motto), very often in verse, celebrating the dead person's primary qualities – here the poet admits that although their legend is verse, it may not be appropriate for a tomb; ***hearse*** a wooden structure placed over the coffin of a nobleman during a funeral service, usually decorated with tapers, and often having epitaphs pinned to it.

[31] **And if no piece of chronicle we prove**
'And even if our story is not of sufficient interest as the subject of a long history.'

[32] **We'll build in sonnets pretty rooms**
involves a pun on the Italian word *stanza*, which means both 'room' (i.e. bedroom) and 'sonnet' (little sounds): thus, the poet and his mistress, in their bedroom, will construct fine verses out of their amorous sighs.

[33–4] **As well . . . as half-acre tombs**
'The ashes of even the greatest men are as fittingly contained in a well-wrought urn as in a monumental tomb.'

[35] **these hymns**
(a) their own sonnets – i.e. their death has canonised them, and their sonnets (love songs) have now become hymns (sacred songs); (b) the hymns of all who invoke them (i.e. by repeating the poet's work: his poems/his lovemaking).

[35–6] **approve . . . for love**
approve sanction, confirm; ***canonise*** to admit formally to a list of saints, regard as a saint.

[37] **You**
the lovers; ***reverend*** sacred: cf. 'The Sun Rising', line 11 and note.

[38] **hermitage**
(a) a hermit's abode or monastery;

(b) solitary retreat (with implications of being a place of quiet communion with God, away from the profane 'rage' of the world).

[39] **rage**
not 'anger', but a state of unrest, inability to find peace.

[40] **did . . . contract**
(a) reduced; (b) epitomised.

[40–1] **drove . . . your eyes**
drove (a) urged, usually by force or threat; (b) chased or frightened (e.g. animals or enemy troops) from a large area into a small area in order to kill or capture: the direct object of the verb is 'Countries, towns, courts' (line 44); *glasses* the pupils of the eyes, in which the countries, towns and courts are reflected in miniature (cf. 'The Good-Morrow', stanzas 2 and 3): note how, after the preposterous circling of the argument, the poem returns the reader to the subject of the first stanza, but from a very different point of view!

[42–3] **(So made . . . epitomise)**
epitomise condense; thus, 'Thereby making your eyes both mirrors (that see the world in miniature) and spies (that report on the triviality of the world).'

[44] **beg**
the implicit subject of 'beg' is still 'all' from line 35; but it is also the Countries/towns/courts; *above* heaven, where the poet and his mistress are because they are saints.

[45] **pattern**
ideal example on which everyone should model themselves.

6 / *A Valediction: Forbidding Mourning*

As virtuous men pass mildly 'way
  And whisper to their souls to go,
Whilst some of their sad friends do say
  'The breath goes now' and some say 'no',

So let us melt, and make no noise,
  No tear-floods nor sigh-tempests move:
'Twere profanation of our joys
  To tell the laity our love.

Moving o' th'earth brings harms and fears:
  Men reckon what it did and meant.
But trepidation of the spheres,
  Though greater far, is innocent.

Dull sublunary lovers' love
  (Whose soul is sense) cannot admit
Absence, because it doth remove
Those things which elemented it.

But we, by a love so much refined
  That ourselves know not what it is,
Inter-assurèd of the mind,
  Care less eyes, lips, and hands to miss.

Our two souls, therefore, which are one,
  Though I must go, endure not yet
A breach, but an expansion,
  Like gold to airy thinness beat.

If they be two, they are two so
  As stiff twin compasses are two:
Thy soul, the fixed foot, makes no show
  To move, but doth, if th'other do.

And though it in the centre sit,
  Yet when the other far doth roam,
It leans and hearkens after it
  And grows erect as it comes home.

Such wilt thou be to me who must,
  Like th'other foot, obliquely run:
Thy firmness makes my circle just,
And makes me end where I begun.

A valedictory poem in nine stanzas, each of four iambic tetrameters, rhyming *a b a b*. According to Izaak Walton, Donne wrote it for his wife before going to France in 1611.

The poem is remarkable for the way in which it moves from one conceit to another – for example, from the opening, in which the parting of two lovers is likened to the soul of a good man leaving him at the moment of death, to likening the effects produced by their parting not to the upheaval caused by an earthquake – which would, of course, be felt by ordinary lovers – but rather to innocuous cosmic agitations which only they are sufficiently sensitive to feel. The poem is most famous for the image of the compass in the last three stanzas.

The argument is extremely complex. In the first two stanzas, the poet likens the act of parting to something as difficult to perceive as the exact moment of death; in stanzas four and five, he contrasts their love with that of those who require sensual contact; in the final three stanzas, there appears the celebrated but faulty image of the compass.

Title
A valediction is a poem about leave-taking (from Latin *vale* = farewell; *dicere* = to say). Izaak Walton (1593–1683) was a friend of both Donne and Henry King. He is best

known today for *The Compleat Angler* (1653/5), a rambling meditation on the pleasures of fishing. His biography of Donne was published in 1640.

[1] **As virtuous . . . away**
note that the entire first stanza consists of an analogy: ***As*** in the same way as.

[4] **and some say 'no'**
'no, not yet': the point being that it is impossible to say exactly when a good man dies, so gently does he make the transition *from* life *to* death (which for a good man is eternal life); i.e. death – and, by extension, also 'parting' – is being envisaged as something *positive*.

[5] **So let us melt**
the second stanza describes the application of the analogy; ***melt*** is ambivalent, as it can mean either (a) separate or (b) dissolve, i.e. become one – the poet is urging that he and his mistress part/become one with equally little 'noise'.

[6] **No tear-floods, nor sigh-tempests move**
'And not give way either to floods of tears or to sobbing or sighing.'

[7–8] **'Twere profanation . . . our love**
profanation an abuse of something sacred (i.e. of their love); ***laity*** the people of a religious faith in contrast to its clergy – thus, 'It would desecrate our love to allow those outside its sacred joys to know of it.'

[9–16]
The third and fourth stanzas offer further analogies.

[9] **Moving o' th'earth brings**
An earthquake causes; ***harms*** physical damage or hurt.

[10] **reckon**
consider (it ominous).

[11–12] **But trepidation . . . innocent**
trepidation (a) tremulous agitation; (b) oscillation (with specific reference to the function of the 'sphere' hypothesised by the Arab astronomer Thabet hen Korrah [*c*.950] in order to account for the oscillation caused by the rotary shift of the world's axis – i.e. a sphere that did not exist in the planetary system devised by Ptolemy in the second century AD); ***spheres*** (a) planetary spheres; the stanza is drawing a distinction between earthquakes which, though they cause great harm, pale into insignificance in astronomical terms, and the movement of heavenly bodies, which, though of much greater import, causes no harm; ***innocent*** (a) cannot cause any hurt (see 'The Flea', line 20 and note); (b) free from moral guilt (because it cannot cause suffering) – thus, 'Although the tremulous movement of the spheres is on an infinitely greater scale than a mere earthquake, it is harmless' (i.e. it cannot disturb the love between the poet and his mistress).

[13] **Dull sublunary lovers' love**
sublunary beneath the moon; inferior, subject to change. The moon was synonymous with 'change', because of both its ever-changing phases and its effect on tides – thus, 'The love of dull and changeable lovers'.

[14] **(Whose soul is sense) cannot admit**
sense sensual (i.e. 'Whose soul is sense' is a paradox); ***admit*** bear, stand; thus, 'Those whose innermost essence is dependent on outer (sensual) stimulation cannot bear to be parted from one another.'

[15–16] **Absence . . . elemented it**
absence note the pun on sense; ***Those things*** sensual contact; ***elemented it*** made it possible, in the sense of the different kinds of sensual contact (seeing, touch, etc.) which combine in 'dull sublunary love'. Note how the dull sublunary lovers are being compared with 'earthquakes', which make a great deal of noise, cause a great deal of fear and harm, but are, in cosmic terms, of little import; in contrast, the poet implies, he and his mistress should model themselves on the movement of heavenly bodies, which brings no suffering to human beings.

[17–24]
stanzas five and six are concerned with a further application.
[17] **refined**
the word implies refining either by fire or by a chemical (or alchemical) process.
[18] **ourselves**
i.e. we ourselves (do not know).
[19] **Inter-assurèd**
mutally confident in the fidelity of one another's mind, with possible connotations of being bound by legal contract.
[20] **Care less... miss**
'do not care if we miss the sensual contact provided by eyes, lips, and hands (because we are tied by much deeper love)'.
[21] **which are one**
as borne out by the previous argument, especially lines 5 and 17–18.
[22–3] **Though I must go, endure not yet/A breach**
note how the poet has delayed saying that he is responsible for the parting until the sixth stanza; ***must*** (a) because of some worldly commitment (see introductory note); (b) because ordained by the heavenly bodies referred to in stanza three. What is its value here?; ***endure not yet*** none the less, do not suffer; ***breach*** parting, separation.
[23] **expansion**
Their love is not altered in essence by their parting, but only in extension (i.e. the geographical distance between them).
[24] **Like gold to airy thinness beat**
gold can be beaten into extremely thin 'leaf' – one ounce of gold will make approximately 250 square feet of gold leaf (that is: 25 × 10 feet); ***beat*** probably rhymes with 'yet'. Note also that the chemical symbol for gold is a circle with a dot in the centre; this may be a deliberate anticipation of the compass image in line 26.
[25] **so**
in the same way.
[26] **stiff twin compasses**
This celebrated image does not originate with Donne – it is found, for example, and used almost identically, in one of the madrigals of Giovanni Batista Guarini (1537–1612) some of whose works were known in England in the early seventeenth century (see Guarini, *Rime*, XCVI, Venice, 1598).
[27–8] **Thy soul... To move**
note how the two legs of the compass are likened not to bodies, but to *souls*; thus, 'Although thy soul does not appear to move'.
[29] **it**
the fixed foot.
[30] **when the other far doth roam**
when as long as, all the time that; ***other*** the moving leg of the compass (i.e. the poet's soul, which is about to roam far on his travels).
[31] **It leans and hearkens after it**
this line is confusing. The first ***It*** is the fixed foot (representing the mistress); ***hearkens*** listens attentively, in the sense of inwardly following the poet as he travels; the second ***it*** is the moving foot, referring back to 'it' in line 29.
[32] **And grows erect as it comes home**
erect seems to refer to the 'fixed foot' of the compass, and thus the mistress; if so, it is in the sense of 'look up proudly at the returning poet'. It has always been assumed that there is a sexual pun on 'erect', but this fits clumsily into the syntax of all known versions. It is, of course, possible that the text is corrupt, and that lines 31–2 should read something like 'That [i.e. the moving foot] leans and hearkens after it [i.e. the fixed foot] and grows erect as it comes home', but no text justifies the emendments.
[33] **Such wilt thou be to me**
i.e. his mistress will still be the centre of his thoughts and world during his forthcoming travels.
[34] **obliquely run**
follow a curved path, not a straight line – i.e. his journeyings.
[35] **Thy firmness makes my circle just**
(a) 'Your fidelity makes my circle

perfect'; (b) 'Your fidelity makes it possible for me to justify my journey': – i.e. he feels free to travel only because he knows his mistress is faithful.

[36] **And makes me end where I begun** refers to the completion by a compass of a circle, the circle being an age-old symbol of perfection.

7 / *Song*

Go, and catch a falling star;
   Get with child a mandrake root;
Tell me where all past years are,
   Or who cleft the Devil's foot!
Teach me to hear mermaids singing,
   Or to keep off envy's stinging,
      And find
      What wind
Serves to advance an honest mind.

If thou be'st borne to strange sights,
   Things invisible to see,
Ride ten thousand days and nights,
   Till age snow white hairs on thee.
Thou, when thou return'st, wilt tell me
   All strange wonders that befell thee,
      And swear
      Nowhere
Lives a woman true and fair.

If thou find'st one, let me know:
   Such a pilgrimage were sweet!
Yet do not – I would not go,
   Though at next door we might meet.
Though she were true when you met her,
   And last till you write your letter,
      Yet she
      Will be
False, ere I come, to two or three!

The basic device of an impossible task is Petrarchan; it was usually employed to underline the impossibility of measuring the poet's love for his mistress. Donne's 'Song' parodies this tradition: note how the poem's subject is revealed only at the end of the second stanza.

The poem is in three nine-line stanzas, rhyming *a b a b / c c d d d*. The first four lines are heptasyllabic (an amphimacer followed by two iambs); lines five and six are trochaic tetrameters, and these are followed by two iambic monometers and an irregular iambic tetrameter. It may have been written to an already familiar 'air' or tune; it was certainly set to music in Donne's time.

[1] **falling star**
a meteor or mass of matter from outer space which has been ignited on entering the earth's atmosphere – clearly, impossible to catch.

[2] **get with child**
make pregnant; ***mandrake root*** a mandrake is a plant with purple or white flowers and yellow fruit, found in the Mediterranean; a considerable mythology surrounded it in the seventeenth century. Its forked root was thought to resemble a human being, and the shrieks which it was said to let out when plucked were reputed to kill all who heard them – hence a further joke on the impossibility of making it pregnant.

[3] **past years**
the impossibility of recovering 'times past' was a favourite conceit in late medieval and Renaissance poetry. The most famous examples are Sonnet 299 by the Italian poet Francesco Petrarca (Petrarch, 1304–74) and the 'Ballade des Dames du Temps Jadis' by the French poet François Villon (1431–89).

[4] **cleft**
The Devil's foot was said to be cloven like a goat's.

[5] **mermaids singing**
Whereas the first four lines refer to tasks which have no function other than to emphasise impossibility, this line and the next refer to different kinds of desires that the poet might have, were they not equally impossible; thus, no matter how delightful it would be to hear mermaids singing, one can't.

[6] **to keep off envy's stinging**
to be untroubled by envious thoughts.

[7–9] **wind**
pronounced to rhyme with find and mind. The wind may be taken literally ('which wind mades one honest?') or metaphorically; ***advance*** (a) to promote; (b) to bring about; the sense of the lines is therefore ambiguous: (a) 'find out if there is any way of making someone more honest' (i.e. they already are honest); (b) 'find out if there is any way of making someone honest' (i.e. someone who was not previously honest).

[10] **be'st borne to**
(a) are used to; (b) have an inclination to (see).

[13] **age**
old age; ***snow*** a verb, in the sense of 'to scatter like snow'.

[14] **wilt**
will be able to.

[15] **strange wonders**
the extraordinary events; ***befell*** happened to.

[16–18] **true and fair**
the implication is that faithful women are never beautiful, and beautiful women are never faithful – the joke being that if beauty is defined by the lust it occasions (if it does not arouse desire, it is not beauty), then it must surrender to the lust it arouses in order to be certain of itself (note that the last line of the stanza is only heptasyllabic).

[19–20] **If thou . . . sweet**
For a moment the poet entertains the possibility that 'a woman true and fair' could exist, and imagines visiting her as a pilgrimage – in other words, such a woman is an ideal equivalent to the Virgin Mary; ***sweet*** in the sense

that such a pilgrimage would be highly agreeable.

[21] **Yet do not**
On second thoughts, there is no need to tell me you have met such a woman.

[22] **Though . . . meet**
even if she lived as close as in the next house to mine.

[24] **last**
remain true (faithful) until the friend writes a letter telling the poet about her.

[27] **False, ere I come**
the poet assumes that even such a woman would betray him (i.e. sleep with two or three men) before he had time to make his pilgrimage: remember that he is hypothesising that she lives next door to him!

8/ *The Relic*

When my grave's broke up again
Some second guest to entertain
(For graves have learned that woman-head,
To be to more than one a bed),
And he that digs it spies
A bracelet of bright hair about the bone,
Will he not let's alone
And think that there a loving couple lies,
Who hoped that this device might be some way
To make their souls, at the last busy day,
Meet at this grave, and make a little stay?

If this fall in a time or land
Where mis-devotion doth command,
Then he that digs us up will bring
Us to the Bishop, and the King,
To make us relics; then
Thou shalt be a Mary Magdalen, and I
A something else thereby –
All women shall adore us, and some men.
And, since at such time, miracles are sought,
I would have that age by this paper taught
What miracles we harmless lovers wrought.

First, we loved well and faithfully,
Yet knew not what we loved, nor why:
Difference of sex we never knew,

Than our guardian angels do;
Coming and going, we
Perchance might kiss, but not betwixt those meals;
Our hands ne'er touched the seals
Which nature, injured by late laws, sets free.
These miracles we did; but now, alas,
All measure, and all language, I should pass,
Should I tell what a miracle she was.

A poem in three stanzas, each of eleven lines in iambic tetrameters, trimeters and pentameters, rhyming *a a b b / c d d c / e e e*. It may be read as a continuation of another poem, 'The Funeral', in which the poet asks whoever has charge of his burial to take care to bury him with the 'wreath of hair' which he wears tied around his arm, as he is a martyr to his love. But 'The Relic' is both more intense and more interesting, and can be fully enjoyed on its own.

The poet is imagining a time, several years after his death, when someone comes to break up his grave and notices the ringlet of fair hair around one of his bones. In the first stanza, he asks that his bones be not disturbed; in the second, reflecting that this might happen at a time when the country has reverted to Catholicism, he imagines his bones being venerated as relics; in the third, he outlines the special nature of the love that existed between him and his mistress which would justify them being considered as relics.

[1] **grave's**
grave is; ***broke up again*** in urban communities it was sometimes necessary to dig a grave up after a set number of years and send the bones to a charnel house (a building or room where bones were stored) in order to make space for the recently deceased.

[2] **guest**
note the choice of word, implying that Death is a host – a commonplace.

[3–4] **(For graves have learned... one a bed)**
This gratuitous gibe at women seems almost out of place in this poem, which provides a strong reason for considering it as a sequel to 'The Funeral', for it is more in keeping with the tone of that poem. One could also, of course, see it as anticipating the reference to Mary Magdalene (see note to line 17); ***that womanhead*** like women, the neologism being a pun on 'maidenhead' (virginity); ***to be to more*** to be always more.

[5] **he that digs it spies**
he a gravedigger, a typical medieval and Renaissance character employed in poems and drama to reflect upon life (cf. *Hamlet*, V. i); ***spies*** sees.

[6] **bracelet of bright hair**
bright fair, or even golden, as in Renaissance paintings of Mary Magdalene – i.e. a token of his mistress's hair, worn in memory of his love for her (as he had asked in 'The Funeral').

[7] **let's alone**
let leave, so 'leave us alone': although it is elided, the 'us' is important, as it assumes the identity of the poet and his one-time mistress (cf. line 15 below).

[9] **device**
the wreath of hair.

[10] **the last busy day**
the Resurrection, when souls will have to find and rejoin their bodies, and all the separated parts thereof (cf. 'Holy Sonnet 4', p. 70).

[11] **Meet at . . . a little stay**
Because they are bound one to another in this way, the souls of the poet and his one-time mistress will have to meet 'at this grave' at the Resurrection, when they will be able to enjoy one another's company one last time.

[12–13] **If this fall . . . doth command**
mis-devotion refers to Roman Catholic belief in (a) the veneration of saints who could work miracles; and (b) relics – thus, 'If this should happen at a time or in a country in which Roman Catholicism is the dominant religion'. In one of his longer poems, 'The Second Anniversary', Donne describes the worship of saints as 'mis-devotion', since prayers, in his view, should be addressed directly to God.

[15] **the Bishop, and the King**
It was sufficient for relics to be approved as genuine by a bishop, but a king's open veneration would invest them with even higher authority.

[16] **relics**
objects esteemed or venerated because of their association with a saint or martyr; the use of relics was abandoned by the Church of England.

[17] **Mary Magdalen**(e)
She was cured of demonic possession by Jesus (Luke 8: 2), who had a special affection for her (John 11: 5; 12: 3); she is often identified with the repentant 'sinner' (i.e. prostitute) who anointed Jesus's feet with ointment (Luke 7: 37).

[18] **A something else thereby**
(a) anything you like to imagine; (b) some other relic; (c) one of Mary Magdalene's lovers, before her repentance; (d) a Jesus Christ (note the metrical parallel) – this last sense is clearly intended, and is deliberately shocking. For this reason it is important to note that Donne suggests this could happen only in an age of mis-devotion or false idolatry; ***thereby*** by association. The association of Christ and Mary Magdalene as lovers is not original to Donne, but would have been no less provocative for that.

[19] **All women . . . some men**
Roman Catholicism allowed the veneration of relics, but not their adoration; the verb deliberately exaggerates. Note the suggestion that all women are gullible, whereas only some men are.

[20] **at such time . . . are sought**
at such time in the event of the remains of the poet and his mistress's hair being taken to a bishop and considered relics; ***miracles*** according to St Thomas Aquinas, God 'honours relics by working miracles in their presence' (*Summa Theologica*, III, 9.25.6), and a miracle would have been particularly eagerly awaited at the moment of consecration.

[21] **that age by this paper taught**
that age the time when the poet's grave is opened up; ***this paper*** this poem.

[22] **harmless lovers wrought**
harmless (a) free from guilt; (b) did no one any harm (cf. 'The Canonisation', stanza 2); ***wrought*** (a) produced as a result of artistry or effort; (b) produced as a result of our excitement.

[24] **what**
what (we loved) in each other.

[25–6] **Difference of sex . . . angels do**
Angels were said to be sexless; the line thus clearly glorifies Platonic love.

[27] **coming and going**
meeting and parting.

[28] **Perchance . . . those meals**
Perchance might kiss might possibly kiss; ***meals*** the love-feast [*agape*] of the early Christians (cf. Herbert, 'Love [3]', p. 240); thus, their kisses on meeting and parting, sanctioned by the Bible (e.g. 1 Corinthians 16: 20), are described as 'meals' (i.e. as entirely satisfying), for which reason they sought no other or greater pleasure between each such kiss.

[29] **ne'er touched the seals**
ne'er never; ***seals*** metaphorical seals preventing access to their sexual organs.

[30] **Which nature . . . sets free**
injured injuriously affected, impaired,

or marred; ***late law*** (a) the rule of law, which replaced the state of nature; (b) perhaps also a reference to the seventh of the Ten Commandments ('You shall not commit adultery': Exodus 20: 14), implying that the poet's mistress was a married woman. The opposition of nature and a restraining law seems to be modelled on Arthur Golding's 1567 translation of the story of Myrrha, who justifies her incestuous love for her father in these words: 'In happy case they are/That may do so without offence; but man's malicious care/Hath made a bridle for itself, and spiteful laws restrain/The things that nature setteth free' (*Metamorphoses*, 10. 329 ff.).

[31] **miracles**
the 'miracles' (note the plural!) being that they did not consummate their love, in spite of repeated opportunity to do so – this was not, of course, the kind of miracle referred to in line 20.

[32–3] **All measure . . . she was**
the poet would be exceeding all bounds, and even the resources of language, if he were to describe what a miracle his mistress was! The joke is that he could have been sure of this only had he seen her naked (cf. 'Elegy 19'), thereby casting doubt on what he has been saying.

9/ *The Apparition*

When, by thy scorn, O murdress, I am dead,
   And that thou thinkst thee free
From all solicitatíon from me,
Then shall my ghost come to thy bed
And thee, fained vestal, in worse arms shall see.
Then thy sick taper will begin to wink,
And he, whose thou art then, being tired before,
Will, if thou stir or pinch to wake him, think
         Thou call'st for more,
And in false sleep will from thee shrink.
And then, poor aspen wretch, neglected thou
Bathed in a cold, quicksílver sweat wilt lie,
      A verier ghost than I.
What I will say, I will not tell thee now,
Lest that preserve thee – and since my love is spent,
I had rather thou shouldst painfully repent
Than, by my threat'nings, rest still innocent.

This poem draws upon at least three Petrarchan conventions: the poet imagining that his unrequited love will result in his death; the punishment of a mistress for her obduracy; and the rejected lover's desire for revenge. But Donne brings them together in such a way that one does not know whether to be more impressed by the sharp tone or the even sharper wit.

A single-stanza poem of seventeen lines, in iambic tetrameters, varied with trimeters and one dimeter, rhyming *a b b a b / c d c d c / e f f e / g g g*. The poet imagines that he has died as a result of being spurned by his mistress, and that his ghost has returned to visit her as she lies in her new lover's arms, in order to punish her for abandoning him.

[1] **by thy scorn**
as a result of the poet being spurned (by his mistress).

[2–3] **thou thinkst . . . from me**
free no longer subject to something, usually something unpleasant; ***solicitation*** (six syllables) urgent or pestering entreaties; thus, 'you think that you no longer have to put up with my demands'.

[5] **fained vestal . . . worse arms**
fained (a) willing, eager, but also a pun on (b) 'feigned' pretended, fraudulent (perhaps because she has pleaded her virginity as an excuse for not loving him); ***vestal*** originally, a virgin consecrated to Vesta, the Roman goddess of the hearth, whose duty was to tend the sacred fire which burned on her altar, never allowing it to go out; hence, any chaste woman – ***a fained vestal*** is thus a paradox, as a vestal should not be 'eager' (i.e. for sex); ***worse arms*** the arms of her new lover, 'worse' in the sense of not as loving as the poet's.

[6] **sick taper . . . wink**
taper a small candle used as a bedside light; also a frequent symbol of the soul – it is ***sick*** (a) because it 'winks' (i.e. burns badly) in the presence of a ghost; (b) because the woman's soul is sick – first with yearning for her true lover, the poet; and second because it is now engaged to an inferior man (the mistress's new lover).

[7] **whose thou art then, being tired before**
note how the phrase reduces the ex-mistress to an object, and assumes that she has already taken a new lover; ***being tired before*** exhausted quickly, because he has briefly made love to her.

[8] **stir**
try to rouse (her new lover).

[10] **false sleep . . . shrink**
note how the adjective takes up the pun from line 5; thus, 'your new lover will shrink away from what he thinks are your requests for more love-making, pretending to be asleep' – the implication is, of course, that the poet would not have been so easily exhausted, nor so reluctant to engage in further lovemaking.

[11] **aspen wretch, neglected thou**
aspen (literally) a kind of poplar, a tree whose leaves flutter in the lightest breeze; here 'pale and trembling'; ***wretch*** a base or despicable person; ***neglected thou*** neglected now in your turn – just as she neglected the poet.

[12] **a cold quicksilver sweat**
quicksilver mercury; thus, 'she will lie in such fear (of the poet's ghost) that she will produce large drops of mercury-like sweat' – mercury was best known as a cure for syphilis.

[13] **a verier ghost**
even more like a ghost than the poet; more dead than alive.

[15] **Lest that preserve thee . . . spent**
that by telling you what I shall say; thus, 'to prevent you being able to defend yourself against the ghost and what it shall say by being fore-warned'; ***spent*** exhausted – i.e. the poet no longer loves her.

[16–17] **I had rather . . . still innocent**
the poet would prefer his ex-mistress to continue her affair with her new lover and so suffer the painful repentance he wants from her rather than, by heeding his threats, casting her new lover aside and so becoming once more as innocent as a virgin.

10 / *To Sir Henry Wotton*

Sir! More than kisses, letters mingle souls,
For thus friends absent speak. This ease controls
The tediousness of my life. But for these
I could ideate nothing which could please,
But I should wither in one day, and pass
To a bottle of hay, that am a lock of grass.
Life is a voyage, and in our life's ways
Countries, courts, towns are rocks or remoras:
They break or stop all ships – yet our state's such
That though than pitch they stain worse, we must touch.
If in the furnace of the even line
Or under th'adverse icy poles thou pine,
Thou know'st two temperate regions girded in:
Dwell there. But O, what refuge canst thou win
Parched in the court, and in the country frozen?
Shall cities, built of both extremes, be chosen?
Can dung, or garlic, be a perfume? or can
A scorpion, or torpedo, cure a man?
Cities are worst of all three – of all three
(O knotty riddle!) each is worst equally!
Cities are sepulchres: they who dwell there
Are carcasses, as if none such they were.
And courts are theatres, where some men play
Princes, some slaves, all to one end, and of one clay.
The country is a desert, where no good
Gained (as habits, not born) is understood.
There men become beasts, and prone to more evils:
In cities blocks, and in a lewd court devils.
As in the first chaos, confusedly,
Each element's qualities were in th'other three.
So pride, lust, covetise, being several
To these three places, yet all are in all,
And mingled thus, their issue's incestuous.
Falsehood is denizened. Virtue is barbarous.
Let no man say then, 'Virtue's flinty wall
Shall block vice in me, I'll do none, but know all.'
Men are sponges, which to pour out, receive;

Who know false play, rather than lose, deceive.
For in best understanding sin began:
Angels sinned first, then devils, and then man.
Only perchance beasts sin not – wretched we
Are beasts in all but white integrity.
I think if men which in these places live
Durst look for themselves, and themselves retrieve,
They would like strangers greet themselves, seeing then
Utopian youth grown old Italian.
  Be then thine own home, and in thyself dwell;
Inn anywhere, continuance maketh hell.
And seeing the snail, which everywhere doth roam,
Carrying his own house still, still is at home,
Follow – for he is easy-paced – this snail:
Be thine own palace, or the world's thy gaol.
And in the world's sea, do not like cork sleep
Upon the water's face, nor in the deep
Sink like a lead without a line – but, as
Fishes glide, leaving no print where they pass,
Nor making sound, so closely thy course go,
Let men dispute whether thou breathe or no.
Only in this one thing, be no Galenist. To make
Court's hot ambitions wholesome, do not take
A dram of country's dullness; do not add
Correctives, but, as chemics, purge the bad.
  But, Sir, I advise not you, I rather do
Say o'er those lessons which I learned of you,
Whom, free from German schisms, and lightness
Of France, and fair Italy's faithlessness,
Having from these sucked all they had of worth
And brought home that *faith* which you carried forth,
I throughly love. But if myself I've won
To know my rules, I have, and you have,

Donne.

The Renaissance tradition of verse epistles began with Petrarch and flourished throughout the period. Donne wrote some forty such epistles, most of which were collected under the subtitle 'Letters to Several Personages [= various people]'. This epistle was written about 1597–8, when both Donne and Wotton were looking for appointments at the court of Elizabeth I. Grierson (1912/1971) has argued that it was written as part of a literary debate among friends of the

Earl of Essex on the subject of 'Which kind of life is best, that at Court, that in the City, or that in the Country?'.

It consists of seventy iambic lines rhyming in couplets. Lines 1–6 provide an amusingly deferential introduction; lines 7–46 outline Donne's equal abhorrence of country, court, and town life; lines 47–62 offer the addressee advice on how to live; and lines 62–70 serve as an ambivalent complimentary conclusion.

Henry Wotton (1568–1639) studied at New College Oxford, where he and Donne, who was four years younger, met and became friends. Between 1589 and 1594 he travelled widely on the Continent. He then went on to study law at the Middle Temple; he became secretary to the Earl of Essex, whom he accompanied, along with Donne, on expeditions to Cadiz (1596) and the Azores (1597). He was knighted in 1603; the following year he was appointed Ambassador to Venice. He became Provost at Eton (1624–39) and published *Elements of Architecture* (1624); his poems were published posthumously as *Reliquiae Wottonianae* (1651), which includes at least two works of a high quality: 'Character of a Happy Life' and 'On His Mistress, the Queen of Bohemia'. Izaak Walton wrote a 'Life' of him (1670), in which there is a witty definition: 'An ambassador is an honest man, sent to lie abroad for the good of his country'.

The debate in which Wotton and Donne took part was provoked by two epigrams from *The Greek Anthology*, paraphrased by Nicholas Grimald in *Tottel's Miscellany* (1557), and again in Puttenham's *Art of English Poesy* (1589). It was a popular subject in the Renaissance: Shakespeare refers to it in *As You Like It*; cf. also Donne's 'Canonisation', line 44. A copy of Bacon's contribution to the debate was found among Wotton's papers – it begins 'The world's a bubble', a very neat encapsulation of one of the epigrams.

The verse epistle is an essentially *literary* genre. Although at least some of the views that Donne advances in this epistle also appear in other works of his, they should not be questioned too closely for their sincerity. The aim is to reformulate the commonplaces of a debate so as to startle the reader into admiration. It may be interesting to compare this poem with Polonius's advice to Laertes (*Hamlet*, I, iii, 55–81).

[1–2] **kisses**
the normal way in which early followers of Christ would greet one another: cf. 'Greet one another with a holy kiss of peace' (1 Corinthians 16: 20); thus, 'more than kisses' is suggestive of a mark of even greater bonding (but *not* with any sexual implications); ***letters*** cf. two remarks by Donne in his prose letters: (a) (letters) are the means 'by which we deliver over our affections and assurances of friendship, and the best faculties of our souls' (*Letters to Severall Persons of Honour*: a facsimile of 1st edn of 1651 [Delmar, NY, 1977], p. 23); (b) 'our letters are our selves and in them absent friends meet' (*ibid.*, p. 240); ***thus*** by means of letters; ***speak*** note the importance of speech for Donne; ***ease*** relief: cf. the notion of 'purging' later in the poem (line 62); ***controls*** (a) relieves, or modifies; but perhaps also, ironically, (b) limits.

[3] **tediousness of my life**
(a) a common sentiment whose literary expression culminated in Burton's *Anatomy of Melancholy* (1621); (b) also a reference to a popular subgenre of poetry; the *taedium vitae* – e.g. Shakespeare's 'Tired with all these, for restful death I cry' (Sonnet 66); ***But for these*** were it not (for the opportunity provided by writing) letters.

[4] **ideate**
to form an idea of – cf. 'that form of a state which Plato ideated' (*Pseudo-Martyr*, p. 4); ***please*** give pleasure.
[5–6] **But**
And; ***wither*** dry up – cf. 'For [those who do evil] will soon be cut down like the grass and will wither like a green herb' (Psalm 37: 2); ***pass*** become, be transformed into; ***bottle*** in the sixteenth century meant 'bundle' (cf. *A Midsummer Night's Dream*, IV, i, 30); ***lock*** a very small quantity, such as a handful, of hay or straw; implicitly, '*only* a lock of grass'; ***grass*** cf. the second Isaiah: 'all humankind is grass' (Isaiah 40: 6); also Psalm 90: 5–6; 103: 15): the lines are a witty adaptation of a biblical commonplace.
[7] **Life is a voyage**
a secular commonplace that begins with the writers of classical Greece and Rome, but was popularised by Petrarch (1304–74) and subsequent French Renaissance sonneteers (e.g. Ronsard), especially as a storm-tossed sea-voyage: cf. Spenser, *Amoretti*, 63: 'After long storms'; ***our life's ways*** the obstacles we come up against in life.
[8] **Countries, courts, towns**
i.e. as places in which to live; ***courts*** the small circles of privileged officials and friends who surround various monarchs; ***rocks*** i.e. rocks on which the individual is 'shipwrecked'; ***remoras*** sucking-fish (Latin name *Echeneis remora*); according to Pliny (*Natural History*, 9, 79) a remora, by attaching itself to a ship, was able to bring it to a standstill. The *OED* gives 1567 as the first instance of the word in English; by 1604 it had also come to mean 'an obstacle, hindrance, impediment'.
[9] **break**
i.e. break individuals upon the 'rocks', as if the individual were a ship; ***yet*** but; ***state's*** natural condition is.
[10] **though than pitch, etc.**
though they stain worse than pitch; ***pitch*** a thick and very dark brown sticky substance produced by distilling tar or turpentine, used for sealing the joints between the wooden planks of a boat or ship to make it waterproof; 'pitch' will ***stain*** anything (hands, clothes) which it 'touches' – cf. the proverb: 'He that touches pitch shall be defiled' (Ecclesiasticus 13: 1); but here ***stain*** the rocks and remoras, i.e. the obstacles which individuals inevitably ('we must touch') come up against in life; ***must touch*** cannot avoid coming up against such obstacles.
[11] **furnace**
an oven used for heating, especially metals, to very high temperatures; here, extreme climatic heat; ***even line*** the equator, because it is midway between the poles: possibly occasioned by the poet's experience in Cadiz (south-west corner of Spain) or the Azores (islands in the North Atlantic) which, though not near the equator, have a much warmer climate than England.
[12] **adverse**
(a) hostile to human life; (b) at opposite extremes of the globe: north and south; ***pine*** to waste away with longing (e.g. for a temperate climate), or sickness caused by adverse conditions.
[13] **two temperate regions**
temperate (a) moderate, having a mild climate; (b) showing moderation and self-restraint – thus the regions in both the northern and southern hemispheres which, placed between an extremely cold pole and an extremely hot equator, enjoy a temperate climate: i.e. most of Europe and, of course, England; ***girded in*** squeezed in – as if at the waist, by a tight-fitting dress.
[14] **win**
obtain as 'prize' (e.g. for official duties).
[15] **Parched**
as if the court were a desert; ***and*** or; ***country*** as if the country were an Arctic or Antarctic wasteland.
[16] **Shall cites . . . chosen**
'Would you prefer to live in cities, in which equally abhorrent extremes are encountered?'

[17] **dung**
the (strong-smelling) excrement of an animal or *human*; ***garlic*** a small bulbous plant with a very strong smell, and a strong flavour when used in cooking, i.e. for *human* consumption; but not the kind of smell one would employ in making perfume! Note how the two images reduce city life to an exotic (rather than a basic) foodstuff and its digestive end.

[18] **scorpion**
a small insect with large claws and a jointed tail that can be bent over its head to inject a poisoned sting into prey held by the claws; their sting could be fatal, and they were proverbially associated with treachery. Donne may also have been poking fun at another commonplace: 'To a man [struck by a] scorpion, ashes of scorpions burned, drunk in wine, is remedy' (cf. the theory of Galen, lines 59–62); ***torpedo*** a ray, a flat fish that gives off an electric shock if touched.

[19] **Cities**
known as unsafe places, filled with crime and vice; this means 'Cities are the worst of the three'.

[20] **knotty**
puzzling, difficult to explain; ***worst equally*** equally and extremely bad or unpleasant.

[21] **sepulchres**
tombs cut in rock or stone (i.e. houses!).

[22] **carcasses**
the bodies of dead animals; ***as if . . . they were*** (live in cities) as if they were not carcasses of exactly the same kind as those around them.

[23] **theatres**
the image of life as a 'play' was a commonplace: e.g. Jaques, 'All the world's a stage' (*As You Like It*, II, vii, 139–66).

[24] **one end**
the 'one' is ambivalent: (a) the applause of the audience; (b) their own death; ***clay*** the material out of which God formed man: cf. Job's complaint to the Lord: 'I am formed out of clay' (Job 33: 6); also 'Lord, you are our father: we are the clay, you are the potter' (Isaiah 64: 8); in Genesis, man is made out of the dust of the ground (2: 7); note that the line is an Alexandrine, as is line 59.

[25–6] **country**
i.e. anywhere away from London, even another town which had not the same entertainment to offer as the capital; ***desert*** a wilderness where nothing grows; ***no good/gained*** nothing good that is acquired by any means is ***understood*** – i.e. is apprehended for its deepest import; ***as habits, not born*** just as social habits which are, by definition, acquired and not innate – i.e. in the country, deprived of the society necessary for the acquisition of civilised habits, one cannot understand and so learn from any experience.

[27] **beasts**
a commonplace: although it was written three or four years later, Hamlet's Act IV soliloquy offers an example:

> What is a man
> If his chief good and market [use] of his time
> Be but to sleep and feed? A beast, no more.
> (*Hamlet*, IV, iv, 33–5)

[27] **more evils**
i.e. even greater evils than those committed by wild animals.

[28] **blocks**
(a) blockheads, idiots; but also (b) logs of wood, a material much used in construction at the time; ***lewd court lewd*** lascivious: the sometimes loose morals of court life have always provided a focus for gossip; ***devils*** i.e. devil-may-care rakes, whose morality was 'devilish': i.e. in cities men 'only' become blockheads/logs; at court, 'only' devils – to be a beast (i e. without speech or reason) is an even worse fate.

[29] **first chaos**
i.e. the 'formless void' out of which God created the world: see Genesis 1.

[30] **element's qualities**
essential aspects of the characteristic of each condition: i.e. city, court, and country life.
[31] **pride**
arrogance: by its position, refers back to 'cities'; ***lust*** refers to 'courts', and ***covetise*** covetousness – i.e. in the country, all one can do is 'covet' what those in town enjoy: but cf. the Tenth Commandment: 'You shall not covet your neighbour's house; [nor] his wife, nor his servant, nor his maid, nor his ox, ass, nor anything that belongs to him' (Exodus 20: 17); ***several*** distinctive features, and thus found only in one or other.
[32] **yet**
and yet (all of these vices can be found in all conditions).
[33] **mingled thus**
mixed in this way (i.e. as in a chaos); ***issue*** (a) literally, offspring or children; (b) outcome, inevitable product: note how God created a world from the original chaos; all that is produced from this 'secondary' chaos ***is incestuous*** (a) the product of sexual union between closely related partners (i.e. the sins of cities, courts, the country, are all very closely related); (b) etymologically, 'un-chaste', i.e. vicious or lewd.
[34] **Falsehood is denizened**
falsity has become a naturalised citizen – i.e. though foreign, has become a natural part of society; ***barbarous*** something pertaining to barbarians, i.e. foreigners with primitive habits – Virtue does not pertain to the three conditions described.
[35] **Virtue's flinty wall**
flinty wall the 'speaker' clearly means: a wall made out of a hard unyielding stone; but note the irony: flint chips easily, thus a flinty wall would be one from which one little chip after another will gradually fall away – i.e. a rotten wall.
[36] **block vice in me**
i. e. 'my wall of Virtue will protect me from vice': but note pun: 'lock' in me = (the rottenness of the wall) ***seals*** vice in me; ***I'll do none, but know all*** 'I'll do nothing vicious, but will only watch and experience the vice of others' – this, as the sequel makes clear, is only self-delusion.
[37] **to pour out, receive**
i.e. just as a sponge must absorb water before water can be squeezed from it, so men will first lap up a vice and then reveal it.
[38] **Who know . . . deceive**
Those who know how to play falsely, if faced by the prospect of losing, will not hesitate to cheat.
[39] **best understanding**
highest spiritual understanding possible: cf. note to line 26.
[40] **Angels sinned first . . .**
Lucifer, the brightest of angels, was the first to sin; having sinned, he fell from Paradise (along with other rebellious angels), became the Devil, and tempted man to sin: this is, of course, expounded at length in Milton's *Paradise Lost* (1667) – i.e. written some seventy years after this epistle.
[41] **perchance**
maybe, perhaps; ***wretched*** (a) pitiable, pitiful; (b) unfortunate; (c) contemptible.
[42] **in all but white integrity**
in everything except purest innocence, moral rectitude, wholeness.
[43] **these places**
i.e. cities, courts, the country.
[44] **Durst**
dared to; ***look for themselves***: i.e. their real 'self' is lost: note that some MSS. give 'in' in place of 'for', which emphasises the notion that the real self is an 'inner self'; ***retrieve*** recover possession of (themselves, their 'inner' selves).
[45] **strangers**
i.e. they would greet their real selves as if they were strangers; ***seeing then*** since, or given that.
[46] **Utopian**
idealistic: the word comes from Sir Thomas More's *Utopia* (1516), which concerns the search for the best possible form of government; ***grown*** *has* or *is* grown; ***old Italian*** i.e. devious and treacherous.

[47] **in thy self dwell**
cf. 'For as every man is a little world, so every man is his own house, and dwells in himself; and in this house, God dwells too' (*Sermons*, VI, 251).
[48] **Inn**
a verb meaning to take temporary lodgings (as opposed to living in a permanent home); an 'inn' (substantive) is a house where travellers can find accommodation for one or two nights; ***continuance*** settling permanently anywhere, or at any occupation.
[49] **the snail**
(a) a slug-like mollusc with a spiral shell into which it can withdraw at night or when endangered; (b) a symbol of self-sufficiency, because of this ability; (c) scholastic philosophy described the spiral shell as evidence of God's existence, because of its perfect spiral ascension to its true centre.
[50] **still is at home**
is always at home.
[51] **easy-paced**
snails move slowly, proverbially.
[52] **or**
or if not; ***gaol*** prison.
[53] **the world's sea**
the 'sea' that is this world; ***sleep*** lie floating and bobbing: note how the verb (a) refers forward to the following image (sea-*bed*), and (b) underlines the metaphorical application of the 'sea'.
[54] **face**
surface; but note the personification.
[55] **a lead without a line**
a lead weight used for testing the depth of water; without the rope/string attached to it that one needs to pull the weight back up to the surface in order to ascertain the depth, the lead sinks to the *bed* of the sea; ***but as*** but in the same way as.
[56] **glide**
advance with a smooth, continuous movement, e.g. like a fish through the water; ***leaving*** *neither* leaving; ***print*** (a) footprint; (b) distinguishing mark.
[57] **Nor making sound**
nor making any sound; ***closely*** i.e. keep yourself to yourself so guardedly.
[58] **dispute**
be left uncertain, argue.
[59] **Galenist**
a follower of Claudius Galen (second century AD), a doctor who held that sickness was caused by either an excess or a deficiency of one or other of the 'humours' (hot, cold, moist, dry), and that the purpose of medicine was to 'correct' the balance (compare homeopathy, founded in the eighteenth century): note that the line is an Alexandrine, causing a heavy stress on the phrase 'one thing', which anticipates the following joke.
[60] **Court's hot ambitions**
(a) feverish striving after court appointment; (b) lustfully catering to the loose morals of the women at court.
[61] **dram**
a very small amount; the word comes from 'drachm' = the scales of an apothecary (i.e. on which he would measure the medicine needed to cure a pox); ***country's dullness*** (a) having fallen from court favour, be forced into dull exile in the country; (b) having contracted the pox (i.e. syphilis, a venereal disease), be forced to go into voluntary exile: cf. Donne, 'the barbarousness and insipid dullness of the country' (*Letters*, p. 63).
[62] **Correctives**
i.e. in the manner of Galen – do not think that if you fall prey to one 'sickness', you need only apply another 'ill' (remedy) to find your cure; ***chemics*** alchemists who believed one could purify base matter until it was transformed into pure gold: especially followers of Paracelsus (1493–1541): 'chemists' who argued that just as one can purify metals, so one can 'purge' a sickness; here ***purge the bad*** avoid the bad influences you will meet at court.
[63] **But, Sir**
the conclusion to this epistle designedly departs a little from its

ostensible subject, but note the 'implicit' connection – according to Donne, Wotton has already shown himself capable of rising above the evil ways of cities and courts, thus his return to England constitutes a willingness to live in the 'country' but *after* having 'understood' and learned from the courts and cities of all Europe; ***advise*** it might have seemed presumptuous for a younger man from an inferior level of society to give advice to an older man.

[64] **Say o'er**
repeat – i.e. having formulated a series of 'precepts', Donne gives the addressee/reader credit for them; ***I learned of*** i.e. just as Wotton has learned the true 'worth' of life from his travels, so Donne has learned this *from* Wotton.

[65] **German schisms**
(a) the quarrelsome temper of Germans; (b) the Reformation: when Martin Luther (1483–1546) attracted a number of followers and split (schism) from the Catholic Church.

[65–6] **lightness of France**
either laxness of French morals, or lack of honour among Frenchmen.

[66] **Italy's faithlessness**
treachery of Italians; but might also refer to lax morals, as many young Englishmen were beginning to travel to Europe as the 'finishing school' of their education: the 'Grand Tour'. Venice was visited by most travellers, and was notorious for its courtesans (euphemism for prostitutes) – Wotton had travelled in Germany, France and Italy in 1589–94.

[67] **from these sucked**
having learned from Germany, France and Italy; ***worth*** of *real* value (compare the implicit 'real' inner self) – it was usual for young aristocrats to bring back from their travels valuable paintings, furniture, decorative arms, etc.

[68] **brought home**
(a) returned to England with; (b) more fully understood, as a result of your travels/these precepts; ***faith*** (a) Christian faith and the ability to rest 'innocently' in his faith; (b) true virtue which had successfully resisted all temptations while abroad in Europe; ***carried forth*** the faith/virtue with which he left England at the outset of his travels

[69] **throughly**
wholly, completely; ***won*** (a) convinced; (b) won back from his previously erring ways.

[70] **rules**
i.e. the precepts set out in the poem; ***I have . . . Donne*** punning on his own name: (a) ***I*** have done [i.e. finished]; (b) ***you*** have Donne [i.e. as your friend].

11/ *Holy Sonnet 4 (7)*

At the round earth's imagined corners, blow
Your trumpets, Angels! and arise, arise
From death, you numberless infinities
Of souls! And to your scattered bodies go –

All whom the flood did, and fire shall o'erthrow,
All whom war, dearth, age, agues, tyrannies,

Despair, law, chance, hath slain, and you whose eyes
Shall behold God, and never taste death's woe.

But let them sleep, Lord, and me mourn a space,
For, if above all these my sins abound,
'Tis late to ask abundance of thy grace,
When we are there. Here, on this lowly ground,

Teach me how to repent, for that's as good
As if thou'dst sealed my pardon with thy blood.

This Petrarchan sonnet in iambic pentameters, rhyming *a b b a / a b b a / c d c d / e e*, was probably composed about 1609 – i.e. several years before Donne was ordained a deacon. It borrows heavily from the Book of Revelation, the last book in the New Testament.

The poet, reflecting on his unworthiness to be admitted to heaven, is thinking of all those who will have to face God on the day of the Last Judgement. In the octave, he imagines the situation; in the sestet, he meditates on what it might mean for him.

A Petrarchan sonnet is one divided into an octave rhyming *a b b a, a b b a,* and a variously rhyming sestet (here *c d c d, e e*), a form adopted by Francesco Petrarca (1304–74) in the sonnets incorporated in his *Rime Sparse*, a work which set the pattern of lyric poetry for the next two hundred and fifty years.

'Holy Sonnets' is the largest single subdivision of the 'Divine Poems', which consists of (a) a remarkable sonnet sequence of seven sonnets called 'La Corona', in which the last line of each sonnet is repeated as the first line of the next, and the final line of the seventh sonnet is identical to the first line of the first, making it a perfect 'crown' of praise addressed to Christ, although it is modelled on the prayers addressed by Catholics to the Virgin Mary; (b) the nineteen 'holy sonnets', and (c) a litany, several occasional poems, three hymns, and two Latin poems. Helen Gardner has argued that the 1633 sequence of twelve holy sonnets represents a sequence, broken up by Grierson in his edition. It is a convincing argument, and the primary numbering here refers to her edition; the number in brackets is that adopted by Grierson.

Gardner argues that the first six sonnets in the 1633 edition have to do with death and judgement; the next three, with atonement; and the last three, with the love man owes to God.

[1–2] **At the . . . Angels**
imagined in the sense, as 'imagined' by the various authors of the New Testament. The situation fuses two separate scenes, both of which describe God's Last Judgement: (a) 'And after these things I saw four angels standing on the four corners of the earth' (Revelation 7: 1); (b) 'for the trumpet shall sound, and the dead shall be raised incorruptible' (1 Corinthians 15: 52).

[2–4] **arise . . . go**
numberless infinities/Of souls the innumerable and immeasurable (i.e. too many either to count or to measure) souls of the dead, as

described further in the second quatrain (lines 5–8); ***scattered bodies*** bodies dispersed, for any reason, after death; at the Last Judgement, the souls of the blessed are to rejoin their scattered bodies (cf. 'The Relic', lines 10–11).

[5] **All whom . . . o'erthrow**

flood the Flood described in Genesis 6–8, which God sends to punish the wicked; ***fire*** the fire which will consume everything on 'the day of the Lord', i.e. the Last Judgement (see 2 Peter 3: 10; also Revelation 8, 9).

[6–7] **All whom war . . . hath slain**

Donne catalogues first impersonal deaths (line 6) and then individual deaths (line 7); ***dearth*** scarcity, i.e. famine; ***agues*** fevers, diseases; ***Despair*** those who have committed suicide; ***law*** those executed in accordance with the law, presumably for crimes committed; ***chance*** accidents – i.e. all those who have been killed in any of a variety of ways (cf. 'Holy Sonnet 6', lines 9–10).

[7–8] **you whose eyes ... death's woe**

death's woe the body's return to dust; the phrase refers to the righteous who are alive on the last day and will never taste death (cf. Luke 9: 27).

[9] **But let . . . a space**

the poem hinges on this line: ***let them sleep*** refers to all other people, and 'sleep' is used in a spiritual sense – cf. 'Awake, you who sleep! Rise from the dead and Christ shall give you light' (Ephesians 50: 14); ***mourn*** '[and let me] feel grief or lament for someone who is dead': the poet is not mourning all those who have died in the ways he has listed, but mourning for his own spiritual 'death'; ***a space*** for a certain time; thus, 'let them sleep, for from their sleep they will arise, but I must mourn, at least for the time being, as I see no such certainty for me'.

[10] **For if . . . abound**

above more than; ***abound*** to be so numerous as to be on the point of overflowing; the poet is conjecturing that his sins may be more (or worse) than the sins of those who have died in the ways he has described.

[11–12] **'Tis late . . . are there**

late too late; ***abundance*** large and almost superfluous quantity, so large as to be overflowing (cf. 'abound' in previous line); ***grace*** God's grace or favour; ***there*** before God, on the day of the Last Judgement. The poet is pointing out that if his sins are more numerous than the sins of others who have died, then, on the day of the Last Judgement, it will be too late for him to ask God's forgiveness. Note the tone of these lines: in line 11, a playful hypothesis (if), couched in terms too vague to convince us that the poet really believes it; followed by a sudden shift of tone in line 12, where the simplicity of the syntax suggests that the poet is entirely sincere; ***this lowly ground*** while the poet is still alive, here, on earth.

[13–14] **Teach me . . . thy blood**

sealed (a) as in a legal contract; (b) a theological term, meaning marked by a seal which reserves the individual for a particular destination: derived from Revelation 7: 4–8: 'And I heard how many had been sealed . . . ' (cf. Jonson, *Underwood*, 47); thus, 'if the poet could learn truly to repent, this would be equivalent to the pardon Christ promised to all by his sacrifice'.

12 / *Holy Sonnet 5 (9)*

If poisonous minerals, and if that tree,
Whose fruit threw death on else immortal us;
If lecherous goats, if serpents envious
Cannot be damned, alas, why should I be?

Why should intent, or reason, born in me,
Make sins, else equal, ín me móre heinous?
And mercy being easy and glorious
To God, in his stern wrath why threatens he?

But who am I, that dare dispute with thee,
O God? O, of thine only worthy blood
And my tears make a heavenly Lethean flood,
And drown in it my sins' black memory!

That thou remember them some claim as debt:
I think it mercy if thou wilt forget.

This sonnet is a mix of an English sonnet (three quatrains plus final couplet) and a Petrarchan sonnet (octave plus sestet). It rhymes *a b b a / a b b a / a c c a / d d.* In the octave, Donne sets up a conflict between the innate characteristics of man and those of God. Being heir to original sin, a man cannot help but sin. But at the same time, one of the defining attributes of God is his mercy. In the next four lines the poet shows his contrition, against which he juxtaposes an apparent paradox between the concepts of remembering and forgetting.

The poem is remarkable for the way in which it moves from histrionic rhetoric, through a sudden and unexpected show of apparently sincere contrition, to the rhetorical individualism of the ending.

At the heart of this sonnet is the question of innate properties, and thus an exploration of the nature not only of man, but also of God. Note how it proceeds by way of rhetorical questions to its ending which, though no less rhetorical, provides very much the same kind of contrition and submission as Job shows after he has seen God: 'Before this, I knew of you only what I had been told about you, but now I have seen you with my own eyes' (Job 42: 5).

[1–2] **poisonous minerals**
such as white sublimate or arsenic; *that tree* the Tree of Knowledge of Good and Evil, which grew in the Garden of Eden: although these lines anticipate the opening – and a major aspect of the theme – of Milton's *Paradise Lost* (1667), it is not known whether Milton ever read Donne's poem; ***fruit*** the fruit of the Tree of Knowledge of Good and Evil opened Eve's eyes and made her conscious of her 'nakedness'; ***threw*** an unexpected verb – (a) propel through the air; reminiscent of the thunderbolt of Zeus; (b) compel something forcibly (on to someone else); (c) in the sense of 'discarded' or 'got rid of'; ***else*** otherwise.

[3] **lecherous goats**
goats were traditionally reputed to be lecherous and lascivious. The notion goes back to Antiquity – satyrs had the lower body, legs and horns of a

goat, and the upper body of a man; so did Pan, to whom there are very few references in Greek mythology, but he features prominently in English pastoral; ***serpents envious*** the notion that the serpent 'envied' the happiness of Adam and Eve, developed by Milton (*Paradise Lost*, 4, 358–92), goes back to the Lord's words to the serpent that had tempted Eve: 'I shall put enmity between you and [Eve], between your offspring and hers: they shall strike at your head, and you shall strike at their heel' (Genesis 3: 15) – to follow someone closely and enviously is to 'kick at their heels'.

[4] **Cannot be damned**
cannot, (a) because it is the nature of a poisonous mineral to be poisonous, of the fruit of the Tree of Knowledge of Good and Evil to open a human being's eyes to Good and Evil, of a goat to be lecherous, and of a snake, to be envious; (b) because only an animal invested with choice (i.e. a human animal) can incur damnation.

[5–6] **intent**
intention; ***born in me*** (a) born along with the poet, and thus a part of his innate nature; (b) that springs from inside the poet, and thus constitutes his essential self; (c) punning on 'borne' = carried within the poet, and thus constituting the burden the poet has to bear, in the same way as Christ says: 'Anyone who wishes to become a follower of mine, he must leave his own self behind; he must take up his cross and follow me' (Matthew 16: 24); ***else equal*** equal in all other respects; ***ín me móre heinous*** note how the natural stress would fall on 'in', emphasising the notion that the poet's sins are *innate*: this would hold even if the reader also wanted to stress the 'me'; ***heinous*** utterly hateful, odious or wicked; it is worth noting that one of its most significant uses in the Bible comes from the Book of Job, during Job's final evaluation of his case, in which he refers to any lustful coveting of a married man's wife as a heinous crime, 'to be punished by the judges' (Job 31: 11).

[7] **And mercy**
i.e. And (why should) mercy; ***mercy*** is one of God's innate characteristics: 'The Lord is long-suffering and of great mercy, and will forgive iniquity and transgression' (Numbers 14: 18; also Psalm 25: 10); thus ***easy*** natural, because *innate* to God, and therefore not something that will cause him any effort in showing; ***glorious*** i.e. to show mercy is to be glorious – cf. the psalm of thanksgiving: 'Sing loudly the honour of the Lord's name. Make his praise glorious! . . . Blessed be God, who has not turned away my prayer, nor withdrawn his mercy' (Psalm 66: 2, 20).

[8] **stern wrath**
cf. Job's certainty that the wicked will 'drink of the wrath of the Almighty' (Job 21: 20); note, however, that although the Lord is often quickly roused to wrath (e.g. Deuteronomy 29: 20), his 'anger only lasts for a moment' (Psalm 30: 5) – see the prayer of Habbakuk: 'O Lord, I have heard of all your deeds; I have seen all your work. At the mid-point of my life you did make yourself known, and in your wrath you did remember your mercy' (Habakkuk 3: 2); ***why threatens he?*** this is the question that the reader asks of the Lord's final manifestation to Job (Job 38–41): why does the Lord need to threaten Job so terribly? Job's reply is significant: he concedes the greatness of the Lord: 'I have spoken of things I did not understand . . . I melt away and repent in dust and ashes' (Job 42: 2–6).

[9] **But who am I . . . thee**
this is the sense of Job's final admission that the Lord's purpose is utterly incomprehensible by a human being; ***dispute*** the whole of the Book of Job consists of a dispute with his three friends and, finally, with the Lord.

[10] **thine only worthy blood**
'the blood of you who alone are worthy' – note how this implies a switch from 'the Lord' of the Old Testament to Christ, in the 'New Testament'. Christ was the only son of

God (John 1: 14) – cf. 'No man comes to the Father [i.e. God] except through me [Christ]' (John 14: 6), and 'Whosoever eats my body and drinks my blood will have eternal life' (John 6: 54).

[11] **my tears**
nothing before this has suggested the poet's 'contrition', i.e. his complete penitence (both regretting and wishing to atone for his sins); note how the 'blood' and the 'tears' commingle – i.e. Christ's mercy calls for penitence; ***heavenly Lethean flood heavenly*** divinely wrought; ***Lethean*** Lethe is the river of Hades, from which the shades of the dead drink and so forget their past life; ***flood*** an overflowing of water beyond its normal confines; thus: '[of your infinite mercy make] your blood and my tears combine to produce an overflowing of penitence that will eventually allow me to forget my sins completely'.

[12] **drown in it**
it the river Lethe; ***my sin's black memory*** the baneful memory of my sins; thus: 'drown the hateful memory of my sins so that they are forgotten for ever'.

[13–14] **remember**
cf. the plea made by one of the criminals between whom Christ was crucified: 'Lord, remember me when you arrive in your kingdom' (Luke 23: 42); ***debt*** payment owed for faithful service; ***mercy*** (a) compassion and forbearance; (b) kindness – cf. the prayer of the faithful, 'Lord have mercy on us'. 'Remember, O Lord, your tender mercy and your loving kindness, that you have always shown. Do not remember either the sins or offences of my youth, but as you are merciful, remember me because of your own goodness' (Psalm 25: 6–7); see also the Lord's promise to Jeremiah: 'I shall forgive their evil ways, and shall no longer remember their sin' (Jeremiah 31: 34), quoted by St Paul in his Letter to the Hebrews, 8: 12.

---

13 / *Holy Sonnet 6 (10):*

Death, be not proud, though some have callèd thee
Mighty and dreadful, for thou art not so:
For those whom thou think'st thou dost overthrow
Die not, poor Death, nor yet canst thou kill me.

From rest and sleep, which but thy pictures be,
Much pleasure, then from thee much more must flow,
And soonest our best men with thee do go,
Rest of their bones, and souls' delivery.

Thou'rt slave to fate, chance, kings, and desperate men,
And dost with poison, war, and sickness dwell,

And poppy or charms can make us sleep as well,
And better than thy stroke: why swell'st thou then?

One short sleep past, we wake eternally,
And death shall be no more: Death, thou shalt die.

This is perhaps the best-known of Donne's holy sonnets. It is an English sonnet in irregular iambic pentameters, probably written about 1609, and rhyming *a b b a / a b b a / c d d c / e e.*

The poem should be read in the light of the frequent motif of the *memento mori*, a pictorial reminder of death, usually a skull either in the middle of a still life or even engraved on a ring or other piece of jewellery. Here, the poet is meditating on the power with which the idea of Death grips the mind; he reminds himself, in the first two stanzas, that humankind has been promised salvation and, in the third, that it is not Death who decides human destiny.

The extent to which the *memento mori* (=remember [that you have] to die) infused life at the time may be seen in 'The Ambassadors' (1533), a well-known painting by Hans Holbein, in which two young men stand facing the viewer: it appears to be an 'official' portrait; closer examination reveals no fewer than four evident reminders of death.

An English sonnet is one in which three quatrains (here, *a b b a, a b b a, c d d c*) are followed by a final couplet, in which the whole poem is resolved – Shakespeare's sonnets are the most familiar example of the form.

[1] **proud**
Death is told not to be proud just because some people have called it 'mighty and dreadful' (line 2).

[2] **not so**
not mighty and dreadful.

[3] **thou think'st thou dost**
you think you do; ***overthrow*** demolish, in the sense of 'kill'.

[4] **Die not, poor Death**
Die not because their souls will be either resurrected or sent to eternal damnation; ***poor*** powerless, pitiful.

[5–6] **From rest . . . must flow**
the image of rest and sleep as 'pictures' of death is a conventional conceit derived from Petrarch: cf. Samuel Daniel, sonnet 45, 'Care charmer sleep', line 2); ***pleasure*** comes from rest and sleep; thus, if rest and sleep can provide so much pleasure, and they are only an imitation of Death, then a great deal more pleasure must be derived from Death itself.

[7] **soonest . . . go**
with thee with Death; the line is perhaps a reference to the proverb 'Only the good die young' (cf. 'A Valediction: Forbidding Mourning', lines 1–2).

[8] **Rest of . . . delivery**
giving rest to their bones, and delivery (liberation from their body) to their soul.

[9] **Thou art . . . desperate men**
slave to subject to; ***fate*** destiny or Providence; ***chance*** fatal accidents; ***kings*** the possible tyrannies of kings; ***desperate men*** men who commit suicide (i.e. those who commit suicide make 'Death' subject to them): cf. 'Holy Sonnet 4', lines 6–7.

[10] **dost . . . dwell**
(literally) does live, lives; i.e. Death is the inevitable companion of poison, war and sickness.

[11] **poppy or charms**
poppy the juice of the poppy is a narcotic; ***charms*** magic, perhaps hypnosis.

[12] **stroke . . . swell'st**
stroke blow, i.e. the fact or moment of death; ***why swell'st thou*** 'why do you puff yourself up with pride?'
[13] **wake eternally**
wake to eternal life.
[14] **death shall be . . . die**
there is sound biblical authority for this paradox: cf. St Paul's words about the Resurrection: 'For just as we die because of our union with Adam [i.e. we all carry the burden of original sin], so all who unite with Christ will be raised to eternal life, each in his own time . . . Christ will overcome [cf. 'overthrow', line 3] all churches and temples and congregations, and the last enemy to be defeated by him before the world ends will be Death' (1 Corinthians 15: 22–6), and 'When the last trumpet blasts, in an instant we shall all be transformed from body into spirit . . . what dies will become immortal, thereby fulfilling the prophecy "Death will be destroyed and victory complete!" Then shall we ask, "Death, where was your victory? Death, where was that power of yours to hurt?"' (1 Corinthians 15: 51–5, *reversing* the prophecy given in Hosea 13: 14).

14 / *Holy Sonnet 10 (14)*

Batter my heart, three-personed God, for you
As yet but knock, breathe, shine, and seek to mend.
That I may rise and stand, o'erthrow me, and bend
Your force to break, blow, burn, and make me new.

I, like an usurped town, t'another due,
Labour to admit you – but oh, to no end!
Reason, your viceroy in me, me should defend,
But is captived, and proves weak or untrue.

Yet dearly I love you and would be lovèd fain,
But am betrothed unto your enemy.
Divorce me, untie, or break that knot again,
Take me to you, imprison me, for I,

Except you enthrall me, never shall be free,
Nor ever chaste, except you ravish me.

This is one of Donne's richest and most arresting poems. Not only is its imagery extraordinarily powerful, but its logic is unusually ambivalent, even by his standards. It is an English sonnet in iambic pentameters, rhyming *a b b a / a b b a / c d c d / e e*, and was most probably written about 1609.

The poet, struggling to bring God into his life, calls upon God to reveal himself more forcefully to him, as no matter how hard he tries he cannot free himself from the bonds in which he finds himself. Note how each stanza develops its own imagery, and also the daring paradox of the final couplet.

[1] **Batter . . . God**
batter knock violently or heavily; ***three-personed God*** God as Trinity (Father, Son, and Holy Spirit).

[2] **knock . . . seek to mend**
knock cf. Christ's message to the Laodiceans: 'I chide and chasten all those whom I love. Give up your sinful ways and take heed! For I am always standing at the door and *knocking*. If anyone hears my voice and opens the door, I shall enter his house and eat with him' (Revelation 3: 20); ***breathe*** to whisper or speak softly; ***shine*** cf. the prayer 'Bring us back to you, O God almighty; shine your face on us [i.e. show us mercy] and we shall be saved' (Psalm 80: 7), and 'the light shines in the darkness and the darkness [here, the poet] cannot understand it' (John 1: 5): various interpretations of this run of verbs have been offered – notably (a) that they refer to the Trinity: the theme of calling upon God (as King of Love) to break open an individual's locked door is found in medieval mystical verse; the breathing refers to the Holy Spirit; the shining refers to Christ as Son (i.e. Sun); (b) that they refer to metalworking in which knocking is hammering; breathing is blowing upon the metal to cool it (a procedure which the metalworker would use when shaping the metal); shining is burnishing (shining metal by means of friction); ***mend*** remove the defects, correct what is faulty.

[3] **rise . . . bend**
rise (a) as a true Christian; (b) at the Resurrection; ***o'erthrow*** overthrow, i.e. to cast down from prosperity and bring to ruin – a paradox, given that it follows immediately on 'rise' and 'stand'; ***bend*** direct.

[4] **break . . . new**
blow in the sense of (a) fashion into shape or (b) inject with the Holy Spirit; ***burn*** baptism by fire (Matthew 3: 11); ***new*** cf. St Paul's words about Christian living: 'You must make your hearts and minds completely new, and refashion yourself as if you were a New Man, modelled on Christ, and must reveal this in all your actions' (Ephesians 4: 23–4); and Christ's assertion that 'no one will see the Kingdom of God unless he is born again' (John 3: 3).

[5] **usurped town . . . due**
usurped appropriated wrongfully, i.e. by force or contrivance; ***to another due*** properly belonging to another (i.e. the poet's allegiances *should* belong to God) – the central image in the second stanza is a town, here symbolising the poet's self.

[6] **Labour . . . end**
Labour strive or work hard; ***to no end*** to no avail – no matter how hard the poet tries, he can't 'admit' – i.e. allow – God into his life.

[7] **Reason . . . defend**
Reason is seen as God's viceroy (the governor of a country, acting in the name of a non-resident ruler); ***should defend*** should have defended me (against the enemy which usurped power).

[8] **captived . . . untrue**
captived a prisoner of the enemy; ***and*** and therefore; ***untrue*** false reason, i.e. error.

[9] **Yet . . . fain**
Yet in spite of the situation described (note how the 'yet' hints at a *volta* in the argument, in which case the sonnet is as much 'Petrarchan' as 'English'); ***fain*** willingly, with pleasure – i.e. the poet strongly wants to be loved by God. The scansion is difficult – the line looks like a hexameter, but is probably meant to read: 'Yet dearl'I love you, 'n'would be lovèd fain'; note how all the verbs in the second stanza have to do with *union*.

[10] **betrothed ... enemy**
betrothed engaged; ***enemy*** (a) the world – there is no reason to suppose that the poet meant either Satan or Sin, as neither of these concepts plays any part in the poem; or (b), perhaps more specifically, a woman: note how the *imagery* of the stanza is entirely related to the language of worldly love.

[11] **Divorce me ... knot again**
both this and the following line are addressed to God; ***divorce*** cancel a union; ***untie*** cancel a bond; ***break (a) knot*** refers to taking a young woman's virginity; thus (paradoxically) 'make me a virgin once more': the relationship between God and the Israelites was often likened to one between a husband and wife: e.g. God's promise, according to Hosea: 'Israel, I shall [once again] make you my wife' (Hosea 2: 19); so too was the relationship between Christ and his Church – cf. John's vision: 'For the time has come for the wedding of the Lamb, and his bride [i.e. the Heavenly Jerusalem] has prepared herself for him' (Revelation 19: 7–9; 21: 9–10) – here, the poet is seeking 'divorce' from God's 'enemy'; i.e. the annulling of an 'old' contract (cf. Herbert, 'Redemption', p. 200).

[12] **Take me ... imprison**
note how the phrase 'break that knot again' from the previous line is *also* the first in a new sequence of three ideas: ***take me to you*** accept me as yours; the motif of possession plays on the image 'The Lord possessed me in the beginning of his way' (Proverbs 8: 22); note that the motif of imprisonment *reverses* the traditional image (e.g. 'Set me free from my prison so that I may praise thy name': Psalm 142: 7); their combination (i.e. imagery of imprisonment and possession) is found in Christian mysticism.

[13–14] **Except ... ravish me**
Except unless, ***enthrall*** (a) hold in thrall, i.e. enslave; (b) enchant; ***ravish*** (a) seize violently and carry off (i.e. enslave); (b) violate, i.e. rape; note the outrageous paradox. On the sensual/sexual nature of divine possession, cf. the mystical visions of St Teresa of Avila (1515–82), who wrote: 'As the angel withdrew [his spear with a tip of fire], he left me ablaze with a love of God.' This moment of 'transverberation' is brilliantly illustrated by the Italian sculptor Gianlorenzo Bernini (1598–1680) in his 'The Ecstasy of St Teresa' in the Cornaro Chapel, Santa Maria della Vittoria, Rome.

15 / *Good Friday, 1613: Riding Westward*

Let man's soul be a sphere, and then, in this,
The intelligence that moves, devotion is;
And as the other spheres, by being grown
Subject to foreign motions, lose their own,
And being by others hurried every day,
Scarce in a year their natural form obey,
Pleasure or business, so, our souls admit
For their first mover, and are whirled by it.
Hence is't that I am carried towards the west
This day, when my soul's form bends toward the east.

There I should see a sun by rising set,
And by that setting endless day beget:
But that Christ on this Cross did rise and fall,
Sin had eternally benighted all.

Yet dare I almost be glad I do not see
That spectacle of too much weight for me.
Who sees God's face, that is self life, must die.
What a death were it then to see God die?
It made his own lieutenant Nature shrink,
It made his footstool crack, and the sun wink.
Could I behold those hands which span the poles.
And turn all spheres at once, pierced with those holes?
Could I behold that endless height which is
Zenith to us and t'our antipodes,
Humbled below us? Or that blood which is
The seat of all our souls, if not of his,
Make dirt of dust, or that flesh which was worn
By God for his apparel, ragg'd and torn?
If on these things I durst not look, durst I
Upon his miserable mother cast mine eye,
Who was God's partner here, and furnished thus
Half of that sacrifice which ransomed us?

Though these things, as I ride, be from mine eye,
They are present yet unto my memory
For that looks towards them; and thou look'st towards me,
O saviour, as thou hang'st upon the tree:
I turn my back to thee but to receive
Corrections, till thy mercies bid thee leave.
O think me worth thine anger, punish me,
Burn off my rusts and my deformity,
Restore thine image, so much, by thy grace,
That thou mayst know me, and I'll turn my face.

A meditative poem of forty-two lines in iambic pentameters, rhyming in couplets. It was almost certainly written on or about the day in question, when Donne left Sir Henry Goodyer's house in Warwickshire, in the English Midlands, to go to Sir Edward Herbert's home in Wales.

The action may be divided into three parts: in lines 1–14 (apart from the rhyme-scheme, a self-contained sonnet), the poet reflects on the paradox of travelling westward on a day when he is thinking of Christ's crucifixion, which occurred in the Holy Land (i.e. to the *east*); in lines 15–32, he reminds himself that the crucifixion was so awesome that he should perhaps be glad that it is not more vivid in his mind; in lines 33–42, he asks Christ to correct those defects in his character which cause his image to be so faint.

This poem is one of a group of six occasional poems – i.e. poems written to celebrate a particular occasion.

Title
Good Friday the day on which Christians celebrate Christ's crucifixion, death, and descent into hell; three days later, he rose from the dead and ascended into heaven, where he took his place at the right hand of God, an event celebrated on Easter Sunday; 'Good' here means 'holy' (from 'God, godly'), but in the specific sense of announcing a 'good' tiding or news – in ritual terms, Christ must 'die' before he can be 'resurrected'; the 'death' thus announces the 'resurrection', which Christians see as a 'new birth' and thus celebrate it with joy.

[1–2] **Let . . . devotion is**
Let allow or imagine that: a term much used in logic and mathematics, or as an introduction to a syllogism (a kind of argument in which the individual seeks to draw a conclusion from two or more assumed premisses or propositions; ***be*** is; ***in this*** i.e. in the sphere of man's (more specifically, the poet's) soul; ***intelligence*** (a) the faculty of understanding; (b) angel – not in the popular sense, but meaning the 'pure intelligence' which allows a sphere (or any other body) to 'move'; thus, in the same way as every heavenly sphere is moved by the angel (intelligence) inside it, so every human soul is moved by devotion; ***moves*** animates, directs, guides, or allows a person to act.

[3–4] **other spheres . . . their own**
other planets or heavenly bodies; ***by being grown*** because they have become; ***subject to foreign motions*** subject to the movements of other heavenly bodies; ***their own*** their own motion or movement.

[5–6] **And being by others . . . obey**
others i.e. other heavenly bodies; ***hurried*** perturbed or agitated; ***Scarce*** rarely; ***natural form*** their own course or guiding principle: the view expressed in these lines was widespread in the seventeenth century; it was based on the astronomical system devised by Nicolaus Copernicus (1473–1543), a Polish astronomer often called the father of modern astronomy.

[7–8] **Pleasure . . . whirled by it**
so in the same way, go too (do); ***admit*** allow (pleasure or business) to enter them; ***For*** as, in the capacity of; ***first mover*** God; ***whirled*** guided in an agitated fashion; ***it*** pleasure or business: thus, lines 3–8: 'In the same way as every heavenly body is so affected by the movements of other bodies that it is thrown off its natural course to such an extent that rarely, in any year, does it subscribe to its own motion, so too do our souls allow pleasure and business to divert them from their true course and act as their guiding principle.'

[9–10] **I am carried . . . east**
carried because riding a horse or, perhaps, in a carriage; ***west*** (a) the poet is, literally, travelling west; (b) the sun sets in the west, and is thus, by extension, suggestive of death (i.e. thoughts of Christ's crucifixion); ***This day*** Good Friday – see note to Title; ***soul's form*** not, as one might imagine, the 'outer shape' of the soul (which would be the body), but the soul's *essence*, that which defines or 'forms' it; ***bends*** (a) directs its course; (b) bows; ***toward the east*** (a) in the direction of the rising sun, and thus the Holy Land; (b) thoughts of Christ's resurrection.

[11] **sun**
Christ; ***set*** die; thus, ***by rising set*** die by being raised on the Cross.

[12] **by that setting . . . beget**
that setting Christ's death; *endless day* eternal life, promised by Christ to all humankind ('For God so loved the world that he gave the world his only Son, so that everyone who believes in Christ will have eternal life': John 3: 16); *beget* bring about, give rise to – thus, 'by his death bring about eternal life'.

[13–14] **But that Christ . . . benighted all**
But that Unless; *this Cross* (a) the Cross on which the poet is meditating; (b) the symbol of Christianity as a paradox (cf. lines 11–12); *benighted* cast every one into eternal night; thus, 'If Christ had not on this Cross died and been resurrected, Sin would have cast mankind into perpetual darkness.'

[15–16] **Yet dare I . . . for me**
'In spite of the promise of eternal life offered by thoughts about the crucifixion and Resurrection, the poet is almost glad that he cannot witness the scene itself, which would have been too powerful an experience to be borne.'

[17] **Who sees . . . must die**
that is self life that is 'Life' itself – cf. the Lord's words to Moses: 'My face you cannot see, for no mortal man may see me and live' (Exodus 33: 20).

[18] **What a death . . . die**
If to see God's *living* face is to die, then how much more certain a death it is to see Christ crucified.

[19] **Lieutenant**
God's closest subordinate (i.e. Nature); *shrink* show fear.

[20] **footstool crack . . . sun wink**
footstool the world – cf. God's assertion: 'Heaven is my throne and earth my footstool' (Isaiah 66: 1); *crack . . . sun wink* the crucifixion was immediately followed by an earthquake and an eclipse (see Matthew 27: 51, 45); *sun wink* (a) an eclipse ('From midday a darkness fell over the whole land, which lasted until three in the afternoon': Matthew 27: 45); (b) Christ 'descended into hell, and on the third day rose again' – i.e. he went into 'eclipse' for three days.

[21–2] **Could I behold . . . those holes**
those hands the hands of God – cf. the psalm of praise: 'The sea is his and he made it, and his hands formed the dry land' (Psalm 95: 5); *span the poles* God holds the whole world in his hands; *tune* give movement and thus music to: the reference is to the so-called 'music of the spheres': Pythagoras, noting that pitch depends on the rapidity of vibration, and that the planets move at different speeds, concluded that their movement must cause vibration, and hence music: a treatise by Johan Kepler (1571–1630) popularised the theory; *at once* at the same time; *those holes* the stigmata, the wounds caused by the nails which held Jesus to the Cross: note how the imagery in the succeeding questions becomes increasingly vivid.

[24–5] **Zenith . . . antipodes**
endless height (a) heaven; (b) Christ – i.e. the highest ideal a person can have; *Zenith* highest point in the sky above an observer; *antipodes* those people living on the opposite side of the earth from the observer: the point being that wherever you are, Christ is always the 'highest' ideal; *humbled below us* treated like a common criminal – Christ was crucified between two criminals (Luke 23: 32–3).

[25–8] **The seat of all our souls . . . ragg'd and torn**
that blood the blood (a) that dripped from Christ's wounds as he hung from the Cross; (b) that Christ shed for all Christians by his humiliation and death; it is the *seat of our souls* by virtue of the Mass or Communion (cf. 'Drink all of this, for this is my blood of the New Testament, which is shed for you and for many for the remission of sins', from 'The Order of Holy Communion' from *The Book of Common Prayer*); *if not of his* Christ, as Son of God, derived his immortality from his Father; *make dirt of dust* refers to

Christ's blood dripping on the dry ground and turning it into dirt or mud; ***that flesh*** Christ's flesh; ***worn/By God*** (a) Christ is the bodily manifestation of God; but also (b) note how the body is seen as the garment of the inner man; ***ragg'd and torn*** bruised and wounded by his beating, scourging and the soldier's spear – cf. Mark 15: 15 and John 19: 34. Medieval and Renaissance artists would often show Christ's wounds in extreme detail in order to emphasise his suffering (e.g. Matthias Grünewald's altarpiece, now at Colmar in eastern France).

[29] **durst**
dare.

[30–2] **miserable mother . . . ransomed us**
miserable in a state of *extreme distress*; ***God's partner*** Mary, the mother of Christ, is viewed as an almost equally venerable figure in Catholicism; the notion is alien to Protestantism and thus reflects Donne's continued adherence to aspects of Catholicism as late as 1613, long after his conversion to the Church of England; ***furnished*** supplied, provided; ***Half of that sacrifice which ransomed us*** deliberately ambiguous in order to avoid censure: (a) in the sense that Mary was one of Christ's two parents, and thus provided 'half' of Christ; (b) in the sense that by her suffering at the Cross, Mary has a half share in Christ's sacrifice (i.e. crucifixion), which ***ransomed*** (i.e. redeemed or saved) humankind.

[33] **be from**
lie outside his view because (a) these events belong to the distant past; (b) he is looking away from the scene of them – i.e. west, not east.

[34] **memory**
(a) memory; (b) inner eye.

[35] **that**
the poet's memory/inner eye; ***thou*** Christ.

[36] **tree**
the Cross on which Christ was crucified, a common image in the Middle Ages and Renaissance – cf. 'Christ carried our sins in his own body on the *tree*, so that we could stop living in sin and begin to live in righteousness. By his wounds you have been healed' (1 Peter 2: 24) – note how 'wounds' refers us back to 'ragg'd and torn' in line 28.

[37–8] **I turn my back to thee, . . . bid thee leave**
turn my back (a) literally, because he is riding westward; and (b) metaphorically – even though the poet's image of Christ is not as vivid as he thinks it ought to be; ***but*** only; ***Corrections*** correcting punishment, usually by blows, with specific reference to the 'correction' necessary to turn the poet's soul away from pleasure and business to God (lines 7–8); ***till thy mercies bid thee leave*** until in your infinite mercy you stop, because you consider the correction sufficient.

[39] **worth thine anger**
because, were the poet *not* worth God's anger, God would not seek to give him a desire for eternal life, thus making his damnation inevitable: thus, lines 37–9 suggest that the poet is looking away from Christ not only because he is afraid of allowing the full image of the crucifixion to enter his thoughts, but also to see if Christ loves him sufficiently to make him 'turn his face' – the idea inverts the image of a child who, having been punished, sulks until he has been reassured of a parent's affection; here the unpunished poet seeks the punishment to reassure himself of Christ's love for him.

[40] **Burn off . . . deformity**
Burn refers to Christ the Son or 'Sun'; ***rusts*** just as iron becomes rusted when it is exposed to the elements, so the poet has become rusty by being turned to the world – here, moral corrosion, corruption obtained while 'looking away' from Christ; ***deformity***, because not naturally inclined to God; thus, moral deformity.

[41] **Restore thine image**
(a) make vivid once again that image

of your sufferings upon the Cross so that the poet can accept Christ's sacrifice; (b) revive again the divine image in me: remember that man is made in God's 'image' (Genesis 1: 26); ***so much*** to such an extent.

[42] **That thou may'st know me** ambivalent (a) 'that you may see your image in me'; (b) 'that you will recognise me as one of your creatures' (which would signal the poet's salvation); ***turn my face*** the concept of 'turning' (i.e. turning again to God after a period of falling away, or even for the first time) is central to the Old Testament (e.g. 'Turn us again, O God, and cause thy face to shine; and we shall be saved': Psalm 80: 3). It is less common in the New Testament, but it does appear – e.g. 'And the hand of the Lord was with them: and a great number believed, and turned unto the Lord' (Acts 11: 21); here, (a) metaphorically, in this sense, but also (b) in the sense 'I shall be ready to receive all the correction you consider necessary': cf. the expression, derived from Christ's teaching (Matthew 5: 39), 'turn the other cheek'.

16 / *Hymn to God my God, in my Sickness*

Since I am coming to that holy room
Where, with thy choir of saints for evermore,
I shall be made thy music, as I come
I tune the instrument here at the door,
And what I must do then, think now before.

Whilst my physicians by their love are grown
Cosmographers, and I their map, who lie
Flat on this bed, that by them may be shown
That this is my south-west discovery
Per fretum febris, by these straits to die,

I joy that in these straits I see my West;
For though their currents yield return to none,
What shall my West hurt me? As west and east
In all flat maps (and I am one) are one,
So Death doth touch the Resurrection.

Is the Pacific Sea my home? Or are
The eastern riches? Is Jerusalem?
Anyan, and Magellan, and Gibraltar,
All straits, and none but straits, are ways to them,
Whether where Japhet dwelt, or Cham, or Shem.

We think that Paradise and Calvary,
  Christ's Cross and Adam's tree, stood in one place;
Look, Lord, and find both Adams met in me;
  As the first Adam's sweat surrounds my face,
  May the last Adam's blood my soul embrace.

So, in his purple wrapped, receive me, Lord,
  By these His thorns give me His other crown;
And as to others' souls I preached thy word,
  Be this my text, my sermon to mine own:
  'Therefore, that he may raise, the Lord throws down'.

This is the penultimate of three hymns with which 'Divine Poems' ends. It is a meditative prayer in iambic pentameters, divided in six stanzas, each rhyming *a b a b b*. It was probably written in 1623, at the time when Donne was suffering from the fever which he describes in his prose *Devotions*, although Izaak Walton, who published a biography of Donne in 1640, ascribes it to the period of the latter's final sickness in March 1631.

The poet is reflecting on his sickness, and possibly imminent death. The first stanza is introductory: in stanzas 2–4, he puns on the Latin word *fretum*, which can mean both 'raging heat' (i.e. the poet's fever) and 'straits' – a geographical term, and also sufferings. In the last two stanzas, he develops the argument by reference to the cyclical history told in the Bible.

[1] **holy room**
i.e. heaven.

[2] **thy choir . . . evermore**
thy your, i.e. God's; the idea of a choir comes from Revelation 5: 11 ('and I heard the voice of many angels round about the throne . . .'); ***saints*** (a) any true believer in Christ, the original meaning of the word, as in Revelation 5: 8 and Romans 1: 7; (b) outstanding examples of Christian living, as in Catholic tradition; ***evermore*** eternity.

[3] **thy music**
a notion probably derived from the expression 'instruments of righteousness': cf. St Paul's teaching: 'Do not allow any part of yourselves to become instruments of sin. On the contrary, surrender yourselves so completely to God, as is fitting for all those who have been saved from death and given new life, that you become instruments of righteousness' (Romans 6: 13); 'instruments' suggests 'musical instruments' and thus 'music'.

[4] **I tune . . . at the door**
tune correct the intonation of a musical instrument; ***instrument*** the poet (a) as a musical instrument; (b) as a minister of the Church, i.e. God's instrument; ***door*** the door separating death and everlasting life (see Revelation 4: 1).

[5] **must do . . . before**
must do will be doing (by virtue of his situation [he is sick and thinks he is going to die], not because of any compulsion), i.e. surrendering himself entirely to God's judgement; thus, 'while I am still alive, I am reflecting on what I shall be doing after my death'.

[6–7] **physicians . . . map**
physicians doctors; ***by their love*** so much is their love; ***cosmographers*** map-makers and geographers; ***I their***

map because he is a microcosm, a 'small world'. The image thus suggests an equation between the doctors attending the poet and God (a) as divine physician; (b) as supreme representative of the macrocosm or 'large world' – death is the absorption of the microcosm by the macrocosm.

[8] **by them may be shown**
I may be shown by them; the joke is that the earthly physicians can only 'read' the poet's illness in the same way as they would read a map; they cannot cure it.

[9] **south-west discovery**
south the tropics, and thus heat; ***west*** where the sun sets, and thus death: hence, ***south-west*** 'death by heat [i.e. fever]'; ***discovery*** in the sense of revelation, something suddenly understood.

[10] ***per fretum febris*** **. . . to die**
The key phrase in the poem, involving a double pun: ***fretum*** (Latin) (a) raging heat; (b) straits, where 'straits' are (a) narrow passages, between two land masses, separating two large bodies of water; (b) rigorous conditions, sufferings (e.g. of an illness). The phrase can thus mean either (a) 'by the raging heat of the fever' or (b) 'by the sufferings caused by fevers'; ***to die*** there may be an oblique reference here to the Portuguese explorer Ferdinand Magellan (1480–1521), who sailed south-west through the Straits of Magellan (between the South American continent and Tierra del Fuego [= land of fire]), only to die in the Philippines.

[11] **joy . . . West**
The poet is joyful because he is looking forward to his resurrection; ***West*** i.e. his death – note that this is the main clause of the sentence which begins at line 6.

[12] **For though . . . none**
currents a reference to the strong currents normally met with in straits; ***yield return to none*** allow no one to sail or swim against their currents.

[13–15] **What shall . . . Resurrection**
What shall . . . either (a) 'What? is it possible that (my death) will . . . ?'; (b) 'In what way would . . . ?'; (c) 'How could . . . ?'; ***west and east . . . are one*** on a globe, the extreme 'west' becomes the extreme 'east' – the same is true of a 'flat map'; ***touch*** in the sense of adjoining or meeting without overlapping; ***Resurrection*** Christ's Resurrection, celebrated on Easter Sunday, only two days after Good Friday.

[16–17] **Pacific Sea . . . Jerusalem**
Three images of peace and serenity, i.e. of earthly paradises: ***Pacific Sea*** the Pacific Ocean (from Latin ***pax*** = peace); ***Eastern riches*** the fabled land of Cathay; ***Jerusalem*** (a) vision of peace (Hebrew); (b) the 'heavenly Jerusalem' of Revelation 21: 10–27; 22: 1–5.

[18] **Anyan . . . Gibraltar**
three straits: (a) ***Anyan*** literally, the straits dividing eastern Asia and North America, now called the Bering Strait, but the reference is not so much to these geographical waters as, metaphorically, to the passage which was thought to connect the North Atlantic and Pacific Oceans; (b) ***Magellan*** see note to line 10; (c) ***Gibraltar*** the straits connecting the Atlantic and the Mediterranean. The first two thus represent northern and southern passages to the East; the third, to Jerusalem.

[19] **straits**
ambivalent: (a) the earthly paradises referred to in lines 16–17 can be attained only by passing through 'straits'; (b) it is only by suffering that an individual will get to heaven.

[20] **Whether . . . Shem**
Japhet, Cham, and Shem the three sons of Noah (the first two are usually called Japheth and Ham), said to have peopled Europe, Africa, and Asia respectively.

[21–2] **We think . . . one place**
Paradise the Garden of Eden (Genesis 2, 3), where ***Adam's tree*** (i.e. the Tree of the Knowledge of Good and Evil) stood; ***Calvary*** the Latinised name for the site where Jesus was crucified

(Luke 23: 33 – the original Greek means 'skull', which in Hebrew is 'golgotha'). Although there is no biblical authority for locating them in one place, *The Golden Legend*, a medieval manual of religious lore (lives of saints, etc.), still widely read in the early seventeenth century, states that Christ died 'in the same place' that Adam was buried.

[23] **both Adams met in me**
The two Adams are Adam (Genesis 2–4) and Christ (cf. 'The first Adam was a human being, but the last Adam is the life-giving Spirit': 1 Corinthians 15: 45; also Romans 5: 12–21); they are 'met' in the poet, because he is the descendant of the one and has also partaken of Christ's blood at Mass or Holy Communion.

[24] **Adam's sweat surrounds**
cf. 'You shall gain your bread by the sweat of your brow' (Genesis 3: 19); ***surrounds*** covers.

[25] **May . . . embrace**
blood the blood (wine) taken at his last Communion; ***embrace*** eagerly accept for myself; thus, 'I pray that my soul can receive the blood of Christ' (i.e. so that he can die in peace).

[26] **in his purple wrapped**
cf. 'They dressed [Christ] in purple and, after plaiting a crown of thorns, they placed it on his head' (Mark 15: 17) – but here Christ's cloak is metaphorical; it refers to the purple blood/wine of the poet's last Communion – note the inversion of seeing the inner as outer, i.e. the blood is seen as 'wrapping' the individual (soul).

[27] **By these . . . other crown**
thorns Christ's crown of thorns, symbolising his suffering, just as the poet is suffering; ***His other crown*** Christ's crown of glory – cf. 'When the chief Shepherd [i.e. Christ] appears, you will be given the unfading crown of glory' (1 Peter 5: 4).

[28] **And as to others' . . .**
Donne was Dean of St Paul's Cathedral, where he preached some remarkable sermons – thus, 'Just as I preached your Word to others . . . '

[29] **Be**
let this be; ***my text . . . mine own*** sermons usually develop a biblical text; the last line of the poem is the 'text' upon which the poet bases his last sermon to his own soul.

[30] **Therefore . . . throws down**
that in order that; thus, 'The Lord throws down in order that he may raise': the text is not biblical, but of Donne's own devising; compare it with 'Holy Sonnet 10: "Batter my heart"', line 3. The point of the text is that just as the Bible traces man's history from the Fall (Adam's expulsion from the Garden of Eden for disobedience) to Christ's Resurrection (with which the Gospels end) and the heavenly Jerusalem (with which the Book of Revelation ends), so Donne must die (i.e. 'fall') before he can be 'raised'.

17 / *A Hymn to God the Father*

Wilt Thou forgive that sin where I begun,
  Which is my sin, though it were done before?
Wilt Thou forgive those sins through which I run,
  And do them still, though still I do deplore?
    When Thou hast done, Thou hast not done,
      For I have more.

Wilt Thou forgive that sin by which I've won
   Others to sin, and made my sin their door?
Wilt Thou forgive that sin which I did shun
   A year or two, but wallowed in a score?
      When Thou hast done, Thou hast not done,
         For I have more.

I have a sin of fear that when I've spun
   My last thread I shall perish on the shore;
Swear by Thy self, that at my death Thy son
   Shall shine as he shines now, and heretofore;
      And, having done that, Thou hast done,
         I have no more.

This is the last poem in the collection: a prayer in iambic metre, in three stanzas composed of four pentameters followed by a tetrameter and a dimeter, each rhyming *a b a b a b*. Izaak Walton ascribes it to Donne's final sickness, but it may well have been written earlier.

The poet asks God to forgive his sins. Note the sequence of sins which Donne lists, and the way in which he puns on his own name in the penultimate line of each stanza, and that of his wife (More) in the last.

[1–2] **Wilt thou . . . before**
Wilt thou Will you? ***that sin where I begun*** original sin (i.e. the state of sin in which all men and women find themselves as a result of the disobedience of Adam and Eve) – thus, ***done before*** by Adam and inherited by all human beings at birth (***where I begun***) and therefore, also, the poet's sin.
[3–4] **those sins . . . I deplore**
run ran; i.e. the various sins which the poet has committed, and still commits, even though he deplores them.
[5–6] **When thou . . . more**
these lines make a pun on both the poet's name (done = Donne) and the maiden name of his wife (more = Ann More, whom Donne married in December 1601). Thus, 'When (a) you [i.e. God] have forgiven my sins;' (b) 'When you have Donne [i.e. received Donne's soul], you (a) have not finished, (b) do not have Donne's soul, because (a) I have more sins, (b) I am still committed to Ann More' – and she, therefore, still has the poet's soul.
[7–8] **that sin . . . door**
that sin not specified, but perhaps (a) licentious living; (b) licentious poetry; ***their door*** i.e. the poet's sins have tempted others to sin in similar fashion.
[9] **shun**
to avoid deliberately.
[10] **wallowed in a score**
wallow (lit.) roll about in an indolent manner – here, to indulge immoderately; thus, to wallow in sin = to take an improper delight in; ***score*** twenty (years); thus, 'Will you forgive that sin which I was able to resist for some years, but which, once I had committed it, I was unable to stop myself from indulging in it for some twenty years' – this may be seen as worldly pleasure or, more specifically, as his carnal love for Ann More.
[11–12] **a sin of fear . . . the shore**
fear is a sin because it represents a

lack of faith; ***thread*** a reference to the expression 'thread of life' (an image derived from classical mythology rather than the Bible); thus, ***spun my last thread*** the poet is afraid that he is about to die; ***perish on the shore*** die on the beach, i.e. from exhaustion after a shipwreck. Note the implicit parallel between life and a sea-voyage, and death and regaining land; the phrase, of course, is metaphorical, but it represents an original reformulation of an otherwise tired Petrarchan conceit; ***shore*** earth, as opposed to heaven; thus, 'I shall not make it to [i.e. be allowed to enter] heaven'.

[13] **by thy self . . . heretofore**

by thy self i.e. God is to promise, in his own name, the most powerful promise possible – cf. God's promise to Abraham: 'By my own name, I promise you that I shall richly bless you' (Genesis 22: 16); also 'When God made his promise to Abraham, he wanted to impress Abraham by the power of his vow, and so made it in his own name' (Hebrews 6: 13); ***thy son*** your son, Christ, with a pun on 'sun'; ***shine as he shines now*** shine as brightly as he is shining in the poet's vision of Christ, even as he is reciting his prayer/writing his poem; ***heretofore*** (as he has done) up to this time.

[14–15] **having done that . . . no more**

having done that having sworn by your own name; ***I have no more*** (a) I have no further fear; (b) I have no further sins; (c) I can no longer be attached to (Ann) More because, by his promise, God has made Donne entirely his.

BEN JONSON

(1572–1637)

1616 *Works* (first folio: Part 1, Epigrams)
1640 *Works* (Part 2, *The Forest* and *The Underwood;* published posthumously)

Ben Jonson was born in London, a month after his father's death. Though his grandfather was supposedly a gentleman of some standing, the family declined under Queen Mary. Jonson's stepfather was a bricklayer. As a child he first attended school in St Martin's Church, then went to Westminster. At about the age of sixteen he was put to work in his stepfather's business. Three years later he volunteered to fight with the army in Flanders, returning to civilian life in 1592. At some point during the next three years he married Anne Lewis; his first son, called Benjamin after his father, was born in 1596. A daughter also seems to have been born to the couple, though her date of birth is not known.

The next stage in Jonson's life, as playwright, was crucial. In July 1597 he was employed by Philip Henslowe, the leading theatre proprietor and manager at the time, to write for the theatre; later that same year he was imprisoned for his contribution to a play that was judged seditious. In the following year, however, his first important comedy, *Every Man in His Humour,* was acted by the Lord Chamberlain's Men, with Shakespeare in a leading role, and we may assume that their friendship dated from that time. Unfortunately, in the same year Jonson killed a fellow actor in a duel and was once again imprisoned. By claiming immunity from imprisonment as a member of the minor clergy he was able to gain release, but he lost all his goods and was permanently branded. At this time he converted to Roman Catholicism. During the first five years of his career as a dramatist, Jonson contributed to and wrote a substantial number of plays. In 1603, however, he suffered two blows: his son Benjamin died at the age of seven, and he was called before the Privy Council, accused of treason and of practising Roman Catholicism. Nevertheless, during this same year he created the first in a long line of royal entertainments for the court of James I. Despite these successes at court, he was imprisoned once again in 1605 because of a supposed slur against the king in his play *Eastward Ho*, written in collaboration with George Chapman. This time the intercession of powerful friends among the nobility was responsible for his freedom.

Though Jonson continued to encounter difficulties – including being cited once more for practising Roman Catholicism and for a peripheral involvement with the conspirators in the Gunpowder Plot against King James I – he continued to produce masques for the court and plays for the theatre during the next seven years. In 1610 he seems to have returned to the Church of England, and in 1612–13 he travelled to France as tutor to the son of Sir Walter Raleigh, apparently with mixed results. Jonson's greatest plays were written during this period, between his third release from prison and the definitive end of his political problems. His career reached a high point when he was awarded an annual pension of one hundred marks by King James in February 1616; in the same year the first folio volume of his *Works* was published. Oxford University awarded him an honorary MA degree on 17 July 1619. A further honour was accorded him on 5 October 1621, when he was nominated to the Office of Master of the Revels. In October 1623 Jonson became associated with Gresham College as a lecturer; in the same month, a fire in his lodgings destroyed a large number of books and manuscripts from his extensive and valuable library.

His life was frequently marked by this curious pattern of good and bad fortune in the same year. After the death of King James (1625), for instance, he continued to enjoy favour during the reign of King Charles I; but in 1628, though he was appointed chronologer of the City of London (a sinecure that meant income rather than recognition of special abilities), he also suffered a stroke that left him partially paralysed. Fortunately, two years later, his royal pension was increased to one hundred pounds per year and an annual cask of Canary wine was granted him from the cellars at Whitehall. He continued to present or publish plays and entertainments for the next four years. Towards the end of 1635, his only remaining son died;

two years later, on 6 August 1637, Jonson died in Westminster and was buried three days later in Westminster Abbey. In 1640–41 the second folio of his *Works* was published.

Context

Despite his familiarity with the nobility and his ability to move in upper-class society with some ease, Jonson thought of the great poets of the past as the real aristocrats and those most worthy of his respect. Unlike Donne, who remained an amateur poet and a writer of verses addressed to the narrow confines of his own personal circle, Jonson became a public poet, and his prestige was such that he gave the profession of poetry as a vocation a new meaning. He exhibited the ideal of the poet as a truly educated and learned man, intimately familiar with the literature of Graeco-Roman Antiquity, but no antiquarian. He saw the great minds of the past as his real contemporaries. Aware of the seamier side of aristocratic behaviour, he confined his praise to a select few among the living.

Nevertheless, no small part of the meaning of Jonson's work is tied up with his relationship with the upper class and his ambiguous position as a famous public figure who wrote in support of aristocratic ideals, yet could not participate in them fully as a person. For that reason, some recent scholars have focused on the complex role he played in a society built on a system of patronage that sanctioned his success as a writer of court masques, theatre plays, and epistolary verses while forcing him to address an audience of patrons who placed him under considerable strain to maintain his status. Jonson was, above all, a man who presented himself self-consciously as a poet and had to return to classical models in order to re-create the conditions that would allow him to follow his profession.

Genre

Jonson was the author of a large number of plays and other public entertainments that prove his versatility. He was, moreover, the master of numerous poetic forms, including epigram, satire, epistle, ode, song, sonnet, and epithalamion. By temperament he seems to have been drawn to two main types of poetry: the epigram, based principally, though not exclusively, on the example of the Roman writer Martial; and the short lyric, where he frequently excels in combining both elegance and simplicity. Unlike Donne, he made very few metrical experiments (and, indeed, seems to have disapproved vehemently of Donne's deliberate irregularities), tending to write in even, though seldom monotonous, iambic rhythms.

Many of Jonson's poems are addressed to friends and fellow intellectuals. Though he wrote some famous love poems, he was not primarily a love poet; and he rarely attempted certain popular forms such as the sonnet. He was a brilliant composer of songs, however, and a number of his lyrics were set to music. Some of the best-known were either written for or included in his comedies.

Jonson supervised the publication of his poetry, which he clearly valued even more than the plays. Such attention was unusual at the time. Plays were likely to be considered entertainment rather than serious literature, and aristocrats who wrote poems avoided giving any indication that they would like to see them in print, since publication might suggest a demeaning connection with those who had to earn money from their writings. But Jonson was proud of his achievement, and gave it weight by appealing to the example of the Ancient Greeks and Romans. It may well be said that in so doing he redefined and enhanced the dignity of the English writer by daring to call his collected writings his *Works* (a translation of the Latin *Opera*, usually applied to the venerable writings of classical authors), exactly as though he were a classical author himself. Such audacity was not lost on his contemporaries, but it finally earned him the respect he considered his due. Jonson's greatest contribution to the genre of poetry may well have been his insistence on the gravity, seriousness, and social importance of the poet as professional spokesman for his society.

Critical Reception

In a certain sense, Jonson's influence was more enduring – at least as far as the next century and a half was concerned – than Donne's. While Donne and his followers were out of fashion by the last third of the seventeenth century, the so-called 'Sons of Ben' were being increasingly admired and taken as models for the style that emerged after 1660 as neoclassicism and lasted almost to the end of the following century. Jonson's reputation took a different turn, however, in the nineteenth century. His poetry began to seem less relevant to the needs of a generation of poets and readers more interested in originality and turbulence of emotion than in equanimity and social grace. His comedies were appreciated by William Hazlitt and Samuel Taylor Coleridge at the beginning of the century, but by its end he was being criticised by J.A. Symonds for a lack of romantic temperament. By the beginning of the twentieth century, thanks to A.C. Swinburne's 1889 study, it was Jonson's plays that continued to hold interest for those few people who actually read much beyond a famous poem or two. This neglect of the poetry was reinforced by an emerging preference for the Metaphysical poets during the 1920s and 1930s, notwithstanding the fact that T.S. Eliot, who was largely responsible for the vogue of Donne, also wrote admiringly of his contemporary, Jonson, and called for a total reassessment of Jonson's achievements in a 1919 essay.

A monograph devoted exclusively to Jonson the poet (as distinguished from the dramatist), G.B. Johnston's *Ben Jonson: Poet* (New York, 1945), appeared only a quarter-century later; since then, there have been a number of book-length studies of the poems. Even so, Jonson tends to appear somewhat limited to late-twentieth-century readers. He offers neither the complexity of the Metaphysicals nor the mythopoeic range of the Romantics, and his social models, exemplary as they are of an essentially aristocratic culture, may seem quaint or even pernicious in a world dominated by democratic and egalitarian ideals. Nevertheless, recent critics have not lacked new insights into the poetry. Studies of the allusiveness of the poems reveal another kind of depth, and an interweaving of multiple strands of often surprising intricacy. Jonson's difficult position between the aristocracy and the middle class represents a source of intellectual complexity which, while it is different from the complexity of Donne's poetry, has attracted the interest of younger scholars fascinated with the social and ideological forms of power that are among his less-explored themes. Moreover, for some readers, Jonson's verse engages many fresh questions concerning class and gender relationships that have direct relevance to contemporary problems.

Further Reading

Editions

Ben Jonson, ed. C.H. Herford and Percy and Evelyn Simpson, 11 vols (Oxford, 1925–52) is the standard edition of the complete works, but is cumbersome to use; *The Complete Poetry of Ben Jonson*, ed. William B. Hunter (New York, 1963) is more convenient, as is *The Complete Poems*, ed. George Parfitt (Harmondsworth, 1975), which includes helpful annotations. J.D. Fleeman, ed., *The Complete English Poems* (New Haven, CT, 1982) contains some notes.

The Oxford Authors series volume of *Ben Jonson*, ed. Ian Donaldson (Oxford, 1985) provides a modernised text; it is a revision of his 1975 Oxford Standard Authors edition, and has the most up-to-date text and useful notes.

Critical Studies

There are a number of books devoted principally or exclusively to the plays. Monograph-length studies exclusively concerned with Jonson the poet are Wesley Trimpi, *Ben Jonson's Poems: A study of the plain style* (Stanford, CA, 1962); J.G. Nichols, *The Poetry of Ben Jonson* (London, 1969); Judith Kegan Gardiner, *Craftsmanship in Context: The development of Ben Jonson's poetry* (The Hague, 1975); George Parfitt, *Ben Jonson: Public poet and private man* (London, 1976); Richard S. Peterson, *Imitation and Praise in the Poems of Ben Jonson* (New Haven, CT, and London, 1981); Sara J. van den Berg, *The Action of Ben Jonson's Poetry* (Newark, NJ, 1987); Robert C. Evans, *Ben Jonson and the Poetics of Patronage* (Lewisburg, PA, London and Toronto, ON, 1988); and Michael McCanles, *Jonsonian Discriminations: The Humanist poet and the praise of true nobility* (Toronto, ON, 1991), which covers all the poems.

D. Heyward Brock, *A Ben Jonson Companion* (Bloomington, IN and Brighton, 1983) provides information on all aspects of Jonson's life, work and career in encyclopaedia form. Another handbook is David C. Judkins, *The Nondramatic Works of Ben Jonson: A reference guide* (Boston, MA, 1982). Mario di Cesare and Ephim Fogel, eds, *A Concordance to the Poems of Ben Jonson* (Ithaca, NY and London, 1978) is a useful tool. For bibliography, see D.H. Craig, *Ben Jonson: The critical heritage, 1599–1798* (London, 1990), which collects the major texts, and for later criticism and scholarship, Samuel A. and Dorothy R. Tannenbaum, *Ben Jonson: A concise bibliography* (New York, 1938; supplement, 1947; reprinted Port Washington, NY, 1967), supplemented in turn by Heyward Brock and James M. Welsh, *Ben Jonson: A quadricentennial bibliography, 1947–72* (Metuchen, NJ, 1974). The following list concentrates on publications after 1972.

Two recent biographies are Rosalind Miles, *Ben Jonson, His Life and Work* (London and New York, 1986) and David Riggs, *Ben Jonson, A Life* (Cambridge, MA, and London, 1989). Frank W. Bradbrook, 'Ben Jonson's poetry', in Boris Ford, ed., *The New Pelican Guide to English Literature, III: From Donne to Marvell* (Harmondsworth, 1982), pp. 159–70 is a succinct introduction to the poet; Robert H. Ray, 'Ben Jonson and the metaphysical poets: continuity in a survey course', in Sidney Gottlieb, ed., *Approaches to Teaching the Metaphysical Poets* (New York, 1990), pp. 89–95 offers suggestions for introducing Jonson to the current generation of students.

The complex social relationships between poetry, audience, patronage and friendship, so prominent in Jonson's work, are discussed at length in Robert C. Evans, 'Literature as equipment for living: Ben Jonson and the poetics of patronage', *College Language Association Journal*, **30** (1987), 379–94; 'Strategic debris: Jonson's satires on Inigo Jones in the context of Renaissance patronage', *Renaissance Papers*, **26** (1986), 69–81; and, especially, *Ben Jonson and the Poetics of Patronage* (Cranbury, NJ, 1989). See also Robert Wiltenburg, '"What need hast thou of me? or of my Muse?" Jonson and Cecil, politician and poet', in Claude J. Summers and Ted-Larry Pebworth, eds, *'The muses commonweale': Poetry and politics in the seventeenth century* (Columbia, MO, 1988); W.H. Herendeen, 'Like a circle bounded in itself:

Jonson, Camden, and the strategies of praise', *Journal of Medieval and Renaissance Studies*, **11** (1981), 137–67; Richard Helgerson, *Self Crowned Laureates: Spenser, Jonson, Milton and the literary system* (Berkeley, CA, 1983); Richard Finkelstein, 'Ben Jonson's Ciceronian rhetoric of friendship', *Journal of Medieval and Renaissance Studies*, **16** (1986), 103–24; Stanley Fish, 'Author readers: Jonson's community of the same', *Representations*, **7** (1984), 26–58; Jonathan Goldberg, *James I and the Politics of Literature: Jonson, Shakespeare, Donne, and their contemporaries* (Baltimore, MD, 1983) and also his 'The poet's authority: Spenser, Jonson, and James VI and I' *Genre*, **15** (1982), 81–99.

A special issue of *Studies in the Literary Imagination*, **6** (1973), *Ben Jonson: quadricentennial essays*, includes essays on Jonson's verse by Ian Donaldson, William Kerrigan, Edward Partridge and Richard S. Peterson. The more recent Claude J. Summers and Ted-Larry Pebworth, eds, *Classic and Cavalier: Essays on Jonson and the sons of Ben* (Pittsburgh, PA, 1982) also contains a number of good essays on the poetry.

For readings of individual poems, see W.D. Kay, 'The Christian Wisdom of Ben Jonson's "On My First Sonne"', *SEL*, **11** (1971), 125–36; G.W. Pigman III, 'Suppressed grief in Jonson's funeral poetry', *ELR*, **13** (1983), 203–20; Mary Ellen Rickey, 'Jonson's "On My First Sonne"', *Explicator*, **41** (1983), 19–21; Peter Hyland, 'The failure of stoicism: a reading of Ben Jonson's "On My First Sonne"', *Concerning Poetry*, **17** (1984), 35–42; Ilona Bell, 'The most retired and inmost parts of Jonson's "On My First Sonne"', *College Language Association Journal*, **29** (1985), 171–84; Don W. Der, 'Jonson's "On My First Sonne"', *Explicator*, **44** (1986), 16–18; Joshua Scodel, 'Genre and occasion in Jonson's "On My First Sonne"', *SP*, **86** (1989), 235–59; H.W. Matalene, 'Patriarchal fatherhood in Ben Jonson's Epigram 45', in David G. Allen and Robert A. White, eds, *Traditions and Innovations: Essays on British literature of the Middle Ages and the Renaissance* (Newark, NJ, 1990), pp. 102–12; Ann Lauinger, '"It Makes the Father, Lesse, to Rue": Resistance to consolation in Jonson's "On My First Daughter"', *SP*, **86** (1989), 219–34; Charles R. Forker, 'The Maid's Tragedy and Jonson's epitaph "On My First Daughter"'. *Notes and Queries*, **30** (1983), 150–51; Leanore Lieblein, 'Jonson's epigrams, 76', *Explicator*, **37** (1979), 5–6 ('To Lucy, Countess of Bedford'); Lawrence Venuti, 'Why

Jonson wrote not of love', *Journal of Medieval and Renaissance Studies,* **12** (1982), 195–220; Anthony Miller, 'Jonson's praise of Shakespeare and Cicero's De Oratore, III.vii', *Notes and Queries,* **38** (1991), 82–3 ('To the Memory of... Shakespeare'); Roger A. Gognard, 'Jonson's "Inviting a Friend to Supper"', *Explicator,* **37** (1979), 3–4; Meredith Goulding, 'A case for the epigram: Ben Jonson's "Inviting a Friend to Supper"', *Sydney Studies in English,* **8** (1982–3), 16–25; Robert C. Evans, '"Inviting a Friend to Supper": Ben Jonson, friendship, and the poetics of patronage', in Allen and White (see above), pp. 113–26; Bruce Thomas Boehrer, 'Renaissance overeating: the sad case of Ben Jonson' *PMLA,* **105** (1990), 1071–82 (mostly tongue-in-cheek); Michael C. Schoenfeldt, '"The mysteries of manners, armes, and arts": "Inviting a Friend to Supper" and "To Penshurst"', in Claude J. Summers and Ted-Larry Pebworth, eds (see above), pp. 62–79; P. Cubeta, 'A Jonsonian ideal: "To Penshurst"', *PQ,* **42** (1963), 14–24; G.E. Wilson, 'Jonson's use of the Bible and the Great Chain of Being in "To Penshurst"', *SEL,* **8** (1968), 77–89; Carole E. Newlands, 'Statius' Villa poems and Ben Jonson's "To Penshurst": The shaping of a tradition', *Classical and Modern Literature,* **8** (1988), 291–300; Richard Harp, 'Jonson's "To Penshurst": the country house as church', *John Donne Journal,* **7** (1988), 73–89; and, especially, Don E. Wayne, *Penshurst: The semiotics of place and the poetics of history* (Madison, WI, 1984); see also Harold Toliver, '"Householding and the poet's vocation": Jonson and after', *ES,* **66** (1985), 113–22; M. Van Deusen, 'Criticism and Ben Jonson's "To Celia"', *EIC,* **7** (1957), 95–103; A.D.P. Brown, 'Drink to me, Celia', *MLR,* **54** (1959), 554–7; Alan J. Peacock, 'Ben Jonson, Celia, and Ovid', *Notes and Queries,* **33** (1986), 381–4; Robert C. Evans, '"Men That Are Safe, and Sure": Jonson's "Tribe of Ben" epistle in its patronage context', *Renaissance and Reformation/Renaissance et Reforme,* **9** (1985), 235–54; William E. Cain, 'Self and others in two poems by Ben Jonson', *SP,* **80** (1983), 163–82; William A. McQueen, 'Jonson's Christmas clay', *ANQ,* **4** (1991), 13–17; P.J. Klemp, '"Sunke in That Dead Sea of Life": Fulke Greville in Jonson's Cary–Morison Ode', *Sidney Newsletter,* **5** (1984), 10–16; Timothy Cook, 'Possible recollections of Spenser in Jonson's "Immortal Memory" Ode', *Notes and Queries,* **32** (1985), 4, 487; W. Scott Blanchard, 'Ut Encyclopedia Poesis: Ben Jonson's Cary–Morison

Ode and the "Spheare" of "Humanitie"', *SP*, **87** (1990), 194–220; James A. Stewart and Stanley Riddell, 'Jonson reads "The Ruines of Time"', *SP*, **87** (1990), 427–55.

From *Epigrams*

18 / *To the Reader*

Pray thee, take care, that tak'st my book in hand,
To read it well – that is, to understand.

An iambic pentameter couplet that serves as introduction to Jonson's whole book. The majority of the poems in the volume are in this metrical style, which, in the form of the closed couplet, became increasingly dominant around 1660.

[1] **Pray thee**
I implore you; ***that tak'st . . . hand*** (a) you who pick up this book; (b) you who take care of it – note the repetition of 'take' and the implied play on the two senses of 'care': (a) be careful; (b) be attentive.

[2] **To . . . understand**
not simply to look at it but also take it to heart; Jonson seems to imply that his book, (a) like a child, needs both protection and understanding; (b) should be studied and heeded, not simply perused.

19 / *To My Book*

It will be looked for, book, when some but see
Thy title, *Epigrams*, and named of me,
Thou should'st be bold, licentious, full of gall,
Wormwood and sulphur, sharp and toothed withal;
Become a petulant thing, hurl ink and wit
As mad-men stones, not caring whom they hit.
Deceive their malice, who could wish it so.
And by thy wiser temper, let men know
Thou art not covetous of least self-fame
Made from the hazard of another's shame,
Much less with lewd, profane, and beastly phrase
To catch the world's loose laughter or vain gaze.
He that departs with his own honesty
For vulgar praise doth it too dearly buy.

The author's address to his book, expressing his concern for its reception, was a feature in the work of a number of ancient authors, such as Catullus or Ovid. Here it serves as a warning against those who might deliberately misread or misrepresent what Jonson has to say; the poem may also be classified as an 'apology' or defence of the author's intentions.

[1–3] **It . . . see**
Many who see the title and name of the author of this book will expect it to be. . .
[2] **named of me**
(a) said to be by me; (a) adorned with my name on the title-page.
[3] **Thou should'st be**
i.e. will expect my book to be (continues the idea from line 1); ***bold*** shameless; ***licentious*** indecent; ***gall*** rancour.
[4] **wormwood and sulphur**
bitter and bad-smelling substances; ***sharp and toothed*** biting and aggressive in satirical tone; ***withal*** in addition.
[5] **petulant**
insolently rude; ***hurl . . . wit*** The phrase suggests an author who simply throws words on to paper, but also one who besmirches others' reputations with (ink)stains.
[6] **As . . . stones**
as madmen hurl stones.
[7] **Deceive . . . malice**
disappoint their unfavourable expectations; ***who . . . so*** whoever they are who expect you to be typical of irresponsible satire.
[8] **wiser temper**
more moderate tone and attitude; ***temper*** character, temperament.
[9–10] **covetous . . . shame**
not in the least desirous of calling attention to yourself or becoming well known at the expense of those whom you attack.
[10] **hazard**
perhaps an allusion to the winning of an opening 'set' in the game of real tennis, therefore competing with another in order to defeat him.
[12] **loose . . . gaze**
The author's book is not intended as mere entertainment for the vulgar, nor as a means of gaining the author empty prestige.
[13] **departs with**
gives us, renounces; ***honesty*** Jonson emphasises the traditional character of the satirist or epigrammatist as a man who speaks his mind openly, whatever the consequences, in attacking obvious vice. Though Jonson's main model is the Roman poet Martial, famous for his epigrams, he also has in mind the satires of Horace and Juvenal. The *Epigrams* were published at a time of intense satirical activity in verse (John Donne, Joseph Hall and John Marston made important contributions), and Jonson seeks here to differentiate himself from more extreme contemporary practitioners of the genre.
[14] **vulgar praise**
the praise of the undiscerning crowd; ***doth . . . buy*** pays too high a price.

20 / *On My First Daughter*

Here lies, to each her parents' ruth,
Mary, the daughter of their youth;
Yet all heaven's gifts, being heaven's due,
It makes the father less to rue.
At six months' end, she parted hence
With safety of her innocence,
Whose soul heaven's Queen (whose name she bears),
In comfort of her mother's tears,
Hath placed amongst her virgin-train,
Where, while that severed doth remain,
This grave partakes the fleshly birth,
Which cover lightly, gentle earth.

One of two elegies written for Jonson's children. This one, in tetrameter couplets, echoes in its last line the formulaic closing line of the poems in the *Greek Anthology*, an ancient collection of short Greek poems.

[1] **Here lies**
The traditional opening of an epitaph or inscription on a tombstone; ***ruth*** (a) sorrow, distress; (b) remorse; (c) ruin.
[2] **Mary**
Some scholars think that this 'daughter of their youth' may have been the Jonsons' first child. Others, pointing to the references to the Virgin Mary in lines 7 f., think that she might have been born during Ben Jonson's Roman Catholic period (after 1598); ***daughter... youth*** an ambivalent phrase that could be taken to mean (a) born early in their marriage; or (b) the offspring of their youthful hopes. Infant mortality was common in this period.
[3] **heaven's gifts... due**
It was a commonplace to speak of children as a gift from God, but gifts imply the recipient's obligation to give something to the giver in return, hence the daughter was 'heaven's due', i.e. (a) what is owed to heaven; (b) due to return to heaven, whence she came.
[4] **father less to rue**
(a) regret less that she has died; (b) not wish that he had done otherwise. Note that the grief affects both parents, but the father alone finds some consolation in the lines that follow.
[6] **With... innocence**
(a) for ever safe from doing harm because too young to sin; (b) safe, in her ignorance of evil, from knowing suffering or sorrow.
[7] **heaven's Queen**
the Virgin Mary, mother of Jesus and, in the Roman Catholic tradition, patroness of virginal innocence.
[8] **In... tears**
The consolation for the mother is that the child is now in the company of the Virgin Mary in heaven.
[9] **virgin-train**
The deceased child is imagined as an attendant among those who accompany Mary in her heavenly entourage.
[10] **Where**
heaven; ***that severed*** that which has been severed, i.e. the child's soul, which now resides in heaven.
[11] **grave partakes**
The grave has the body as its share, with a suggestion in ***partake*** (to share

in a meal) of the commonplace image of a *devouring* grave; ***the fleshly birth*** the body, a gift of the earth, which returns to its donor, just as the soul, the gift of God, returns to its source.

[12] **Which . . . earth**
A frequent elegiac closing in Greek or Roman epitaphs. The tone of this last line suggests that the earth is a tender and delicate custodian of the infant body.

21 / *On Margaret Ratcliffe*

Marble, weep, for thou dost cover
A dead beauty underneath thee
Rich as nature could bequeath thee.
Grant, then, no rude hand remove her.
All the gazers on the skies
Read not in fair heaven's story
Expresser truth or truer glory,
Than they might in her bright eyes.
Rare as wonder was her wit
And like nectar ever flowing,
Till time, strong by her bestowing,
Conquered hath both life and it –
Life, whose grief was out of fashion
In these times. Few so have rued
Fate in a brother. To conclude,
For wit, feature, and true passion,
Earth, thou hast not such another.

An acrostic in iambic tetrameter, the initial letters of which spell out the name of the deceased. Margaret Ratcliffe was a young woman admired for her beauty and other qualities enumerated in this epitaph (which was not placed on her tombstone). She was maid of honour to the queen, who had her buried as a nobleman's daughter upon her death in November 1599 at the age of twenty-four.

[1] **Marble**
Margaret's tombstone. Literary epitaphs imitate the sort of sentiment that might be carved on the headstone of a grave. Usually, however, an epitaph is addressed to an onlooker, not to the stone itself; ***weep*** a command which is obviously impossible, especially addressed to a mute and unfeeling stone. The phrase suggests, hyperbolically, the extreme sadness of the occasion.

[2] **beauty**
beautiful person.

[3] **Rich**
i.e. rich in admirable qualities; ***nature***

. . . bequeath the grave is imagined to be the heir of all that nature produces, and Margaret as the precious behest.
[4] **rude**
(a) unmannerly; (b) insensitive, uncultured.
[5] **gazers**
astrologers or learned astronomers.
[6] **fair heaven's story**
(a) the mythological figures associated with the constellations and stars; (b) the influence of the stars on the lives of human beings.
[7] **expresser**
(a) more evident, better framed or constructed; (b) truer; ***glory*** splendour of light, in addition to the more usual meaning.
[8] **they might in**
they might read in.
[9] **Rare**
(a) uncommonly excellent; (b) seldom present elsewhere; ***wonder*** a wonderful thing or event; ***wit*** intelligence.
[10] **nectar**
(a) the drink of the gods; (b) the substance collected by bees from plants.
[11–15] **Till . . . fashion**
Margaret died of grief for her brother, Sir Alexander Ratcliffe, killed fighting in Ireland. In a letter a contemporary observer notes that she 'hath pined in such strange manner, as voluntarily she has gone about to starve herself and by two days together hath received no sustenance . . .'. Her extreme expression of grief for her brother's death is presented as admirable because it is so unusual an instance of fidelity to the memory of a loved one.
[11] **strong . . . bestowing**
as she grew weak because of her grief, time (i.e. death) grew strong; ***bestowing*** (a) expenditure; (b) granting or giving something to someone else; (c) employment.
[12] **it**
her wit.
[14] **rued**
grieved for.
[15] **Fate**
a tragic death.
[16–17] **wit . . . another**
The concluding lines sum up Margaret's qualities, both reasserting and justifying the claims made in line 3.
[16] **feature**
physical beauty; ***true passion*** (a) true love; (b) true suffering.
[17] **Earth . . . another**
(a) the world can offer no one to replace her; (b) no grave holds a more admirable person. Note that the last word rhymes with 'brother' in the middle of line 14, but is otherwise isolated; the unpaired final line also has 'not such another' to match it.

22 / *On Giles and Joan*

Who says that Giles and Joan at discord be?
   Th'observing neighbours no such mood can see.
Indeed, poor Giles repents he married ever.
   But that, his Joan doth too; and Giles would never
By his free will be in Joan's company.
   No more would Joan he should. Giles riseth early
And, having got him out of doors, is glad.

The like is Joan, but turning home is sad –
And so is Joan. Oft-times, when Giles doth find
Harsh sights at home, Giles wisheth he were blind.
All this doth Joan. Or that his long-yearned life
Were quite out-spun. The like wish hath his wife.
The children that he keeps Giles swears are none
Of his begetting, and so swears his Joan.
In all affections she concurreth still.
If, now, with man and wife, to will and nill
The selfsame things a note of concord be,
I know no couple better can agree.

An elaboration of three lines from an epigram by Martial (8.35).

[1] **at discord be**
don't get along.
[3] **repents . . . ever**
regrets ever marrying.
[4] **that**
i.e. that he married her; ***doth too*** i.e. she shares his regret.
[6] **No more would . . . should**
She doesn't want him in her company either.
[7] **him**
himself.
[8] **The like is Joan**
Joan is also glad; ***turning*** returning; ***is sad*** i.e. Giles is sad to [re]turn home.
[10] **Harsh**
very unpleasant.
[11–12] **that . . . out-spun**
i.e. often wishes that he were dead; ***long-yearned*** long-yarned; according to Greek mythology, the three Fates wove, measured, and cut a different length of thread or yarn to determine the extent of a person's life; ***quite out-spun*** over, finished; ***like wish*** same wish.
[13] **children . . . begetting**
i.e. he claims that some other man is the father of his children; ***keeps*** rears, maintains.
[15] **affections**
(a) passions; (b) preferences; ***concurreth still*** continues to agree.
[16] **If . . . agree**
i.e. if sharing the same likes and dislikes is the evidence that a couple get along, then no husband and wife agree more with one another than these two; ***will and nill*** want and not want.

23 / *On My First Son*

Farewell, thou child of my right hand and joy.
My sin was too much hope of thee, loved boy.
Seven years thou'ert lent to me, and I thee pay,
Exacted by thy fate, on the just day.
O, could I lose all father now! For why
Will man lament the state he should envy?

To have so soon scaped world's and flesh's rage,
And, if no other misery, yet age?
Rest in soft peace and, asked, say: here doth lie
Ben. Jonson his best piece of poetry,
For whose sake, henceforth, all his vows be such
As what he loves may never like too much.

This touching poem, one of Jonson's best-known elegies, is both personal lament and self-accusation of the kind that one often expresses in trying to account for one's feelings about the loss of a loved one. Jonson told William Drummond, a Scottish poet whom he visited at a later date, that he was away from home and had a prescient vision of his young son's death which was confirmed upon his return. However, nothing of that experience seems to be reflected in the poem, which combines intense personal regret with a sense of detachment and irony towards a doting parent.

[1] **right hand**
The son was called Benjamin, a name meaning 'of the right hand' – that is, 'dexterous' or 'fortunate'.

[2] **sin**
Though loving one's child cannot be thought truly a sin, Jonson has in mind the sin of presumption, i.e. too great a trust in transient things; ***hope*** (a) too great an expectation that Benjamin would survive to adulthood; (b) too much confidence in the permanence of an earthly creature. In an age of high infant mortality, a child's death was not an unusual event.

[3] **Seven years**
The child died of the Plague at the age of seven; ***Thou'ert*** you were; ***lent*** as in Epigram 22, 'On My First Daughter', Jonson thinks of children as a gift or loan from God, not as permanent possessions; ***I thee pay*** I repay God for you (as a loan).

[4] **Exacted . . . fate**
Fate (the time when one is destined to die) is described in terms of a loan which has come due – ***exact*** demand (a) payment of a loan or (b) surrender of an object; ***just day*** (a) precise or very day a loan is due; (b) the day of death or judgement, when God exercises his justice; apparently little Benjamin died on his seventh birthday – hence at exactly seven years old.

[5] **could . . . now**
If only I could now forget that I was ever a father.

[6] **Will . . . envy**
Why do men mourn for a death (i.e. state) that is really a desirable liberation from the sorrows of this life?

[7] **scaped**
escaped; ***world's and flesh's*** i.e. two of the three traditional sources of sinful temptation in this life: the world, the flesh, and the Devil; ***rage*** (a) madness; (b) violent passion.

[8] **if . . . age**
if you have not escaped all suffering, at least you won't have to put up with the miseries of old age.

[9] **and asked**
Of course the dead child cannot answer; part of the convention of the epitaph is that it anticipates the questions of those who gaze at the grave of the deceased.

[10] **Jonson his**
Jonson's; ***best . . . poetry*** his best conception.

[11] **whose**
Jonson's; ***henceforth, all*** from now on, may all.

[11–12] **vows . . . much**
i.e. may his desires – vows = (a) wishes; (b) promises, expectations – not cause him to become too attached to ('like too much') the things he loves.

24 / *On Lucy, Countess of Bedford*

This morning, timely rapt with holy fire,
  I thought to form unto my zealous Muse
What kind of creature I could most desire
  To honour, serve, and love, as Poets use.
I meant to make her fair and free and wise,
  Of greatest blood and yet more good than great.
I meant the day-star should not brighter rise
  Nor lend like influence from his lucent seat.
I meant she should be courteous, facile, sweet,
  Hating that solemn vice of greatness, pride.
I meant each softest virtue there should meet,
  Fit in that softer bosom to reside.
Only a learned and a manly soul
  I purposed her, that should, with even powers,
The rock, the spindle, and the shears control
  Of destiny, and spin her own free hours.
Such when I meant to feign and wished to see,
  My Muse bade, Bedford write, and that was she.

Jonson wrote many tributes to friends and patrons, but this one stands out not only because its subject was a prominent supporter of several famous poets of the period but also because it illustrates Jonson's ability to combine compliment to a great lady with irony towards himself as poet.

Title
The Countess of Bedford (1581–1627) was a friend and patroness of several literary men, including Jonson and John Donne, who also addressed poems to her. She was both beautiful and talented – prominent at court, a collector of paintings, and a lover of gardens.
[1] **timely**
early; ***rapt*** entranced, inspired; ***holy fire*** i.e. inspiration; cf. Plato's *Ion* for the most famous account of poetic inspiration as a sort of fiery frenzy caused by a god.
[2] **to form unto**
to depict for; ***zealous*** eager, full of passionate ardour; ***Muse*** one of the nine Greek goddesses who preside over poetry and the arts; here the inspirer is probably either Erato (love poetry) or Euterpe (lyric poetry); sometimes, however, the beloved

woman is herself said to be the poet's Muse.

[4] **as Poets use**
as poets are accustomed to doing.

[5] **make her fair**
depict her as a beautiful woman; ***free*** generous (especially as a patroness of the arts).

[6] **of greatest blood**
The Countess was the daughter of Sir John Harington, godson of Queen Elizabeth. Her piety, for which she was renowned in later life, was especially pronounced after she recovered from a grave illness in 1612; ***more good than great*** i.e. her goodness and virtue are more prominent features of her character than her aristocratic rank or pride of birth and wealth.

[7] **I meant . . .**
I meant to say that; ***day-star*** (a) Venus (the morning-star); (b) the sun; ***should not*** would not or could not.

[8] **lend like influence**
(a) affect the earth as much; (b) have as much (astrological) influence on human actions as she has had by her presence on earth; ***lucent seat*** the brilliance of the planet Venus (also called Lucifer, the light-bearer) when it rises at morning in the east.

[9] **facile**
(a) courteous; (b) easy of access or behaviour.

[10] **solemn**
impressive, awe-inspiring; ***greatness*** high rank in society.

[12] **Fit**
suitable; ***bosom to reside*** i.e. remain in her heart.

[13] **learned and manly soul**
intellectual and governing powers were thought to be masculine in character.

[14] **purposed**
(a) intended for; (b) proposed for; ***even powers*** (a) with equanimity; (b) even-handedly.

[15] **rock . . . shears**
These are the attributes of the three Fates: Clotho, who manages the distaff (or rock) and spins the thread of life; Lachesis, who winds it on the spindle, determining its length; and Atropos who, with her shears, cuts it off. In other words, Lucy is one who is in control of her own life and can 'spin her own free hours'.

[17] **Such . . . see**
When I wished to portray and actually see such a person.

[18] **My Muse . . . she**
Perhaps an echo of the famous closing line of Sir Philip Sidney's first sonnet in *Astrophil and Stella* ('"Fool!", said my muse to me, "look in thy heart and write"'); ***bade*** commanded me to (past tense of bid); ***that*** the woman he has been describing.

25 / *To the Same [Sir Henry Goodyere]*

When I would know thee *Goodyere*, my thought looks
  Upon thy well-made choice of friends and books.
Then do I love thee and behold thy ends
  In making thy friends books and thy books friends.
Now, I must give thy life and deed the voice
  Attending such a study, such a choice.
Where, though't be love that to thy praise doth move,
It was a knowledge that begat that love.

Sir Henry Goodyere, a friend of both Jonson and Donne, was a Gentleman of the Privy Chamber to James I. This is the second of two epigrams addressed to him. Jonson's praise of his friend's learning is meant to suggest the openness in his personal relationship with others. The poem might be said to illustrate the saying 'To know him is to love him'.

[1] **would**
wish to.
[1–2] **looks/Upon**
considers.
[2] **friends and books**
Both of great importance in Jonson's life as well as the subjects of many of his poems.
[3] **ends**
purpose, goal.
[5] **give . . . voice**
i.e. celebrate your achievements in a poem.
[6] **Attending**
that goes along with or is appropriate for.
[7] **Where**
i.e. in this poem; ***though't*** though it; ***love . . . move*** love that causes me to praise you.
[8] **It . . . love**
(a) 'It was my knowledge of your character that made me love you'; (b) 'It was your knowledge of books that made me love you'; ***begat*** fathered, caused to exist (past tense of beget).

26/ *On English Monsieur*

Would you believe, when you this Monsieur see,
  That his whole body should speak French, not he?
That so much scarf of France and hat and feather
  And shoe and tie and garter should come hither
And land on one whose face durst never be
  Toward the sea farther than halfway tree?
That he, untravelled, should be French so much
  As Frenchmen in his company should seem Dutch?
Or had his father – when he did him get –
  The French disease, with which he labours yet?
Or hung some Monsieur's picture on the wall
  By which his dam conceived him, clothes and all?
Or is it some French statue? No, 't doth move
  And stoop and cringe. O, then, it needs must prove
The new French-tailor's motion, monthly made
  Daily to turn in Paul's and help the trade.

A satirical portrait of a courtier who affects foreign ways; a generation earlier, Englishmen were more inclined to ape 'Italian' manners. Jonson's portrayal is similar to the 'characters'or brief prose sketches of such types published in collections like those of Sir Thomas Overbury or Joseph Hall. These sharp pictures of Elizabethan and Jacobean personality traits were modelled, in turn, on the writings of the ancient Greek author Theophrastus.

[1] **Monsieur**
the French word implied a somewhat higher social status during this period than its English equivalent, 'Master' (or 'Mr'); it is used here to suggest a Frenchman.
[2] **body . . . French**
The Englishman who affects a Gallic appearance does so through what we would now call 'body language', but the irony is that such would-be Frenchmen seldom spoke French well, if at all.
[3] **scarf of France**
The various items of apparel enumerated were popular imports from the Continent. Note the rhythmic effect of the repeated 'and', which implies a piling up of separate pieces of clothing rather than an integration of them into a unified appearance.
[5] **durst**
dared.
[6] **halfway tree**
apparently a tree or landmark of some sort that stood halfway between London and Dover.
[7–8] **he . . . seem Dutch**
or, as one would say now, 'more French than the French', to describe a person who imitates another nationality too thoroughly; ***as*** that.
[9] **French disease**
syphilis [*Morbus gallicus*] or venereal disease; ***labours yet*** (a) still suffers; (b) still makes love, though infected; ***he*** the Monsieur.
[11–12] **hung . . . clothes and all**
a witty reference to the popular notion that a woman's offspring could be influenced by whatever she had seen, heard or eaten at the time of conception.
[13] **'t**
it; note the use of the pronoun, implying that the English Monsieur is more thing than person.
[14] **stoop and cringe**
abject and self-debasing behaviour typical of a pretender; ***prove*** turn out to be.
[15] **tailor's motion**
puppet or mechanical doll, dressed by a tailor.
[16] **Paul's**
The forecourt of St Paul's Cathedral was a popular place for persons of fashion to display their new clothes.

27 / *To John Donne*

Who shall doubt, Donne, whe'er I a poet be,
   When I dare send my epigrams to thee?
That so alone canst judge, so alone does make,
   And, in thy censures, evenly does take
As free simplicity to disavow
   As thou has best authority to allow.

Read all I send; and if I find but one
Marked by thy hand, and with the better stone,
My title's sealed. Those that for claps do write,
Let puisnes', porters', players' praise delight;
And, till they burst, their backs, like asses', load.
A man should seek great glory and not broad.

Jonson wrote two epigrams addressed to his contemporary and fellow poet. This one, in iambic pentameter couplets, illustrates his ability to compliment himself and, at the same time, praise his addressee. Though the two poets wrote in very different styles, and Jonson had some reservations about his friend's metrical practice, the sincerity of this poem is not in doubt.

[1] **whe'er**
'whether', pronounced as one syllable to preserve the metre.
[2] **dare send**
implying that Donne was a very severe and discerning critic.
[3] **That . . . make**
who are alone as good a judge of poetry as a maker of verses.
[4] **censures**
critical judgements; ***evenly*** even-handedly, equitably, impartially.
[5] **free simplicity**
(a) open sincerity; (b) unadorned plainness; (c) naturalness; ***disavow*** refuse to acknowledge as correct; criticise as wrong.
[6] **best authority to allow**
i.e. Donne can allow departures from poetic norms and rules because, as a poet himself, he was such a brilliant breaker of them.
[8] **the better stone**
The Romans marked days they considered particularly good with a white stone.
[9] **My title's sealed**
(a) a deed of title, stamped with a seal to indicate acceptance; (b) his claim to the title of poet is assured – a similar idea is to be found in the Roman satirist Persius (*Satires*, 2.1) and in Martial (9.3, 5); ***claps*** applause, approval.
[10] **Let puisnes' . . . praise delight**
i.e. let the praise of puisnes . . . delight them. Note the satirical effect of the alliterating 'p' sounds, which suggests explosion or bursting; ***puisne*** (pronounced 'puny') novice or underling; ***porter*** (a) doorkeeper or janitor; (b) a person hired to carry burdens or luggage; ***players*** actors or theatrical performers – all are, presumably, poor judges of quality in poetry.
[11] **And . . . load**
i.e. load them (with praises) like asses' backs until they collapse under the burden (however, ***burst*** also implies a swelling up with excessive pride).
[12] **great glory . . . broad**
i.e. the quality of the glory one earns is more important than how widespread it is.

28 / *Inviting a Friend to Supper*

Tonight, grave sir, both my poor house and I
Do equally desire your company;
Not that we think us worthy such a guest,
But that your worth will dignify our feast
With those that come, whose grace may make that seem
Something, which, else, could hope for no esteem.
It is the fair acceptance, Sir, creates
The entertainment perfect, not the cates.
Yet shall you have, to rectify your palate,
An olive, capers, or some better salad
Ushering the mutton; with a short-legged hen,
If we can get her, full of eggs; and then
Lemons and wine for sauce; to these, a coney
Is not to be despaired of, for our money;
And, though fowl, now, be scarce, yet there are clerks,
The sky not falling, think we may have larks.
I'll tell you of more – and lie – so you will come:
Of partridge, pheasant, woodcock, of which some
May yet be there, and godwit, if we can,
Knat, rail, and ruff too. How so ere, my man
Shall read a piece of Virgil, Tacitus,
Livy or of some better book to us,
Of which we'll speak our minds, amidst our meat;
And I'll profess no verses to repeat.
To this, if ought appear, which I not know of,
That will the pastry, not my paper, show of.
Digestive cheese and fruit there sure will be,
But that, which most doth take my Muse and me,
Is a pure cup of rich Canary-wine
(Which is the Mermaid's now but shall be mine)
Of which had Horace or Anacreon tasted,
Their lives – as do their lines – till now had lasted.
Tobacco, Nectar, or the Thespian spring
Are all but Luther's beer, to this I sing.
Of this we will sup free but moderately,
And we will have no Poley, or Parrot by,
Nor shall our cups make any guilty men,
But, at our parting, we will be as when
We innocently met. No simple word,
That shall be uttered at our mirthful board,

Shall make us sad next morning or afright
The liberty that we'll enjoy tonight.

A particularly apt example of Jonson's neoclassical style, this poem in iambic pentameter couplets is based on a number of Greek and Roman models, including poems or lines from poems by Anacreon, Catullus, Horace, Juvenal and, especially, Martial, which might be called 'dinner-proposal' verse. Apart from the elegance and calculated politeness of the invitation, this tradition usually includes a great deal of wit and even satire, along with an implied set of moral standards that the meal and its presentation suggest. Jonson's poem has been much admired for these qualities in the past, but recent critics have also seen in it a tension between political power and amicable deference, or conspicuous consumption and social inferiority – that is, a conflict between Jonson's prestige or pretensions as a poet and his middle-class origins.

Title
Friend (a) a beloved person; (b) a person who can perform a service for or assist one in some way; ***Supper*** A meal can stand for an occasion to display one's opulence and to offer largesse to others, but it can also be a subtle mode of control, since the guest, by accepting the invitation, is placed under an obligation to repay his host either in kind or in quality.

[1] **grave**
serious, learned; the familiar tone of the poem suggests that a friendly and somewhat light-hearted compliment is intended, but some scholars suggest that a truly learned friend, such as Jonson's old teacher William Camden, might be intended; ***poor*** the adjective implies modesty and self-deprecation; the poet's residence is not a grand one (such as an aristocrat might own – see 'To Penshurst') and he has not the means to offer a truly magnificent banquet; ***house*** i.e. household, including family and servants.

[2] **equally**
The guest will be as eagerly awaited by the rest of the house as by its master, making the invitation sound all the more persuasive.

[3] **we . . . us**
Not a formal or 'royal' use of the plural pronoun referring to the poet alone but a literal reference to the whole household taken collectively.

[4] **worth**
Note the echo of 'worthy' from the preceding verse; the compliment made to the guest suggests that his visit will be considered not only out of the ordinary but also something of a favour to the hosts, since he is their superior.

[5] **those that come**
An invitation such as this one was never extended to the individual alone but to his entourage as well.

[5–6] **whose grace . . . esteem**
i.e. the prestige of the guests will make the supper take on an importance that it would not otherwise possess; note the way Jonson gracefully implies that he is indebted to his guest rather than that the guest will be indebted to him for accepting; ***make that*** make the supper; ***else*** otherwise.

[7–8] **It . . . cates**
Martial (5.78.16) has 'you will make the wine a good one by drinking it'; ***fair acceptance*** favourable response to the invitation; ***creates*** makes; ***cates*** food; observe, however, that this complimentary style also makes the guest responsible for the success of the feast by accepting, and for its failure by refusing.

[9] **rectify**
(a) to make right or correct; (b) to clear (the palate) in preparation for the

main course; (c) to remove impurities (in chemistry).

[10] **salad**
Pronounced 'sallet' at this time.

[11] **short-legged hen**
Probably a smaller variety, such as a bantam or Cornish fowl; note the sense of plenty, despite the diminutive size of the bird, suggested by the possibility of her being 'full of eggs'; cf. also Shakespeare's *2 Henry IV*, v, i, 25, where two such hens are part of Falstaff's dinner.

[13] **coney**
a rabbit or hare.

[14] **despaired of**
Note the comic expression of hope, applicable to both host and guest.

[15] **clerks**
learned men.

[16] **The sky ... larks**
A witty turn on the proverbial phrase 'When the sky falls, we shall have larks' – meaning, of course, never; here Jonson suggests that the wait will not be quite so long; ***larks*** small songbirds, eaten as a delicacy.

[17] **lie**
This amusing admission is translated from Martial, 11.52.13 ('I will lie so that you'll come').

[18] **partridge, pheasant, woodcock**
All edible gamebirds, usually reserved for aristocratic tables.

[19] **May yet be there**
Note the coy suggestion without any real commitment actually to serve such delicacies; ***godwit*** another gamebird, found in marshes, similar to a curlew.

[20] **Knat**
a kind of snipe of the sandpiper family (also called ***knot***); ***rail*** an edible gamebird belonging to the *Rallidae* species; ***ruff*** another variety of sandpiper, the male of which bears a ruff and ear-tufts during the breeding season; in Jonson's comedy *The Alchemist*, however, Sir Epicure Mammon considers knat and godwit more suited to his servant than himself (II,ii,80–81); ***my man*** Possibly Richard Brome, Jonson's assistant.

[21] **Virgil**
Author of the *Aeneid*, the greatest Roman epic poet; ***Tacitus*** Roman historian, particularly famous for his prose style.

[22] **Livy**
An earlier Roman historian, author of a history of Rome from the time of its founding; ***some better book*** i.e. (a) some book even greater than those mentioned; or (b) some book more suited to the occasion or the tastes of the guest.

[23] **Of which ... meat**
Reading at table was a common practice in Antiquity and also, in Jonson's time, at the king's and some aristocrats' tables; but Juvenal (Satire 11, 179–81), whom Jonson may be recalling at this point, suggests that intellectual fare will make up for the paucity of food at his table; here the suggestion is of two kinds of nourishment – bodily and intellectual.

[24] **profess**
(a) promise; (b) swear; ***no verses to repeat*** i.e. he promises not to bore the guest by reciting his own poetry.

[25] **To this**
concerning this subject; ***ought*** any.

[26] **pastry ... show of**
Since paper was expensive, pastry-cooks used whatever scraps they could find to line the bottoms of pies; an old joke thus had it that bad poets should fear the pastry chef. Note the mock modesty of the poet towards his own poetry – i.e. the guest may be surprised by the pastry, but not by having to sit through a recitation of Jonson's verses. Martial (5.78.25; 1.52.16 f.) likewise assures his guests that he will not read or recite to them.

[27] **Digestive cheese**
i.e. to be served after the main course as an aid to digestion.

[28] **take my Muse and me**
(a) inspire me to write poetry; (b) intoxicate me.

[29] **Canary-wine**
A much-appreciated wine, originally from the Canary Islands.

[30] **Mermaid's**
The Mermaid was a famous tavern in Broad Street, Cheapside, London, which Jonson and his friends favoured and frequented; ***shall be mine*** because he will procure a stock of his favourite wine from his favourite tavern to honour his guest.
[31] **Horace . . . Anacreon**
Horace (first century BC) was the most famous of Roman lyric poets and a model, as was the Greek lyricist Anacreon (sixth century BC), for many of Jonson's own poems; both wrote in praise of wine, and of its salutary effect on poetry and longevity.
[33] **Tobacco**
included among the beverages because Elizabethans spoke of *drinking* rather than of smoking it; it was thought to have certain medical properties; ***Nectar*** in Greek mythology, the drink of the Olympian gods; ***Thespian spring*** a spring sacred to the Muses at the foot of Mount Helicon and, more generally, a symbol of poetic inspiration.
[34] **Luther's beer**
i.e. German beer, made with hops rather than with malt and yeast alone, like English ale, and therefore considered weaker and inferior; ***to this I sing*** i.e. compared to the Mermaid's Canary wine that the poet is praising.
[35] **free**
(a) without restraint or limit; (b) generously; (c) without paying; ***moderately*** note the humour of the seeming contradiction – the wine will not cost anything (Jonson, as Poet Laureate, received a cask of wine as compensation for his duties), but both host and guests will need to exercise self-restraint.
[36] **Poley or Parrot**
There are two witty references here: Polly is a common name for a parrot (the implication is that there will be no one around to report verbatim, like a parrot, what was discussed), but these were also the names of two government spies, Robert Poley and another informer, who appears in contemporary records as Parrot but whose first name is unknown. The poet reassures his guest that nothing they say at dinner will be repeated elsewhere, whether by a parrot or by spies; ***by*** nearby.
[37] **our cups**
our drinking together; ***make . . . men*** nor will host and guest incriminate anyone else by what they say.
[41] **afright**
disturb, disrupt.
[42] **liberty**
(a) freedom of speech; (b) openness and friendship; (c) liberality, generosity; cf. Martial's description of his dinner party (10.47.21–4), where sentiments very similar to those in lines 37–42 are discussed, which Jonson is obviously imitating.

29 / *To Mary, Lady Wroth*

Madam, had all antiquity been lost,
All history sealèd up and fables crossed
That we had left us, nor by time nor place
Least mention of a nymph, a Muse, a Grace,
But even their names were to be made anew,
Who could not but create them all from you?

He that but saw you wear the wheaten hat
Would call you more than Ceres, if not that;
And, dressed in shepherd's 'tire, who would not say
You were the bright Oenone, Flora, or May?
If dancing, all would cry the Idalian queen
Were leading forth the Graces on the green;
And, armèd to the chase, so bare her bow,
Diana alone so hit and hunted so.
There's none so dull that for your style would ask
That saw you put on Pallas' plumèd casque;
Or, keeping your due state, that would not cry
There Juno sat – and yet no peacock by.
So are you nature's index, and restore
In yourself all treasure lost of the age before.

A complimentary poem praising its addressee in pentameter couplets; Lady Mary was a patroness of letters as well as a friend and fellow poet. Jonson was well acquainted with the Wroths and addressed several poems to them, including a long one to Sir Robert and three shorter epigrams to his wife. She participated in some of his masques at court, and his comedy *The Alchemist* (1610) was dedicated to her.

[1] **antiquity**
(a) ancient civilisations, particularly those of Greece and Rome; (b) their records or works of art and literature.
[2] **sealèd up**
i.e. kept from view, locked away or hidden; ***fables*** (a) stories, accounts; (b) mythological or legendary tales; ***crossed*** cancelled, marked or crossed out.
[3] **That**
so that; ***nor . . . nor*** neither . . . nor.
[4] **Least**
the least; ***a nymph, a Muse, a Grace*** The names of these three varieties of classical feminine deities or semi-divine beings, which figure so often in Greek and Roman mythology, were also used poetically during the Renaissance to describe women noted for loveliness or other inspiring qualities.
[5] **But even . . . anew**
i.e. so that even their names had to be reinvented.
[6] **create them . . . you**
The poet goes further than those who would describe the lady as a Muse or Grace; in a deft reversal of convention he implies that Lady Mary's qualities make her the model for the goddesses rather than they the model for her (the compliment is, of course, deliberately extravagant).
[7] **wheaten**
straw.
[8] **Ceres**
the Roman goddess of grains and agriculture; a spring festival was held in her honour.
[9] **'tire**
attire, apparel.
[10] **Oenone**
a nymph with the gift of prophecy who dwelt on Mount Ida and was married to the Trojan prince Paris in his guise as a shepherd before he deserted her for Helen; ***Flora*** Roman goddess of flowers and springtime, wife of the west wind, Zephyr. Her

festival was celebrated in April and May.
May
(a) Maia, classical goddess of spring growth, mother of Mercury; (b) the month of May, imagined as a goddess.
[11] **Idalian queen**
Venus, classical goddess of love and grace.
[12] **Graces**
the three sister goddesses (Aglaia, Thalia, Euphrosyne), bestowers of beauty and charm, always depicted as exquisitely lovely women; ***green*** grassy ground or spot.
[13] **armèd to**
armed for; ***chase*** hunt; ***bare*** archaic past tense of bear (bore, carried); ***bow*** i.e. bow and arrows, the accoutrements of the goddess of the hunt, but also implying the erotic passion induced by the arrows of Venus or her son Cupid.
[14] **Diana**
the Roman virgin goddess of the hunt, patroness of wild animals and the forest; ***hit*** i.e. with her arrows.
[15] **There's none . . . casque**
i.e. no one, however obtuse, could fail to desire your intellectual gifts for himself or herself; ***dull*** slow of understanding; ***style*** (a) manner of performing an action; (b) manner of writing (with a *stylus* or pen); ***ask*** want for oneself.
[16] **Pallas**
Athena, classical goddess of wisdom; ***plumèd casque*** helmet with a plume mounted on it, normally an attribute of Athena associated with her warlike character; here, however, it is perhaps more of a 'thinking cap', with the 'plume' understood as the pen with which she writes.
[17] **keeping your due state**
maintaining your proper public dignity as an aristocrat and a great lady.
[18] **Juno**
Roman goddess, wife of Jupiter and emblem of dignity and sovereignty; ***peacock*** emblem of vanity, sometimes associated with Juno; ***by*** alongside, next to her.
[19] **index**
guiding principle.
[19–20] **restore . . . age before**
The concluding phrase combines two separate ideas: on the one hand, Lady Mary is said to contain within herself all that was best in the culture of classical Antiquity, so that if knowledge of the past and everything it produced were lost, its treasures could be restored by taking her as the pattern for creating new ones; on the other, she is described as though she might lead in a new Golden Age, that time of harmony which was lost to later generations of humankind.

30 / *Epitaph on S[alomon] P[avy], a Child of Q[ueen] El[izabeth's] Chapel*

Weep with me all you that read
   This little story,
And know, for whom a tear you shed,
   Death's self is sorry.
'Twas a child that so did thrive
   In grace and feature,
As heaven and nature seemed to strive
   Which owned the creature.

Years he numbered scarce thirteen
When Fates turned cruel,
Yet three filled zodiacs had he been
The stage's jewel
And did act (what now we moan)
Old men so duly
As, sooth, the Parcae thought him one,
He played so truly.
So, by error, to his fate
They all consented;
But viewing him since (alas, too late)
They have repented
And have sought (to give new birth)
In baths to steep him;
But, being so much too good for Earth,
Heaven vows to keep him.

An elegy in the form of an epitaph or inscription supposed to be carved on the tomb of the deceased, Salomon Pavy (who died at the age of thirteen in 1602), this poem combines both lament for the death of a young boy and witty appreciation of the roles he played in the theatre. It consists of a quatrain-like rhyme scheme consisting of a line of tetrameter followed by a line of dimeter, rhyming *a b a b / c d c d*, etc.

[3–4] **And know . . . sorry**
i.e. know that Death itself is sorry for him for whom you are weeping.
[5] **'Twas**
he was; ***thrive*** turn out well.
[6] **In grace and feature**
both in his actions and in his physical appearance.
[7] **heaven and nature**
i.e. both the spiritual and the physical realms lay claim to him; note, however, that they only 'seem' to ***strive*** (dispute, fight with one another). Eventually, Jonson implies, heaven and nature are both ruled by the same divine purpose, though human understanding is unable to grasp it.
[8] **which owned the creature**
i.e. over whether he should be taken to heaven now, because of his perfection, or allowed to remain on earth and grow to full manhood.
[9] **numbered**
counted (in age).
[10] **Fates turned cruel**
The three Fates (Clotho, Lachesis and Atropos) were classical goddesses who determined the course of human life; in this case their 'cruelty' consisted of cutting off Salomon's life at an early age.
[11] **three filled zodiacs**
three full years on the stage; however, 'zodiac' also suggests that his life during that time included the full range of human experience.
[12] **stage's jewel**
i.e. he was a 'star' of the theatre.
[13] **act**
portray on stage; ***moan*** bemoan, lament, regret.
[14] **old men**
Apparently Salomon Pavy excelled in portraying elderly characters; ***duly*** properly, realistically.

[15] **sooth**
truth, in fact; ***Parcae*** (Latin) another name for the Fates; ***one*** an old man.
[16] **played so truly**
acted out his part so convincingly.
[17] **by error**
The conceit consists of imagining that the Fates mistook him for a man who had lived a full life, so excellent was his acting; ***fate*** death.
[19] **viewing him since**
i.e. now that he is dead and no longer acting, so that his true age is evident.
[22] **In baths to steep him**
to revive him by placing him in a bath that restores a deceased person to life, such as the one Jupiter used to bring back the dead Pelops in classical myth; ***steep*** soak in water, but here also soak in tears (both those of the mourners and those of the Fates themselves). In addition to the pagan classical references, Jonson is probably implying the ritual of baptism with water, a symbol of spiritual rebirth and a reminder for Christians that death itself is really a birth into a new, more perfect life in the hereafter.
[24] **Heaven vows to keep him**
The concluding line settles the conflict in line 7.

From *The Forest*

31 / *Why I Write Not of Love*

Some act of Love's bound to rehearse,
I thought to bind him in my verse;
Which, when he felt, 'Away' (quoth he),
'Can poets hope to fetter me?
It is enough, they once did get
Mars, and my Mother, in their net;
I wear not these, my wings, in vain.'
With which, he fled me and again
Into my rhymes could ne'er be got
By any art. Then wonder not
That, since, my numbers are so cold,
When Love is fled and I grow old.

Though he wrote some of the most famous love poems in the English language, Jonson had a somewhat detached and often humorous attitude towards his efforts. This poem in tetrameter couplets serves as the introduction to the whole section Jonson labelled 'The Forest'. Compare it with 'My Picture Left in Scotland', which has some of the same self-deprecatory tone.

[1–2] **Some . . . verse**
A mock-complaint as old as Ovid's *Amores* ('Loves'), which open with an apology for writing love poetry rather than heroic verse, and continued in a different vein by Sir Philip Sidney in *Astrophil and Stella* and Edmund Spenser in *The Shepherd's Calendar*; ***bound . . . bind*** note the parallel frustrations of love and the art of writing

verse, to each of which the dual meaning of ***bind*** is applicable – (a) the obligations of convention and the constraints of form, on the one hand; and (b) the inevitability of passion and the necessary observance of social rules – including those conventionally associated with the behaviour of lovers – on the other.

[4–6]
In Homer's *Odyssey* the story is told of Hephaestus (Vulcan) trapping his wife Aphrodite (Venus) and her lover, Ares (Mars) in a net after being informed of their relationship by Apollo, god of poetry; Eros (Love), as son of Aphrodite, therefore holds poets responsible for his mother's being held up to ridicule.

[7] **wings**
Cupid is traditionally depicted as an infant boy with angel-like wings.

[9] **ne'er**
never.

[10] **art**
(a) craft; (b) trick; (c) skill in poetry; ***wonder not*** do not be surprised (or amazed).

[11] **That, since**
that ever since then; ***numbers*** verses; ***cold*** (a) pedantic, dull; (b) lacking in passion.

[12] **Love is fled**
(a) no woman will love him; (b) he can no longer write love poetry; ***old*** Jonson was in his late thirties.

32 / *To Penshurst*

Thou art not, Penshurst, built to envious show
  Of touch or marble nor canst boast a row
Of polished pillars or a roof of gold.
  Thou hast no lantern whereof tales are told
Or stair or courts, but stand'st an ancient pile,
  And these grudged at, art reverenced the while.
Thou joy'st in better marks of soil, of air,
  Of wood, of water; therein thou art fair.
Thou hast thy walks, for health as well as sport;
  Thy Mount, to which the Dryads do resort,
Where Pan and Bacchus their high feasts have made
  Beneath the broad beech and the chestnut shade;
That taller tree, which of a nut was set
  At his great birth, where all the Muses met.
There, in the writhèd bark, are cut the names
  Of many a Sylvan, taken with his flames;
And thence, the ruddy Satyrs oft provoke
  The lighter Fauns to reach thy Lady's oak.
Thy copse, too – named of Gamage – thou hast there,
  That never fails to serve thee seasoned deer
When thou wouldst feast or exercise thy friends.

The lower land that to the river bends
Thy sheep, thy bullocks, kine, and calves do feed;
The middle grounds thy mares and horses breed.
Each bank doth yield thee coneys, and the tops,
Fertile of wood – Ashour and Sydney's copse –
To crown thy open table doth provide
The purpled pheasant with the speckled side.
The painted partridge lies in every field
And, for thy mess, is willing to be killed.
And if the high swollen Medway fail thy dish,
Thou hast thy ponds that pay thee tribute fish:
Fat, agèd carps that run into thy net
And pikes, now weary their own kind to eat,
As loath the second draught or cast to stay,
Officiously, at first, themselves betray;
Bright eels that emulate them and leap on land
Before the fisher or into his hand.
Then hath thy orchard fruit, thy garden flowers,
Fresh as the air and new as are the hours.
The early cherry, with the later plum,
Fig, grape, and quince, each in his time doth come.
The blushing apricot and woolly peach
Hang on thy walls that every child may reach.
And though thy walls be of the country-stone,
They're reared with no man's ruin, no man's groan.
There's none that dwell about them wish them down,
But all come in, the farmer and the clown –
And no one empty-handed – to salute
Thy lord and Lady, though they have no suit.
Some bring a capon, some a rural cake,
Some nuts, some apples, some that think they make
The better cheeses bring 'em or else send
By their ripe daughters, whom they would commend
This way to husbands and whose baskets bear
An emblem of themselves in plum or pear.
But what can this (more than express their love)
Add to thy free provisions, far above
The need of such whose liberal board doth flow
With all that hospitality doth know,
Where comes no guest but is allowed to eat
Without his fear and of thy lord's own meat,

Where the same beer and bread and self-same wine
 That is his Lordship's shall be also mine,
And I not fain to sit (as some, this day,
 At great men's tables) and yet dine away?
Here no man tells my cups nor, standing by,
 A waiter doth my gluttony envy
But gives me what I call and lets me eat.
 He knows, below, he shall find plenty of meat.
Thy tables hoard not up for the next day,
 Nor, when I take my lodging, need I pray
For fire or lights or livery. All is there,
 As if thou, then, were mine, or I reigned here.
There's nothing I can wish, for which I stay.
 That found King James, when hunting late this way
With his brave son, the Prince, they saw thy fires
 Shine bright on every hearth as the desires
Of thy Penates had been set on flame
 To entertain them or the country came,
With all their zeal, to warm their welcome here.
 What (great, I will not say, but) sudden cheer
Did'st thou, then, make 'em, and what praise was heaped
 On thy good lady then, who, therein, reaped
The just reward of her high huswifery:
 To have her linen, plate, and all things nigh,
When she was far, and not a room but dressed
 As if it had expected such a guest!
These, Penshurst, are thy praise and yet not all.
 Thy lady's noble, fruitful, chaste withal,
His children thy great lord may call his own –
 A fortune, in this age, but rarely known.
They are and have been taught religion. Thence
 Their gentler spirits have sucked innocence.
Each morn and even, they are taught to pray
 With the whole household, and may, every day,
Read in their virtuous parents' noble parts
 The mysteries of manners, arms, and arts.
Now, Penshurst, they that will proportion thee
 With other edifices, when they see
Those proud, ambitious heaps, and nothing else,
 May say, their lords have built, but thy lord dwells.

This 'country-house poem', one of Jonson's best-known works, is usually considered to be the model for a whole tradition, including such later poets as Carew, Waller, Marvell and Pope, of descriptive pieces in praise of an aristocratic estate. It is unusual in that the poet addresses the place rather than its owners. The estate had belonged since the mid sixteenth century to the famous Sidney family, who were prominent in the courts of both Elizabeth I and James I. Four of the Sidneys were poets – Sir Philip, the most famous and author of *Astrophil and Stella*; his sister, Mary Countess of Pembroke, best known for her metrical versions of the Psalms; his brother, Sir Robert; and his niece, Lady Mary Wroth, Sir Robert's daughter. The estate that Jonson praises belonged to Sir Robert.

Penshurst is made to personify the qualities that its masters are praised, indirectly, for possessing. It is depicted as a place where everything good and natural is in abundance; the estate is a sort of utopia, presented to an audience that shares the background, values and goals of the poet and the subjects of the poem. It is not a seat of sumptuous and ostentatious consumption, characterised by idleness, frivolity or irresponsibility. Everything is integrated into an order that is productive and caring. The house regulates and promotes the relations of man to man and of man to nature. Yet, as the poet intimates, it is easier for man and nature to be in harmony than for man to get along with man. It is notable that most of the positive characteristics are assigned to the natural landscape, the negative to human actions. The architecture and setting of Penshurst serve to rectify the relationship of man to man. Throughout the poem, sincerity and communal values are opposed to grand spectacle and isolation. Recent commentators have noted that real conditions on seventeenth-century estates were rather different from those depicted here, and there has been some controversy about the meaning of a poem in which those realities are overlooked (although they are present, at least implicitly, in the comparison between Penshurst and other (inferior) contemporary estates).

The poem, in pentameter couplets, consists of four main parts: (1) an eight-line opening section in which other houses are compared unfavourably with Penshurst; (2) a passage (lines 9–44) describing the surrounding environment; (3) a depiction (lines 45–88) of the way life is lived inside the house; (4) a conclusion (lines 89–102) in which the virtues of house and family are summed up. The style is typical of Jonson at his most classical; it derives from late Roman models, urbane yet plain and simple, emphasising brevity, clarity and certainty of thought, orderly arrangement, and interest in empirical detail.

Emilia Lanier's 'The Description of Cookham' (p. 154), contemporary with or perhaps even earlier than Jonson's poem, seems to be a totally independent work which neither influenced nor was influenced by it. In any event, Lanier's country-house poem was totally ignored by literary historians until very recently, and it seems to have had no impact whatsoever on later poets.

Title

Penshurst Penshurst Place, near Tonbridge in Kent, was built in an earlier period and was not one of the newer houses constructed by administrators who had risen to power and great wealth during the later sixteenth century; these estates, which were emblems of recently acquired dynastic power, were often characterised by elements and styles imitated from neoclassical Italian architecture – marble floors and columns, embellished ceilings, lanterns, great central staircases, and extensive, symmetrically designed and positioned courtyards. But the Sidney family had not owned it for much more than half a century. Originally built in Gothic style by a London merchant in the medieval period, Penshurst was given to Sir William Sidney by Edward VI in 1552.

[1] **built to**
created for; ***envious show*** ostentatious display provoking envy in others.

[2] **touch**
touchstone, a form of basalt or black marble; ***boast*** claim proudly.

[4] **lantern**
A tower with glass windows that allows light to shine into the room below; ***whereof tales are told*** outstanding architectural features of country houses were often as much the object of visitors' journeys and interest as the inhabitants themselves.

[5] **pile**
(a) a castle or stronghold; (b) a massive or impressive group of buildings – Penshurst was built around 1340 and was not, therefore, a work of sumptuous or elaborate architecture.

[6] **these grudged at, art reverenced the while**
i.e. 'while these things [pillars, roof, lantern] are the object of envy, you [Penshurst], though you lack them, are paid the deepest respect'; ***grudged at*** begrudged, envied, admired reluctantly.

[7] **joy'st in**
(a) enjoy; (b) rejoice in, delight in; ***marks*** (a) qualities; (b) characteristics – the quality of the air was a major factor in the choice of a favourable site for a house.

[8] **Therein . . . fair**
i.e. Penshurst is not distinguished for its architecture so much as for the healthiness of its environment.

[9] **sport**
(a) recreation; (b) hunting.

[10–18] **Where . . . oak**
Imitates a passage from Martial (9.61.11–16), in which the poet describes a stand of trees Julius Caesar planted on his Tartessus estate.

[10] **Thy Mount**
A rise in the park grounds at Penshurst is still so designated; ***dryads*** tree nymphs (in Greek mythology).

[11] **Pan**
a Greek nature god; ***Bacchus*** Dionysus, the Greek god of wine, often associated with natural forces and, especially, with revelry and feasting. The figure of Pan that was popular during the Renaissance was a tamer version of the wild deity of the Greeks; he symbolised the rural and the rustic in their picturesque aspects, and was presented as an image of natural man, unaffected by civilisation or refined manners.

[13–14] **taller . . . birth**
This oak tree, which grew from an acorn planted (***of a nut was set***) the day Sir Philip Sidney was born (30 November 1554), can still be seen today; the passage also recalls Suetonius' description, in his *Life of Virgil*, of a poplar planted at Virgil's birth.

[14] **where . . . met**
where can refer either to the oak or to Sir Philip Sidney's birth; if it refers to the tree, the phrase implies that it is a place that has been particularly inspirational; if to the birth, it praises Sir Philip the poet as gifted from birth with his multiple talents; ***Muses*** the Greek goddesses, usually nine in number, who foster and inspire various arts.

[15] **writhèd**
The bark of an oak often has a twisted texture, especially as it grows older. The carving of the name of a beloved person in the bark of a tree was common practice then, as now. See Carew's 'A Rapture' (p. 274) and Marvell's 'The Garden' (p. 499) for other references to this practice.

[16] **sylvan**
(a) a forest-dweller (from the Roman wood-spirit Silvanus); (b) a rural lover; ***his flames*** love-passion (either that of the 'sylvan' himself or that described in Philip Sidney's poetry).

[17] **thence**
to the tree; ***ruddy*** red-faced, hence rustic in complexion; ***ruddy Satyrs*** in Greek mythology, rough, primitive creatures, half-man, half-goat, who

were symbolic of the lower appetites and often depicted as attendants of Bacchus; ***provoke*** challenge, as in a race.

[18] **lighter**

(a) fleeter of foot, faster; (b) smaller or less ponderous; ***Faun*** an ancient Italian deity of fields and herds, usually depicted as half-man, half-goat, like the satyr; ***Lady's oak*** Barbara Gamage, Lady Leicester, who married Sir Robert Sidney in 1584, was said to have gone into labour under this tree. She bore him at least ten children.

[19–20] **copse . . . deer**

Barbara Gamage often fed the deer in this grove, which came to bear her name; ***serve thee*** i.e. the household at Penshurst is provided with its venison from this part of the park – note the complementarity: Lady Sidney fed the deer, which in turn 'fed' her table; ***seasoned*** (a) in the proper season; (b) well seasoned with spices.

[21] **exercise thy friends**

i.e. by giving guests the opportunity to hunt deer, so that the estate grounds provide both sport and food.

[22–4] **lower land . . . breed**

The domesticated stock is contrasted with the wild game mentioned both before and after these lines.

[23] **kine**

cows (an archaic plural); ***bullocks*** bulls; ***do feed*** the subject is 'land' ('do', in south-western dialect, is a third-person singular form).

[25] **coneys**

hares or rabbits; ***tops*** the upper parts of the river banks.

[26] **fertile**

abundant in, full; ***Ashour*** Ashour's Wood, still in existence on the east bank of the Medway river; ***Sidney's copse*** probably part of the north-east extension of Ashour.

[27] **open**

available to all; ***doth provide*** the subject is 'tops'.

[28] **purpled**

brightly coloured.

[29] **painted partridge**

A literal translation of Martial's phrase (3.58.15).

[30] **mess**

meal; ***is willing*** The notion that animals offer themselves up willingly to their hunters is part of the Golden Age myth, and reflects the belief that nature exists to serve humanity; here it suggests that all things are conscious of the needs of the great house and its occupants.

[31] **swollen Medway**

a river whose rapid waters were notorious for being difficult to fish in.

[32] **tribute**

(a) something contributed voluntarily as due; (b) a service rendered to show respect or gratitude; (c) a large tax imposed by a landlord.

[33] **run into thy net**

see line 30.

[34] **weary . . . eat**

Pikes were thought to be the cannibals of the fish world.

[35] **loath**

reluctant; ***second draught or cast to stay*** i.e. the fish do not wish to wait for the fisherman to cast his line a second time, but bite the hook the first time it is in the water; ***draught or cast*** the throwing out of a fishing line; ***stay*** prevent.

[36] **Officiously**

(a) obligingly; (b) dutifully; (c) according to office or purpose.

[37] **emulate**

(a) imitate; (b) rival, vie with.

[42] **quince**

a fruit resembling a large yellow apple.

[43] **blushing**

rosy-coloured, hence ripe; ***woolly*** ripe peaches are covered with a fine fuzz.

[44] **hang on thy walls**

i.e. the fruit trees are grown as espaliers, trained to climb flat against the walls.

[45] **walls**

In May 1612 walls were built on the estate using local stone; if this line is an allusion to that construction, then the poem was composed sometime after that date.

[46] **wish them down**
i.e. because they prevent no one from entering.
[48–71] **But all . . . the next day**
These lines are based on an epigram of Martial (3.58.33–44).
[48] **clown**
rustic or peasant.
[49–50] **salute . . . suit**
i.e. they bring gifts when they come, even though they have no favours to ask.
[51] **capon**
a castrated male chicken, considered a table delicacy because of its excellent meat.
[53] **'em**
their superior cheeses.
[54–6] **ripe daughters . . . pear**
i.e. the marriageable daughters of the region, whom the lord of the estate was often responsible for seeing properly matched with husbands, bring ripe fruit that reflects their own sexual and social maturation.
[56] **emblem**
a typical representative. During the period, so-called 'emblem-books', which consisted of symbolic images accompanied by a short explanatory text, were popular. The fruit, as image of the young women, suggests the fundamental harmony between nature and humanity that prevails on the estate.
[58] **free provisions**
generous stock of food, bounteous supply. The household already has all it needs, hence these gifts are purely symbolic.
[59] **liberal board**
a table from which guests may take what they want.
[61–2] **guest . . . mine**
Jonson once complained that aristocrats tended to serve food of inferior quality to guests of lower social status.
[65] **fain**
desirous, wishing; ***sit*** be seated at table.
[65–6] **as some . . . tables**
i.e these days, some guests are so poorly seated or ignored by their hosts that they feel out of place. Other poets, such as Robert Herrick and Thomas Carew, praise liberality and courtesy to guests. Compare Jonson's 'Conversations with William Drummond' (lines 316 ff.); when Jonson, dining at Salisbury's table, was asked what displeased him, he replied: 'You promised I should dine with you, but I do not', because he was not served the same food as his host was eating; ***dine away*** forced to eat as if he were sitting at another table, or in another room, or even in another place altogether.
[69] **what I call**
what I ask for.
[71] **hoard not up**
i.e. they do not keep food back to serve as leftovers the next day.
[73] **livery**
(a) provisions; (b) appointments; (c) allowance.
[76] **that found**
[the king] found that to be true . . . ***King James*** a room at Penshurst is still known as 'King James's room'.
[76–88] **when hunting . . . a guest**
Royal visits could be ruinously expensive, since they involved a large number of people in the monarch's entourage; the point of this passage is that the king, who dropped in at Penshurst unexpectedly, found the house well prepared for a royal visit, even though he arrived without warning.
[77] **the Prince**
Prince Henry died in November 1612; since Jonson seems to speak of him here as still living, most scholars would date the poem sometime before then.
[78] **as the**
as if the.
[79] **Penates**
the Roman household gods, minor deities who protected hearth and home and were given their own altar within it.
[80] **entertain**
welcome as guests; ***or the*** or as though

the; ***country*** all the inhabitants of the countryside.
[82] **sudden**
prompt; ***cheer*** hospitable entertainment.
[83] **make 'em**
i.e. provide for the royal party.
[85] **high huswifery**
excellent management of the estate. Aristocratic ladies had considerable say over the running of their households.
[86] **nigh**
nearby, ready.
[87] **was far**
was not there. In other words, the household was so efficiently organised that it did not require the presence of its mistress.
[90] **fruitful**
alluding to the many children born to Lady Leicester; see note to line 18 above; ***withal*** in addition, besides.
[91] **great lord**
Sir Robert Sidney (1563–1626), younger brother of Sir Philip Sidney and father of Lady Mary Wroth, all three poets. He was knighted in 1586 for valour in battle at Zutphen, became Baron Sidney of Penshurst, Viscount Lisle (1605), and, after Jonson's poem was published, Earl of Leicester (1618). By describing Sidney as 'thy great lord', the poet implies that he rules his domain with the kind of respect and care that characterise stewardship at its best; ***may call his own*** The court of King James was marked by a certain licentiousness and sexual liberty. Sir Robert is fortunate in knowing that the children born to his wife were not the fruit of extramarital affairs because he pays proper attention to his spouse and household, and therefore has no need to worry about her fidelity to him.
[94] **sucked innocence**
i.e. imbibed innocence just as they drank their mother's milk.
[97] **noble parts**
aristocratic bearing or aspect.
[98] **mysteries**
(a) skills developed for a profession; (b) religious truths.
[99] **proportion**
compare.
[100] **ambitious heaps**
monumental castles or estates.
[102] **built . . . dwells**
Echoes an epigram of Martial (12.1.8): 'How well you do not dwell'. The construction of impressive estates was one of the ways the aristocracy sought to increase prestige; Penshurst is praised because it is liveable in and comfortable rather than ostentatious, and those who dwell there benefit from an architecture designed for the practical activities of a fully functioning household.

33 / *Song: To Celia*

Drink to me only with thine eyes,
    And I will pledge with mine;
Or leave a kiss but in the cup,
    And I'll not look for wine.
The thirst that from the soul doth rise
    Doth ask a drink divine;
But might I of Jove's Nectar sup,
    I would not change for thine.

I sent thee, late, a rosy wreath,
  Not so much honouring thee,
As giving it a hope that there
  It could not withered be.
But thou thereon did'st only breathe
  And sent'st it back to me;
Since when, it grows and smells, I swear,
  Not of itself, but thee.

A poem in alternating tetrameter and pentameter verses with an unusual rhyme-scheme of *a b c b* / *a b c b* / *d e f e* / *d e f e*. This famous song was set to music during Jonson's lifetime. It consists mainly of scattered phrases translated from Flavius Philostratus, a Greek sophist of the second century AD, whose work Jonson liked enough to draw on as a source in several other works.

The song divides metrically and thematically into two equal sections. In the first half the poet compliments Celia by honouring her with a poetic toast; in the second, with a poetic wreath. Each suggests that the lady can bestow a kind of divine quality on her admirer. Her kiss is a drink of immortality for the soul; her breath can revive the rose, that most transitory of flowers.

Title
Celia The name means 'heavenly one' in Latin. The identity of the lady is uncertain; indeed, she may have been purely imaginary.
[1] **only . . . eyes**
i.e. as opposed to proposing a toast aloud.
[2] **pledge**
give assurance to someone in the act of drinking.
[3–4] **kiss . . . wine**
The comparison of kisses to wine is an ancient and familiar poetic figure; since both 'intoxicate' the recipient, the lover need not seek inebriation in drink if his lips touch the same cup as his beloved's have touched.
[5–6] **thirst . . . rise**
The notion of the soul as thirsting for the divine is as old as the biblical psalms (cf. Psalm 42: 'As the deer thirst for a stream of cool water, so I thirst for you, O God'), but the context here is rather more secular in tone, since the 'drink divine' is the glance of the lady.
[6] **ask**
demand, call for, require.
[7] **Jove's nectar**
Nectar was served to the Greek and Roman gods in lieu of wine, just as ambrosia took the place of food for them; ***sup*** consume at a meal.
[8] **change for thine**
i.e. he would not trade Jove's nectar for the 'drink divine' that is her kiss (***change*** exchange, trade).
[9] **late**
(a) recently (as in the phrase 'of late'); (b) tardily.
[9–12] **I sent . . . withered be**
i.e. the wreath of roses was intended not so much as an acknowledgement of Celia's beauty as a means of allowing it to benefit from her life-bestowing presence and breath. Note the reversal of the usual situation, as presented in Waller's 'Go, lovely rose' (p. 294). The rose is sent to the lady not in order to emphasise the fragility of her beauty but to be enhanced by it.
[11] **it**
the 'rosy wreath'.

From *The Underwood*

34 / *My Picture Left in Scotland*

I now think Love is rather deaf than blind,
For else it could not be
That she,
Whom I adore so much, should so slight me
And cast my love behind.
I'm sure my language to her was as sweet
And every close did meet
In sentence of as subtle feet
As hath the youngest He
That sits in shadow of Apollo's tree.
Oh, but my conscious fears
That fly my thoughts between
Tell me that she hath seen
My hundreds of grey hairs,
Told seven and forty years,
Read so much waste as she cannot embrace
My mountain belly and my rocky face,
And all these, through her eyes, have stopped her ears.

The lady referred to in this amusing poem is unknown, and may simply be a rhetorically necessary reference. Jonson visited William Drummond, a fellow poet, in Scotland in 1619. The form is very unusual – trimeter, tetrameter and pentameter lines, in an irregular rhyming pattern: *a b b b a c c c b b / d e e d d f f e.*

[1] **deaf than blind**
Cupid (Eros or Amor, the god of love) is often depicted as a winged male infant bearing bow and arrows and blindfolded; love is usually said to be blind because lovers overlook the most obvious flaws in those to whom they are attracted. Jonson's witty variation suggests that lovers are equally undiscriminating in what they choose to hear.

[7] **close**
(a) concluding passage of a speech; (b) the concluding strain of a musical phrase; *did meet* i.e. reached its close.

[8] **sentence**
(a) verbal phrase; (b) a short or pithy saying; (c) a complete musical phrase; *feet* metrical rhythm.

[9] **As hath the youngest He**
as the youngest poet is capable of producing.

[10] **sits . . . Apollo's tree**
i.e. that writes poetry or sings songs. Apollo was the god of both; his tree is the laurel, with whose leaves poets were crowned in recognition of their achievement.

[12] **fly . . . between**
that interrupt my thoughts.

[15] **told . . . years**
(a) she has *counted* his forty-seven years (Jonson's age); (b) his grey hair has *betrayed* his age; *told* enumerated.

[16] **Read**
i.e. read between the lines of his verses, and deduced his age and appearance from what he has written there; ***so much waste*** a pun on 'waist' (his 'mountain belly' in the next line) and 'waste', i.e. the effects of old age on his body and his cragged ('rocky') features. Jonson became rather rotund in his later years.
[17] **all these . . . ears**
The last line is an ironic answer to the opening verses; the poet's failure to attract the lady is explained by the fact that his unattractive appearance belies the mellifluous qualities of his poetry.

35 / *An Epistle to Master Arthur Squib*

What I am not and what I fain would be,
  Whilst I inform myself, I would teach thee,
My gentle Arthur, that it might be said
  One lesson we have both learned and well read.
I neither am – nor art thou – one of those
  That harkens to a jack's pulse when it goes,
Nor ever trusted to that friendship yet
  Was issue of the Tavern or the Spit.
Much less a name would we bring up or nurse
  That could but claim a kindred from the purse.
Those are poor ties, depend on those false ends;
  'Tis virtue alone, or nothing, that knits friends.
And, as within your office you do take
  No piece of money but you know or make
Inquiry of the worth, so must we do:
  First weigh a friend, then touch and try him too.
For there are many slips and counterfeits.
  Deceit is fruitful. Men have masks and nets,
But these with wearing will themselves unfold.
  They cannot last; no lie grew ever old.
Turn him and see his threads; look if he be
  Friend to himself that would be friend to thee,
For that is first required: a man be his own.
  But he that's too much that is friend of none.
Then rest and a friend's value understand;
  It is a richer purchase than of land.

A tribute to a friend that is also a kind of moral essay on friendship itself.

Title
Arthur Squib Jonson's friend, a teller in the Exchequer, whom he addressed in this and another poem.
[1] **fain**
willingly.
[4] **well read**
(a) understood; (b) studied.
[6] **harkens**
listens attentively, sympathetically, or respectfully; ***jack's pulse*** a mechanical metal figure of a man with a large hammer that strikes the hours on a clock; i.e. a 'yes-man', someone who agrees unquestioningly with the opinions or moods of another; also, a token friend.
[7] **was issue of**
i.e. which was the result of the kind of fellowship one strikes up in taverns and public houses.
[8] **Tavern or the Spit**
well-known London public drinking houses (pubs).
[9] **nurse**
(a) cultivate; (b) hold in one's heart and mind.
[10] **kindred . . . purse**
i.e. is a friend only so long as his tavern bill is being paid by someone.
[11] **ties, depend**
those ties are poor that depend on; ***false ends*** hypocritical purposes.
[12] **virtue alone**
Another proverbial saying calls virtue the basis of friendship.
[13] **office**
(a) profession, line of duty; (b) his booth in the Exchequer.
[13–15] **take . . . worth**
i.e. you accept no coins or bills until you have determined that they are worth their face value. These lines are perhaps an elaboration of a sentiment in Plutarch's *How to Tell a Flatterer*, 2, and *Of Having Many Friends*, 3.
[16] **touch and try**
Precious metals were tested (tried) by placing them in contact with a touchstone, which would react with them if they were genuine.
[17] **slips**
(a) small twigs or shoots used for grafting on to other plants (cf. 'fruitful' in the following line); (b) counterfeit coins.
[18] **masks and nets**
i.e. masks to conceal their true intentions and nets to catch the unwary in.
[19] **unfold**
reveal.
[20] **no lie . . . old**
a proverbial saying from classical Antiquity; an example is in Seneca's *Epistles*, 79.18.
[21] **Turn . . . threads**
Tapestries and carpets look very different on their reverse sides, where the threads that make up the pattern are revealed; note the possible further meaning of 'unfold' – to examine the inside of a fabric – in line 19.
[22] **Friend to himself . . . to thee**
another commonplace notion, also found in Seneca's *Epistles*, 6.7.
[23] **be his own**
be his own person, not controlled by anyone else.
[24] **too much that**
too much his own person.
[26] **richer purchase**
a final proverbial phrase – better a true friend than a rich farm; ***purchase*** acquisition.

36 / *An Epistle Answering to One that Asked to be Sealed of the Tribe of Ben*

Men that are safe and sure in all they do
Care not what trials they are put unto;
They meet the fire, the test, as martyrs would,
And, though opinion stamp them not, are gold.
I could say more of such but that I fly
To speak myself out too ambitiously
And, showing so weak an act to vulgar eyes,
Put conscience and my right to compromise.
Let those that merely talk and never think,
That live in the wild anarchy of drink,
Subject to quarrel only; or else such
As make it their proficiency how much
They've glutted in and lechered out that week,
That never yet did friend or friendship seek
But for a sealing – let these men protest,
Or th'other, on their borders, that will jest
On all souls that are absent, even the dead,
Like flies or worms, with man's corrupt parts fed;
That to speak well think it above all sin
Of any company but that they are in,
Call every night to supper in these fits
And are receivèd for the covey of wits;
That censure all the town and all th'affairs
And know whose ignorance is more than theirs.
Let these men have their ways and take their times
To vent their libels and to issue rhymes.
I have no portion in them, nor their deal
Of news they get to strew out the long meal.
I study other friendship – and more one
Than these can ever be – or else wish none.
What is't to me whether the French design
Be or be not to get the Valtelline?
Or the States' ships sent forth belike to meet
Some hopes of Spain in their West-Indian fleet?
Whether the Dispensation yet be sent
Or that the match from Spain was ever meant?
I wish all well and pray high heaven conspire
My prince's safety and my king's desire.

But if, for honour, we must draw the sword
　And force back that which will not be restored,
I have a body yet that spirit draws
　To live or fall a carcass in the cause.
So far without inquiry what the States
　Brunsfield and Mansfield do this year, my fates
Shall carry me at call; and I'll be well,
　Though I do neither hear these news nor tell
Of Spain or France or were not pricked down one
　Of the late mystery of reception,
Although my fame to his not underhears
　That guides the motions and directs the bears.
But that's a blow by which in time I may
　Lose all my credit with my Christmas clay
And animated Porc'lane of the Court.
　Aye, and for this neglect, the coarser sort
Of earthen jars there may molest me too.
　Well, with mine own frail pitcher, what to do
I have decreed: keep it from waves and press,
　Lest it be jostled, cracked, make nought or less.
Live to that point I will for which I am man
　And dwell as in my centre, as I can,
Still looking, too, and ever loving heaven,
　With reverence using all the gifts thence given.
'Mongst which, if I have any friendships sent
　Such as are square, well-tagged, and permanent,
Nor built with canvas, paper, and false lights –
　As are the glorious scenes at the great sights –
And that there be no fevery heats nor colds,
　Oily expansions, or shrunk duty folds,
But all so clear and led by reason's flame
　As but to stumble in her sight were shame.
These I will honour, love, embrace, and serve
　And free it from all question to preserve.
So short you read my character and theirs
　I would call mine, to which not many stairs
Are asked to climb. First, give me faith who know
　Myself a little. I will take you so,
As you have writ yourself. Now, stand, and then,
　Sir, you are sealèd of the Tribe of Ben.

A poem consisting of iambic pentameter couplets in the form of a letter to someone who had expressed a desire to become one of the group (or 'tribe' of his literary associates) that met regularly with Jonson in the Apollo room at the Devil Tavern in Fleet Street. Dating from 1623, it is the poet's reaction to his failure to be included among those involved in official preparations for Prince Charles's expected arrival from Spain.

Title
Tribe of Ben An allusion to the Book of Revelation 7: 3–8, in which the angels from the earth's four corners 'seal' or place a mark 'on the foreheads of the servants of our God'. Members of the tribe of Benjamin were preserved from the wrath of God because of their virtue, and twelve thousand of them were so 'sealed'. The reference is at least partly humorous.

[1] **safe**
confident; ***sure in*** convinced of the rightness of.

[2] **what trials . . . put unto**
what tortures they are subjected to.

[3–4] **meet . . . gold**
Proverbial (and here, slightly comic) characteristics of stoic sufferers; ***martyrs*** those willing to suffer or die for their beliefs. Note that the 'l' in 'would' was pronounced at this time.

[3] **meet**
stand up to; ***fire*** (a) burning at the stake; (b) trial by fire or testing the purity of something or someone by seeing if it can withstand flames; ***test*** i.e. the test of endurance under duress typically inflicted upon martyrs or on certain metals.

[4] **though opinion stamp them not**
though what they do is not widely approved of; ***stamp*** (a) make coins (e.g. of gold); (b) mark an object as genuine; (c) test as true or false; ***gold*** (a) incorruptible, long-enduring; (b) of great value; (c) morally excellent.

[5] **fly**
(a) avoid; (b) refuse.

[6] **speak . . . out**
express myself; ***ambitiously*** (a) vehemently; (b) indulging in too much self-praise.

[7] **showing . . . act**
(a) displaying such human weaknesses in general; (b) going too far by speaking too 'ambitiously'; ***vulgar*** (a) unrefined; (b) unappreciative.

[8] **put . . . compromise**
i.e. go against his own conscience and renounce his own right to speak the truth.

[9] **merely talk**
cf. Jonson's *Discoveries*, 343 ff.: 'But you shall see some so abound with words without any seasoning or taste of matter, in so profound a security, as while they are speaking, for the most part they confess to speak they know not what.'

[10–11] **wild . . . quarrel only**
the belligerent and uncontrollable acts of an intoxicated person.

[11] **subject to**
ruled by.

[11–13] **such . . . lechered out**
those who brag of their capacity for food and drink, and of their sexual prowess.

[12] **proficiency**
special talent.

[14–15] **friendship seek . . . sealing**
i.e. seek to be friends with Ben Jonson in order to enjoy the prestige of belonging to his circle.

[16] **th'other . . . borders**
the other kind, close to them in character.

[16–17] **jest . . . dead**
speak disparagingly of persons absent or even deceased; ***souls*** (a) persons; (b) spirits as opposed to bodies.

[18] **like flies . . . fed**
i.e. the talk of these backbiters is fed only by men's defects, as maggots feed only on putrefying bodies.

[19–20] **to speak . . . in**
i.e. think it wrong to speak well of those who are absent but all right to flatter those who are present.

[21] **call**
come; ***fits*** disposition to criticise others.

[22] **are received . . . wits**
are welcomed into the company of 'brilliant conversationalists'; ***covey*** a small flock (normally applied to birds); ***wits*** intellectuals.
[23] **censure**
criticise; ***affairs*** goings-on.
[24] **know . . . theirs**
An ironic remark: though the backbiters are ignorant, they can always find someone more ignorant than they to criticise.
[26] **vent**
express; ***libels*** unwarranted verbal attacks; ***issue*** (a) put forth; (b) proclaim; (c) publish.
[27] **portion**
share; ***deal*** an indefinite amount.
[28] **strew out**
scatter throughout.
[29] **study**
am interested in, speak of; ***more one*** more of a friendship.
[30] **wish none**
wish to have none.
[31] **design**
scheme, plan.
[32] **Valtelline**
The Valtellina is a valley in Lombardy; it was an important strategic site in Italy, and was held by various forces – the Spanish in 1621, the French in 1624 – and underwent further occupations thereafter.
[33] **States' ships**
The Dutch fleet; Dutch and Spanish shipping interests began to clash after war between them resumed in 1621; ***belike*** probably; ***to meet*** to compete with.
[34] **hopes**
ambitions; the Spanish fleet had been weakened by storms before leaving the West Indies in 1622.
[35] **Dispensation**
permission from the Pope in Rome, granted in April 1623, to allow Prince Charles, heir to the throne, to marry the Infanta or Spanish princess.
[36] **match**
the proposed marriage, which was controversial in both countries.
[37] **conspire**
(a) intend, plan; (b) bring about.
[40] **force back . . . restored**
Frederick, son-in-law of King James I, was defeated and the Palatinate was invaded by Spain in 1620; English sentiments for his restoration ran high at this time.
[41] **I have . . . cause**
i.e. despite his age, he is still willing to risk his life in battle should it become necessary; Jonson had served in the army as a young man; ***yet*** still.
[44] **Brunsfield**
Probably Christian of Brunswick, who attempted to aid Frederick in 1621; ***Mansfield*** Ernst, Graf von Mansfeld, who led Frederick's army.
[45] **carry me at all**
i.e. I will do whatever fate decrees.
[47] **pricked down**
chosen to be, designated as.
[48] **late . . . reception**
Plans were being made for elaborate ceremonies to receive the Infanta in 1623; Jonson is referring to the activities of his former theatrical collaborator, now his rival, architect and stage designer Inigo Jones; ***late*** recent; ***mystery*** ritual, sacred rite (ironic).
[49] **his**
Inigo Jones's; ***not underhears*** is not inferior (apparently a word – based on 'to hear' in the sense of 'to be spoken of, well or ill' – invented by Jonson, who was no longer a partner with Jones in creating entertainments or spectacles for the court).
[50] **that guides . . . bears**
i.e. Jones is described deprecatingly as doing no more than direct the movements of puppets (***motions***) and trained bears.
[51] **blow**
(a) the damage to his reputation resulting from his ceasing to participate in court entertainments; (b) Inigo Jones's triumph over him; (c) the physical damage resulting from the collision of a harder with a more fragile surface (see the following notes); ***in time*** eventually.

[52] **credit**
artistic reputation; ***Christmas clay*** (a) the material out of which Jonson shaped his masques and other court entertainments for Twelfth Night (Christmas time), including not only language, costumes, sets and props but also the aristocratic participants in the spectacle; (b) material from which jars are made.
[53] **animated Porc'lane**
the nobility who took part in the masques, here described ironically as having the brilliant, smooth surface of porcelain (i.e. clay sculptures fired and hardened) but also the brittleness of beautiful things that are easily broken.
[54–5] **coarser sort/of earthen jars**
the various hangers-on at court who are likely to ***molest*** (i.e. bother) a person of importance like Jonson for favours.
[56] **mine own frail pitcher**
his body, which he often described as a vessel or barrel because of his great size, girth and weight (20 stone, or about 280 pounds) during this period; the lines that follow are a complex and elaborate series of metaphors based on the image of court aristocrats as fine porcelain containers and himself as a round jug.
[57–8] **keep it . . . less**
An allusion to Aesop's fable about two pots, one of brass, the other of clay, floating on a river: the clay pot answers an invitation from the other to join it in a journey, but expresses a fear of banging against it in transit and being irreparably shattered; the poem contains a number of other echoes from Cicero, Seneca, Horace and Plutarch, dealing with both drinking and sailing vessels.
[57] **press**
crowds.
[59] **point**
(a) the direction on a compass; (b) the navel, centre of the body, which stands for mortal birth and human fragility; ***centre*** (a) his rotund middle; (b) his proper place in the universe.
[61] **looking to**
(a) praying to; (b) trusting to.
[63] **friendships sent**
in exchange for the gifts sent by heaven (with a play on 'ship' as the vessel in which things are sent).
[64] **square**
(a) honest, sincere; (b) well-constructed, with a good sail (of a ship); (c) solid, well-founded; ***well-tagged*** (a) properly appointed or dressed; (b) having proper ropes or rigging (as with a well-trimmed or appointed ship); (c) well-fastened or tied together.
[65] **canvas . . . false lights**
Materials used for creating a theatrical spectacle or stage illusion.
[66] **glorious scenes . . . great sights**
Referring both to the spectacles presented to the court and to the spectacle of the court itself, with the implication that both are mere appearances with little substance behind them.
[67] **fevery heats nor colds**
periods of excessive ardour or of estrangements in the friendship.
[68] **Oily expansions**
attempts at ingratiating oneself with another by exaggerated professions of loyalty or love; ***shrunk duty folds*** renunciation of commitment or obligation (***fold*** handclasp or embrace). Both terms may be applied to dangers in personal or group relationships, and to the effects of extreme heat and cold on stage scenery, which can expand or shrink, sag or stretch if it is not properly attended to.
[69] **reason's flame**
the light of reason; but Jonson also refers to the problems of moving about on a dim stage with only candlelight as guide (the court theatres were indoors and needed artificial lighting, unlike popular outdoor theatres such as the Globe).
[70] **stumble**
(a) lose sight of reason or falter in a relationship; (b) trip over something while performing on stage.
[71] **These**
the precepts just enumerated.
[72] **it**
his 'frail vessel'; ***from all question to preserve*** from all dangers to its safety.

[73] **short**
briefly; ***read*** (a) read in the poem; (b) understand to be his character.
[73–4] **theirs/I would call mine**
the characters of the others 'sealed in his tribe'.
[75] **give me faith**
(a) trust me; (b) give me your word; ***who*** refers to 'I' in the preceding line.
[76] **so**
exactly.
[77] **writ yourself**
(a) signed or sworn your character to be; (b) portrayed yourself as being (***writ*** written). Jonson has written about his character (in this poem), and he now invites this new tribesman to write about himself with the same sincerity (the 'tribe of Ben' consisted mainly of poets and authors).
[77–8] **Now . . . Ben**
Note the closing, which imitates a formal swearing-in or initiation ceremony.

37 | *To the Immortal Memory and Friendship of that Noble Pair, Sir Lucius Cary and Sir Henry Morison*

The Turn
Brave infant of Saguntum clear
Thy coming forth in that great year,
When the prodigious Hannibal did crown
His rage with razing your immortal town,
Thou, looking then about,
E're thou were half got out,
Wise child, did'st hastily return
And mad'st thy mother's womb thine urn.
How summed a circle didst thou leave mankind
Of deepest lore, could we the centre find!
The Counterturn
Did wiser Nature draw thee back
From out the horror of that sack,
Where shame, faith, honour, and regard of right
Lay trampled on, the deeds of death and night
Urged, hurried forth, and hurled
Upon th'affrighted world,
Sword, fire, and famine, with fell fury met,
And all on utmost ruin set,
As, could they but life's miseries foresee,
No doubt all infants would return like thee?

The Stand

For what is life, if measured by the space,
Not by the act;
Or maskèd man, if valued by his face
Above his fact?
Here's one outlived his peers
And told forth fourscore years.
He vexed time and busied the whole State,
Troubled both foes and friends,
But ever to no ends.
What did this stirrer but die late?
How well at twenty had he fallen or stood!
For three of his fourscore, he did no good.

The Turn

He entered well, by virtuous parts
Got up, and thrived with honest arts.
He purchased friends and fame and honours then
And had his noble name advanced with men.
But weary of that flight,
He stooped in all men's sight
To sordid flatteries, acts of strife,
And sunk in that dead sea of life
So deep, as he did then death's waters sup,
But that the cork of title buoyed him up.

The Counterturn

Alas, but Morison fell young.
He never fell; thou fall'st, my tongue.
He stood, a soldier to the last right end,
A perfect patriot and a noble friend
But most a virtuous son.
All offices were done
By him, so ample, full, and round
In weight, in measure, number, sound,
As though his age imperfect might appear.
His life was of humanity the sphere.

The Stand

Go, now, and tell out days summed up with fears
And make them years;
Produce thy mass of miseries on the stage
To swell thine age;
Repeat of things a throng

To show thou hast been long,
Not lived. For life doth her great actions spell
By what was done and wrought
In season and so brought
To light. Her measures are: how well
Each syllable answered and was formed, how fair.
These make the lines of life, and that's her air.

The Turn

It is not growing like a tree
In bulk doth make man better be,
Or standing long an oak, three hundred year,
To fall a log, at last, dry, bald, and sere.
A lily of a day
Is fairer far in May,
Although it fall and die that night;
It was the plant and flower of light.
In small proportions we just beauties see,
And in short measures, life may perfect be.

The Counterturn

Call, noble Lucius, then, for wine,
And let thy looks with gladness shine.
Accept this garland; plant it on thy head
And think, nay, know, thy Morison's not dead.
He leaped the present age
Possessed with holy rage
To see that bright eternal day
Of which we priests and poets say
Such truths as we expect for happy men,
And there he lives with memory, and Ben.

The Stand

Jonson, who sung this of him, ere he went
Himself to rest
Or taste a part of that full joy he meant
To have expressed
In this bright Asterism,
Where it were friendship's schism
(Were not his Lucius long with us to tarry)
To separate these twi-
Lights, the Dioscuri,
And keep the one half from his Harry.

But fate doth so alternate the design,
Whilst that in heav'n, this light on earth must shine.

The Turn

And shine as you exalted are,
Two names of friendship but one star,
Of hearts the union, and those not by chance
Made or indentured or leased out t'advance
The profits for a time.
No pleasures vain did chime
Of rhymes or riots at your feasts,
Orgies of drink or feigned protests,
But simple love of greatness and of good
That knits brave minds and manners, more than blood.

The Counterturn

This made you first to know the Why
You liked, then, after, to apply
That liking and approach so one the t'other,
Till either grew a portion of the other,
Each stylèd by his end
The copy of his friend.
You lived to be the great surnames
And titles by which all made claims
Unto the virtue. Nothing perfect done
But as a Cary or a Morison.

The Stand

And such a force the fair example had,
As they that saw
The good and durst not practise it, were glad
That such a law
Was left yet to mankind,
Where they might read and find
Friendship in deed was written, not in words,
And with the heart, not pen,
Of two so early men,
Whose lines her rolls were and records,
Who, ere the first down bloomèd on the chin,
Had sowed these fruits and got the harvest in.

This poem, the first great example of a Pindaric ode in English, celebrates the lives of two young friends, one of whom died early. Of Greek origin, the ode is a highly formal and organised form of lyric poem composed to commemorate some significant public occasion or person. Pindar (522–442 BC) was the most famous of its practitioners, and his verses were designed to be sung and danced in a choral performance. The typical structure of a Pindaric ode is tripartite, consisting of three repeated stanzaic patterns – *strophe, antistrophe* and *epode* – each of which is in a complex pattern of varying length and metre. Though each stanzaic pattern is distinct, it is exactly repeated throughout the poem in the same sequence of triads. The poetry itself is characterised by unusual images, startling shifts in subject matter, and abrupt transitions. In tone it is highly charged emotionally, and exalted in diction and manner. Jonson translates strophe, antistrophe and epode as 'turn', 'counterturn' and 'stand', influenced, no doubt, by the Italian writer Scaliger's *volta, rivolta* and *stanza*. Sir Lucius Cary (1610?–43) was himself the author of a later elegy on Jonson and son of Sir Henry Cary, a friend of the poet. Sir Henry Morison, son of Sir Richard Morison, died, probably of smallpox, in 1629, around the time of his twenty-first birthday. Other contemporary references to the pair confirm their outstanding and precocious intellectual abilities.

[1] **Brave . . . Saguntum**
The story of the infant of Saguntum, a town in Spain captured and destroyed by Hannibal in 219 BC, thus beginning the Second Punic War, is told by Pliny, *Natural History*, 7,3.40–42. He relates how, in that year, an infant returned to the womb; ***Brave*** (a) splendid, excellent; (b) courageous; ***clear*** (a) brilliant, shining; (b) noble; (c) famous (all meanings of Latin *clarus*); some, however, read the word not as an adjective but as a verb, i.e. clarify, explain.

[3] **prodigious Hannibal**
A rendering of Horace's epithet for the Carthaginian general in his *Odes*, 3.6.36.

[8] **womb . . . urn**
The association of 'womb' and 'tomb' is frequent in English because they rhyme; here the idea of a paradoxical conjunction, though not the rhyme, is preserved; ***urn*** funeral or burial urn, hence tomb.

[9] **summed**
complete; ***circle*** (a) the life cycle from birth to death; (b) the traditional emblem of perfection, prominent in Renaissance philosophy, poetry, painting and architecture.

[12] **sack**
destruction and plundering of a city by an army.

[18] **fell**
fierce, savage.

[19] **life's miseries**
Compare with 'On My First Son', lines 6–8.

[21–2] **measured . . . act**
An echo of the Roman moralist Seneca (*Epistles*, 93–4), who insists that life should be judged by performance rather than by long duration.

[23] **face**
appearance (cf. also the character by that name in Jonson's comedy *The Alchemist*).

[24] **fact**
deeds (from Latin *factum*, 'thing done').

[25–32] **Here's one . . . good**
Another echo of Seneca (93.3): 'What good does this older man derive from his eighty years of living idly? He has not lived but merely tarried in life for a time. He has not died late in his life; he has simply spent a long time dying. You say that he has lived eighty years? That depends on when you date his death.' Whether or not Jonson has any particular person in mind is not clear, but it could be Sir Edward Coke, the famous judge and jurist dismissed from the Chief Justiceship in 1616, who was approaching the age of eighty at this time; though this age is mentioned in Seneca and may simply

be derived from that source, along with the example of the man who has outlived his usefulness.

[26] **told forth**
counted out; ***fourscore*** eighty (a score is twenty).

[31] **stirrer**
agitator; ***twenty*** Morison's probable age at death.

[32] **three of his fourscore**
that is, he did little good during the last sixty of his eighty years of life, and would have done better to have died at the age of twenty.

[38] **stooped**
the plummeting attack of a falcon or other bird of prey; used here in a moral sense of the failure to maintain a high level of rectitude.

[40] **dead sea**
a metaphor that perhaps alludes to the Dead Sea of biblical fame but is probably based, once more, on Seneca (67.4), who uses it of an existence that is not disturbed by ill fortune.

[42] **cork of title buoyed**
i.e. he was kept in the public eye (buoyed up) by the prestige (cork) of his public title.

[43] **Alas . . . young**
Follows Seneca (*Epistles*, 93.4) speaking of the death of a young friend 'in the bloom of his manhood'.

[43] **fell**
'died'.

[44] **fell**
failed morally; ***fall'st, my tongue*** fail as a poet to speak fully or adequately of Cary's character. In this stanza and the next Jonson plays on multiple senses of falling and failure.

[45] **stood**
remained courageous and morally upright as a good soldier.

[49] **round**
complete, perfect.

[50] **weight . . . sound**
Cf. The Book of Wisdom 11: 21: 'But by measure and number and weight you ordered all things'.

[52] **humanity . . . sphere**
the exemplary or more perfect form of humanity.

[53–9] **Go . . . lived**
These lines possibly refer, in a self-accusatory mood, to Ben Jonson himself.

[53] **tell**
count; ***summed up*** filled out, as in line 9 above.

[57] **Repeat of**
(a) say again, reiterate; (b) celebrate.

[58–9] **To show . . . long**
A paraphrase of the same passage from Seneca (93.4) alluded to in line 43.

[59] **spell**
(a) discover; (b) denote, make public.

[61–2] **brought/To light**
Refers both to childbirth and to publication.

[62] **measures**
(a) criteria; (b) units of music; (c) units of poetry.

[63] **syllabe**
The French form of syllable, frequently used by Jonson.

[64] **lines**
(a) lineaments, delineations; (b) the threads spun by the three Fates.

[65] **tree**
An image suggested by Seneca (93.4).

[72] **flower of light**
the lily (a) a flower that lasts only while there is daylight; (b) a flower associated with Easter and the resurrection of Christ, the 'Light of the World' (John 1: 4–5).

[73–4] **In small . . . perfect be**
Inspired by Seneca (93), who says that a short man can be a perfect person; likewise, a short life can also be perfect.

[77] **garland**
The present poem.

[78–84] **And think . . . and Ben**
Once more, suggested by Seneca (93. 5), who says that a person whose life is remembered never dies entirely. See also Milton's 'Lycidas', p. 397, line 165: 'For Lycidas, your sorrow, is not dead.').

[81] **bright eternal day**
the afterlife, heaven.

[92–3] **twi-/Lights**
twin lights, i.e. the constellation

Gemini, the Dioscuri. Castor and Pollux were twin gods who regularly exchanged places; while one dwelt on earth, the other resided in the underworld.
[95] **alternate**
(a) alter; (b) reverse.
[98] **star**
It was mistakenly thought that the twin stars of Gemini never shone simultaneously.
[99–101] **not by chance . . . times**
i.e. their affection was not simply bestowed at random, nor merely made to serve temporary or selfish ends.
[103] **riots**
wild behaviour.
[104] **feigned protests**
hypocritical talk.
[105] **of greatness, and of good**
Frequently conjoined in Jonson's poetry.
[107–10] **This made . . . the other**
Compare with Jonson's praise of Sir Henry Goodyere, p. 107.
[112] **copy**
(a) duplicate, reproduction; (b) pattern, example; (c) fullness, abundance (*copia* in Latin).
[114] **titles**
(a) just claim to land or property; (b) the surnames of the two young men.
[115] **Unto**
for.
[117] **force**
power.
[119] **durst**
dared.
[120] **law**
i.e. of behaviour.
[125] **so early men**
i.e. who had so many remarkable intellectual and moral achievements at an early age.
[126] **lines**
See above, line 64; ***rolls*** (a) scrolls; (b) official record; ***records*** pronounced as though it were the verb form.
[127] **ere**
before; ***first down bloomed*** the early signs of a beard.
[128] **sowed . . . harvest in**
Note the final reference to the themes of abundance and fertility. The concluding lines imply that the quality of the seed sowed determines the character of the harvest. This last image suggests the kind of responsibility typical of the landed gentry.

38 / *To the Memory of My Beloved, the Author Mr William Shakespeare: And What He Hath Left Us*

To draw no envy, Shakespeare, on thy name,
   Am I thus ample to thy book and fame,
While I confess thy writings to be such
   As neither man nor Muse can praise too much.
'Tis true and all men's suffrage. But these ways
   Were not the paths I meant unto thy praise,
For seeliest ignorance on these may light,
   Which, when it sounds, at best but echoes right;
Or blind affection, which doth ne'er advance
   The truth but gropes and urgeth all by chance;

Or crafty malice, might pretend this praise
   And thinks to ruin where it seemed to raise.
These are, as some infamous bawd or whore
   Should praise a matron. What could hurt her more?
But thou art proof against them, and indeed
   Above th'ill fortune of them or the need.
I, therefore, will begin: Soul of the Age!
   The applause, delight, the wonder of our stage!
My Shakespeare, rise. I will not lodge thee by
   Chaucer, or Spenser, or bid Beaumont lie
A little further to make thee a room.
   Thou art a monument without a tomb
And art alive still, while thy book doth live
   And we have wits to read and praise to give.
That I not mix thee so, my brain excuses;
   I mean with great, but disproportioned, Muses.
For if I thought my judgement were of years,
   I should commit thee surely with thy peers
And tell how far thou didst our Lyly outshine,
   Or sporting Kyd, or Marlowe's mighty line.
And though thou hadst small Latin and less Greek,
   From thence to honour thee I would not seek
For names but call forth thundering Aeschylus,
   Euripides, and Sophocles to us,
Pacuvius, Accius, him of Cordova dead,
   To life again to hear thy buskin tread
And shake a stage. Or, when thy socks were on,
   Leave thee alone, for the comparison
Of all that insolent Greece or haughty Rome
   Sent forth or since did from their ashes come.
Triumph, my Britain, thou hast one to show
   To whom all scenes of Europe homage owe.
He was not of an age, but for all time!
   And all the Muses still were in their prime
When, like Apollo, he came forth to warm
   Our ears or, like a Mercury, to charm!
Nature herself was proud of his designs
   And joyed to wear the dressing of his lines,
Which were so richly spun and woven so fit
   As, since, she will vouchsafe no other wit.
The merry Greek, tart Aristophanes,

Neat Terence, witty Plautus, now not please
But antiquated and deserted lie,
As they were not of nature's family.
Yet must I not give nature all: thy art,
My gentle Shakespeare, must enjoy a part.
For though the poet's matter nature be,
His art doth give the fashion; and that he
Who casts to write a living line must sweat
(Such as thine are) and strike the second heat
Upon the Muses' anvil, turn the same
(And himself with it) that he thinks to frame,
Or for the laurel he may gain a scorn,
For a good poet's made, as well as born,
And such were thou. Look how the father's face
Lives in his issue; even so, the face
Of Shakespeare's mind and manners brightly shines
In his well-turnèd and true-filèd lines,
In each of which he seems to shake a lance,
As brandished at the eyes of ignorance.
Sweet Swan of Avon! What a sight it were
To see thee in our waters yet appear
And make those flights upon the banks of Thames
That so did take Eliza and our James!
But stay; I see thee in the hemisphere
Advanced, and made a constellation there!
Shine forth, thou star of poets, and with rage
Or influence chide or cheer the drooping stage,
Which, since thy flight from hence, hath mourned like night
And despairs day, but for thy volume's light.

This eulogy of a friend, fellow dramatist and theatrical mentor was published in the first folio edition of Shakespeare's works (1623). The surprisingly bold claims that Jonson makes for Shakespeare's greatness, addressed to a public that was accustomed to fulsome praise and eulogistic exaggeration, were fully vindicated by the subsequent history of Shakespeare's reputation. Indeed, the very difficulty that Jonson faced in speaking of his older contemporary in such superlative terms is implied in the poem itself.

It consists of pentameter couplets, opening with a sixteen-line introduction and apology for the eulogy that follows (lines 17–46), a celebration of Shakespeare's stature and a declaration that his genius surpasses even that of the greatest ancient writers. The remaining lines explore, in terms of Jonson's theory of the relationship between nature and art, the contributions of each to Shakespeare's achievement (lines 47–70) and culminate in an apotheosis which places him, in classical fashion, as a constellation in the heavens (lines 71–80).

[1–2] **To draw . . . fame**
i.e. I do not praise you and your work so highly in order to make others envy you.
[1] **draw envy . . . on thy name**
make your name a target for envy.
[2] **ample**
speaking highly, fully enough to suit your greatness; ***book and fame*** Jonson distinguishes between 'fame', which may or may not be deserved, and the works ('book'), which are truly worthy of praise.
[3–4] **While I confess . . . much**
i.e. though some might accuse him of praising Shakespeare excessively, Jonson does not think it possible to praise his writings enough.
[4] **man nor Muse**
Jonson also distinguishes between ordinary readers ('man') and other writers or poets; ***Muse*** i.e. person inspired by the Muses.
[5] **suffrage**
(a) collective opinion; (b) consent, approval.
[6] **unto**
to; ***thy praise*** praise of you.
[7] **seeliest**
(a) most ill-informed; (b) simplest, most innocent; ***these*** i.e. the 'ways' and 'paths'; ***light*** land.
[8] **it**
ignorance; ***sounds*** resounds, utters a sound; ***at best but echoes right*** i.e. when ignorant praise hits the mark, it is only because it repeats the judgements of more informed persons.
[9] **blind affection**
personal bias, based upon friendship or love.
[10] **grope**
attempt to find by feeling about without seeing (because 'blind'); ***urgeth*** (a) hastens or presses forward; (b) advocates or advises earnestly; ***by chance*** without plan or design, at random.
[11–12] **Or crafty malice . . . raise**
The poet shifts to the opposite of the ignorant praise he speaks of in the preceding lines, the kind of calculated, exaggerated praise that makes its object look inadequate.
[11] **crafty malice**
hatred carefully disguised as praise; ***pretend this praise*** pretend that this (poem) is praise.
[12] **think**
intend; ***ruin where it seemed to raise*** note that 'ruin' and 'raise' can refer to both buildings or monuments and to reputations (raise = erect an architectural structure).
[13] **These**
practices; ***as some*** as though some; ***bawd*** (a) a procurer or go-between for sexual services or debauchery; (b) a woman who runs a house of prostitution.
[14] **matron**
a respectable family woman; ***her*** the matron.
[15] **proof**
(a) the condition of having successfully stood a test; armed defence against an enemy; (b) witness, testimony, evidence; (c) check, barrier.
[16] **ill fortune of them or the need**
i.e. you cannot be harmed by what they say (whether in ignorance or in malice) nor need them to sustain your fame.
[17] **therefore**
Jonson is concluding his apology for venturing to praise Shakespeare in the highest terms by assuming that he has made his case and can now launch into the main part of the poem. ***Soul of the Age*** (a) leading spirit of his times; (b) the animating principle of his era; (c) the immortal aspect of his age, destined to survive it.
[19] **lodge**
(a) provide with temporary habitation; (b) lay to rest; (c) place in the memory; (d) cast something so as to cause it to be caught or stuck in place.
[20] **Chaucer or Spenser**
the greatest of Shakespeare's precursors, Geoffrey Chaucer (*c.*1340–1400) and Edmund Spenser (*c.*1552–99); ***bid*** entreat, ask pressingly; ***Beaumont*** Francis Beaumont (*c.*1584–1616), dramatist and collaborator with John Fletcher in plays that were more popular even than Shakespeare's. All

three were buried in Westminster Abbey, unlike Shakespeare, who was buried in the parish church of Stratford-upon-Avon.

[21] **to make thee a room**
make you room; Jonson is referring to the opening lines of an 'Elegy on Shakespeare' by William Basse: 'Renowned Spenser, lie a thought more nigh/ To learnèd Chaucer, and rare Beaumont lie/ A little nearer Spenser to make room/ For Shakespeare in your threefold, fourfold tomb.'

[22] **monument without a tomb**
Jonson is playing on the multiple meanings of monument: (a) sepulchre; (b) written document, record; (c) an enduring evidence or example; (d) a structure or edifice commemorating a notable person or event.

[23–4] **And art alive . . . praise to give**
Though it was conventional praise to say that a poet would last as long as the English language was read, Jonson's point is also that a poet's memory is kept alive by those who praise and understand him, thus further justifying the kind of eulogy this poem represents.

[25] **mix thee so**
i.e. with Chaucer, Spenser and Beaumont; ***my brain excuses*** i.e. he refuses to rank Shakespeare with them on logical and rational grounds rather than because of his personal attachment to him.

[26] **great, but disproportioned, Muses**
In other words these other poets, though greatly inspired, were still not of the same stature as Shakespeare; ***disproportioned*** not to be compared to, out of proportion with; ***Muses*** (a) poets; (b) the geniuses of individual poets.

[27] **of years**
(a) sufficiently mature; (b) concerned with a long period of time (and thus extended back to the ancients).

[28] **commit**
(a) unite, join with; (b) match; ***peers*** not the three English playwrights whose names follow immediately, but the six ancient tragedians of lines 33–5.

[29] **our Lyly**
John Lyly (pronounced 'lily'; *c.*1554–1606) was the most fashionable English writer of the 1580s, best known for his prose romance *Euphues*, characterised by its highly artificial prose style, and his plays. Jonson speaks of him as *our* (i.e. native, English) 'lily' by way of compliment, since that flower was often associated with light (see the Cary–Morison ode, line 72), delicacy, and exceptional fairness or purity; note, however, that Shakespeare is said to ***outshine*** him (i.e. surpass this 'flower' of dramatic art in splendour and excellence).

[30] **sporting Kyd**
Jonson puns on the name of this second dramatist, Thomas Kyd (1558–94), author of *The Spanish Tragedy* (*c.*1590), the first of a long succession of revenge plays, by characterising him, somewhat curiously, as 'sporting' (i.e. playful, lively, sportive) and as a 'kid' (i.e. young goat); ***Marlowe*** Christopher Marlowe (1564–93), author of *The Tragical History of Dr Faustus* (*c.*1589–92) and the greatest of Shakespeare's English predecessors. ***Marlowe's mighty line*** Marlowe, who made blank verse into a supple dramatic instrument, was particularly admired for the grandeur and magnificence of his poetic style; this phrase has been called one of Jonson's finest critical pronouncements on another poet. Each of these three dramatists was an important influence on Shakespeare, though he surpassed the greatest qualities of each.

[31] **small Latin and less Greek**
one of the most famous – or notorious – lines in the poem; however, it is obviously meant to be complimentary and echoes a line from the 'Poetic Art' of the learned Italian Renaissance poet Antonio Minturno, suggesting that Shakespeare's limited education in these ancient languages did not

prevent him from matching the greatest achievements of their dramatic poets; actually, scholars have demonstrated that Shakespeare's grammar-school education equipped him with a surprisingly large stock of classical learning, at least by comparison with the attainments of twentieth-century undergraduates; ***small*** little; ***and less*** and even less.

[32] **From thence**
from among his English predecessors.

[32–3] **seek/For**
have trouble finding.

[33] **call forth**
(a) evoke; (b) call up from the dead; (c) recall to memory; (d) bring back on to the stage; ***thundering Aeschylus*** (*c.* 524–c.455 BC), the earliest of the three great Greek tragedians, admired for the grandeur of his poetic language and spectacular dramatic style.

[34] **Euripides and Sophocles**
the other great fifth-century Greek dramatists, who lived from *c.*485 to *c.*407 BC and *c.*497 to *c.*406 BC respectively.

[35] **Pacuvius, Accius**
two Roman dramatists whose tragedies have been lost but whose high reputation Jonson was aware of from Horace's mention of them in *Epistles*, 2.1.56; ***him of Cordova dead*** Seneca the poet, Roman author of tragedies that were of considerable influence on English Renaissance dramatists.

[36] **thy buskin tread**
i.e. to watch Shakespeare act out (or, at least, create and present) tragic roles on the stage; ***buskin*** a high, thick-soled boot worn by actors in Greek tragedy; ***tread*** step or walk with grandeur.

[37] **shake a stage**
an obvious pun on Shakespeare's name, but it also suggests a parallel between him and *thundering* Aeschylus; the earliest surviving example, however, is in the unfriendly mention of the dramatist in rival Robert Greene's *Groat's-worth of Wit* (1592), where he is called a 'Shake-scene'; ***socks*** low-heeled shoes worn by Greek comic actors (from Latin *socci*).

[38] **Leave thee alone . . . comparison**
compare no one with you (i.e. Shakespeare's comedy is incomparable and surpasses even the greatest comic writers of Antiquity).

[39] **insolent Greece or haughty Rome**
a somewhat tempered assessment of the proud achievement of these ancient civilisations, based on a phrase from Seneca.

[40] **sent forth**
gave the world; ***since . . . ashes come*** has been recovered in recent times by scholars and archaeologists.

[41] **Triumph**
be elated, glory in one's victory.

[41–2] **one to show . . . homage owe**
In speaking of Shakespeare as a playwright greater than any other produced by a modern European nation, Jonson is also asserting a claim for the importance of English literature, which need no longer stand in the shadow of French, Italian and Spanish achievements; ***scenes*** stages (from Greek *skene*).

[43] **not of an age . . . all time**
i.e. Shakespeare was not simply the greatest dramatist of his generation but one who will be regarded as great for centuries to come.

[44] **Muses . . . prime**
Shakespeare began to write for the London stage at a time when Elizabethan literature had already reached a high degree of excellence.

[45–6] **Like Apollo . . . charm**
Apollo was the classical god of inspiration and prophecy; Mercury was the Roman god of eloquence.

[47] **designs**
his artistic ideas and their execution.

[48] **joyed**
took pleasure, rejoiced; ***wear . . . lines*** i.e. Shakespeare's embellishment of nature was an enhancement that complemented rather than detracted from the natural; ***dressing*** (a) clothing; (b) ornamentation.

[49] **richly spun and woven so fit**
applicable both to the fabric out of which beautiful and suitable clothing is made and to well-written, appropriately combined verses.
[50] **As**
that, so that; ***since*** subsequently; ***vouchsafe*** (a) permit or allow; (b) acknowledge; ***wit*** genius, talent.
[51] **merry Greek**
i.e. as writer of comedies; ***tart*** (a) biting, sharp; (b) satirical; ***Aristophanes*** Greek dramatist (*c*.435–*c*.385 BC) of satiric comedies, the greatest of the authors of Old Comedy and more of an influence on Jonson than on Shakespeare.
[52] **neat**
(a) clear and to the point; (b) clever; ***Terence*** one of the two Roman writers of comedies whose plays have survived; ***Plautus*** the other Roman comic dramatist. Both imitated the 'New Comedy' of the Greek playwright Menander, and were the chief models for a great number of Renaissance comedies; ***now not please*** are no longer popular.
[53] **antiquated**
(a) obsolete; (b) old-fashioned.
[54] **As**
as though; ***not of nature's family*** i.e. their plays now seem artificial and untrue to nature.
[55] **nature . . . art**
Jonson is distinguishing here between inborn, intuitive talent and creative facility, on the one hand, and study, training and careful craftsmanship, on the other.
[56] **gentle**
(a) aristocratic in birth or bearing, belonging to the class of gentlemen; (b) like a gentleman in character – noble, generous, courteous. Shakespeare purchased a coat of arms from the College of Heralds in 1596 and subsequently had the right to be styled a gentleman, but Jonson's argument is that he was a 'natural' gentleman who possessed true nobility even without a coat of arms; ***enjoy a part*** i.e. must receive credit for contributing to his greatness.
[57] **poet's matter nature be**
though nature is the subject of poetry.
[58] **art . . . fashion**
art gives form to nature and makes it into something higher; ***that he*** that poet.
[59] **casts**
(a) intends or plans to write; (b) form metal into a shape; ***living line*** poetry that possesses life and energy; ***sweat*** labour, work hard.
[60–2] **strike the second heat . . . frame**
Jonson's imagery is taken from foundry work and the blacksmith's shop, where a piece of iron is heated, struck repeatedly with the hammer, reheated, turned, and beaten into shape.
[61] **Muses' anvil**
Note that Jonson depicts the Muses as associated more with the crafting of form than with the passive reception of inspired subject matter; ***the same*** the living line (or piece of iron).
[62] **And himself with it**
i.e. the poet who exercises the craft of poetry must submit himself to the same discipline that shapes (or 'frames') his ideas.
[63] **Or for the laurel . . . scorn**
otherwise, instead of praise for his poetry he will receive only disdain.
[64] **a good poet's . . . born**
Jonson is challenging the old saying that 'a poet is born, not made'.
[65] **such wert thou**
i.e. Shakespeare was a born poet, but he also worked hard to perfect his natural gifts.
[65–6] **the father's face . . . issue**
it was commonplace to describe a poet's writings as his offspring or children.
[66] **race**
posterity.
[68] **well-turnèd and well-filèd lines**
Jonson returns to the imagery of metalworking.
[69] **shake a lance**
another pun on Shakespeare's name (see line 37 above); the main privilege of a gentleman was the right to bear

arms, but the arms Shakespeare bears here are brandished, in his poetry, against ignorance. Note, in addition, that the tip of a lance is forged, shaped, and turned on an anvil.

[71] **Sweet Swan**
Poets were often compared to swans; Jonson used the imagery more extensively in another poem, the 'Ode' to Hugh Holland, where the poet is also transformed into a constellation (Cygnus); ***Avon*** the river flowing through Stratford, Shakespeare's place of birth.

[72–3] **our waters . . . Thames**
the theatres were located on or near the banks of the river.

[74] **Eliza and our James**
Queen Elizabeth I and James I.

[75] **But stay**
but wait!; ***in the hemisphere*** in the heavens.

[76] **Advanced**
rising in the sky, as do some constellations during the course of the evening. Metaphorically, Jonson refers to the rising prominence of Shakespeare's reputation, but he is drawing principally on the classical image of apotheosis, usually applied to mythological figures or to the Caesars, who were said to mount into the sky after death and become stars.

[77–8] **with rage . . . drooping stage**
i.e. the star of Shakespeare is asked to shed its influence (a technical, astrological term – stars were thought to affect human actions by the flow of an ethereal fluid) on the decline (the adjective 'drooping' was a term also applied to a star sinking on the horizon) of the present theatre, and either vigorously ('with rage' – certain stars of violent influence were said to 'rage') scold the current generation of dramatists or prompt them to new heights.

[79] **thy flight from hence**
Shakespeare retired from the London stage to Stratford towards the end of his life, but Jonson is doubtless referring to his death.

[80] **despairs day**
despairs of seeing the dawn; ***thy volume's light*** (a) the brilliance of Shakespeare's plays, collected in the folio edition; (b) Shakespeare's book as the guiding light or model for all playwrights.

39 / *Song*

Still to be neat, still to be dressed
As you were going to a feast;
Still to be powdered, still perfumed –
Lady, it is to be presumed,
Though art's hid causes are not found,
All is not sweet, all is not sound.

Give me a look, give me a face
That makes simplicity a grace:
Robes loosely flowing, hair as free –
Such sweet neglect more taketh me
Than all th'adulteries of art.
They strike mine eyes but not my heart.

A song from Jonson's comedy *Epicoene, or The Silent Woman* in two stanzas of three tetrameter couplets each. In the context of the play, which is about a deception organised by a nephew in order to gain his uncle's inheritance, this song has something of an ironic twist, since the 'silent woman' of its title is actually a boy disguised as a woman. The subject may be compared with Herrick's 'Delight in Disorder' (p. 250), which may well have been inspired by Jonson's example.

[2] **As you**
as if you; ***feast*** pronounced 'fest' at the time.

[5] **art's hid causes**
the unseen technique or means that produces a particular effect or appearance; ***art*** here, the enhancements of dress; ***found*** found out, discovered, apparent.

[6] **sound**
wholesome, free from flaws.

[8] **simplicity a grace**
This phrase could be taken as the ideal of Jonson's brand of neoclassicism.

[10] **sweet neglect**
an oxymoron that reveals, curiously enough, the self-consciousness that lies behind this cultivation of a 'natural' look; ***taketh me*** (a) attracts me, engages me; (b) charms me, captivates me.

[11] **adulteries**
(a) adulterations, the substituting of one substance for another without acknowledgement; (b) taints.

[12] **strike . . . heart**
The poet is suggesting not simplicity for its own sake but an approach to simplicity that is artful in its own way; the poem is about presenting the *appearance* of neglectfulness and freedom, a process which is not altogether free of calculation but is more interesting to the onlooker than mere ornament for its own sake. Note the two senses of ***strike*** (a) catch the attention; (b) penetrate to the seat of the emotions.

EMILIA LANIER

(1569–1645)

1611 *Salve Deus Rex Judaeorum*

Not a great deal is known about Emilia Lanier (or Aemilia Lanyer, as her name was formerly spelt). Records of the activities of seventeenth-century women who were not of the nobility or publicly prominent in some way are sadly sporadic and unpredictable. In Lanier's case much information comes from the journals of a doctor and astrologer called Simon Forman, whom she consulted in the late 1590s. Other information has been garnered from legal documents. She was the daughter of Baptista Bassani, an Italian musician whose service in the English court began sometime in the mid sixteenth century. All we know of her mother, Margaret, is that she was buried in 1587. Emilia herself was baptised at St Botolph's, Bishopsgate on 27 January 1569. From her poetry we learn that in her early years she was associated in some way with the Countess Dowager of Kent, perhaps as a servant in her household. Forman noted that she had been the mistress of Henry Carey, first Lord Hunsdon and Queen Elizabeth's Lord Chancellor (d. 1596), and was married on 18 October 1592, as a 'cover' for her pregnancy, to Captain Alfonso Lanier, a civil servant who also came from a musical family. She seems to have been in frequent financial straits, especially after her husband's death in 1613. *Salve Deus Rex Judaeorum,* her only volume, was entered in the Stationer's Register on 2 October 1610 and published in 1611. Perhaps the publication was intended to attract support from aristocratic patrons. She opened a school for noblemen and gentlemen's children, but seems to have had recurrent financial difficulties until her death. Her burial at Clerkenwell was on 3 April 1645. She had at least two children and two grandchildren.

Context

Lanier's poetry is unique in a number of striking ways. At a time when it was unusual for women, even among the aristocracy, to attempt literary forms at all, much less to publish, her polish and competence as a poet demonstrate a talent developed independently of the official world of letters, yet certainly a match for any number of established writers of the period. Though her achievement is a somewhat isolated one, it is noteworthy in revealing an otherwise hidden point of view – that of Protestant feminine religious ideals contemporary with the better-known works of Donne or Herbert. All her poems are written in praise of virtuous women, and they draw on the feminine allegories of the biblical tradition, including the 'bride of Christ' metaphor for the Church. Hers is the first serious attempt by an Englishwoman to write a whole book of poetry in praise of women. She develops a vision of woman that places the feminine at the very heart of Christianity, thus making women the agents of God's will rather than, as was often asserted, of the Devil.

Genre

The book consists of three sections – a dedication to Queen Anne, Princess Elizabeth, and a series of virtuous women; the title poem, 'Salve Deus Rex Judaeorum'; and, finally, 'The Description of Cookham'. Lanier attempts to rehabilitate the image and reputation of woman by countering conventional misogyny with portraits of the most prominent and learned aristocratic ladies of England in the tradition of the 'Book of Good Women'. Like her contemporary male counterparts, she writes in what may seem to modern ears fulsome terms, but the encomium was a generally accepted literary posture at the time, and her combination of praise with the central doctrines of the Christian spiritual life – humility, charity, patience, as opposed to public power or military valour – gives her work an original cast, especially in so far as she portrays Christ as surrounded by women.

Critical Reception

Emilia Lanier is a recent discovery, and her place in English literature is not yet fully established, but it is obvious that her poetry is of more than merely historical significance. She was first brought to the attention of scholars by historian A.L. Rowse, who claimed (on very slender evidence) that she was Shakespeare's mistress and the 'dark lady' of his sonnets. His arguments have found little support, but the reprinting of Lanier's book, which survives in only nine copies, has had the merit of making it available to literary critics who have grasped the significance of her achievement as an important voice in her own right.

Further Reading

Editions

The Poems of Shakespeare's Dark Lady, ed. A.L. Rowse (New York, 1979), the first modern edition, contains information about Lanier's life (apart from the controversial identification of her as Shakespeare's 'dark lady'), but no notes on the poems. It has been superseded by *The Poems of Aemilia Lanyer*, ed. Susanne Woods (London and New York, 1993). 'The Description of Cookham' is also printed in *Kissing the Rod: An anthology of seventeenth-century women's verse*, ed. Germaine Greer, Susan Hastings, *et al.* (New York and London, 1988), pp. 44–53, with an introduction and notes.

Critical Studies

The best introduction to Lanier's work as a whole, apart from the editions cited above, is Barbara Lewalski, 'Of God and good women: the poems of Aemilia Lanyer', in *Silent But for the Word: Tudor women as patrons, translators, and writers of religious works*, ed. Margaret Hannay (Kent, OH, 1985), pp. 203–24. The same author has also provided important biographical information on the two women who figure prominently in 'The Description of Cookham' in 'Re-writing patriarchy and patronage: Margaret Clifford, Anne Clifford, and Aemilia Lanyer', *Yearbook of English*

Studies, **21** (1991), 87–106; and compares Lanier's to the topographical poems of Jonson, Lovelace and Marvell in 'The lady of the country-house poem', in *The Fashioning and Functioning of the British Country House*, ed. Gervase Jackson-Stops *et al*. (Hanover, NH, 1989), pp. 261–7. Aliki Barnstone, 'Women and the garden: Andrew Marvell, Emilia Lanier, and Emily Dickinson', *Women and Literature*, **2** (1982), 147–67 also compares her with later poets; while Lynette McGrath, 'Metaphoric subversions: feasts and mirrors in Aemelia Lanier's *Salve Deus Rex Judaeorum*', *Lit: Literature Interpretation Theory*, **3** (1991), 101–13 offers a reading of the poet's 'subversive' feminist strategy. Elaine V. Beilin has a chapter, 'The feminization of praise: Aemilia Lanyer', in her *Redeeming Eve: Women writers of the English Renaissance* (Princeton, NJ, 1987), pp. 177–207, in which she compares Lanier with Donne and Jonson, and describes *Salve Rex Deus Judaeorum* as a book about women 'as the heroic protectors of the Christian spirit'. She also notes a millenarian strain in Lanier that foresees 'the establishment on earth of God's will through the particular agency of women'.

40 / *The Description of Cookham*

Farewell, sweet Cookham, where I first obtained
Grace from that grace where perfect grace remained,
And where the Muses gave their full consent
I should have power the virtuous to content,
Where princely palace willed me to indite
The sacred story of the soul's delight.
Farewell, sweet place, where virtue then did rest
And all delights did harbour in her breast;
Never shall my sad eyes again behold
Those pleasures which my thoughts did then unfold.
Yet you, great lady, mistress of that place
From whose desires did spring this work of grace,
Vouchsafe to think upon those pleasures past
As fleeting worldly joys that could not last
Or as dim shadows of celestial pleasures,
Which are desired above all earthly treasures.
Oh how, methought, against you thither came,

Each part did seem some new delight to frame!
The house received all ornaments to grace it
And would endure no foulness to deface it.
The walks put on their summer liveries,
And all things else did hold like similies:
The trees with leaves, with fruits, with flowers clad
Embraced each other, seeming to be glad,
Turning themselves to beauteous canopies
To shade the bright sun from your brighter eyes;
The crystal streams with silver spangles graced,
While by the glorious sun they were embraced;
The little birds in chirping notes did sing
To entertain both you and that sweet spring;
And Philomela, with her sundry lays,
Both you and that delightful place did praise.
Oh how, methought, each plant, each flower, each tree
Set forth their beauties then to welcome thee!
The very hills right humbly did descend
When you to tread upon them did intend,
And, as you set your feet, they still did rise,
Glad that they could receive so rich a prize.
The gentle winds did take delight to be
Among those woods that were so graced by thee.
And in sad murmur uttered pleasing sound
That pleasure in that place might more abound.
The swelling banks delivered all their pride
When such a Phoenix once they had espied.
Each arbour, bank, each seat, each stately tree
Thought themselves honoured in supporting thee.
The pretty birds would oft come to attend thee,
Yet fly away for fear they should offend thee.
The little creatures in the burrow by
Would come abroad to sport them in your eye;
Yet fearful of the bow in your fair hand,
Would run away when you did make a stand.
Now let me come unto that stately tree
Wherein such goodly prospects you did see,
That oak that did in height his fellows pass
As much as lofty trees, low growing grass,
Much like a comely cedar, straight and tall,
Whose beauteous stature far exceeded all.

How often did you visit this fair tree,
Which, seeming joyful in receiving thee,
Would like a palm tree spread his arms abroad,
Desirous that you there should make abode;
Whose fair green leaves, much like a comely veil,
Defended Phoebus when he would assail;
Whose pleasing boughs did yield a cool, fresh air,
Joying his happiness when you were there;
Where, being seated, you might plainly see
Hills, vales, and woods, as if on bended knee
They had appeared, your honour to salute,
Or to prefer some strange unlooked-for suit,
All interlaced with brooks and crystal springs –
A prospect fit to please the eyes of kings –
And thirteen shires appeared all in your sight.
Europe could not afford much more delight!
What was there then but gave you all content,
While you the time in meditation spent
Of their creator's power, which there you saw
In all his creatures held a perfect law,
And in their beauties did you plain descry
His beauty, wisdom, grace, love, majesty?
In these sweet woods how often did you walk
With Christ and his apostles there to talk,
Placing his Holy Writ in some fair tree
To meditate what you therein did see.
With Moses you did mount his holy hill
To know his pleasure and perform his will;
With lovely David you did often sing
His holy hymns to Heaven's eternal King,
And in sweet music did your soul delight
To sound his praises morning, noon, and night.
With blessed Joseph you did often feed
Your pined brethren when they stood in need;
And that sweet lady – sprung from Clifford's race,
Of noble Bedford's blood fair stem of grace,
To honourable Dorset now espoused,
In whose fair breast true virtue then was housed –
Oh, what delight did my weak spirits find
In those pure parts of her well-framed mind!
And yet it grieves me that I cannot be

Near unto her whose virtues did agree
With those fair ornaments of outward beauty
Which did enforce from all both love and duty.
Unconstant Fortune, thou art most to blame,
Who casts us down into so low a frame,
Where our great friends we cannot daily see,
So great a difference is there in degree.
Many are placèd in those orbs of state,
Parters in honour, so ordained by Fate,
Nearer in show, yet farther off in love,
In which the lowest always are above.
But whither am I carried in conceit,
My wit too weak to conster of the great?
Why not? Although we are but born of earth,
We may behold the heavens, despising death;
And loving Heaven that is so far above
May in the end vouchsafe us entire love.
Therefore, sweet memory, do thou retain
Those pleasures past which will not turn again.
Remember beauteous Dorset's former sports,
So far from being touched by ill reports,
Wherein myself did always bear a part
While reverend love presented my true heart.
Those recreations let me bear in mind
Which her sweet youth and noble thoughts did find,
Whereof deprived, I evermore must grieve,
Hating blind Fortune, careless to relieve.
And you, sweet Cookham, whom these ladies leave,
I now must tell the grief you did conceive
At their departure when they went away,
How everything retained a sad dismay.
Nay, long before, when once an inkling came,
Methought each thing did unto sorrow frame:
The trees that were so glorious in our view
Forsook both flowers and fruit, when once they knew
Of your depart; their very leaves did wither,
Changing their colours as they grew together.
But when they saw this had no power to stay you,
They often wept – though, speechless, could not pray you,
Letting their tears in your fair bosoms fall
As if they said, 'Why will ye leave us all?'

This being vain, they cast their leaves away,
Hoping that pity would have made you stay.
Their frozen tops, like age's hoary hairs,
Shows their disasters, languishing in fears.
A swarthy riveled rine all over spread,
Their dying bodies half alive, half dead.
But your occasions called you so away
That nothing there had power to make you stay;
Yet did I see a noble grateful mind,
Requiting each according to their kind,
Forgetting not to turn and take your leave
Of these sad creatures, powerless to receive
Your favour, when with grief you did depart,
Placing their former pleasures in your heart,
Giving great charge to noble memory
There to preserve their love continually.
But specially the love of that fair tree
That first and last you did vouchsafe to see –
In which it pleased you oft to take the air
With noble Dorset, then a virgin fair,
Where many a learned book was read and scanned –
To this fair tree, taking me by the hand,
You did repeat the pleasures which had passed,
Seeming to grieve they could no longer last;
And with a chaste, yet loving kiss took leave,
Of which sweet kiss I did it soon bereave,
Scorning a senseless creature should possess
So rare a favour, so great happiness.
No other kiss it could receive from me,
For fear to give back what it took of thee.
So I, ungrateful creature, did deceive it
Of that which you vouchsafed in love to leave it;
And though it often had given me much content,
Yet this great wrong I never could repent,
But of the happiest made it most forlorn
To show that nothing's free from Fortune's scorn,
While all the rest with this most beauteous tree
Made their sad consort sorrow's harmony.
The flowers that on the banks and walks did grow
Crept in the ground, the grass did weep for woe.
The winds and waters seemed to chide together

Because you went away, they knew not whither;
And those sweet brooks that ran so fair and clear
With grief and trouble wrinkled did appear.
Those pretty birds that wonted were to sing
Now neither sing, nor chirp, nor use their wing;
But with their tender feet, on some bare spray,
Warble forth sorrow and their own dismay.
Fair Philomela leaves her mournful ditty,
Drowned in dead sleep, yet can procure no pity.
Each arbour, bank, each seat, each stately tree
Looks bare and desolate now for want of thee,
Turning green tresses into frosty grey,
While in cold grief they wither all away.
The sun grew weak; his beams no comfort gave,
While all green things did make the earth their grave.
Each briar, each bramble, when you went away,
Caught fast your clothes, thinking to make you stay.
Delightful Echo, wonted to reply
To our last words, did now for sorrow die.
The house cast off each garment that might grace it,
Putting on dust and cobwebs to deface it.
All desolation then there did appear
When you were going whom they held so dear.
This last farewell to Cookham here I give;
When I am dead, thy name in this may live
Wherein I have performed her noble hest
Whose virtues lodge in my unworthy breast
And ever shall, so long as life remains,
Tying my heart to her by those rich chains.

'The Description of Cookham', a topological encomium in pentameter couplets, can be dated sometime between the marriage of Lady Anne Clifford in February 1609 and the date of entry of the book in the Stationer's Register (October 1610). The exact nature of Lanier's relationship with the Cliffords is not clear, and the only record of her association with the family is the poem itself. (Neither the date of this poem nor the exact date of Jonson's 'To Penshurst' (p. 119), usually considered the first of a long tradition of 'country-house' poetry, is known; it is possible that Lanier's is the earlier. In any case, her verses may owe something to the themes of exile and the sympathy of nature in Virgil (Eclogue I) and in late-sixteenth-century Italian poetry. Her poem may possibly claim precedence over 'To Penshurst' as the first country-house poem, but it had no influence on the development of that tradition. Its significance lies elsewhere, however, and it retains its importance in the history of literature independently of Jonson's poem. Cookham is depicted as a specifically feminine rather than merely aristocratic paradise, and it establishes a quasi-mythical image of woman as a creative and fostering presence independently of any particular social status. Lanier's poem is also distinct in its religious perspective, lacking in Jonson's more obviously secular emphasis. Its uniqueness is a consequence not of a conscious effort to vary an established literary theme but of its resolutely feminine perspective.

The two women celebrated in the poem were themselves unusually self-assured and strong-willed. Margaret Russell Clifford was well read (though she knew no language other than English) and had an interest in alchemy. Her husband, George, third Earl of Cumberland, was an active man, concerned with the future of his properties (the couple had no son) and a notorious philanderer. As a consequence, he was separated from his wife, who was tireless in ensuring that their daughter Anne eventually received the estates which were her due, though she had been bypassed in favour of her uncle and his heirs. The couple were reconciled only on his deathbed. The Cliffords' estrangement seems to have strengthened the ties between mother and daughter; both women were clearly intelligent, deeply religious, and fully determined to resist the domination of a male-centred society. Emilia Lanier seems to have regarded herself in a client–patron relationship to them, and certainly their personality is reflected in her book. The dates of the stay at Cookham are difficult to determine, though there are some indications that mother and daughter resided there after the Cliffords' separation.

The poem may be divided into three parts. The first, lines 1–98, recalls the past pleasures of the speaker's sojourn at Cookham. The second, lines 99–127, consists of the poet's protest against ill fortune and the separations caused by social distinctions, ending with a return to memory for consolation. The third, lines 128–210, depicts the effect on the landscape of the ladies' departure and ends with the poet's farewell to the place.

Title

Cookham A royal manor near Maidenhead that was the property of the crown until the early nineteenth century. At the time described in the poem it was held by Lord William Russell of Thornhaugh, the brother of Margaret Clifford, Countess of Cumberland, to whom the poem is addressed and who sometimes stayed there.

[1] **where . . . first obtained**

Lanier seems to suggest that her earliest poetic inspiration came from a sojourn or visit to Cookham, though the exact nature of her experiences there is unknown, apart from the information provided in this poem.

[2] **Grace . . . grace**

The poem plays on an extraordinary number of senses of the word 'grace', which had both religious and secular connotations at this time: (a) pleasing quality; (b) favour; (c) gratitude; (d) the condition or fact of being favoured (by God or man); privilege or dispensation; (e) permission to do something; (f) a mark of divine favour; (g) one's appointed fate or destiny, good or bad luck, share of Providence; (h) divine influence which sanctifies and renews; (i) virtue in general or an individual virtue, divine in origin (such as inspiration); (j) a courtesy title used for a countess or duchess (as in the phrase 'your grace'). A reading of the line, therefore, might be 'I first received favour from that person [the countess] whose qualities and virtues are perfect'; but it could also be understood as 'I received grace from God in that attractive place [Cookham] where an unspoiled, Eden-like natural environment still remained'; but numerous other possibilities and nuances are equally likely, since the source and character of the grace could be both human and divine, natural and supernatural, applied to the place or to the owner of that place.

[3] **Muses . . . consent**
It was unusual for a woman to write, much less publish, poetry during this period; the poet refers to her three-part poem 'Salve Deus Rex Judaeorum' ('Hail, God, King of the Jews'), which consists of a narrative of Christ's Passion in which women figure prominently as Christian exemplars; it is dedicated to the Countess of Cumberland, as well as to other prominent women.

[4] **virtuous . . . content**
The poet claims to have received the support and approbation of such ladies as the Countess of Cumberland and other aristocratic women named in her volume.

[5] **princely palace**
the house at Cookham estate; ***willed*** (a) gave me the will; (b) [those who were at Cookham] commanded or encouraged her; ***indite*** tell, recite.

[6] **sacred story**
refers to the title poem of the volume, 'Salve Deus Rex Judaeorum'; ***soul's delight*** Christ; but another reading of this phrase is possible, i.e. 'The story of the delight of the soul in Christ's redeeming grace'.

[7] **harbour . . . breast**
i.e. sheltered either (a) in the heart of the estate ('her' referring to the 'princely palace' above) or (b) in the heart of the Countess of Cumberland.

[11] **great lady**
the dedicatee of the poem, Margaret Clifford, Countess of Cumberland, (1560?–1616), daughter of the third Earl of Bedford; she was estranged from her husband, who was accused of adultery; ***place*** i.e. Cookham.

[12] **work of grace**
(a) Cookham or (b) Lanier's poetry.

[13] **Vouchsafe**
deign or condescend.

[14] **fleeting . . . joys**
a traditional Christian attitude towards all earthly pleasures, even virtuous ones, is that one cannot trust them to last.

[15] **dim . . . pleasure**
a second way of thinking about earthly pleasures was to see them as a foretaste of those to come after death.

[17] **methought**
it seemed to me; ***against you thither*** i.e. to welcome your arrival there.

[18] **Each part**
every part of the estate; ***to frame*** to fashion or form; but there is an implied pun on the word taken in an architectural sense (the house 'frames' the pleasures that are experienced within it or its grounds).

[19] **received**
accepted willingly.

[20] **endure**
allow.

[21] **walks**
The pathways on the estate, especially in the gardens; ***liveries*** clothing or uniforms worn by servants.

[24–74] **The trees . . . more delight**
This lengthy passage, with its depiction of the cordial welcome the natural world offers its visitor, reflects a poetic commonplace of the period that is also at the centre of Jonson's 'To Penshurst' (p. 119); the perfect harmony between landscape and the dweller, whom all living things in it honour and serve, suggests an Edenic or a paradisal state, one of the meanings of the 'grace' referred to in line 2. Scholars have pointed to the influence of Spenser's 'Mutabilitie Cantos' (*Faerie Queene*, 4.7.7, 8–13); in fact, Spenser's *Four Hymns* (1596) were dedicated to the Countess of Cumberland and her sister, the Countess of Warwick, so the image of the court of nature with a woman at its centre may well have been inspired by them.

[23] **similies**
similarities, similitudes.

[24–5] **Embraced each . . . canopies**
i.e. formed a canopy overhead where their branches met.

[26] **bright sun . . . brighter eyes**
a commonplace of love poetry – the beautiful woman's eyes are brighter

than the sun – but here given an unusual turn in that the phrase is ambiguous, meaning that the trees either (a) shade the lady's eyes from the sun, or (b) protect the sun from the greater brilliance of the lady's eyes.

[27] **spangles**
brilliant points of reflected light.

[31] **Philomela**
the nightingale; although it is the male nightingale that sings, Greek myth tells the story of Philomela and her sister Procne, abused by the husband of the former, who were turned into a nightingale and a swallow after seeking revenge on him. The best-known version of the story is Ovid's, in *Metamorphoses*, 6.401–674. Though Philomela as an alternative name for the nightingale appears frequently in the poetry of this period, the myth of the mistreated woman has a special point in the work of a writer who protested against literary misogyny; ***lays*** songs.

[33] **methought**
it seemed to me.

[35–8] **When you . . . prize**
a conceit suggesting the bowing and rising of the landscape as a servant might pay obeisance to the mistress.

[35] **right**
quite, completely.

[38] **receive**
(a) welcome as guest; (b) accept as gift.

[41] **sad**
(a) serious, dignified; (b) sorrowful.

[43] **swelling banks delivered**
The image of the 'pregnant' bank is familiar from John Donne's 'The Ecstasy', where it also occurs, but here the word 'delivered' suggests a birth as well. Again, a commonplace image takes on a fresh appropriateness in the feminine perspective of the poem.

[44] **Phoenix**
(a) the bird of classical myth that expires in flames and then rises again from its ashes; (b) a person of unusual or unique qualities, one of a kind; (c) Queen Elizabeth I (occasionally designated in this way).

[45] **arbour**
a bower or shady retreat.

[49] **burrow**
(a) an underground dwelling-place; (b) a secluded place.

[50] **come abroad**
emerge; ***sport them*** frolic, play.

[51–2] **Bow . . . stand**
It was not unusual for women at this time to engage in archery; ***make a stand*** get in position to shoot.

[53] **unto**
to.

[54] **goodly prospects**
beautiful vistas or perspectives (gained by climbing on to its branches).

[55] **pass**
surpass.

[57] **comely**
handsome, attractive; there may be an oblique reference here to Psalm 92: 8–15.

[61] **spread his arms abroad**
spread out its branches.

[62] **make abode**
i.e. climb into its branches.

[64] **Defended**
protected from, warded off by providing shade; ***Phoebus*** (a) the sun; (b) the Greek god of the sun; ***assail*** i.e. by shining too brightly or with too much heat. Note, however, the image of protectiveness from masculine brutality and overbearingness.

[66] **Joying**
(a) having the use or benefit of; (b) enjoying.

[68] **bended knee**
another image of obeisance that emphasises the theme of nature as servant; in this domestic realm, however, nature willingly submits to the feminine graces of the mistress it serves rather than yielding to the domination of a masculine conqueror.

[69] **your honour to salute**
(a) to greet a great lady ('her honour'); (b) to acknowledge her prestige.

[70] **prefer**
submit for acceptance; ***unlooked-for***

unexpected because there seems to be nothing lacking in the plenitude of nature; ***suit*** request.

[73] **shires**
country regions or districts under local administration rather than entire counties, as the word would now be understood.

[75] **What was . . . content**
i.e. there was nothing there that did not content you.

[76] **meditation**
The countess was a deeply religious woman; the practice of systematic meditation had been popular since the mid sixteenth century among both Catholics and Protestants. In the following lines we learn of the specific object of her meditation: the revelation of the works of God in nature.

[78] **held a perfect law**
Natural creatures, unlike human beings, obey God's law perfectly.

[81–2] **walk . . . apostles**
i.e. (a) by reading in the Holy Scriptures, or (b) by imagining their company and putting herself in a religious frame of mind.

[83–4] **Placing . . . see**
The countess set her Bible in the branches of a tree in lieu of a bookstand. However, 'therein' may refer both to the book she is reading and to the tree, an example of the natural order created by God, in which it is supported.

[85] **Moses**
The great leader of the Israelites out of their slavery in Egypt received the tablets on which the law (the Ten Commandments) was inscribed on Mount Sinai (Exodus 19–20).

[87] **David**
(a) The famous King of Israel in the Old Testament, who was said to be the author of the Psalms; (b) The Book of Psalms itself.

[91] **Joseph**
alluding to Genesis 47: 12.

[92] **pined**
in pain, afflicted.

[93] **that sweet lady**
Anne Clifford, the countess's only surviving child; she was tutored by Samuel Daniel, a well-known contemporary poet.

[94] **stem**
in the sense of a genealogical chart or family tree; a family line.

[95] **Dorset now espoused**
Anne Clifford married Richard Sackville, third Earl of Dorset, on 25 February 1609.

[102] **enforce**
produce, effect, compel by moral force.

[103] **Unconstant**
inconstant, unpredictable.

[104] **low a frame**
debased condition, lowly status.

[105] **great friends**
'great' not only in the sense of 'close' friends but also because of their social prominence and rank (i.e. friends from among the nobility).

[106] **difference in degree**
Lanier laments the fact that class structure separates her from the companions she cares most about.

[107] **orbs of state**
orbits or realms of power and government authority.

[108] **parters**
(a) dividers, separators; (b) departers.

[109] **Nearer in show**
i.e. physically close in appearance but distant in emotions.

[110] **lowest always are above**
i.e. the lowest in rank love the highest more than they are loved in return.

[111] **conceit**
(a) overweening opinion of oneself; (b) frame of mind, personal opinion; (c) fanciful speculation.

[112] **conster of**
construe, understand.

[113–16] **Why not? . . . love**
The centre of the poem is a muted protest against the barriers of class-consciousness; Lanier was evidently too aware of her own intellectual prowess to be comfortable with the idea that she was vastly inferior to those of higher social rank than she.

[118] **turn**
return.

[119] **sports**
games of all sorts and even participation in theatrical presentations, as well as sport in the modern sense.
[120] **ill reports**
unfavourable comments or criticisms.
[121] **Wherein myself . . . part**
i.e. she was involved in the games Lady Anne played, not in the 'ill reports'.
[123] **Those recreations . . . mind**
Let me bear those recreations in mind.
[128ff.]
These lines are an extensive example of what John Ruskin called the 'pathetic fallacy', the attribution of human feelings to nature. The technique is, however, one of the most frequently used in poetry, and here the change from summer to autumn, which evidently occurred while they were still resident, is seen as a reaction to the departure of the countess and her entourage.
[128] **conceive**
feel.
[131] **inkling**
hint.
[132] **unto sorrow frame**
took on a sorrowful appearance.
[136] **depart**
departure.
[137] **stay**
prevent.
[138] **pray**
beg.
[143] **hoary**
white.
[144] **disasters**
ill fortune, bad luck.
[145] **swarthy riveled rine**
(a) the dark, wrinkled bark of a tree; (b) dark, crazed frost or ice.
[149] **noble . . . mind**
i.e. the countess's.
[150] **Requiting**
rewarding, compensating.
[161] **scanned**
examined or discussed minutely.
[165–72] **And with . . . leave it**
i.e. the speaker, who could not bid farewell to her lady with a kiss, stole one from the tree. The passage illustrates a point concerning the necessary distance enforced by social rank.
[166] **I . . . bereave**
i.e. she kissed the tree where the countess had kissed it.
[171] **deceive it**
rob it.
[174] **great wrong . . . repent**
i.e. she imagines that in kissing the tree she has taken from it the token of affection for the place left by the countess's parting gesture.
[175–6] **happiest . . . scorn**
an extension of the original conceit. The tree was happiest because the departing lady bestowed her affection on it, but the poet took away the kiss it had been given with the excuse that she was teaching it the uncertainties of existence in this world.
[178] **consort**
(a) concert; (b) an ensemble of musical instruments.
[179–204]
The landscape in mourning is a familiar theme in Elizabethan poetry, particularly in Spenser (*The Shepherd's Calendar*) and in Shakespeare (Sonnets 12 and 73).
[181] **chide**
(a) complain; (b) rebuke.
[185] **wonted**
accustomed.
[189] **ditty**
song, tune.
[197–9] **briar . . . stay**
The pathetic fallacy is here extended, through this conceit, to the physical realm.
[205–10] **This last farewell . . . chains**
The final lines of the poem take up the common Renaissance theme of fame bestowed by the poet on the beloved, though here it is given to a place rather than a person. The conclusion suggests that the bond between the countess and the poet, who could not have held a very high position in her household, will be sealed by the poem

and their shared experience of a special place. Thus the poem serves not only to establish the claim to fame of Cookham but also the claim to a close relationship, despite the barrier of class, with a woman that Emilia Lanier seems to have admired greatly.

LADY MARY WROTH

(1586 or 1587–1653)

1621 *The Countess of Montgomery's Urania* (with *Pamphilia to Amphilanthus)*

Mary Sidney, Lady Wroth was born on 18 October 1586 or 1587, the daughter of Barbara Gamage and Sir Robert Sidney. The Sidneys were among the best-known and most respected aristocratic families of their time; Mary's uncle was the famous Sir Philip Sidney, a universally admired author, gentleman and soldier, and two other members of her family were also poets. Her childhood was spent at the same Penshurst that is the subject of Ben Jonson's poem (p. 119). As a member of a family prominent in both Elizabeth I's and James I's courts she performed, in her early years, in dances and masques before both monarchs. In 1603 she was married to the recently knighted Sir Robert Wroth, who continued to be host on several occasions to King James and Prince Henry, and thus to keep his wife at the centre of court activities. In addition to her aristocratic connections, she became friendly with a number of prominent writers as both patron and fellow author, following in the footsteps of her aunt, Mary Countess of Pembroke. She was personally acquainted with Ben Jonson, who addressed poems to both her and her husband, and in whose masques she performed. Her husband died in 1614, shortly after the birth of their son, who lived for only two years. At this point she found herself in a difficult position, with an estate heavily charged with debt. After her son's death even that was taken from her, and she continued to be plagued with debt until 1628.

In 1621 she published a volume containing a long prose romance, *The Countess of Montgomery's Urania* (modelled after her uncle Philip Sidney's *Arcadia*) and a sonnet sequence, *Pamphilia to Amphilanthus*. Claims that the narrative slandered certain living persons caused the volume to be withdrawn in the same year. Indeed, given the scandals that characterised the court of James I – including Lady Mary's own affair with her cousin William, Earl of Pembroke (a union which resulted in two children) – it is not unlikely that a number of episodes depicting licentious behaviour would have struck contemporaries as troublesome reminders of the past. In any case she had left the court by this time, and spent the last decades of her life in the country, where she died in the 1650s.

Context

Mary Sidney Wroth was known, at least in her prime, as a patroness of letters, though much of her reputation may have been the result of family ties rather than direct financial support. She was a close friend of Ben Jonson, who addressed her in two poems and showed other evidence of his admiration for her both as a person and as a writer. Yet her writings were never given the kind of circulation that would have led to influence on other women authors; and the forms she chose, obviously in imitation of the preceding generation of Sidneys, were not likely to offer later poets useful models. Her remarkable talents, even for a woman of high social standing and undeniable intellectual and artistic gifts, were not enough to ensure her influence. Only by mid-century, when the admittedly eccentric though interesting efforts of Margaret Cavendish, Duchess of Newcastle, were published, did a woman writer dare to put forward her efforts with the same claim to seriousness that was routinely allowed male authors.

Genre

Pamphilia to Amphilanthus was the first sonnet sequence published by a woman in England. Though cycles of this sort were thoroughly out of fashion by the 1620s, Lady Mary used that situation to her advantage, since it allowed her to experiment. She was the first poet to reverse the traditional roles of lover and beloved in such a sequence, and the first to offer a perspective on love from a feminine point of view – the woman as poet replacing the woman as muse. The main theme of the sonnets is the nature of constancy on the woman's part; the usual language of courtship and descriptions of the physical appearance of the beloved are absent. The real focus of the sonnets emerges towards the end of the sequence, when the poet turns to divine themes. In this respect Wroth's sequence is more like Petrarch's, which moves from human to heavenly love, than like those of her Elizabethan precursors, which rarely – if ever – transcend the realm of human erotic experience.

Critical Reception

Lady Mary Wroth's writings are a recent discovery, and her place in English literature has been obscured by centuries of neglect, though Frederick Rowton did include her in an anthology of women poets published in 1848. Apart from their own literary merit, her sonnets have a certain historical significance; by the time she published them the sequence was out of vogue, and hers is the last of a tradition that stretches back to her uncle's *Astrophil and Stella*. Though she brings little in imagery or style that is new to the sonnet form, her unusual perspective brings to it a certain freshness. It is that perspective which has drawn the attention of recent critics, who see in her a poet worthy of a place among the better minor poets of the era. Beginning with Josephine A. Roberts's 1979 essay, there has been a steady stream of articles and books devoted to Wroth's work.

Further Reading

Editions

Pamphilia to Amphilanthus, ed. Gary Waller (Salzburg, 1977) is a pioneering edition of the sonnet sequence, now superseded by *The Poems of Lady Mary Wroth*, ed. Josephine A. Roberts (Baton Rouge, LA, 1983), the standard scholarly edition, which contains an indispensable introduction.

Critical Studies

In the brief period since interest in Wroth began, a lively body of criticism has begun to emerge, beginning with Josephine A. Roberts, 'Lady Mary Wroth's sonnets: a labyrinth of the mind', *Journal of Women's Studies in Literature*, **1** (1979), 319–29 and 'The biographical problem of *Pamphilia to Amphilanthus*', *Tulsa Studies in Women's Literature*, **1** (1982), 43–53. Both these essays overlap with the introduction to her edition of the poems. For a short general account, see Margaret Patterson Hannay, 'Lady Mary Wroth', in *British Women Writers: A critical reference guide*, ed. Janet Todd (New York, 1989), pp. 740–43. Elaine V. Beilin, '"The onely perfect vertue": constancy in Mary Wroth's *Pamphilia to Amphilanthus*', *Spenser Studies*, **2** (1981), 229–45, identifies the theme of constancy in the speaker as central to the whole cycle, and writes of constancy as a heroic feminine virtue in 'Heroic virtue: Mary Wroth's *Urania* and *Pamphilia to Amphilanthus*', ch. 8 of *Redeeming Eve: Women writers in the Renaissance* (Princeton, NJ, 1987). Sandra Yeager, '"She who still constant lov'd": *Pamphilia to Amphilanthus* as Lady Wroth's indictment of male codes of love', *Sidney Newsletter*, **10** (1990), 88–9 sees Wroth's ideal of love as marital and mutual. Jeff Masten, '"Shall I turne blabb?": circulation, gender, and subjectivity in Mary Wroth's sonnets', in *Reading Mary Wroth: Representing alternatives in early modern England*, ed. Naomi J. Miller and Gary Waller (Knoxville, TN, 1991), pp. 67–87, analyses the privacy and antitheatricality of Wroth's poetic universe. Her effort to reclaim poetic invention for women is the subject of Nona Fienberg, 'Mary Wroth and the invention of female poetic subjectivity', in Naomi J. Miller and Gary Waller, eds (see above), pp. 175–90. Maureen Quilligan examines some of the poems outside the sonnet sequence in 'The constant subject: instability and female authority in Wroth's Urania poems', in *Soliciting Interpretation: Literary theory and seventeenth-century English poetry*, ed. Elizabeth D. Harvey and Katherine Eisaman Maus (Chicago, 1990), pp. 307–35.

A number of essays place Wroth's work in the context of Renaissance poetry generally, or in relation to specific poets. May Nelson Paulissen, *The Love Sonnets of Lady Mary Wroth: A critical introduction* (Salzburg, 1982) places the sequence in the context of Renaissance poetic forms and themes, but does not offer much in the way of analysis of individual poems. Gary Waller, who edited an early edition of the sonnets, has described the difficulties faced by Renaissance women in writing and publishing in his 'Struggling into discourse: the emergence of Renaissance women's writing', in *Silent But For the Word: Tudor women as patrons, translators, and writers of religious works*, ed. Margaret Patterson Hannay (Kent, OH, 1985), pp. 238–56, and examines Wroth's Petrarchan elements in 'Reopening the canon', ch. 8 of *English Poetry of the Sixteenth Century* (London, 1986). Janet MacArthur, '"A Sydney, though unnamed": Lady Mary Wroth and her poetical progenitors', *English Studies in Canada*, **15** (1989), 12–20 also studies Wroth's precursors, including those of the Sidney family. Likewise, Naomi J. Miller, 'Rewriting lyric fictions: the role of the Lady in Lady Mary Wroth's *Pamphilia to Amphilanthus*', in *The Renaissance Englishwoman in Print: Counterbalancing the canon*, ed. Anne M. Haselkorn and Betty S. Travitsky (Amherst, MA, 1990), pp. 295–310 compares Wroth's sequence with those of her uncle Philip and father Robert Sidney. Ann Rosalind Jones, 'Feminine pastoral as heroic martyrdom', ch. 4 of *The Currency of Eros: Women's love lyric in Europe, 1540–1620* (Bloomington, IN, 1990) offers an interesting comparison of Wroth with Italian Renaissance poet Gaspara Stampa, and she is compared with another Italian woman poet in Ann Rosalind Jones, 'Designing women: the self as spectacle in Mary Wroth and Veronica Franco', in Naomi J. Miller and Gary Waller, eds (see above), pp. 135–53.

There is a helpful annotated bibliography of work on Wroth in Naomi J. Miller and Gary Waller, eds (see above), pp. 229–34. This important volume also contains essays on Lady Mary's narrative and dramatic works.

From *Pamphilia to Amphilanthus*

Pamphilia (her name in Greek means, roughly, 'all-loving') and Amphilanthus ('lover of two') are characters in Wroth's long romance *Urania*. Her sonnet sequence, however, is presented as an independent work. Of the one hundred and three poems of the cycle, the first fifty-five consist of eight groups of six sonnets, each concluded by a song. They are followed by a series of songs and sonnets in no particular order, and the whole is ended with a corona or crown of fourteen sonnets, linked by first and last lines into a perfect circle in praise of love. The corona begins with sonnet 77; the whole sequence ends with sonnet 103. The sonnets have a variety of different rhyme-schemes.

41 / *When Night's Black Mantle*

When night's black mantle could most darkness prove,
  And sleep, death's image, did my senses hire
  From knowledge of myself, then thoughts did move
  Swifter than those most swiftness need require.

In sleep, a chariot drawn by wing'd desire
  I saw, where sat bright Venus, Queen of Love
  And, at her feet, her son, still adding fire
  To burning hearts which she did hold above.

But one heart, flaming more than all the rest,
  The goddess held and put it to my breast.
  'Dear son, now shut', said she. 'Thus must we win'.

He her obeyed and martyred my poor heart.
  I, waking, hoped as dreams it would depart,
  Yet since, O me, a lover I have been.

This introductory sonnet of the sequence omits the encounter with or depiction of the beloved that begins most cycles, and focuses instead on the speaker's inner disposition. Wroth's sonnets are unusual in that they vary the rhyme-scheme of the octave (first eight lines, usually invariable in the Italian form) as well as the sestet (the remaining six, with variable rhyme-scheme). The rhyme scheme of this one is *a b a b* / *b a b a* / *c c d e e d*.

[1] **black mantle**
black covering; a common metaphor – compare Chaucer's 'Merchant's Tale', line 554: 'Night with his mantle that is dark and rude/Gan overspread the hemisphere about'; ***could most darkness prove*** showed itself at its darkest.
[2] **did my senses hire**
engaged my senses temporarily.
[3] **From knowledge of myself**
(a) made me unconscious; (b) took

away my capacity for self-awareness (and, by extension, control).
[4] **Swifter than those most swiftness need require**
i.e. moved even more swiftly than those thoughts that require utmost speed.
[5] **chariot**
Petrarch's 'Triumph of Love' also has a dream sequence depicting a processional victory and is probably the prototype of this image; ***wing'd desire*** Venus's chariot is often depicted as drawn by doves (see Ovid's *Metamorphoses*, 14.597; the motif also appears in Sir Philip Sidney's *Astrophil and Stella*, sonnet 79, line 4).
[7] **her son**
Cupid, Roman god of love, or his Greek counterpart, Eros; ***fire*** desire.
[8] **burning**
filled with passion; ***above*** on display, as captives were displayed during a triumphal procession.
[11] **shut**
set free; ***win*** vanquish, overcome.
[12] **martyred**
tormented.
[13] **as**
like.

42 / *When Everyone to Pleasing Pastime Hies*

When everyone to pleasing pastime hies,
Some hunt, some hawk, some play, while some delight
In sweet discourse, and music shows joy's might,
Yet I my thoughts do far above these prize.
The joy which I take is that free from eyes
I sit, and wonder at this daylike night,
So to dispose themselves, as void of right,
And leave true pleasure for poor vanities.
When others hunt, my thoughts I have in chase;
If hawk, my mind at wishèd end doth fly;
Discourse, I with my spirit talk and cry;
While others music choose as greatest grace.
O God, say I, can these fond pleasures move?
Or music be but in sweet thoughts of love?

A sonnet on the Petrarchan theme of pleasures of the lover's meditative solitude; it is closer to the traditional form with its 'embracing rhymes', but extends them to the sestet: *a b b a / a b b a / c d d c / e e.*

[1] **hies**
hastens.
[2] **hunt . . . hawk**
typical aristocratic activities (***hawk*** to practise falconry, the art of training birds of prey to hunt); ***play*** engage in various recreations suitable for both men and women.
[3] **discourse**
conversation; ***shows joy's might*** i.e. is

expressive of the intensity of joy felt everywhere.

[4] **I . . . prize**
I prize my thoughts far above these things.

[5] **free from eyes**
i.e. unobserved by others.

[6] **wonder**
to be struck by surprise; ***daylike night*** the blindness of those who participate in the daylight pastimes listed above.

[7] **So to dispose themselves**
put themselves in such a frame of mind or condition; ***as void of right*** as if lacking all power or privilege.

[8] **leave true pleasure for poor vanities**
i.e. those who indulge in various pastimes seek empty activities instead of true pleasure.

[9] **my thoughts . . . in chase**
i.e. she pursues her thoughts while others pursue their hunting quarry.

[10] **mind at wished end doth fly**
her mind reaches the conclusions she seeks.

[11] **I . . . talk and cry**
i.e. she converses with and expresses her feelings with herself.

[12] **as greatest grace**
as being the most pleasing or possessing the greatest charm.

[13] **These**
i.e. hunting, hawking and discoursing; ***fond*** foolish; ***move*** affect the feelings.

[14] **music be . . . of love**
i.e. is there any music other than that heard when one thinks about love? Note that music is treated separately from the other activities as the only one that can be enjoyed without company (other than that of the musicians). The speaker's solitary contemplation is, nevertheless, superior even to music. The sonnet contrasts the pleasures of retirement and meditation with the emptiness of a search for pleasures in superficial activities and the company of the crowd.

43 / *False Hope, Which Feeds*

False hope, which feeds but to destroy and spill
   What it first breeds, unnatural to the birth
   Of thine own womb, conceiving but to kill,
   And plenty gives to make the greater dearth,
So tyrants do, who, falsely ruling earth,
   Outwardly grace them and with profit's fill
   Advance those who appointed are to death
   To make their greater fall to please their will.
Thus shadow they their wicked vile intent,
   Colouring evil with a show of good;
   While in fair shows their malice so is spent,
   Hope kills the heart, and tyrants shed the blood.

For hope, deluding, brings us to the pride
Of our desires the farther down to slide.

A sonnet with an interesting rhyme-scheme that suggests the Shakespearian form, but with the second stanza made into a mirror-image of the first: *a b a b| b a b a | c d c d | e e.* The two organising metaphors – abortion and tyranny – depict two related kinds of violence against the integrity of maternal love and public trust.

[1] **spill**
put an end to life.
[2] **breeds**
conceives.
[2–3] **unnatural . . . womb**
an image of miscarriage; while the imagery of pregnancy (see *Astrophil and Stella,* sonnet 1, line 13) appears occasionally among the male sonneteers, this phrase gives a deeper sense of involvement and loss because it is written by a woman.
[4] **plenty gives . . . dearth**
and provides abundant life only to make its destructive loss seem the greater.
[5] **tyrants**
This political metaphor is given additional point by the conventional description of love or the unresponsive beloved as a tyrant.
[6] **grace them**
(a) appear benevolent (them, i.e. themselves); (b) bestow favour on (them, i.e. 'those' in the following line); ***profit*** (a) progress, advancement; (b) advantage, benefit; ***fill*** full extent.
[7] **Advance**
promote; ***appointed*** secretly destined.
[8] **their greater fall**
those deceptively rewarded by tyrants; ***their will*** the tyrants'.
[9] **shadow they**
they conceal, obscure.
[10] **show**
(a) appearance; (b) display.
[11] **fair shows**
pageantry, spectacles; ***so*** thus; ***spent*** used, exhausted.
[13] **pride**
(a) exalted position; (b) magnificence, ostentation; (c) sexual desire ('heat' in animals).
[14] **slide**
(a) fall precipitously from a great height (usually used to describe the fall of a tragic hero); (b) lose one's foothold.

44 / *If Ever Love Had Force*

If ever love had force in human breast,
If ever he could move in pensive heart,
Or if that he such power could but impart
To breed those flames whose heat brings joy's unrest,
Then look on me; I am to these addressed.
I am the soul that feels the greatest smart;
I am that heartless trunk of heart's depart;
And I that one by love and grief oppressed.

None ever felt the truth of love's great miss
  Of eyes till I deprivèd was of bliss,
  For had he seen, he must have pity showed;
I should not have been made this stage of woe,
  Where sad disasters have their open show.
  O, no! more pity he had sure bestowed.

A sonnet whose rhyme-scheme is closer to the traditional Petrarch form: *a b b a / a b b a / c c d / e e d.*

[1] **force**
power.
[3] **if that he . . . impart**
if he could but send such power; ***impart*** (a) share; (b) communicate.
[5] **Then look on me**
i.e. if all these things have ever been true, then look at me to see an example; ***addressed*** (a) made ready; (b) delivered up.
[6] **smart**
pain, hurt.
[7] **heartless**
(a) callous, unfeeling; (b) lacking a heart (because it has left); ***depart*** departure.
[8] **love and grief**
a linking of opposites common in love poetry from Catullus (e.g. 'I hate and I love') to Petrarch (e.g. 'I freeze and I burn').
[9] **truth**
aptness; the Roman poet Propertius wrote a love poem ('Whoever first depicted Love as a boy') in which he praised the aptness of the traditional allegorical image of Cupid; ***miss*** loss, lack; Cupid or Amor was often depicted as sightless; cf. the old saying 'Love is blind'.
[11] **he**
love.
[12] **stage of woe**
(a) sad period of life; (b) tragic theatrical setting. Wroth uses the imagery of dramatic tragedy in the concluding couplet of 'False hope, which feeds'.
[14] **sure**
surely; ***bestowed*** given.

45 / *In This Strange Labyrinth*

In this strange Labyrinth, how shall I turn?
  Ways are on all sides, while the way I miss:
  If to the right hand, there in love I burn;
  Let me go forward, therein danger is;
If to the left, suspicion hinders bliss;
  Let me turn back, shame cries I ought return
  Nor faint, though crosses which my fortunes kiss.
  Stand still is harder, although sure to mourn.

Thus let me take the right or left-hand way,
  Go forward, or stand still, or back retire.
  I must these doubts endure, without allay
  Or help, but travail find for my best hire.
Yet that which most my troubled sense doth move,
Is to leave all and take the thread of Love.

The rhyme-scheme uses the same 'reverse' pattern as 'False Hope, Which Feeds': *a b a b / b a b a / c d c d / e e.*

[1] **strange Labyrinth**
cf. Petrarch, sonnet 211, line 14: 'I have entered the labyrinth from which I see no escape.' The image was taken up afterwards by numerous sonneteers. The original labyrinth of Greek myth held the murderous Minotaur in its centre; the hero Theseus found and killed him. Thanks to a long thread provided by Ariadne, who had fallen in love with him, he was able to find his way out and escape; ***how shall I turn?*** (a) which way shall I turn?; (b) how shall I return?

[2] **Ways . . . way**
A labyrinth consists of many possible paths, but only one is the right one.

[3] **right hand**
The right side was associated with good fortune and fulfilment.

[4] **go forward**
i.e. openly avow her love, act in too forward a manner.

[5] **left**
associated with evil or bad fortune; the word 'sinister' means 'left side' in Latin, hence the left way is suspect.

[6] **Let me**
if I; ***ought return*** ought to return.

[7] **Nor**
and not; ***faint*** (a) grow weak; (b) lose courage; ***though*** though I encounter; ***crosses*** (a) intersections of paths in the labyrinth; (b) afflictions or trials; ***fortunes*** (a) the turns and courses that accompany a person in life; (b) destiny; ***kiss*** (a) come into contact, touch, or collide with; (b) greet; (c) press to the lips. The speaker's fortunes lead her to the kiss of affliction rather than affection.

[8] **Stand still**
to stand still; ***although*** although I am; ***mourn*** feel sorrow or regret.

[11] **I . . . endure**
I must endure these doubts; ***allay*** abatement, relief.

[12] **travail**
pronounced 'travel' – mental pain or suffering; ***find*** (a) discover; (b) receive; ***hire*** compensation, payment.

[13] **that which . . . move**
that which my troubled mind is most inclined to do.

[14] **leave all**
abandon everything else; ***take the thread of Love*** an allusion to the myth of Theseus and Ariadne (see line 1). Note that Ariadne's 'thread of love' allowed Theseus to leave the labyrinth safely.

46 / *My Muse Now Happy*

My muse now happy, lay thyself to rest;
  Sleep in the quiet of a faithful love.
  Write you no more, but let these fancies move
  Some other hearts; wake not to new unrest.
But if you study, be those thoughts addressed
  To truth, which shall eternal goodness prove –
  Enjoying of true joy, the most and best,
  The endless gain which never will remove.
Leave the discourse of Venus and her son
  To young beginners, and their brains inspire
  With stories of great love, and from that fire
  Get heat to write the fortunes they have won,
And thus leave off; what's past shows you can love:
Now let your constancy your honour prove.

The concluding sonnet of the sequence; it has the same rhyme-scheme as 'When Everyone to Pleasing Pastime Hies'.

[1] **My muse now happy**
Now that my muse is happy; the muse is not the beloved, as it is frequently in love poetry written by men, but the usual goddess of poetic inspiration; ***thyself*** the poet (not the muse), the opening phrase is addressed not to the muse but to the speaker herself.
[2] **faithful love**
The sequence is about the fidelity of Pamphilia, not the consummation of her love.
[3] **these fancies**
(a) the passions of love; (b) these poems.
[5] **study**
meditate.
[6] **prove**
(a) prove to be; (b) confirm or test.
[7–8] **Enjoying . . . gain**
enjoying the unending increase of true joy.
[8] **gain**
(a) increase in value; (b) profit, possession; ***remove*** go away.
[9] **discourse of Venus and her son**
talk of love; her 'son' is, of course, Cupid or Amor, but there may be an intended pun on 'sun', a word frequently used for the loved one who gives the light of life to the beloved.
[10] **their brains inspire**
(a) let the muse inspire the brains of young beginning poets; (b) let younger writers be inspired by the stories of her great love.
[12] **heat**
(a) love passion; (b) poetic fire or inspiration; ***write*** write of; ***fortunes*** (a) great riches (of love); (b) good luck or adventures in love.
[13] **leave off**
quit (writing); ***what's past*** (a) her behaviour as a lover; (b) the story told in the previous sonnets of the sequence; ***shows*** note the strength of this verb, which emphasises that the poet has said all she needs to say.
[14] **constancy**
fidelity in love; i.e. it is her faithfulness to a sometimes unfaithful lover

that will demonstrate her worthiness. The sequence is unusual in its concentration on faithfulness and steadfastness, particularly in view of the commonplaces of male poets that depict women as fickle and forever changing in affections (cf. Donne's 'Go, and Catch a Falling Star', p. 56).

HENRY KING

(1592–1669)

1624 probable composition of 'An Exequy'
1657 *Poems, Elegies, Paradoxes, and Sonnets* (unauthorised)

◇

Henry King was the son of John King, a widely esteemed Bishop of London who was a close friend of Donne. With his younger brother John he attended Westminster School, where he was a contemporary of George Herbert, then went on to Christ Church Oxford. The two brothers took their DD together in 1625, and both joined the Church.

After his father's death, Henry also became a close friend of Donne. Indeed, it was to King that Donne entrusted many of his manuscripts at the time of his final sickness. Other friends included Izaak Walton (Donne's biographer) and Ben Jonson. King became a celebrated preacher until his career was interrupted by the growing civil unrest of the late 1630s. He was deprived of his bishopric during the Civil War.

He married Anne Berkeley in the early 1620s; she died in January 1624. His most famous poem celebrates his love for her.

Context

Like Donne before him, King showed no interest in publishing his verse. He was a monarchist and High Churchman who always lived in busy towns and on the fringes of court life (in Colchester, Oxford, London). He appears to have written both secular and religious verse intermittently from about 1612 to about the time when an unauthorised edition of his verse appeared in 1657 – during the Protectorate of Oliver Cromwell: further evidence, incidentally, that the time of Cromwell saw less rigorous censorship than the period of so-called Charles I's rule.

Genre

Far and away King's most famous work is the elegy he wrote in memory of his wife. It was most probably written shortly after her death in 1624 during the last year of James I's reign – i.e. before the growing political troubles occasioned by Charles I's attempt to rule without Parliament (1629–40). It thus almost certainly antedates any of Herbert's poems.

As most of King's poems are meditations on public rather than private concerns, the 'Exequy' cannot be described as typical of his work. Nevertheless, his tribute to his young wife has long been recognised as one of the outstanding English elegies. The felicity of its conceits and its sudden unexpected images make it not only one of his best works, but also a kind of poem not attempted by his greater contemporaries.

The 'Exequy' is clearly influenced by Donne in its blend of seriousness and paradoxical conceits, and by Jonson; but it shows a more sustained intensity in its grief than the latter's 'On My First Son' (p. 104). However, the poem must be judged not on its 'sincerity' but on its intrinsic beauty and craftsmanship.

Critical Reception

King's poems received only modest attention in the later seventeenth century. The revival of interest in his older friend, John Donne, brought him to the attention of modern readers once more. The 'Exequy' has been highly admired, and is his main claim to poetic fame. In spite of various critical efforts to secure him a wider readership, his other work still remains largely neglected. It used to be said of him that he wrote like a bishop, and the remark seems to have deterred interest in his work.

Further Reading

Edition

The standard edition is *The Poems of Henry King*, ed. Margaret Crum (Oxford, 1965).

Critical Studies

Ronald Berman, *Henry King and the Seventeenth Century* (London, 1964) is still the best introduction, an invaluable study which includes extensive consideration of 'An Exequy'.

Cleanth Brooks offers a thoughtful reading of the poem in 'Need Clio quarrel with her sister muses? The claims of literature and history', in John M. Wallace, ed., *The Golden and the Brazen World: Papers in literature and history, 1650–1800* (Berkeley, CA, 1985), pp. 1–15. See also the same author's 'The poet's sincerity: Henry King', in *Historical Evidence and the reading of seventeenth-century poetry* (Columbia, MO, 1991), pp. 7–22. Joseph Summers devotes some interesting pages to King in 'Gentlemen at home and at church: Henry King and George Herbert', ch. 3 of *The Heirs of Donne and Jonson* (New York and London, 1970), pp. 75–86.

Recent comparative studies include Del Chessell, 'A constant shaping pressure: mortality in poetry', *The Critical Review*, **26** (1984), 3–17, which compares 'An Exequy' with Donne's 'Hymn to God my God'; and Antoon Van Velzen, 'Two versions of the funeral elegy: Henry King's "The Exequy" and Thomas Carew's "...Elegie Upon...Donne"', *Comitatus: A Journal of Medieval and Renaissance Studies*, **15** (1984), 45–57, which compares it with Thomas Carew's 'An Elegy upon the Death of the Dean of Paul's, Doctor John Donne' (see p. 284).

For further bibliographical material, see William McCarron and Robert Shenk, *Lesser Metaphysical Poets: A bibliography, 1961–1980*, 'Checklists in the Humanities and Education' no. 7 (San Antonio, TX, 1983).

47 / *An Exequy to His Matchless Never to be Forgotten Friend*

Accept, thou shrine of my dead saint,
Instead of dirges, this complaint;
And for sweet flowers to crown thy hearse,
Receive a strew of weeping verse
From thy grieved friend, whom thou might'st see
Quite melted into tears for thee.

Dear loss! since thy untimely fate
My task hath been to meditate
On thee, on thee. Thou art the book,
The library whereon I look,
Though almost blind. For thee, loved clay,
I languish out, not live, the day,
Using no other exercise
But what I practise with mine eyes;
By which wet glasses I find out
How lazily time creeps about
To one that mourns: this, only this,
My exercise and business is.
So I compute the weary hours
With sighs dissolved into showers.
Nor wonder if my time go thus
Backward and most preposterous.
Thou hast benighted me. Thy set
This eve of blackness did beget,
Who wast my day, though overcast
Before thou hadst thy noontide passed.
And I remember must in tears,
Thou scarce hadst seen so many years
As day tells hours. By thy clear sun
My love and fortune first did run,
But thou wilt never more appear
Folded within my hemisphere,
Since both thy light and motion
Like a fled star is fallen and gone,
And 'twixt me and my soul's dear wish
An earth now interposed is,
Which such a strange eclipse doth make
As ne'er was read in almanac.
I could allow thee for a time
To darken me and my sad clime.
Were it a month, a year, or ten,
I would thy exile live till then,
And all that space my mirth adjourn,
So thou wouldst promise to return,
And putting off thy ashy shroud,
At length disperse this sorrow's cloud.
But woe is me! the longest date

Too narrow is to calculate
These empty hopes! Never shall I
Be so much blest as to descry
A glimpse of thee, till that day come
Which shall the earth to cinders doom,
And a fierce fever must calcine
The body of this world, like thine –
My little world! That fit of fire
Once off, our bodies shall aspire
To our souls' bliss. Then we shall rise
And view ourselves with clearer eyes
In that calm region where no night
Can hide us from each other's sight.
   Meantime, thou hast her, earth: much good
May my harm do thee. Since it stood
With heaven's will I might not call
Her longer mine, I give thee all
My short-lived right and interest
In her whom, living, I loved best;
With a most free and bounteous grief
I give thee what I could not keep.
Be kind to her, and prithee look
Thou write into thy doomsday book
Each parcel of this rarity
Which in thy casket shrined doth lie.
See that thou make thy reckoning straight,
And yield her back again by weight,
For thou must audit on thy trust
Each grain and atom of this dust,
As thou wilt answer Him that lent,
Not gave thee, my dear monument.
   So close the ground, and 'bout her shade
Black curtains draw; my bride is laid.
   Sleep on, my love, in thy cold bed,
Never to be disquieted!
My last good-night! Thou wilt not wake
Till I thy fate shall overtake;
Till age, or grief, or sickness must
Marry my body to that dust
It so much loves; and fill the room
My heart keeps empty in thy tomb.

Stay for me there! I will not fail
To meet thee in that hollow vale,
And think not much of my delay:
I am already on the way,
And follow thee with all the speed
Desire can make, or sorrows breed.
Each minute is a short degree,
And every hour a step t'wards thee.
At night when I betake to rest,
Next morn I rise nearer my west
Of life, almost by eight hours' sail,
Than when sleep breathed his drowsy gale.
  Thus from the sun my bottom steers,
And my day's compass downward bears;
Nor labour I to stem the tide
Through which to thee I swiftly glide.
  'Tis true, with shame and grief I yield:
Thou, like the van, first took'st the field,
And gotten hast the victory
In thus adventuring to die
Before me, whose more years might crave
A just precedence in the grave.
But hark! My pulse like a soft drum
Beats my approach, tells thee I come.
And slow howe'er my marches be,
I shall at last sit down by thee.
  The thought of this bids me go on,
And wait my dissolution
With hope and comfort. Dear (forgive
The crime!), I am content to live
Divided, with but half a heart,
Till we shall meet and *never* part.

This lament for a dearly loved wife surely stands as one of the supreme examples of the genre. A highly personal address to the deceased, it expresses private rather than public grief and, in contrast to other great English elegies – e.g. Milton's 'Lycidas' (1638) (p. 393), Shelley's *Adonais* (1821) or Tennyson's *In Memoriam* (1850) – it contains no pastoral element, no wish for fame, no questioning of larger issues. It expresses very simply, but with extreme boldness for a Churchman, a very deep love for a departed wife. It hinges on the poet's certainty that he will meet his wife again in Paradise; indeed, that Paradise *is* this reunion.

The poem consists of 120 iambic tetrameters, rhyming in couplets. Lines 1–6 are addressed to the grave of the poet's dead wife; 7–60 are addressed to his deceased wife; 61–78 to the earth that covers her grave; 79–80 to the gravedigger; and 83–120 once again to his wife.

Title
Exequy usually a funeral rite (in modern English, used only in plural: exequies); from Latin *exsequias*, funeral procession; here, more specifically a verse meditation in honour of someone recently deceased: note how the poet's train of thoughts reflects the idea of 'procession' implicit in the word 'exequy'; ***Matchless*** without an equal, i.e. supremely excellent; ***Friend*** in the Old English sense, a kinsman, although Samuel Johnson's definition – 'One joined to another in mutual benevolence and intimacy' (*Dictionary*, 1755) – succinctly expresses the sense; the 'friend' in question was the poet's wife, Anne, who died in 1624.

[1] **shrine**
a casket or tomb, usually holding the relics of a saint; often highly decorated; ***dead saint*** the poet's wife; ***saint*** a pious Christian (cf. Milton's 'my late espoused saint' (p. 415), line 1).

[2] **dirges**
songs of mourning sung at a burial; ***complaint*** (a) a lament; (b) an expression of injustice suffered (here, the injustice of having been deprived of his wife) – a popular Renaissance form in which the poet bewails the vicissitudes of life.

[3] **for**
instead of; ***sweet*** sweet-smelling; ***crown*** form the uppermost decoration of; ***hearse*** a vehicle used to carry the coffin at a funeral.

[4] **strew**
something (e.g. flowers, sand) scattered over a surface (e.g. a grave) – it is a common verb (to strew), but rare as a substantive; ***weeping*** very sad, reflecting the poet's tears.

[5] **grieved**
feeling deep sorrow (cf. 'complaint' in line 2); ***might'st see*** might be able to see, (a) if you cared to look or were not dead; (b) from heaven.

[6] **Quite**
entirely; ***melted*** (a) the friend (i.e. the poet) has been moved to tears; but also (b) he has been transformed into a liquid state, he has 'become' tears; perhaps also an oblique reference to the myth of Niobe. Having seven sons and seven daughters, she boasted of being greater than Leto, who had only two children, Apollo and Artemis. The latter killed all her children, and as Niobe began to weep, she was turned to stone (Ovid, *Metamorphoses*, 6.146–312).

[7] **Dear loss!**
an evident oxymoron: 'dear' beloved; 'loss' dead; ***untimely fate*** premature death – note that this, too, is an oxymoron, as 'fate' is that which cannot be altered and cannot, therefore, come 'untimely' or before it is due.

[8] **task**
work, usually imposed by a superior on an inferior; here, undertaken willingly; ***meditate*** exercise the mind in contemplation of a spiritual kind; meditation was a spiritual discipline – it involved visualising a scene (usually to do with the life of Christ) so as to integrate the spiritual truth it represented. Although the finest example is *The Spiritual Exercises* by Ignatius Loyola (1491–1556), founder of the Catholic 'Society of Jesus' (the Jesuits), meditation was a common practice amongst High Church Anglicans such as King.

[9] **On thee**
note the effect of the repetition – the first suggests the poet's dead wife, whom he addresses; the second suggests an image of his wife, very much alive in his imagination; ***book*** this is probably a daring reference to 'the book of life' (i.e. God's law) referred to in both the Old Testament (e.g. Psalm 69: 12; Daniel 12: 1) and

the New (e.g. Philippians 4: 3; Revelation 3: 5).

[10] **library**
i.e. in not only both meanings suggested in note to previous line, but in innumerable other ways as well.

[11] **blind**
if this poem was indeed written in or shortly after 1624, the blindness was not 'literal' – i.e. it must mean blinded by (a) tears; (b) grief; (c) the brightness of his wife as 'sun' – see line 29; ***clay*** Adam was formed out of the dust of the ground (Genesis 2: 7), but in Job and elsewhere the word is 'clay' – e.g. 'I also am formed out of the clay' (Job 33: 6), and 'we are the clay, and thou [= God] our potter' (Isaiah 64: 8); thus all men and women are formed out of clay: 'loved clay', i.e. Anne.

[12] **languish out**
exist in a state of inertia, i.e. passively, with the implication that this is because the poet has lost someone dear to him; note that a cult of melancholy developed in the late Elizabethan and early Jacobean period, culminating in the publication of Burton's *The Anatomy of Melancholy* in 1621, three years before Anne's death; ***not live*** contrast with expression 'seize the day' [*carpe diem*].

[13] **Using . . . exercise**
not just a reference to physical exercise, but 'performing no other activity'.

[14] **practise . . . eyes**
activity implies 'practice' (i.e. doing something, especially habitually) – i.e. the poet can only weep.

[15] **wet glasses**
the eyeballs (not spectacles), moistened by tears.

[16–17] **lazily time creeps about**
in a popular Renaissance subgenre, a male lover chides his mistress for lying in bed late into the morning: e.g. Herrick, 'Corinna's Going a-Maying' (p. 252): here King inverts the tradition; ***to one that mourns*** i.e. in contrast to a happy lover; ***this*** mourning his wife: the repetition emphasises two aspects: *his* weeping, and his missing *her*.

[18] **exercise**
in the sense of 'spiritual exercise', i.e. time set aside daily for meditation; ***business*** necessary but self-imposed task.

[19] **compute**
determine by calculation; ***weary hours*** note how the poet collapses the meaning 'hours which bring only weariness to me' into a phrase in which 'hours' are given human attributes – an example of the 'pathetic fallacy' identified by John Ruskin (*Modern Painters*, 1856); note how this arises from his 'projecting' his own weariness into the hours.

[20] **sighs . . . showers**
showers tears – note the implication that a sigh is only the 'solid' form of a tear; cf. 'melted' in line 6.

[21] **Nor wonder**
Nor do I wonder; ***thus*** in this way.

[22] **Backward**
i.e. instead of accepting the flow of time, the poet dwells on a time in the past, increasingly distant from his present position; ***preposterous*** contrary to nature, absurd: in Latin the word has the literal meaning of reversed, 'hindside placed forward'.

[23] **benighted**
caused me to fall into a state of intellectual, moral and social darkness; ***set*** setting (as of the sun), i.e. death.

[24] **eve of blackness**
just as the setting of the sun precedes evening, so the death of Anne precedes a state of darkness; ***beget*** occasion, give rise to.

[25] **day**
likening a woman to the day was a commonplace of Renaissance verse: e.g. Shakespeare, 'Shall I compare thee to a summer's day?' (Sonnet 18); ***though overcast*** though your day was clouded over: punning on 'overcast' as overthrown, i.e. killed = died.

[26] **noontide**
i.e. half the allotted span of life (three score years and ten – cf. Psalm 90: 10): thirty-five years, or before Anne had reached her thirty-fifth birthday.

[27] **remember must**
must remember, in the sense of 'only to think that ... makes the poet weep'.
[28–9] **tells**
has (twenty-four hours): i.e. Anne was barely twenty-five when she died; ***sun*** a commonplace in Renaissance verse: e.g. Sidney, *Astrophil and Stella*, 7.
[30] **run**
prosper.
[32] **hemisphere**
within the 180 degrees of the poet's vision.
[33] **light**
the 'light' that Anne (figuratively) cast around her; ***motion*** movement, especially that of a star or planet.
[34] **a fled star**
a star that has dipped below the horizon of the night sky; ***gone*** disappeared from sight – note how the continued existence of the star is assumed (i.e. the poet imagines Anne as living on in heaven).
[35] **'twixt**
between; ***dear wish*** most coveted desire – i.e. to join his wife in death/heaven.
[36] **earth**
the earth that covers his wife's coffin; ***interposed*** come between.
[37] **eclipse**
a favourite image of King's: an eclipse of the moon occurs when the earth comes between the sun and the moon, thereby depriving the latter of light – the eclipse is 'strange' because it is the earth (in line 36) that has come between the poet and his desire.
[38] **almanac**
annual calendar giving astrological and other predictions for the coming year – i.e. the eclipse described by the poet could not be found in any astrological calendar.
[39] **I could allow...**
the poet continues the image of the eclipse.
[40] **darken**
i.e. by eclipse; ***clime*** mood.
[42] **I would**
I would bear with; ***thy exile*** (a) his wife's 'exile' in death; (b) the poet's 'exile' from his wife – i.e. he imagines his continuing separation from his wife as a period of long absence from his native country; note that classical Greek and Roman writers saw exile as almost worse than death.
[43] **that space**
i.e. the intervening *time* is imagined as space (because the poet is referring to the spatial metaphor of 'exile'); ***mirth*** (a) all thoughts of happiness; (b) the happiness he imagines will arise from reunion with his wife; ***adjourn*** put off, postpone.
[44] **So**
if; ***return*** i.e. from death/exile; the word may also involve a deliberate reversal of the Lord's decree to Adam: 'You will return to dust' (Genesis 3: 19).
[45] **ashy shroud**
the earth/ashes that cover (i.e. shroud, conceal from sight) the coffin – cf. 'earth to earth, ashes to ashes, dust to dust', a phrase from 'The Order for the Burial of the Dead' from *The Book of Common Prayer* (1552).
[46] **disperse**
scatter, drive or send off in different directions – note how this refers back to 'overcast' in line 25; ***this sorrow's cloud*** i.e. the metaphorical cloud of the poet's grief.
[47–9] **longest date**
the time between that in which the poet is writing and an unimaginably distant future; ***narrow*** small or constricting; ***calculate*** i.e. to give the poet hope of seeing his wife again; ***empty hopes*** i.e. no amount of time would suffice for the poet to measure (calculate) the longed-for pleasure (empty hopes) of seeing his wife again in life – note how further to the paradox implicit in these lines, an 'empty hope' is also an oxymoron.
[50] **descry**
succeed in catching sight of.
[51–2] **till that day come ... to cinders doom**
the day referred to is the day of the Last Judgement (often called *doomsday*),

when all those whose names are not written in the Book of Life are thrown into a fire which will burn the whole world to 'cinders' (i.e. 'ashes', see line 45) before a new heaven and a new earth appear (the New Jerusalem) in which only the just (i.e. the faithful) will live with God (Revelation 20–21).

[53–4] **And a fierce fever . . . of this world**

fever (a) heat; (b) high bodily temperature caused by sickness – i.e. (a) a fierce conflagration must reduce the world (earth) to calcium oxide (ashes); cf. 'But the day of the Lord will come like a thief at night; then the heavens shall pass away with a great noise, the elements shall melt with fierce heat, along with the earth, and everything on it burn up' (2 Peter 3: 10); (b) my sickness [i.e. the poet's longing to see his wife again] will consume his own body (i.e. his world); ***this world*** (a) the globe, earth; (b) the poet's body as 'microcosm'; ***like thine*** i.e. in the same way as his wife's body was returned to ashes.

[55] **My little world**

i.e. his wife is a 'microcosm' of the poet, just as the poet is a microcosm of the world.

[55–7] **That fit of fire/Once off**

When the conflagration/mortal fever is over – note how the verb 'fit' makes light of death; ***our bodies . . . bliss*** the Gospel promises that the bodies of 'good Christians' will rise from the dead to live with Christ, their 'bliss' or perfect happiness – note how the reunion of man and wife is daringly equated with the soul's reunion with Christ; note also the implicit parallel with the myth of the phoenix: a unique Egyptian or Arabian bird which, at the end of its allotted life, makes a nest amongst spices, sings its own dirge, then sets fire to itself by flapping its own wings; burnt to ashes, it then rises again with new life.

[59] **that calm region**

heaven, Paradise; ***night*** the night of 'death'.

[61–2] **thou hast her, earth**

the poet addresses the ground in which his wife lies – note the paradox implicit in this new juxtaposition of 'realism' (his wife is dead; the poet can be addressing only the earth that covers her) and 'fantasy': the personification of 'earth'; ***my harm*** the grief suffered by the poet.

[62–3] **stood/With**

i.e. since it was decreed by or was the will of heaven.

[64] **Her longer mine**

her mine any longer.

[64–5] **give . . . right . . . interest**

all terms to do with property.

[66] **living**

i.e. when his wife was still alive.

[67] **free and bounteous**

adjectives usually used of love or generosity of spirit; here applied to 'grief'.

[69] **kind**

(a) gentle; (b) of the same substance – note how the earth is constrained to model itself on the 'gentler' earth of his wife; ***prithee look*** please be certain that.

[70] **thy doomsday book**

the Book of those destined for everlasting life.

[71] **each parcel**

every part or aspect; ***rarity*** rare or saintly (person).

[72] **thy casket shrined**

the space occupied by the coffin, but with a secondary reference to the casket or coffin in which the poet's wife lies; 'casket' would usually signify an urn in which a person's ashes might be kept after cremation.

[73] **make thy reckoning straight**

the poet cautions the earth to ensure that it keeps an accurate account of what it has been entrusted with, so that when the day of the Last Judgement comes, it can surrender Anne to everlasting life.

[74] **by weight**

i.e. physically, exactly as Anne was in life.

[75] **audit on thy trust**

be held responsible for, calculate

honestly (looking forward to lines 77–8).

[77–8] **As thou wilt**
Because you will have to; ***Him*** God; ***lent,/Not gave*** i.e. God entrusts the (God-fearing) dead to the ground for the latter to take care of until the day of final Resurrection; ***dear monument*** (a) the body of his wife; (b) her tomb.

[79–80] **So close the ground . . . laid**
'bout about; ***shade*** a word used to describe the ghostly forms of the dead in the underworld of classical Greece and Rome – here, Anne's dead body; ***Black curtains*** emphasises the death – note how the curtains one might draw around a person who has died at home are here applied to the earth 'closing' (i.e. being piled) on her body; ***my bride is laid*** (a) my bride is prepared (to go to heaven, but also with implicit, though probably unconscious, sexual innuendo); (b) 'in which' Anne lies.

[82] **disquieted**
'quiet' is repose, peace; 'quietus' is release from life, death; thus, Anne can never now be shaken from the peace she enjoys.

[83] **wake**
i.e. at the Last Judgement.

[84] **overtake**
come suddenly upon the same fate as Anne – i.e. 'die'.

[86] **Marry**
unite; ***dust*** i.e. the same plot of ground in which his wife lies buried – it was, and continues to be, common for man and wife to share the same plot.

[87–8] **and fill the room/ . . . in thy tomb**
an astonishing image – the 'room' in the tomb is the space created by the poet's longing to be reunited with his wife.

[89] **Stay for me there**
i.e. he asks her to wait until he can join her in death, as though they might be reunited in a second marriage – note the way in which his appeal exploits absurdity (being dead, Anne can do nothing but wait) to achieve a genuinely moving effect.

[90] **hollow vale**
Anne's grave, a 'vale' (valley) because it is a dip in the ground – the 1657 edition has 'hallow', which would underline the sacredness of the space occupied by Anne's grave.

[94] **Desire**
the speed with which 'desires' travel is proverbial; ***breed*** give rise to, occasion – note that 'breed' is usually used of 'giving life to'; here the purpose is to attain *death* more quickly.

[95] **minute**
(a) a unit of time; (b) a unit of spatial measurement on the globe, i.e. 'degree' of longitude or latitude.

[97] **betake**
commit (myself) to go, decide to go.

[98–9] **my west/Of life**
'west' being where the sun sets, the phrase means 'my death': cf. Donne, 'Good Friday, 1613', (p. 79), lines 9–12.

[99] **sail**
life as a sea-voyage fraught with storms is an age-old literary metaphor, popularised by Petrarch – e.g. Spenser: 'After long storms and tempests sad assay' (*Amoretti*, 63).

[100] **drowsy gale**
here King provides an unexpected twist to the metaphor – the 'gales' are usually life's difficulties; here the difficulties of either (a) a dream; or (b) a sleepless night.

[101] **from the sun**
away from the sun; ***bottom*** (a) the hull of a ship (continuing the image begun in line 99); (b) fundamental essence or character.

[102] **compass**
probably not the magnetic instrument used for navigation, but (a) extent or limit of what is visible, the horizon (i.e. the bounds of the poet's life); (b) any circular arc; ***downward*** (a) i.e. towards death; (b) being a circular movement, the poet seeks death in order to rise again.

[103] **Nor labour I to stem**
nor do I make any effort to reverse or, more specifically, swim against (the tide of life towards death).

[104] **Through ... glide**
float, like a boat ploughing 'through' the surface of the sea.
[105] **yield**
(a) confess; (b) surrender to the fact.
[106] **van**
vanguard, i.e. the front troops of an army; ***took'st the field*** advanced on the field of battle.
[107] **gotten hast**
has got or won; ***victory*** victory over death: cf. St Paul's explanation of how the dead are raised to eternal life: 'O Death, where is your victory? O Death, where is your sting?' (1 Corinthians 15: 55).
[108] **adventuring**
(a) advancing bravely; (b) preparing oneself for something that is to come – cf. 'advent'.
[109] **more years**
i.e. the poet is older than Anne – his greater age gives him the right to ***crave*** (a) demand with authority; (b) more fervently desire.
[110] **precedence**
the right to a superior position in a social hierarchy or ceremony – i.e. the poet thinks he should have died first.
[111–12] **a soft drum ... I come**
an unexpected continuation of the military conceit – note that the soft drumbeat could also be that of his own pulse; ***approach*** i.e. to death.
[113] **slow howe'er**
however slow; ***marches*** (a) physical progression towards death; (b) musical march (which is slow, because it is mourning for Anne).
[114] **sit**
another daring verb, pregnant with religious overtones: (a) the phrase from the Creed: 'The third day he rose again according to the Scriptures. He ascended into Heaven, where he sits at the right hand of his Father' (*Book of Common Prayer*); cf. lines 55–7 above; cf. also (b) the last line of Herbert, 'Love (3)' (p. 241) and note.
[115] **bids**
commands; ***go on*** continue in his march towards death.
[116] **dissolution**
i.e. dissolution in death: cf. 'melted/dissolved', lines 6, 20 – note again the ambivalence: Christians are exhorted to meet death with hope of eternal life in heaven.
[118] **the crime**
the crime being the poet's content.
[119] **Divided, with but half a heart**
note again the surprise – by 'divided', we immediately understand the physical separation that exists between the poet and his deceased wife; then King tells us it also refers to him having only half a heart, an unexpected reference to the Platonic idea of the soul.
[120] **Till we shall meet ...**
i.e. on the day of the Last Judgement.

GEORGE HERBERT

(1593–1633)

1633 *The Temple* (posthumous)

◇

George Herbert was born into an aristocratic family which moved at the very centre of literary, Church and court life during the reigns of Elizabeth I and James I. His mother, Magdalen, was a friend and patroness of John Donne; the two young men became close friends. An elder brother, Edward, became Lord Herbert of Cherbury, and he too was a poet; another brother became Master of Revels.

George studied at Westminster School from 1605 to 1609, then at Trinity College Cambridge; he was there when Prince Henry, the heir to the throne, died in 1612. He contributed two Latin poems to a volume commemorating this event. In 1616 he was made a Fellow of Trinity College, and from 1620 to 1628 he was Public Orator at Cambridge University. In 1624 he became Member of Parliament for Montgomery, in Wales, and two years later he became a deacon, thereby signalling the end of his hopes of state office. In 1627 his mother died (her funeral sermon was preached by Donne – the published version was accompanied by commemorative poems, including one by Herbert, in Latin). Two years later, he married Jane Danvers. The following year, several months after assuming a post at Bemerton Rectory, near Salisbury, he took holy orders. In 1633, just before his fortieth birthday, he died of consumption (tuberculosis).

In short, his life was relatively uneventful. His talents gave him a right to expect state office, and there can be no doubt that this is what he wanted. But after repeated disappointments he joined the Church, and most of the English poems that make up *The Temple* were probably written in the last three years of his life. He entrusted the manuscript to Nicholas Ferrar, the remarkable leader of a small religious community which he established at Little Gidding,* with instructions to publish it or destroy it as he saw fit. Ferrar published it very shortly after the poet's death, though not without difficulty with the censor. It became enormously popular, going through some thirteen editions between 1633 and 1680. Herbert's first biographer was Izaak Walton, who published his study of the poet's life, with comments on the works, in 1674.

Context

Herbert was a whole generation younger than Donne, a gentle scholarly man who stayed on at Cambridge University to become a Fellow and subsequently Public Orator long after most of his contemporaries had hurried to London for court preferment. Although he was certainly ambitious for the highest public office – with his background and, perhaps, also his personality, nothing less would have been acceptable – only his talent made him suitable for this. His health was delicate, and it is unlikely that he could have coped with the pressures of state affairs at a particularly difficult time in English history.

Herbert came of age during the early years of James I's reign, when both the king and Parliament were fiercely disputing what each considered their inalienable rights. Although James I had been brought up in the Presbyterian Church, he relied so heavily on Church of England support for his government that the country gradually slid towards High Church practices that were virtually indistinguishable from Catholicism – this was why the censor only reluctantly allowed Ferrar permission to publish *The Temple* after Herbert's death. The debate between opposing factions was keen – an introvert like Herbert could not help but be confused by the upheaval in all walks of life. The world of religious submission and aristocratic privilege into which he was born was being questioned daily – both by Puritans calling for another reformation of the Church of England and by Members of Parliament calling for extensive constitutional reforms and a greater say in government. It was an age that

* 'Little Gidding' is the title of the last of the *Four Quartets* (1944) by T.S. Eliot, who also greatly admired Ferrar.

promoted extreme opinions and had little time for one man's meditations, no matter how well they can be seen to reflect the greater debate of the time.

From about the mid 1620s, when Herbert was in his early thirties, he seems to have realised that his hopes of a political career were slim. He became a deacon. His solution was characteristic: to retire to the country where, if his poetry is to be believed, he found greater contentment than he had known during his earlier, more ambitious years. There can be little doubt that *The Temple,* written in his late thirties, is the product of a deliberate retirement from the world after a failure to achieve a political post. But one should resist any simplification this suggests, for more is to be gained from seeing Herbert's works as a vivid personal commentary on the intensity with which individuals wrestled with religious concerns at the time. It used to be argued that his works represent the expression of true Christian submission. More recently, it has been shown that they also reveal a crisis of faith.

Genre

Although Herbert is still best known as a 'Metaphysical poet', the term sits very uncomfortably on his work. While a great many of the characteristics of Donne's work can be found in Herbert's poems (formal variety, great immediacy, startling conceits), their tone is quite different. A more appropriate term might be 'meditative verse' (Martz, 1954) or 'devotional verse'.

The Temple is unique in English literature. Sadly, we know very little about how Herbert composed it, or how he came to choose the sequence of the poems it comprises – about 180, of varying length, in three sections: (1) 'The Church Porch', consisting of one long poem; (2) 'The Church', the main body of poems; and 'The Church Militant', another long poem followed by a short 'envoi' or final hymn of praise. All the poems in this anthology are from the central section and concern a wide range of subjects to do with church service, the church year, the parts of a church, etc. While most reveal the poet's struggle to achieve the kind of belief to which he aspired, one never doubts that his belief was both constant and very deeply rooted (although this view has recently been questioned by Barbara Harman). Like Donne, Herbert plays with metaphors and even argument, but his works display a more gentle personality – even in his anger, he is deeply submissive. His works still retain their immediacy and can be fully enjoyed for both their thought and their craftsmanship, quite apart from the religious views they express.

Critical Reception

The popularity of Herbert's poems is attested to by the many times his volume was reprinted – thirteen editions between 1633 and 1709 – as well as by Izaak Walton's biography (1670) and his marked influence upon other poets, such as Crashaw and Vaughan.

In spite of the admiration of William Cowper (1731–1800) and John Wesley (1703–91), his reputation declined in the eighteenth century until an edition of his works published in 1799 caught the imagination of some of the Romantic poets.

Coleridge praised him in his *Biographia Literaria* (1817), ch. 19, and later (1835–6) published a two-volume edition of his works with notes. Herbert's sacred subjects and accessible style assured his verse a relatively wide readership throughout the nineteenth century – some thirty separate editions appeared.

The renewed interest in Donne that arose from Grierson's 1912 edition of the poet's works did not immediately affect Herbert's reputation. Indeed, not until Hutchinson's edition of Herbert's works in 1941 was interest really rekindled. A number of seminal studies appeared in the 1950s and early 1960s, and his reputation has continued to grow as critics become more aware of his unique voice.

Jonathan Post (1984) has divided recent criticism neatly into three phases. The first includes studies by Rosamond Tuve, Louis Martz, Joseph Summers, and others, whose views constitute, essentially, a refinement of 'Coleridge's perception'; they examine the poetry as an expression of an essentially religious experience. The second group includes critics like Arnold Stein, Helen Vendler and Stanley Fish, who, writing in the wake of New Criticism, eschew religious issues in favour of analysing textual complexities and rhetorical strategies. Most recently, a number of studies have appeared which are characterised by their advancement of a particular view; *The Temple*, 'like the hall of Appleton House,* [changes] shape with the entrance of each reader': notable among these recent critics are Heather Asals, Barbara Harman, Richard Strier and Diana Benet.

Further Reading

Editions

The standard work is still *Works of George Herbert*, ed. F.E. Hutchinson, rev. edn (Oxford, 1945), although both *The English Poems of George Herbert*, ed. C.A. Patrides, 'Everyman Classics' (London, 1974) and *George Herbert and Henry Vaughan*, ed. Louis L. Martz, 'Oxford Authors' (Oxford, 1986) are more useful for most purposes: the Everyman edition is especially useful for its bibliography. The Norton Critical Edition, *George Herbert and the Seventeenth-Century Religious Poets*, ed. Mario Di Cesare (New York, 1978) includes some useful essays.

Critical Studies

A good introductory study is Stanley Stewart, *George Herbert*, 'Twayne' (Boston, MA, 1986). Useful collections of essays include John R. Roberts, ed., *Essential Articles for the Study of George Herbert's Poetry* (Hamden, CT, 1979); Claude J. Summers and Ted-Larry Pebworth, eds, *'Too Rich to Clothe the Sunne': Essays on George Herbert* (Pittsburgh, PA, 1980); and Edmund Miller and Robert DiYanni, eds, *Like Season'd Timber: New essays on George Herbert* (New York, 1987); the latter has a very helpful article by Charles A. Hutter on Herbert and the Emblematic Tradition. For an invaluable overview of critical reception of Herbert from the seventeenth century to modern times, see C.A. Patrides, *George Herbert: The critical heritage* (London, 1983).

* 'Upon Appleton House' is a poem by Andrew Marvell, too long for inclusion in this anthology.

Amongst the seminal studies, mention must be made of Rosamond Tuve's ground-breaking work *A Reading of George Herbert* (Chicago, 1952); J.H. Summers, *George Herbert: His religion and art* (London, 1954); Louis L. Martz, *The Poetry of Meditation: A study of English religious literature of the seventeenth century* (New Haven, CT, 1954); and T.S. Eliot's short but pertinent essay in the 'Writers and Their Work' series: *George Herbert* (London, 1962). Earl Miner, *The Metaphysical Mode from Donne to Cowley* (Princeton, NJ, 1969) includes an especially useful chapter on 'The Flower'. Arnold Stein, *George Herbert's Lyrics* (Baltimore, MD, 1968) is difficult, but still one of the best accounts of Herbert's major works. Helen Vendler is especially strong in relating the poetry to the poet in *The Poetry of George Herbert* (Cambridge, MA, 1974). Stanley E. Fish, *The Living Temple: George Herbert and catechizing* (Berkeley and Los Angeles, CA, 1978) continues to offer provocative insights.

Recent trends in Herbert criticism are too disparate to categorise easily. Especially thoughtful are Heather Asals, *Equivocal Predication: George Herbert's way to God* (Toronto, ON, 1981), Barbara Leah Harman, *Costly Monuments: Representations of the self in George Herbert's poetry* (Cambridge, MA, 1982), which argues – somewhat controversially – that Herbert's religious conviction was much less certain than it appears; Richard Strier, *Love Known: Theology and experience in George Herbert's poetry* (Chicago, 1983), which explores the theme of justification by faith; and Diana Benet, *Secretary of Praise: The poetic vocation of George Herbert* (Columbia, MO, 1984), which explores the themes of grace and charity. For invaluable assessments of these studies, see Jonathan F.S. Post, 'Reforming *The Temple*: Recent criticism of George Herbert', *John Donne Journal*, **3** (1984), 221–47; Marion White Singleton, *God's Courtier: Configuring a different grace in George Herbert's 'Temple'* (Cambridge, 1987); and Robert H. Ray, 'Recent studies in Herbert: 1974–1986', *ELR*, **18** (1988), 460–75.

Some of the more provocative recent accounts of individual poems include Dennis H. Burden, 'George Herbert's "Redemption"', *RES*, **34** (1983), 446–51; Judy Z. Kronenfeld, 'Probing the relation between poetry and ideology: Herbert's "The Windows"', *John Donne Journal*, **2** (1983), 55–80; Anne Williams, 'Gracious accommodations: George Herbert's "Love (III)"',

MP, **82** (1984), 13–22 – she argues that this well-known poem is not so much an allegory as an appeal 'to private, imagined experience'; and Ilona Bell, 'Revision and revelation in Herbert's "Affliction (I)"', *John Donne Journal*, **3** (1984), 73–96.

The standard biography is now Amy M. Charles, *A Life of George Herbert* (Ithaca, NY, 1977), but no biography will ever displace Izaak Walton's almost contemporary account, 'The Life of Mr. George Herbert' (1670).

Further research should begin with John R. Roberts, *George Herbert: An annotated bibliography of modern criticism: 1905–1984* (Columbia, MO, 1988), an indispensable aid; and Mario A. Di Cesare and Rigo Magnani, *A Concordance to the Complete Writings of George Herbert* (Ithaca, NY, 1977). The *George Herbert Journal*, ed. Sidney Gottlieb (from 1978) is another useful resource.

48 / *The Agony*

Philosophers have measured mountains,
Fathomed the depths of seas, of states, and kings,
Walked with a staff to heaven, and traced fountains.
But there are two vast spacious things
The which to measure it doth more behove –
Yet few there are that sound them: Sin and Love.

Who would know Sin, let him repair
Unto Mount Olivet. There shall he see
A man so wrung with pains that all his hair,
His skin, his garments, bloody be.
Sin is that press and vice which forceth pain
To hunt his cruel food through every vein.

Who knows not Love, let him assay
And taste that juice which on the cross a pike
Did set again abroach – then let him say
If ever he did taste the like.
Love is that liquor sweet and most divine
Which my God feels as blood – but I, as wine.

'Agony' (from the Greek word *agonia* = [a] a physical contest, e.g. *Olympiakoi agones* = Olympic games; [b] a mental conflict) is the word used to describe Christ's struggle with himself in the Garden of Gethsemane just before his arrest, which led to his trial and crucifixion: 'Then, being in an agony, he prayed more earnestly, until his sweat turned to drops of blood that fell on the dry ground' (Luke 22: 44; cf. also Matthew 26); here, it refers to the struggle faced by all Christians when they seek to understand the nature of human sin and the depth of Christ's love.

This strikingly visual emblematic poem should be read in the light of those Renaissance and early Baroque conventions in the depiction of Christ's crucifixion which emphasise his suffering. It is in three stanzas of six lines of iambic tetrameters and pentameters, rhyming *a b a b c c*. The first stanza describes how man, in his quest for human knowledge, fails to explore two more pressing issues: the nature of sin and love. The second is concerned with sin; the third, with love.

Christ's 'Agony' was a frequent subject of Renaissance painting – e.g. Giovanni Bellini, 'The Agony in the Garden', *c.*1465 (National Gallery, London), or Albrecht Dürer, 'Christ on the Mount of Olives', 1515 (ink drawing, Albertina, Vienna).

[1] **Philosophers**
not to be taken literally; here it means simply scholars, or learned men; ***measured*** ascertained the height of – the verb implies that mountains can be fully known merely by ascertaining their height.

[2] **Fathomed**
(a) literally: measured the depth of water by means of a weighted line; and (b) figuratively: penetrated a subject sufficiently deeply to understand it fully – note how the literal sense applies to 'seas'; the figurative to the 'states' and 'kings'.

[3] **Walked with a staff**
a reference to Jacob's prayer to God upon returning to his country to face his brother Esau, whom he had cheated of his birthright: 'I am not worthy of the unfailing love that you have shown me, for I am only your servant. When I crossed the Jordan, I had only my staff [walking stick] to call my own, and now I have prospered to such an extent that a division has opened up in my following' (Genesis 32: 10) – thus, ***staff*** (a) the meagreness of human resources; also (b) help from God; ***heaven*** (a) clearly not Herbert's idea of heaven, if it can be arrived at so easily; (b) Jacob's return to the homeland from which he fled is symbolic of man's fall from grace/heaven and his ever-present possibility of regaining it; ***traced*** ascertained by investigation, sought out; ***fountains*** in a figurative sense, the 'source' of any subject studied by the scholars; thus ***traced fountains*** discovered the essence of a subject by investigation. But note: just as the philosophers' heaven is not Heaven, so the fountains they discover are not the Water of Life.

[4] **spacious**
not tautologous – it means 'characterised by greatness, breadth, or comprehensiveness of character' (*OED*).

[5] **The which . . . behove**
which it is more appropriate, proper or necessary to 'measure'.

[6] **sound**
fathom, i.e. to measure depth of water with a weighted 'sounding' line.

[7] **Who would know**
'Whoever really wants to know what Sin is' – the phrase implies not only seeking full knowledge, but also understanding of its awful, awe-inspiring nature and consequences.

[7–8] **repair/Unto Mount Olivet**
repair go; ***Mount Olivet*** the Mount of Olives, a range of limestone mountains to the east of Jerusalem, (a) on which Christ foretells the difficulties

and persecutions which his followers must be prepared to face, and warns his disciples to be wary of false prophets and alert for true signs of the coming of the Son of Man and the end of time (Mark 13) – this sermon is a prologue to the story of Christ's Passion or 'agony' (Mark 14 ff., Luke 22: 39 ff.); (b) the Mount of Olives is also the site of Christ's ascension (Acts 1: 12). The Garden of Gethsemane was situated on the Mount of Olives – Gethsemane means 'oil-press' (a press designed to squeeze the oil from olives). Herbert's phrase is thus polyvalent, as he is contracting two different events into one: (a) *Christ's 'agony'*, which is usually set in the Garden of Gethsemane (Mark 14: 32; Matthew 26: 36–9) or simply on the Mount of Olives (Luke 22: 39–44) – it is here that Christ prays: 'Father, if it be thy will, take this cup from me. Yet not my will but thine be done.' According to Luke, an angel thereupon appears to him, and Christ prays in an agony, or in even greater anguish, 'until his sweat turned to drops of blood that fell on the dry ground'. But the phrase (as the sequel makes clear) also points to (b) *the crucifixion* which took place at Golgotha or Calvary (respectively, Hebrew and Latin for 'skull'), whose location remains uncertain (Mark 15: 22; Luke 23: 33). Herbert was not the first to suggest that it too occurred on the Mount of Olives, but the powerful description of Christ's suffering is particularly striking. The phrase thus implies: (a) that to know what Sin is, one must re-experience both Christ's agony in the Garden of Gethsemane *and* his suffering at the crucifixion – i.e. two different aspects of Christ's Love.

[8] **There shall he see**
the sense demands that the 'seeing' is figurative, but note that Herbert is implying that the crucifixion is an eternally present event.

[9–10] **A man so wrung with pains**
wrung twisted; the ***man*** Christ, traditionally identified with the 'man of sorrows' mentioned in Isaiah 53: 3. The pains are not only the physical pains of the crucifixion, but the accumulated sorrows of Christ's ministry; ***bloody be*** the emphasis on the suffering recalls such powerful works as Matthias Grünewald's 'Crucifixion' on the Isenheim altar-piece, 1512–15, now in Colmar, France.

[11] **Sin**
(a) the world's sin at the time of Christ; (b) every individual's sin – i.e. at the time Herbert was writing; ***press and vice press***, i.e. a wine-press – cf. Gethsemane = oil-press; also a reference to 'the great winepress of the wrath of God' at the end of Time (Revelation 14: 19–20); ***vice*** a device to hold something firmly in place while it is being worked on, e.g. by a carpenter or blacksmith; ***his cruel food*** the food of Sin's cruelty, Christ's blood – i.e. 'sin' is to make Christ suffer; note the implications for all those who drink 'Christ's blood' at Communion/Mass.

[13] **Who knows not Love**
Whoever has not experienced Love; ***assay*** attempt, try.

[14] **juice**
Christ's blood; ***pike*** spear – i.e. the spear used by the soldier who pierced Christ's side to ascertain that he was dead (John 19: 34).

[15] **abroach**
to pierce (e.g. a cask of wine); thus, 'to cause once more to flow': many paintings of the crucifixion illustrate Christ's blood spurting from the wound as if it were bursting from a leaking cask: e.g. Fra Angelico, 'The Crucifixion', *c.*1443 (Metropolitan, New York).

[16] **the like**
i.e. such a sweet and most divine liquor.

[18] **feels**
experiences – God sacrifices his blood; Herbert is spiritually intoxicated by wine.

49 / *Redemption*

Having been tenant long to a rich Lord,
   Not thriving, I resolvèd to be bold
   And make a suit unto him, to afford
A new small-rented lease, and cancel th'old.
In heaven at his manor I him sought:
   They told me there that he was lately gone,
   About some land which he had dearly bought
Long since on earth, to take possession.
I straight returned and, knowing his great birth,
   Sought him accordingly in great resorts:
   In cities, theatres, gardens, parks, and courts.
At length I heard a ragged noise and mirth
Of thieves and murderers: there I him espied,
Who straight *'Your suit is granted'* said – and died.

This English sonnet, composed of three iambic quatrains followed by a couplet and rhyming *a b a b / c d c d / e f e f / g g*, is one of the best examples of Herbert's parabolic or parable poems.

The poet imagines himself as a tenant who rents his home from a wealthy 'Lord' (i.e. Christ) and wants to change the conditions of his lease. He goes to heaven to look for Christ, only to discover that the latter has recently moved to a property on earth which he has purchased at considerable expense. In the third quatrain, while searching the fashionable places where he expects to find Christ, his attention is suddenly caught by a group of criminals, amongst whom is Christ – who thereupon dies.

This sonnet is placed between poems on 'Good Friday' and 'Sepulchre', which is followed by 'Easter'; it is, therefore, intended to be read in the light of the crucifixion story – indeed, its original title was 'The Passion'. Various explanations have been offered for the old and new leases, on which the poem is based; on the essential point, however, there is little disagreement. The house in which the poet has lived is a much grander one than the one he now seeks – the grander home represents (a) the views expressed by Richard Hooker in his 'judicious' study *Of the Laws of Ecclesiastical Polity* (1593), which outlines the principle of 'original contract' as the basis of sovereignty; it influenced a whole generation of moderate clerics who valued tradition and unity; (b) the Protestant belief that a person is justified (i.e. earns a place in heaven) by their actions; and (c) it may also refer to Herbert's earlier interest in rising to state office through a High Church appointment. The smaller home into which he wants to move represents (a) the conservative views of Nicholas Ferrar (1592–1637), leader of a small religious group which met at Little Gidding, whose ideas are characterised by a Protestant simplicity; Herbert bequeathed his manuscript of *The Temple* to Ferrar; (b) a greater interest in the Pauline view that a place in heaven is earned by faith and grace alone; and (c) satisfaction with his unworldly retreat at Bemerton, in Wiltshire, where he lived during the last years of his life.

Headnote
a ***parable*** a short story designed to illustrate a moral or religious lesson. Christ made great use of parables in his conversations with his disciples and others (e.g. 'the parable of the prodigal son': Luke 15: 11–32).

[1] **a rich lord**
(a) a wealthy lord from whom the poet rents a house; (b) Christ in majesty.

[2] **not thriving**
(a) the poet's affairs are not prospering or doing well; (b) the poet's soul is not developing fully; ***to be bold*** i.e. to come to a decision.

[3] **make a suit**
to petition or ask; ***to afford*** to (have to) allow [the poet to cancel the old lease and take out a new one].

[4] **small-rented lease**
a house with a smaller rent. The over-expensive house stands for an over-majestic image of Christ; ***th'old*** refers to the 'legal' contract which binds the tenant to his landlord; here, it refers to High Church practices; the image may be compared with the one in the third stanza of Donne's 'Batter my heart' (p. 77).

[5] **manor**
cf. Christ's words 'In my father's house are many mansions' (John 14: 2).

[6–7] **lately gone/About**
recently left to attend or look after.

[7] **dearly bought**
(a) bought at great expense; (b) bought because he very much wanted such a house.

[8] **long since**
a long time previously; ***take possession*** i.e. Christ had owned the property on 'earth' for some time, but was now resolved to inhabit it – note that this decision coincides with the poet's resolution 'to be bold'.

[9] **returned**
i.e. back to (his home on) earth; ***his great birth*** Christ was, of course, the son of God; note also the signs and portents of his advent (see Matthew 1, 2), including the visit of the three kings.

[10] **resorts**
places frequented by the wealthy for purposes of pleasure; see the following line.

[12] **ragged**
here, jarring; ***mirth*** laughter.

[13] **thieves and murderers**
the image is shocking: Christ told his disciples to look after the poor, not to look after criminals. The reference is to three men who featured in the story of the crucifixion. The Jewish leaders handed Christ over to Pontius Pilate at the time of the Passover, a festival when it was customary for the Roman Governor to release a prisoner chosen by the people of Israel. The crowd called to have Barabbas released and for Jesus Christ to be crucified – according to Mark, Barabbas was a *murderer* (Mark 15: 6); Christ was crucified between two *thieves* (Matthew 27: 38, 44; Mark 15: 27); ***espied*** saw.

[14] **straight**
immediately.

50 / *Easter Wings*

Lord, who createdst man in wealth and store,
Though foolishly he lost the same,
Decaying more and more,
Till he became
Most poor,
With thee
O let me rise
As larks, harmoniously,
And sing this day thy victories;
Then shall the fall further the flight in me.

My tender age in sorrow did begin:
And still with sicknesses and shame
Thou didst so punish sin
That I became
Most thin.
With thee
Let me combine,
And feel this day thy victory:
For, if I imp my wing on thine,
Affliction shall advance the flight in me.

Herbert's best-known pattern poem; it is preceded by 'Easter' and followed by two poems on 'Holy Baptism'. In iambic metre, beginning with a pentameter and losing one foot each line (pentameter→tetrameter→trimeter→dimeter→monometer), and then repeating this in reverse, gaining one foot each line: each stanza rhymes *a b a b a* / *c d c d c*.

The poem's form resembles a pair of wings, such as those that angels have in paintings and other illustrations. More specifically, the wings, which recall Christ's Resurrection, symbolise the poet's prayer that his thoughts might fly upwards until he is united in spirit with Christ.

Herbert wrote a number of pattern poems in which the visual form is a vital and integral part of the poem's meaning. 'Easter Wings' should be read in the light of the words of hope offered by God's promise to Isaiah: 'God will immeasurably increase the spiritual strength of all those who put their trust in him and believe that he will help them: however far they have to walk, their limbs will not grow weak; when they want to run they will not grow tired; they will be able to soar upwards as if on the wings of an eagle' (Isaiah 40: 31).

Note how the form of the first stanza imitates the movement from the spiritual wholeness symbolised by the Garden of Eden as depicted in Genesis, the first book in the Bible, through the spiritual poverty of Israel at the time of Christ, to the final victory of the second coming described in Revelation, the last book in the Christian Bible; and how the second stanza applies this to the poet's own life, which proceeds from the spiritual wholeness of childhood, through the spiritual emptiness of his life as a courtier, to the desire for renewed wholeness through union with Christ in the final lines.

[1] **wealth**
spiritual riches – i.e. the state of spiritual wholeness enjoyed by man when he lived in the Garden of Eden/earthly delights (see Genesis 2–4); ***store*** spiritual abundance.

[2] **foolishly he lost the same**
cf. the story of the Fall: tempted by the serpent, Eve foolishly ate the fruit of the Tree of Knowledge of Good and Evil and persuaded Adam to do likewise, for which they were expelled from Eden, thereby losing its 'wealth and store' (Genesis 2–4).

[3–5] **Till he . . . poor**
poor deficient – a major theme of the prophetic books of the Bible is that the Jews were constantly straying away from God; the idea that man decayed 'more and more' until, by the time of Christ, he had become spiritually deficient: (a) a reference to the Jewish religious leaders' refusal to recognise Christ as the 'prince of peace'; also (b) a reference to the 'servant of the Lord who underwent great suffering' prophesied by Isaiah (Isaiah 9: 1–7; 52: 13–53: 12) or the Messiah (i.e. chosen leader) whose significance the Angel Gabriel explained to Daniel (Daniel 9: 20–27); both are equated with Herbert's own situation.

[6–9] **With thee . . . thy victories**
thee Christ; ***larks*** European songbirds that are noted for singing while flying high in the air: a frequent motif of Renaissance love poetry; ***rise*** a reference to God's promise to Malachi that the Day of the Lord is imminent: 'The day is fast approaching when the wicked shall burn like straw. But for those of you who fear my name, my power to save you will rise within you like the sun, and heal you like the beams of the sun' (Malachi 4: 1–2) – note that Malachi is the last book in the Old Testament; ***sing*** praise, sing in praise; ***this day*** Easter Sunday, which commemorates the Resurrection; ***victories*** (a) Christ's victory over the world, achieved through resisting temptation to sin (Luke 4: 1–13) and putting his spiritual mission above all worldly concerns – i.e. accepting his crucifixion; (b) Christ's victory over death – i.e. his Resurrection; cf. man's possibility of similar victories: 'everyone who believes in God is able to defeat the world' (1 Peter 5: 4); also: 'all who believe in Christ will be raised to eternal life' (1 Corinthians 15: 22).

[10] **the fall**
the Fall, described by Saint Augustine as a *felix culpa* (happy sin) because it made Christ's incarnation necessary, and this in turn gave man the possibility of winning eternal life; line 10 is clearly paradoxical (to rise through a fall).

[11] **tender age**
childhood; ***sorrow*** probably refers to the death of the poet's father in 1596 (when he was three) and, by analogy, the 'death' of God in his life during his adolescence.

[12–15] **sicknesses/sin**
the poet seems to subscribe to the Deuteronomic view that if man is afflicted, it must be because he has sinned; ***sin*** probably the poet's ambition to attain a powerful position at court; ***thin*** spiritually thin, insubstantial.

[17–18] **combine**
unite, join as one substance through faith and communion; ***feel*** experience, in the sense of 'make the experience my own'; ***victory*** see note to line 9.

[19–20] **imp**
a term used in falconry (the breeding and training of hawks), meaning to engraft feathers in the damaged wing of an injured hawk to restore its ability to fly; the image suggests that Christ 'requires' the help of man's faith;

Affliction (a) the poet's sense of his own shortcomings; (b) his yearning for Christ; ***flight*** (a) escape from worldly concerns; (b) ability to fly upwards – i.e. to 'spiritual concerns' or heaven.

51/ *Affliction (1)*

When first thou didst entice to thee my heart,
    I thought the service brave:
So many joys I writ down for my part,
    Besides what I might have
Out of my stock of natural delights,
Augmented with thy gracious benefits.

I lookèd on thy furniture so fine
    And made it fine to me.
Thy glorious household stuff did me entwine,
    And 'tice me unto thee.
Such stars I counted mine: both heaven and earth
Paid me my wages in a world of mirth.

What pleasures could I want, whose king I served,
    Where joys my fellows were?
Thus argued into hopes, my thoughts reserved
    No place for grief or fear.
Therefore my sudden soul caught at the place
And made her youth and fierceness seek thy face.

At first thou gav'st me milk and sweetnesses:
    I had my wish and way.
My days were strawed with flowers and happiness:
    There was no month but May.
But with my years sorrow did twist and grow
And made a party unawares for woe.

My flesh began unto my soul in pain:
    'Sicknesses cleave my bones.
Consuming agues dwell in every vein
    And tune my breath to groans.'
Sorrow was all my soul: I scarce believed –
Till grief did tell me roundly – that I lived.

When I got health, thou took'st away my life
        And more, for my friends die.
My mirth and edge was lost: a blunted knife
        Was of more use than I.
Thus thin and lean, without a fence or friend,
I was blown through with every storm and wind.

Whereas my birth and spirit rather took
        The way that takes the town,
Thou didst betray me to a lingering book
        And wrap me in a gown.
I was entangled in the world of strife
Before I had the power to change my life.

Yet, for I threatened oft the siege to raise,
        Not simpering all mine age,
Thou often didst with academic praise
        Melt and dissolve my rage.
I took thy sweetened pill, till I came where
I could not go away, nor persevere.

Yet lest perchance I should too happy be
        In my unhappiness,
Turning my purge to food, thou throwest me
        Into more sicknesses.
Thus doth thy power cross-bias me, not making
Thine own gift good, yet me from my ways taking.

Now I am here, what thou wilt do with me
        None of my books will show.
I read, and sigh, and wish I were a tree,
        For sure then I should grow
To fruit or shade: at least some bird would trust
Her household to me, and I should be just.

Yet, though thou troublest me, I must be meek;
        In weakness must be stout.
Well, I will change the service, and go seek
        Some other master out.
Ah, my dear God! 'though I am clean forgot,
Let me not love thee, if I love thee not.

A poem in eleven stanzas of six iambic lines – the first four are alternating pentameters and trimeters rhyming *a b a b*, followed by a couplet *c c* – in which the poet, while recalling various stages of his life, not only lays bare the paradoxical relation that can exist between a longing for spiritual wholeness and sensuality, but also plays upon the usual meanings ascribed to 'sickness' and 'health'.

The poems that immediately precede 'Affliction (1)' are two poems called 'Holy Baptism', the second of which ends 'The growth of flesh is but a blister/Childhood is health'; this is followed by 'Nature', in which the poet begins: 'Full of rebellion I would die' before appealing to God to 'smooth [his] rugged heart'; then comes 'Sin (1)', which sets the care with which a child is educated against the ease with which sin can enter its heart.

The three poems following 'Affliction (1)' are: 'Repentance', 'Faith', and 'Prayer (1)'. The poem thus describes a growing consciousness of sin.

[1] **entice**
attract by means of an offer of pleasure or reward: ***thou*** Christ, but note how the identity is left vague – it could refer here to a woman, a male friend, or God, an ambiguity which continues through much of the poem.

[2] **service**
answering to the poet's personal need (i.e. by 'attracting' the poet to him) – note the irony; the phrase suggests that *God* serves *him*, which in turn suggests that he is inflated; ***brave*** wonderful.

[3] **writ down for my part**
writ wrote, but here, 'calculated would accrue to me'.

[4] **might have**
i.e. could or would have been able to expect.

[5] **Out of . . . natural delights**
stock store, abundance, sum; ***delights*** the poet's qualities, which he enjoys as a consequence of his own nature – thus 'as a result of the sum of my own personal merits'.

[6] **Augmented**
increased; ***benefits*** (a) good deeds; (b) payments made to one in need.

[7] **furniture**
God's furniture, i.e. the stars, planets, etc. (see line 11); ***fine*** exquisitely fashioned, excellent, wonderful.

[8] **fine**
acceptable.

[9] **household stuff**
(a) the 'furniture' of the preceding line; (b) God's/Christ's personal qualities; ***entwine*** enfold, embrace – i.e. 'Your glorious qualities so fascinated me that they took me in their arms'.

[10] **'tice**
entice (see line 1 and note).

[11] **stars**
i.e. a part of God's furniture; ***counted*** considered – the phrase further indicates the poet's inflation: he is describing a feeling of *over*excitement.

[12] **wages**
(a) contrast with 'benefits' in line 6; (b) cf. the biblical phrase 'the wages of sin is death' (Romans 6: 23) – note, however, that there is no evidence of the poet 'serving' but only of *receiving* 'service'; ***world of mirth*** (a) the poet was uncontrollably happy to feel himself united with God; but note the irony implicit in the phrase (a further indication of the poet's inflation).

[13–14] **want**
lack; ***whose king*** ironic: the king of pleasures (whom the poet serves) is not a definition of God; ***fellows*** companions.

[15–16] **Thus argued . . . or fear**
'In this way my mind was persuaded [i.e. enticed] into such [false] hopes that I did not think I had anything to grieve about or fear' – the words 'grief' and 'fear' imply that he should have been grieving at having strayed from a right-minded reverence for the Lord, and afraid of punishment for his inflation.

[17] **Therefore**
precisely for this reason (because he had no grief or fear) – an illogical, and thus unsatisfactory/unresolved *volta*; ***sudden*** impetuous, suggesting immaturity; ***caught*** snatched at but turned away (perhaps out of grief or fear?); ***the place*** see line 16 – i.e. a 'place' which is 'no place'.
[18] **made**
note how it is the poet's immature, overardent and 'feminine' soul that causes him to seek God.
[19] **gav'st**
gavest, gave; ***milk*** etc. note how God is invested with *maternal* properties – cf. the femininity of the soul in the previous line.
[21] **strawed**
strewn.
[22] **May**
in northern Europe, a month associated with the onset of summer pleasures, especially lovemaking and courtship; ***no month but*** only May, an eternal May.
[23] **with my years**
As I grew older; ***sorrow*** cf. the use of this word in 'Easter Wings', line 11; ***twist*** in the sense of a knife twisting inside him, or something twisting itself around him (cf. 'entwine' in line 9).
[24] **Made a party**
made [of me] (a) a person; (b) a faction which, by definition, is opposed by another (i.e. a person divided); ***unawares for*** unaware of, unprepared for, not ready to deal with; ***woe*** an even deeper sorrow than that of line 23.
[25] **began**
i.e. began *to complain;* ***in pain*** can refer to both the flesh and the soul.
[26] **cleave**
to divide; thus: 'sicknesses are causing [my bones] to break or fracture'.
[27] **Consuming agues**
devastating fevers.
[28] **tune**
'correct' the musical pitch of the poet's voice until it becomes a groan – the word is a pun on 'turn' (i.e. 'correct' in the sense of punish).
[29] **Sorrow . . . soul**
'My entire soul was wretched'.
[30] **roundly**
bluntly.
[31–2] **When I got health . . . my friends die**
perhaps the most ambiguous lines in the poem. The poet does not regain his health at this moment; he is describing a change in his understanding of the meaning of health – here it means only the *premonition of what health is* arising out of his experience of grief in the preceding line, i.e. something akin to pangs of conscience; ***took'st away my life*** i.e. the poet can no longer enjoy his previous 'life' of pleasure; therefore his friends 'die' (i.e. lose interest in him).
[33] **edge**
trenchant wit, ability to cause hurt or distress.
[35] **thin and lean**
presumably figuratively, as in the subsequent phrases; ***fence*** the word derives from 'defence', i.e. a structure whose purpose is to defend; here, probably meaning something more akin to 'bulwark' than to a garden fence – i.e. anything to protect him from the perils or storms of life.
[36] **blown through**
i.e. the poet is devoid of substance.
[37–40] **Whereas . . . gown**
spirit natural, masculine inclination; ***lingering*** because (a) a book takes a long time to read; and (b) books cause one to linger over them; ***gown*** an academic gown, as worn by university teachers. Here the poet is giving a second account of his spiritual odyssey – now he says it was his own inclination that led him to pursue the pleasures of *the town* (i.e. a life of dalliance, drink and gambling), and that 'God' misled him ('betray', line 39) into taking up a life of academic study.
[41–2] **I was entangled . . . life**
these lines seem to echo the first four, but the following verse makes it clear

that they are ambivalent; ***entangled*** cf. 'entwine' (line 9); ***the world of strife strife*** struggle, conflict, dispute; appears to refer to the outside world of struggle for advancement; but also (see next stanza) refers to the conflicts and disputes of academic (i.e. theological) debate – note how the poet still thinks he has the power to change his life at this stage.

[43–4] **for**
because; ***oft*** often; ***the siege to raise*** i.e. to renounce his desire for God (cf. Donne, 'Batter my heart' (p. 77), stanza 2); ***simpering*** (a) smile weakly, affectedly; (b) smirk with self-satisfaction, thus 'But, because I often threatened to give up trying to get close to you, not wishing to smile affectedly all my life (as if I had knowledge of something about which I was in fact ignorant).'

[45] **academic praise**
(a) praise of the poet's academic abilities; but (as the sequel makes clear), this praise was entirely imagined by the poet, hence (b) specious praise.

[46] **my rage**
(a) the poet's rage against other academic opinions; (b) his rage at not being able to discover God by academic reasoning.

[47] **sweetened pill**
i.e. the academic praise in line 45.

[48] **I could not . . . persevere**
i.e. until he discovered that he had come to a spiritual standstill.

[49] **Yet, lest . . . happy be**
'But, in order that I might not become too happy'; ***happy*** because the poet is blinded by God's praise.

[50] **unhappiness**
the reality of his situation, caused by his inability to move either backwards or forwards.

[51–2] **Turning my purge . . . more sicknesses**
my purge lit. (spiritual) cleansing; here, the process of coming to a standstill (thereby requiring the poet to find some 'other' way out of his impasse); ***food*** bad food – i.e. the praise that the poet imagines is coming from God, whereas it is really imagined by himself; ***throwest*** throws; the poet is once again accusing God of misleading him, i.e. giving him bad food that sinks him into further 'sickness'.

[53–4] **power**
cf. the poet's 'power' in line 42; ***cross-bias*** i.e. God's bias, inclination or purpose, which runs counter to – is opposed to – the poet's inclination or desire; ***not making . . . taking good*** cf. God's delight at the end of each stage of the Creation ('And God saw that it was good': Genesis 1: 10); the poet is accusing God not only of withholding one of his defining attributes (i.e. what God gives *should* be good) but of acting just sufficiently to mislead the poet, thereby defeating both their purposes – note how the poet assumes that God's purpose is to 'reward' him; ***from my ways taking*** diverting me from my intended way of life.

[55] **here**
still in a complete impasse, still ignorant of God's intentions towards him.

[57] **tree**
a symbol of growth.

[58] **sure**
certainly.

[59] **fruit or shade**
to serve a purpose: a fruit can be eaten; shade provides shelter.

[60] **household**
the bird would build her nest in the tree – a bird is a common symbol of the soul; ***and I should be just*** (a) and I would look after what I was entrusted with justly; (b) and I would be justified, in the sense 'have been given a *raison d'être*'.

[61] **troublest me**
cause me distress; ***I must be meek*** I must submit to this humbly.

[62] **weakness**
(a) the exhaustion caused by his impasse; (b) the weakness of man compared to God; ***stout*** resolute.

[63–4] **I will change . . . master out**
these lines are deliberately ambivalent: (a) they represent the poet's

continued rage and his determination to find a new master; (b) finally realising that it is his own idea of God that is at fault, the poet determines to 'serve' another 'master' – i.e. God as God would have himself seen.
[65] **though I am clean forgot**
(a) even after confessing his error, the poet still feels that God has forgotten him: is this ironic?; (b) even though you choose to ignore me completely.
[66] **Let me not love thee . . . thee not**
'Let me not love you at all, if it is not your true self that I love.'

52 / *Jordan (1)*

Who says that fictions only and false hair
Become a verse? Is there in truth no beauty?
Is all good structure in a winding stair?
May no lines pass, except they do their duty
  Not to a true, but painted chair?

Is it no verse, except enchanted groves
And sudden arbours shadow coarse-spun lines?
Must purling streams refresh a lover's loves?
Must all be veiled, while he that reads, divines,
  Catching the sense at two removes?

Shepherds are honest people: let *them* sing!
Riddle who list, for me, and pull for prime!
I envy no man's nightingale or spring!
Nor let them punish me with loss of rhyme,
  Who plainly say, '*My God, My King*.'

This poem may be read as (a) an indictment of secular lyric verse, (b) a defence of religious verse, or (c) a meditation on a *rite of passage* facing the poet. It is composed of three five-line stanzas, in which the first four lines are pentameters and the last is a tetrameter, rhyming *a b a b a*; its form would seem to have been intended as a declaration of independence against the ubiquitous sonnet.

Two basic ideas combine in the title: (a) a *regressive* movement indicative of a period of introversion necessary before one is able to make a future step (cf. the French saying '*reculer pour mieux sauter*' = step back in order to jump further). Jacob, when he left his father, crossed the Jordan with nothing but a staff and, after many years, finally prospered (Genesis 32: 10); and (b) a *progressive* movement – i.e. a *rite of passage* from a state with which one is no longer satisfied to another: (a) it was on crossing the Jordan that the Israelites came into their 'promised land' (Numbers 32: 20–23; Joshua 3); (b) Christ's mission started when he was baptised by John the Baptist in the Jordan (Luke 3; 4: 1) – significantly, both these meanings meet in the Order of Baptism: cf. '[Thou] didst safely lead . . . thy people through the Red Sea, figuring thereby the Holy Baptism: and by the Baptism of . . . Christ did sanctify the flood Jordan, and all other waters to the mystical washing away of sin' (*The Book of Common Prayer*): cf. also 2 Kings 5: 9–10).

[1] **fictions**
(a) elaborate and exaggerated poetical conceits; (b) things made by men (*fictionem* = fashioned by hand); ***false hair*** a wig: a contrast with hair as symbol of spiritual strength – cf. the story of Samson (Judges 13–16), also St Paul's description of a woman's hair as 'a glory' (1 Corinthians 11: 15). See Donne, 'Elegy 19' (p. 38), line 16 and note.

[2] **Become**
are suitable as material for – the question is clearly ironic, as are the following questions; ***truth*** (a) as opposed to fiction; (b) Christ: cf. 'I am the way, I am the truth, and I am life: no one comes to the Father except by me' (John 14: 6); also 'Only if you follow my teachings can you call yourselves my disciples: only in this way can you know the truth, and this truth will set you free' (John 8: 32).

[3] **good structure . . . winding stair**
stair staircase: the image tacitly contrasts the 'winding' staircases of late-Renaissance architecture with the 'straight' ladder that led to heaven in Jacob's dream (Genesis 28: 12).

[4–5] **lines**
lines of poetry; ***pass*** be accepted or applauded; ***except*** unless; ***do their duty . . . to*** serve; ***a true*** (chair) (a) the throne of Christ/God: cf. 'Those who invite me into their hearts shall sit beside me on my throne, just as I sit beside my father on his throne' (Revelation 3: 21); (b) heaven (Matthew 5: 34); ***a painted chair*** the throne of a monarch, i.e. a garish imitation of a 'true' throne (cf. the death of Herod, who dies because he mimics God on his throne: Acts 12: 20–21) – note that the distinction the poet is making is not biblical but Platonic: cf. the Platonic idea, as described in *The Republic*, especially books 6, in which he outlines his theory, and 7, in which he illustrates it by means of the famous image of the cave.

[6–7] **no verse**
not poetry; ***except*** unless; ***enchanted groves groves*** small woods; ***enchanted*** because, in pastoral poetry, events occasioned by magic frequently occur in small woods; ***sudden arbours*** unexpected clearings in a small wood, or a shaded spot in a large garden – frequently used in pastoral poems of the sixteenth and early seventeenth centuries; ***shadow coarse-spun lines*** disguise the fact that the quality of the poetry is crude (coarse) – the poet is implicitly contrasting such groves and arbours with places such as the mountainside on which Christ preached his most famous sermon (Matthew 5–7), or the Garden of Gethsemane, in which Christ prays on the night of his arrest (Matthew 26: 36–46).

[8] **purling**
fast-flowing, babbling; the poet is contrasting the love that forms the subject of love poetry (i.e. *eros* or love between two human beings) with the love of God (*caritas*, i.e. charity [see 1 Corinthians 13: 1–13], and *agape*, a mystical love feast [see 'Love (3)' below]): cf. Christ's two commandments (to love God, and to love one's neighbour as oneself: Matthew 22: 37–40); and 'God is Love, and whoever lives with love of God in his heart lives in union with God' (1 John 4: 16).

[9] **veiled**
i.e. not transparently clear – the phrase refers back to St Paul's epistle: 'What we see now is like the dim image in a mirror' (i.e. 'through a glass darkly': 1 Corinthians 13: 12);

while he that reads, divines so that the reader has to guess (at the poem's meaning).

[10] **Catching**
understanding; ***two removes*** i.e. between (a) an outer reality and the pastoral description of it; and (b) the pastoral description and the sense intended by the poet.

[11] **Shepherds**
pastoral verse, by definition, is mainly concerned with shepherds, or with princes/princesses disguised as shepherds/shepherdesses; such shepherds contrast with the shepherds who went to admire Christ on the day of his birth (Luke 2: 8–20); ***let* them *sing*** i.e. let them do as they like (and, by implication, the poet demands the right to write as he wants): the phrase contrasts with the praises sung to God by the shepherds in Luke 2: 20.

[12] **Riddle who list**
let anyone who wants to write riddling (i.e. Metaphysical) poetry; ***for me*** for all I care, as far as I'm concerned; ***pull for prime*** literally refers to a player drawing for a winning hand in primero, a card game; figuratively 'and that's enough of the subject!'

[13] **envy not**
do not envy/begrudge; ***nightingale or spring*** nightingales and spring (the season, though there may also be a reference to a fountain) are often mentioned in Elizabethan love poetry – here they contrast with 'Holy Spirit' and Christ's Resurrection, and thus emphasise Herbert's rejection of fanciful secular poetry.

[14] **punish**
accuse; ***with loss of rhyme*** (a) for my less fanciful rhymes; (b) for being out of harmony with my subject matter.

[15] ***My God, My King***
i.e. God and Christ – the image implies a contrast with the idealised mistress of secular verse.

53 / *The Windows*

Lord, how can man preach thy eternal word?
He is a brittle, crazy glass,
Yet in thy temple, thou dost him afford –
This glorious and transcendent place! –
To be a window through thy grace.

But when thou dost anneal in glass thy story,
Making thy life to shine within
The holy Preacher's, then the light and glory
More reverend grows, and more doth win,
Which else shows wat'rish, bleak, and thin.

Doctrine *and* life! Colours and light in one!
When they combine and mingle bring
A strong regard and awe, but speech alone
Doth vanish like a flaring thing
And in the ear, not conscience, ring.

In *The Temple* there are several poems devoted to aspects of a church building: notably 'The Altar' (a pattern poem: the first in the main section) and 'The Church Floor', which immediately precedes 'The Windows', in which the floor-slabs are seen as representing the virtues of Patience, Humility, Confidence and Charity.

'The Windows' is a meditative poem in three five-line stanzas; the first four lines are alternating pentameters and tetrameters, the fifth is a further tetrameter, with each stanza rhyming *a b a b b*. In the first stanza, the poet likens man to a pane of stained glass; in the second, he describes how the stained glass adds considerably to the meaning of the Gospel message; in the last, he contrasts the way in which mere speech is soon forgotten, leaving a speech deepened by the life that glows within the glass resounding in man's consciousness.

The poem derives from an impression created by the light cast by the sun coming through a stained-glass window – i.e. a window composed of small, thick pieces of variously coloured glass, held together by lead. From the twelfth century, different sections of a stained-glass window often illustrated typologically related scenes (e.g. the bottom half would be a scene from the Old Testament; the upper half, a 'corresponding' scene from the New Testament). Stained-glass windows were used not only in cathedrals, but also in small parish churches.

[1] **preach**
Herbert was ordained a priest in September 1630; the phrase recalls St Paul's emphasis on his own mission to preach the 'Gospel' (the good news): e.g. Acts 20: 24; but it is also general, in the sense that all who believe must also defend their belief.

[2] **crazy**
(a) made up of irregular pieces; (b) madly impetuous – note how both 'irregular' and 'impetuous' contrast with 'eternal' in line 1.

[3–4] **afford**
allow (man to be a 'window'); ***This*** In this; ***place*** the church in which the poet is; the syntax of lines 3–5 is unusual: 'in' must announce 'To be a window'; the clause in line 4 qualifies 'temple' in line 3.

[5] **through**
(a) by; (b) through (which God's grace does shine).

[6] **anneal**
to heat glass until it becomes molten, when colours can be added to it, and then allow it to cool slowly; here, also to fix 'with fire'; ***thy story*** most scenes in a stained-glass window of a Christian church relate either to the life of Christ, or to scenes from the Old Testament (i.e. 'types') which anticipate moments from the life of Christ.

[7] **thy life**
Christ's life, his life-giving spirit; ***within*** i.e. Christ's story comes to life in the preacher's sermons.

[8] **Preacher's**
i.e. Christ's life illumines the preacher's life, and thus allows the latter to illustrate his (Christ's) message: ***preacher*** (a) the vicar, who preaches a sermon each week; (b) the artist who illustrated the scene in the window and/or 'fixed' it in glass (and, by extension, also applies to the poet as God's craftsman); ***the light and glory*** i.e. of (a) the preacher's life, words or message; (b) the artist's/poet's life/message.

[9] **more doth win**
is better able to convince the listener of the truth of what is said.

[10] **Which else . . . thin**
'Which otherwise would appear insubstantial, tedious or dismal, and unconvincing.'

[11] **Doctrine and life . . . in one**
The church windows contain Christ's doctrine and life, where *life* (a) Christ's biographical story, told in

colours and light; and (b) Christ's spirit: cf. 'I am the way, and the truth, and the life: no one goes to the Father in heaven, except by way of me' (John 14: 6), conveyed in colours brightened by the fire of the sun/son.

[12] **mingle**
become so mingled that they are inseparable; ***bring*** bring about, cause.

[13] **but**
whereas.

[14] **vanish**
is gone (so quickly); ***flaring thing*** a torch (blown out by the wind).

[15] **conscience**
note the use of this word, on which the whole poem revolves – not conscience as in 'guilty conscience', but conscience as the listener's ability to understand spirit with spirit: cf. 'The blood of goats and bulls and the ashes of a heifer, sprinkled on those who have defiled themselves, may restore their bodily purity. Then how much more will the blood of Christ, who offered himself, blameless as he was, to God through the eternal spirit, purify our conscience from dead actions so that we can worship the living God' (Hebrews 9: 13–14); also 'We know that the son of God has come and has *given us understanding so that we may know the One who is true.* We are in the One who is true, as we are in Jesus Christ. He is the true God and this is eternal life' (1 John 5: 20); ***ring*** resound.

54 / *Denial*

When my devotions could not pierce
Thy silent ears;
Then was my heart broken, as was my verse:
My breast was full of fears
And disorder:

My bent thoughts, like a brittle bow,
Did fly asunder:
Each took his way; some would to pleasures go,
Some to the wars and thunder
Of alarms.

As good go anywhere, they say,
As to benumb
Both knees and heart, in crying night and day,
Come, come, my God, O come –
But no hearing.

O that thou shouldst give dust a tongue
To cry to thee,
And then not hear it crying! All day long
My heart was in my knee –
But no hearing.

Therefore my soul lay out of sight,
Untuned, unstrung:
My feeble spirit, unable to look right,
Like a nipped blossom, hung
Discontented.

O cheer and tune my heartless breast,
Defer no time;
That so thy favours granting my request,
They and my mind may chime
And mend my rhyme.

This prayer, which is also a meditation on prayer, has an especially striking form in that it also plays upon the possibility of formlessness. It is in six stanzas, each of five iambic lines: tetrameter, dimeter, pentameter, trimeter, and dimeter. The first four lines rhyme *a b a b*, the last line does not rhyme except in the last verse (*b*).

This poem was almost certainly inspired by the Litany, in which the subject prays: 'We sinners beseech you to *hear* us, O Lord God. . . . That it may please you to give us an heart to love and dread you, and diligently to live following your commandments; . . . that it may please you to bring into the way of truth all those who have erred or are mistaken;. . . that it may please you to make us truly repent, to forgive us all our sins, our negligence and ignorance, and to endue us with the grace of your Holy Spirit so that we amend our lives according to your Holy Word' (*Book of Common Prayer*).

[1] **devotions**
supplications, prayers.

[3] **verse**
a frequently encountered metaphor for divine Creation, because the poet, too, creates order out of chaos. The implication is that the poet's verse is 'whole' only when he is at one with God; ***broken*** also in the sense of irregular; because it jars, the ear rejects it.

[4] **breast**
refers back to 'heart'.

[5] **disorder**
note how the 'disorder' or chaos in the poet's heart is reflected in the final *unrhymed* line of each of the first five stanzas.

[6–7] **bent . . . fly asunder**
bent (a) curved, i.e. not straight; (b) determined, in the sense that the poet's devotions were *over*purposive; (c) unwholesome, dishonest; ***fly asunder*** instead of flying in a straight line to their mark (God), his thoughts fly asunder – i.e. in different directions at once; ***brittle bow*** bows are traditionally made out of willow, a

particularly flexible wood. A brittle bow is one in danger of snapping, i.e. breaking 'asunder'.

[8] **Each took his way**
i.e. each thought went off in its own direction. Some went to seek pleasure, etc.

[10] **alarms**
calls to battle.

[11] **As good go anywhere . . . as to benumb**
'Better to go off in any direction than deaden or make insensible.'

[13] **crying**
A great many Psalms are about the psalmist 'crying' to the Lord: e.g. 'Let my prayer come before thee: incline thy ear unto my cry' (Psalm 88: 2); 'The righteous cry, and the Lord heareth, and delivereth them out of all their troubles' (Psalm 34: 17). See also below, line 17.

[14] ***Come, come,* etc.**
A frequent introductory appeal to both prayers and hymns: e.g. 'Come, O Creator Spirit, come / And make within our hearts thy home; / To us thy grace celestial give, / Who of thy breathing move and live' (Hymn 152).

[15] **no hearing**
i.e. God is not listening. The line must be read in the light of frequent references in the New Testament to the need for one to 'hear' God: e.g. 'So then faith cometh by hearing, and hearing by the word of God' (Romans 10: 17).

[16] **dust**
Adam, the first man, was made out of dust (Genesis 3: 19).

[17] **cry**
cf. 'Hear my prayer, O Lord, and let my cry come unto thee' (Psalm 102: 1).

[19] **My heart**
i.e. although the poet's supplication is sincere.

[20] **no hearing**
cf. line 15: but here the phrase is ambivalent: (a) God is not listening; (b) (my heart was in my knee) but not in my hearing.

[21] **out of sight**
i.e. out of God's sight.

[22] **Untuned**
implies a musical instrument; ***unstrung*** either a musical instrument or a bow.

[25] **Discontented**
note how this refers to the implication of line 3; see above. Content or happiness can be found only with God.

[26] **heartless**
because out of God's sight.

[27] **Defer no time**
Defer put off until later time, postpone; thus, 'Do not delay'.

[28] **That so . . .**
So that his prayers (request) should meet God's favour, or coincide with his favour, thereby ensuring God's mercy.

[29] **chime**
sound (like church bells) in harmony.

[30] **mend my rhyme**
(a) thereby making the poet's prayers 'rhyme' (with God's blessing); (b) thereby correcting the poet's verse.

55 / *Vanity (1)*

The fleet Astronomer can bore
And thread the spheres with his quick-piercing mind.
He views their stations, walks from door to door,
Surveys as if he had designed
To make a purchase there: he sees their dances
And knoweth, long before,
Both their full-éyed aspécts, and secret glances.

The nimble Diver with his side
Cuts through the working waves that he may fetch
His dearly-earnèd pearl, which God did hide
On purpose from the vent'rous wretch
That he might save his life, and also hers,
Who with excessive pride
Her own destruction, and his danger, wears.

The subtle Chymick can divest
And strip the creature naked till he find
The callow principles within their nest:
There he imparts to them his mind,
Admitted to their bed-chamber, before
They appear trim and dressed
To ordinary suitors at the door.

What hath not man sought out and found
But his dear God? Who yet his glorious law
Embosoms in us, mellowing the ground
With showers and frosts, with love and awe,
So that we need not say, Where's this command?
Poor man, thou searchest round
To find out *death*, but missest *life* at hand.

A meditative poem in four seven-line stanzas, each composed of alternating iambic tetrameters and pentameters; the second and third lines are pentameters, the sixth a trimeter, and the whole rhymes *a b a b c a c*. The title is a reference to the text: 'Vanity, vanity, said the religious leader, life is vanity [i.e empty of meaning]' (Ecclesiastes 1: 2).

The first three stanzas represent different activities, each of which is ambivalent. On the one hand, the poem depicts men so preoccupied with their chosen professions that they fail to understand their primary duty to love God;

on the other, each of the activities symbolises man's eternal quest for God – the astronomer understands the secrets of the world; the diver risks his life in order to bring a pearl of great price to the surface; and the man of science discovers the vital principles of other living creatures. The last stanza reminds the reader that engaging in symbolic activity is not the same as discovering God for oneself.

[1] **fleet**
swift-minded, nimble-eyed; ***bore*** penetrate to the centre of (a subject).
[2] **thread**
(a) pick one's way through (e.g. a maze or a crowded place); (b) understand the relation of each star, planet, system or galaxy to its apparent neighbour; (c) connect together as if by a thread; *quick-piercing* (a) life-penetrating; (b) like a needle.
[3] **stations**
positions; ***walks from door to door*** figuratively, as if each 'sphere' was something displayed in a shop window.
[4] **had designed**
intended.
[5] **there**
in that particular shop; ***dances*** rhythmical movements around some centre – with oblique reference to (a) the idiomatic expression 'to lead someone a dance' = to cause someone a great deal of trouble, usually for no purpose; (b) the so-called 'dance of the spheres', a phrase synonymous with 'music of the spheres'.
[6] **long before**
before long, i.e. very quickly or immediately.
[7] **full-éyed**
open to view, i.e. obvious; ***secret glances*** those secrets which they reveal only to those who search diligently to know them.
[8] **Diver**
a person who dives, e.g. for pearls.
[9] **working**
heaving.
[10] **dearly-earnèd**
hard-earned, earned with great effort; ***pearl*** in the Bible, an ornament of great value – cf. Christ's parable: 'The Kingdom of heaven is like this. A man spends his life looking for a pearl of great price. One day, he finds exactly what he has been seeking, and so he sells everything he has in order to buy it' (Matthew 13: 45); ***God did hide*** not literally, but in the sense that by placing pearls within oysters on the seashore, he made it difficult for man to obtain them.
[11] **vent'rous**
(venturous) venturesome, disposed to take risks; ***wretch*** unhappy or miserable (as man is if he cannot find his pearl, i.e. does not know God).
[12] **That he . . . also hers**
That God might save the diver's life, and also that of the pearl (by allowing it to be brought to light, and thus accorded value) – note how the pearl is feminine, like the soul.
[13] **Who with . . . pride**
it is the pearl whose pride is 'excessive', because it does not want to be brought to the surface: note the implicit parallel with man, who does not want to know God.
[14] **destruction . . . wears**
wears carries as an attribute; thus, 'demands that she be left on the seabed [i.e. equivalent to damnation, as its value would thus never be discovered] and requires that man put himself in danger in order to obtain her'.
[15] **subtle Chymick**
(a) intelligent or sharp-minded chemist or man of science; (b) God, as Creator; ***divest*** remove the clothing or covering from something: cf. 'For what people consider wisdom is nonsense in God's eyes . . . for the Lord knows that the ideas of academics are worthless' (1 Corinthians 3: 19–20, quoting Psalm 94: 11).
[16] **the creature**
(a) the pearl; (b) man.
[17] **callow principles**
principles in their 'naked' or featherless state; ***their nest*** refers back to

'callow' as 'featherless', like a young bird – thus, 'the deepest principles within the soul'.
[18] **There**
in the 'nest' or soul; ***he*** (a) the man of science; (b) God; ***imparts*** gives a part of, communicates with.
[19] **Admitted to their bed-chamber**
this clause belongs between 'There' and 'he imparts' in the previous line: ***their*** refers to the principles – thus, 'There, once permitted into the nest or bed-chamber [i.e. soul] of the principles, he imparts . . .'
[20] **They**
the principles (which have now been explained by the man of science); ***trim*** free of any unsightly quality; ***dressed*** fit to appear in public view.
[21] **ordinary suitors**
laymen, people who have no understanding of science; ***the door*** the door between (a) the soul and the individual as he presents himself to the world; (b) God's mysterious ways and the world.
[22–3] **What hath not . . . dear God?**
'What is it that man has searched for and found if it is not his most precious God?' (cf. 'pearl of great price'/the 'callow principles'); ***yet*** still; ***law*** cf. the 'principles' of the preceding lines.
[24] **embosoms in us**
(God) puts into our bosoms (i.e. breasts, hearts); ***mellowing*** softening and enriching; ***ground*** man, who would be 'hard' and 'infertile' without God's love.
[25] **showers**
light rain is necessary for any plant to grow; ***frosts*** cause death to many plants: note how 'showers' corresponds to 'love', and 'frosts' to 'awe'.
[26] **this command**
i.e. the commandment to seek out God: cf. Christ's promise: 'Ask, and you will receive; seek, and you will find; knock, and the door will be opened to you' (Matthew 6: 7; Luke 11: 9).
[27] **round**
in a roundabout manner, not to the purpose.
[28] **To find out**
only to find; ***death*** i.e. 'not discovering the pearl of great price'; ***but*** and; ***life*** i.e. life *in Christ*, eternal life; ***at hand*** which is right next to you, i.e. which can be achieved without having to dive (as for a pearl) or experiment (like the man of science) simply by turning one's full attention to Christ, as one cannot 'serve two masters': 'Set your thoughts entirely on God, asking yourselves what he wants of you, and he will provide you with all your needs' (Matthew 6: 33): cf. 'Man', line 29.

56 / *Affliction (4)*

Broken in pieces all asunder,
        Lord, hunt me not,
        A thing forgot;
Once a poor creature, now a wonder –
    A wonder tortured in the space
    Betwixt this world and that of grace.

My thoughts are all a case of knives,
Wounding my heart
With scattered smart,
As wat'ring pots give flowers their lives:
Nothing their fury can control
While they do wound and pink my soul.

All my attendants are at strife,
Quitting their place
Unto my face.
Nothing performs the task of life:
The el'ments are let loose to fight
And, while I live, try out their right.

O help, my God! Let not their plot
Kill them and me
And also thee
Who art my life! Dissolve the knot
As the sun scatters by his light
All the rebellions of the night.

Then shall those powers, which work for grief,
Enter thy pay
And day by day
Labour thy praise and my relief,
With care and courage building me
Till I reach heav'n and, much more, thee.

A prayer in five six-line stanzas, each composed of iambic tetrameters, with two dimeters, and rhyming *a b b a c c*. The poet, unable to focus his thoughts on Christ, prays to have the grief and affliction removed so that he can once again find Christ in his prayers.

[1] **asunder**
broken in pieces; the phrase, being tautologous, emphasises the idea, which refers not only to the poet's physical but also to his spiritual health (i.e. wholeness).
[2–3] **hunt**
chase, with a pun on 'chasten' (i.e. punish): 'hunt'/'forgot' is a paradox (God can't be 'hunting' the poet if he has forgotten him).
[3] **thing forgot**
the poet has become a ***thing*** because, having lost his spiritual wholeness, he has lost his defining human attribute; ***forgot*** because he can have lost his defining human attribute only if God has forgotten him.
[4] **poor creature**
man as a feeble creature (without God); ***A wonder*** *not* something 'wonderful', but a 'freak', something

to be wondered at or about; *wonder . . . space* note the opposition between a 'state' (wonder) and 'space' (line 5).

[5] **tortured**
greatly tormented, i.e. afflicted.

[6] **that of grace**
the world of grace (i.e. a state).

[7–8] **a case of knives**
literally a box or chest for knives – but note how the phrase has a surprising aggressivity.

[9] **scattered smart**
scattered in various different places; ***smart*** severe pain(s).

[10] **As wat'ring pots . . . their lives**
pots cans, i.e. with which to water plants: a startling example of analogy by contrast: knives/water; wounding/nurturing; man/flower.

[11] **their**
refers to the 'knives' from line 7.

[12] **pink**
to pierce slightly, a term used in fencing.

[13–15] **my attendants . . . face**
the ***attendants*** those 'thoughts' (cf. line 7) which 'attend' on him and whose position (i.e. ***their place***) or function is to serve the poet in his service of God, whereas all the poet can experience is ***strife***, i.e. turmoil, confusion; ***Unto my face*** the image is of 'servants' impertinently refusing to do their work, even when told to do so by their master.

[16] **Nothing**
i.e. none of the poet's faculties or talents; ***the task of life*** cf. Christ's reminder that one cannot be the servant of two masters: 'Do not worry about where your food, or your drink, or your clothes will come from, for these things alone do not ensure life. . . . But set all your thoughts on finding the Kingdom of God, asking yourselves what he requires of you' (Matthew 6: 24–34).

[17] **el'ments**
(= elements) i.e. earth, water, air and fire, considered the basic elements of all matter.

[18] **try out their right**
compete with one another to see which has the most 'right' (i.e. rightful authority/primacy or might/power) over the others.

[19] **their plot**
further develops the dominant metaphor of the previous stanza.

[20–1] **them**
the poet is concerned about his 'attendants' (i.e. thoughts), precisely because they should be a valuable part of him; ***thee*** i.e. by ousting God from the poet's concerns.

[22] **life**
Christ ('I am the way, and the truth, and the life': John 14: 6); ***Dissolve the knot*** undo the knot – the knot is caused by the thoughts that have become tightly intertwined.

[23–4] **As the sun . . . of the night**
pun on sun/son [i.e. Christ]: thus, (a) as the rising sun scatters the fantasies or nightmares that one might have had during the night; (b) as Christ scatters the rebellious thoughts inspired and encouraged by Satan and sin.

[25] **powers, which work for grief**
powers i.e. the poet's spiritual energy (which, misplaced because forgotten by God, has led him into considerable grief or pain: cf. 'The Flower', line 5.

[26–7] **thy pay**
Christ's or God's service; ***day by day*** day after day or increasingly.

[28] **Labour**
work for or towards; ***relief*** alleviation from pain or distress.

[29] **courage**
note how the subject of this sentence is still 'powers' (i.e. the poet's rediscovered spiritual energy will rebuild the exhausted soul of the poet with both 'care' and also 'courage' (i.e. patient insistence in the face of possibly slow progress).

[30] **much more**
even more importantly.

57 / *Man*

My God, I heard this day
That none doth build a stately habitation
But he that means to dwell therein.
What house more stately hath there been,
Or can be, than is man? to whose creation
All things are in decay.

For man is every thing
And more. He is a tree, yet bears mo' fruit;
A beast, yet is or should be more.
Reason and speech we only bring.
Parrots may thank us if they are not mute:
They go upon the score.

Man is all symmetry,
Full of proportions, one limb to another,
And all to all the world besides.
Each part may call the farthest, brother.
For head with foot hath private amity,
And both, with moons and tides.

Nothing hath got so far
But man hath caught and kept it as his prey.
His eyes dismount the highest star.
He is in little all the sphere.
Herbs gladly cure our flesh, because that they
Find their acquaintance there.

For us the winds do blow,
The earth doth rest, heav'n move, and fountains flow.
Nothing we see but means our good,
As our delight or as our treasure.
The whole is either our cupboard of food
Or cabinet of pleasure.

The stars have us to bed.
Night draws the curtain which the sun withdraws,
Music and light attend our head.
All things unto our flesh are kind
In their descent and being; to our mind
In their ascent and cause.

Each thing is full of duty.
Waters united are our navigation,
Distinguishèd, our habitation.
Below, our drink; above, our meat:
Both are our cleanliness. Hath *one* such beauty?
Then how are all things neat!

More servants wait on man
Than he'll take notice of: in every path
He treads down that which doth befriend him.
When sickness makes him pale and wan –
O mighty Love! – man is one world and hath
Another to attend him.

Since then, my God, thou hast
So brave a palace built, O dwell in it
That it may dwell with thee at last!
Till then, afford us so much wit
That, as the world serves us, we may serve thee
And, both, thy servants be.

At first reading this appears to be a hymn in which the poet, by praising man, celebrates God; closer examination of its ambivalence reveals that it is much more centrally concerned with man's nothingness without God, and man's greatness when his thoughts are directed towards God. It is in nine stanzas, each of six iambic lines: the first and last are trimeters, the second and fifth are pentameters, the two central lines are tetrameters; rhyming *a b c a b c*. The poet wonders at the greatness of man, whom he likens to a magnificent house, fit for the Lord to dwell in.

Even though influence is doubtful, it is interesting to compare this poem with the description of man's power by the Chorus in Sophocles, *Antigone*, lines 332–75.

[2] **habitation**
home – i.e. a large country house – cf. various biblical uses of ***house*** (a) *heaven* (cf. 'the house of the Lord': Psalm 23: 6); (b) *the Israelites or chosen people* (cf. 'the house of Israel': Jeremiah 2: 4); (c) *house* cf. Moses's reminder to the Israelites not to forget God: 'Take care to keep the Lord's commandments, as I order you today. When you have eaten and are full, and have built goodly houses and dwelt therein, and when your herds and flocks and your silver and your gold and everything you have has been multiplied [in the Promised Land], be sure not to become proud or to forget the Lord your God who brought you from your slavery in Egypt' (Deuteronomy 8: 11–14); (d) *man* cf. St Paul's words: 'We are Christ's house if we persevere in our faith in him' (Hebrews 3: 3); 'Come to the lord as living stones with which to build a spiritual temple for him' (1 Peter 2: 5); also 'You are now members of

God's family. The foundations of your house were laid by the apostles, and Christ is its corner-stone. He holds it together, transforming it into a temple dedicated to the Lord. You have become God's *habitation*, in which his spirit lives' (Ephesians 2: 19–22); but the word is also disturbingly ambivalent – cf. the parable of the evil spirit: 'When a man gets rid of his evil spirit, it will roam around looking for another place to live, and if it can't find one, it will have another look at its original home. If it finds it empty, clean and tidy, it will be so pleased that it will invite seven other spirits far worse than itself to *dwell* in its home. And once they have settled in, the man is in a far worse state than he was initially' (Matthew 12: 43–5).

[3] **dwell therein**
this phrase produces further ambivalence: (a) the primary reference is, of course, to Christ – cf. St Paul's prayer 'That Christ may *dwell* in your hearts by faith' (Ephesians 3: 17); but it also recalls (b) the curse on Judas: 'For it is written in the book of Psalms, "May his *habitation* be desolate for ever, and let no man *dwell therein*"' (Acts 1: 20, quoting Psalm 69: 25): i.e. Christ 'dwells' in man, but man is also Judas.

[4–5] **hath there been/Or can be**
has ever been or ever will be; ***to*** compared to.

[6] **All things are in decay**
the rest of the world exists in a lesser or lower state – cf. God's words to Adam: 'You must have a great many children so that your descendants will live all over the world and bring it under their control. For all kinds of grain and every kind of fruit, the fish, birds and all other wild animals are yours, with which to do as you like' (Genesis 1: 28).

[7] **every thing**
i.e. the most important creature.

[8] **tree, . . . no fruit**
tree an ambivalent symbol of growth – cf. Christ's parable: 'Every tree is known by the fruit it bears. Just as a good tree does not bear bad fruit, nor does a poor tree bear good fruit, . . . so a good person engenders good from the *treasure* of good things in his heart, and a bad person brings about evil because his *treasure* is corrupt' (Luke 6: 43–5); ***mo' fruit*** (a) more; (b) but note how the eye also reads 'no'; cf. the story of Christ who, on returning from Bethany, went to see if a fig tree had any fruit on it. But when he saw there were no ripe figs, for it was not the season for them, he cursed the tree. Later he used this story as an example to his disciples to be always ready for his second coming (Mark 11: 12–14; 13: 28–31).

[9] **beast**
cf. the psalm on the justice of God: 'I was as foolish as a *beast* before you; I could not understand your holy ways' (Psalm 73: 22); ***should be*** note the implicit irony; ***more*** (should understand God) better.

[10] **we only bring**
alone distinguish us (from beasts), as Aristotle said.

[11] **Parrots**
birds celebrated for their ability to mimic the human voice; but the reference may be more general – i.e. to people who just mimic the thoughts/language of others; ***may*** might; ***are not mute*** if they were not really dumb; thus, 'if they were able to formulate language for themselves'.

[12] **go upon the score**
live only on credit (i.e. man taught parrots how to speak): the entire metaphor implies that just as parrots owe their ability to mimic to man, so man owes his language to God: it thus suggests that language itself is not an achievement of which man can legitimately be proud.

[13–14] **symmetry . . . proportions**
a commonplace of Renaissance belief – note that it derives from classical philosophy rather than the Bible.

[15] **all to all the world besides**
the 'proportions' of man correspond to the 'proportions' of the world in which he lives: cf. Genesis.

[16] **part**
limb; ***the farthest*** the limb most remote from the original.
[17–18] **For**
note the ambivalence in this application; ***private*** secret; ***amity*** friendship; ***both*** i.e. both head and foot are connected with moons and tides – an astrological belief; ***moons and tides*** Renaissance symbols of change and inconstancy; cf. Shakespeare: 'Swear not by the ... inconstant moon' (*Romeo and Juliet*, II, ii, 109); ***tides*** cf. Spenser: 'One day I wrote her name upon the strand/But came the waves and washed it away' (*Amoretti*, 75).
[19–20] **Nothing hath go so far**
no animal has been able to run so fast (that man has not been able to catch it); but note the ambivalence of ***prey***: cf. Isaiah's indignation at those who have made widows their prey (Isaiah 10: 2) and contrast with St Paul's reminder, with reference to the race of life: 'I run as directly as I can towards my goal, which is to attain God's blessing through Jesus Christ' (Philippians 3: 14) – contrast *prey* and *goal*.
[21] **dismount . . . star**
(a) bring the highest star down to earth, by means of a telescope; (b) belittle Christ, who is the 'bright morning star' (Revelation 22: 16).
[22] **in little**
(a) in miniature – i.e. a microcosm; but also (b) a pusillanimous imitation of what he ought to aspire to; ***all the sphere*** the entire world, i.e. the macrocosm.
[23] **herbs**
medicinal plants; ***cure our flesh*** repair our bodily ills – the point being that man should be equally concerned with his spiritual shortcomings; ***gladly*** so naturally that it would seem to be with pleasure; ***because that*** because.
[24] **acquaintance**
being aware of or knowing slightly – cf. 'All flesh is grass' (Isaiah 40: 6); i.e. the 'herbs' cure our 'flesh' because they recognise something akin to themselves in our flesh: a tenet central to so-called Hermetic philosophy; e.g. 'Whatsoever is without a man, the same is also within him' (Valentine Weigel, *Astrologie Theologized*, London, 1649, p. 7) – the point is that man should not be satisfied with being 'acquainted' with plants, but should seek greater 'acquaintance' with Christ/God.
[25–6] **For us . . .**
cf. the Israelites' hymn of praise to God after passing through the Red Sea: 'You blew on the sea and the flowing waters were parted into a wall on either side, leaving the ground dry between' (Exodus 15: 8) – in other words, the winds blow (etc.) for those who are on the way to their Promised Land.
[27] **Nothing we see . . . our good**
(a) everything we see exists for us; everything we see is a means by which we can attain our good/goal in Christ – this phrase should be set against such moments as Christ's conversation with the rich man:

'Why do you call me good? Jesus asked. 'No one is good, except God alone. Have you followed the commandments?' The man replied: 'Yes, I have done so as long as I can remember.' 'Then you must do one thing more: sell all you have and give it to the poor.' The man was disconcerted, and Jesus continued: 'It is more difficult for a rich man to enter the Kingdom of Heaven than it is for a camel to pass through the eye of a needle. . . . Whoever leaves behind all that he most treasures in order to find the Kingdom of God will receive still more in this lifetime, and eternal life in the next.' (Luke 18: 18–29)

The point is that we mistake earthly pleasures for a spiritual goal.
[28] **delight**
contrast the self-evident meaning of 'delight' here with 'Make me follow your commandments, for in them I delight' (Psalm 119: 35); ***treasure*** cf. 'Your heart will always be where you

think your treasure lies. Do not store up treasure for yourselves here on earth, where it is subject to moths and rust and thieves, but set your mind on preparing treasure for yourselves in heaven, where there are neither moths, nor rust, nor thieves' (Matthew 6: 16–18); and 'It is better to be poor and to fear the Lord, than to have great treasure and to be in difficulties' (Proverbs 15: 16).

[29] **The whole**
the whole world; ***either*** (a) either; (b) both; ***food*** cf. 'Do not worry about where your food, or your drink, or your clothes will come from, for these things alone do not ensure life. . . . But set all your thoughts on finding the Kingdom of God, asking yourselves what he requires of you, and he will provide you with all your needs' (Matthew 6: 24–34); cf. also 'Vanity (1)', line 28 and note; ***pleasure*** cf. 'I decided to enjoy myself, but discovered this was not possible for me. Laughter gives us no lasting pleasure, and what we call pleasure is of short duration' (Ecclesiastes 2: 1–2).

[31] **stars**
created by God (Genesis 1: 16); ***have us to bed*** look after us when we sleep.

[32] **Night**
(a) night, as created by God (Genesis 1: 5); but also (b) the time of darkness – i.e. spiritual ignorance (cf. 'The light shone in the darkness but the darkness did not understand it': John 1: 5); ***the curtain*** the curtain of night – cf. 'He spread the sky around him as if it were a curtain, or as if he were making a tent in which to live' (Isaiah 40: 22).

[33] **Music and light**
i.e. when the sun wakes us . . . ; ***music*** the 'dawn chorus' of birds that sing at first light; ***light*** of the sun; ***attend*** surround, look after; ***our head*** our mind.

[34–5] **All things . . . being**
unto to; ***are kind*** are kin, are related (cf. lines 17, 22, 24 – the idea is borrowed from Hermetic philosophy); ***their descent and being*** because they, like us, descend from, and exist only because of, God.

[35–6] **to our mind . . . ascent and cause**
all things are related to our minds because it is by way of our prayers that we ascend to their origin, which is God.

[37] **full of duty**
(a) has its proper function; (b) obeys its duty towards God – cf. 'Let us hear the conclusion of the whole matter: Fear God, and keep his commandments: for this is the whole *duty* of man. For he is going to judge everything we do, whether it be for good or for evil, even those things we have done surreptitiously' (Ecclesiastes 12: 13–14).

[38–9] **Waters united . . . navigation**
Waters united i.e. where rivers meet the sea, on both of which we travel; but contrast such commerce with the waters that God 'divided' in order that Moses and the Israelites could cross the Red Sea on foot and so reach the Promised Land (Exodus 14: 21: see lines 25–6 and note, above); ***Distinguished*** (a) *waters* distinguished – cf. the waters that God 'divided' at the Creation: the waters 'above the firmament' being heaven (i.e. our *eternal* habitation: Genesis 1: 9–10); (b) 'our habitation [here on earth] is distinguished' – given the ambivalence that exists in the entire picture of man painted by Herbert in this poem, this is surely ironic.

[40] **Below**
on earth; ***drink*** (a) drink, as a less dense form of food; (b) intoxication (through alcohol, hubris or spiritual blindness); ***above*** in heaven; ***meat*** (a) more substantial 'spiritual food' (cf. the parable in which Christ tells his disciples to be like watchful servants, for their master will make them sit down to eat *meat*, and he will serve them: Luke 12: 35–40; cf. also 'Love (3)', line 17 and note; also (b) our 'meet' (i.e. just deserts – punishment for hubris); note further that 'meat and drink' represent a perfect offering

(see Numbers 29) and are, of course, a reference to the 'body and blood' of Christ remembered at Holy Communion/Mass.

[41] **are**

(a) literal, 'are'; (b) ironic, meaning 'should be'; ***our cleanliness*** ordinary water cleans the body; the 'spiritual' water of baptism cleans the soul.

[42] **Hath *one* such beauty?**

beauty symmetrical perfection; thus (a) 'one' contrasts with 'all' in the following line – i.e. if such beauty exists in only one thing, there will be much more beauty in many things; but also (b) 'one' contrasts with 'Both' – i.e. how can man be clean if he washes only in (ordinary) water?; (c) 'one'; i.e. man – this question is even more ironic, as the answer (judging from Herbert's argument) is clearly 'no': man falls short in his 'duty' towards God.

[43] **Then how are all things neat!**

neat clean, properly ordered, cleverly arranged; thus (a) if such symmetrical perfection exists, then things really are both clean and well ordered; but also (b) an implicit question: if such symmetry is not truly evident here on earth, the exclamation is ironic.

[43] **servants**

figuratively, (a) all things that could contribute to man's welfare; (b) thoughts or prayers that could 'serve' to put man into closer communion with Christ or God.

[44] **Than he'll**

(a) than he can (man lives in such abundance); (b) than he does (man does not use the resources, e.g. prayer, available to him); (c) than he will (man is stubborn); ***take notice of*** notice and use to best effect.

[45] **treads down**

the verb 'tread' is used in the Bible to describe physical treading or trampling on (e.g. the Lord trod or trampled on his enemies or those of his people who forsook him, as upon a winepress: Isaiah 63: 3–6); it is contrasted with 'walk' as in the phrase 'to walk with God' (Genesis 5: 22; 17: 1) which signifies not only being *befriended* by God, but also complete submission to him (see Vaughan, 'The Retreat' (p. 529), line 22 and note) – the inversion implicit in Herbert's phrase is the poem's culminating irony.

[46] **sickness**

sickness of the soul, i.e. distance from God; ***wan*** weary-looking (like someone who has struggled too long with a problem).

[47] **O mighty Love**

the *volta* – the phrase suggests that God's love is mysterious beyond the comprehension of man, as it tolerates all man's shortcomings.

[48] **man is . . . attend him**

one world (a) a microcosm; (b) a kind of world that does not appear to act either rationally or even for its own good; ***Another*** (a) a macrocosm, i.e. God; (b) a world with quite other concerns; ***attend*** (a) serve – note the inversion of the traditional view: man was created in order to serve God: here, God serves man; cf. Christ's reminder 'Ask, and you will receive; seek, and you will find; knock, and the door will be opened to you' (Luke 11: 9).

[49] **then**

thus, in this way.

[50] **brave**

(a) splendid, glorious, but also (b) ostentatious, showy; ***a palace*** i.e. man; ***O dwell in it*** (a) live in it, because the palace would/could be an appropriate habitation for God or Christ; (b) live in it, because man has need of you if he is to translate his vain ostentation into appropriate action: cf. St Paul's reminder that Christ has given each of us an individual gift, according to our deserts, the purpose of which is to increase the community of believers 'so that, united in faith and understanding of the Holy Spirit, we each aspire to manhood measured by nothing less than the full stature of Christ' (Ephesians 4: 13).

[51] **dwell with thee**

(a) live according to your precepts,

here on earth; (b) prepare ourselves to live with you in Paradise; ***at last*** (a) finally (i.e. after a long period of transgression); (b) when man dies, at the end of his life or on the final Day of Judgement; (c) for ever.
[52] **afford us so much wit**
'grant that we may have sufficient intelligence to grasp'.

[53] **as the world . . . serve thee**
(a) in the same way as the world offers us its service, so we may offer you ours; (b) in the same way as we make use of the world to further ourselves, you will make use of us in order to advance yourself.
[54] **And, both**
And thus/in this way both the world and man may become your servants.

58 / *Mortification*

How soon doth man decay!
When clothes are taken from a chest of sweets
To swaddle infants whose young breath
Scarce knows the way,
Those clouts are little winding sheets
Which do consign and send them unto death.

When boys go first to bed,
They step into their voluntary graves.
Sleep binds them fast: only their breath
Makes them not dead:
Successive nights like rolling waves
Convey them quickly, who are bound for death.

When youth is frank and free
And calls for music, while his veins do swell
All day exchanging mirth and breath
In company,
That music summons to the knell
Which shall befriend him at the hour of death.

When man grows staid and wise,
Getting a house and home where he may move
Within the circle of his breath,
Schooling his eyes,
That dumb inclosure maketh love
Unto the coffin that attends his death.

When age grows low and weak,
Marking his grave and thawing every year
Till all do melt and drown his breath
When he would speak,
A chair or litter shows the bier
Which shall convey him to the house of death.

Man, ere he is aware,
Hath put together a solemnity
And dressed his hearse while he has breath
As yet to spare:
Yet Lord, instruct us so to die,
That all these dyings may be life in death!

This extraordinary meditation is in six stanzas, each of six iambic lines (trimeter, pentameter, tetrameter, dimeter, tetrameter, pentameter), rhyming *a b c a b c*, with the same *c* rhymes 'breath'/'death' used throughout the poem. Each of the central five stanzas deals with a different phase in a man's life, in which the the central image is of the omnipresence of death.

The title refers to the Catholic practice, continued by the more conservative wing of the Church of England to which Herbert adhered, of bringing the body and passions into subjection by means of self-denial or self-discipline. The poem is both a *Vanitas,* a poem on the vanity or emptiness of human life without God, and a *Mementum Mori,* a work in which the poet or artist, by reminding himself of his approaching death, prepares himself to face it. It might be subtitled 'The Five Ages of Man' and be compared with Jaques's speech 'All the world's a stage', which outlines seven ages, from Shakespeare's *As You Like It* (II, vii, 138–65).

[1] **How soon . . . decay!**
How quickly man declines (in quality, power and energy).

[2] **sweets**
dried flowers, leaves and spices, used to keep clothes fresh-smelling: equivalent to what is now called potpourri.

[3] **swaddle**
wrap tightly around (swaddling bands/clothes = a wide bandage of linen or soft cloth wrapped tightly around a child); ***breath*** breathing.

[4] **Scarce knows the way**
is still very weak and uncertain (because the infant is still not breathing/has not learned to breathe regularly).

[5] **clouts**
clothes; here, an infant's clothes; ***winding sheets*** linen sheets in which a corpse is 'wound' or wrapped before being sent for burial.

[6] **consign**
commit, deliver, earmark, destine (for).

[7] **go first to bed**
the first time a boy goes to bed by himself.

[8] **voluntary**
created by the boys' deliberate choice or action; self-induced.

[9] **binds**
note the verb, suggesting imprisonment.

[10] **Makes them**
indicates that they are.

[11] **like rolling waves**
life as a sea-voyage was a traditional Petrarchan conceit – e.g. Petrarch, Sonnet 189.
[13] **frank**
still free from self-consciousness; ***free*** still able to do as it likes, because it has not yet assumed any responsibilities.
[14] **music**
e.g. music played on a lute, traditionally used to accompany love songs; ***veins do swell*** i.e. as a result of drinking too much beer, wine or other alcohol.
[15] **mirth**
laughter; ***breath*** idle conversation.
[17] **music**
(a) the music referred to in line 14; (b) the music of laughter and idle conversation; ***summons to*** calls upon, requires the young man to attend; ***knell*** the sound of a church-bell, esp. one announcing a death, or rung at a funeral.
[18] **befriend**
the notion of death 'befriending' man is not biblical; it stems from medieval Christianity; the 'bell' befriends the dying man (a) by keeping him company in a crisis, and (b) by summoning others to pray for him.
[19] **staid**
sober, steady, reliable – i.e. when the young man becomes an adult.
[20–1] **move/Within . . . his breath**
live during his lifetime.
[22] **Schooling his eyes**
studying – the phrase indicates that the poem is specifically concerned with a scholar, such as Herbert was.
[23–4] **dumb inclosure**
the house or home – note again the implicit suggestion of something that 'imprisons'; ***maketh love/Unto*** seeks the special attention of, seeks reciprocal attention or affection from; ***attends*** waits for, is waiting for.
[25] **When age grows low**
When a man grows bent with age, losing his height.
[26] **Marking**
observing carefully – note how it is the man's 'age' (i.e. the life allotted him) which marks the grave, not the man; ***thawing*** usually, releasing a liquid from a frozen into its natural state; here, weakening (the man, the man's faculties), with the implication that life is not man's natural state.
[27] **all**
everything and everyone; ***do melt*** usually, change from solid to liquid by heat; here, becomes confused together by his weakening senses; ***drown his breath*** make his voice imperceptible.
[29] **chair or litter**
chair the chair on which an old man sits, a little to the side of a family gathering or a party; ***litter*** a small vehicle containing a bed or chair used to carry the sick and elderly, either carried by four servants or, on wheels, pulled by an animal; ***shows*** heralds, announces – i.e. resembles, makes one think of; ***bier*** moveable stand on which a corpse, or coffin, rests; often the bier was carried, the coffin resting on the bier.
[30] **the house of death**
here, the (man's) grave.
[31] **ere**
before; ***aware*** aware of what is happening (as described in the poem).
[32] **Hath put together a solemnity**
has constructed his life as a solemn ceremony (such as a funeral procession).
[33] **dressed his hearse**
decorated the vehicle used to carry his own coffin.
[33–4] **while he has breath . . . spare**
while he still has more than enough life in him.
[35] **so to die**
to die in this manner.
[36] **That all these dyings . . .**
So that all these dyings (i.e. reminders of death: see note to 'title') may give us true life (because lived in the full knowledge of death) in death (i.e. during our 'lives' here on earth, which are as 'death' when compared to 'eternal life' in Paradise).

59 / *Jordan (2)*

When first my lines of heavenly joys made mention,
Such was their lustre, they did so excel,
That I sought out quaint words and trim invention:
My thoughts began to burnish, sprout, and swell,
Curling with metaphors a plain intention,
Decking the sense, as if it were to sell.

Thousands of notions in my brain did run,
Offering their service, if I were not sped,
I often blotted what I had begun:
This was not quick enough, and that was dead.
Nothing could seem too rich to clothe the sun,
Much less those joys which trample on his head.

As flames do work and wind, when they ascend,
So did I weave my self into the sense.
But while I bustled, I might hear a friend
Whisper, *How wide is all this long pretence!*
There is in love a sweetness ready-penned:
Copy out only that, and save expense.

This is perhaps Herbert's best-known parody (or 'sacred parody') – the original to which it refers is, of course, the first sonnet of Sidney's *Astrophil and Stella,* in which the poet describes how he anguished over the best way to approach his subject until he realised that all he had to do was 'look in [his] heart and write'. Herbert's original title was – not surprisingly – 'Invention'.

The poem is in three six-line stanzas of iambic pentameters, rhyming *a b a b a b*. In the first stanza, the poet describes how he began to write poetry; in the second, the nature of the frustrations he encountered; in the last, his enthusiasm until a friend suggests that he adopt a much more natural approach.

Title
see note to 'Jordan (1)', above; ***invention*** see note to line 3.

[1] **When first . . . made mention**
'When I first began to write of the joys of heaven in my verse.'

[2] **their**
refers to the impression made on the poet by the heavenly joys; ***lustre*** (a) radiant beauty; (b) surface brilliance; ***did so excel*** the impression was so brilliant – note how the poem's conclusion is anticipated in this phrase; the poet, however, does not understand this at this stage.

[3] **quaint words . . . trim invention**
quaint ingeniously or cunningly contrived; elaborate; ***invention*** a word

belonging to the subject of rhetoric, describing the selection of the subject by exercise of the intellect or imagination – sometimes also applied to the process of creating an original and striking argument; ***trim*** (a) suitable, proper, fine; and (b) having a smart outward appearance: hence often used ironically.

[4] **burnish, sprout, and swell**
burnish to shine or gleam as if polished by friction; ***sprout*** to appear (through the soil) and grow rapidly; ***swell*** to arise and grow in the mind.

[5] **Curling . . . plain intention**
curling the word suggests *over*-decorating; ***metaphors*** contrasts here with *sacred* analogy (i.e. analogy derived from the Bible – metaphor is to profane verse what analogy is to sacred verse); the line as a whole suggests that the poet's original idea is buried by being over-elaborated.

[6] **Decking**
to cover or adorn in order to appear beautiful.

[7–8] **Thousands of notions . . .**
Thousands of ideas ran through my mind; ***offering their service . . .*** whenever I was not completely satisfied with an idea, another would present itself as a possible alternative – the implication being that once one starts trying to improve an idea, one will never be satisfied.

[9] **blotted**
erased, because not satisfied with.

[10] **not quick enough**
quick vital, living; thus, not sufficiently vivid or lively; ***dead*** i.e. a cliché or platitude.

[11] **rich**
elaborate or brilliant; ***the sun*** note (a) how this refers back to 'lustre' in line 2; (b) the pun on 'son', here Christ – thus, 'Nothing seemed too brilliant a metaphor by which to describe Christ.'

[12] **Much less those joys which trample on his head**
joys the joys of discovering a quaint metaphor – note how such joys contrast with those mentioned in line 1; ***trample on*** refers back to 'decking', but implies brutally treading – this verb is used in the Bible to describe physical trampling (e.g. the Lord trod or trampled on his enemies or those of his people who forsook him, as upon a wine-press: Isaiah 63: 3–6): by implication, the poet's would-be joys are not joys to Christ; ***his head*** Christ's head; thus, 'Least of all those joys which (in fact) brutally take away the natural lustre of Christ's head'.

[13–14] **As flames . . . into the sense**
flames reflect (a) the poet's passionate involvement in the task of finding the most vivid image; (b) the sacrifice of his true 'self'; ***work*** behave; ***weave*** with implications that the poet is contorting himself by his effort, adapting himself to his art rather than allowing his art to express his true self.

[15] **bustled**
was fussily engaged (in this activity); ***might hear*** ambiguous: (a) might have heard; (b) could hear; ***friend*** note that Christ called his disciples 'friends' (John 15: 14).

[16] **wide**
deviating from the aim; missing the mark – note how it refers back to 'Curling' in line 5; ***pretence*** self-deception.

[17] **Love**
(a) divine love; (b) Christ: cf. St Paul's farewell: 'Set your heart on becoming whole . . . and the God of love and of peace will be with you' (2 Corinthians 13: 11); ***ready-penned*** already written (cf. line 2).

[18] **save expense**
save save yourself; ***expense*** (a) 'expensive' adornment (as in trim, decking, rich); (b) the waste of misapplied effort (cf. Shakespeare, Sonnet 129).

60 / *The Collar*

I struck the board and cried 'No more!
I will abroad.
What? Shall I ever sigh and pine?
My lines and life are free – free as the road,
Loose as the wind, as large as store.
Shall I be still in suit?
Have I no harvest but a thorn
To let me blood, and not restore
What I have lost with cordial fruit?
Sure there was wine
Before my sighs did dry it; there was corn
Before my tears did drown it.
Is the year only lost to me?
Have I no bays to crown it?
No flowers, no garlands gay? – All blasted?
All wasted?
Not so, my heart – but there is fruit,
And thou hast hands.
Recover all thy sigh-blown age
On double pleasures: leave thy cold dispute
Of what is fit, and not. Forsake thy cage,
Thy rope of sands,
Which petty thoughts have made, and made to thee
Good cable to enforce and draw
And be thy law,
While thou didst wink and wouldst not see.
Away, Take Heed!
I will abroad.
Call in thy death's head there: tie up thy fears!
He that forbears
To suit and serve his need,
Deserves his load.'
But as I raved and grew more fierce and wild
At every word,
Me thoughts I heard one calling, *'Child!'*
And I replied *'My Lord.'*

The title of this poem involves a two- or even three-way pun: 'collar' = (a) the stiff collar worn by clerics, an emblem of constraint; it has recently been suggested by D.B.J. Randall (*SP*, **81** [1984], 473–95) that it also refers to the iron collar used to confine animals, slaves, sinners and madmen; (b) 'choler' – in the seventeenth century, choler [sometimes spelt 'collar'] was both a medical condition and its effect, and referred to an outburst of uncontrollable anger; and perhaps (c) 'caller' – i.e. one who calls upon another. The poem – which, until the closing lines, is a parody of meditative verse – vividly describes various facets of the poet's pent-up irritation with his own religiosity. The irregular pattern of both its rhyme-scheme and its metre (dimeters, trimeters, tetrameters and pentameters) contributes to reinforce the angry, bitter, almost hysterical tone.

[1] **board**
(a) usually, a table spread with food; (b) here, the Communion table which, in the Prayer Book used in Herbert's time, was called 'God's board' – 'No more' thus represents a decision to abandon his faith.

[2] **abroad**
the sense here is figurative – the word implies that even in his 'choler' or anger, the poet conceives his faith as his 'home country', and any activity undertaken outside adherence to the Church as a foreign country.

[3] **sigh and pine**
traditionally, in late-sixteenth-century English verse, words used to describe a male poet's yearning for his mistress – here, used of a longing for God, of whom the poet is now tired.

[4] **lines**
note the irregular metres of the poem's lines – dimeters, trimeters, tetrameters and pentameters; ***free*** i.e. the poet affirms that just as he is not subservient to anyone, so his poetry is not subservient to any tradition.

[4] **free as the road**
the three phrases in lines 4 and 5 are all ambivalent, for although the poet is affirming his independence, they all carry specific connotations – ***free*** open to all comers; but for ***road***, cf. 'I am the way, and the truth, and the life' (John 14: 6).

[5] **loose as the wind**
loose (a) state of being unrestrained; (b) unreliable, vague, dissolute; ***wind*** ambivalent – (a) traditionally associated with God: e.g. 'he brings forth the wind out of his treasures' (Jeremiah 10: 13); but also (b) an 'ill wind' – e.g. the epistle in which St Paul tells his listeners that only if they become 'united in faith and understanding of the Holy Spirit, and aspire to manhood measured by nothing less than the full stature of Christ' can they hope to avoid being 'tossed to and fro like a ship in a storm, or blown this way and that with the shifting wind of doctrines devised by men determined to exploit them' (Ephesians 4: 13–14); ***large as store large*** (a) ample, generous; (b) of wide range, without any specific aim; ***store*** ambivalent – (a) God's plenty, as we know it: cf. Peter's warning 'But God has ordained that the heavens and the earth as we know them are being kept in store, in order to be destroyed by fire on the day when he will come to judge and condemn those who have forsaken him' (2 Peter 3: 7), and Timothy's stipulation that the rich should be careful to do good, 'so as to ensure that they have a store of good deeds in heaven that will secure their future and guarantee them eternal life' (1 Timothy 6: 19).

[6] **still in suit**
always waiting on or asking favours from another person.

[7] **harvest . . . blood**
harvest used figuratively, to describe the result of or reward for the poet's faith; ***thorn*** (a) the stiff, pointed part of a shrub, which can inflict pain – cf. the Lord's sentence on Adam after discovering Eve's crime: 'Because of what you did, a curse lies on the ground. All your life you will have to work hard to weed out the thorns and thistles that will hinder you, if you are

to produce the food you need' (Genesis 3: 17–18); also (b) Christ's crown of thorns (Mark 15: 17) which, of course, carries the implication of being a pain that 'saves'.

[8–9] **let me blood**
make me bleed; ***and not restore*** without [me] being able to restore; ***cordial*** restorative; ***cordial fruit*** the fruit of man's work – the bread and wine that are consumed at 'God's board', representing the body and blood of Christ.

[10–11] **Sure there was . . . dry it**
sighs i.e. the sighs that caused the poet to want to go 'abroad'; thus, 'there must have been wine before my sighs caused it to lose its taste.'

[11–12] **there was corn . . . drown it**
tears as 'sighs' in preceding line; thus, 'there must have been bread before my tears caused it to become inedible'; ***corn*** wheat, used to make the Communion bread or wafer.

[13] **Is the year . . .**
'Am I the only person who achieves nothing each year?'

[14] **bays**
laurels, being associated with Apollo, were a traditional symbol of poetic achievement; ***to crown it*** to signal that I have achieved something.

[15] **flowers, garlands**
symbols of pastoral or earthly success; ***All blasted?*** 'Have all my achievements been destroyed?'

[17] **Not so, my heart – but . . .**
'My heart, however, is not wasted [i.e. dried up], and . . . '

[17–18] **fruit . . . hands**
fruit fruit to be enjoyed by his heart, with an oblique reference to the Fall – i.e. to tasting of forbidden pleasures; ***hands*** Adam was punished for tasting of the fruit of the Tree of Knowledge of Good and Evil by having 'to till the ground' – i.e. to work with his hands.

[19] **Recover**
retrieve, or stop feeling the effects of; ***sigh-blown age*** as a result of all his sighing (yearning for God), the poet has aged prematurely.

[20] **double**
to enjoy oneself is one pleasure; to be able to do something forbidden that one wants to do 'doubles' the pleasure; ***cold dispute*** the ***dispute*** refers to him having been torn by conflicting desires; it is ***cold*** because it is already past.

[21] **fit**
appropriate or proper for him to do; ***Forsake thy cage*** Leave your self-created prison; i.e. 'slip your collar'.

[22] **rope of sands**
the poet feels that he is bound with a rope; it is envisaged as being made of sand because each grain of sand is something of infinitesimal size, but many grains of sand make something of considerable weight – in other words, he is tied (only) by a large quantity of minute considerations: cf. the proverb: 'A stone is heavy, and the sand weighty; but a fool's anger is heavier than either of them' (Proverbs 27: 3).

[23–4] **petty**
unimportant, of no consequence (i.e. like a single grain of sand); ***made to thee . . . Good cable*** caused the rope of sands to appear to you as if it were strong rope; ***enforce and draw*** to reinforce the hold the rope of sands has on you, and to make you feel you want to be tied.

[25] **law**
cf. St Paul's reminder: 'the new covenant consists not of a written law but of spirit, for laws always signal death, whereas spirit engenders life' (2 Corinthians 3: 6).

[26] **wink and wouldst not see**
close your eyes deliberately so as not to see.

[27] **Away, Take Heed!**
Take Heed note the implicit ambivalence: (a) the poet is urging himself to leave, to 'take heed' of the signs of his imprisonment; but also (b) a personification of his cautious conscience (cf. the words of Christ 'Take heed therefore that the light which is in thee be not darkness': Luke 11: 35) – the phrase occurs frequently in both

the Old and New Testaments: thus the poet is distancing himself from all warnings (i.e. 'I do not want to hear any more advice to "take heed"').

[28] **I will abroad**
the 'will' is emphatic.

[29] **Call in thy death's head**
Call in the poet tells Take Heed that he has no use for such devices as his ***death's head***; in the seventeenth century, a skull was a common symbol of the frailty of life and the transience of human endeavour, often used in paintings, called *memento mori* (= remember you must die), whose purpose was to exhort the viewer to 'take heed'; ***tie up*** keep your warnings to yourself, an ironic reference to the 'rope of sands'/'Good cable'; ***fears*** the fears occasioned by the death's head.

[30–2] **He that forbears ... load**
forbears abstains or refrains from (doing something); ***suit*** satisfy, meet the demands of; ***serve*** meet (the needs of), satisfy; ***need*** (a) requirements; (2) desires: the phrase thus means 'He that abstains from responding to and satisfying his desires deserves to be burdened by them' – note how Herbert deliberately employs words that have another sense: ***forbearance*** means curbing one's more *hasty* tendencies; for ***suit***, see line 6; ***serve*** to serve the Lord (see 'Love (3)', line 16); ***load*** must be read – indeed, the entire poem should be read – in the context of St Paul's reminder to the Galatians: 'For if a man imagines he is someone important, he is deluding himself. Each one of us must examine our own conduct and assess his achievement not in comparison with anyone else's, but according to his own talent. For everyone has his own burden to bear' (Galatians 6: 3–5).

[33] **raved ... wild thoughts**
cf. 'Beware of false prophets who come to you with the appearance of sheep, but are nothing but ravening [i.e. wild and savage] wolves' (Matthew 7: 15).

[34] **word**
note the ambiguity: at every 'word' of (a) the poem; (b) his own 'raving'.

[35] **Me thoughts**
I thought, it seemed to me – cf. the 'still, small voice' with which God spoke to Elijah (1 Kings 19: 12); ***one*** someone (i.e. Christ).

---

61 / *The Pulley*

When God at first made man,
Having a glass of blessings standing by,
'Let us', said He, 'pour on him all we can:
Let the world's riches, which dispersèd lie,
Contract into a span.'

So Strength first made a way;
Then Beauty flowed, then Wisdom, Honour, Pleasure.
When almost all was out, God made a stay,
Perceiving that, alone of all his treasure,
Rest in the bottom lay.

'For if I should', said He,
'Bestow this jewel also on my creature,
He would adore my gifts instead of me,
And rest in Nature, not the God of Nature:
So both should losers be.

'Yet let him keep the rest –
But keep them with repining restlessness.
Let him be rich and weary, that at least,
If goodness lead him not, yet weariness
May toss him to my breast.'

The title of this poem refers to a block of wood through which a rope is passed in such a way as to enable the block to take a greater strain than the loose end of the rope, thus enabling a person to lift a weight that might otherwise be too heavy. The poem implies that man holds the pulley rope. Note that the significance of the title does not become apparent until the last line.

The poem is in four five-line stanzas, the outer lines of which are trimeters, the three inner ones pentameters; the whole rhyming *a b a b a*. It is based on a well-wrought pun on the word 'rest'. Almost the whole poem consists of thoughts attributed to God. In the first stanza, the poet tells how God determined to pour all his blessings on man; the second specifies what these are; in the third, God wonders whether it would be wise to allow man rest; in the last, God explains why he decided not to give rest to man.

[2] **glass of blessings**
a vial or small glass container with God's various 'blessings' (i.e. God's gifts, divine favours, some of which are mentioned in lines 6–7, 10), – chemists and doctors both used 'vials'; so too did alchemists; ***standing by*** close at hand.

[3] **pour**
cf. the Lord's words: 'For I shall pour out water for he who is thirsty and rain on the parched land. I shall pour out my spirit on your children and my blessing on your offspring' (Isaiah 44: 3).

[5] **contract**
join together; ***span*** the distance between the tip of the thumb and the tip of the little finger – approximately nine inches; here, used to indicate a small space entirely contained by the hand of God.

[6–7] **Strength, Beauty, Wisdom, Honour, Pleasure**
the blessings mentioned in line 2; ***made a way*** 'Strength was the first to make its way out of' – i.e. to be poured from the vial.

[8] **almost all**
i.e. almost all the blessings, with a possible pun on 'all' as the most important of the blessings (i.e. rest, see line 10); ***made a stay*** (a) stopped what he was doing; (b) put a lid on the glass.

[9] **treasure**
cf. 'Wisdom and knowledge are the assurance of salvation; the fear of the Lord is [Zion's] treasure' (Isaiah 33: 6).

[10] **Rest**
the condition of enjoying or ability to enjoy rest, relaxation; but Herbert clearly means 'absolute Rest' – i.e.

complete freedom from care or anxiety about anything beyond what can be enjoyed with his human senses, intelligence and moral sense; ***bottom*** the bottom of the vial: note how it lies at the bottom of the stanza.

[12] **jewel**
i.e. Rest is perhaps the greatest of God's blessings (see line 8 and note); ***my creature*** because created by God (see Genesis 1: 26–30; 2: 7).

[13] **adore my gifts**
i.e. adore those gifts that God has already poured from his vial: Strength, Beauty, Wisdom, Honour, Pleasure; if man were also given Rest, he would in time lose all desire to seek God, and would thus adore God's various gifts instead of God – because, freed from all anxiety, he would lose all concept of God.

[14] **rest in Nature**
be content with Nature (i.e. the natural world of his senses, intelligence and moral sense); ***not the God of Nature*** and not be content with God, who created the world.

[15] **So**
with the result that; ***losers*** man would be a 'loser' from such a situation because he would lose his possibility of knowing God; note Herbert's echo of the biblical position that God requires man just as much as man requires God.

[16] **the rest**
i.e. Strength, Beauty, Wisdom, etc. (see lines 6–7).

[17] **repining**
fretting, discontented; ***restlessness*** inability to find any rest, condition of being forever anxious about something.

[18] **weary**
not 'tired', but *dispirited* (i.e. lacking the spirit of God), sick with impatience; ***that at least*** so that, if nothing else will.

[19] **goodness**
note Herbert's assumption that 'goodness' could (perhaps should) lead man to God – by goodness, he presumably meant a model Christian life; ***weariness*** man's utter inability to find any rest (outside God) – his ever-present yearning for something beyond himself.

[20] **toss**
(a) throw lightly or carelessly; (b) jerk something upwards that lies cradled in a blanket by pulling on its four corners; (c) roll around, in a bed, restlessly.

62 / *The Flower*

How fresh, O Lord, how sweet and clean
Are thy returns! even as the flowers in spring
To which, besides their own demean,
The late-past frosts tributes of pleasure bring.
Grief melts away
Like snow in May
As if there were no such cold thing.

Who would have thought my shrivelled heart
Could have recovered greenness? It was gone
Quite underground, as flowers depart
To see their mother-root when they have blown:
Where they together
All the hard weather,
Dead to the world, keep house unknown.

These are thy wonders, *Lord of Power*:
Killing and quick'ning, bringing down to hell
And up to heaven in an hour,
Making a chiming of a passing-bell.
We say amiss
This or that is:
Thy word is all, if we could spell.

O that I once past changing were,
Fast in thy Paradise, where no flower can wither!
Many a spring I shoot up fair,
Off'ring at heaven, growing and groaning thither:
Nor doth my flower
Want a spring-shower,
My sins and I joining together.

But while I grow in a straight line,
Still upwards bent as if heav'n were mine own,
Thy anger comes and I decline:
What frost to that? What pole is not the zone
Where all things burn
When thou dost turn
And the least frown of thine is shown?

And now in age I bud again.
After so many deaths I live and write:
I once more smell the dew and rain
And relish versing. O my only light!
It cannot be
That I am he
On whom thy tempests fell all night.

These are thy wonders, *Lord of Love*:
To make us see we are but flowers that glide,
Which when we once can find and prove
Thou hast a garden for us where to bide,
Who would be more,
Swelling through store,
Forfeit their Paradise by their pride.

In this meditative poem, the poet likens not only the renewals of his experience of Christ to the seasonal reappearance of a flower, but himself to a flower that can blossom only in Christ's love.

It is in seven stanzas, each of seven iambic lines: the first four lines have alternating tetrameters and pentameters; the next two are dimeters; the final line is another tetrameter.

[1] **sweet**
sweet-smelling, fragrant, highly gratifying; ***clean*** cleansing, purifying.
[2] **returns**
those moments when Christ/God, who has not shown himself to the poet for a long time, reveals himself again; ***even as*** just like.
[3–4] **besides their own demean**
apart from bringing the beauty of their own appearance; ***To which . . . The late-past frosts tributes of pleasure bring*** 'The recently ended frosts bring offering of pleasure to the spring' – i.e. admitting their submission to the spring.
[5] **Grief**
cf. 'Affliction (4)', stanza 5.
[7] **no such cold thing**
i.e. as grief ('snow in May' is only the analogy).
[8] **shrivelled**
(a) because God has not revealed himself to the poet for a long time; (b) from the cold occasioned by his grief.
[11] **their mother-root**
i.e. the roots of the flower, into which it recedes after it has bloomed or blossomed (***when they have blown***); ***mother-root*** because the flower grows from the root.
[13] **All the hard weather**
throughout the cold weather of winter.
[14] **keep house unknown**
remain invisible to the eye (because underground).
[16–17] **killing and quick'ning**
killing (i.e. a flower, after it has bloomed) and quickening (= giving it life again once it has returned to its root); ***hell/heaven***: used figuratively (***hell*** = underground; ***heaven*** = the sweetness of spring) as well as more literally.
[18] **chiming of a passing-bell**
a ***passing-bell*** is a church-bell sounded at regular, monotonous intervals on one note, to signal the death of a parishioner; ***chiming*** ringing several bells, pitched differently, to produce a pleasing tune.
[19] **We say amiss**
we are wrong to say.
[21] **if we could spell**
i.e. if only we could understand it.
[22] **once past changing were**
could be for ever free from having to undergo changes.
[23] **Fast**
secure.
[24] **spring**
used here figuratively; ***shoot up*** to sprout, burst into bud; ***fair*** properly and beautifully (like a flower).
[25] **Off'ring**
(Offering) aiming, looking; ***groaning thither*** struggling towards heaven.

[27] **Want**
lack.
[28] **sins and I joining together**
i.e. by the poet responding to his sins with tears of remorse, providing the 'spring-showers' of line 27.
[29] **a straight line**
i.e. not deviating from God.
[31] **decline**
'die' (like a flower, i.e. falling away from the vertical growth).
[32–3] **What frost to that?**
'What is frost compared to this?' ***pole*** both poles (North and South) are places of extreme cold (frost); ***the zone/ Where all things burn*** hell.
[34] **When thou dost turn**
note the irony – the poet seeks God, but when God 'turns' towards him it is in anger, perhaps because of the inflation implicit in line 30 ('as if heav'n were mine own').
[35] **the least frown... is shown**
'You are revealed as being in the slightest way displeased'.
[36] **in age**
i.e. in 'old age' (Herbert was only in his late thirties when he wrote this poem); ***bud*** burst into flower, after a spiritual 'winter'.
[38] **the dew and rain**
literally, as a flower might; figuratively, God's nurturing goodness.
[39] **relish**
take a delight in; ***versing*** writing poetry.
[42] **tempests... night**
note how the imagery of cold/winter is replaced by the more common imagery of tempest/night, thereby collapsing seasonal change (winter/ spring) into daily recommitment.
[44] **see**
understand; ***glide*** pass away unnoticed.
[45] **when we once can find and prove**
once we are able to discover (i.e. understand) this and know for certain (***prove*** to have absolute faith in).
[46] **a garden for us**
i.e. Paradise, but also the terrestrial paradise of complete faith; ***where to bide*** where to wait.
[47] **Who would be more**
Whoever seeks to be more (than a 'contented flower').
[48] **Swelling through store**
swollen with abundance (cf. inflation in line 30).
[49] **Forfeit**
will lose; ***by*** as a result of.

63 / *Love (3)*

Love bade me welcome: yet my soul drew back,
    Guilty of dust and sin.
But quick-eyed Love, observing me grow slack
    From my first entrance in,
Drew nearer to me, sweetly questioning,
    If I lacked any thing.

'A guest', I answered, 'worthy to be here':
    Love said, 'You shall be he.'
'I the unkind, ungrateful? Ah my dear,
    I cannot look on thee.'

Love took my hand, and smiling did reply,
  'Who made the eyes but I?'

'Truth Lord, but I have marred them: let my shame
  Go where it doth deserve.'
'And know you not', says Love, 'who bore the blame?'
  'My dear, then I will serve.'
'You must sit down', says Love, 'and taste my meat':
  So I did sit and eat.

This is the last poem in *The Temple*, which finishes with a reference to the 'four last things': Death, Judgement, Hell, and Heaven; slightly modifying this traditional sequence, Herbert's last five poems are 'Death', 'Doomsday', 'Judgement', 'Heaven', and 'Love (3)': note the omission of 'Hell' and the decision to follow 'Judgement' with 'Heaven' and then 'Love'.

The poem celebrates 'the wedding-supper of the Lamb' (cf. Revelation 19: 9) which will take place in heaven, but clearly it is also making an implicit reference to the sacrament of Holy Communion/the Mass. It is about a final acceptance of Christ. There are three six-line stanzas, of alternating iambic pentameters and trimeters, rhyming *a b a b c c*. Note how the few metrical irregularities usually highlight a specially important word.

This final poem should be read in the light of two parables from different gospels:
1. *The Parable of the Wedding Feast*: Speaking to the chief priests and Pharisees, Jesus once likened the Kingdom of Heaven to a king who had prepared a feast for his son's wedding, but found no one willing to attend. So he called his servants and told them to go out into the streets and invite everyone they could find to the wedding. The servants did so, and finally the hall was packed with guests. But when the king came in, he noticed one man who was not dressed for a wedding and asked him: 'Why did you come without your wedding clothes?' When the man had nothing to say, the king told his attendants to bind him hand and foot and turn him out into the dark, the place of wailing and grinding of teeth. '"For", the king explained, "though many are invited, few are chosen"' (Matthew 22: 2–14).
2. *The Parable of the Watchful Servants*: One day, Jesus told his disciples to be always ready, with belts fastened and lamps alight. 'Be like men who wait for their master's return from a wedding-party: happy are those servants whom the master finds on the alert when he comes. For I tell you that the master shall gird himself, and make his servants *sit down to eat meat*, and he will serve them' (Luke 12: 35–40); cf. 'Man', line 34 and note.

[1] **Love**
Christ: cf. 'love is from God. Everyone who loves is a child of God and knows God, . . . For God is love; and his love was disclosed to us in this, that he sent his only Son into the world to bring us life' (1 John 4: 7–9); ***welcome***: as there were very few inns in the seventeenth century, it was a common practice for travellers to seek hospitality at any house on their way; the poem may be referring to this tradition.

[2] **Guilty of dust and sin**
in Christian teaching, man is born of dust (Genesis 2: 7) and, because he is the heir of Adam's Fall (i.e. knowledge of evil), also sin: see Genesis 3.
[3–4] **quick-eyed**
quick (a) rapid; (b) penetrating – cf. 'For the word of God is quick and powerful, sharper than any two-edged sword; it can even divide soul and spirit' (Hebrews 4: 12); ***observing me grow slack . . . entrance in*** seeing me back away; ***slack*** suggests that firm purpose is 'taut'; thus, slack = 'insufficiently firm of purpose'.
[6] **lacked**
note that this 'lack' contrasts with the plenitude symbolised in the final line.
[7] **A guest . . . worthy to be here**
the poet, in the sense that he feels unworthy to be present at the heavenly feast.
[8] **Love said, 'You shall be he'**
he (a) the guest; but also (b) Christ – cf. St Paul's reminder that Christ has given each of us an individual gift, according to our deserts, the purpose of which is to increase the community of believers 'so that, united in faith and understanding of the Holy Spirit, we each aspire to manhood measured by nothing less than the full stature of Christ. We are no longer to be children, tossed by the waves and whirled about by every fresh gust of teaching, dupes of crafty rogues and their deceitful schemes. No, let us speak the truth in love; so shall we fully grow up into Christ' (Ephesians 4: 13–15).
[9] **unkind, ungrateful**
unkind lacking a natural inclination to goodness (i.e. unable to come to Christ of his sole volition); ***ungrateful*** not responding with proper gratitude to Christ (i.e. his Mercy).
[12] **Who made the eyes but I?**
cf. Psalm 94, in which the psalmist reprimands those who justify their wrong-doing by thinking that 'Yahweh is not looking' by reminding them: 'Does he that planted the ear not hear, he that moulded the eye not see?' (verse 9).
[13–14] **marred**
here, hindered (i.e. not allowed his eyes to see/receive Christ) – cf. Christ's rebuke of his disciples: 'Do you still not understand? Are your minds closed? You have eyes: can you not see?' (Mark 8: 17–18), with a possible reference to the eyes of Adam and Eve being 'opened' to a knowledge of good and evil (Genesis 3: 7). Here, of course, it would mean being 'opened' to Christ – cf. 'As in Adam all men die, so in Christ all will be brought to life' (1 Corinthians 15: 22); ***let my shame/Go where it doth deserve shame*** (a) the consequence of sin (Genesis 2: 25; 3: 10); (b) cf. 'we must throw off every encumbrance, every sin to which we cling, and run with resolution the race for which we are entered, our eyes fixed on Jesus, on whom faith depends from start to finish: Jesus who, for the sake of the joy that lay ahead of him, *endured the cross, making light of the shame*, and has taken his seat at the right hand of the throne of God' (Hebrews 12: 1–2); ***where it doth deserve*** (a) the place of wailing and grinding of teeth – cf. Matthew 22: 13; (b) where it is 'thrown off' by acceptance of Christ's sacrifice and love.
[15–16] **who bore the blame**
Christ, by virtue of his Passion; ***serve*** cf. Luke 12: 37.
[17] **meat**
(a) the body and blood of Christ, celebrated at Communion – a reference also to the *agape* or 'love-feast' held by the early Christians to commemorate Christ's Last Supper: cf. Paul's exhortation: 'That Christ dwell in your hearts with love [love of Christ = *agape*] . . . so that you come to know the breadth and height and depth of the love [*agape*] of Christ' (Ephesians 3: 17, 19).

ROBERT HERRICK

(1591–1674)

1648 *Hesperides* with *His Noble Numbers*

Robert Herrick was born in London and baptised on 24 August 1591, the seventh and last child of Nicholas Herrick, who died a year later. At the age of sixteen he was apprenticed to his uncle, a prosperous London goldsmith; he went on to study at Cambridge, graduating in 1613, then taking his MA in 1620 and holy orders in 1623. Since he was in touch with a number of prominent men of letters in the 1620s, he probably returned to London, where the circle of intellectual and artistic friends he made at Cambridge was further enlarged. In 1627 he accompanied the Duke of Buckingham as chaplain for an expedition to the Ile de Ré. Two years later he was appointed to Dean Prior, a parish in Devonshire, in the West Country. He ran into difficulties during the Civil War and was removed from his parish in 1646; he did not return until after Charles II was restored to the throne. Though he does not seem to have been terribly fond of Devonshire, he remained there, unmarried, until his death in 1674. His one book, *Hesperides*, contains some 1,400 poems, most of them very brief; a large number were doubtless written earlier, perhaps as much as a quarter-century.

Context

Herrick' s poetry gives one the impression of a *bon-vivant*, devil-may-care sort of person, but his true temperament is perhaps better suggested by the name of his housemaid, Prudence. A witty man in company, he seems to have been much appreciated by friends and acquaintances from his early London years until his death. He was not in favour with the Puritans, however, and despite his personal discretion he was dismissed from his parish when they came to power. Their instincts were, perhaps, correct. Much of Herrick's verse has a distinctly Epicurean ring with its celebration of nature, wine, women and song. A great admirer of Ben Jonson, whom he knew personally, he caught the spirit of classicism and of the Ancient Greek and Roman lyric as completely as any writer in the century, his master included. His limitations are obvious. The religious verse collected in *His Noble Numbers* does not reveal him at his best, and he seems to have had no talent for narrative or the long poem. Apart from a poem of medium length, such as his masterpiece, 'Corinna's Going a-Maying', he succeeds most in writing pithy, light-hearted (though not necessarily light-headed) poems of extreme brevity. Whatever he writes, however, nearly always shows a high concern for art, craftsmanship and polish. Subjected to close analysis, even the slightest of his poems, though seemingly tossed off, reveals the care with which they have all been constructed.

Genre

For a poetry that appeals to such a narrow range of sensibility, Herrick's is surprisingly varied. It draws not only on classical authors such as Anacreon, Horace, Ovid and Martial – who were Jonson's models – but also on the world of folktale and English fairy lore, the Bible and Fathers of the Church, older English poetry and Italian madrigals. Some of the forms in which he wrote include epigram, satire, elegy, love lyric, epithalamion or marriage song, complimentary poems and occasional poems of all sorts. Herrick evokes church festivals and rural feasts, pagan festivals and Christian devotional ritual, superstitions, oral traditions, charms, recipes, gossip, and local goings-on in the same fluent and mellifluous breath.

Critical Reception

Herrick's poems circulated fairly widely in manuscript before his one and only collection was published, and many continued to be republished in mid-century collections after it appeared. It was not until the nineteenth century, however, that real interest in him was revived; a select edition was published in 1810 and a full one in 1823. From that time until the present, more or less complete editions of his poetry have appeared regularly. The first scholarly account of Herrick (by Nathan Drake) appeared in 1804, and despite a few negative reactions, critics during the nineteenth century were mostly appreciative of his qualities. In fact, the basic lines of disagreement established by Romantic and Victorian critics continued well into the twentieth century – arguments concerning his poetic stature, his alleged unevenness, his 'pagan' perspective, his religious lyrics, and so on. He is one of a handful of absolute lyricists in English, and the author of at least one major lyric, 'Corinna's Going a-Maying'. Though some modern critics, such as F.R. Leavis and T.S. Eliot, have considered him not quite of the very first rank, more recent critics have disagreed, pointing to the essential unity of his book and its larger implications, taken as a whole. If his reputation will probably never rise higher than it has in the twentieth century, it can at least be said that the peculiar appeal of his poetry is perennial, despite its seemingly limited range. His irrepressible wit and *joie de vivre* are as appealing now as they have ever been.

Further Reading

Editions

The Poetical Works of Robert Herrick, ed. L.C. Martin (Oxford, 1956) is the standard edition, but *The Complete Poetry of Robert Herrick*, ed. J. Max Patrick (Garden City, NY, 1963) is a reliable and very convenient edition with fuller notes.

Critical Studies

Roger B. Rollin, *Robert Herrick*. rev. edn (New York, Toronto, ON, and Oxford, 1992) is an important account of Herrick's life and works, and an excellent introduction. Herrick has attracted a number of fine studies in recent years, a fact that is all the more surprising considering the seemingly limited range of his verse. Sydney Musgrove's brief but pioneering monograph *The Universe of Robert Herrick* (Auckland, 1950; reprinted Folcroft,

PA, 1971) is still worth reading, but it has been followed by a number of more ambitious accounts of *Hesperides*, in particular A. Leigh DeNeef's *'This Poetick Liturgie': Robert Herrick's ceremonial mode* (Durham, NC, 1974), an important examination of the 'poetic rituals' in *Hesperides*, and Robert H. Deming, *Ceremony and Art: Robert Herrick's poetry* (The Hague, 1974), which approaches the poetry through its courtly, pastoral, realistic and artistic ceremonial or ritualistic and festive elements, with an extensive treatment of social themes. Ann Baynes Coiro, *Robert Herrick's 'Hesperides' and the Epigram Book Tradition* (Baltimore, MD, 1988) is the only attempt to give a thoroughgoing account of the structure of Herrick's book.

Interesting shorter treatments are Joseph H. Summers, 'Gentlemen of the court and of art', in *The Heirs of Donne and Jonson* (New York, 1970), pp. 41–75, a succinct, balanced account; Austin Warren, 'Herrick revisited', *MQR*, **15** (1976), 245–67, the last word of a distinguished critic and scholar; and A.B. Chambers, 'Herrick and the trans-shifting of time', *SP*, **72** (1975), 85–114, which sees the metamorphic theme as contributing to Herrick's complex union of classical and Christian elements. Achsah Guibbory, 'The Temple of Hesperides and Anglican–Puritan controversy', in Claude J. Summers and Ted-Larry Pebworth, eds, *'The muses common-weale': Poetry and politics in the seventeenth century* (Columbia, MO, 1988), pp. 135–147; and Anthony Low, 'Robert Herrick: the religion of pleasure', in *Love's Architecture: Devotional modes in seventeenth-century English poetry* (New York, 1978), pp. 208–34 attempt to define Herrick's unique religious perspective. For an account of Martial's influence on Herrick, see Gordon Barden, *The Classics and English Renaissance Poetry* (New Haven, CT and London, 1978), pp. 180–94. A useful collection of essays on a wide variety of topics, including a helpful annotated selected bibliography, is Roger B. Rollin and J. Max Patrick, eds, *'Trust to Good Verses': Herrick tercentenary essays* (Pittsburgh, PA, 1978).

For treatments of individual poems, see Barbara H. Smith, *Poetic Closure: A study of how poems end* (Chicago and London, 1968), pp. 108–32 (analyses 'To the Virgins' and 'Argument of His Book'); A. Leigh DeNeef, 'Herrick's "Argument" and Thomas Bastard', *SCN*, **29** (1971), 9–10.

For Corinna, see Cleanth Brooks, 'What does poetry communicate?', in *The Well-Wrought Urn* (New York, 1947), pp. 62–9 (a classic analysis of 'Corinna's Going a-Maying', the basis for all later discussions); and, on the same poem, Frederick H. Candelaria, 'Ronsard and Herrick', *Notes and Queries*, n.s. 5 (1958), 286–7; J. Rea, 'Persephone in "Corinna's Going A-Maying"', *CE*, **26** (1965), 544–6; Phyllis Brooks Toback, 'Herrick's "Corinna's Going A-Maying" and the epithalamic tradition', *SCN*, **24** (1966), 13; Edward Le Comte, 'Herrick's Corinna', *Names: Journal of the American Name Society*, 33 (1985), 292–5; Mary Ellen Rickey, 'Herrick's "Corinna's Going a Maying"', *Explicator*, **40** (1982), 16–17.

Hugh Richmond, *The School of Love: The evolution of the Stuart love lyric* (Princeton, NJ, 1964) contains a good analysis of 'To the Virgins'. See also Virginia R. Mollenkott, '"Gather Ye Rosebuds": an expanded interpretation', *C&L*, **23** (1974), 47–8; and Sarah Gilead, 'Ungathering "Gather Ye Rosebuds": Herrick's misreading of carpe diem', *Criticism*, **27** (1985), 133–53; 'To the Virgins, To Make Much of Time' is also discussed in Madonne M. Miner, 'Gender, reading and misreadings', *Reader: Essays in reader oriented theory, criticism, and pedagogy*, **13** (1985), 10–18.

For Julia, see Ann Baynes Coiro, 'Herrick's "Julia" poems', *John Donne Journal*, **6** (1987), 67–89; Leo Spitzer, 'Herrick's "Delight in Disorder"', *MLN*, **76** (1961), 209–14; reprinted in *Essays on English and American Literature*, ed. Anna Hatcher (Princeton, NJ, 1962), pp. 132–8; R.J. Ross, 'Herrick's Julia in silks', *EIC*, **15** (1965), 171–80; Dale B.J. Randall, 'The Roman vibrations of Julia's clothes', *English Language Notes*, **21** (1984), 10–16; Robert F. Fleissner, '"Julia's Clothes" Retailored', *Cahiers Elisabéthains*, **28** (1985), 73–6. Still a highly readable biography is Marchette Chute, *Two Gentle Men: The lives of George Herbert and Robert Herrick* (New York, 1959; London, 1960).

64 / *The Argument of His Book*

I sing of brooks, of blossoms, birds, and bowers,
Of April, May, of June, and July flowers.
I sing of Maypoles, hock carts, wassails, wakes,
Of bridegrooms, brides, and of their bridal cakes.
I write of youth, of love, and have access
By these to sing of cleanly wantonness.
I sing of dews, of rains, and, piece by piece,
Of balm, of oil, of spice, and ambergris.
I sing of times trans-shifting, and I write
How roses first came red and lilies white.
I write of groves, of twilights, and I sing
The court of Mab and of the fairy king.
I write of hell; I sing (and ever shall)
Of heaven, and hope to have it after all.

Herrick's introduction offers a summary of his main themes in pentameter couplets. The Garden of the Hesperides, alluded to in the title of the book, was a mythological sacred grove containing golden fruit and presided over by the goddess Juno. It is also a kind of Garden of Eden to which poetry and imagination are the means of access. Most of his poetic themes are therefore pastoral in nature, connected with the rural landscape and the activities of the countryside rather than with urban or sophisticated courtly life.

Title
Argument subject; ***His Book*** Herrick's poetry was published in one book as two parts, *Hesperides* (for the non-religious poems) and *His Noble Numbers* (for the religious ones); this poem serves as introduction to the whole.

[1] **I sing of**
'I tell of' – a traditional formula for opening a long poem, though this poem was obviously meant to be read or recited rather than sung; nevertheless, lyric poetry implies, by its nature, at least a suggestion of some sort of musical connection; ***brooks . . . bowers*** i.e. subjects having to do with nature (***bower*** a space enclosed by leafy branches; a shady recess).

[2] **April . . . July**
the blooming season in England; ***July*** pronounced to rhyme with 'truly'.

[3] **Maypoles . . . wakes**
various social customs practised in rural communities during the period; ***Maypole*** a tall pole, painted with varicoloured spiral stripes and decorated with flowers, placed in an open space as the focal point of May Day festivities; ***hock cart*** the celebration wagon that carried home the last fruits of the harvest; ***wassail*** a salutation used in presenting a cup or drinking a person's health (literally 'be fortunate' or 'be of good health'); ***wake*** a parish festival.

[6] **by**
by means of (youth and love); ***cleanly wantonness*** chaste unchastity, an oxymoron with not a few ambiguities – ***cleanly*** (a) spiritually or morally innocent, pure, sinless; but also (b) clever, neatly executed, elegant in language, artful; ***wantonness*** (a) lust,

lasciviousness or naughtiness; (b) revelry, extravagance of behaviour or language; (c) whim, unrestrained licence of imagination. As a priest of the Church of England, Herrick defends his subject matter by reminding his reader that this poetry is a celebration of innocence and natural freedom.

[7] **piece by piece**
in succession.

[8] **balm**
any aromatic fragrance or ointment; ***ambergris*** a wax-like, fragrant excretion from whales used in perfume-making.

[9] **times trans-shifting**
(a) the changing of the various seasons; (b) the temporary nature of all things subject to time (***times*** time's); (c) metamorphosis (a classical theme, derived principally from Ovid, the Roman author of *Metamorphoses*); (d) changes in circumstances (***trans-shifting*** moving across or away).

[10] **came**
became, came to be; stories of this sort, which deal with the causes or origins of things, are called 'aetiological' and are frequent in myth, legend and fable.

[12] **Mab . . . fairy king**
Herrick wrote a number of poems on English fairies; Queen Mab also appears in Milton's 'L'Allegro' (see p. 371, line 102 and note).

[13–14] **I write . . . after all**
A reference to the poems on religious themes in *His Noble Numbers*.

[13] **after all**
(a) when life is over; (b) in spite of any sins he may have committed.

65 / *The Vine*

I dreamed this mortal part of mine
Was metamorphosed to a vine,
Which, crawling one and every way,
Enthralled my dainty Lucia.
Methought her long small legs and thighs
I, with my tendrils, did surprise:
Her belly, buttocks, and her waist
By my soft nervelets were embraced.
About her head I writhing hung,
And with rich clusters (hid among
The leaves) her temples I behung,
So that my Lucia seemed to me
Young Bacchus ravished by his tree.
My curls about her neck did crawl,
And arms and hands they did enthral,
So that she could not freely stir
(All parts there made one prisoner).

But when I crept with leaves to hide
Those parts which maids keep unespied,
Such fleeting pleasures there I took,
That with the fancy I awoke
And found (Ah, me!) this flesh of mine
More like a stock than like a vine.

A humorous, self-deprecating poem in tetrameter couplets that sums up the probable extent of the poet's erotic experiences.

[1] **mortal part**
his body.
[4] **Enthralled**
(a) imprisoned, captured; (b) captivated, held spellbound; ***Lucia*** pronounced as three syllables.
[8] **nervelets**
tendrils.
[9–11] **About . . . behung**
Note the triple rhyme.
[11] **behung**
overhung, festooned.
[14] **Bacchus**
The Graeco-Roman god of wine, revelry and licentiousness; ***tree*** the grape vine, associated with Bacchus.
[19] **unespied**
unseen (out of modesty).
[20] **fleeting pleasures**
brief, like all sexual pleasures.
[21] **fancy**
image or imagined situation.
[22] **flesh of mine**
(a) his body; (b) his penis.
[23] **stock**
(a) the hardened stalk or stem of a plant (with sexual implications); (b) a block of wood, hence something lifeless, motionless or void of sensation; (c) the lower part of a grape vine that is left after the harvest, when the upper branches have been cut away.

66 / *Delight in Disorder*

A sweet disorder in the dress
Kindles in clothes a wantonness.
A lawn about the shoulders thrown
Into a fine distraction;
An erring lace, which here and there
Enthrals the crimson stomacher;
A cuff neglectful and, thereby,
Ribbons to flow confusedly;
A winning wave, deserving note,
In the tempestuous petticoat;
A careless shoestring, in whose tie
I see a wild civility,
Do more bewitch me than when art
Is too precise in every part.

A short lyric in tetrameter couplets that recalls lines in Jonson's 'Still to be neat' (p. 149), which probably inspired it.

[1] **sweet disorder**
Note the oxymoron; ***dress*** apparel, clothing.
[2] **kindles**
(a) sets on fire; (b) encourages, suggests; (c) impassions (observe that the passion is attributed to the clothing, not to the onlooker); ***wantonness*** (a) lust, lasciviousness or naughtiness; (b) revelry, extravagance of behaviour or language; (c) whim, unrestrained licence of imagination (as in 'The Argument of His Book', note to line 6 above).
[3] **lawn**
a kind of fine linen, used here as a shawl.
[3–4] **thrown/Into . . .**
merely tossed over the shoulders.
[4] **fine distraction**
another oxymoron; ***fine*** (a) perfect, excellent, accomplished; (b) delicate, subtle, refined; (c) ornate, showy; (d) good-looking, handsome; ***distraction*** (a) a pulling asunder, stretching, or dispersion; (b) diversion of the mind or attention; (c) disorder or confusion caused by conflicting forces or emotions – observe how the word can be applied to the physical disposition of the shawl as well as the mental disposition of the onlooker.
[5] **erring**
(a) deviating from the right moral course or conduct; (b) wandering in a physical sense, moving aimlessly.
[6] **Enthrals**
(a) enslaves, holds in bondage; (b) captivates, holds spellbound by pleasing qualities; ***stomacher*** a covering for the chest, often ornamented or decorated with jewels, and worn by women under the bodice lacing.
[7] **cuff**
cuffs were not always attached to the end of the sleeve but were often separate strips of linen worn around the wrist and under the sleeve; ***neglectful*** unattended to, carelessly worn; ***thereby*** (a) attached to; (b) as a result; (c) in addition.
[9] **winning**
(a) alluring, attractive; (b) conquering, triumphing; (c) contending; ***note*** (a) attention; (b) renown.
[10] **tempestuous**
(a) resembling a tempest; (b) impetuous, passionate; ***petticoat*** an ornamented skirt, worn on the outside (rather than inside, like the present-day slip).
[11] **careless**
(a) untied, unattended to; (b) without care or concern.
[12] **wild civility**
yet another oxymoron; ***wild*** (a) untamed, natural; (b) ill-mannered, improperly behaved; ***civility*** (a) urbanity, proper behaviour, refinement of culture or manners; (b) thoughtfulness towards others.
[13] **bewitch**
echoes 'enthral' in sense (b); ***art*** as opposed to nature or natural behaviour – (a) use of artificial expedients; (b) skill in dressing for display; (c) studied conduct or actions, cunning, artfulness.
[14] **precise**
(a) perfect, complete; (b) exact, meticulous, correct; (c) strict, puritanical.

67 / *Corinna's Going a-Maying*

Get up! get up for shame! the blooming morn
Upon her wings presents the god unshorn!
See how Aurora throws her fair
Fresh quilted colours through the air!
Get up, sweet slug-a-bed, and see
The dew bespangling herb and tree!
Each flower has wept and bowed toward the east
Above an hour since, yet you not dressed –
Nay, not so much as out of bed?
When all the birds have matins said
And sung their thankful hymns, 'tis sin,
Nay, profanation to keep in,
Whenas a thousand virgins on this day
Spring, sooner than the lark, to fetch in May.

Rise and put on your foliage and be seen
To come forth like the springtime, fresh and green
And sweet as Flora. Take no care
For jewels for your gown or hair;
Fear not; the leaves will strew
Gems in abundance upon you;
Besides, the childhood of the day has kept,
Against you come, some orient pearls unwept.
Come, and receive them while the light
Hangs on the dew-locks of the night,
And Titan, on the eastern hill,
Retires himself or else stands still
Till you come forth. Wash, dress, be brief in praying;
Few beads are best when once we go a-Maying.

Come my Corinna, come, and, coming, mark
How each field turns a street, each street a park
Made green and trimmed with trees, see how
Devotion gives each house a bough
Or branch; each porch, each door ere this,
An ark, a tabernacle is,
Made up of whitethorn neatly interwove,
As if here were those cooler shades of love.

Can such delights be in the street
And open fields, and we not see 't?
Come, we'll abroad, and let's obey
The proclamation made for May
And sin no more, as we have done, by staying,
But my Corinna, come, let's go a-Maying.

There's not a budding boy or girl this day
But is got up and gone to bring in May.
A deal of youth, ere this, is come
Back and with whitethorn laden home.
Some have dispatched their cakes and cream
Before that we have left to dream,
And some have wept and wooed and plighted troth
And chose their priest, ere we can cast off sloth.
Many a green-gown has been given,
Many a kiss, both odd and even;
Many a glance, too, has been sent
From out the eye, love's firmament;
Many a jest told of the keys betraying
This night, and locks picked, yet we're not
a-Maying.

Come, let us go while we are in our prime
And take the harmless folly of the time.
We shall grow old apace and die
Before we know our liberty.
Our life is short, and our days run
As fast away as does the sun;
And, as a vapour or a drop of rain,
Once lost, can ne'er be found again,
So when or you or I are made
A fable, song, or fleeting shade,
All love, all liking, all delight
Lies drowned with us in endless night.
Then while time serves and we are but decaying,
Come, my Corinna, come, let's go a-Maying.

Herrick's most famous poem and one of the major lyrics of the English language, this piece illustrates the classical theme of *carpe diem*, 'seize the day', a popular motif in Renaissance poetry in imitation of poets like Horace, from whom the phrase derives and whose light-hearted advice to enjoy the present and live for today is very much taken to heart in Herrick's non-religious poetry. The unabashed pleasure he takes in the celebration of spring and the natural world does not clash in any way with Herrick's religious convictions, though it could not have gone down very well with his Puritan contemporaries. The stanzaic form consists of seven rhyming couplets of varying line lengths. The first, fourth and seventh couplets are pentameters; the others, enclosed by them, are tetrameters.

Title
Corinna The name occurs with some frequency in Greek and Latin poetry, and is used here for a girl who was doubtless imaginary; ***a-Maying*** the May Day celebrations were a remnant of pagan practices that survive in various attenuated forms in modern times; they were essentially fertility rites, performed to ensure the success of the crops by invoking the tutelary gods and goddesses of the spring.

[1] **Get up**
The speaker is to be imagined as addressing the sleeping girl from outside her bedroom window and inviting her to join him there (normally, a lover would seek entry to her room for a less 'innocent' purpose than a stroll through the landscape); ***blooming morn*** the dawn.

[2] **her wings**
a personification of morning as a bird, but also an allusion to Aurora, the goddess of the dawn, who flies in bearing the sun, i.e. ***the god unshorn***; ***unshorn*** (a) untrimmed, uncropped (the sun's rays are imagined as flowing hair); (b) not reduced or diminished, not deprived of anything; (c) unharvested (crops or fields) – this last meaning ties in with the following images of the growth, plenty, and as yet unharvested bounty of nature.

[4] **quilted colours**
multicoloured hues, like a patchwork quilt; but note, as well, that Aurora has thrown *off* her quilt, as the speaker is inviting the sleeping girl to do.

[5] **slug-a-bed**
a lazy person who sleeps too late; since *slug* (or sluggard) is a slow, lazy person in a pejorative sense, the phrase ***sweet slug-a-bed*** is something of an oxymoron.

[6] **bespangling**
sprinkling with small glittering objects, another indication of the early hour – not only has the morning dew not yet evaporated, but the early-morning sun strikes it obliquely and causes it to gleam.

[7] **Each flower . . . east**
as though they were saying morning prayers to the rising sun (in the east); ***wept*** (a) expressed remorse for their sins; (b) shed the dew that hung on them from the cool night.

[8] **Above . . . since**
i.e. at least an hour ago.

[10] **matins**
(a) the morning call or song of birds; (b) public morning prayers in the Church of England.

[11] **hymns**
continuing the double sense of ***matins***; ***sin*** a humorous suggestion of neglect of public and sacred duty (***matins*** also meant a morning duty, occupation or performance).

[12] **profanation**
Though the custom of welcoming in May was a survival of pagan times and regarded as a secular ceremony, Herrick pretends that it is still part of sacred ritual; ***keep in*** stay in.

[13] **Whenas**
Seeing that; ***virgins*** unmarried girls.

[14] **Spring**
Jump up vigorously (like the lark), with a pun on the season; ***to fetch in May*** (a) to meet and escort the spring on its arrival; (b) to celebrate the fertility of the season by making love.

[15] **foliage**
(a) clothes; (b) pristine appearance, like the leaves on the trees; note the

suggestion of naturalness even in dress.

[17] **Flora**
the Roman goddess of flowers and personification of Nature's power to produce them.

[19–20] **leaves . . . upon you**
i.e. by scattering dew on her.

[21] **childhood**
early morning; ***kept*** reserved.

[22] **Against you come**
In preparation for your coming; ***orient pearls unwept*** some unevaporated dew, here compared with precious jewels from the East.

[24] **dew-locks**
an image rich in meanings; it suggests (a) the dew-soaked hair of the god of Night, whose departure is held back by the hesitation of the light; (b) dew held back by the sluicegate of night, about to be opened by the rising sun; (c) moisture locked up during the night and about to be released at dawn.

[25] **Titan**
the sun personified as Sol, the sun-god of Roman mythology.

[26] **Retires himself**
Withdraws or hides himself.

[28] **beads**
(a) prayers, religious devotions; (b) the rosary, a string of one hundred and sixty-five beads, each representing a prayer in a repetitive sequence and serving to keep track of one's place in it.

[30] **turns**
(a) turns into, becomes; (b) faces.

[31] **trimmed**
decorated, ornamented.

[32] **Devotion**
Careful attention (but with a religious overtone suggesting worship of the spring goddess).

[33] **ere this**
before this moment.

[34] **ark**
a wooden box containing the tables of the law in the Old Testament; it was kept in the holiest part of the temple; ***tabernacle*** (a) a portable sanctuary, consisting of a curtained tent containing the Ark of the Covenant, which accompanied the Israelites during their wanderings in the desert; (b) an ornamented enclosure where the consecrated host (in Roman Catholic ritual) is kept; (c) a temporary place of worship or meeting-house used by Protestant Nonconformists.

[35] **whitethorn**
a form of hawthorn, a small, thorny tree bearing white blossoms; ***interwove*** interwoven.

[36] **As if here . . . love**
The love that is celebrated on May Day is not the wild, passionate variety but the more stately, public and ceremonial presence of a natural force that pervades the whole world at springtime.

[38] **see 't**
see it (the whole scene).

[39] **we'll abroad**
we'll go outside.

[40] **proclamation**
(a) the command to go forth and celebrate the season (see also, in Genesis 1, the Creator's command to the world: 'Be fertile and multiply'); (b) the public ceremonies acknowledging the arrival of May.

[41] **sin no more**
Compare with the biblical 'Go, and sin no more' (John 8: 11) and line 11 above.

[43] **budding**
(a) beginning to grow or develop; (b) coming forth, emerging.

[44] **got up**
(a) arisen; and, possibly, (b) appropriately adorned or clothed for the season.

[45] **deal of youth**
a large number of young people; ***ere this*** before now.

[47] **dispatched**
eaten up completely.

[49] **wept . . . troth**
Three stages of falling in love: (a) weeping or expressing frustrated longing for the beloved; (b) wooing; (c) plighting troth or promising to love faithfully.

[50] **chose their priest**
to marry them; ***ere . . . sloth*** before we have overcome our laziness.
[51] **green-gown . . . given**
i.e. by rolling the girl on the grass in sport so that her gown is stained green, a euphemism for making love with a girl.
[52] **odd and even**
i.e. a kiss returned or not.
[54] **From out the eye**
It was believed that sight emanated from beams in the eye which met the object viewed; ***firmament*** (a) firm foundation; (b) the outermost heavenly sphere where the fixed stars are placed; (c) the heaven where God dwells.
[55] **jest**
(a) an idle tale; (b) a trivial or merry story; ***keys betraying*** i.e. the lover was given access to the girl's room by being provided with a secret key.
[56] **locks picked**
i.e. the lover opened the door and entered the room without being given a key.
[57] **prime**
(a) six o'clock, the first hour of the day, or at sunrise; (b) the beginning or first age of something; (c) the spring-time of life, from about age twenty-one to twenty-eight; (d) the period of greatest vigour, before strength and beauty begin to wane.
[58] **harmless folly**
an attack on Puritanism, which disapproved of such 'pagan' practices as bringing in May; the poet argues that these activities are indeed folly, but not evil or particularly licentious; ***folly*** (a) foolishness; (b) lewdness; (c) wickedness, mischief or harm; (d) sin or wrong-doing; they are offered as current popular practice (***of the time***) without any particular moral implications.
[59] **apace**
quickly.
[60] **liberty**
(a) exemption from tyrannical or despotic control; (b) freedom from the bondage of sin or the law; (c) release from captivity (including remaining indoors); (d) power to do as one likes; (e) freedom of behaviour or speech.
[65–6] **you or I . . . shade**
i.e. after we have died and remain only as memories; ***fable*** story; ***fleeting shade*** ghost; this sentiment is frequently expressed in Greek and Roman poetry – the lovers will soon be no more than names in a tale or song.
[67–8] **All . . . night**
A paraphrase of 'once our brief sun is extinguished, our night will be one long sleep', lines 3–4 of 'Vivamus, mea Lesbia atque amemus' ('Lesbia, let us live and love'), a poem by the Roman poet Catullus.
[69] **serves**
(a) profits, is useful; (b) assists, waits on, or obeys someone; (c) is available; (d) is profitable, usable towards some end; ***decaying*** (a) growing older; (b) slowly moving towards death.

68 / *To the Virgins, To Make Much of Time*

Gather ye rosebuds while ye may,
Old time is still a-flying;
And this same flower that smiles today,
Tomorrow will be dying.

The glorious lamp of heaven, the sun,
The higher he's a-getting,
The sooner will his race be run,
And nearer he's to setting.

That age is best which is the first,
When youth and blood are warmer;
But being spent, the worse, and worst
Times still succeed the former.

Then be not coy, but use your time,
And while ye may, go marry;
For having lost but once your prime,
You may for ever tarry.

A classic example, in four tetrameter quatrains rhyming *a b a b*, of the *carpe diem* theme, inspired by Horace and other Roman poets in imagery, phrase and sentiment.

Title
Virgins young, unmarried girls; ***Make . . . Time*** (a) use their time wisely; (b) take seriously the fact that time passes.

[1] **rosebuds**
Since the rose is often evoked in poetry as a flower that is beautiful for no more than a day, the poet advises young girls to pluck rosebuds (i.e. roses that have not yet bloomed), which will last a little longer. Rosebuds are also symbolic of the young virgins themselves.

[3] **smiles**
blooms, is happy in its beauty.

[5] **glorious lamp of heaven**
a familiar epithet for the sun in poetry.

[9] **age . . . first**
It was thought that the earliest age of humankind was the Golden Age, a time when people lived in harmony with nature and the gods, and that our subsequent history is one of gradual decline from perfection.

[10] **warmer**
(a) more vigorous, agile; (b) more passionate; heat and fire were thought to be present in the blood in varying degrees.

[11] **spent**
used up, exhausted.

[13] **coy**
(a) shy; (b) not responding readily to a man's advances; ***use your time*** i.e. take advantage of your youth.

[14] **marry**
Greek and Roman poets often urged young girls to enjoy the fruits of love while they were young, but Herrick's

advice is characterised by a certain propriety that his models do not often express.

[15] **prime**
See 'Corinna's Going a-Maying', line 57 and note.

[16] **tarry**
(a) wait for someone to marry you; (b) await death alone.

69 / *Upon Julia's Clothes*

Whenas in silks my Julia goes,
Then, then, methinks, how sweetly flows
That liquefaction of her clothes.

Next, when I cast mine eyes and see
That brave vibration each way free,
Oh, how that glittering taketh me!

A poem in the form of two monorhyming tetrameter triplets, another piece possibly inspired by Jonson's 'Still to be neat' (p. 149) but emphasising the positive aspects of natural attractiveness.

[1] **Whenas**
Whenever; ***in silks*** wearing silk garments, which were considered exotic and luxurious imports.

[2] **methinks**
it appears to me, seems to me.

[3] **liquefaction**
A brilliant choice of word, with multiple implications: (a) turning into a liquid; (b) dissolution; (c) release from stiffness and restraint – the silks defy both the properties of solid matter and the purpose of clothes (to conceal the body), but they also suggest openness, freedom, unconventionality, easiness, and an ability to move readily from one state to another.

[5] **brave**
(a) splendid, showy; (b) excellent, handsome; (c) daring; ***vibration*** (a) any quivering or tremulous motion or movement up and down or from side to side; and, possibly, the later sense of (b) vacillation or variation in respect to opinion or conduct; contemporary science held that physical vibrations were transmitted internally by way of the nerves – thus Julia's vibrations move the poet's emotions not only figuratively but literally.

[6] **glittering**
(a) tremulous or varying display of light; (b) showiness, splendour of appearance, brilliance; ***taketh*** (a) strikes, draws attention, catches the eye; (b) captures, enthrals, engages; (c) delights, charms, excites a liking in – note that Herrick's central theme is the old one of the lover who is 'enslaved' by the freedom of the lady's motions.

70 / *Upon the Nipples of Julia's Breast*

Have ye beheld (with much delight)
A red rose peeping through a white?
Or else a cherry (double graced)
Within a lily's centred place?
Or ever marked the pretty beam
A strawberry shows half drowned in cream?
Or seen rich rubies blushing through
A pure, smooth pearl – and orient too?
So like to this, nay, all the rest,
Is each neat niplet of her breast.

A brief poem in the '*blason*' tradition of praising a single aspect of a woman's body.

[2] **red rose peeping**
a red rose showing through the petals of a white rose or, less probably, the delicate reddishness at the centre of the freshly blooming white petals.
[3] **double graced**
by its own beauty and that of the surrounding lily.
[5] **beam**
a gleam of colour, such as a ray of sunlight shining through a cloud. Note that this is the only image of the four that one might possibly experience; the rest are largely imaginative.
[7] **blushing through**
Herrick may mean that the colour of the ruby is reflected by the polished surface of the pearl.
[8] **orient**
a brilliant or precious pearl from the Indian seas.
[10] **neat**
(a) clean, pure; (b) clear, bright; (c) elegant, precisely placed; ***niplet*** (a) small nipple; (b) little bit (nip).

71 / *The Funeral Rites of the Rose*

The rose was sick and, smiling, died
And (being to be sanctified)
About the bed, there sighing stood
The sweet and flowery sisterhood.
Some hung the head, while some did bring
(To wash her) water from the spring.
Some laid her forth, while other wept,
But all a solemn fast there kept.
The holy sisters some among
The sacred dirge and trental sung.

But ah! what sweets smelled everywhere,
As heaven had spent all perfumes there.
At last, when prayers for the dead
And rites were all accomplishèd,
They, weeping, spread a lawny loom
And closed her up, as in a tomb.

The rose is the traditional symbol of fragility and transitoriness, particularly in relation to love and feminine beauty, but it has also been associated with the divine and the holy (i.e. Dante's mystic rose in *The Divine Comedy*). This whimsical account in tetrameter couplets suggests all these themes, but it also presents a natural world that has a kind of sanctity and charitableness, cares for itself, and leads to holiness. It presents a small image of Herrick's view of the nature he celebrates.

[1] **smiling**
flowers are often said to 'smile' metaphorically.
[2] **being to be**
about to be; ***sanctified*** (a) taken up to heaven; (b) declared a saint.
[3] **bed**
(a) deathbed; (b) flower bed.
[4] **sisterhood**
(a) surrounding flowers; (b) nuns.
[5] **hung the head**
in mourning.
[6] **to wash her**
i.e. to prepare her body for burial; ***spring*** (a) river or fountain; (b) season of rain showers.
[7] **laid her forth**
laid out the corpse; ***other*** others.
[8] **solemn fast**
abstention from food in honour of the dead.
[9] **holy sisters some among**
some from among the 'nuns'.
[10] **dirge**
song sung at the burial; ***trental*** an elegy or dirge, originally a set of thirty requiem Masses.
[12] **spent**
exhausted.
[15] **lawny**
(a) made of fine linen; (b) made of grass; ***loom*** (a) web, shroud; (b) loam (? as a pun).

72 / *His Prayer to Ben Jonson*

When I a verse shall make,
Know I have prayed thee,
For old religion's sake,
Saint Ben, to aid me.

Make the way smooth for me
When I, thy Herrick,

Honouring thee, on my knee,
Offer my lyric.

Candles I'll give thee
And a new altar;
And thou Saint Ben shall be
Writ in my psalter.

In this amusing little poem, consisting of three trimeter quatrains rhyming *a b a b* with feminine rhymes in every other verse, Herrick pays a tribute to his old friend and master Ben Jonson, with a typical jocular touch that exaggerates yet graciously acknowledges his influence.

Title
Prayer Herrick offers this mock-prayer in a spirit of fun, but he is serious to the extent that he esteemed Jonson's person and poetry very highly.
[2] **I have prayed thee**
(a) prayed to you; (b) begged you. Jonson is made to play a role that combines the intercessory powers of the Roman Catholic saint with the inspiring powers of the poetic Muse. It was believed that one could pray to saints not as divinities but as sympathetic listeners in heaven who might pray to God on one's behalf.
[3] **old religion's sake**
i.e. out of respect for the 'old' religion (i.e. Roman Catholicism), with which Herrick, as a High Churchman and a man with a lifelong interest in rituals and folklore, had some sympathy.
[4] **Saint Ben**
Since Jonson was not particularly noted for his piety, it is obvious that this 'canonisation' or designation of sainthood is the consequence of his poetic achievement.
[6] **thy Herrick**
The expression parodies the intimacy of the language of prayer.
[7] **on my knee**
One goes down on one knee before a person, on two to pray before God.
[8] **Offer my lyric**
an appropriate thing to offer a 'saint' whose inspiration has made it come into being.
[8–10] **Candles . . . altar**
Although it was considered permissible to make an offering gesture before a shrine honouring a saint, Herrick's attitude is more appropriate for a worshipper before the shrine of a pagan god, to whom such inducements were often proffered in a quasi-contractual fashion in return for requested favours. The poem is an amusing illustration of Herrick's way of combining classical and Christian modes.
[12] **psalter**
an edition of the Psalms arranged for devotional recitation or singing; here understood more generally as a book of liturgical hymns or prayers. To enter the name of a dead person into the psalter would be to declare him or her an official saint – in other words, to canonise them, as Herrick implies Jonson should be honoured among poets.

73 / *Upon His Verses*

What offspring other men have got,
The how, where, when I question not.
These are the children I have left,
Adopted some, none got by theft.
But all are touched (like lawful plate),
And no verse illegitimate.

This epigrammatic piece in three tetrameter couplets is a defence of Herrick's originality despite his obvious dependence on classical and other models.

[1] **offspring**
(a) children, progeny; (b) figuratively, the products of the imagination; ***have got*** (a) begotten, caused to be conceived; (b) possess.
[2] **how, where, when**
The traditional questions one poses concerning the cause or origin of things.
[3] **these**
i.e. these poems; ***I have left*** (a) that still remain to me; (b) that I have brought into the world; (c) that will survive my death.
[4] **Adopted**
An adopted child, though not biologically related to the adoptive parents, is considered by law to have the same rights and relationship as physical offspring; Herrick is referring to those poems which are imitated or translated from other poets and distinguishing his 'adoptions' (i.e. making them his own by reimagining them) from mere theft (i.e. plagiarism); imitation of ancient poets was considered an honourable, even prestigious practice throughout the century and even later; ***theft*** fairies were said to steal newborn children from their cradles.
[5] **touched**
(a) tested for quality or genuineness (gold or silver) by being rubbed against a touchstone; (b) officially stamped to indicate that the gold or silver is of standard fineness; and, possibly, (c) submitted, in the case of an engraving or reproduction of a picture, to the original artist for his approval; ***lawful*** (a) sanctioned, recognised by law (as in 'lawful heir'); (b) designated or approved by law (as in 'lawful money'); (c) legitimate (as in 'lawful matrimony' or 'lawful offspring'; ***plate*** (a) a piece of money, precious metal; (b) an authorised engraving; (c) tableware, dishes, etc.
[6] **verse illegitimate**
Note the turn from metaphor (children) to literal subject (poetry) which, as a defence of poetic practice, echoes the opening 'Argument of His Book' and anticipates the moral defence advanced in 'To His Book's End'.

74 / *The Pillar of Fame*

Fame's pillar here, at last, we set
Out-during marble, brass, or jet,
Charmed and enchanted so,
As to withstand the blow
Of overthrow.
Nor shall the seas
Or outrages
Of storms o'erbear
What we uprear.
Though kingdoms fall.
This pillar never shall
Decline or waste at all
But stand forever by his own
Firm and well-fixed foundation.

A 'shaped poem' (see Herbert's 'Easter Wings', (p. 202) in diminishing and expanding lines of tetrameter, trimeter and dimeter couplets. It echoes the motif of everlasting renown in the Roman poet Horace's 'Exegi monumentum' and Shakespeare's Sonnets (see the note for Waller's 'Of English Verse' [p. 307] line 13, where the opposing sentiment is expressed). The Romans erected commemorative columns to celebrate the achievements of famous men.

[2] **Out-during**
outlasting (out-enduring); ***jet*** black marble. See also the poems of Horace (*Odes* 1.30) and Shakespeare (Sonnet 55) mentioned in the introduction.

[3] **Charmed**
protected by magic; ***enchanted*** preserved by a spell.

[14] **foundation**
pronounced in four syllables.

75 / *To His Book's End*

To his book's end this last line he'd have placed:
Jocund his muse was, but his life was chaste.

Herrick's last words of apology for his poetic content in a single pentameter couplet.

[1] **To his book's end**
(a) to the last page of the book; (b) to express the purpose of the book; (c) for the sake of his book – the ending of the book is both a final statement of its author's purpose in writing it and

a defence of that purpose; ***he'd have*** he would like to have, he insists on having.

[2] **Jocund**

mirthful, jolly, glad, sprightly, light-hearted, pleasant; ***muse*** (a) inspiration; (b) imagination; ***his life was chaste*** i.e. (a) he never indulged literally in the activities his poetry describes; (b) he remained sexually pure – Herrick's avowed purpose in his book is to celebrate life and its pleasures in opposition to the narrower and somewhat dour outlook of his Puritan contemporaries.

THOMAS CAREW

(1594 or 1595–1640)

1640 *Poems*
1642 *Poems* (2nd edn, posthumous)
1651 *Poems. With a Maske.*

Thomas Carew (probably pronounced 'Carey') was born sometime during the twelve months between June 1594 and June 1595, presumably at his parents' estate at West Wickham, Kent. In 1598 the family moved to London. In 1608 he matriculated at Merton College Oxford, taking his BA on 31 January 1611; the following year he received a BA from Cambridge and began to study law. A year later his family suffered financial difficulties, and Thomas became secretary to Sir Dudley Carleton, English Ambassador to Venice, where, during a year-and-a-half-long stay, he learned Italian. Unfortunately, Carew managed to offend his employer during a subsequent embassy to The Hague, and he returned home to seek his fortune at court after further attempts to secure another position failed. In 1619 he accompanied Sir Edward Herbert (also a poet) on an embassy to Paris and became a close friend of John Crofts, whose estate was celebrated in several poems. During this time he began to associate with Jonson and his 'tribe', and to seek his fortune at court. After a scheme to marry a widow failed in late 1624, he finally succeeded in obtaining a position at court as a steward in the royal household, where he became well known as a witty poet and courtier. He was able to live a life of some ease from that time on, though he had a reputation for scandalous behaviour and licentious writings that seems to have caused him problems throughout his career. He participated in the expedition against Scotland that King Charles I led in 1639 (The First Bishops' War); and he died, perhaps from the physical hardships he encountered in it, in the early spring of 1640.

Context

Carew was influenced by both Ben Jonson and John Donne, as well as by the sonneteers of the late Elizabethan period, French and Italian poets of the sixteenth and early seventeenth centuries, and the Latin love poets of Antiquity. However, his poetry mostly reflects his own literary personality: witty, detached and worldly. He seems to have been a careful craftsman, drawing on the example of his master Jonson, no doubt, to create verses that read smoothly but conceal the labour invested in them. Like Donne, he makes use of surprising images and metaphors, and enjoys deflating the exaggerations of Petrarchan conventions, but he does so with a more even and courtly tone. Though he is usually grouped along with Suckling and Lovelace as a 'Cavalier' poet, and with them and others as a 'Son of Ben', he was a great admirer of Donne. His poems, however, are overwhelmingly secular and avoid, for the most part, any very weighty topics; the religious tradition – with the exception of a few poems, supposedly composed when he thought he was dying – has little place in his work.

Genre

Carew was almost exclusively a lyric poet. The author of at least 130 poems which include – surprisingly – translations from the Psalms, he favoured the rhyming couplet, iambic rhythms, and the six-line stanza. He wrote an almost equal number of poems in tetrameter and pentameter. He was also the author of a masque, *Coelum Britannicum*, performed in 1634.

Critical Reception

Carew was little published during his lifetime, but his poems circulated, like many others, in manuscript and gained him a reputation for salaciousness (based mostly, it seems, on 'A Rapture'), though they were extremely popular during the last decade of his life. The posthumous edition of his poems was denounced in the House of Commons, but Carew continued to influence later poets. Interest in him declined towards the end of the century, but eighteenth-century poets admired him for the regularity of his metre, the precision of his craft, the even civility of his tone, and the smoothness of his style. Alexander Pope drew on his poetry and considered him one of the fore-runners of the Augustan style, though he called him 'a bad Waller'. (Perhaps it was the 'Metaphysical' element that he found objectionable, though it was the versification that he criticised.) Carew fared even less well with nineteenth-century readers, and it was not until the revival of interest in the Metaphysical poets around 1920 that some of his earlier stature was recovered. Even so, his writings have attracted only a modest body of criticism and scholarship.

Further Reading

Edition

The Poems of Thomas Carew with His Masque Coelum Britannicum, ed. Dunlap Rhodes (Oxford, 1949; reprinted 1970). The standard edition.

Critical Studies

F.R. Leavis, *Revaluation: Tradition and development in English poetry* (London, 1936; reprinted 1959) made a key reassessment of Carew's place in English poetry which helped to establish him in the canon of important, albeit minor, followers of Donne and Jonson. Edward I. Selig, *The Flourishing Wreath: A study of Thomas Carew's poetry* (New Haven, CT, 1958; reprinted Hamden, CT, 1970) is a spirited defence of the poet and a thorough study of his genres that presents Carew as an excellent poet within the limitations of his language, style and genre. Lynn Sadler, *Thomas Carew* (Boston, MA, 1979) is a more recent monograph that offers general coverage of the life and works; it includes an annotated bibliography. L.L. Martz, 'Thomas Carew: the Cavalier world', in *The Wit of Love: Donne, Carew, Crashaw, Marvell* (South Bend, IN, 1969), pp. 61–110, is a briefer but equally important account.

A number of essays, while not exclusively devoted to Carew, are helpful for showing his relationship to contemporary writers and thinkers: R.A. Blanshard emphasises his originality in 'Thomas Carew and the Cavalier poets'. *Transactions of the Wisconsin Academy of Sciences, Arts, and Letters,* **43** (1954), 97–106, and 'Thomas Carew's Master Figures', *BUSE,* **3** (1957), 214–27. Carew's debt to Jonson is explored by the same author in 'Carew and Jonson', *SP,* **52** (1955), 195–211. Robin Skelton, *Cavalier Poets* (London, 1960) presents Carew as the quintessential cavalier; while Hugh M. Richmond, *The School of Love: The evolution of the Stuart love lyric* (Princeton, NJ, 1964) places Carew within the traditions and context of the seventeenth-century love lyric, and discusses several individual poems; as do Joseph H. Summers, *The Heirs of Donne and Jonson* (New York and London, 1970) and Earl Miner, *The Cavalier Mode from Jonson to Cotton* (Princeton, NJ, 1971). An interesting and fresh perspective is offered by Donald Bruce. 'The war poets of 1639: Carew, Suckling and Lovelace', *Contemporary Review,* **259** (1991), 309–14.

On Carew as love poet, see, in addition to Richmond, G.A.E. Parfitt, 'The poetry of Thomas Carew'. *RMS,* **12** (1968), 56–67; and A.J. Smith, 'The failure of love: love lyrics after Donne', *Stratford-upon-Avon Studies,* **11** (1970), 41–71. Bruce King, 'The strategy of Carew's wit', *Review of English Literature,* **5** (1964), 42–51; D.F. Rauber, 'Carew redivivus', *Texas Studies in Language and Literature,* **13** (1971), 17–28; and Diana Benet, 'Carew's monarchy of wit', in Claude J. Summers and Ted-Larry Pebworth, eds, *'The muses common-weale': Poetry and politics in the seventeenth century* (Columbia, MO, 1988), pp. 80–91, emphasise the intellectual element in Carew's poetry. Some neglected political aspects are covered in Kevin Sharpe, 'Cavalier critic? The ethics and politics of Thomas Carew's poetry', in Kevin Sharpe and Steven N. Zwicker, eds, *Politics of Discourse: The literature and history of seventeenth-century England* (Berkeley, CA, 1987), pp. 117–46. Reid Barbour, '"Wee, of th'Adult'rate Mixture Not Complaine": Thomas Carew and poetic hybridity', *John Donne Journal,* **7** (1988), 91–113 looks at his eclecticism; and Anthony Low, 'The "Turning Wheele": Carew, Jonson, Donne (and the First) Law of Motion', *John Donne Journal,* **1** (1982), 1–2, 69–80, links him with his two great mentors.

On 'A Rapture', see Paula Johnson, 'Carew's "A Rapture": the dynamics of fantasy', *SEL*, **16** (1976), 145–55; Renee Hannaford, '"My Unwashed Muse": sexual play and sociability in Carew's "A Rapture"', *English Language Notes*, **27** (1989), 32–9; Margaret J.M. Ezell, 'Thomas Carew and the erotic law of nature', *Explorations in Renaissance Culture*, **14**, (1988), 99–114. For critical analysis of other poems included in this anthology, see Renee Hannaford, '"Express'd by Mee": Carew on Donne and Jonson', *SP*, **84** (1987), 61–79; Michael R. Parker, 'Diamond's dust: Carew, King, and the legacy of Donne', in Claude J. Summers and Ted-Larry Pebworth, eds, *The Eagle and the Dove: Reassessing John Donne* (Columbia, MO, 1986), pp. 191–200; Sydney Gottlieb, 'Elegies upon the author: defining, defending, and surviving Donne', *John Donne Journal*, **2** (1983), 23–38; Antoon Van Velzen, 'Two versions of the funeral elegy: Henry King's "The Exequy" and Thomas Carew's "...Elegie Upon...Donne"', *Comitatus*, **15** (1984), 45–57; Elizabeth K. Hill. 'Carew and corsets: feminine imagery in the elegy on Donne', *Greyfriar*, **24** (1983), 35–46.

76 / *A Song*

Ask me no more where Jove bestows,
When June is past, the fading rose,
For in your beauty's orient deep
These flowers, as in their causes, sleep.

Ask me no more whither doth stray
The golden atoms of the day,
For in pure love heaven did prepare
Those powders to enrich your hair.

Ask me no more whither doth haste
The nightingale when May is past,
For in your sweet dividing throat
She winters and keeps warm her note.

Ask me no more where those stars light
That downwards fall in dead of night,
For in your eyes they sit and there
Fixèd become as in their sphere.

Ask me no more if east or west
The phoenix builds her spicy nest,
For unto you at last she flies
And in your fragrant bosom dies.

Carew's most famous poem is a series of hyperbolic comparisons typical of the Petrarchan tradition of compliment to a beautiful lady. Frequently echoed, answered and satirised by contemporaries, it is an example of Carew's seemingly casual tone and stylish elegance, which conceal carefully crafted and measured lines. The lady addressed in this poem is paid extravagant compliments, but the tetrameter stanzas, rhyming in couplets, preserve the wit and 'Cavalier' tone of the compliments.

[1] **no more**
no longer; ***Jove*** the ruler of the gods in classical mythology, but here simply the deity generally; ***bestows*** lodges or stows away for safekeeping.

[2] **June is past**
Roses seldom survive summer warmth.

[3] **orient**
(a) source or east (where the sun rises); (b) the brilliance of her beauty; (c) pearly or pearl-like (from 'orient pearl'); ***deep*** (a) as noun, depths; (b) as adverb, deep down.

[4] **as in their causes**
Carew is alluding to the Aristotelian doctrine of the four causes (material, efficient, formal and final, as described in *Physics*, 2.2.3 and *Metaphysics*, 1.3–7) which bring a thing into existence. Her beauty is the means, substance, destiny and form of the rose's beauty.

[5] **whither doth stray**
where are lost.

[6] **golden atoms**
(a) particles of dust visible in a sunbeam; (b) the smallest portions of light, conceived of as a stream of tiny particles.

[7] **prepare**
provide.

[8] **powders**
tiny bits of sparkling matter sprinkled on the hair to give it radiance; ***enrich*** (a) make more beautiful in appearance; (b) give a golden appearance, therefore one of preciousness and wealth. Note the contrast of the lady's dawn-like loveliness with the fading of the rose and sunset.

[9] **haste**
depart hastily.

[10] **nightingale . . . past**
Nightingales rarely sing after springtime.

[11] **dividing throat**
The reference is to musical practice in the period, which consisted of the improvised execution by a singer of rapid, florid passages that embellished or 'divided' up the slower notes of the main melody.

[12] **winters**
protects from the winter cold; ***her note*** the nightingale's song.

[13] **light**
descend to earth, land (like a bird).

[14] **that downwards fall**
The reference is, of course, to 'falling' stars.

[16] **Fixèd . . . sphere**
In Ptolemaic astronomy, the stars were fixed or attached to a series of concentric rotating crystalline spheres; the falling stars have thus left their heavenly spheres and found a new place in the lady's brilliant eyes. The image is a familiar Petrarchan conceit.

[18] **phoenix . . . nest**
The phoenix was a mythical bird which lived its life cycle of five or six centuries in the Arabian desert and was consumed to ashes on a funeral pyre of aromatic wood ignited by the sun and fanned by its wings, after which it arose rejuvenated. Note the pattern of cyclical return to youth and beauty implied by these images.

[19] **she**
Perhaps Carew makes the phoenix feminine in order to imply an identity between the bird and the lady addressed; in this way he also avoids a different kind of erotic innuendo in the final line.

77 | *To Saxham*

Though frost and snow locked from mine eyes
That beauty which without door lies,
Thy gardens, orchards, walks, that so
I might not all thy pleasures know,
Yet, Saxham, thou within thy gate
Art of thyself so delicate,
So full of native sweets that bless
Thy roof with inward happiness,
As neither from nor to thy store
Winter takes aught, or spring adds more.
The cold and frozen air had starved
Much poor, if not by thee preserved,
Whose prayers have made thy table blest
With plenty far above the rest.
The season hardly did afford
Coarse cates unto thy neighbours' board,
Yet thou hadst dainties as the sky
Had only been thy volary;
Or else the birds, fearing the snow
Might to another deluge grow,
The pheasant, partridge, and the lark
Flew to thy house as to the ark.
The willing ox, of himself, came
Home to the slaughter with the lamb,
And every beast did thither bring

Himself to be an offering.
The scaly herd more pleasure took,
Bathed in thy dish, than in the brook.
Water, earth, air did all conspire
To pay their tributes to thy fire,
Whose cherishing flames themselves divide
Through every room, where they deride
The night and cold abroad, whilst they,
Like suns within, keep endless day.
Those cheerful beams send forth their light
To all that wander in the night
And seem to beckon from aloof
The weary pilgrim to thy roof,
Where if, refreshed, he will away,
He's fairly welcome; or, if stay,
Far more, which he shall hearty find
Both from the master and the hind.
The stranger's welcome each man there
Stamped on his cheerful brow doth wear,
Nor doth this welcome or his cheer
Grow less 'cause he stays longer here.
There's none observes (much less repines)
How often this man sups or dines.
Thou hast no porter at the door
T'examine or keep back the poor,
Nor locks nor bolts; thy gates have been
Made only to let strangers in.
Untaught to shut, they do not fear
To stand wide open all the year,
Careless who enters, for they know
Thou never didst deserve a foe;
And as for thieves, thy bounty's such,
They cannot steal, thou giv'st so much.

The estate in Suffolk of Sir John Crofts (1563–1628) and his family, for whom Carew wrote a number of poems, was usually known as Little Saxham. The poem – like its model, Jonson's 'To Penshurst' (p. 119) – celebrates the estate as an extension of those who dwell in it, and glorifies the ideal of aristocratic generosity and hospitality. Like its predecessor it is in couplets, though tetrameter rather than pentameter. Furthermore, the poem is set in winter, unlike most other 'country-house' poems, and focuses on the great house as a refuge from an unfriendly world.

[1] **mine**
my.
[2] **without door**
out of doors.
[4] **I might not**
I am not able (because of the weather).
[6] **of thyself**
in yourself; ***delicate*** delightful.
[7] **native sweets**
sweet things that come from or belong to you by nature.
[9] **store**
abundance.
[10] **Winter . . . adds more**
i.e. the seasons have no effect on the pleasures and plenty offered to those dwelling in Little Saxham.
[11–12] **starved . . . poor**
Part of the responsibility of the landed gentry was to help feed the poor of the parish.
[13] **Whose prayers**
i.e. the prayers of the poor, who seek in this way to compensate the Crofts family for its attention to their needs.
[14] **the rest**
other country estates.
[15] **afford**
provide.
[16] **Coarse cates**
crude or very basic foodstuff; 'cates' usually implies table delicacies; ***board*** dinner table.
[17] **dainties**
gourmet delicacies; ***as*** as though.
[18] **volary**
aviary or fowl-coop.
[19–22] **fearing . . . ark**
i.e. like the animals that were gathered in Noah's ark (Genesis 7) to escape the forty days and forty nights of rain that caused the great flood, the birds seek refuge from the snowstorm on the estate.
[23–4] **ox . . . lamb**
Traditional sacrificial animals in Graeco-Roman and Hebrew religious ritual.
[26] **offering**
The various animals come to the house willing to be food for its tables; compare 'To Penshurst' (p. 120), lines 29–38. Note the quasi-religious suggestion of a solemn sacrifice.
[27] **scaly herd**
fish (a periphrasis that became part of eighteenth-century poetic diction).
[29] **Water, earth, air**
three of the four classical elements.
[30] **tributes**
offerings or gifts acknowledging superiority, esteem or affection; ***fire*** the fourth of the classical elements. In the cold season everything in the household revolves around the hearth and its fire.
[31–3] **cherishing . . . cold abroad**
The fire and the hearth were the centre of Roman households and, as symbolised by the Temple of Vesta in the forum, of Rome herself; flames that might otherwise be destructive when they expand are here viewed as protective, even caressing.
[33] **abroad**
outside.
[35] **beams**
the glow from the house, visible from afar.
[36] **light . . . night**
a traditional Christian image of salvation or guidance (see Matthew 5: 16).
[37] **aloof**
far away, at some distance.
[38] **pilgrim**
traveller; but note, once again, a quasi-religious implication.
[39–42] **Where . . . hind**
i.e. the unexpected visitor is welcome whether he chooses to stop just long enough to get warm, eat something, and catch his breath, or to stay longer and enjoy the generous hospitality of the whole household; ***hind*** servant.
[43] **stranger's welcome**
a welcome for the stranger; ***each man there*** each man of the household.
[45] **cheer**
kindly welcome or reception.
[47–8] **none observes . . . dines**
Compare 'To Penshurst' (p. 121), lines 67–8.
[47] **repines**
grudges, expresses discontent, complains.
[49] **porter**
a person employed to carry things in

and out of the house; here, primarily, a doorman.
[50] **examine**
interrogate.
[53] **Untaught**
incapable of.
[55] **Careless**
unconcerned, indifferent to.
[57] **bounty**
(a) generosity; (b) abundance.

78 / *A Rapture*

I will enjoy thee now, my Celia, come
And fly with me to Love's Elysium.
The giant, Honour, that keeps cowards out
Is but a masquer; and the servile rout
Of baser subjects only bend in vain
To the vast idol, whilst the nobler train
Of valiant soldiers daily sail between
The huge Colossus' legs and pass unseen
Unto the blissful shore. Be bold and wise,
And we shall enter. The grim Swiss denies
Only tame fools a passage that not know
He is but form and only frights in show
The duller eyes that look from far. Draw near,
And thou shalt scorn what we were wont to fear.
We shall see how the stalking pageant goes
With borrowed legs, a heavy load to those
That made and bear him, not, as we once thought,
The seed of gods but a weak model wrought
By greedy men that seek t'enclose the common
And within private arms impale free woman.
   Come, then, and mounted on the wings of Love,
We'll cut the flitting air and soar above
The monster's head and in the noblest seats
Of those blest shades quench and renew our heats.
There shall the Queen of Love, and Innocence,
Beauty, and Nature banish all offence
From our close ivy-twines. There I'll behold
Thy barèd snow and thy unbraided gold;
There my enfranchised hand on every side
Shall o'er thy naked, polished ivory slide.

No curtain there, though of transparent lawn,
Shall be before thy virgin-treasure drawn;
But the rich mine, to the enquiring eye
Exposed, shall ready still for mintage lie,
And we will coin young Cupids. There a bed
of roses and fresh myrtles shall be spread
Under the cooler shade of cypress groves,
Our pillows of the down of Venus' doves,
Whereon our panting limbs we'll gently lay
In the faint respites of our active play,
That so our slumbers may in dreams have leisure
To tell the nimble fancy our past pleasure;
And so our souls, that cannot be embraced,
Shall the embraces of our bodies taste.
Meanwhile the bubbling stream shall court the shore;
Th'enamoured chirping wood-choir shall adore
In varied tunes the deity of Love;
The gentle blasts of western winds shall move
The trembling leaves and through their close boughs breathe
Still music, whilst we rest ourselves beneath
Their dancing shade; till a soft murmur, sent
From souls entranced in am'rous languishment,
Rouse us and shoot into our veins fresh fire,
Till we in their sweet ecstasy expire.
    Then, as the empty bee that lately bore
Into the common treasure all her store
Flies 'bout the painted field with nimble wing,
Deflow'ring the fresh virgins of the spring,
So will I rifle all the sweets that dwell
In my delicious paradise, and swell
My bag with honey, drawn forth by the power
Of fervent kisses, from each spicy flower.
I'll seize the rose-buds in their perfumed bed,
The violet knots, like curious mazes spread
O'er all the garden, taste the ripened cherries,
The warm firm apples, tipped with coral berries.
Then will I visit, with a wandering kiss,
The vale of lilies and the bower of bliss;
And, where the beauteous region doth divide
Into two milky ways, my lips shall slide
Down those smooth alleys, wearing as I go

A tract for lovers on the printed snow.
Thence, climbing o'er the swelling Apennine
Retire into thy grove of eglantine,
Where I will all those ravished sweets distil
Through love's alembic; and with chemic skill
From the mixed mass one sovereign balm derive,
Then bring that great elixir to thy hive.
   Now in more subtile wreaths I will entwine
My sin'wy thighs, my legs and arms, with thine.
Thou like a sea of milk shalt lie displayed,
Whilst I the smooth, calm ocëan invade
With such a tempest as when Jove of old
Fell down on Danaë in a storm of gold.
Yet my tall pine shall in the Cyprian strait
Ride safe at anchor and unlade her freight.
My rudder, with thy bold hand, like a tried
And skilful pilot, thou shalt steer, and guide
My bark into love's channel, where it shall
Dance, as the bounding waves do rise or fall.
Then shall thy circling arms embrace and clip
My willing body, and thy balmy lip
Bathe me in juice of kisses, whose perfume,
Like a religious incense, shall consume,
And send up holy vapours to those powers
That bless our loves and crown our sportful hours,
That with such halcyon calmness fix our souls
In steadfast peace as no affright controls.
There no rude sounds shake us with sudden starts.
No jealous ears, when we unrip our hearts,
Suck our discourse in; no observing spies
This blush, that glance, traduce; no envious eyes
Watch our close meetings; nor are we betrayed
To rivals by the bribèd chambermaid.
No wedlock bonds unwreathe our twisted loves.
We seek no midnight arbour, no dark groves
To hide our kisses; there the hated name
Of husband, wife, lust, modest, chaste, or shame
Are vain and empty words, whose very sound
Was never heard in the Elysian ground.
All things are lawful there that may delight
Nature or unrestrainèd appetite.

Like and enjoy, to will and act is one;
We only sin when Love's rites are not done.
The Roman Lucrece there reads the divine
Lectures of love's great master, Aretine,
And knows as well as Lais how to move
Her pliant body in the act of love.
To quench the burning ravisher, she hurls
Her limbs into a thousand winding curls
And studies artful postures, such as be
Carved on the bark of every neighb'ring tree
By learnèd hands that so adorned the rind
Of those fair plants, which as they lay entwined
Have fanned their glowing fires. The Grecian Dame,
That in her endless web toiled for a name
As fruitless as her work, doth there display
Herself before the Youth of Ithaca
And th'amorous sport of gamesome nights prefer
Before dull dreams of the lost Traveller.
Daphne hath broke her bark and that swift foot,
Which th'angry gods had fastened with a root
To the fixed earth, doth now unfettered run
To meet th'embraces of the youthful sun.
She hangs upon him like his Delphic lyre;
Her kisses blow the old and breathe new fire.
Full of her god, she sings inspirèd lays,
Sweet odes of love such as deserve the bays,
Which she herself was. Next her, Laura lies
In Petrarch's learnèd arms, drying those eyes
That did in such sweet smooth-paced numbers flow
As made the world enamoured of his woe.
These and then thousand beauties more that died
Slave to the tyrant now enlarged deride
His cancelled laws and, for their time mis-spent,
Pay into Love's exchequer double rent.
Come, then, my Celia, we'll no more forbear
To taste our joys, struck with a panic fear,
But will depose from his imperious sway
This proud usurper and walk free as they
With necks unyoked; nor is it just that he
Should fetter your soft sex with chastity,
Which Nature made unapt for abstinence,

When yet this false impostor can dispense
With human justice and with sacred right
And, maugre both their laws, command me fight
With rivals or with em'lous loves that dare
Equal with thine their mistress' eyes or hair.
If thou complain of wrong and call my sword
To carve out thy revenge, upon that word
He bids me fight and kill or else he brands,
With marks of infamy, my coward hands;
And yet Religion bids from bloodshed fly
And damns me for that act. Then tell me why
  This goblin Honour, which the world adores,
  Should make men atheists and not women whores.

Carew's most famous erotic poem recalls Donne's 'Elegy 19' (p. 38), but it also seems to be inspired by the neo-Latin Renaissance poet Johannes Secundus (author of *Basia* – 'Kisses'). Like Marvell's 'To His Coy Mistress' (p. 462) it is a poem of seduction, in which various arguments are offered to entice the addressee to yield to the speaker, though we are not told whether or not they are successful.

The poem, in pentameter couplets, consists of six sections. The opening is an appeal to Celia to come to the poet and ignore any qualms she might have about her 'honour' (lines 1–20). This is followed by a rather detailed description of proposed lovemaking (lines 21–54), which is further elaborated in a following section, a long simile based on the bee and its activity (lines 55–78). This, in turn, is succeeded by another long simile whose basis is a storm-tossed ship (lines 79–114); this ends in a transition to the next section (lines 115–46), a rewriting of mythological and literary figures as they might appear in 'Love's Elysium'. Finally, the poem closes with a third appeal, which concludes with an argument that free love helps to preserve religious values.

Title
Rapture (a) the act of carrying off a woman; (b) transport of mind, mental exaltation, ecstatic delight.

[1] **enjoy**
take pleasure of someone in a sexual sense; ***Celia*** the heavenly lady – a name, doubtless fictitious and perhaps suggested by Jonson's 'To Celia' (p. 126); Carew addresses her in several poems.

[2] **fly**
(a) flee, escape; (b) take wing, rise; ***Elysium*** in Greek mythology, the dwelling-place of the blessed after death.

[3] **Honour**
(a) chastity or sexual purity, regarded as the greatest virtue in a woman; (b) good name or reputation for chastity.

[4] **masquer**
a pretender, a masquerader.

[6] **train**
artillery, vehicles and men who follow the attacking front ranks in a battle siege.

[8] **Colossus**
(a) an enormous statue, one of the seven wonders of the ancient world, that stood at the entrance to the harbour of Rhodes in the third century

BC, between whose legs ships sailed; (b) any very large person.
[9] **blissful shore**
Elysium.
[10] **grim Swiss**
i.e. the Swiss guard, mercenary soldiers from Switzerland who hired themselves out to monarchs (and especially to the Pope) as a bodyguard.
[12] **but form . . . show**
like the 'masquer' above; the royal bodyguard usually wear more elaborate uniforms than combat soldiers.
[13] **draw near**
(a) come closer and inspect the Swiss guard; (b) come nearer the speaker, the would-be lover.
[15] **stalking pageant**
a stage machine or other contrivance, such as a stage giant.
[18] **seed of gods**
In mythology giants are said to be descended from gods; ***weak model*** a powerless representation.
[19] **greedy man**
(a) theatrical producers who, to make more money from a play, introduce spectacular stage effects; (b) husbands or rivals who try to monopolise a woman for their own pleasure by appealing to honour; ***the common*** (a) that which should be shared by many; (b) undivided or unfenced land belonging to the community as a whole.
[20] **private arms**
only one man's embrace; ***impale*** (a) enclose with a fence or stakes; (b) thrust a pointed stake through the body (with sexual implications); ***free*** (a) meant to live unconfined or unencumbered; (b) meant to have many lovers, to be free in a sexual sense.
[24] **blest shades**
(a) the blessed spirits dwelling in Elysium; (b) lovers who have 'died' (i.e. consummated their love) and are now dwelling in a lovers' paradise; ***quench and renew our heats*** satisfy and further induce sexual appetite.
[25] **Queen of Love**
Venus; ***Innocence*** (a) freedom from guilt; (b) freedom from artifice or deception; (c) harmlessness.
[27] **close ivy-twines**
embraces; ivy was sacred to the Greek god Dionysus; here it suggests licence and the rejection of inhibition.
[28] **barèd snow**
the whiteness of her naked skin; ***unbraided gold*** her hair, after it has been let down.
[29] **enfranchised**
(a) allowed personal freedom; (b) released from confinement; (c) admitted to certain privileges.
[30] **ivory**
her body; pale skin was a mark of beauty.
[31] **though of transparent lawn**
not even one made of transparent fabric.
[32] **virgin-treasure**
her hitherto untouched body.
[33] **rich mine**
the hidden physical endowments of a beautiful woman were frequently compared with a mine of precious metals; compare Donne's 'Elegy 19' (p. 38), lines 29 ff.; ***enquiring*** investigating.
[34] **mintage**
(a) the making of metal into coins; (b) the stamping of a likeness on a piece of metal. The point of the metaphor is that the value of the metal is increased once it has been so modified – note also the sexual implications of 'stamping a likeness'.
[35] **coin young Cupids**
(a) make love; (b) create offspring; (c) mint money (Cupid-like figures occasionally appeared on ancient coins). 'To coin' could also mean 'to wedge something in a crevice or corner'.
[36] **myrtles**
associated with Venus, as roses are with love.
[37] **cypress**
also associated with Venus.
[38] **down of Venus' doves**
Venus is sometimes depicted driving a chariot drawn by doves.
[39] **panting**
from heightened sexual desire rather than physical exertion.

[40] **faint respites . . . play**
The respites are 'faint' because they do not satisfy completely; ***active play*** vigorous foreplay.
[42] **tell the nimble fancy**
transmit residual impressions of the senses to the imagination during sleep, according to the theories of the era.
[43–4] **souls . . . taste**
A reversal of the usual relationship between soul and body, but not unlike Donne's argument in 'The Ecstasy', where he notes that the unity of two souls can only be read in the 'book' of the body.
[45] **bubbling stream**
a typical feature of the pastoral landscape, perhaps with a sexual implication as well; ***court*** (a) woo, make love to; (b) lap against the bank.
[46] **enamoured chirping wood-choir**
love-struck birds of the forest, a traditional image in love poetry; ***adore*** as though they were pagan priests or monks singing to Venus or Cupid.
[47] **western winds**
the winds of springtime.
[52] **am'rous languishment**
the lassitude following the sexual act.
[53] **shoot into our veins fresh fire**
Though the phrase is largely metaphorical it is based on Renaissance physiology, which interpreted desire in terms of a fiery mixture in the blood.
[54] **in their sweet ecstasy expire**
reach sexual climax.
[55–62] **Then . . . spicy flower**
This conceit comparing sexual foreplay with the activity of a bee was popular with other poets of the period, including Herrick and Suckling. Note, however, that the parallel is meant to be witty but not necessarily exact. Carew is aware, for instance, that worker bees are female (line 56: 'her store'), but in his analogy they play a masculine role.
[55–6] **that lately bore . . . store**
the bee has just deposited her nectar-filled sac in the hive, and is returning to the field of flowers to gather more.
[57] **painted**
multicoloured (with flowers).
[58] **Deflow'ring**
(a) collecting nectar; (b) violating; (c) depriving a woman of her virginity. Since bees do not truly harm or change the flowers they visit but, on the contrary, help them to reproduce by assisting in pollination, there is perhaps a further dimension to the analogy; ***fresh virgins*** the new, unpollinated flowers.
[59] **rifle**
plunder or take everything of value after searching thoroughly; ***sweets*** sexual pleasures.
[60] **paradise**
her body.
[60–2] **swell . . . kisses**
The description suggests the excitation of the penis.
[62] **spicy**
fragrant.
[63] **rose-buds**
(a) girls in their youthful beauty; (b) the pleasures of love; ***perfumed bed*** (a) a flower bed; (b) a boudoir; (c) the woman's body in which such pleasures reside.
[64] **violet knots**
flower beds laid out in a design, thus perhaps a conceit for the boudoir or bed; the phrase is in apposition with 'perfumed bed' in the preceding line. It is possible, however, that the 'knots' refer to veins, in which case there is a double metaphor: flower bed = boudoir = body. Critics have often confessed their failure to find a one-to-one correlation in these analogies, though the images are common in love poetry of the era. Thus gathering 'rosebuds' for Herrick is a metaphor for enjoying the pleasures of youth, and the feminine body was frequently compared to a garden; ***curious*** skilfully or carefully arranged.
[65] **the ripened cherries**
the lips.
[66] **apples**
the breasts; ***berries*** the nipples.
[68] **vale of lilies . . . bower of bliss**
the bosom (see the Song of Songs 2:

16) and the midriff; lily-white bosoms were frequently admired by contemporary poets; the 'bower of bliss' is an allusion to Spenser, *Faerie Queene*, 2.12, where a garden of earthly delights is described under that name.

[70] **milky ways**
the thighs.

[72] **tract**
(a) trail, path; (b) treatise.

[73] **swelling Apennine**
the *mons Veneris*.

[74] **grove of eglantine**
the pudenda (***eglantine*** sweetbriar).

[75] **ravished**
stolen, seized.

[76] **alembic**
(a) a gourd-shaped beaker used for distillation, especially in alchemy; (b) the penis.

[77] **sovereign**
extremely efficacious in healing; ***balm*** a medicinal ointment; ***derive*** extract.

[78] **elixir**
a distillation or extract capable of prolonging life indefinitely; ***hive*** the *mons Veneris* – the metaphor was a common one in the Renaissance, but note that here it serves to complete this extended comparison of the bee's and the lover's activities.

[79–90] **Now . . . fall**
The metaphor shifts to another popular analogy: the lover as ship (compare Sir Thomas Wyatt's 'My Galley Chargèd With Forgetfulness').

[79] **subtile**
(a) ingeniously contrived; (b) fine, delicate.

[80] **sin'wy**
sinewy, strong, well-developed.

[81] **sea of milk**
because of her fair skin, much admired in women.

[82] **ocean**
pronounced as three syllables; 'ocean' is the object of 'invade'.

[83] **tempest**
sighs (compare Donne, 'A Valediction: Forbidding Mourning' (p. 52), line 6).

[83–4] **Jove . . . gold**
Jupiter, in love with Danaë, a mortal woman whose father had locked her away to prevent her from bearing a son, visited her in a shower of gold; their offspring was the hero Perseus.

[85] **my tall pine**
(a) the mainmast of the ship, often used synecdochically in poetry for the whole ship; (b) the erect penis; ***Cyprian strait*** the female genitalia – the island of Cyprus was the birthplace of Venus, goddess of love.

[86] **ride safe . . . freight**
an obvious reference to sexual climax; ***unlade*** take the cargo out of a ship.

[87] **rudder**
penis.

[89] **bark**
ship; ***love's channel*** the Cyprian strait of line 85.

[90] **dance . . . fall**
The sexual metaphor is obvious.

[91] **clip**
hold in a tight grasp.

[92] **balmy**
delicately and deliciously fragrant or soft and soothing.

[94] **religious incense**
the fragrant smoke produced by burning aromatic gums and spices associated with solemn ceremonies; it usually symbolises prayers rising to heaven; ***consume*** burn.

[96] **sportful hours**
playful erotic interludes.

[97] **halcyon**
calm, quiet (like the variety of kingfisher by that name which supposedly possessed the power to calm the seas).

[98] **as no affright controls**
that no terror can overcome.

[100] **unrip**
open up.

[101] **Suck our discourse in**
hear and register our conversation.

[102] **traduce**
speak evil of.

[103] **close**
(a) secret; (b) intimate.

[105] **wedlock . . . loves**
There are two ways of construing this phrase as it might apply in a time when marriages still tended to be political or pragmatic rather than

romantic: (a) neither of us is married, hence there is no legal impediment to our loving; (b) our embrace is not spoiled by our being married to one another (a paradox, since one set of bonds unwinds another).

[106] **no midnight arbour, no dark groves**
typical meeting-places of illicit lovers.

[110] **never heard . . . Elysian ground**
It was a commonplace of the so-called 'courtly love' tradition that true love was not possible within the legal constraints of official wedlock, but Carew may also have a witty point in mind, based on the biblical statement that there are no marriages in heaven (Luke 20: 34–5).

[111–13] **All things . . . one**
This description is true of the traditional notion of heaven, where there is no longer a conflict between desire and fulfilment, body and spirit, but here it is applied to the earthly 'heaven' of love's Elysium.

[114] **We only sin . . . done**
The conclusion is that in such a heaven, where it is impossible to commit a sin, one can sin only by omission. From an orthodox point of view, of course, the whole argument is spurious, since it is a fleshly, not a spiritual, realm of which the poet speaks.

[115] **Roman Lucrece**
Lucretia, wife of Collatinus, was for the Ancient Romans the exemplar of the chaste woman; raped by Tarquin after rejecting his advances, she committed suicide rather than be shamed.

[115–16] **divine . . . Aretine**
Pietro Aretino (1492–1556) was notorious for his sonnets, written to accompany a series of erotic engravings; he was known to Elizabethans as 'the divine Aretine'.

[117] **Lais**
at least three courtesans bore this name in Ancient Greece; the most celebrated lived in the fifth century BC.

[119] **burning ravisher**
presumably a reference to Tarquin, but also an ironic description of Lais's clients.

[121] **studies**
investigates, explores; ***artful*** (a) dexterous; (b) ingenious.

[123] **learnèd**
The art of the woodcut, a source of many book illustrations, consisted of skilfully carving out a block of wood in a reversed image; however, 'learnèd' here is probably ironic; ***rind*** bark.

[124] **they**
the lovers in the forest.

[125] **Grecian Dame . . . Traveller**
Odysseus' wife Penelope, famous for her fidelity to her missing husband (the 'lost Traveller' of line 130), refused to consider remarriage and put off choosing from her importunate suitors with the excuse that she had not finished weaving a funeral shroud for her father-in-law (the 'endless web' of line 126); what she wove by day, however, she unwove at night in order to delay her decision indefinitely.

[127–9] **doth there . . . prefer**
i.e. is depicted (contrary to the usual version of her story) in 'Love's Elysium' as arousing the suitors rather than longing in dreams for her husband's return.

[131–9] **Daphne . . . was**
The story of Daphne, told by Ovid, *Metamorphoses*, 1. 452–567, was of a river nymph who refused to have anything to do with men. Pursued by an amorous Apollo, she prayed to the goddess Gaia (Earth) for help, and was accordingly turned into a laurel tree. Here, however, she yields to and receives inspiration from Apollo ('the youthful sun' of line 134), god of the lyre and of poetry ('inspirèd lays', line 137) whose symbol was the laurel tree, from which crowns were fashioned ('bays', line 138) for the heads of poets victorious in contests. Daphne's name means 'laurel' in Greek.

[135] **Kisses . . . fire**
Her kisses satisfy Apollo's (the sun's) old passion (fire) and provoke a new one.

[137] **Full of her god**
(a) inspired by; (b) sexually satisfied by.

[139–42] **Laura . . . woe**
Laura (note the transition from 'laurel') was the woman loved by the Italian poet Francesco Petrarca (Petrarch) (1304–74); she died in 1348 but never yielded to his passion. His famous sonnet cycle recounts his love for her in a series of 366 poems, divided into two sections devoted to her before and after her death. Petrarca was considered the most learned (line 140) man of his time.

[141] **numbers**
verses.

[144] **tyrant**
Honour; ***enlarged*** set free, given liberty.

[145] **cancelled**
annulled, rendered void.

[146] **Love's exchequer**
a conceit inspired by Donne, 'Elegy 18', lines 91–4. The Exchequer is the royal or national treasury, along with the offices and officials that manage and collect revenue; ***rent*** tax paid in tribute.

[147] **forbear**
refrain, keep from.

[148] **panic**
the adjective refers to the Greek god Pan, who overcame enemies by means of a shout that induced unreasoning terror into them. However, since Pan was also associated with natural instincts and lack of restraint, the 'panic fear' might also be taken to imply fear of erotic licence.

[149] **depose**
unseat a ruler.

[150] **usurper**
Honour, who has unlawfully seized Love's ruling power; ***they*** joys (line 148).

[151] **necks unyoked**
slaves and prisoners were sometimes chained around the neck.

[152] **soft sex**
womankind.

[153] **unapt for abstinence**
Satirists and moralists had often claimed that women were naturally lustful; the contention was hotly debated during the sixteenth-century 'Querelle des Femmes' or dispute over the nature of women. Carew turns this dubious proposition to his own comic purposes (compare with Donne's 'Go, and catch a falling star' [p. 56]).

[154] **false impostor**
Honour.

[156] **maugre**
despite.

[157] **rivals or with em'lous loves**
The code of honour also required men to fight duels for the sake of their ladies or challenge rivals to their love, either verbally or physically; ***em'lous*** emulous, driven by the spirit of rivalry or imitation.

[158] **Equal**
equate.

[159] **call my sword**
(a) call for me to take up my sword; (b) provoke an erection.

[161] **fight and kill**
(a) do battle with and slay Honour; (b) engage in sexual activity.

[163] **And yet religion . . . act**
The final argument of the poem turns on a paradox: the code of honour in love flies in the face of Christian moral precepts that enjoin men not to perform acts of violence against one another.

[165] **goblin**
a mischievous and ugly demon.

[166] **make men atheists**
i.e. by making them go against the most fundamental of religious precepts; ***and not women whores*** i.e. why should not women be free to love any and all men as often as they wish? The spuriousness of the argument, based on a rather loose interpretation of what is meant by 'Religion', is part of its humour.

79 / *An Elegy upon the Death of the Dean of Paul's, Doctor John Donne*

Can we not force from widowed poetry,
Now thou art dead, great Donne, one elegy
To crown thy hearse? Why yet dare we not trust,
Though with unkneaded dough-baked prose, thy dust,
Such as th'unscissored churchman, from the flower
Of fading rhetoric, short-lived as his hour,
Dry as the sand that measures it, should lay
Upon thy ashes on the funeral day?
Have we no voice, no tune? Didst thou dispense
Through all our language both the words and sense?
'Tis a sad truth. The pulpit may her plain
And sober Christian precepts still retain;
Doctrines it may and wholesome uses frame,
Grave homilies and lectures; but the flame
Of thy brave soul – that shot such heat and light
As burnt our earth and made our darkness bright,
Committed holy rapes upon our will,
Did through the eye the melting heart distil
And the deep knowledge of dark truths so teach
As sense might judge what fancy could not reach,
Must be desired for ever. So the fire
That fills with spirit and heat the Delphic choir,
Which, kindled first by thy Promethean breath,
Glowed here awhile, lies quenched now in thy death.
The Muses' garden, with pedantic weeds
O'erspread, was purged by thee; the lazy seeds
Of servile imitation thrown away
And fresh invention planted. Thou didst pay
The debts of our penurious, bankrupt age:
Licentious thefts that make poetic rage
A mimic fury, when our souls must be
Possessed, or with Anacreon's ecstasy
Or Pindar's, not their own. The subtle cheat
Of sly exchanges and the juggling feat
Of two-edged words – or whatsoever wrong
By ours was done the Greek or Latin tongue –
Thou hast redeemed and opened us a mine
Of rich and pregnant fancy, drawn a line

Of masculine expression, which had good
Old Orpheus seen or all the ancient brood
Our superstitious fools admire and hold
Their lead more precious than thy burnished gold,
Thou hadst been their exchequer, and no more
They each in other's dust had raked for ore.
Thou shalt yield no precedence but of time
And the blind fate of language whose tuned chime
More charms the outward sense, yet thou may'st
claim
From so great disadvantage greater fame,
Since to the awe of thy imperious wit
Our stubborn language bends, made only fit
With her tough thick-rubbed hoops to gird about
Thy giant fancy, which had proved too stout
For their soft melting phrases. As in time
They had the start, so did they cull the prime
Buds of invention many a hundred year
And left the rifled fields, besides the fear
To touch their harvest. Yet, from those bare lands
Of what is purely thine, thy only hands
(And that thy smallest work) have gleanèd more
Than all those times and tongues could reap before.
But thou art gone, and thy strict laws will be
Too hard for libertines in poetry.
They will repeal the goodly exiled train
Of gods and goddesses, which in thy just reign
Were banished nobler poems. Now with these,
The silenced tales o'th' *Metamorphoses*
Shall stuff their lines and swell the windy page,
Till verse, refined by thee, in this last age
Turn ballad-rhyme or those old idols be
Adored again with new apostasy.
O pardon me, that break with untuned verse
The reverend silence that attends thy hearse,
Whose awful solemn murmurs were to thee
More than these faint lines a loud elegy,
That did proclaim in a dumb eloquence
The death of all the arts, whose influence,
Grown feeble, in these panting numbers lies
Gasping short-winded accents and so dies.

So doth the swiftly turning wheel not stand
In th' instant we withdraw the moving hand,
But some small time maintain a faint weak course
By virtue of the first impulsive force;
And so, whilst I cast on thy funeral pile
Thy crown of bays, oh, let it crack awhile
And spit disdain, till the devouring flashes
Suck all the moisture up, then turn to ashes.
  I will not draw thee envy to engross
All thy perfections or weep all our loss.
Those are too num'rous for an elegy,
And this too great to be expressed by me.
Though every pen should share a distinct part,
Yet art thou theme enough to tire all art;
Let others carve the rest; it shall suffice
I on thy tomb this epitaph incise:

Here lies a king that ruled as he thought fit
The universal monarchy of wit;
Here lie two flamens, and both those the best:
Apollo's first, at last, the true God's priest.

Carew's eulogy in iambic pentameter couplets was one of several published in the posthumous 1633 edition of Donne's poetry. It is not only a fine tribute in imitation of Donne's style but a remarkably apt account of the main strengths of his poetry, and his major innovations.

[1] **force**
produce under great pressure or strain; ***widowed poetry*** The implication is that Donne was married to poetry.
[2] **Now thou art dead**
Donne died on 31 March 1631.
[3–8] **Why yet . . . day?**
a complicated sentence, in imitation of Donne's own style; in very approximate paraphrase, it means something like: 'Why are we afraid to commemorate Donne's death, albeit with hastily assembled, unpoetic, and soon-forgotten words such as a novice preacher might speak at his funeral?'
[3–4] **dare we not trust . . . thy dust**
(a) is it because we cannot admit that you are truly dead? (b) is it because we are afraid to entrust your reputation to whatever inadequate tribute we might produce?
[3] **unkneaded dough-baked prose**
(a) inadequately prepared; (b) superfluous ('unkneaded' = unneeded); (c) formless, tedious language.
[4] **unscissored**
(a) unkempt, uncombed; (b) unedited, unrevised (speech); (c) untonsured (tonsure is an initiatory ritual for the priesthood consisting of shaving the head or cutting a lock of hair), therefore an incompletely ordained clergyman.
[4–5] **flower of fading rhetoric**
The 'flower of rhetoric', referring to

figures of speech, is a conventional phrase; such prose would be composed of clichés. There is perhaps a pun on 'flower' = flour, extending the image of dough in line 4.

[6] **short-lived**
Flowers are the usual emblem of a brief existence.

[7] **Dry**
boring; ***sand that measures*** in an hour-glass; ***it*** the 'hour' or time on earth of line 6.

[9–10] **Didst thou dispense . . . sense?**
(a) 'Were you the only one who could provide our language with words and meaning?'; (b) 'Has your death caused language to be relieved of all words and sense?'; ***dispense*** (a) distribute; (b) do away with.

[14–21] **the flame . . . for ever**
A tribute to Donne's great eloquence and fame as a preacher; Carew draws on contemporary theories of physiology and vision to describe Donne's effect on his listeners, whose hearts were 'fired up' and transformed by the fire and light of his sermons, just as baser metals are 'distilled' (line 18) in the alchemist's alembic into their essences, and lead the alchemist to greater knowledge of himself.

[15] **brave**
(a) intrepid, courageous; (b) splendid.

[17] **Committed holy rapes**
persuaded us to good religious practice with its eloquence (the oxymoron probably alludes to Donne's 'Batter my heart' [p. 77]).

[19] **dark**
hidden, obscure, or unknown.

[20] **sense might judge . . . reach**
i.e. conveyed a knowledge that even imagination (fancy) could not attain.

[21] **desired for ever**
will be missed from now on.

[22] **Delphic choir**
(a) those prophets inspired by the Greek god Apollo from his shrine in Delphi; (b) poets (since Apollo was also the god of poetry).

[23] **Promethean breath**
The Titan Prometheus was responsible, in Greek myth, for endowing humanity with the gift of fire.

[25] **Muses' garden**
poetry; ***pedantic weeds*** i.e. Donne banished the mere display of learning for its own sake in poetry.

[26–8] **lazy seeds . . . planted**
Carew praises Donne's innovative style, which rejuvenated a poetry that had become too dependent on well-worn Petrarchan conventions.

[29] **debts of . . . age**
Beginning with the manifesto of a group of French men of letters who called themselves 'The Pleiad', sixteenth-century poets felt that they had to 'pillage' Greek and Latin language and literature in order to make their native writings measure up to the standards of greatness set by past literary achievements.

[30] **Licentious**
unwarranted, illegal; ***rage*** inspiration.

[31] **fury**
poetic madness or inspiration.

[32] **Possessed**
inspired as though by a god.

[32–3] **or with . . . Or Pindar's**
i.e. their inspiration comes second-hand from ancient poets, either from Anacreon (sixth century BC Greek lyric poet) or Pindar (*c*.518–*c*.438 BC, Greek poet particularly famous for his odes). Since both these poets were prominently imitated by Ben Jonson, it is possible that the criticism extends to him; though Carew has often been spoken of as a 'Son of Ben', he was not an uncritical admirer of the older poet. Nevertheless, it is more probable that the target is any number of minor writers of the period, or simply a general tendency among all of them.

[32] **ecstasy**
poetic inspiration.

[33] **subtle cheat**
clever deception.

[34] **sly exchanges**
perhaps the importation of Latin and Greek words, a widespread practice during the Renaissance intended to compensate for the poverty of native vocabulary.

[34–5] **juggling feat/Of two-edged words**
(a) punning on words in both their Latin or Greek and their English senses; (b) overuse of puns.
[35–6] **whatsoever wrong . . . Latin tongue**
Men of letters during this period often wrote poems in Latin or even Greek; Carew may mean to suggest that these literary efforts did little to enhance the languages in which they were written. Another possible meaning is that extensive borrowing from Greek or Latin and misuse of words derived from them have debased the classical languages. In any case, it is clear from the context that the poet is attacking the unoriginality that results from a literary climate of affectation and second-hand inspiration.
[37] **redeemed**
paid off the debts of line 29.
[38] **pregnant fancy**
abundant imagination.
[38–9] **drawn a line/Of masculine expression**
Carew's characterisation of Donne's style has been much admired for its succinctness and accuracy; ***masculine*** strongly personalised rather than passively imitative, complex rather than simple, drawing on science and philosophy rather than merely decorative and conventional in description.
[40] **Orpheus**
son of Apollo and archetypal poet-singer in Greek myth; ***ancient brood*** Greek and Roman writers (the object of 'admire' in line 41).
[41] **superstitious fools**
imitators of the Greeks and Romans who worship them with a quasi-religious fervour.
[42] **lead . . . gold**
the usual extremes of base and precious metals.
[43] **their exchequer**
see the note to 'A Rapture', line 146; 'their' refers to 'the ancient brood' of line 40.
[44] **had raked for ore**
i.e. had Orpheus and the ancient writers seen Donne's poetry, they would have imitated him.
[45] **yield no precedence**
acknowledge no superior precursor or previous claimant to his title; ***but of time*** except for the historical accident that causes some to be born before others.
[46] **blind fate of language**
i.e. a poet cannot choose which language he will be born into; ***tuned chime*** regular, smooth and musical verse.
[48] **so great disadvantage**
the handicap of writing in English, as compared with writing in Latin or Greek.
[49] **awe of thy imperious wit**
Note the metaphors of absolute rule (***imperious*** absolute, overmastering) in line 45, this line, and line 95.
[50] **bends**
(a) submits, is made to conform; (b) bows in respect.
[51] **hoops**
used to strengthen wooden barrels; the image is suggested by the bending of the language in the preceding line.
[52] **fancy**
poetic imagination; ***stout*** powerful, strong.
[53] **soft melting phrases**
the 'feminine' lines to which is opposed Donne's 'masculine expression' in line 39.
[54] **they**
the Ancient Greek and Roman poets.
[55–7] **cull the prime . . . harvest**
It was often lamented that the ancient poets had exhausted the entire stock of literary themes, leaving later poets no alternative but to imitate them.
[55] **invention**
the first part of rhetoric, consisting of the discovery of a subject to write about.
[57] **touch their harvest**
challenge the ancient poets by writing on the same themes as they.
[58–60] **Of what . . . before**
i.e. your bare hands alone, in the course of your least exertions, have collected more from those fields that

belong exclusively to you than all your ancient precursors could gather with their harvesting tools (note the opposition of 'glean' – to gather with one's bare hands – and 'reap' – to gather with a scythe).

[61] **strict laws**
because Donne's wit rules 'imperiously'.

[62] **libertines**
those who hold free or loose opinions about religion; here, by extension, those who are less disciplined in poetry.

[63] **They**
the libertines.

[63–4] **repeal**
recall from exile.

[63–4] **train/Of gods and goddesses**
use of Greek and Roman gods as mere verbal decoration in English poetry.

[65] **banished**
banished from, not allowed to appear in; ***these*** = gods and goddesses.

[66] ***Metamorphoses***
Ovid's famous book, long a major source of information about Greek and Roman mythology.

[67] **their lines**
those of the libertines; ***windy*** full of insubstantial words.

[68–70] **Till verse, refined by thee . . . apostasy**
Carew seems to think that the high standards set by Donne will not be maintained, and poetry will inevitably decline after his death.

[68] **this last age**
(a) the present; (b) the end of time, when the world is in decline.

[69] **ballad-rhyme**
popular narratives, in undignified verse, of sensational or crudely reported events; ***idols*** the classical gods and goddesses.

[71–8] **O pardon . . . dies**
Carew returns to the theme of his opening by recognising the inadequacy of his elegy to praise Donne sufficiently or to halt the inevitable decline of poetry that will follow his death.

[71] **untuned verse**
(a) irregular, disorderly; (b) deliberately rough, in Donne's style.

[73] **awful**
full of awe.

[75] **dumb**
silent.

[77] **these panting numbers**
the breathless verses of this poem (short-winded from trying to keep up with their model?).

[79] **swiftly turning . . . force**
A Donne-like analogy that draws attention to the tendency of all things to lose momentum once their motivating force is withdrawn; ironically, Carew's elegy was published at about the time of Milton's earliest poetry – hardly evidence of a decline.

[80] **moving hand**
the hand that moves it.

[81] **maintain a faint weak course**
continue to turn.

[82] **impulsive**
impelling.

[83] **pile**
pyre.

[84] **crown of bays**
(a) the imagined laurel wreath placed on the head of a poet in recognition of his greatness (in imitation of the victory crownings practised by the Ancient Greeks); (b) this elegy; ***crack*** (a) crackle (while burning); (b) utter a pronouncement.

[85] **spit disdain**
i.e. at the present state of poetry – the moisture within leaves tends to explode when they are tossed on the fire.

[87] **draw the envy**
(a) attract envy; (b) make others desire; ***to engross*** (a) to magnify; (b) to write large.

[89] **Those**
Donne's perfections; ***too num'rous*** (a) too many; (b) poetic (numbers = verse).

[90] **this**
our loss.

[91] **Though every pen . . . part**
though every writer should take part in praising you by writing his own tribute.

[92] **tire**
(a) attire, dress up; (b) exhaust, wear out.

[94] **incise**
engrave, carve.

[95] **king**
Note that Carew makes explicit in this line a metaphor of absolute rule implied throughout the poem, especially in lines 45 and 49.

[96] **monarchy**
kingdom; *wit* human understanding, intellect, mind.

[97] **flamens**
priests in pagan Rome devoted to the service of a particular deity.

[98] **Apollo's first . . . priest**
Donne was two 'priests' at different stages of his career – he served Apollo, god of poetry, as a young courtier before becoming a priest of the Church of England in later years.

EDMUND WALLER

(1606–87)

1645–68	*Poems*
1685	*Divine Poems*
1690	*Poems* (Part Two, posthumous)

Born in March 1606 at Coleshill, Hertfordshire, Edmund Waller was educated at Eton and King's College, Cambridge, but he never finished a degree course, opting in his teens for a political career. He was a Member of Parliament for Amersham, Ilchester, and Chipping Wycombe during the reigns of James I and Charles I and later, during the Long Parliament, for St Ives. He was involved in a conspiracy against Parliament in support of the king, arrested, and banished. In 1643 he married a second time (his first wife had died in 1634) and went to live in France. He continued to support the Royalist cause in Paris at great expense to himself, but was allowed to return to England in 1651, his sentence revoked. There he lived quietly until the monarchy was restored in 1660. In 1661 he became MP for Hastings, where he maintained a stance of tolerance towards Nonconformists, whom he frequently defended. He became something of a fixture in the House of Commons for the next twenty-five years and died at Hall Barn, surrounded by his family, on 21 October 1687.

Context

Waller has been accused of political opportunism for changing sides during Cromwell's reign; he even wrote 'A Panegyric to my Lord Protector' which earned him the office of Commissioner of Trade in 1655. Distasteful as his behaviour may appear, he seems to have learned from his experiences and was liked, even respected, throughout his career. Perhaps it is enough to say that he was a brilliant survivor who made up for his lack of character with a certain social agility.

Genre and Critical Reception

Waller was primarily a lyricist, though he was also a prolific writer of narrative, political and satirical verse. He was much admired for his sophistication during his own lifetime. His lyrics were set to music by Henry Lawes and other prominent composers. Later he was regarded as a literary reformer who brought to poetry the same kind of moderation that characterised his politics. His main achievement was his balanced and smooth style; his use of the 'heroic' or closed couplet established it as the form of choice for the next hundred years. He continued to be esteemed by readers of Samuel Johnson's generation in the later eighteenth century, but then his reputation declined, and it has not really recovered since. One poem, 'Go, Lovely Rose', has kept his name alive, and it remains among his few truly memorable poems in English. With the exception of one or two other lyrics, most of his verses strike modern readers as trite and lacking in poetic vigour, despite the prestige they once enjoyed. However, Ezra Pound paid Waller's lyrical gifts a prominent tribute in the twentieth century by offering a paraphrase of 'Go, Lovely Rose' as the climax ('Envoi') of his 1922 sequence 'Hugh Selwyn Mauberly'. More recently, Waller's political poetry has attracted the interest of scholars.

Further Reading

Edition

Poetical Works, ed. G. Thorn-Drury (London, 1893; New York, 1904) is still the only comprehensive edition. There are selections in Hugh Maclean, ed., *Ben Jonson and the Cavalier Poets* (New York and London, 1974), pp. 231–51.

Critical Studies

Despite the small amount of commentary devoted to Waller, he is the subject of two very useful books. A.W. Allison, *Toward an Augustan Poetic* (Lexington, KY, 1962), studies the influence of his language, style and versification on later poets; and W.L. Chernaik, *The Poetry of Limitation* (New Haven, CT, 1968) is a comprehensive examination of most of his poetry, with a fine appreciation of both its virtues and its limitations. Ruth C. Wallerstein, 'The development of the rhetoric and metre of the heroic couplet, especially in 1625–1645', *PMLA*, **50** (1935), 166–209, is a pioneering investigation of his contribution to neoclassical metrics; later, George Williamson, 'The rhetorical pattern of neo-classical wit', in *Seventeenth-Century Contexts* (Chicago, 1961) did the same for his style. F.W. Bateson offers 'A word for Waller' in his *English Poetry: A critical introduction* (New York, 1966). Ruth Nevo has examined some of his post-Restoration political poems in *The Dial of Virtue: A study of poems on affairs of state in the seventeenth century* (Princeton, NJ, 1963); while Hugh M. Richmond, in 'The intangible mistress'. *MP*, **56** (1959), 217–23, and 'The fate of Edmund Waller', *SAQ*, **60** (1961), 230–38, wrote of his love poetry. Waller is also discussed in the same author's *The School of Love: The evolution of the Stuart love lyric* (Princeton, NJ, 1964).

There are a few good essays on individual poems. Earl Miner, *The Cavalier Mode from Jonson to Cotton* (Princeton, NJ, 1971), is persuasive on 'Go, Lovely Rose' (pp. 39–41) and 'On St James's Park' (pp. 24–37), as is A.B. Chambers, 'Waller and King Charles in St James's Park', in *Andrew Marvell and Edmund Waller: Seventeenth-century praise and Restoration satire* (University Park, PA and London, 1991), pp. 57–84. Richard Hillyer, 'Better read than dead: Waller's "Of English Verse"', *Restoration: Studies in English Literary Culture, 1660–1700,* **14** (1990), 33–43 offers a close reading of another frequently anthologised poem.

80 / *Song*

Go, lovely rose!
Tell her that wastes her time and me
That now she knows,
When I resemble her to thee,
How sweet and fair she seems to be.

Tell her that's young
And shuns to have her graces spied,
That hadst thou sprung
In deserts, where no men abide,
Thou must have uncommended died.

Small is the worth
Of beauty from the light retired;
Bid her come forth,
Suffer herself to be desired,
And not blush so to be admired.

Then die, that she
The common fate of all things rare
May read in thee:
How small a part of time they share
That are so wondrous sweet and fair!

An apt confirmation of a truism which states that a poet need write only one truly fine poem in order to be remembered. This song was given a musical setting by the composer Henry Lawes. Its opening lines suggest the medieval device of the 'envoi', a concluding stanza (and, later, an entire poem) beginning with the word 'go', addressed to the poem itself, asking it to bear its message of the poet's love to his lady. Waller combines that motif with the ancient image of the rose as a symbol of fragile feminine beauty and the transitory nature of all earthly things in a delicate lyric of four stanzas, rhyming *a b a b b*; the first and third lines are dimeters, the rest are tetrameters.

[1] **Go, lovely rose**
Probably a translation of 'I felix rosa' (Go, happy rose), a phrase from the Roman poet Martial.

[2] **wastes her time and me**
a witty play on three different senses of 'waste': (a) the lady is misusing her youth and youthful beauty by not accepting the poet's proffered love – is wasting away (declining in beauty), like the rose; (b) she is 'wasting her time' in the usual sense; (c) she is making the poet 'waste away' as he pines with unrequited love (a conventional complaint of lovers, whose health is supposed to suffer when their desires are unfulfilled).

[4] **resemble**
compare.
[5] **seems**
Note the force of this word; the lady's seeming possession of the same attributes as the rose will be challenged in the remaining lines of the poem.
[7] **shuns**
(a) shies away from; (b) prevents; ***graces*** physical beauty, particularly unclothed; ***spied*** perceived (but with a suggestion of revealing something normally hidden).
[8] **sprung**
(a) grown; (b) bloomed.
[9] **deserts**
desolate places devoid of humans or human habitation – not, as in the current sense, an arid plain with scanty vegetation; ***abide*** dwell.
[10] **must have**
would have necessarily; ***uncommended*** unnoticed, unappreciated and unpraised.
[12] **retired**
withdrawn, held back.
[13] **Bid**
request.
[14] **Suffer**
allow, permit.
[16] **that**
so that.
[17] **common fate**
i.e. not simply mortality but the tendency of roses to wither or fade rapidly after attaining their fullest beauty; ***rare*** (a) especially fine or excellent; (b) precious.
[18] **read**
discern; note that it is the rose which the lady will 'read', rather than the poem.
[19] **they**
those things.
[20] **wondrous**
wondrously, marvellously.

81/ *On a Girdle*

That which her slender waist confined,
Shall now my joyful temples bind;
No monarch but would give his crown,
His arms might do what this has done.

It was my heaven's extremest sphere,
The pale which held that lovely deer;
My joy, my grief, my hope, my love
Did all within this circle move!

A narrow compass, and yet there
Dwelt all that's good, and all that's fair!
Give me but what this ribbon bound,
Take all the rest the sun goes round!

An example, in three tetrameter stanzas rhyming *a a b b*, of Waller's gallant style, in which simple elegance and compliment disguise the fact that the speaker's interest in the lady is primarily confined to her sexual attractiveness. See Lovelace's 'Gratiana Dancing and Singing' (p. 330) for another example of astronomical metaphors.

Title
Girdle a sash or belt worn round the waist.
[1] **confined**
held close, embraced.
[2] **my joyful temples bind**
i.e. he will wear it tied round his head like a victory crown, perhaps to display it as the trophy of his amorous success.
[4] **arms**
possibly a pun on arms = weapons of conquest, in which case the girdle, by implication, would be like the spoils of war; ***do what this has done*** encircle her waist.
[5] **my heaven**
(a) the lady; (b) his love; ***extremest sphere*** outermost sphere, alluding to the notion that the heavens consisted of a nest of concentric spheres, of which the last defined the realm of the fixed stars, which were beyond corruption and change. Note the play on the old parallel between macrocosm (i.e. the great world or universe) and microcosm (i.e. the little world of human nature; the human body).
[6] **pale**
enclosure, wall or fence; ***deer*** his mistress (a pun on 'dear').
[8] **all . . . move**
a discreet way of describing the locus of his physical attraction.
[9] **compass**
(a) enclosed or delimited space; (b) range of interest.
[10] **good**
(a) virtuous; (b) desirable, of value; (c) pleasurable.
[11] **ribbon**
the girdle.
[12] **all . . . goes round**
i.e. the world; the image presupposes a Ptolemaic scheme of the universe, in which the sun orbits around the earth.

82 / *On St James's Park, As Lately Improved by His Majesty*

Of the first paradise there's nothing found.
Plants set by heaven are vanished, and the ground,
Yet the description lasts. Who knows the fate
Of lines that shall this paradise relate?
  Instead of rivers rolling by the side
Of Eden's garden, here flows in the tide;
The sea, which always served his empire, now
Pays tribute to our prince's pleasure too.
Of famous cities we the founders know,
But rivers, old as seas to which they go,
Are nature's bounty. 'Tis of more renown
To make a river than to build a town.

For future shade, young trees upon the banks
Of the new stream appear in even ranks;
The voice of Orpheus or Amphion's hand
In better order could not make them stand.
May they increase as fast and spread their boughs
As the high fame of their great owner grows!
May he live long enough to see them all
Dark shadows cast and, as his palace, tall!
Methinks I see the love that shall be made,
The lovers walking in that amorous shade,
The gallants dancing by the river's side:
They bathe in summer and in winter slide.
Methinks I hear the music in the boats
And the loud echo which returns the notes,
While overhead a flock of new-sprung fowl
Hangs in the air and does the sun control,
Darkening the sky; they hover o'er and shroud
The wanton sailors with a feathered cloud.
Beneath, a shoal of silver fishes glides
And plays about the gilded barges' sides.
The ladies, angling in the crystal lake,
Feast on the waters with the prey they take;
At once victorious with their lines and eyes,
They make the fishes and the men their prize.
A thousand Cupids on the billows ride,
And sea-nymphs enter with the swelling tide,
From Thetis sent as spies to make report
And tell the wonders of her sovereign's court.
All that can, living, feed the greedy eye
Or dead, the palate, here you may descry –
The choicest things that furnished Noah's ark
Or Peter's sheet, inhabiting this park,
All with a border of rich fruit-trees crowned,
Whose loaded branches hide the lofty mound.
Such various ways the spacious alleys lead,
My doubtful Muse knows not what path to tread.
Yonder, the harvest of cold months laid up
Gives a fresh coolness to the royal cup.
There ice, like crystal, firm and never lost,
Tempers hot July with December's frost,
Winter's dark prison, whence he cannot fly,

Though the warm spring, his enemy, draws nigh.
Strange, that extremes should thus preserve the snow
High on the Alps or in deep caves below.
  Here, a well-polished Mall gives us the joy
To see our prince his matchless force employ.
His manly posture and his graceful mien,
Vigour and youth in all his motions seen,
His shape so lovely and his limbs so strong
Confirm our hopes we shall obey him long.
No sooner has he touched the flying ball
But 'tis already more than half the Mall,
And such a fury from his arm has got
As from a smoking culverin 'twere shot.
  Near this, my Muse, what most delights her, sees
A living gallery of agèd trees:
Bold sons of earth that thrust their arms so high
As if once more they would invade the sky.
In such green palaces the first kings reigned,
Slept in their shades, and angels entertained.
With such old counsellors they did advise,
And, by frequenting sacred groves, grew wise.
Free from the impediments of light and noise,
Man, thus retired, his nobler thoughts employs.
Here Charles contrives the ordering of his states.
Here he resolves his neighbouring princes' fates:
What nation shall have peace, where war be made
Determined is in this oraculous shade;
The world, from India to the frozen north,
Concerned in what this solitude brings forth.
His fancy, objects from his view receives;
The prospect, thought and contemplation gives.
That seat of empire here salutes his eye,
To which three kingdoms do themselves apply:
The structure by a prelate raised, Whitehall,
Built with the fortune of Rome's capitol.
Both, disproportioned to the present state
Of their proud founders, were approved by fate.
From hence he does that antique pile behold
Where royal heads receive the sacred gold.
It gives them crowns and does their ashes keep;
There made like gods, like mortals there they sleep.

Making the circle of their reign complete,
Those suns of empire, where they rise, they set.
When others fell, this, standing, did presage
The crown should triumph over popular rage;
Hard by that house, where all our ills were shaped,
The auspicious temple stood and yet escaped.
So snow on Ætna does unmelted lie,
Whence rolling flames and scattered cinders fly.
The distant country in the ruin shares;
What falls from heaven the burning mountain spares.
Next, that capacious hall he sees, the room
Where the whole nation does for justice come,
Under whose large roof flourishes the gown,
And judges grave, on high tribunals, frown.
Here, like the people's pastor he does go,
His flock subjected to his view below,
On which, reflecting in his mighty mind,
No private passion does indulgence find.
The pleasures of his youth suspended are
And made a sacrifice to public care.
Here, free from court compliances, he walks
And with himself, his best adviser, talks –
How peaceful olive may his temples shade
For mending laws and for restoring trade,
Or how his brows may be with laurel charged
For nations conquered and our bounds enlarged.
Of ancient prudence here, he ruminates,
Of rising kingdoms and of falling states;
What ruling arts gave great Augustus fame,
And how Alcides purchased such a name.
His eyes, upon his native palace bent
Close by, suggest a greater argument.
His thoughts rise higher when he does reflect
On what the world may from that star expect
Which at his birth appeared, to let us see
Day, for his sake, could with the night agree,
A prince on whom such different lights did smile,
Born the divided world to reconcile!
Whatever heaven or high extracted blood
Could promise or foretell, he will make good,
Reform these nations and improve them more
Than this fair park from what it was before.

St James's Park is a triangular plot of ground next to the palace of the same name, bordered on the north by the broad avenue of the Mall and on the south by Birdcage Walk. On its eastern border are the government offices at Whitehall, on its west Buckingham Palace and its gardens. It is the easternmost of the series of four contiguous royal parks that stretch three miles from Whitehall, just west of the Thames, to Kensington. St James's was originally a marsh; it was turned into a deer park and recreation area, with bowling green and tennis court, by Henry VIII. Immediately after assuming rule, Charles II transformed it into a pleasure garden with the help of Louis XIV's celebrated garden planner, André Le Nôtre. In the nineteenth century it was further modified by John Nash. Its most prominent features are the lake and the broad Mall that connects Buckingham Palace with Whitehall.

Waller's poem belongs to the topographical tradition of Jonson's 'To Penshurst' (p. 119) and Lanier's 'The Description of Cookham' (p. 154), though unlike them it describes an urban and royal setting rather than a country estate. As a consequence the poem is more overtly political, though its recommendations to the new king are carefully subordinated to themes based on the biblical description of Eden, Virgil's *Eclogues* (particularly the prophetic Fourth Eclogue, which foresees the emergence of a new golden age), and the pastoral tradition in general. Its more immediate parallels are such mid-century poems as John Denham's 'Cooper's Hill' and Andrew Marvell's 'Upon Appleton House', but its most distinguished successor was to be Alexander Pope's 'Windsor Forest', which evokes some of its same themes and imagery, though with a different political focus. Waller's poem uses Charles's improvements in the park as the occasion to suggest a course of action for his monarch to reform his entire realm. Unfortunately, Waller's hopes were not to be realised. Charles II turned out to be more interested in bodily pleasures than in the body politic.

The poem is written in closed iambic pentameter couplets and may be divided into five sections: a four-line introduction comparing the park to Eden, followed by eight lines in praise of the lake; a segment describing the activities in the park; a portrait of the king at play there; and a long final section that expresses Waller's hopes for Charles's leadership of the nation.

[1] **the first paradise**
the Garden of Eden, where the Creator placed the first man and woman, as recounted in Genesis 2: 8.

[2] **Plants set by heaven**
See Genesis 2: 9: 'Out of the ground the Lord God made various trees grow'; ***and the ground*** The exact location of Eden was debated well into the nineteenth century.

[3] **the description lasts**
Eden is described not only in the Bible but in much subsequent literature, where it is evoked as a harmonious, unspoiled environment perfectly suited to basic human needs.

[4] **Of lines**
this poem; ***this paradise*** St James's Park; ***relate*** tell about.

[5–6] **rivers . . . garden**
According to Genesis 2: 10–14, the single river that ran through Eden, irrigating it, divided into four branches.

[6] **here . . . tide**
A new canal allowed the waters from the Thames to flow into the park. The Thames is a tidal river which not only flows into the sea but also receives water from it when its flow changes direction.

[8] **The sea . . . pleasure too**
Shipping had become an important component of British power during the sixteenth century, and London developed into a major port, rivalling and eventually displacing Venice. The personified sea is imagined, through the reversal that causes the waters to

flow into the park, as paying homage to Charles and contributing to his recreation there, just as in the past it has provided the means for British prosperity through mercantile and naval activity.

[9] **founders**
London's founder is unknown, unlike Rome's (the mythical Romulus).

[10] **rivers . . . go**
The image of the river flowing into the sea, very popular in the period, is an ancient figure of the tribute paid by a subordinate to a superior or of the individual soul, after death, flowing into eternity.

[11] **nature's bounty**
i.e. a gift of nature.

[11–12] **more renown . . . a town**
The conceit is meant to suggest that Charles, by creating the new stream that feeds water into the park, may boast of a greater achievement than the mere founding of a city, since normally nature alone creates rivers. These lines speak of the necessity for a monarch to admit new internal improvements as well as encourage outward expansion. Charles does not simply receive honours from abroad but also gives himself honour by improving his own realm.

[14] **even ranks**
The trees, planted in this orderly fashion as though to give tribute to the monarch, also stand for the necessity of establishing early an order that will later reach full maturity.

[15] **Orpheus**
the son of Apollo; his music made trees move in sympathy; ***Amphion*** mythological son of Zeus; his music moved the stones into place for the walls of Thebes. Note that both these figures from Greek mythology were poets as well; Waller may be implying that his hortatory poetry is also capable of bringing about future order (Amphion was also the founder of a town).

[20] **Dark shadows**
Not an ominous note of things to come but a feature of the pastoral landscape, which provides protection from the sun's heat, as is hinted at in line 22; ***his palace*** Buckingham Palace, at the end of the Mall.

[22] **amorous**
(a) suitable for lovers; (b) caringly provided for human beings.

[23] **gallants**
fashionable men or lovers.

[24] **bathe . . . slide**
The river serves for swimming in summer and skating in winter.

[25] **Methinks I hear**
I seem to hear.

[27] **new-sprung fowl**
birds from the game preserve that have recently flown up.

[28–30] **Hangs . . . cloud**
The fowl fly in formations so thick that they blot out the sun over the lake; like the river, they seem to offer their services to those who enjoy the park; ***wanton sailors*** couples who sail boats on the lake for pleasure (***wanton*** (a) sportive, merry; (b) amorous).

[31] **shoal**
a large number of fish.

[32] **gilded barges**
ornate pleasure-boats.

[33] **angling**
(a) fishing with hook and bait; (b) attracting the attention of men by their glances.

[34] **Feast . . . prey**
(a) eat the fish they catch, while still in the boat; (b) enjoy the company of the men they attract to their boats; see the next verses, 35–36. Also, note the sea-nymphs in the lines that follow.

[37–8] **A thousand Cupids . . . sea-nymphs**
i.e. an erotic atmosphere pervades the lake. Note how this highly artificial conceit suggests the typical iconography of the time (as displayed in the Marie de' Médicis series painted by Rubens, for instance); Waller is monumentalising this small body of water, like a Baroque painter, by depicting it as haunted by the presence of innumerable minor deities associated with sexual desire. The scene portrayed is more elegant, however, than libidinous.

[39] **Thetis**
(a) a minor sea deity, mother of Achilles by her mortal husband Peleus, one of the heroes sailing on the ship *Argo* whose attention she attracted by displaying her divine charms as she swam in the water alongside; (b) the sea itself.

[39–40] **spies . . . court**
Note that the nymphs are presumably sent to admire and report rather than to carry out some hostile purpose; ***her sovereign*** Charles II, whose subject Thetis is. One is reminded that the sea, coming in with the river-tide, was also said to bear tribute in the earlier lines of the poem; ***wonders*** (a) marvellous devices or works of art; (b) great accomplishments.

[41] **living . . . the palate**
Note the double appeal to eye and taste, which parallels the visual and gustatory feasting of the ladies in the gilded barges of line 32; ***descry*** discover.

[43] **furnished Noah's ark**
Noah's ark was large enough to contain every zoological specimen on earth, male and female, to save all living creatures from the universal flood (Genesis 6–8); 'choicest things' (i.e. most carefully selected for quality) and 'furnished' suggest, however, that Noah's pantry as well as his menagerie is meant. Furthermore, the diners aboard the ark would presumably have been fed from the surrounding sea as well.

[44] **Peter's sheet**
an allusion to the biblical episode in Acts 10: 9–16 and 11: 5–10 – the hungry St Peter's vision of 'a large sheet coming down, lowered to the ground by its four corners', in which were all the animals of the earth, from which he was commanded to choose his food. The ark and the sheet provide two images of plenty, one from the Old Testament, the other from the New. The park, according to the contemporary witness of Samuel Pepys, contained a number of wild animals. Both passages suggest a new order supplanting a previous one: Noah and his family survive after the wicked have perished in the Flood, and Peter begins his mission to the Gentiles by setting aside the strictures of traditional Jewish law. Doubtless some sort of parallel with the restoration of the monarchy after the Commonwealth is implied.

[47] **alleys**
bordered walks.

[48] **doubtful**
hesitant; ***Muse . . . tread*** i.e. he doesn't know what aspect to describe next. The theme of plenty is extended from the animals in the park to the variety of its spatial design.

[49] **harvest of cold months**
ice.

[49–56] **laid up . . . deep caves below**
The 'lofty mound' of line 46 covers a hollowed-out cave where ice, collected in winter, is kept cold through the summer in the depths of the earth. The passage presents the park as a place that can contain the extremes of heat and cold, summer and winter (as the lake serves to entertain both bathers and skaters) and offer cool refreshment to Charles's 'royal cup' after his exertions at games in the park, described in the following lines.

The mound, which combines the loftiness of the Alps and the depth of the caves while it keeps ice from being 'lost' (melting), is one of the 'wonders' alluded to in line 40. Like the canal that brings the sea within range of the court, it mediates between nature and humanity, and brings together extremes.

[52] **July**
in this period, pronounced to rhyme with 'truly'.

[57] **well-polished Mall**
a smooth alley in which pall-mall was played – a hardwood ball was driven with a mallet through an iron ring suspended at the other end of the alley. The player who managed to do this with the fewest strokes was the winner.

[59] **mien**
facial expression.

[62] **obey him long**
(a) because the beauty of his person, combining grace and vigour, makes him a worthy model; (b) because, given his excellent state of health, he should live to rule for a long time.
[65] **fury**
impetuous force. Charles's recreational energy is supposed to foreshadow his success in war.
[66] **culverin**
a large, very long cannon with a narrow bore and a long firing range.
[69–70] **Bold sons of earth . . . sky**
The trees are described as though they were Titans – in Greek myth the older generation of gods, born of Earth and Sky, who invaded Olympus and attempted to dethrone Zeus.
[71–2] **green palaces . . . angels entertained**
This couplet combines reminiscences of the pagan 'Golden Age' (associated with the rule of Saturn and the Titans) and of the era of an Old Testament patriarch such as Abraham, who was visited by and entertained the Lord and two angels. Waller may also have in mind Britain's druidic past, which was said to have held trees sacred and drawn wisdom from them.
[75–6] **Free . . . employs**
This couplet concludes a brief vision of the park as a typical pastoral retreat, but it also stands for the kind of government the poet hopes will emerge from the new monarch.
[77] **contrives**
devises, plans; ***his states*** the three estates of clergy, commonalty and nobility; however, another meaning – the conditions of Charles's mind and body – may also be implied.
[78] **resolves**
decides.
[80] **oraculous**
oracular; i.e. a place where one receives divine wisdom. The doctrine of the divine right of kings, closely associated with the Stuart monarchs, may also be hinted at in this otherwise hyperbolic description of the meditative park grounds where the king would find peace and solitude for making important decisions.
[83–5] **His fancy . . . eye**
fancy imagination; the couplet describes, in terms of mid-seventeenth-century psychology, the orderly workings of the monarch's mind; the fancy is made up of stored sense impressions; ***prospect*** perspective, view; Charles's imagination is fed not only by the tranquillity of the park but by the government buildings visible from it; from that perspective 'the seat of empire' that affects the 'world, from India to the frozen north' (line 81) – Westminster Abbey, Parliament, and Whitehall – 'salutes' (i.e. strikes) his eye (line 85).
[86] **three kingdoms**
England, Scotland and Ireland; ***themselves apply*** make application, seek information or aid; note the parallel with the sea-nymphs, representatives of Thetis, who also 'apply' in this sense to Charles's government.
[87] **Whitehall**
Whitehall Palace. It dates back to the thirteenth century and was the London residence of the Archbishop of York. Rebuilt by Cardinal Wolsey in the early sixteenth century, it was later appropriated by Henry VIII for the royal offices. It was subsequently expanded under James I, Charles I and Charles II (in 1661, the date of Waller's poem), only to be destroyed by fire in 1698. Today the site is occupied by government buildings.
[88] **Built . . . capitol**
Like the Capitol in Rome, Whitehall was first built for private use and turned into a public building ('fortune' = fate), as the following couplet explains.
[89] **disproportioned**
appropriated; see the note to line 87; ***proud founders*** The Capitol in Rome was completed by Tarquin the Proud; Whitehall received its magnificence from the equally proud Cardinal Wolsey. Both were fated to be humbled and have their property seized because of their tyrannous or overambitious behaviour.

[91] **antique pile**
ancient architectural structure.
[92] **Where royal heads . . . gold**
Westminster Abbey, where the monarchs of England are crowned. Since the king is the head of both Church and state, the gold with which he is crowned is doubly sacred.
[93] **does their ashes keep**
British monarchs are also buried in Westminster Abbey.
[94] **made like gods . . . sleep**
Note the paradox; the monarchs, quasi-deified during their reigns, become icons of human mortality in their burial. The lines are a subtle warning – like those alluding to Tarquin and Wolsey – of the common fate of all men, including the most powerful, such as Cromwell, who had died only three years earlier; though his name is not mentioned, the poem alludes to him, albeit indirectly (and prudently, since Waller had supported him) at several points.
[95] **circle of their reign complete**
The secular reign of the monarch is perfected by the sacred context of its beginning and end. 'Complete' was pronounced, French-style, to rhyme with 'set'.
[96] **suns of empire**
The sun as symbol of the monarch is an ancient image; it was prominent in the reign of Charles's contemporary, the French king Louis XIV, styled the 'sun-king'. Here the figure is a reminder of both the glory and the mortality of the ruler.
[97] **others fell**
other buildings and institutions; though the House of Lords was abolished, the head of the Church (Charles I) executed, and the Book of Common Prayer banned, the Abbey itself escaped physical damage.
[98] **popular rage**
the destructive rebellion of the people during the Civil War and Commonwealth period. The Abbey stands for the permanence of England's sacred and political institutions.
[99] **Hard by that house**
Westminster Abbey is near the House of Commons, where the 'ills' of Cromwell's reign, the execution of Charles I and the rule of Parliament, were first planned ('shaped').
[100] **auspicious**
(a) fortunate; (b) giving promise of a fortunate issue; ***temple*** Westminster Abbey.
[101] **Ætna**
the famous volcano on Sicily.
[102–4] **Whence . . . spares**
i.e. the hot ashes and debris hurled from the erupting volcano burn the countryside but fail to disturb the snow on the mountainside. The image of Ætna echoes the mount in the park that holds the ice from summer heat, as the Abbey encloses the emblems of a monarchy safe from the fiery destruction of revolution. The destruction of stained glass, organs, altars and decorations, both interior and exterior, characterised one stage of the Civil War.
[105] **capacious hall**
Westminster Hall, originally part of Westminster Palace, which was replaced by the present Houses of Parliament after the fire of 1834; it is the largest open-timber hall in Europe, and the place where the High Court once sat.
[108] **frown**
look severe, impressively impartial as interpreters of the law.
[109] **people's pastor**
A medal created for the coronation represented the young king as a shepherd guarding his flock; the image of Charles, head of both Church and state, as pastor is therefore doubly appropriate, but it also continues the pastoral mode of the poem as a whole.
[110] **subjected**
submissive; ***his view below*** i.e. his view from below (in the park) allows him to share his flock's perspective in dispensing justice.
[112–14] **private passion . . . public care**
Unfortunately, Waller's hope that

Charles II would prove to be a monarch who could set aside or sacrifice his youthful pleasures and personal concerns for the sake of his subjects was not fulfilled; ***public care*** serious attention to the needs of the kingdom.

[115] **court compliances**
conforming in manners to the demands of his courtly environment; the park is a retreat from the pomp and rituals of the palace.

[117] **olive**
the emblem of peace, whether the leaves are offered on their branch or woven into a crown.

[118] **mending**
reforming.

[119] **brows**
head; ***laurel charged*** crowned with laurel leaves, like a conqueror or winner of a prize or contest; 'charged', however, also bears a sense of heavy responsibility. As a symbol of achievement and ambition, the laurel leaves are the opposite of the olive.

[120] **bounds**
national boundaries (with a hint of imperial ambitions).

[121] **ancient prudence**
i.e. he meditates on the precepts of the Greek and Roman philosophers who counselled prudence in war and government.

[121] **rising . . . states**
Waller is speaking of the usually cyclical view of the emergence and decline of great empires, whose history should serve as object lesson for Charles's decisions; but he may have something more specific in mind in his distinction between 'kingdom' and 'state', since the new regime would be characterised as the former, while the defunct government of Cromwell it replaced could only be described as the latter.

[123] **ruling arts**
skill in governing; ***Augustus*** the first Roman emperor, Octavian, who initiated the period of Augustan Peace after the long civil wars that destroyed the Ancient Roman Republic.

[124] **Alcides**
Hercules, the greatest of the Greek heroes; ***purchased*** earned. Though Augustus did wage war earlier in his career, he was best known in subsequent history as the bringer of a lasting peace; Hercules, whose valour came as a result of his successful completion of the twelve labours enjoined upon him, stands as a complementary, if not opposed, figure; one teaches how to maintain peace, the other how to behave in times of peril. Hercules was considered the archetype of the active monarch who protects his kingdom.

[125] **native palace**
St James's Palace, where Charles was born. After twelve years in exile, the daily sight of his birthplace would have been especially moving for the returning monarch.

[126] **argument**
theme.

[128] **that star**
(a) the rising star of Charles's fortune, now that he has returned; (b) an unusual phenomenon that marked the future king's birth was the appearance of a star around noon on that day. The scene was portrayed on a medal commemorating the event, and John Dryden mentions it in his poem 'Astraea Redux'. It is perhaps meant to suggest the Star of Bethlehem, which marked the birth of Christ.

[130] **Day . . . night agree**
Yet another example of the reconciliation of opposites in the person of the king, as heat and cold are united in the park.

[132] **divided world**
i.e. the restoration of the monarchy with Charles's return brought together the Parliamentarian and Royalist factions that had torn the kingdom apart.

[133–4] **Whatever heaven . . . make good**
a further hint of even greater achievements, echoing the utopian vision of Virgil's Fourth Eclogue and its

prediction of a new era of universal peace and prosperity.
[135–6] **Reform . . . before** The final couplet is an exhortation addressed directly to the king, making explicit the indirect recommendations in the rest of the poem; ***nations*** (a) the three realms of the British king's domain; (b) the nations of Europe.

83 / *Of English Verse*

Poets may boast, as safely vain,
Their works shall with the world remain;
Both, bound together, live or die,
The verses and the prophecy.

But who can hope his lines should long
Last in a daily changing tongue?
While they are new, envy prevails,
And, as that dies, our language fails.

When architects have done their part,
The matter may betray their art;
Time, if we use ill-chosen stone,
Soon brings a well-built palace down.

Poets that lasting marble seek
Must carve in Latin or in Greek.
We write in sand; our language grows,
And, like the tide, our work o'erflows.

Chaucer his sense can only boast,
The glory of his numbers lost!
Years have defaced his matchless strain,
And yet he did not sing in vain.

The beauties which adorned that age,
The shining subjects of his rage,
Hoping they should immortal prove,
Rewarded with success his love.

This was the generous poet's scope
And all an English pen can hope,
To make the fair approve his flame
That can so far extend their fame.

Verse, thus designed, has no ill fate,
If it arrive but at the date
Of fading beauty, if it prove
But as long-lived as present love.

A variation on the *carpe diem* theme ('seize the day'), in which Waller seems to argue, discreetly, that poetry need serve no purpose higher than that of gaining a woman's love. What seems to be a serious discourse on the problem of writing in English turns out to be a ruse for making a witty and perhaps self-deprecating point about the modest aims of the Cavalier or court poet. The quatrains, in tetrameter couplets, contribute to this balanced tone.

[1] **as safely vain**
i.e. Poets may predict (in vain) that their poems will last (though it is unlikely) because they will be dead by the time they are proved wrong.
[2] **with the world remain**
last long after the death of the authors.
[3–4] **bound together... prophecy**
The prophecy will last no longer than the poems.
[7] **envy prevails**
That is, if the poems are truly good, rivals will speak ill of them out of jealousy.
[8] **that**
envy; by the time hostile criticism has finally ceased and the poems can be esteemed for their own artistic merit, the language has changed so radically that they can no longer be appreciated.
[10] **matter**
materials of which a building is constructed; ***art*** skill or ingenuity of construction or design.
[13] **lasting marble**
an ironic allusion to a famous ode of the Roman poet Horace ('*Exegi monumentum*', *Odes*, 1.30) or, rather, the tradition it inspired (e.g. Shakespeare's Sonnet 55: 'Not marble, nor the gilded monuments/Of princes shall outlive this powerful rhyme').
[14] **Latin... Greek**
The classical languages were still the models for all serious composition. The ability to write poetry in Latin or even in Greek was fostered at grammar school and was, indeed, the focus of the curriculum. The Latin of Cicero, promoted by Renaissance humanists as a model, was imitated closely, so that the language seemed not to have changed in sixteen centuries, while writers of English were already becoming aware of differences between their language and that of Shakespeare a half-century earlier. The French Academy had provided a model for the stabilising and perfecting of a language, and scholars speculated about the nature of language throughout the century.
[17–18] **Chaucer... lost**
There had been several attempts to discover the metrical principles of Chaucer's verse, but no one had succeeded in reconstructing them. Towards the end of the century, John Dryden published modernised versions of some of the *Canterbury Tales*.
[17] **his sense can only boast**
Chaucer's fame is now based on the

meaning rather than on the artistic merits of his poetry.

[18] **numbers**
metrical principles, versification.

[19] **strain**
(a) offspring, progeny; (b) melody; (c) tone or turn of expression.

[20] **in vain**
suggesting an alternative to the 'safely vain' boasts of the opening line.

[21] **beauties**
lovely women; ***adorned*** made famous, added lustre to.

[22] **shining**
brilliant; ***subjects*** objects; ***rage*** passion, love frenzy.

[24] **Rewarded . . . love**
i.e. gave him their love so that he would immortalise them in his verses.

[25] **generous**
(a) high-spirited, gallant; (b) munificent.

[26] **English pen**
as opposed to one who writes in Latin or Greek.

[27] **fair**
lady; ***approve his flame*** yield to his passion.

[28] **that**
(a) pen (= poet); (b) flame (i.e. love expressed in poetry).

[30] **If**
though; ***arrive but at*** last until.

[31] **as present love**
These last words suggest that the ladies are deceived in thinking that the poet will make their names immortal, since their fame will last no longer than his verses. Waller's poem, therefore, belongs at least indirectly to the line of poems of seduction that offer a dubious premiss in order to persuade the lady to offer her favours.

SIR JOHN SUCKLING

(1609–42)

1646 *Fragmenta Aurea*
1658 *Fragmenta Aurea* (enlarged; posthumous)
1659 *The Last Remains of Sir John Suckling*

Suckling was baptised on 10 February 1609, so he must have been born shortly before that date in Twickenham, Middlesex. Little is known of his early schooling; he matriculated at Trinity College Cambridge in 1623, but does not seem to have taken a degree. He studied law for a short time, but his father's death in 1627 and his subsequent inheritance of the extensive family estates brought that career to a halt. Later that year, he seems to have taken up a military career and spent several years in active service on the Continent. Knighted in 1630, he accompanied the embassy to Gustavus Adolphus of Germany in 1632 and had a private audience with the king immediately afterwards, an indication of a relationship with and commitment to his monarch that was to characterise most of his career. The main consequence of his return, however, was the opportunity to indulge himself by gambling away a good part of his patrimony. Perhaps for this reason he began the unsuccessful courtship of a wealthy heiress, Anne Willoughby. Suckling's next years were filled with vicissitudes and further quarrels, not all of them unprovoked; from 1635 onwards, however, he did enjoy a relationship with Mary Bulkeley, who was apparently the 'Aglaura' addressed in a number of his poems and letters, and inspired a play by that name. Nevertheless, he was to be no more successful in wooing her than he had been with others, despite his reputation as a witty and generally attractive – if financially irresponsible – person.

Suckling's most productive period as a writer was 1637–8, but this intensive activity was halted in 1639, when he joined King Charles's forces in their attempt to put down a series of revolts in the North. After a number of failures in countering the growing revolt in Scotland the royal army was forced to retreat, and Suckling returned home to continue supporting the king's cause against the growing power of Parliament. As a consequence of his subsequent involvement in an army plot, Sir John was found guilty of high treason by the Commons and forced to flee to France in 1641. He continued to support the king even after his flight but died abroad not long afterwards – according to some reports, by suicide.

Context

Suckling's life and personality correspond to a certain pattern, even if his refusal to take much of life seriously seems to contradict his passionate devotion to the monarchy. Indeed, his behaviour was later taken to be exemplary of the standard courtier figure, one who took his loyalties seriously but little else, who always performed with ease and naturalness in all that he did and never showed any sign of strain or effort. His devotion to the royal cause, however, could be understood as a gesture of commitment to the things that really matter, such as maintaining a stable social order and political responsibility. Indeed, the writings of Suckling's last four years reveal a turn away from the elegant devil-may-care attitude of the early poetry to a concern with social relationships and the sophisticated, urbane world of intellectual society in the city or the learned gentry in the country. Short as his life was, it points to the transition from narrower literary concerns focused on the interests of a courtly or noble audience to the broader kind of literate society characteristic of the eighteenth century.

Genre and Critical Reception

Though he wrote a few plays and some elegant prose, including a short essay and some interesting letters, Suckling's reputation is entirely based on a handful of poems. His forte is the short, witty, uncomplicated yet sophisticated love lyric, and it is his achievement in this poetry that has been the basis of his reputation. Within five years of his death, Suckling's poetry was gathered into a volume and published. The collection was popular enough to be given a second edition two years later. His reputation was especially high with the poets of the Restoration, and those who admired his example hoped to maintain something of his tone and style. By the middle of the eighteenth century, however, the mood changed – he was judged to be deficient both in the craft of metre and in interesting subject matter. But his polished simplicity and directness continued to win him readers, so that by the middle of the following century he was admired once more for the very same qualities that had characterised what Alexander Pope called 'the mob of gentlemen who wrote with ease'. His reputation, despite some doubts and qualifications, remained strong enough in the twentieth century to ensure his place in standard anthologies of English poetry. No one doubts that he is a minor poet, but no one would deny him a permanent place among those writers who have had something memorable to say in verse and have the craftsmanship and fluency to say it well. It has been said that Suckling combines the witty and colloquial language of Donne with the directness and simplicity of Jonson; if his total achievement is not high, it is still great enough to place at least a handful of his best poems among the most familiar in the language.

Further Reading

Edition

The Works of Sir John Suckling: The non-dramatic works, ed. Thomas Clayton (Oxford, 1971) is the definitive edition.

Critical Studies

Charles L. Squier, *Sir John Suckling* (Boston, MA, 1978) is the only monograph devoted entirely to Suckling and his works. Criticism devoted to the poet is quite sparse. F.O. Henderson, 'Traditions of *Précieux* and *Libertin* in Suckling's poetry', *ELH*, **4** (1937), 274–98 is still helpful in demonstrating his relationship to contemporary French poetry. F.H. Candelans, 'Ovid and the indifferent lovers', *RN* **13** (1960), 294–7, identifies an Ovidian theme. J.H. Summers, 'Gentlemen of the court and of art: Suckling . . . ', in *The Heirs of Donne and Jonson* (New York and London, 1970 pp. 41–51); Geoffrey Walton, 'The Cavalier poets', in Boris Ford, ed., *New Pelican Guide to English Literature, III: From Donne to Marvell* (Harmondsworth, 1982), pp. 205–18; Michael P. Parker, '"All are not born (Sir) to the Bay": "Jack" Suckling, "Tom" Carew, and the making of a poet', *ELR*, **12** (1982), 341–68; Gerald W. Morton, 'Mildmay Fane's satiric poem on John Suckling', *Notes and Queries*, **38** (1991), 85–6; and Bruce Donald, 'The war poets of 1639: Carew, Suckling and Lovelace', *Contemporary Review*, **259** (1991), 309–14, relate him to his fellow Cavaliers, while Bruce Donald, 'Why Millamant studied Sir John Suckling', *Notes and Queries*, **34** (1987), 334–5; T.N. Corns, W.A. Speck and J.A. Downie, 'Archetypal mystification: polemic and reality in English political literature, 1640–1750', *Eighteenth-Century Life*, **7** (1982), 1–27; and John Wilders, 'Rochester and the Metaphysicals', in Jeremy Treglown, ed., *Spirit of Wit: Reconsiderations of Rochester* (Hamden, CT, 1982), pp. 42–57, consider his relationship to later writers.

R.A. Anselment, '"Men Most of All Enjoy, When Least They Do": the love poetry of John Suckling', *TSLL*, **14** (1972), 17–32; Thomas Clayton, '"At Bottom a Criticism of Life": Suckling and the poetry of low seriousness', in Claude J. Summers and Ted-Larry Pebworth, eds, *Classic and Cavalier: Essays on Jonson and the Sons of Ben* (Pittsburgh, PA, 1982), pp. 217–41, are helpful for assessing Suckling from a more positive perspective than usual. One of the rare examples of sustained analysis of a Suckling poem is L.A. Beaurline, '"Why So Pale and Wan": an essay in critical method', *TSLL*, **4** (1962), 553–63.

84 / *Song*

Why so pale and wan, fond lover?
Prithee, why so pale?
Will, when looking well can't move her,
Looking ill prevail?
Prithee, why so pale?

Why so dull and mute, young sinner?
Prithee, why so mute?
Will, when speaking well can't win her,
Saying nothing do't?
Prithee, why so mute?

Quit, quit, for shame; this will not move,
This cannot take her.
If of herself she will not love,
Nothing can make her.
The devil take her!

One of Suckling's most popular pieces, this poem typifies the witty, sceptical posture that is associated with the Cavalier manner. It consists of four alternating tetrameter and trimeter lines followed by a trimeter verse that echoes the first line of each stanza, rhyming *a b a b b*.

[1] **wan**
unhealthily pale, sickly; ***fond*** (a) infatuated, doting; (b) foolish, silly; (c) insipid, sickly in flavour.
[2] **Prithee**
I pray thee, I ask you.
[3–4] **Will . . . prevail?**
i.e. 'If she is not attracted to you by your healthy appearance, how do you expect your sickly appearance to change her feelings towards you?' Note the ironic opposition between 'lover' and 'move her', paralleled by 'sinner' and 'win her' in the next stanza; ***prevail*** succeed in making her love you.
[6] **dull**
(a) senseless, inanimate; (b) foolish, fatuous; (c) lacking in wit or humour; ***sinner*** the young man addressed is a sinner because either (a) he has transgressed against the rules of conduct proper to a lover and offended the lady he is courting; or (b) he is a would-be rogue or seducer of women who looks comically incapable of carrying out his ambitions.
[8] **speaking well**
(a) speaking pleasingly and with grace; (b) speaking persuasively.
[11] **quit**
give up; ***this*** his behaviour; ***move*** persuade, affect someone.
[12] **take her**
attract her, take her fancy.
[13] **of herself**
according to her own inclinations or desires.
[15] **devil take her!**
forget about her! Let her go to hell! This comic shift in tone typifies the Cavalier ideal of not taking such things as the conventions of love too seriously.

85 / *Out upon It!*

Out upon it! I have loved
Three whole days together
And am like to love three more,
If it hold fair weather.

Time shall moult away his wings,
Ere he shall discover
In the whole wide world again
Such a constant lover.

But a pox upon't is, no praise
There is due at all to me:
Love with me had made no stays
Had it any been but she.

Had it any been but she,
And that very very face,
There had been at least ere this
A dozen dozen in her place.

The usual authority for the text of this poem is the 1659 volume of Suckling's works, but his most recent editor, Thomas Clayton, has demonstrated that it is unreliable. The version given below is based on the Clayton edition of the works.

It consists of four quatrains of alternating tetrameter and trimeter lines, the second and fourth lines rhyming (except for stanza three, which rhymes *a b a b*). The poem illustrates perfectly the natural ease and colloquial humour of Suckling's best work.

[1] **Out upon it!**
Enough of this!
[2] **whole days together**
three entire days in succession; see the proverb 'After three days men grow weary of a wench, a guest, and weather rainy.'
[4] **fair weather**
if conditions continue to be favourable (if the lady continues to respond with the same fervour as before).

[5] **Time shall moult . . . wings**
Time is traditionally depicted as a winged figure; ***moult*** to shed feathers, as birds do periodically.
[8] **constant lover**
Constancy (i.e. fidelity) in love was spoken of ironically and with comic scepticism throughout the century (cf. Donne's 'Go, and catch a falling star' [p. 56]; here the poet suggests humorously that his remaining

faithful for three days is virtually unprecedented.

[9–10] **But a pox upon't . . . to me**
'Curse it! I'm sorry to say that I can't even take any credit for it.'

[11] **stays**
(a) pause or suspension of action; (b) delay or waiting period; (c) control, self-restraint.

[12] **Had it**
had his lover.

[14] **that very very face**
that face and no other. The poet's specifying what in particular kept him interested in the lady for so 'long' is part of the somewhat comic compliment he pays her in this poem. Note the parallel repetitions that contrast the lady of line 14 with her imagined rivals in the last line.

[15] **ere this**
before now.

[16] **A dozen dozen . . . place**
The exaggeration of the number of women the poet would have been capable of loving within three days serves to make his claim of a lengthy commitment to one lady seem all the more complimentary.

86 / *A Ballad upon a Wedding*

I tell thee, Dick, where I have been,
Where I the rarest things have seen,
   Oh, things beyond compare!
Such sights again cannot be found
In any part of English ground,
   Be it at wake or fair.

At Charing Cross, hard by the way
Where we, thou know'st, do sell our hay,
   There is a house with stairs;
And there did I see coming down
Such folk as are not in our town,
   Forty, at least, in pairs.

Amongst the rest, one pest'lent fine
(His beard no bigger, though, than thine)
   Walked on before the rest.
Our landlord looks like nothing to him;
The King (God bless him), 'twould undo him,
   Should he go still so dressed.

At Course-a-park, without all doubt,
He should have first been taken out
   By all the maids i'th' town;

Though lusty Roger there had been,
Or little George upon the Green,
   Or Vincent of the Crown.

But wot you what? The youth was going
To make an end of all his wooing;
   The Parson for him stayed;
Yet by his leave, for all his haste,
He did not wish so much all past,
   Perchance, as did the maid.

The maid (and thereby hangs a tale,
For such a maid no Whitsun-ale
   Could ever yet produce),
No grape that's kindly ripe could be
So round, so plump, so soft as she,
   Nor half so full of juice.

Her fingers were so small, the ring
Would not stay on which they did bring,
   It was too wide a peck;
And to say truth (for out it must),
It looked like the great collar (just)
   About our young colt's neck.

Her feet beneath her petticoat
Like little mice stole in and out,
   As if they feared the light;
But oh, she dances such a way,
No sun upon an Easter day
   Is half so fine a sight!

He would have kissed her once or twice,
But she would not; she was so nice,
   She would not do't in sight;
And then she looked as who should say,
'I will do what I list today,
   And you shall do't at night.'

Her cheeks so rare a white was on,
No daisy makes comparison
(Who sees them is undone);
For streaks of red were mingled there,
Such as are on a Katherine Pear
(The side that's next the sun).

Her mouth so small when she doth speak,
Thou'dst swear her teeth her words did break
That they might passage get;
But she so handles still the matter,
They come as good as ours or better
And are not spoiled one whit.

Her lips were red, and one was thin,
Compared to that was next her chin
(Some bee had stung it newly);
But, Dick, her eyes so guard her face,
I durst no more upon her gaze
Than on the sun in July.

If wishing should be any sin,
The parson self had guilty been
(She looked that day so purely);
And did the youth so oft the feat
At night, as some did in conceit,
It would have spoiled him, surely.

Passion o' me, how I run on!
There's that that would be thought upon,
I trow, besides the bride:
The business of the kitchen great;
For it is fit that men should eat,
Nor was it there denied.

Just in the nick the cook knocked thrice,
And all the waiters in a trice
His summon did obey;
Each serving man, with dish in hand,
Marched boldly up, like our trainband,
Presented, and away.

When all the meat was on the table,
What man of knife or teeth was able
   To stay to be entreated?
And this the very reason was:
Before the parson could say grace,
   The company was seated.

Now hats fly off, and youths carouse;
Healths first go round and then the house;
   The bride's came thick and thick;
And when 'twas named another's health,
Perhaps he made it hers by stealth.
   (And who could help it, Dick?)

O' th' sudden up they rise and dance,
Then sit again, and sigh and glance,
   Then dance again and kiss;
Thus several ways the time did pass,
Whilst every woman wished her place,
   And every man wished his.

By this time all were stol'n aside
To counsel and undress the bride,
   But that he must not know;
But yet 'twas thought he guessed her mind
And did not mean to stay behind
   Above an hour or so.

When in he came, Dick, there she lay
Like new-fall'n snow melting away
   ('Twas time, I trow, to part);
Kisses were now the only stay,
Which soon she gave, as who should say,
   'God b'w'y', with all my heart.'

But just as heavens would have, to cross it,
In came the bridemaids with the posset;
   The bridegroom eat in spite;
For had he left the women to't,
It would have cost two hours to do't,
   Which were too much that night.

At length the candle's out, and now
All that they had not done, they do;
  What that is, who can tell?
But I believe it was no more
Than thou and I have done before
  With Bridget and with Nell.

The title suggests the kind of popular poem or song, printed on a single large sheet and sold in the streets, that celebrated important events. The speaker and his addressee are apparently rustics from the West Country (Devonshire or Somerset). The main point of this burlesque epithalamion, or wedding song, is the contrast between city and country manners, yet when the impressive manners and display of the ceremony are over, the speaker concludes, all weddings come down to the same thing in the end. The metre and stanza – two lines of tetrameter followed by a trimeter line, with the same pattern repeated and rhyming *a a b c c b* – is reminiscent of popular ballad form.

[1] **I tell thee, Dick**
The speaker is a provincial recounting his experiences to a friend back home, perhaps in the West Country.

[2] **rarest**
of uncommon interest or excellence.

[6] **wake**
an annual festival held by the parish or village, originally in honour of its patron saint, not the vigil before a funeral; *fair* a seasonal festival, usually of somewhat wider scope and including some business activity.

[7] **Charing Cross**
site near the Haymarket in London, a centre of activity from as far back as medieval times.

[9] **a house with stairs**
This feature would suggest grandeur and magnificence to a man like the speaker, who probably dwells in a small farm-cottage.

[13] **one**
one man; *pest'lent* pestilent, i.e. (here) surpassingly, extremely (a humorously colloquial expression); *fine* of elegant demeanour and dress.

[16] **landlord**
owner of the land they farm as tenants.

[17] **The King (God bless him)**
Observe the naive respect for the monarch, whom the speaker comically compares, unfavourably, to the bridegroom; *undo him* bankrupt him.

[18] **still**
all the time.

[19] **Course-a-park**
a country game in which a girl called out to one of the participating boys to chase her.

[20] **taken out**
chosen.

[22–4] **Roger . . . George . . . Vincent**
Obviously the most admirable boys of the village; a proverb ran 'As good as George of Green'; 'Roger' has sexual connotations, and 'Vincent' (Latin *vincere*) implies a victory of some sort.

[22] **lusty**
merry; but the modern sexual sense is perhaps also implied.

[25] **wot you what?**
do you know what?

[26] **make an end**
conclude, i.e. get married.

[27] **Parson**
a clergyman attached to a parish, especially in the country.

[28] **by his leave**
with his permission, usually employed ironically to gain permission for something that the addressee would hesitate to grant.

[29] **all past**
get it over with.
[30] **Perchance**
perhaps (an ironic note of speculation on the speaker's part); *maid* maiden or virgin, the bride-to-be.
[31] **thereby hangs a tale**
about that there is something to tell (a common phrase).
[32] **Whitsun-ale**
a country festival that featured ale-drinking, celebrated at Whitsuntide, the seventh Sunday after Easter.
[33] **produce**
have to show, attract.
[36] **full of juice**
full of life and energy.
[38] **Would not stay on which they would bring**
which they would bring would not stay on.
[39] **too wide a peck**
too large by a great deal (*peck* a considerable number).
[40] **out it must**
I must say it (a common expression).
[41] **just**
exactly; the size of the ring, which implies its great price, impresses the speaker even more than the daintiness of the bride's fingers.
[43] **petticoat**
skirt, whether worn as an inner or outer garment.
[44] **stole**
crept.
[47] **No sun upon an Easter day**
according to folklore, the sun was said to dance on Easter Sunday to celebrate Christ's Resurrection.
[50] **nice**
proper.
[51] **in sight**
in public.
[52] **as who should**
like someone who might.
[53] **list**
please, want.
[54] **do't**
Note the sly ambiguity of the bride's response.
[57] **is undone**
loses his heart, falls in love with her.
[59] **Katherine Pear**
an early-ripening variety.
[61] **Her mouth so small**
her mouth was opened so slightly (a sign of feminine elegance).
[62] **her teeth her words did break**
interrupted her speech, disturbed her articulation.
[66] **spoiled**
garbled, poorly enunciated; *one whit* one bit.
[69] **Some bee had stung it newly**
a common conceit for a pouting lower lip, considered a desirable feature.
[70] **her eyes . . . sun in July**
a variant of the Petrarchan conceit comparing the brilliance of the lady's eyes to the sun's; *July* pronounced 'Julie'.
[73] **parson self**
parson himself.
[75] **purely**
perfect.
[76–7] **did the youth . . . conceit**
if the groom made love as much that night as the other men at the wedding did in their imaginations; *conceit* imagination, fancy.
[78] **spoiled him**
exhausted him.
[79] **Passion o' me**
Shame on me!; *run on* talk too much.
[80–81] **There's that that . . . bride**
There's more to tell about than the bride.
[81] **I trow**
I suppose.
[82] **business**
activity.
[85] **in the nick**
in the nick of time.
[86] **trice**
instant.
[87] **summons**
orders.
[89] **trainband**
trained company of citizen soldiers.
[90] **Presented, and away**
presented their dishes and left.
[91] **meat**
meal, food.
[93] **stay to be entreated**
wait until asked to be seated.

[98] **Healths first go round and then the house**
i.e. after all have had a turn to toast, the house seems to turn around because of their intoxication.
[99] **The bride's**
her health, toasted repeatedly.
[101] **he made it hers by stealth**
i.e. when someone else was toasted, perhaps he himself drank secretly to the bride.
[103] **O' th' sudden**
All of a sudden.
[111] **he**
the bridegroom.
[114] **Above an hour or so**
i.e. the bridegroom was too impatient to wait more than an hour for the undressing ceremony to be finished.
[117] **part**
depart.
[118] **stay**
delay.
[119] **as who should**
like someone who wanted to.
[120] **God b'w'y'**
goodbye (both are contractions of 'God be with you').
[121] **heavens . . . cross it**
as fate would have it.
[122] **posset**
a bedtime hot-milk drink, sweetened and spiced, and curdled with wine or ale.
[123] **eat**
ate; ***in spite*** despite his desire to do something else.
[124] **to't**
alone to take care of everything.
[125] **cost**
taken.
[132] **Bridget . . . Nell**
the names of two local village girls.

RICHARD LOVELACE

(1618–57)

1649 *Lucasta*
1659 *Posthume Poems of Richard Lovelace, Esq.*

Described by one seventeenth-century biographer as a soldier, gentleman, lover and poet, Lovelace was, even more than Suckling, the model courtier. He was born in 1618, the descendant of a family of professional soldiers, near London or, possibly, in Holland, while his father was serving in the Dutch military service. Both his parents died while he was still young. He was educated at Charterhouse and then Oxford, where he was much admired by contemporaries for his amiable character and handsome features. When King Charles I and his queen came to Oxford in 1636, they were so impressed with this young man of eighteen that they had the MA conferred on him during their visit. After leaving Oxford, he spent some time at the court before taking part in the two disastrous expeditions of 1639 to Scotland, where he may have met Suckling; then he returned to his estates in Kent. Always loyal to the monarchy, he presented a Royalist petition to the House of Commons, which responded by imprisoning him in London for two months. It was there that he wrote his celebrated 'To Althea, from Prison'.

After his release he went to the Continent. He spent the next four years fighting in wars abroad, and was eventually promoted to the rank of colonel. In 1648 he was imprisoned again, probably on trumped-up charges; during this second incarceration he put together his first volume of poetry, which was published in 1649. Released in the same year, he was obliged to sell off much of his estates; but he was also helped by the generosity of friends like Charles Cotton (see p. 333), even as he had himself been a patron of others. The exact date and manner of his death are not certain; he died sometime between 1657 and 1659. As the incarnation of the Caroline Cavalier ideal, he suffered the consequences of the fall of the monarchy and the spirit that informed it.

Context

Richard Lovelace is often linked with Sir John Suckling, though they appear to have had a personal rather than a literary relationship. As poets, however, they had in common a certain style that has led scholars to speak of both as 'Cavalier poets' or – not entirely accurately – as among the 'Sons of Ben' [Jonson]. In fact Lovelace is not much like Suckling, and the influence of Donne's early poems is as evident in his verse as that of Jonson. Even more than Suckling, Lovelace was the model courtier; certainly he had the good looks, the witty style, and the appealing personality that were felt to be the hallmarks of such a figure. He was scholarly, cultured and intelligent, with wide-ranging interests. He numbered musicians and painters, as well as writers, among his many friends, at least some of whom were of a very different political persuasion from his own. He was curious about many things beyond the traditional gentlemanly occupations of falconry, hunting and the military, including languages, painting, music, theatre, and the other arts.

Genre

Lovelace's poetry is characterised by that simplicity which is said to be the hallmark of the Cavalier style. This directness of diction and ease of expression serve him admirably in the handful of poems by which he is known, but his grace and wit, never completely absent from any of his writing, are not enough to make the remaining poetry seem more than the occasional pieces many of them doubtless were. He is at his best when his natural lyric gift is applied to matters of deep conviction and personal commitment, such as are evident in his two most famous songs.

Critical Reception

Though 'To Althea' was being read and referred to as early as the mid 1640s and reprinted throughout the following decades of the seventeenth century, Lovelace's reputation was not as high as that of his fellow Cavalier poets during the century and a half following his death. Seemingly ignored during much of the eighteenth century, except for a few attempts at revival during the second half, his poetry as a whole was not resuscitated until well into the nineteenth. Even in the twentieth century his reputation did not benefit greatly from the revival of interest in Donne and Jonson, with whom he was compared unfavourably. Yet his celebrated poems to Lucasta and Althea maintained a kind of underground existence during all these years, so that phrases from them have passed into the stock of proverbial expressions. If Lovelace is unlikely ever to be perceived as more than a minor poet, he nevertheless achieved what very few writers of a century crowded with poets could claim: a few of his words have become a permanent part of the English language.

Further Reading

Edition

The standard edition still remains *Poems*, ed. C.H. Wilkinson (Oxford, 1925, 1953).

Critical Studies

Of the earlier accounts, C.H. Hartmann, *The Cavalier Spirit and Its Influence on the Life and Work of Richard Lovelace* (London, 1925) is still useful. More recent general studies are R. Skelton, *The Cavalier Poets* (London, 1960; New York, 1970); Earl Miner, *The Cavalier Mode from Jonson to Cotton* (Princeton, NJ, 1971); Geoffrey Walton, 'The Cavalier poets', in Boris Ford, ed., *The New Pelican Guide to English Literature, III: From Donne to Marvell* (Harmondsworth, 1982); Manfred Weidhorn, *Richard Lovelace* (New York, 1970) gives a comprehensive account of the life and works; Donald Bruce, 'The war poets of 1639: Carew, Suckling and Lovelace', *Contemporary Review*, **259** (1991), 309–14, offers a new perspective on the Cavalier group.

For essays on individual poems, see C.F. Williamson. 'Two notes on the poems of Lovelace', *MLR*, **52** (1957), 227–9; N.H. Pearson, 'Lovelace's *To Lucasta, Going to the Warres*'. *Explicator*, **7** (1949), Item 58; G.F. Jones, '"Lov'd I Not Honour More": the durability of a literary motif', *CL*, **11** (1959), 131–43; Christopher S. Nassaar, 'Lovelace's "To Lucasta, Going to the Wars"', *Explicator*, **39** (1981), 44–5; A.D. Cousins, 'Lucasta, Gratiana, and the amatory wit of Lovelace', *Parergon*, **6A** (1988), 97–104; Gerald Hammond, 'Richard Lovelace and the uses of obscurity', *Proceedings of the British Academy*, **71** (1985), 203–34; D.C. Allen, 'Richard Lovelace: "The Grasse-Hopper"', in *Image and Meaning: Metaphoric traditions in Renaissance poetry* (Baltimore, MD, 1960; rev. edn 1968), a famous essay on the poem; B. King, 'Green ice and a breast of proof', *CE*, **26** (1965), 511–15; B. King, '*The Grasse-hopper* and Allegory', *Ariel E*, **1** (1970), 71–82; Dale B.J. Randall, 'Reading the light in Lovelace's "The Grass-hopper"', *College Literature*, **16** (1989), 182–9; Cleanth Brooks, 'A pre-Romantic view of nature: Sir Richard Lovelace', in *Historical Evidence and the Reading of Seventeenth-Century Poetry* (Columbia, MO, 1991), pp. 113–28. Brooks's essay is a full reading of the poem which suggests corrections for some of Allen's interpretations.

87 | *To Althea, from Prison*

When Love with unconfinèd wings
Hovers within my gates
And my divine Althea brings
To whisper at the grates;
When I lie tangled in her hair
And fettered to her eye,
The gods that wanton in the air
Know no such liberty.

When flowing cups run swiftly round
With no allaying Thames,
Our careless heads with roses bound,

Our hearts with loyal flames;
When thirsty grief in wine we steep,
When healths and draughts go free,
Fishes that tipple in the deep
Know no such liberty.

When, like committed linnets, I
With shriller throat shall sing
The sweetness, mercy, majesty
And glories of my King;
When I shall voice aloud how good
He is, how great should be,
Enlargèd winds that curl the flood
Know no such liberty.

Stone walls do not a prison make,
Nor iron bars a cage;
Minds innocent and quiet take
That for an hermitage.
If I have freedom in my love,
And in my soul am free,
Angels alone, that soar above,
Enjoy such liberty.

Lovelace's most famous poem consists of three eight-line stanzas of alternating tetrameter and trimeter lines, rhyming *a b a b c d c d*. It is notable for its definitions of liberty and imprisonment, which take on multiple senses as the word is applied to love, fellowship, and political loyalty.

[1] **Love . . . wings**
i.e. not simply love understood in its usual sense but also its conventional representation in Ancient Greek and Roman poetry as Cupid, an infant boy with wings; ***unconfinèd*** free to move anywhere, unfettered, unimprisoned.
[2] **Hovers**
(a) hangs above while flapping the wings (as applied to Cupid); (b) lingers as a presence (as applied more abstractly to love as an emotion); ***within my gates*** i.e. inside the prison where he is incarcerated.
[3] **And my . . . brings**
brings my divine Althea; ***divine*** (a) extraordinarily beautiful or good; (b) held sacred because the object of his love.
[4] **whisper at the grates**
Since he and Althea, who must remain outside his cell, cannot speak in private, they must whisper to one another.
[5] **lie tangled in her hair**
i.e. when he lies with her in an embrace (cf. Milton, 'Lycidas' (p. 395), lines 68–9; 'sport . . . with the tangles of Neaera's hair'); but note that he is also 'imprisoned' in it.
[6] **fettered to her eye**
bound to her by gazing deeply and

affectionately into her eyes. Vision was often understood during this period as a kind of beam emanating from the eye and striking the object seen. For example, Donne speaks of lovers gazing at one another as having 'their eye-beams twisted' and threaded 'upon one double string' ('The Ecstasy', lines 7–8). Lovelace added to this image the notion of being chained.

[7] **wanton**
(a) to play unrestrainedly; (b) to play lasciviously or with erotic abandon. Note that this image recalls that of the god of love in the opening lines.

[8] **liberty**
(a) freedom from captivity; (b) freedom to act as one wishes; (c) unrestrained erotic familiarity.

[9] **flowing**
often filled or overfilled; ***run swiftly round*** are passed around the table.

[10] **allaying**
diluting; ***Thames*** water (from the river Thames, which flows through London); wine mixed with water is, of course, not only less potent but also weaker in flavour.

[11] **careless**
without cares or worries; ***with roses bound*** wearing wreaths of roses; note the attenuated image of enchainment.

[12] **loyal flames**
(a) passionate fellowship; (b) patriotic fervour or fidelity to the king, a quality typical of the Cavalier; note that the companions are bound together both in head and in heart, by their intellectual and political commitment to the king, along with the order he represents, and by their emotional attachment to that order and to one another.

[13] **thirsty grief**
cf. the expression 'to drown one's sorrows in drink'; ***steep*** to soak until suffused by the surrounding liquid, whose colour, flavour, or odour is absorbed.

[14] **healths and draughts go free**
i.e. when toasting and drinking to the health of others is unrestrained.

[15] **tipple**
(a) to drink (any liquid); (b) to drink until intoxicated; ***the deep*** sea.

[16] **liberty**
Observe the rhyme-words in this entire stanza and the way they express apparent opposition ('run swiftly round', 'bound'; 'Thames', 'flames') in the first four lines and similarity or identity in the last four ('steep', 'deep'; 'free', 'liberty').

[17] **committed**
(a) imprisoned, encaged; (b) charged with a duty; ***linnet*** a warm grey or brown songbird whose breast and head (in the male) become crimson in the summer when it is wild but remain the same colour year-round if it is kept captive.

[18] **shriller**
(a) sharper, higher pitched; (b) more poignant; (c) more clearly, brightly; (d) indicative of strife or discomfort; ***throat*** i.e. the sounds that issue from the throat.

[19–20] **sweetness, mercy, majesty/ And glories**
note the paradox: while the first two qualities characterise the humaneness of the king, the third and fourth emphasise those that elevate him above ordinary humanity.

[21] **voice**
express.

[22] **how great should be**
i.e. should properly be regarded as being.

[23] **Enlargèd**
(a) who enjoy absolute freedom because boundless and unrestrained; (b) increased in magnitude or strength; ***curl*** cause to ripple or form waves with high crests; ***flood*** any large body of water, as opposed to land.

[24] **Know**
experience. Note that the poet compares his willingness to proclaim his support for the monarchy with both a small source of sound (the linnet) and a mighty one (the great crashing waves raised by powerful winds), with one imprisoned by men and one unleashed by nature.

[25–6] **Stone walls . . . cage**
These two lines are among the most quoted in the English language; the implication is, as William Blake was later to say, that most manacles or restraints are 'mind-forged' rather than physically imposed.
[27] **innocent**
(a) free of sin or guilt, at ease; (b) harmless to others; ***quiet*** calm, unperturbed.
[28] **That**
the prison; ***hermitage*** (a) literally, the dwelling-place of a hermit, where he can meditate undisturbed; (b) figuratively, any place of retirement where one can enjoy quiet and solitude.
[29] **freedom in my love**
(a) independence in choosing whomever he wishes to love; (b) liberty of action that is the result of loving; (c) frankness, openness; (d) the right to love.
[31] **Angels alone**
i.e. no earthly creature can experience greater freedom; observe the opposition between the liberty of the angels, supernatural beings not bound by the limitations of the material world, and the captivity of the linnet, a natural creature also endowed with the ability to fly; ***soar above*** (a) that fly above our heads, in heaven; (b) that surpass our nature, rise far beyond it.
[32] **Enjoy**
(a) take pleasure in; (b) experience, have the benefit of.

88 / *To Lucasta, Going to the Wars*

Tell me not, sweet, I am unkind
That from the nunnery
Of thy chaste breast and quiet mind,
To war and arms I fly.

True, a new mistress now I chase,
The first foe in the field,
And with a stronger faith embrace
A sword, a horse, a shield.

Yet this inconstancy is such
As you too shall adore;
I could not love thee, dear, so much,
Loved I not honour more.

A love poem in quatrains consisting of tetrameter lines followed by trimeter lines and rhyming *a b a b*. It combines, rather neatly, the two Cavalier ideals of love and valour.

[1] **sweet**
i.e. Lucasta, his mistress; ***unkind*** (a) unloving, cruel, thoughtless; (b) unnatural (by acting against his own best interests).

[2] **nunnery**
(a) convent, residence for nuns, women devoted to a life of chastity and religious devotion; (b) place of refuge and safety, away from the dangers of the world. Cf. Shakespeare, *Hamlet*, III, i, 122: 'Get thee to a nunnery. Why wouldst thou be a breeder of sinners?' The worship that the speaker would practise in this nunnery, however, is not of God but of his mistress.

[3] **chaste . . . mind**
A double compliment is intended here: the breast (or bosom) is a place of refuge and comfort (as in the biblical phrase 'in the bosom of Abraham'), but erotic overtones are implied in these words as well, even if the poet insists on the virtuousness of his mistress ('chaste') and the 'quiet mind' is indicative of the peace of a retirement from the pressures of the world that the poet finds in the company of his lady. In short, why should he give up the company (and love) of a beautiful, virtuous and tranquil woman for the ugly violence of fighting in a war?

[4] **arms**
weapons and armour (deriving from the Latin *arma*).

[5] **new mistress**
i.e. Bellona, the Roman goddess of war; ***chase*** (a) pursue an attractive woman; (b) pursue an enemy in war.

[6] **first foe in the field**
A poetic oxymoron, at least as old as Petrarch's sonnets (fourteenth century), described the beloved lady as the 'sweet foe' or enemy of the lover because she was the cause of the suffering and pain he felt in longing for her (ungranted) favours. Here the poet plays on this conceit by seeking out his literal enemy, who is to be found in the field rather than the boudoir.

[7] **stronger faith**
Again, a play on traditional poetic love language. The 'faith' of the lover, who worships his beloved with religious fervour, refers to his fidelity to the lady of his affections; but the poet admits that he embraces his new mistress, War, with even more passionate fervour; ***embrace*** (a) buckle a shield on to one's arm; (b) adopt as a course of action or belief; (c) clasp in the arms; (d) enjoy sexually.

[8] **sword, horse, shield**
the main components of the arms referred to above; note their opposition to the nunnery, chaste breast and quiet mind of line 3.

[9] **inconstancy**
(a) infidelity to another or to a lover; (b) erratic or irrational behaviour.

[10] **you too**
i.e. the lady will understand his motives in leaving her; ***adore*** (a) treat with the greatest respect or love; (b) worship as a divinity.

[11–12] **I could not . . . more**
These last two lines are extremely well known; note the paradoxical explanation that is offered for the speaker's behaviour – his love for his mistress would be worth much less if he did not value even more his sense of duty to do what is expected of him as a gentleman and subject of his monarch. The word ***honour*** has a number of shades of meaning: (a) high respect accorded because of position or rank; (b) esteem because of personal achievements; (c) glory, fame, reputation, good name; (d) a fine sense of what is right according to some accepted standard of conduct; (e) fidelity to a sworn promise; (f) (of a woman) a reputation for chastity, purity or fidelity as high virtues.

89 / *Gratiana Dancing and Singing*

See with what constant motion,
Even and glorious as the sun,
 Gratiana steers that noble frame,
 Soft as her breast, sweet as her voice,
 That gave each winding law and poise,
 And swifter than the wings of Fame.

She beat the happy pavëment
By such a star made firmament,
 Which now no more the roof envies,
 But swells up high with Atlas even,
 Bearing the brighter, nobler heaven,
 And in her all the deities.

Each step trod out a lover's thought
And the ambitious hopes he brought,
 Chained to her brave feet with such arts,
 Such sweet command and gentle awe
 As, when she ceased, we sighing saw
 The floor lay paved with broken hearts.

So did she move, so did she sing,
Like the harmonious spheres that bring
 Unto their rounds their music's aid,
 Which she performèd such a way,
 As all th'enamoured world will say
 The Graces danced and Apollo played.

An elegant example of the Cavalier style at its best, this lyric in tetrameter lines rhyming *a a b c c b* echoes the gracefulness of its subject with an equally musical rhythm and style.

Title
Gratiana The name is derived from Latin *gratia*, grace; in effect, her name recalls the three Graces of classical mythology, who were often represented as a dancing and singing trio.
[3] **steers that noble frame**
directs her body; ***noble*** splendid, lofty. There is a conceit running throughout the poem comparing Gratiana to one of the angelic 'intelligences' that were thought to guide the seven concentric, transparent spheres surrounding the earth and carrying the planets around as they turned.
[5] **winding**
a sinuous course, full of bends and turns; the Ptolemaic account of the universe had recourse to 'epicycles' or smaller circular movements within the

larger, more regular motions of the planets (wandering bodies, in Greek) in order to give an adequate geometrical explanation for the apparent irregularity of their paths.

[6] **law**
regular pattern of movement; ***poise*** balance.

[8] **By such a star made firmament**
i.e. Gratiana (the star) makes the ground beneath her feet into a new firmament (the eighth sphere, containing the unmoving, fixed stars).

[9] **Which now no more the roof envies**
i.e. the pavement no longer envies the roof its height.

[10] **with Atlas even**
is even with Atlas, the Titan in Greek myth who supported the vault of the heavens on his shoulders or head and hands.

[11] **the brighter, nobler heaven**
The pavement now outshines the upper heavens because it supports Gratiana's resplendent beauty.

[12] **in her**
(a) in Gratiana; or, less likely, (b) in the 'nobler heaven' of the preceding line; ***all the deities*** i.e. she contains within herself not only the three Graces but all the gods.

[13] **trod out**
marked off, followed the path of.

[14] **ambitious hopes**
the lover s hope to possess her.

[15] **brave**
splendid; ***arts*** (a) skill in dancing; (b) elegance of demeanour.

[16] **sweet command and gentle awe**
Note the oxymorons.

[18] **paved with broken hearts**
i.e. (a) like falling stars that have plunged to earth; or (b) made up of the hopes she has trampled underfoot.

[20–21] **the harmonious spheres . . . music's aid**
The motion of the spheres was thought to produce a heavenly music, inaudible to humankind but not to heavenly denizens, such as angels.

[21] **rounds**
orbits.

[24] **Graces**
Usually depicted as attendants to Venus, they gave beauty to young ladies and dispensed gentleness and loveliness wherever they appeared; ***Apollo*** the god of music and, especially, of the lyre.

---

90 / *The Grasshopper*

To My Noble Friend, Mr Charles Cotton

Oh, thou that swing'st upon the waving hair
  Of some well-fillèd oaten beard,
Drunk every night with a delicious tear
  Dropped thee from heav'n, where now th'art reared;

The joys of earth and air are thine entire,
  That with thy feet and wings dost hop and fly;
And when thy poppy works, thou dost retire
  To thy carved acorn bed to lie.

Up with the day, the sun thou welcom'st then,
   Sport'st in the gilt-plats of his beams,
And, all these merry days, mak'st merry men,
   Thyself, and melancholy streams.

But ah, the sickle! golden ears are cropped,
   Ceres and Bacchus bid goodnight;
Sharp frosty fingers all your flow'rs have topped
   And what scythes spared, winds shave off quite.

Poor verdant fool! and now green ice! thy joys,
   Large and as lasting as thy perch of grass,
Bid us lay in 'gainst winter rain and poise
   Their floods with an o'erflowing glass.

Thou best of men and friends! we will create
   A genuine summer in each other's breast
And, spite of this cold time and frozen fate,
   Thaw us a warm seat to our rest.

Our sacred hearths shall burn eternally
   As vestal flames; the North Wind, he
Shall strike his frost-stretched wings, dissolve, and fly
   This Etna in epitome.

Dropping December shall come weeping in,
   Bewail th'usurping of his reign;
But when, in showers of old Greek, we begin,
   Shall cry, he hath his crown again!

Night as clear Hesper shall our tapers whip
   From the light casements where we play,
And the dark hag from her black mantle strip,
   And stick there everlasting day.

Thus richer than untempted kings are we,
   That asking nothing, nothing need.
Though lord of all that seas embrace, yet he
   That wants himself is poor indeed.

A poem of address (or ode in the broader sense) consisting of quatrains of alternating pentameter and tetrameter, rhyming *a b a b*. The poem is based on a Greek poem by Anacreon, with echoes from Aesop's fable of the carefree but improvident grasshopper and the industrious ant who prepares for the coming winter by stockpiling food. In most versions of the story, the grasshopper is rebuffed by the ant after begging for relief from starvation. Lovelace's version, however, is more conspicuously sympathetic to the grasshopper. The political allegory at the heart of the poem suggests that fellowship and generosity of spirit, rather than hoarding, is the key to survival. People, unlike animals, can compensate to some extent for the harshness of the season, whether that be a matter of weather or politics.

Subtitle
Charles Cotton Lovelace's friend was Charles Cotton the elder (not his son, the poet of the same name, who died in 1658), a man known as a delightful conversationalist with friendly manner and gentlemanly charm. He had a fine library and was a friend of writers such as Jonson, Donne and Herrick.

[1–2] **swing'st . . . oaten beard**
The grasshopper is pictured as perched on the swaying tip of an oat stalk (the hair and beard refer to the fine bristles surrounding the grain); ***well-filled*** i.e. the grain is mature and ready to be harvested.

[3] **Drunk**
(a) sated; (b) intoxicated.

[3–4] **tear/Dropped thee from heaven**
a drop of dew which, on this small scale, is more than ample to satisfy his thirst.

[4] **where now th'art reared**
towards which (heaven) you are now lifted (by the swaying stalk); note the suggestion of a Providence from heaven that takes care of the grasshopper's needs.

[7] **poppy**
(a) a bright-coloured flower with four petals, the milk of whose stem has narcotic qualities; (b) an extract from this plant used to induce sleep at bedtime; ***retire*** go to bed.

[8] **carved acorn bed**
The grasshopper is whimsically imagined as going to sleep in a miniature oak bedstead, consisting of the empty cup of an acorn.

[9] **Up with the day . . . welcom'st**
The grasshopper presumably rises with the sun and celebrates the new day by his chirping.

[10] **Sport'st**
plays; ***gilt-plats*** (a) the golden streams of light emanating from the early-morning sun; (b) flat ornaments of gold or other precious metal.

[11–12] **mak'st merry men,/Thyself, and melancholy streams**
i.e. 'you make yourself, men, and melancholy streams merry'; the streams are melancholy because of the languid sounds they make, in contrast to the bright chirping of the grasshopper.

[13] **sickle**
a long, sharp, curved blade affixed to a short handle and used for cutting and gathering cereal crops such as wheat or oats (one has to stoop to use it); ***ears*** the part of a cereal plant that contains its flowers or seeds; however, the cutting off of human ears was also a punishment for certain offences; ***golden*** ripened by the sun; ***cropped*** cut off, reaped.

[14] **Ceres**
the Roman goddess of cereals and grains; ***Bacchus*** the Greek and Roman god of grapes and wine; ***bid*** say.

[15] **sharp frosty fingers**
A typical personification of winter and cold weather; ***topped*** taken off the tops; the subject is 'fingers'.

[16] **scythe**
like a sickle but with a longer handle, so that it can be used standing up; both are traditional symbols of the destructive element of time.

[17] **verdant**
(a) green (the colour of many

grasshoppers); (b) unripe, inexperienced, gullible; ***green ice*** the grasses are coated by the sudden ice, but retain their colour. Notice the contrast of green with 'golden'. Some critics interpret 'poor verdant fool' as referring to Charles I. The grasshopper was associated with royalty in Ancient Greek literature.

[17–18] **thy joys,/Large and as lasting as**
'your joys are no greater nor more lasting than'.

[19] **Bid us**
beseech us to; observe the syntax – the subject of 'bid' is 'joys' in the preceding line. Thus the joys of the present should make one aware of the need to prepare for a less plentiful time. Most scholars think that this poem was written during the Interregnum, when the social ideals of Royalists like Lovelace were difficult to maintain; ***lay in 'gainst*** store up food and drink in anticipation of.

[19–20] **poise/Their floods**
(a) weigh on scales; (b) set in opposition; (c) compensate, with a full glass, for the flood outside; note the suggestion that the delicate balance of the grasshopper on his perch in summer should be matched in winter with a balance of stored supplies and continued pleasure.

[21] **Thou best**
The remainder of the poem is presumably addressed to Charles Cotton.

[22] **summer in each other's breast**
i.e. the warmth of personal friendship will compensate for their exclusion from public life.

[23] **spite of**
despite.

[24] **us**
for ourselves; ***seat*** home, dwelling-place; ***to*** for.

[25–6] **sacred hearths ... vestal flames**
In Greek and Roman times the hearth, presided over by the goddess Hestia or Vesta, was considered holy and the intimate centre of the home; a fire in the Roman forum, from which individual households gathered the sacred flame as part of a special ceremony, was kept perpetually burning by a special group of vestal virgins who tended it. This code of fidelity in friendship was of particular importance to the Cavaliers.

[26] **North Wind**
Boreas, the coldest and fiercest of the winds to blow down on England.

[27] **strike**
(a) spread out suddenly; (b) lower the sails of a ship; ***dissolve*** dissipate; ***fly*** flee.

[28] **Etna**
a famous volcano in Sicily; ***in epitome*** in miniature.

[29] **Dropping December**
i.e. bearing precipitation; ***weeping*** begins with rainy weather.

[30] **Bewail... reign**
The Puritans abolished Christmas festivities in 1642; ***reign*** probably, a pun on 'rain'.

[31] **showers**
abundance, plenty; ***old Greek*** (a) Greek literature, which educated men studied and often quoted to one another – an allusion, among other things, to Cotton's scholarly achievements; (b) the highly esteemed Greek wine favoured by Romans in Antiquity; ***begin*** (a) start to celebrate; (b) start to recite, as in the old days.

[32] **he hath his crown again!**
(a) refers to December (the crowning month of the year) and its festivals, which included various carnival crownings, with a contrast between the celebratory mood of Christmastide, kept alive in the spirits of the exiled Royalists, and the suppression of such festivities by the Puritans; (b) refers to the deposed King Charles I, whose reign has been restored in the minds and hearts of his followers.

[33] **as**
like; ***Hesper*** the morning star; ***tapers*** the candlelight of their night-long vigil (i.e. the wintry period of Parliamentary rule).

[34] **whip**
beat away. The syntax of this line is unusual. It may be paraphrased as follows: 'The tapers shall beat night away, like the clear light of Hesper.'
[34–5] **light casements . . . strip**
Through the windows of their candle-lit room, brilliance and warmth spilling into the night suggest the light-hearted mood of their vigil as they wait for winter to end and dawn to come and strip away the darkness.
[35] **the dark hag**
Hecate, daughter of night (see Shakespeare's *Macbeth*, where the three witches are described as worshippers of Hecate); ***black mantle*** darkness; ***strip*** 'tapers' is the subject.
[36] **stick there**
put permanently in its place; ***everlasting day*** Lovelace expresses his belief that once the Interregnum is over, the monarchy and its more congenial atmosphere will be restored for ever.
[37–8] **untempted kings . . . nothing need**
i.e. the friends are like kings who already have everything and therefore need ask for nothing.
[39] **all that seas embrace**
all territory on the earth.
[40] **wants himself**
(a) lacks control over his own life; (b) cannot enjoy himself; (c) is more anxious for physical possessions than for his spirit. The poem as a whole implies that the self-mastery of the man who knows himself and lives accordingly is superior to the narrow seriousness and severity of the Puritan (or the ant in the fable).

JOHN MILTON

(1608–74)

1629 'On the Morning of Christ's Nativity'
1634 *Comus* (A Masque)
1637 'Lycidas'
1646 *(1645) Poems of Mr John Milton*
1667 *Paradise Lost*
1671 *Paradise Regained* and *Samson Agonistes*

Milton, the greatest epic poet in the English language, was also the versatile and learned author of a wide variety of works in prose and verse. His career may be divided into three periods: a youthful stage of preparation that ended with his leaving Cambridge University and touring Italy; a middle stage of vigorous political activity and a direct participation in the radical government of Oliver Cromwell; and a final stage in which, in obscurity and afflicted with total blindness, he wrote his great masterpieces, *Paradise Lost, Paradise Regained,* and *Samson Agonistes*.

John Milton was born in London on 9 December 1608. His first ten years were not particularly eventful, but Thomas Young, a Scottish Puritan who became his tutor in 1618, may have influenced the religious direction he took as an adult. It was Milton's later adherence to the Puritan party that was to lead him straight into the whirlwind of seventeenth-century politics and to shape his career in ways he could not have anticipated as a young man. In 1625, the year King James I died and was succeeded by his son, Charles I, Milton entered Christ's College Cambridge. In the tranquillity of the university environment, he composed his earliest Latin and English poems. In 1629 he took the BA degree; in the same year he wrote his first great poem, the 'Nativity Ode'. During the next two years he continued to produce a number of minor poems in English, including 'On Shakespeare' and the delightful companion lyrics 'L'Allegro' and 'Il Penseroso'. In 1632 he took the MA degree and left Cambridge to pursue a course of study of his own devising.

Milton's plans at this time were not very clear. It was evident by 1634, the date of his masque *Comus*, that he wished to become a writer, but there was no evident way for him to pursue such a vocation directly. Three years later his mother died, and in the same year a fellow student from Cambridge perished at sea. Asked to contribute an elegy for a volume honouring the late Edward King, Milton produced no token tribute but one of the great poems of the English language, 'Lycidas'. In some sense the experience of writing it represented a turning point for him, as well as for English poetry. The next year he set off for the Continent and visited Florence, Rome and Naples, then returned to England in 1639 via Florence and Geneva. While he was away the disastrous First Bishops' War took place: Charles I attempted to impose an episcopal structure on the Church of Scotland.

After his return, Milton started to teach and sketched first plans for *Paradise Lost*. In the meantime, after the failure of the Second Bishops' War in 1640, Charles I found governing alone increasingly difficult and was obliged to summon the Short and Long Parliaments. Milton embarked on a period of controversy and anti-episcopal polemic which was concerned principally with religious questions but necessarily had political overtones. Further writings included not only *The Reason of Church Government* (1642) but also a pamphlet advocating divorce (1643). The latter may have been suggested by certain difficulties Milton encountered at the beginning of his first marriage, to Mary Powell, in 1642; the Civil War began on 22 August of that year. By 1644, after the Battle of Marston Moor, Oliver Cromwell had emerged as a revolutionary leader. During the same period, Milton was writing two of his most famous prose treatises, *Of Education* and *Areopagitica*, which is often considered a key document in the history of the free press. By 1645 Charles had been defeated at Naseby; Archbishop Laud, much disliked by the Puritans, had been executed; and Milton's first volume of poetry was assembled. In 1647 his father died.

The next year was marked by the beginning of the Second Civil War, which ranged Cromwellian supporters against the combined forces of the Scots, the Irish and the Royalists. On 30 January 1649, after military defeat and capture by the Parliamentarian revolutionaries, Charles I was beheaded, an event that shocked all of Europe. The Long Parliament was purged of all but a group of radicals, called the 'Rump', and Milton, who had now been appointed Latin Secretary, published two pamphlets defending the execution of the king. With the end of the Second Civil War in 1651, Milton's fortunes seemed secure, but in the following year he suffered two losses: his first wife died, and he became totally blind. Nevertheless, he continued to write; Cromwell became Lord Protector in 1653. Besides the polemical works he wrote during this period he also produced a number of sonnets, including the well-known poems on his blindness, on the massacre of a community of Waldensians in Piedmont, and others addressed to various friends. He remarried in 1656; his second wife, Katherine Woodcock, died only two years later, in 1658 – the same year as Oliver Cromwell. By 1659 the end of the Commonwealth was near; Cromwell's son abdicated and the Rump Parliament returned, to be replaced by the reconstituted Long Parliament. Eventually, Charles II, son of the executed monarch, was invited to return, and he was restored to the throne on 29 May 1660. Milton's public and political career was at an end.

Though he was arrested and under threat of execution for treason, the blind and helpless poet was obviously of little danger to the restored regime. He was released and allowed to retire in obscurity. For all that, by 1667 he managed to bring to completion a project that he had long planned – *Paradise Lost*, a verse epic in classical form based on the story of man's fall in Genesis. Only four years later, two more works appeared: *Paradise Regained*, a brief epic based on the temptations of Christ; and *Samson Agonistes*, the Old Testament story of Samson told in the form of a Greek tragedy. The climactic events of the last fourteen years of Milton's life were a second edition of his early poems in 1673, and a second (slightly revised) edition of *Paradise Lost* in the next year, which was also his last. John Milton died at Bunhill Fields on 8 November 1674.

Context

Three years after Milton's birth, the Authorised Version of the Bible, a co-operative project that involved both Anglican and

Puritan scholars, was published. Apart from the impact this translation was subsequently to have on the English language, it was also the last sign of unity between the two Church parties, and the conflict between them was to have important consequences, not only for Milton but for all of England. In 1616 William Shakespeare died; seven years later, when Milton was fourteen, the First Folio edition of his plays was published. Milton's formative years coincided with a period of great literary significance; even as a young man he created some of the most familiar poems in the language. During the Interregnum he played an important political role that kept him from writing much poetry during mid-century, yet if Milton had never completed *Paradise Lost*, he would still have been counted among the important seventeenth-century poets. As a prose writer he ranks among the most significant in the language for such stirring tracts as *Areopagitica* and *Of Education* (both 1644). He was a tremendously learned man, at home with both classical and modern languages and proficient enough in Italian to write creditable poems in it. Most important, he was profoundly original on a number of fronts: theological, literary, political and social. He wrote pioneering treatises on divorce, freedom of the press, government, and religious doctrine. It is no surprise to learn that he was a superb debater on complex intellectual topics, and was best known on the Continent for his victories in controversy. Even his Puritanism was atypical; Milton was too much the individual to be comfortable with any orthodoxy for very long. Above all, he insisted on man's freedom, his rational mind, and his responsibility for his own choices. What characterises all his poetry, even his short poems, is their magnificent sweep, due in no small measure to the mythic grandeur he brought to everything he conceived.

Genre

Milton was the master of a wide range of poetic genres, including full-scale epic in classical style, the shorter epic practised by Renaissance writers, Greek tragedy, the sonnet (of which he composed several in Italian as well as in English), classical odes (in English, Latin and Greek), pastoral elegies, psalms, and other forms, less easily defined, such as the companion poems 'L'Allegro' and 'Il Penseroso'. Few poets have been capable of such versatility, much less of creating some of the greatest English examples of each genre. Even within individual forms, such as the sonnet, Milton shows a remarkable variety of movement – from lyric celebration to elegiac longing to satire to powerful indignation. Moreover, he was the creator of a grand style in blank verse that opened up new possibilities for subsequent poets. Unrhymed iambic pentameter in Shakespearian style was a vehicle that had been perfected for the theatre but was not widely used for other purposes before Milton, who may be said to have redefined – even reinvented – it for his time. He experimented early, in 'Lycidas', with irregularly rhyming lines of varying length, and created a kind of free verse in *Samson Agonistes* to reproduce the effects of classical Greek dramatic metre. He learned a great deal from Italian poets, but never simply by replicating them; he turned everything he took into not only a native but a specifically Miltonic product.

Critical Reception

Both Milton's poetry and his thought are important in the intellectual tradition of the English-speaking peoples. Famous in his lifetime, particularly after the publication of *Paradise Lost*, he was honoured in 1695 with the first annotated scholarly edition of the works of any English poet. Before the end of the century, he was the subject of no fewer than five biographies. His first important critic, John Dryden, spoke of *Paradise Lost* as 'sublime', a word given further currency by Joseph Addison in the early eighteenth century. Milton's influence on the poetry of that century as a whole and well into the next was enormous.

The nineteenth century witnessed not only the maintenance of Milton's position as one of England's greatest writers but also the publication of monumental scholarly works on him and his works. A list of writers who were inspired or influenced by him would include most of the Romantic authors, both major and minor. The most prominent feature of the Romantic interpretation of Milton was its sympathy with the Satan of *Paradise Lost* and the exaltation of its author as an opponent of tyranny. However, though he continued to be read as one of the indisputably major authors, he seems to have affected Victorian writers – with the exception of Matthew Arnold – somewhat less; and in the early twentieth century the moderns found his Latinate diction and long, complex sentences in periodic style a baleful example for poets who were attempting to work towards a more direct, less ornate language. The consequence of this anti-Miltonic stance among such critics as T.S. Eliot, Ezra Pound and F.R. Leavis was to focus more rather than less attention on Milton, and eventually to stimulate a revival of interest in him when Christian pro-Miltonists such as C.S. Lewis argued for his centrality in English literature and thought. However, William Empson and A.J.A. Waldock initiated a fresh controversy over Milton's 'God', and the battleground of Miltonic studies has never quite settled down since. Without necessarily rejecting their perspective, such critics in the Romantic tradition as Harold Bloom championed Milton for his mythopoeic power, but with the more recent emergence of feminist and New Historicist approaches – which have once again challenged traditional interpretations of the poetry – it is certain that Miltonic scholarship will continue to generate controversies into the next century.

Further Reading

Editions

Works of John Milton, ed. F.A. Patterson *et al.*, 20 vols (New York, 1931–40) is still the most complete edition, but it consists of the text alone, without commentary. *John Milton: Complete poems and major prose*, ed. Merritt Y. Hughes (New York, 1957) and *Poetical Works*, ed. John Carey and Alastair Fowler (London, 1968) are one-volume editions with annotations and introductions. The most recent edition is *John Milton*, ed. Stephen Orgel and Jonathan Goldberg, in the Oxford Authors series (Oxford and New York, 1991), with notes.

Critical Studies

The body of commentary dedicated to Milton is formidable, and though by far the bulk of it is concerned with the larger works, even that devoted to the shorter lyric poems is quite considerable. Two handy guides through the bibliographical labyrinth are C.A. Patrides, ed., *An Annotated Critical Bibliography of John Milton* (New York, 1987), which lists important scholarship to 1985; and P.J. Klemp, *The Essential Milton: An annotated bibliography of major modern studies* (Boston, MA, 1989), which offers full descriptions of many books and articles from 1900 to 1987. Students should consult them for more comprehensive coverage of commentary devoted both to general Miltonic topics and to individual poems. The following lists concentrate on more recent publications.

Of the older handbooks containing useful information along the lines of traditional scholarship, see Marjorie Nicolson, *John Milton, A Reader's Guide* (New York, 1963; London, 1964). Later introductions are L. Potter, *A Preface to Milton* (London, 1972); A.S.P. Woodhouse, *The Heavenly Muse: A preface to Milton*, ed. Hugh MacCallum (Toronto, ON, 1972); and David M. Miller, *John Milton: Poetry* (Boston, MA, 1978). For a comprehensive view of the basic religious elements of Milton's intellectual background, see C.A. Patrides, *Milton and the Christian Tradition* (Oxford, 1966; reprinted Hamden, CT, 1979); Timothy J. O'Keeffe, *Milton and the Pauline Tradition: A study of theme and symbolism* (Washington, DC, 1982); and Georgia B. Christopher, *Milton and the Science of the Saints* (Princeton, NJ, 1982). For his political ideas, see Christopher Hill, *Milton and the English Revolution* (London, 1977; New York, 1978); Andrew Milner, *John Milton and the English Revolution* (London, 1983); and Charles R. Geisst, *The Political Thought of John Milton* (London, 1984). An important book on Milton's life in relation to his art is Louis L. Martz, *Poet of Exile: A study of Milton's poetry* (New Haven, CT, 1980).

For the literary environment in which Milton worked, see Richard Helgerson, *Self-Crowned Laureates: Spenser, Jonson, Milton and the literary system* (Berkeley, CA, 1983). The background of the pastoral tradition is examined in Richard Mallette, *Spenser, Milton, and Renaissance Pastoral* (Lewisburg, PA, 1981); and Sukanta Chaudhuri, *Renaissance Pastoral and Its English Developments* (Oxford, 1989), which traces in detail the precursors of Milton and Marvell. The context of Milton's first published volume of 1645–6 is discussed by Cleanth Brooks and John Edward Hardy in their edition of *Poems of Mr John Milton* (New York, 1951); by Gale H. Carrithers, Jr, '*Poems* (1645): on growing up', *Milton Studies*, **15** (1981), 161–79; and by Louis L. Martz, 'The rising poet, 1645', in *The Lyric and Dramatic Milton*, ed. Joseph H. Summers (New York, 1965), pp. 3–33 (also part of *Poet of Exile*).

An extremely useful source for the shorter poetry, with introductions, surveys of criticism and scholarship, and very full annotations for each poem, is A.S.P. Woodhouse and Douglas Bush, *A Variorum Commentary on* The Poems of John Milton, *Volume Two: The minor English poems*, general ed. M.Y. Hughes, 2 parts (New York, 1972). Woodhouse and Bush survey the relevant scholarship for each poem almost up to the date of publication. For a detailed commentary on the earlier poems for novice students, see J.B. Broadbent *et al.*, eds, *Odes, Pastorals, Masques. The Cambridge Milton for Schools and Colleges* (Cambridge, 1975) is a stimulating introduction. The essays on the relevant poems in Rosamond Tuve, *Images and Themes in Five Poems by Milton* (Cambridge, MA, 1958) are still worth consulting; and F.T. Prince, *The Italian Element in Milton's Verse* (Oxford, 1954); and J.B. Leishman, *Milton's Minor Poems*, ed. Geoffrey Tillotson (London, 1969) are still helpful.

In addition to the commentary in Woodhouse and Bush and the criticism surveyed there, an impressive amount of scholarship on the shorter poems has been published in the two decades since. Ralph Waterbury Condee, *Structure in Milton's Poetry: From the foundation to the pinnacles* (University Park, PA and London, 1974) examines the structures of 'Lycidas' and the 'Nativity Ode', among others, in relation to *Paradise Lost*. Don Cameron Allen, *The Harmonious Vision: Studies in Milton's poetry*, enlarged edn (Baltimore, MD and London, 1970) collects his essays on 'L'Allegro' and 'Il Penseroso', and on 'Lycidas'. Clay Hunt, *'Lycidas' and the Italian Critics* (New Haven, CT and London, 1979) shows, through an examination of Italian Renaissance literary theory, that Milton refashioned the pastoral genre to create a new form of 'high lyric'.

Studies of the 'Nativity Ode' up to 1979 are usefully surveyed by I.S. MacLaren, 'Milton's Nativity Ode: the function of poetry and structures of responses in 1629 (with a bibliography of twentieth-century criticism)', *Milton Studies*, **15** (1981), 181–200. Other articles on the poem published in *Milton Studies* are in **18** (1983), 85–102; **21** (1985), 119–35; and **25** (1989), 21–42; see, in *Milton Quarterly*, **15** (1981), 80–88; **17** (1983), 108–21 and **23** (1989), 59–66. Other recent analyses are William Shullenberger, 'Christ as metaphor: figural instruction in Milton's Nativity Ode', *Notre Dame English Journal*, **14** (1981), 41–58; Robert L. Entzminger, 'The epiphanies in Milton's Nativity Ode', *Renaissance Papers*, **21** (1981), 21–31; C.A. Patrides, '"That Great and Indisputable Miracle": the cessation of the oracles', ch. 7 of *Premises and Motifs in Renaissance Thought and Literature* (Princeton, NJ, 1982); Richard Halpern, 'The great instauration: imaginary narratives in Milton's "Nativity Ode"', in Mary Nyquist and Margaret W. Ferguson, eds, *Re-Membering Milton* (New York and London, 1987), pp. 3–24; R.M. Fransson, 'Milton's "On the Morning of Christ's Nativity"', *Explicator*, **48** (1990), 249–51.

Elaine B. Safer and Thomas L. Erskine, eds, *John Milton: 'L'Allegro' and 'Il Penseroso'* (Columbus, MO, 1970) is a collection of important essays on the companion poems. Essays on the poems appear in *Milton Studies*, **9** (1976), 203–19; **7** (1975), 77–99; **18** (1983), 45–62; **24** (1988), 3–15; **26** (1991), 3–24; and in *Milton Quarterly*, **15** (1981), 116–19; **17** (1983), 17–19; **23** (1989), 1–7; Annabel Patterson, '"Forc'd fingers": Milton's early poems and ideological constraint', in Claude J. Summers and Ted-Larry Pebworth, eds, *'The muses common-weale': Poetry and politics in the seventeenth century* (Columbia, MO, 1988), pp. 9–22; M.N.K. Mander, 'The music of *L'Allegro and Il Penseroso*', in Mario A. Di Cesare, ed., *Milton in Italy: Contexts, images, contradictions* (Binghamton, NY, 1991), pp. 281–91.

Two volumes with background materials relevant to 'Lycidas' are Scott Elledge, ed., *Milton's 'Lycidas': Edited to serve as an introduction to criticism* (New York, 1966); and Watson Kirkconnell, *Awake the Courteous Echo: The themes and prosody of Comus, Lycidas, and Paradise Regained in world literature with translations of the major analogues* (Toronto, ON, 1973), both of which collect sources and analogues for 'Lycidas'. See also John Leonard, '"Trembling Ear": the historical moment of *Lycidas*', *Journal of Medieval and Renaissance Studies*, **21** (1991), 59–81 for a recent source study. Paul Alpers, '*Lycidas* and modern criticism', *ELH*, **49** (1982), 468–96 is a survey and critique. C.A. Patrides, ed., *Milton's* Lycidas: *The tradition and the poem*, rev. edn (Columbia, MO, 1983) contains key essays and a detailed bibliography. Other studies include the following: David Shelley Berkeley, *Inwrought with Figure Dim: A reading of Milton's 'Lycidas'* (The Hague and Paris, 1974) presents a typological study of the poem as a statement of Christian salvation of the individual. J. Martin Evans, *The Road from Horton: Looking backwards in 'Lycidas'* (Victoria, Australia, 1983) presents the poem as marking Milton's turn away from the poetry of retirement and contemplation to active participation in the world. Stanley E. Fish, '*Lycidas*: a poem finally anonymous', *Glyph: Johns Hopkins Textual Studies*, **8** (1981), 1–18 re-examines a famous essay by John Crowe Ransom; see also Michael Lieb, 'Scriptural formula and prophetic utterance in *Lycidas*', in *Milton and Scriptural Tradition*, ed. James H. Sims and Leland Ryken (Columbia, MO, 1984), pp. 31–42. Dennis Danielson, ed., *The Cambridge Companion to Milton* (Cambridge and New York, 1989) includes an essay on 'Lycidas'. Studies of more limited aspects, including the celebrated 'two-handed engine' crux, have appeared in *Milton Studies*, **15** (1981), 213–55; **16** (1982), 115–30, 131–40, 141–51; **18** (1983), 3–23; **25** (1989), 43–67, 69–88; **26** (1991), 59–80; and in *Milton Quarterly*, **15** (1981), 37–44; **16** (1982), 83; **17** (1983), 29–38, 42–5, 58–9, 89–91; **18** (1984), 61–2, 69–76, 135; **20** (1986), 44–8; **21** (1987), 6–11; **22** (1988), 127–8; **23** (1989), 89–121.

For Milton's 'On Shakespeare', see Loh, Gei yei Loh, 'A note on Milton's "On Shakespeare"', *Notes and Queries*, **30** (1983), 5, 431; Gerald Hammond, 'Milton's "On Shakespeare"', *Southern Humanities Review*, **20** (1986), 115–24; and Paul Stevens, 'Subversion and wonder in Milton's epitaph "On Shakespeare"', *ELR*, **19** (1989), 375–88. For a comparison of Jonson and Milton on Shakespeare, see Gerald Hammond, 'A justly suspected easiness: reading Shakespeare', in *Fleeting Things: English poets and poems, 1616–1660* (Cambridge, MA and London, 1990), pp. 141–53.

Anna K. Nardo, *Milton's Sonnets and the Ideal Community* (Lincoln, NB, and London, 1979) is a close reading of the sonnets as a unified group of poems pointing to the image of an ideal community. William McCarthy, 'The continuity of

Milton's sonnets', *PMLA*, **92** (1977), 96–109 argues that they form a sequence; and James G. Mengert 'The resistance of Milton's sonnets', *ELR*, **11** (1981), 81–95 examines their perspective on the divine. William L. Stull, '"Why Are Not Sonnets Made of Thee?" A new context for the "Holy Sonnets" of Donne, Herbert, and Milton', *MP*, **80** (1982), 129–35 compares the works of all three poets. Two editions, *The Sonnets of Milton*, ed. John S. Smart (Glasgow, 1921; reprinted Oxford, 1966) and *Milton's Sonnets*, ed. E.A.J. Honigmann (London, 1966) contain commentaries, some of them extensive.

On particular sonnets, some recent commentaries are Jerome Mazzaro, 'Gaining authority: John Milton at sonnets', *Essays in Literature*, **15** (1988), 3–12 ['How Soon Hath Time', 'When I Consider', 'Methought I Saw']; Stephen Booth and Jordan Flyer, 'Milton's "How soon hath time": A Colossus in a cherry-stone', *ELH*, **49** (1982), 449–67; Macon Cheek, 'Of two sonnets of Milton', *Renaissance Papers* (Columbia, SC, 1956) [on 'How Soon Hath Time' and 'When I Consider'].

John J. Glavin, '"The Exercise of Saints": Hopkins, Milton, and patience', *TSLL*, **20** (1978), 139–52; Sidney Greenbaum, 'The poem, the poet, and the reader: an analysis of Milton's sonnet 19', *Language and Speech*, **11** (1978), 116–28; Anthony Easthope, 'Towards the autonomous subject in poetry: Milton "On His Blindness"'; *Proceedings of the Essex Conference on the Sociology of Literature, July 1980, 1642: Literature and power in the seventeenth century*, ed. Francis Barker, Jay Bernstein, *et al.* (Colchester, 1981), pp. 301–14; Gary A. Stringer, 'Milton's "Thorn in the Flesh": Pauline didacticism in Sonnet XIX', *Milton Studies*, **10** (1977), 141–54; Thomas B. Stroup, '"When I Consider": Milton's Sonnet XIX', *SP*, **69** (1972), 242–58; David S. Berkeley, '"Light" in Milton's Sonnet XX', *PQ*, **61** (1982), 208–11; Dixon Fiske, 'Milton in the middle of life: Sonnet XIX', *ELH*, **41** (1974), 37–49; and 'Dating Milton', in *Soliciting Interpretation*, ed. Katharine E. Maus and Elizabeth D. Harvey (Chicago, 1990, pp. 119–220).

Leo Spitzer, 'Understanding Milton', in *Essays on English and American Literature*, ed. Anna Hatcher (Princeton, NJ, 1962), pp. 16–27 ['Methought I Saw']; see also, in *Milton Studies*, **4** (1972), 141–9; **6** (1974), 181–97; **8** (1975), 149–63; **10** (1977), 111–25; **10** (1977), 127–39; **18** (1983), 63–76.

Elizabeth K. Hill, 'A dream in the long valley: some psychological aspects of Milton's last sonnet', *Greyfriar: Siena Studies in Literature*, **26** (1985), 3–13; William B. Hunter, 'Milton and the Waldensians', *SEL*, **11** (1971), 153–64; Nicholas R. Jones, 'The education of the faithful in Milton's Piedmontese sonnet', *Milton Studies*, **10** (1977), 167–76; John R. Knott, 'The biblical matrix of Milton's "On the Late Massacre in Piemont"', *PQ*, **62** (1983), 259–63; Edmund Miller, '"The Late Massacre": Milton's liturgical sonnet', *CP*, **17** (1984), 43–50.

For recent trends in critical approaches to Milton, see Mary Nyquist and Margaret W. Ferguson, eds, *Re-Membering Milton* (see above); Catherine Belsey, *John Milton: Language, gender, power* (Oxford and New York, 1988); Jonathan Goldberg, *Voice Terminal Echo: Postmodernism and English Renaissance texts* (New York and London, 1986); Herman Rapaport, *Milton and the Post-modern* (Lincoln, NB, 1983); R.A. Shoaf, *Milton, Poet of Duality: A study of semiosis in the poetry and the prose* (New Haven, CT, 1985); Maureen Quilligan, *Milton's Spenser: The politics of reading* (Ithaca, NY, 1983).

The fullest, most reliable and up-to-date of the twentieth-century biographies is William R. Parker, *Milton* (Oxford, 1968), 2 vols; but David Masson's massive nineteenth-century *The Life of John Milton* (Cambridge and London, 1859–94), in 7 vols, has information not readily accessible elsewhere.

A unique guide to all aspects of the writer is William B. Hunter, general ed., *A Milton Encyclopedia* (Lewisburg, PA, 1978–83), 9 vols. William Ingram and Kathleen Swaim, *A Concordance to Milton's English Poetry* (Oxford, 1972) is the most complete concordance currently available. Two periodicals, *Milton Quarterly* and *Milton Studies*, are devoted to the poet.

91/ *On the Morning of Christ's Nativity*

1

This is the month, and this the happy morn
Wherein the son of Heaven's eternal King,
Of wedded maid and virgin mother born,
Our great redemption from above did bring;
For so the holy sages once did sing,
   That he our deadly forfeit should release,
And with his Father work us a perpetual peace.

2

That glorious form, that light unsufferable,
And that far-beaming blaze of majesty
Wherewith he wont at Heaven's high council-table
To sit the midst of Trinal Unity,
He laid aside; and here with us to be,
   Forsook the courts of everlasting day
And chose with us a darksome house of mortal clay.

3

Say, heavenly Muse, shall not thy sacred vein
Afford a present to the infant God?
Hast thou no verse, no hymn, or solemn strain,
To welcome him to this his new abode,
Now while the heaven by the sun's team untrod
   Hath took no print of the approaching light,
And all the spangled host keep watch in squadrons bright?

4

See how from far upon the eastern road
The star-led wizards haste with odours sweet:
O run, prevent them with thy humble ode,
And lay it lowly at his blessèd feet;
Have thou the honour first thy Lord to greet,
   And join thy voice unto the angel choir,
From out his secret altar touched with hallowed fire.

The Hymn

1

It was the winter wild
While the Heaven-born child
   All meanly wrapped in the rude manger lies;
Nature in awe to him
Had doffed her gaudy trim
   With her great Master so to sympathise;
It was no season then for her
To wanton with the sun, her lusty paramour.

2

Only with speeches fair
She woos the gentle air
   To hide her guilty front with innocent snow,
And on her naked shame,
Pollute with sinful blame,
   The saintly veil of maiden white to throw,
Confounded that her Maker's eyes
Should look so near upon her foul deformities.

3

But he her fears to cease
Sent down the meek-eyed Peace;
   She, crowned with olive green, came softly sliding
Down through the turning sphere,
His ready harbinger,
   With turtle wing the amorous clouds dividing,
And waving wide her myrtle wand,
She strikes a universal peace through sea and land.

4

No war or battle's sound
Was heard the world around;
   The idle spear and shield were high up-hung;

The hookèd chariot stood
Unstained with hostile blood,
   The trumpet spake not to the armed throng,
And king sat still with awful eye,
As if they surely knew their sovereign Lord was by.

5

But peaceful was the night
Wherein the Prince of light
   His reign of peace upon the earth began;
The winds, with wonder whist,
Smoothly the waters kissed,
   Whispering new joys to the mild ocëan,
Who now hath quite forgot to rave,
While birds of calm sit brooding on the charmèd wave.

6

The stars with deep amaze
Stand fixed in steadfast gaze,
   Bending one way their precious influence,
And will not take their flight
For all the morning light,
   Or Lucifer that often warned them thence;
But in their glimmering orbs did glow
Until their Lord himself bespake, and bid them go.

7

And though the shady gloom
Had given day her room,
   The sun himself withheld his wonted speed
And hid his head for shame
As his inferior flame
   The new-enlightened world no more should need;
He saw a greater Sun appear
Than his bright throne or burning axletree could bear.

8

The shepherds on the lawn,
Or ere the point of dawn,
  Sat simply chatting in a rustic row;
Full little thought they than
That the mighty Pan
  Was kindly come to live with them below;
Perhaps their loves or else their sheep
Was all that did their silly thoughts so busy keep.

9

When such music sweet
Their hearts and ears did greet
  As never was by mortal finger struck,
Divinely warbled voice
Answering the stringed noise,
  As all their souls in blissful rapture took;
The air, such pleasure loath to lose,
With thousand echoes still prolongs each heavenly close.

10

Nature that heard such sound
Beneath the hollow round
  Of Cynthia's seat the airy region thrilling,
Now was almost won
To think her part was done,
  And that her reign had here its last fulfilling;
She knew such harmony alone
Could hold all heaven and earth in happier unïon.

11

At last surrounds their sight
A globe of circular light
  That with long beams the shame-faced night arrayed;
The helmèd cherubim

And sworded seraphim
   Are seen in glittering ranks with wings displayed,
Harping in loud and solemn choir
With unexpressive notes to Heaven's newborn heir.

12

Such music (as 'tis said)
Before was never made,
   But when of old the sons of morning sung,
While the Creator great
His constellations set
   And the well-balanced world on hinges hung,
And cast the dark foundations deep,
And bid the weltering waves their oozy channel keep.

13

Ring out, ye crystal spheres,
Once bless our human ears
   (If ye have power to touch our senses so),
And let your silver chime
Move in melodious time,
   And let the bass of Heaven's deep organ blow,
And with your ninefold harmony
Make up full consort to th'angelic symphony.

14

For if such holy song
Enwrap our fancy long,
   Time will run back and fetch the age of gold;
And speckled Vanity
Will sicken soon and die,
   And leprous Sin will melt from earthly mould,
And Hell itself will pass away,
And leave her dolorous mansions to the peering day.

15

Yea, Truth and Justice then
Will down return to men,
   Th'enamelled arras of the rainbow wearing,
And Mercy set between,
Throned in celestial sheen,
   With radiant feet the tissued clouds down steering;
And Heaven, as at some festival,
Will open wide the gates of her high palace hall.

16

But wisest Fate says no,
This must not yet be so –
   The Babe lies yet in smiling infancy
That on the bitter cross
Must redeem our loss,
   So both himself and us to glorify;
Yet first to those ychained in sleep
The wakeful trump of doom must thunder through the deep.

17

With such a horrid clang
As on Mount Sinai rang
   While the red fire and smouldering clouds outbrake;
The agèd earth, aghast
With terror of that blast,
   Shall from the surface to the centre shake,
When at the world's last session,
The dreadful Judge in middle air shall spread his throne.

18

And then at last our bliss
Full and perfect is,
   But now begins; for from this happy day
Th'old Dragon under ground,

In straiter limits bound,
  Not half so far casts his usurpèd sway,
And wroth to see his kingdom fail,
Swinges the scaly horror of his folded tail.

19

The oracles are dumb;
No voice or hideous hum
  Runs through the archèd roof in words deceiving.
Apollo from his shrine
Can no more divine,
  With hollow shriek, the steep of Delphos leaving.
No nightly trance or breathed spell
Inspires the pale-eyed priest from the prophetic cell.

20

The lonely mountains o'er
And the resounding shore
  A voice of weeping heard and loud lament;
From haunted spring and dale
Edged with the poplar pale,
  The parting Genius is with sighing sent;
With flower-inwoven tresses torn,
The nymphs in twilight shade of tangled thickets mourn.

21

In consecrated earth
And on the holy hearth,
  The Lars and Lemures moan with midnight plaint;
In urns and altars round
A drear and dying sound
  Affrights the Flamens at their service quaint;
And the chill marble seems to sweat,
While each peculiar power forgoes his wonted seat.

22

Peor and Baalim
Forsake their temples dim,
With that twice-battered god of Palestine,
And moonèd Ashtaroth,
Heaven's queen and mother both,
Now sits not girt with tapers' holy shine;
The Libyc Hammon shrinks his horn;
In vain the Tyrian maids their wounded Thammuz mourn.

23

And sullen Moloch, fled,
Hath left, in shadows dread,
His burning idol all of blackest hue;
In vain with cymbals' ring
They call the grisly king
In dismal dance about the furnace blue;
The brutish gods of Nile as fast,
Isis and Orus and the dog Anubis haste.

24

Nor is Osiris seen
In Memphian grove or green,
Trampling the unshowered grass with lowings loud,
Nor can he be at rest
Within his sacred chest;
Naught but profoundest Hell can be his shroud.
In vain with timbrelled anthems dark
The sable-stoled sorcerers bear his worshipped ark.

25

He feels from Judah's land
The dreaded Infant's hand,
The rays of Bethlehem blind his dusky eyn;
Not all the gods beside

Longer dare abide,
Not Typhon huge, ending in snaky twine;
Our Babe, to show his godhead true,
Can in his swaddling bands control the damnèd crew.

26

So when the sun in bed,
Curtained with cloudy red,
Pillows his chin upon an orient wave,
The flocking shadows pale
Troop to th'infernal jail;
Each fettered ghost slips to his several grave;
And the yellow-skirted fays
Fly after the night-steeds, leaving their moon-loved maze.

27

But see! the Virgin blessed
Hath laid her Babe to rest.
Time is our tedious song should here have ending.
Heaven's youngest-teemèd star
Hath fixed her polished car,
Her sleeping Lord with handmaid lamp attending;
And all about the courtly stable
Bright-harnessed angels sit in order serviceable.

Nativity hymns were written by other seventeenth-century poets, including Vaughan, Traherne, Herrick and Crashaw. It was typical practice to present the birth of the Christ child as a contemporary event to which the poet was himself a witness; thus, in Milton's poem, the poet is imagined as a participant in the same actions as the Magi, angelic choirs, and shepherds. His vision presents the conquest of gloom and confusion by light and harmony. This emphasis on the poet's experience of the event suggests the Puritan theme of conversion or election; the transformation of the earth is parallel to the development of the poet's moral understanding and art in the course of the poem. Milton began writing it on Christmas Day 1629, shortly after his twenty-first birthday. It is his first great literary work, and it offers a glimpse of his ambitious programme as a heroic poet.

One of the most striking features of the ode is its reconciliation of pagan and Christian themes. Its tradition may be traced back to Virgil's Fourth Eclogue, which announces the return of the Golden Age; Virgil's poem was admired during the medieval period for its prophetic vision (it was thought to herald the coming of Christ) and imitated frequently during the Renaissance. Milton may have drawn on such Italian poets as Gian Francesco Pico and Torquato Tasso, but it is certain that much of his language, imagery and form was inspired by Edmund Spenser, especially his *Four Hymns*. In its opening stanzas, the very form of Milton's ode is a modification of traditional rhyme royal (*a b a b b c c*) influenced, no doubt, by the Spenserian stanza, which also closes with an Alexandrine instead of a pentameter. The remaining stanzas consist of lines of variable length (two groups of trimeter couplets followed by a pentameter line and concluded by two final lines, a tetrameter and an Alexandrine), rhyming *a a b c c b d d*. Most scholars divide the poem into three movements. The first eight stanzas, including the initial four stanzas of the prelude, describe the setting of Christ's birth. The following nine depict the angelic choir. The final nine describe the flight of the pagan gods. Each movement is organised around a contrast of light with darkness, harmony with disharmony.

[1] **month . . . morn**
25 December, the traditional date for celebrating the birth of Jesus Christ (although the historical Nativity probably occurred in early spring; shepherds are more likely to be watching their flocks during the lambing season).

[2] **Wherein**
when; ***son . . . King*** Jesus Christ.

[3] **wedded maid . . . mother**
According to traditional Christian doctrine, Mary, the mother of Christ, was a virgin who conceived by intervention of God the Holy Spirit (see Luke 1); such paradoxes as 'virgin mother' abound in descriptions of her during the medieval and Renaissance periods; ***maid*** a virgin.

[4] **Our great redemption**
God took on human nature as Jesus Christ in order to free man from the effects of his own transgressions.

[5] **holy sages**
the prophets of the Old Testament, who were thought to have foretold the coming of Christ as Messiah (saviour of the Jewish people); ***sing*** the prophets, both Greek and Hebrew, are often spoken of as poets.

[6] **deadly forfeit**
sin in general, as well as original sin, and the consequences, suffering and death.

[7] **his Father**
Christ is the Son of God, as the second person of the Trinity; ***work us*** obtain for us.

[8] **light unsufferable**
too bright to bear.

[9] **far-beaming blaze**
far-reaching brilliance; the depiction of God as light is of great antiquity, perhaps owing part of its inspiration to Zoroastrian and, later, Neoplatonic doctrines.

[10] **Wherewith**
in which (referring to 'form' in line 8); ***he*** God, that is, Christ as second person of the Trinity; ***wont*** was accustomed; ***Heaven's high council-table*** The Son of God is imagined as sitting in council with the Father and the Holy Spirit, a depiction which Milton was to elaborate almost four decades later in *Paradise Lost*, his epic poem on the Fall of man (or original sin) and his redemption.

[11] **the midst**
in the midst (as the middle member of the Trinity); *Trinal Unity* the mystery of the Trinity, which in Christian doctrine is described as the presence of three persons in one God.

[12] **laid aside**
refers back to 'that glorious form' in line 8; ***here with us*** i.e. by taking on human form.

[13] **Forsook the courts . . . day**
left heaven.

[14] **darksome house of mortal clay**
the human body, often described as a dwelling-place, albeit a dim and fragile one, for the human soul; ***clay*** in Genesis the first man is said to have been shaped by God from clay.

[15] **heavenly muse**
Urania, originally goddess of astronomy, was styled muse of sacred poetry by the French Protestant poet Guillaume du Bartas in his *The Christian Muse* (1574); here she is invoked as an alternative for the pagan muse; ***vein*** style, kind.
[16] **Afford**
provide; ***infant God*** a deliberate paradox that is at the centre of the entire poem – how can the maker of the universe also be a helpless newborn child?
[17] **strain**
melody, song.
[18] **his new abode**
(a) the earth; (b) the body.
[19] **by the sun's team untrod**
In Graeco-Roman mythology Helios, the sun, was a god who drove across the sky each day in a chariot pulled by immortal horses – in other words, it is not yet dawn.
[20] **took**
taken; ***no print*** no sign (but note how 'print' = hoofprint is consonant with the image of the horses who would arrive ahead of the chariot they pull).
[21] **spangled host**
(a) the predawn stars; (b) the host of attendant angels; in either case the 'squadrons bright' form an attendant audience and guard for the birth of the child; ***spangled*** sparkling.
[23] **star-led wizards**
an allusion to the story of the three Magi or wise men who came from the distant East, having understood from the appearance of a new star in the heavens that the King of the Jews had been born, bearing gifts of frankincense, myrrh (both 'sweet odours'), and gold (see Matthew 2: 1–12). The story is recalled on the feast of Epiphany (traditionally celebrated on 6 January).
[24] **O run**
Though logically, this apostrophe should be understood as addressed to the heavenly muse of line 15, it is presumably intended to refer to the poet's command to himself; ***prevent them*** anticipate them, arrive before they do; ***humble ode*** the following 'Hymn', the poet's gift.
[25] **lowly**
The word can be understood (a) as an adverb ('in a humble manner'), modifying 'lay'; (b) as an adjective describing the unworthy poet; (c) as an adjective that refers to the 'humble ode' of the preceding line.
[26] **Have thou . . . greet**
'Be honoured as the first to greet your Lord' (Christ).
[27] **angel choir**
Christmas iconography traditionally depicts a choir of serenading angels around the crib of the infant Jesus.
[28] **secret**
private, hidden; ***From out . . . fire*** [thy voice] touched with the holy fire that comes from within his secret altar. In Isaiah 6: 7, the prophet's lips are purified with the touch of a live coal that an angel takes from the fire at his altar.
[29] **winter wild**
in the the dead of winter, wild, desolate, bitterly cold and thus hostile; this is a description of an English winter. The Christmas scene in paintings and sculpture is often represented as though it took place in Europe.
[31] **meanly**
coarsely, poorly; ***rude*** unadorned, crude; ***manger*** a trough from which livestock eat.
[32] **Nature in awe . . . gaudy trim**
i.e. the trees and landscape were bare of flowers and greenery, as though they had removed their bright apparel ('gaudy trim') out of wonder and respect for the God child.
[33] **her great Master**
Christ as creator and sustainer of nature; ***sympathise*** to suffer with; the notion of a sympathetic nature, which appears to express human feelings, is a common device among poets, but here it takes on a paradoxical sense; earlier pagan hymns for the dead Adonis (and similar vegetation gods) also depict the sympathy of the

natural world for a deity subjected to mortal suffering.

[35–6] **It was no season . . . paramour**
These two lines introduce an extravagant extended metaphor. The sun is imagined as the passionate lover ('paramour') of the earth during the spring, when she wears her finest 'garments' of flowers and vegetation to attract him; in the winter she may be said to dress more plainly, and hence to have less erotic inclinations; the image is perhaps intended to show that Christ replaces the sun as earth's 'lover'; ***wanton*** make love.

[37–9] **with speeches fair/She woos . . . snow**
i.e. earth asks the air to cover her nakedness (***guilty front*** shameful face, manifesting her embarrassment at being so naked and sexually promiscuous); ***innocent*** (i.e. pure, because white) snow.

[41] **Pollute with sinful blame**
The earth is ashamed not only because of her rendezvous with the sun but also because, after the Fall of humankind and the original sin committed by Adam, all of nature was affected; Christ's coming was meant to redeem nature as well as man; ***Pollute*** polluted.

[42] **saintly veil . . . throw**
i.e. the landscape covered with snow is compared with a chaste woman who covers her body in white garments; ***to throw*** the object of the verb is 'naked shame', two lines earlier.

[43] **Confounded**
embarrassed, confused; ***her Maker's eyes*** (a) God's omniscience; (b) the eyes of the newborn Christ. Note that since the infant Christ and the Father-Creator are the same God, it is difficult to know precisely which is intended here.

[44] **foul deformities**
(a) her body, made ugly by winter; (b) her sins.

[45] **he her fears to cease**
to stop her fears, he; ***he*** God, her maker.

[46] **meek-eyed Peace**
alludes to (a) Christ the Messiah as described in Isaiah 9: 6: 'For a child has been born to us, a son given to us, and he will rule us; and he will be called Wonderful, Counsellor, Mighty God, Eternal Father, Prince of Peace'; (b) an allusion to the Peace of Augustus, a lengthy period before and after the birth of Christ when the Roman Empire was free of war; ***meek-eyed*** a poetic epithet indicating kindliness.

[47] **olive green**
the olive branch, a traditional symbol of peace.

[48] **turning sphere**
In Ptolemaic astronomy, the earth was surrounded by a series of concentric spheres that bore the various heavenly bodies and turned to make them orbit.

[49] **His ready harbinger**
the willing forerunner of Christ.

[50] **turtle**
turtledove, a bird sacred to Venus, goddess of love.

[51] **myrtle wand**
the myrtle was also sacred to Venus. The wand and the dove suggest attributes that belong to pagan love, but here they have been transformed into the figure of Peace, who turns the earth's shame into universal concord.

[52] **strikes**
brings about with a wave of her wand.

[55] **high up-hung**
hung up high.

[56] **hookèd chariot**
Roman war chariots had curved blades attached to their axles.

[57] **hostile**
enemy.

[58] **trumpet spake not**
i.e. was not sounded to lead a battle charge.

[59] **aweful**
reverent, full of awe. Note how the awe felt by the shepherds (Luke 2: 9, 17–20) is applied to the kings (Matthew 2: 10–12).

[60] **was by**
was near, present.

[61] **But**
And so.
[62] **Wherein**
during which; ***Prince of light*** In both the Old and New Testaments, the imagery of light is used to describe the Messiah or redeemer. Cf. Isaiah 60, John 1: 1–18.
[63] **His reign... began**
i.e. began his reign of peace upon the earth. Cf. Christ's promise: 'I leave you my peace, a peace that the world cannot give' (John 14: 27).
[64] **wonder**
amazement; ***whist*** hushed, silenced.
[66] **ocëan**
pronounced as three syllables.
[67] **Who**
the mild ocean; ***rave*** (a) rage as though mad; (b) crash loudly.
[68] **birds of calm**
halcyons, kingfishers which, according to legendary accounts, made their nests on the winter seas, which remained calm until their eggs were hatched; ***brooding*** sitting on their nests; ***charmèd wave*** magically still waters.
[69] **stars**
stars, in this stanza, symbolise a lesser light (i.e. spiritual understanding) that must give way before a greater; ***amaze*** amazement.
[71] **Bending... influence**
It was thought that an ether emanating from the stars affected human events.
[74] **Or Lucifer**
i.e. despite the morning light and the warnings of Lucifer (the morning star; not to be confused with Satan, sometimes called by this name, which means 'bearer of light').
[76] **Until their Lord... go**
i.e. until Christ himself commanded the stars to leave.
[77–84] **And though... could bear**
The same argument is now extended to apply to the sun.
[77] **shady gloom**
darkness or night.
[78] **room**
place.
[79] **wonted speed**
usual haste.
[80–2] **hid his head... need**
The conceit here is again based on the imagery of light as a description of Christ; the brilliance of the Christ child's appearance ('new-enlightened world' – with the meaning of spiritual as well as physical light) dims the less powerful sun's beams (inferior flame), which it replaces; the description suggests an eclipse of the sun, usually thought of as a sign of some momentous event.
[83] **He**
the sun; ***Sun*** Son, a frequent pun in English religious poetry.
[84] **axletree**
the axle of a chariot and thus, by extension, the chariot of the sun; ***bear*** (a) endure (because of the brilliance of the Son); (b) convey.
[85] **lawn**
grass.
[86] **Or ere**
just before.
[87] **simply**
(a) plainly; (b) innocently; ***rustic row*** in country style.
[88] **Full little thought they than**
(a) they thought only; however, 'than' was also an alternative spelling for 'then', so that an alternative interpretation = (b) they little realised then.
[89] **the mighty Pan**
in Greek mythology, a nature god, patron of shepherds. Since the Greek word 'pan' means 'all', Christ was, from fairly early times, said to supersede this minor deity as the God who is truly All. There is an interesting conflation of the conventional pastoral shepherds of Greek and Roman literature, the shepherds from the biblical narrative of Christ's birth, the pagan gods Hyperion and Pan, and the Son or All who overwhelms them all; and, finally, Christ as the Good Shepherd. Milton's employment of imagery and figures from pagan Antiquity is conventional and typical of the period, but he also puts it to fresh use

by suggesting a relationship between them and their Christian counterparts, which fulfil and surpass these pagan forerunners.

[90] **kindly**
(a) thoughtfully, caringly; (b) participating in their human nature ('kindly' = according to nature or kind).

[91] **loves**
Love between a shepherd and a shepherdess is the subject of many pastoral poems.

[92] **silly**
(a) innocent; (b) simple, humble; ***Was all . . . busy keep*** was all that occupied their simple minds.

[95] **As never . . . struck**
The phrase belongs to 'music' in line 93; ***struck*** plucked by a finger on a stringed instrument.

[96] **Divinely warbled voice**
the angelic choirs that sang at Christ's birth; Milton's depiction of the Nativity in this and other stanzas is obviously based on Renaissance paintings which show angels singing and playing musical instruments.

[97] **noise**
musical sounds.

[98] **As all . . . took**
i.e. as any that ever captivated their souls in joyful ecstasy.

[99] **loath**
unwilling; observe the syntax of this stanza: 'When such music . . . [then] The air . . . .'

[100] **with thousand**
with a thousand; ***still prolongs*** Note the present tense, which has the effect of making the description more vivid but also extends the echoes of the original Nativity music into the present; ***close*** a concluding musical phrase.

[102–3] **hollow round/Of Cynthia's seat**
Cynthia's seat the moon's sphere; ***thrilling*** quivering. The heavens, in the traditional cosmology, were composed of a series of concentric spheres with the earth at their centre and the sphere containing the moon closest to it. All things under the sphere of the moon were subject to change and decay.

[104–5] **won . . . done**
persuaded that her work was complete.

[106] **her reign**
nature's dominion over all earthly creatures that are subject to her laws.

[107] **harmony**
The entire universe was ordered according to a certain harmonic or mathematical concord, often described as the 'music of the spheres'. Nature recognises that a higher harmony, the divine power above hers, supersedes her own, and that the birth of Christ announces a new union of heaven and earth.

[110] **globe of circular light**
A 'globe of fiery Seraphim' appears in Milton's *Paradise Lost*, 2, 512. See Luke 2: 13: 'Suddenly a great army of heaven's angels appeared . . . '.

[111] **shame-faced**
shy, cowering from the light; ***arrayed*** drove back.

[112] **helmèd**
wearing helmets; ***cherubim*** the second rank of angels.

[113] **sworded**
bearing swords; ***seraphim*** the highest order of angels.

[114] **displayed**
outspread.

[115] **Harping**
singing to the accompaniment of a harp, still common in the seventeenth century.

[116] **unexpressive**
inexpressible; ***notes*** i.e. of music; the harps and wings are the usual appurtenances of angels in paintings; ***heir*** the Christ child.

[119] **Creator great**
God the Father, the great creator of the world, as distinguished from God the Son, saviour of mankind as Christ.

[120] **set**
placed in their positions in their respective spheres.

[121] **well-balanced**
suspended at the centre of the universe; ***hinges*** the axes or two poles

of the globe of the earth. See Job 26: 7: 'He . . . hangs the earth upon nothing'.

[122] **cast**
formed; ***dark*** concealed from normal sight, hidden, or obscure.

[124] **bid**
commanded; ***weltering*** surging, raging; ***oozy channel*** the ocean bed (***oozy*** slimy, muddy).

[119–24] **when . . . keep**
An allusion to Job 38: 2–7 ('Where are the foundations of the world anchored? or who laid its cornerstone when the morning stars sang together and all the sons of God shouted for joy?') and to Genesis 1: 9–10 ('Then God commanded, "Let the water beneath the sky come together in the same place and make the land appear", and so it was done. He called the land "earth" and the water "sea"').

[125] **Ring out**
See the note to lines 102–3 above; the music of the concentric spheres was not audible, but it was essential to the ordering of the whole universe; ***crystal*** clear, transparent.

[126–7]
The unusual character of the event is indicated by this possibility that the music of the spheres might actually be made audible.

[128] **silver chime**
The heavenly music was thought to sound light and clear, like the silvery tones of a bell.

[129] **Move . . . time**
move to the rhythm of the heavenly music.

[130] **bass of Heaven's deep organ**
In some accounts of the music of the spheres, the earth was said originally to have provided the bass notes for the harmonious chords produced by the movement of the heavenly globes, though the earth has been out of tune with the heavens since original sin and the Fall of humankind through Adam; here, however, it is back in harmony with the spheres that surround it as a result of God's descent to earth.

[131] **ninefold harmony**
There were ten heavenly spheres in all, but only the inner nine moved and therefore made music.

[132] **consort**
(a) harmonising or accompanying notes; (b) a group of instruments that accompany human voices; ***symphony*** (a) a blending of sounds together; (b) the choir of angels singing their individual parts.

[134] **Enwrap**
absorb, engross in thought; ***fancy*** (a) a composition in a free or impromptu style; (b) changeful mood, tastes or inclination; (c) imagination; ***long*** for a long time.

[135] **run back and fetch**
reverse and revert to; ***the age of gold*** the primordial time, in Greek and Roman mythology, when humans lived and banqueted in the company of the gods, when people were innocent and there was no suffering or sin (see Hesiod, *Works and Days*, 111–26).

[136] **speckled**
(a) spotted by sin; (b) wearing beauty patches (women in this century began wearing small black pieces of fabric on their faces to contrast with and show off the whiteness of their complexions).

[138] **leprous**
bearing white patches, like the skin of someone afflicted with leprosy; see 'speckled' above; ***earthly mould*** the earth and its creatures.

[140] **dolorous**
sorrowful, painful; ***her dolorous mansions*** hell, in Milton's *Paradise Lost*, is depicted as a dark region in the lower depths that contains palaces constructed by the fallen angels; another possibility is that Milton is describing graves, from which the dead are supposed to rise on Judgement Day; ***peering day*** Once hell passes away, its darkness will be penetrated by the light, or, if the mansions are understood as graves, the graves of the dead will open and admit the light of the sun.

[141] **Yea**
truly; ***Truth and Justice*** There are echoes of both biblical and classical motifs here. See Psalm 85: 10–11; 'Mercy and Truth have come together; righteousness and peace have kissed one another'; and the classical figure of Astraea, goddess of justice, who dwelt on earth during the Golden Age but fled when humans grew corrupt and will return if they ever reform sufficiently. See also lines 157–64 below.
[143] **enamelled**
brilliantly coloured; ***arras*** a hanging tapestry.
[144] **Mercy set between**
i.e. between Truth and Justice; the whole description is reminiscent of religious pageants and allegorical paintings.
[145] **Throned in celestial sheen**
seated in the brilliance of heavenly light; note, however, that Mercy has descended, like God, to earth, where her heavenly origins make her shine with splendour.
[146] **radiant feet . . . steering**
The description, which suggests the details of contemporary paintings, gives the descent of Mercy an active and energetic character as she brings part of the heavens (clouds) down with her; ***tissued*** woven with gold or silver thread; ***steering*** guiding.
[149] **wisest Fate**
i.e. the will of God. Note how the preceding scene, presented with all the gorgeousness of Baroque art, is dismissed as too beautiful and too facile.
[152] **bitter**
harsh, painful; Christ's sacrifice and suffering for the sake of humankind culminated in his crucifixion and death.
[153] **redeem our loss**
The death of Christ, in traditional Christian theology, occurred in order that loss of human innocence and sinlessness (cf. the Golden Age motif above) could be atoned for, and human happiness restored.
[155] **ychained**
chained; the 'y' prefix is an archaic form, used here for poetic effect; ***sleep*** moral sleep.
[156] **wakeful trump**
a reference to the seventh and last trumpet blown on the last day to announce the destruction of the known world (hence 'doom') and the reign of Christ (Revelation 11: 15–19). The image of an angel blowing a trumpet to signal the end of the world is a traditional one in Christian art and literature; ***doom*** (a) judgement; (b) justice; (c) fatal last day.
[157] **clang**
the ringing sound of the trumpet.
[159] **outbrake**
broke out.
[160] **aghast**
extremely frightened (by the sound of the trumpet of doom).
[163] **world's last session**
the Day of Judgement, the last day of history, when all the living and the dead are brought before God to be judged and consigned either to eternal happiness for their good lives or eternal damnation for their sinful ones; ***session*** meeting of a court of law.
[164] **dreadful**
awesome; ***Judge*** God; ***middle air*** among the clouds; ***spread his throne*** set up his throne of authority.
[157–64] **horrid clang . . . dreadful Judge**
See the thunder and trumpet sounds that accompanied the giving of the Ten Commandments to Moses (Exodus 19: 16) and the description Christ gives of the Last Judgement in Matthew 24: 30: 'They will see the Son of man coming in the clouds of heaven with power and great glory'.
[165–7] **And then . . . now begins**
i.e. our happiness will be complete only after the Last Judgement, but today, with the birth of Christ, it has begun.
[168] **old Dragon under ground**
Satan (***Dragon*** serpent, the form he takes in the traditional interpretation

of Genesis 3: 1–14). See Milton's version in *Paradise Lost*, 9, 412 f.; also Revelation 12: 9.

[169] **straiter**
narrower; ***bound*** confined.

[170] **Not half... usurpèd sway**
Christ's birth was a further defeat for Satan, and brought about a greater restriction of his activities in tempting humankind to sin; ***usurpèd*** Satan's power over humankind was not granted him by God but gained through deceit and tyranny (as Milton dramatises his fall from heaven and temptation of Adam and Eve in *Paradise Lost*).

[171] **wroth**
enraged.

[172] **Swinges**
lashes.

[173] **oracles**
(a) the place (such as a cave, underground space or natural chasm) where the gods of pre-Christian belief transmit prophecies of the future; (b) the message predicting the future; (c) the priest or priestess who transmits it; ***dumb*** silent.

[174] **hideous hum**
unearthly or uncannily frightful sound.

[175] **archèd roof**
a description of the shape of most oracular sites; ***words deceiving*** the message of the oracle was always ambiguous and difficult to interpret for those who received it.

[176] **Apollo**
Apollo was, among other things, the chief Greek god of oracles, with a famous shrine at Delphi.

[177] **divine**
predict, foretell.

[178] **With hollow shriek**
The priestess who delivered the oracle usually delivered the god's message in a shriek or a frenzied voice; here the departing oracle makes a sound like an evil spirit being evicted from its lair; ***the steep of Delphos*** The famous Delphic oracle had her shrine in a temple of Apollo on the slopes of Mount Parnassos, just above the town of Delphi; ***leaving*** According to a number of writers – especially the Greek author Plutarch, who wrote during the first century AD – the oracles stopped speaking at about the time of Christ's birth.

[180] **nightly trance**
The oracle usually fell into a trancelike state before delivering the message; ***breathed spell*** The priest's spell (i.e. news, information) was often delivered in heavy pants of breath.

[181–5] **lonely... sent**
The various minor gods of Greek and Roman mythology are forced to abandon the earth at the coming of Christ. Milton resolved the problem of reconciling the pagan gods with the Christian God by translating the former into demons (see *Paradise Lost*, 1, 365–521).

[181] **lonely mountains o'er**
all over the lonely mountains.

[182] **resounding**
echoing.

[184] **haunted**
malevolently occupied by a ghost; here the poet refers to the departing demons.

[185] **poplar pale**
The trembling of the poplar was associated with oracular and prophetic pronouncements.

[186] **Genius**
a local deity.

[187] **flower-inwoven tresses**
The nymphs are often depicted with wreaths of flowers woven into their hair.

[188] **nymphs**
minor goddesses of the woods or waters; ***mourn*** i.e. they are sorrowful because the genius is leaving; ***tangled thickets*** The dense grove conceals the sorrowing deities as they bemoan their departure.

[189] **consecrated earth**
the holy places of the old pagan deities.

[190] **holy hearth**
the altars and shrines for such domestic gods as the lares and penates, who protected the home, were located near the hearth.

[191] **Lars**
Roman deities who protected the home or city; ***Lemures*** spirits of the dead, whose ashes were often kept in urns near the hearth.
[193] **drear**
sorrowful.
[194] **Flamens**
priests who conducted religious rites honouring the above deities; ***service quaint*** rituals that are (a) odd and strange or (b) crafty and cunning.
[195] **chill marble . . . sweat**
Perhaps an allusion to Virgil, *Georgics*, I.480, who describes the sweating of the god's marble statue as a portent of imminent evil.
[196] **peculiar**
individual, particular; ***wonted*** usual, accustomed; ***seat*** dwelling-place.
[197] **Peor**
Baal-Peor, a sun-god worshipped by the Canaanites and Phoenicians. The preceding gods are all Greek or Roman. Beginning with this line, those named are of eastern origins; ***Baalim*** other gods of the same religion (the -im is a plural ending).
[198] **dim**
dark in both the literal and the metaphorical sense.
[199] **twice-battered god of Palestine**
Dagon, the god of the Philistines described in 1 Samuel 5: 4; his image was miraculously broken twice so that only its base remained.
[200–1] **moonèd**
with horns, like those of the moon, on her head; ***moonèd Ashtaroth . . . both*** plural of Ashtoreth or Astarte, the goddess, sometimes called 'creatrix of the gods' or 'queen and mother of the heavens', worshipped by the Caananites and Phoenicians.
[202] **girt**
surrounded; ***tapers*** candles.
[203] **Libyc Hammon**
Ammon, an Egyptian god worshipped, in the form of a ram (hence with horns), in the Libyan desert; ***shrinks*** cowers, pulls back.
[204] **Tyrian Maids . . . Thammuz**
Thammuz (or Adonis, in Greek mythology), another Phoenician god, was killed by a boar but came back to life every year; he was a symbol of summer slain by winter, and his death was commemorated annually with ritual mourning by a chorus of maidens.
[205] **sullen**
gloomy.
[206] **dread**
dreadful, fearful.
[207] **hue**
colour.
[209] **grisly**
(a) causing terror or horror; (b) dark in colour.
[210] **dismal**
fearful, hellish; ***furnace blue*** blue because of the very high temperature of its flames.
[205–10] **Moloch . . . blue**
idol worshipped by the Ammonites, who sacrificed children to him in a ritual fire, accompanied by the noise of cymbals to drown out their cries; he is named in 2 Kings 23: 10 and had the form of a king with a calf's head.
[211] **brutish gods**
Egyptian gods in animal form; ***as fast*** refers to 'haste' in the following line.
[212] **Isis and Orus**
The goddess Isis was the mother of Orus (or Horus), who had the head of a hawk and was the god of light, while she bore a cow's horns and the sun-disc on her own head'; ***Anubis*** son of Osiris and ruler over the dead, depicted with a dog or jackal's head.
[213] **Osiris**
the chief god of Egypt, brother and husband of Isis.
[214] **Memphian**
Memphis was the ancient capital of Egypt.
[215] **Trampling . . . lowings**
Osiris was worshipped in the shape of a bull.
[217] **sacred chest**
According to Herodotus 2.63, Osiris's priests bore his image from one temple to another in a small, gilded wooden box.

[218] **shroud**
Osiris was periodically reborn; now, however, he will be permanently banished to the underworld by the coming of Christ.
[219] **timbrelled anthems**
sacred hymns recited with tambourine accompaniment.
[220] **sable-stoled sorcerers**
the black-robed priests of Osiris; ***ark*** a sacred chest or box, carried in procession.
[221] **Judah's land**
See Matthew 2: 6 ('And you, Bethlehem in the land of Judah, are not the least among the princes of Judah, for out of you will come a ruler who shall rule my people Israel'); the biblical passage alludes to a prophecy announcing the coming of the Messiah from the land of Judah.
[222] **dreaded**
greatly feared, awesome; ***hand*** (a) power, might; (b) authority.
[223] **rays of Bethlehem**
the brilliant light described in the Nativity scene (Luke 2: 9); ***dusky eyn*** blinded or obscured eyes.
[224] **Not all the gods beside**
None of the other gods.
[226] **Typhon**
(a) an Egyptian god, brother and murderer of Osiris; (b) a giant in Greek mythology whose lower body was snakelike.
[227–8] **Our Babe . . . damnèd crew**
While these lines convey the paradoxical power of the divine infant, they also suggest the story of Hercules (or Heracles), who strangled two serpents in his cradle; ***swaddling bands*** cloth wrapped around an infant for clothing; ***damnèd crew*** the accursed company of pagan gods.
[229–33] **So when . . . jail**
The sun is presented, somewhat whimsically, awakening from a bed enclosed with rose-coloured curtains and raising its head on an ocean-pillow. The simile describes the pagan gods as abandoning the earth in the same fashion as ghosts were said to do when the sun began to rise above the waters in the east (see Shakespeare, *A Midsummer Night's Dream*, III, ii, 380–82; *Hamlet*, I, v, 89).
[231] **orient wave**
the eastern waters of the ocean.
[232] **flocking**
coming together in large crowds; ***shadows*** (a) the spirits of the dead, or of the banished gods; (b) the shadows of night overcome by the dawn.
[233] **troop**
march off; ***infernal jail*** the lower depths of the earth or hell, the place where the damned are punished.
[234] **fettered**
enchained; ***slips*** (a) vanishes quickly; (b) escapes without notice; ***several*** separate; ***grave*** The word suggests that the false gods of pagan religion are dead and buried, to be ignored for ever.
[235] **yellow-skirted fays**
fairies or native Celtic–British deities, often said to bless childbirth (see, again, *A Midsummer Night's Dream*, V, i, 408–13).
[236] **night-steeds**
the horses of night, which pull his chariot across the sky; ***moon-loved maze*** the ring in which fairies dance by the light of the moon.
[237–8] **But see! . . . rest**
Note the scene's return to the pastoral calm of the night with which it began.
[239] **tedious**
(a) long; (b) wearisome; (c) exhausted. Is the poet suggesting that the hymn is longer than the infant to whom it is addressed needs to hear? Has it put him to sleep, and thus served to give him rest before entering into the trials of human existence?
[240] **youngest-teemèd**
most newly born.
[241] **fixed her polished car**
The new star that was said to have stopped over the stable at Bethlehem and drawn the three Magi from the East is described as though it had come to wait on the newborn infant; ***car*** chariot.
[242] **handmaid lamp**
The star is like a servant woman

holding a lamp over the head of the sleeping infant.

[243] **courtly stable**
an oxymoron, since a stable is far from being a court, where noblemen might be born; yet the presence of the Christ child and his attendant angels makes this lowly place into the highest domain of mankind.

[244] **in order serviceable**
in ranks, ready to serve their Lord.

92/ *On Shakespeare*

What needs my Shakespeare for his honoured bones
The labour of an age in pilèd stones,
Or that his hallowed relics should be hid
Under a star-ypointing pyramid?
Dear son of memory, great heir of fame,
What need'st thou such weak witness of thy name?
Thou in our wonder and astonishment
Hast built thyself a livelong monument.
For whilst to th'shame of slow-endeavouring art
Thy easy numbers flow, and that each heart
Hath from the leaves of thy unvalued book
Those Delphic lines with deep impression took,
Then thou, our fancy of itself bereaving,
Dost make us marble with too much conceiving;
And so sepulchred in such pomp dost lie,
That kings for such a tomb would wish to die.

This tribute, like Ben Jonson's, was published as part of an edition of Shakespeare's plays, the second folio edition of 1632. Milton's first published English poem, it may have been written as early as 1630 and was originally titled 'An Epitaph on the Admirable Dramatic Poet W. Shakespear'. The frontispiece of the volume was a portrait of the playwright; the monument to the poet in Stratford, where he was born, contains a bust of Shakespeare, though the tomb in the same church is a much simpler affair. Milton's central idea – that Shakespeare's poetry is the greater monument to his memory – is an old one that can be traced back to the Roman poet Horace. The original title reveals that it is the Folio itself that is the monument; therefore, Milton's poem serves the function of the traditional inscription on the marble slab that celebrates the greatness of the man buried beneath it. The tribute is organised around a rather elaborate conceit reminiscent of the Metaphysical style: because Shakespeare's poetry is so profound, it makes those who contemplate it virtually incapable of thought, hence as immobile as a piece of marble; and that is the greatest monument of all to his achievement.

[1] **What needs my Shakespeare** Why should the Shakespeare I admire need . . . ; note the personal note implied by ***my***, which indicates both intimate acquaintance and warm admiration; Milton was too young ever to have had a meaningful personal encounter with Shakespeare – unlike Jonson, who also speaks of 'my Shakespeare'; so this expression of intimacy refers rather to the dramatist's writings; ***honoured bones*** his body, honoured by a magnificent burial and tomb (neither of which was actually provided).

[2] **labour of an age** (a) elaborate workmanship, long in execution; (b) a tomb that is merely a product of his own times and will not last; ***pilèd stones*** though even modest tombs are more carefully constructed than a pile of stones, Milton is implying that even the greatest funerary monument is no better than a heap of rocks.

[3] **hallowed relics** his last remains, hallowed (i.e. held sacred) because of his literary greatness; ***hid*** hidden.

[4] **star-ypointing pyramid** The pyramids, tombs of the Ancient Egyptian pharaohs, were famous examples of an extravagant burial monument; they are described as pointing to the stars both because of their physical shape and because of their symbolic suggestion of the immortality and unchangeableness of the person buried under or within them. Note the archaic 'y-' (not, strictly speaking, a correct form), which suggests pretentiousness as well.

[5] **son of memory** Memory or Mnemosyne was the mother of the Muses, Greek goddesses of inspiration and patrons of the arts; the phrase implies both that Shakespeare's genius was divine in origins and that his name will live on in men's memories for ever; ***heir of fame*** (a) Shakespeare has received fame as his inheritance; (b) he is the famous heir of an ancient literary tradition; (c) the excellence of his poetry gives him a rightful title to everlasting fame.

[6] **such weak witness** i.e. of the sort represented by a marble tomb or pyramid (***witness*** record).

[7] **thou in . . . astonishment** (a) you, to our wonder . . . ; (b) our wonder and astonishment are the monument you have built; there is a possible pun in 'astonishment' (i.e. literally, turn to stone) in anticipation of the lines that follow.

[8] **built thyself . . . monument** Compare with Jonson's 'Thou art a monument without a tomb'.

[9] **whilst to the shame** whilst to the shame of those who make; ***slow-endeavouring art*** laboured and lengthy attempts to write poetry.

[10] **easy numbers** (a) fluent, musical metres; (b) seemingly effortless verses; according to Ben Jonson, Shakespeare was particularly admired by contemporaries for the ease and rapidity with which he wrote his greatest plays; ***and that*** and whilst; ***each heart*** every reader.

[11] **leaves** pages; ***unvalued*** invaluable, priceless.

[12] **Delphic lines** (a) the prophetic utterances of Apollo's oracle at Delphi in Greece; ***Delphic*** inspired by Apollo and therefore pre-eminently poetic, since he was god of prophecy and of poetry; (b) the lines of Shakespeare's plays; ***with deep impression took*** (a) those lines of verse that reflect such deep impressions in the poet; (b) those lines that impress readers so deeply; however, there is also a possible meaning of incising or engraving (the lines have been engraved upon our hearts as epigraphs and tributes are engraved upon marble); ***took*** taken (the past participle belongs to ***Hath*** in line 11); i.e. the whole phrase means 'whilst each heart has taken from the pages of your precious book those Delphic lines with a deep impression . . . '.

[9–12] **For ... took**
A complex and somewhat ambiguous phrase, which may be understood as saying that readers are overwhelmed both by Shakespeare's amazing and seemingly effortless skill in writing verses and by the profundity of thought expressed within them.
[13] **fancy ... bereaving**
i.e. our imagination is so overwhelmed by Shakespeare's that his seems to have stolen our own away from us; ***fancy*** imagination; ***bereaving*** (a) depriving; (b) dispossessing violently.
[14] **make us marble ... conceiving**
i.e. his poetry immobilises our thought by making such demands on our abilities to grasp its profundity; compare Milton's 'Il Penseroso', lines 41–2: 'There held in holy passion still,/Forget thyself to marble'; ***conceiving*** (a) reflecting; (b) forming or admitting ideas into the mind; (c) imagining.
[15] **sepulchred**
buried, entombed (in the minds of his engrossed readers); ***pomp*** grandeur, magnificence.

93 / *L'Allegro*

Hence, loathèd Melancholy,
Of Cerberus and blackest midnight born,
In Stygian cave forlorn
'Mongst horrid shapes, and shrieks, and sights unholy.
Find out some uncouth cell
Where brooding darkness spreads his jealous wings,
And the night-raven sings.
There under ebon shades and low-browed rocks
As ragged as thy locks,
In dark Cimmerian desert ever dwell.
But come, thou goddess fair and free,
In Heaven yclept Euphrosynë,
And by men, heart-easing mirth,
Whom lovely Venus at a birth
With two sister Graces more
To ivy-crownèd Bacchus bore –
Or, whether (as some sager sing),
The frolic wind that breathes the spring,
Zephyr with Aurora playing
As he met her once a-Maying,
There on beds of violets blue
And fresh-blown roses washed in dew,
Filled her with thee, a daughter fair,
So buxom, blithe, and debonair.

Haste thee, nymph, and bring with thee
Jest and youthful jollity,
Quips and cranks, and wanton wiles,
Nods, and becks, and wreathèd smiles
Such as hang on Hebe's cheek
And love to live in dimple sleek,
Sport that wrinkled care derides,
And laughter holding both his sides.
Come and trip it as you go
On the light fantastic toe,
And in thy right hand lead with thee
The Mountain Nymph, sweet Liberty.
And if I give thee honour due,
Mirth, admit me of thy crew
To live with her and live with thee
In unreprovèd pleasures free:
To hear the lark begin his flight
And, singing, startle the dull night
From his watch-tower in the skies
Till the dappled dawn doth rise;
Then to come in spite of sorrow
And at my window bid good-morrow
Through the sweet-briar or the vine
Or the twisted eglantine,
While the cock with lively din
Scatters the rear of darkness thin,
And to the stack or the barn door
Stoutly struts his dames before,
Oft listening how the hounds and horn
Cheerly rouse the slumbering morn,
From the side of some hoar hill
Through the high wood echoing shrill.
Sometime walking not unseen
By hedgerow elms on hillocks green,
Right against the eastern gate
Where the great sun begins his state,
Robed in flames and amber light,
The clouds in thousand liveries dight,
While the ploughman near at hand
Whistles o'er the furrowed land,
And the milkmaid singeth blithe,

And the mower whets his scythe,
And every shepherd tells his tale
Under the hawthorn in the dale.
Straight mine eye hath caught new pleasures
Whilst the landscape round it measures
Russet lawns and fallows grey
Where the nibbling flocks do stray,
Mountains on whose barren breast
The labouring clouds do often rest,
Meadows trim with daisies pied,
Shallow brooks and rivers wide.
Towers and battlements it sees
Bosomed high in tufted trees,
Where perhaps some beauty lies,
The cynosure of neighbouring eyes.
Hard by, a cottage chimney smokes
From betwixt two agèd oaks,
Where Corydon and Thyrsis met
Are at their savoury dinner set
Of herbs and other country messes
Which the neat-handed Phillis dresses;
And then in haste her bower she leaves
With Thestylis to bind the sheaves;
Or, if the earlier season lead
To the tanned haycock in the mead,
Sometimes with secure delight
The upland hamlets will invite,
When the merry bells ring round,
And the jocund rebecks sound
To many a youth and many a maid,
Dancing in the chequered shade;
And young and old come forth to play
On a sunshine holiday,
Till the livelong daylight fail;
Then to the spicy nut-brown ale,
With stories told of many a feat:
How Faery Mab the junkets eat.
She was pinched and pulled, she said
And, by the friar's lantern led,
Tells how the drudging goblin sweat
To earn his cream-bowl duly set,

When, in one night, ere glimpse of morn,
His shadowy flail hath threshed the corn
That ten day-labourers could not end;
Then lies him down the lubber fiend
And, stretched out all the chimney's length,
Basks at the fire his hairy strength;
And crop-full out of doors he flings,
Ere the first cock his matin rings.
Thus done the tales, to bed they creep,
By whispering winds soon lulled asleep.
Towered cities please us then
And the busy hum of men,
Where throngs of knights and barons bold,
In weeds of peace, high triumphs hold
With store of ladies, whose bright eyes
Rain influence and judge the prize
Of wit or arms, while both contend
To win her grace, whom all commend.
There let Hymen oft appear
In saffron robe, with taper clear,
And pomp and feast and revelry,
With mask and antique pageantry –
Such sights as youthful poets dream
On summer eves by haunted stream.
Then to the well-trod stage anon,
If Jonson's learned sock be on
Or sweetest Shakespeare, fancy's child,
Warble his native wood-notes wild,
And ever against eating cares,
Lap me in soft Lydian airs,
Married to immortal verse
Such as the meeting soul may pierce
In notes, with many a winding bout
Of linkèd sweetness long drawn out,
With wanton heed and giddy cunning,
The melting voice through mazes running,
Untwisting all the chains that tie
The hidden soul of harmony,
That Orpheus' self may heave his head
From golden slumber on a bed
Of heaped Elysian flowers and hear

Such strains as would have won the ear
Of Pluto, to have quite set free
His half-regained Eurydicë.
These delights, if thou canst give,
Mirth with thee I mean to live.

'L'Allegro' and its companion poem, 'Il Penseroso', are virtually unique, though not without some relationship to other poetic types. They have elements of the ancient debate form, of the encomium (or poem of praise), and – especially in imagery and style – of pastoral and landscape poetry, such as Virgil's, *Eclogues* and *Georgics*. Yet most verse in the debate tradition – Marvell's 'Dialogue between the Soul and Body' (p. 473) is an example – conducts the argument within the limits of a single poem, not in two independent (albeit complementary) ones. Milton may well have been recalling the poems of 'reply' by Donne and Sir Walter Raleigh to Christopher Marlowe's 'Passionate Shepherd to His Love', especially since he echoes the formula of invitation in both. Still, while each can be read separately without loss of intelligibility, they may be seen as two different perspectives on pleasure, pursued through contrasting but equally valid moods. However, not everyone sees the two poems as evenly balanced; some critics see a progression as one moves from 'L'Allegro' to 'Il Penseroso', and interpret the conclusion of the latter as offering a higher species of delight than mere mirth can provide.

Equally as important for an understanding of the companion poems as their formal and literary character is the intellectual background they presuppose. Their most prominent feature is the tradition of reflection on the 'disease' of melancholia, given monumental expression in Robert Burton's *Anatomy of Melancholy* (first edition 1621). According to the prevalent theory of psychological temperament traceable as far back as the Greek medical writer Galen, the mind and body are subject to various conditions induced by one of the four 'humours': blood, phlegm, choler and bile. Melancholy is caused by a predominance of this last humour, and it can lead to what we would call depression or even madness.

Nevertheless, the poems are not exclusively concerned with a psychological contrast; they draw – albeit somewhat light-heartedly – on another contrast: between the active life and the contemplative life.

Moreover, the two poems define two different types of melancholy: the depressive variety described and dismissed by the 'allegro' or 'lively' man at the opening of 'L'Allegro' and the exultant, meditative variety that is attractive to the 'penseroso' or 'thoughtful' man of 'Il Penseroso'. The debate presented by the two poems is not between frivolous joys and profound sobriety but between two different sources of pleasure.

[1] **loathèd Melancholy**
The mirthful speaker of this poem rejects Melancholy at its very beginning; note the corresponding opening of 'Il Penseroso'.

[2–3] **Of Cerberus... born**
Milton personifies Melancholy in the guise of a Greek or Roman god with denizens of Hades and night as parents; there is, of course, no such figure in classical mythology; ***Cerberus*** the three-headed dog, guard of the classical underworld; his name – appropriately – means 'heart-devouring'. ***Stygian*** of or associated with the Styx ('hateful', in Greek) –

one of the five rivers in Hades that separate it from the world of the living; ***cave*** either the dwelling-place of Cerberus or the birthplace of Melancholy (or both).

[4] **Find out**
seek, run off to; ***uncouth*** desolate, hidden, wild; ***cell*** cavern or other remote dwelling-place.

[6] **brooding**
(a) moody; (b) hovering over like a bird hatching eggs; ***jealous*** i.e. of the light. Note the image of night as a huge black bird, an ancient mythological figure.

[7] **night-raven**
night-owl, night-heron, or other nocturnal bird.

[8] **ebon**
black, like ebony wood; ***shades*** (a) shadows; (b) shade cast by dark (ebony) trees; ***low-browed*** lowering, overhanging (like hair over the forehead; see the next line).

[9] **thy locks**
the unkempt 'hair' of the figure of Melancholy.

[10] **Cimmerian desert**
the desolate realm at the edge of the earth (in classical mythology) that is always dark (***desert*** uninhabited realm).

[11] **Goddess**
unlike Melancholy, an actual figure of Greek mythology; ***free*** (a) courteous, of gentle breeding; untrammelled, uninhibited, at liberty.

[12] **Heaven**
i.e. on Olympus, abode of the principal Greek divinities; ***yclept*** called; ***Euphrosynë*** 'Gladness', one of the three Graces, first named by the Greek poet Hesiod but with different parents from those Milton describes.

[13] **heart-easing**
Note the contrast with Cerberus' name above.

[14] **Venus**
the well-known classical goddess of love; Milton follows a different tradition from Hesiod, for whom Zeus and Eurynome, daughter of Ocean, were the parents of the Graces, who give life its loveliness and were imagined as the companions of the Muses.

[15] **sister Graces more**
Aglaia and Thalia, the other two Graces.

[16] **ivy-crownèd Bacchus**
the Greek god of wine and revelry.

[17] **sager**
(a) wiser or (b) more knowledgeable authorities.

[18] **frolic**
joyous, merry; ***wind*** zephyr, the west wind that blows in early spring; ***breathes*** exhales, brings or escorts in.

[19] **Aurora**
goddess of dawn.

[20] **a-Maying**
i.e. celebrating the springtime by gathering flowers. This alternative – and, for the poet, preferable – account of Euphrosyne's origins is an allegory of the freshness of spring, but it also contrasts with the very different act of Hades, god of the underworld, who carried off Persephone, innocently gathering flowers, to be his bride and queen of his dark realm, where Milton imagines Melancholy to have been born.

[24] **buxom**
(a) joyous; (b) friendly; ***blithe*** merry; ***debonair*** courteous, gentle; all three words are nearly synonymous.

[25] **Haste thee**
hurry; ***nymph*** (a) a semi-divine nature being, imagined as a young maiden; (b) any young maiden.

[27] **Quips**
a clever reply or remark; ***cranks*** imaginative figures of speech; ***wanton wiles*** playful tricks.

[28] **Nod**
sign of greeting; ***beck*** bow or other gesture of salutation; ***wreathèd*** with upcurled lips.

[29] **hang**
linger; ***Hebe*** daughter of Zeus and Hera, cupbearer of the gods (her name means 'youth' in Greek).

[30] **live**
i.e. reside in all vitality; ***sleek*** plump.

[31] **Sport**
pleasant pastime or entertainment; ***derides*** laughs at, scorns.

[32] **Laughter . . . sides**
The two personifications of the preceding line (Sport mocking 'wrinkled Care') are effectively reinforced by this more concrete and vigorous image.
[33] **trip it**
(a) dance [it]; (b) step lightly.
[34] **light fantastic toe**
i.e. with nimble foot; ***fantastic*** (a) impulsive; (b) unusual in behaviour; (c) fanciful.
[36] **Mountain Nymph**
an oread or semi-divine companion of the god Pan, who danced on mountaintops; see also the note to line 25; ***Liberty*** (a) freedom from cares or responsibilities; (b) freedom from 'loathèd Melancholy'.
[38] **admit me of thy crew**
let be among your followers.
[39] **her**
Liberty; ***thee*** Mirth.
[40] **unreprovèd**
irreproachable, blameless; ***free*** (a) refers to 'me' in line 38; (b) refers to 'live' in line 39.
[41] **To hear the lark . . . flight**
Because the lark takes flight in near darkness, it can be more readily heard than seen; note that 'to hear' is parallel with 'to live' in line 39 and 'to come' in line 45, all of which depends on 'admit' in line 38.
[42] **singing**
It is the lark that sings; ***startle*** awaken with a start; ***dull*** (a) sluggish, inactive, sleepy; (b) gloomy, dim, indistinct.
[43] **his**
probably refers to 'lark' in line 41 rather than to 'night' in line 42; the skylark ascends to very great heights.
[44] **dappled**
marked with patches of different colours or shades.
[45] **to come**
Some commentators see this infinitive as referring to l'Allegro, others to the lark. If the former is the subject, he arises and goes to his window to greet the morning; if the latter, it flies down to or past the window and awakens the sleeper; ***in spite of sorrow*** in defiance of, scorning the effects of melancholy.
[46] **bid good-morrow**
greet good morning.
[47–8] **sweet-briar . . . twisted eglantine**
There is some dispute about just which plant is meant, since sweetbriar and eglantine are names for the same plant, a thorny shrub with a rose-flower. However, Milton may be differentiating them by calling the eglantine 'twisted', meaning by that, according to some scholars, honeysuckle. But 'twisted' also has the meaning 'pruned' or 'cut back', so that the interpretation remains inconclusive.
[49] **din**
loud, resounding noise.
[50] **Scatters the rear . . . thin**
like a retreating army, attacked from behind.
[51] **stack**
a pile of grain, hay or straw.
[52] **Stoutly**
manfully, proudly; ***struts*** walks fully erect and with dignity; the description is lightly humorous, though in 'defeating' the 'armies' of the night with his crowing, the cock may feel fully justified in his pride; ***dames before*** in front of his hens.
[53] **Oft listening**
referring back, probably, to line 46 and l'Allegro, who often listens at his window; ***hounds and horn*** of early-morning hunters.
[54] **Cheerly**
cheerfully; ***rouse*** after driving off the night, the day must be roused from sleep.
[55] **hoar**
grey, frost-covered.
[57] **Sometime**
at one time or another; ***walking not unseen*** The speaker has left his house to stroll outside.
[58] **hedgerow elms**
a row of elms planted in a hedge-like line.
[59] **eastern gate**
a common poetic description of the horizon where the sun appears at dawn.

[60] **great sun begins his state**
The sun is portrayed as a monarch in splendour beginning his ceremonial procession.
[62] **liveries dight**
decked out or clad in gorgeous clothing.
[64] **Whistles o'er**
i.e. whistles while he ploughs.
[65] **blithe**
joyfully.
[66] **whets**
puts a sharp edge on; ***scythe*** the long, thin, curved blade used for cutting down or mowing tall grasses.
[67] **tells his tale**
(a) counts his sheep (***tell*** count; ***tale*** tally or total number); (b) recites his story.
[68] **hawthorn**
a variety of thorny shrub or small tree, appreciated for its shade; ***dale*** a river-valley between hills or slopes.
[69] **Straight**
immediately, without delay.
[70] **round it measures**
while it measures (i.e. traverses, scans) the landscape all around.
[71] **Russet lawns**
reddish-brown pastures; ***fallows*** ploughed lands.
[73] **barren breast**
bald summit.
[74] **labouring**
(a) moving slowly and with difficulty; (b) as though about to give birth (to rain).
[75] **trim**
in good condition, neat; ***pied*** multi-coloured.
[77] **battlements**
crenellated decoration on the top of a wall, originally provided for defence; ***it*** his eye.
[78] **Bosomed in**
enclosed in the bosom of; ***tufted*** clustered.
[79] **beauty lies**
lovely lady dwells.
[80] **cynosure**
centre of interest or admiration.
[81] **Hard by**
nearby.
[83] **Corydon and Thyrsis**
common classical names for shepherds or rustics in pastoral poetry.
[85] **messes**
meals or simple rural dishes.
[86] **neat-handed**
(a) skilful; (b) having clean hands; ***Phillis*** another common pastoral name for a rural maiden; ***dresses*** (a) prepares; (b) sets in order; (c) adorns.
[87] **bower**
dwelling, perhaps a cottage.
[88] **Thestylis**
yet another classical name for a rustic; ***bind the sheaves*** tie grain together in sheaves.
[89–90] **if . . . tanned haycock**
If it is too early to bind the sheaves, they will rack or gather up the newly mown hay in the meadow.
[91] **secure**
free from worry.
[92] **upland hamlets**
villages further up the slopes, away from the dale.
[93] **merry bells**
in celebration of a feast day or holiday.
[94] **jocund**
merry; ***rebeck*** an early type of fiddle, often associated with rustics and shepherds (in poetry, at least).
[96] **chequered shade**
i.e. shadows in which spots of light are visible.
[98] **sunshine**
sunny.
[99] **livelong**
long-lasting.
[100] **Then**
It is now evening; ***spicy nut-brown ale*** a drink perhaps consisting of nutmeg, sugar, ale, and other ingredients.
[101] **feat**
notable occurrence or deed.
[102] **Faery Mab**
Queen of the fairies, said to rob dairies in Ben Jonson's *Entertainment at Althorp*. It is probable, in fact, that Milton is drawing on Shakespeare and Jonson or other literary sources rather than on true folklore; ***junkets*** cream cheeses or other cream products.

[103] **She was pinched and pulled**
One of the women recounts her adventures with the meddlesome fairies.
[104] **Friar's Lantern**
the will-o'-the-wisp (Jack-o'-lantern, *ignis fatuus*), a deceptive light that leads people astray, usually in the forest or wilderness.
[105] **drudging**
laborious, hard-working; ***goblin*** a mischievous fairy or demon, but here probably Robin Goodfellow (see Shakespeare, *A Midsummer Night's Dream*, II, i, 33–57), a practical joker and the most famous of the goblins who haunted English country life; ***sweat*** sweated, in the older past-tense form.
[106] **earn his cream-bowl**
usually the traditional fee to Robin for leaving people and things alone, but here, apparently, a payment for actual work done.
[108] **shadowy flail**
insubstantial or invisible flail (an instrument for threshing corn by hand).
[109] **ten day-labourers could not end**
i.e. Robin could thresh more overnight than ten men working all day.
[110] **lubber fiend**
According to the *OED*, 'a beneficent goblin supposed to perform some of the laborious work of a household or farm during the night'; ***lubber*** clumsy or rustic fellow; ***fiend*** goblin or demon.
[112] **hairy strength**
Robin Goodfellow was usually described as hairy.
[113] **crop-full**
his stomach full; ***flings*** rushes precipitately.
[114] **Ere**
before; ***matin*** the first public morning prayer, which was usually announced by the ringing of a bell, here by the cock's crow.
[117] **Towered cities**
The speaker turns from typical country activities and stories to typical urban scenes and events.
[118] **busy hum of men**
i.e. swarming activity, like that of bees around a hive.
[120] **weeds of peace**
unwarlike – therefore rich and gorgeous – apparel or clothing; ***high triumphs hold*** present elaborate festivities or performances on stage.
[121] **store**
abundance.
[121–2] **bright eyes/Rain influence**
The ladies' eyes are compared with stars, which supposedly affected human destiny by raining an ethereal fluid down upon people. See also Milton's 'On the Morning of Christ's Nativity', line 71.
[123] **wit or arms**
i.e. contestants in the tournament competed for the ladies' favours in two different categories: that of clever speech and that of prowess or physical skill.
[124] **grace**
favour; ***whom all commend*** It is the lady, not the contestant, whom all praise.
[125] **There**
i.e. in this same scene; ***Hymen*** the classical god of marriage, often depicted in Roman poetry wearing a saffron-coloured robe and bearing a torch.
[127] **pomp**
ceremonial procession; ***feast*** banquet; ***revelry*** (a) the revels, theatrical entertainments presented at court; (b) boisterous mirth or song.
[128] **mask**
(a) disguise for the face; (b) masque, a form of theatrical presentation at court, characterised by elaborate costumes, sets, choreography and music; ***antique*** (a) ancient; (b) involving allegorical, mythical or medieval themes; ***pageantry*** pageants.
[131] **Then to the well-trod stage**
i.e. the speaker turns to comedy, the more popular public form of entertainment; ***well-trod*** much walked upon; ***anon*** directly, right afterwards.
[132] **If Jonson's learned sock**
If Ben Jonson's comedies are being

performed; ***learned*** Jonson, unlike Shakespeare, had attended university and prided himself on his knowledge of Greek and Roman literature; ***sock*** the slipper worn by Ancient Greek actors in comedies, here standing for comedy itself.

[133] **fancy's child**
Shakespeare is thought to possess imagination as an inborn gift, in contrast with Jonson's acquired learning; the phrase may come from Shakespeare himself ('child of fancy' in *Love's Labour's Lost*, I, i, 171).

[134] **Warble**
i.e. sing softly or sweetly (i.e. write poetry) as easily as a bird; ***native*** natural, without obvious art; ***wood-notes wild*** forest-song; Shakespeare is praised as the author of comedies, which often involve a natural or rural setting. This conception of the dramatist's inherent poetic gift may have been suggested by Jonson's 'To the Memory of... Shakespeare' (p. 146), line 47.

[135] **eating**
The more usual idiom is 'devouring' or 'gnawing' care.

[136] **Lap me**
wrap me, as though in cloth or a garment; ***Lydian airs*** relaxing, delightful melodies; the Lydian was one of the ecclesiastical modes of medieval music, though the name goes back to the Ancient Greek musical system.

[137] **Married to immortal verse**
i.e. with words and music harmoniously joined.

[138] **meeting**
advancing in response, moving forward in welcome; ***pierce*** (a) penetrate; (b) permeate, suffuse.

[139] **bout**
turn or repeating pattern.

[140] **linkèd sweetness**
(a) music closely matched to words; (b) 'the sense variously drawn out from one verse into another' (Milton, 'The Verse', introduction to *Paradise Lost*).

[141] **wanton**
unplanned, spontaneous; ***heed*** attention, care; ***giddy*** moving rapidly from one thing to another or in various directions; ***cunning*** skill.

[142] **melting**
with sensitive feeling or modulation; ***mazes*** labyrinthine paths or directions; note the echo of 'winding' in line 139.

[143] **untwisting**
releasing, relaxing; ***chains*** rules and laws that bind notes or words together.

[144] **soul**
animating principle or essence; the 'soul of harmony' is released by the untying of the 'bondage' of strict rules that keep it from acting freely.

[145] **Orpheus' self**
Orpheus himself; ***heave*** lift with some difficulty.

[147] **Elysian flowers**
i.e. the asphodels growing in the realm of the blessed in the classical underworld.

[148] **strains**
melodies, musical passages.

[149–50] **Pluto... Eurydicë**
Orpheus descended into Hades, the realm of Pluto, god of the underworld, in search of his deceased wife, Eurydice, and so charmed the denizens of the underworld with his music that he succeeded in gaining permission to lead her back to earth, on condition that he did not look back at her before they left Hades. Unfortunately, he could not resist doing so, and lost her a second time. The speaker imagines music so delightful as to equal that which Orpheus sang.

[151–2] **These delights... to live**
These closing lines seem to echo the ending of Christopher Marlowe's 'Passionate Shepherd to His Love': 'If these delights thy mind may move, / Then live with me and be my love.' The same lines were repeated in Sir Walter Raleigh's answer to Marlowe, 'The Nymph's Reply to the Shepherd'. Milton may be alluding to both poems: 'Il Penseroso' ends with a similar formula, and the Marlowe–Raleigh pastoral poems, taken as a complementary pair, could have provided something of a model for his own companion pieces.

94 / *Il Penseroso*

Hence, vain deluding joys,
The brood of folly without father bred,
How little you bestead
Or fill the fixèd mind with all your toys;
Dwell in some idle brain
And fancies fond with gaudy shapes possess,
As thick and numberless
As the gay motes that people the sunbeams
Or likest hovering dreams,
The fickle pensioners of Morpheus' train.
But hail, thou goddess, sage and holy,
Hail divinest Melancholy,
Whose saintly visage is too bright
To hit the sense of human sight,
And therefore to our weaker view,
O'erlaid with black, staid wisdom's hue –
Black, but such as in esteem
Prince Memnon's sister might beseem
Or that starred Ethiop Queen that strove
To set her beauty's praise above
The sea-nymphs, and their powers offended.
Yet thou art higher far descended:
Thee bright-haired Vesta long of yore
To solitary Saturn bore.
His daughter she (in Saturn's reign,
Such mixture was not held a stain),
Oft in glimmering bowers and glades
He met her and in secret shades
Of woody Ida's inmost grove,
Whilst yet there was no fear of Jove.
Come, pensive nun, devout and pure,
Sober, steadfast, and demure,
All in a robe of darkest grain,
Flowing with majestic train
And sable stole of cypress lawn
Over thy decent shoulders drawn.
Come, but keep thy wonted state

With even step and musing gait
And looks commercing with the skies,
Thy rapt soul sitting in thine eyes.
There, held in holy passion still,
Forget thyself to marble, till
With a sad, leaden, downward cast
Thou fix them on the earth as fast
And join with thee calm Peace and Quiet,
Spare Fast, that oft with gods doth diet
And hears the Muses in a ring
Ay round about Jove's altar sing;
And add to these retirèd Leisure,
That in trim gardens takes his pleasure;
But first and chiefest, with thee bring
Him that yon soars on golden wing,
Guiding the fiery-wheelèd throne,
The Cherub Contemplation,
And the mute silence hist along,
'Less Philomel will deign a song
In her sweetest, saddest plight,
Smoothing the rugged brow of night –
While Cynthia checks her dragon-yoke
Gently o'er the accustomed oak –
Sweet bird, that shunn'st the noise of folly,
Most musical, most melancholy!
Thee, chantress, oft the woods among
I woo to hear thy evensong,
And, missing thee, I walk unseen
On the dry, smooth-shaven green
To behold the wandering moon
Riding near her highest noon,
Like one that had been led astray
Through the heaven's wide pathless way
And oft, as if her head she bowed,
Stooping through a fleecy cloud.
Oft on a plat of rising ground,
I hear the far-off curfew sound
Over some wide-watered shore,
Swinging slow with sullen roar;
Or, if the air will not permit,
Some still removèd place will fit,

Where glowing embers through the room
Teach light to counterfeit a gloom,
Far from all resort of mirth,
Save the cricket on the hearth
Or the bellman's drowsy charm
To bless the doors from nightly harm,
Or let my lamp at midnight hour
Be seen in some high, lonely tower,
Where I may oft outwatch the Bear
With thrice-great Hermes, or unsphere
The spirit of Plato, to unfold
What worlds or what vast regions hold
The immortal mind that hath forsook
Her mansion in this fleshly nook,
And of those dæmons that are found
In fire, air, flood, or under ground,
Whose power hath a true consent
With planet or with element.
Sometime let gorgeous tragedy
In sceptred pall come sweeping by,
Presenting Thebes or Pelops' line
Or the tale of Troy divine,
Or what (though rare) of later age
Ennobled hath the buskined stage.
But, O sad virgin, that thy power
Might raise Musæus from his bower
Or bid the soul of Orpheus sing
Such notes as warbled to the string
Drew iron tears down Pluto's cheek
And made hell grant what love did seek;
Or call up him that left half-told
The story of Cambuscan bold,
Of Camball and of Algarsife,
And who had Canace to wife,
That owned the virtuous ring and glass,
And of the wondrous horse of brass
On which the Tartar king did ride;
And if aught else great bards beside
In sage and solemn tunes have sung,
Of tourneys and of trophies hung,
Of forests and enchantments drear,

Where more is meant than meets the ear.
Thus night oft see me in thy pale career,
Till civil-suited morn appear,
Not tricked and frounced, as she was wont
With the Attic boy to hunt,
But kerchiefed in a comely cloud,
While rocking winds are piping loud,
Or ushered with a shower still,
When the gust hath blown his fill,
Ending on the rustling leaves
With minute drops from off the eaves.
And when the sun begins to fling
His flaring beams, me, goddess, bring
To archèd walks of twilight groves
And shadows brown that Sylvan loves,
Of pine or monumental oak
Where the rude axe with heavèd stroke
Was never heard the nymphs to daunt
Or fright them from their hallowed haunt.
There in close covert by some brook,
Where no profaner eye may look,
Hide me from day's garish eye,
While the bee, with honied thigh,
That at her flowery work doth sing,
And the waters murmuring
With such consort as they keep,
Entice the dewy-feathered sleep;
And let some strange, mysterious dream
Wave at his wings, in airy stream
Of lively portraiture displayed,
Softly on my eyelids laid,
And, as I wake, sweet music breathe
Above, about, or underneath,
Sent by some spirit to mortals good
Or the unseen Genius of the Wood.
But let my due feet never fail
To walk the studious cloister's pale
And love the high embowèd roof
With antic pillars' massy proof
And storied windows richly dight,
Casting a dim religious light.

There let the pealing organ blow
To the full-voiced choir below
In service high and anthems clear,
As may with sweetness through mine ear
Dissolve me into ecstasies
And bring all heaven before mine eyes.
And may at last my weary age
Find out the peaceful hermitage,
The hairy gown and mossy cell,
Where I may sit and rightly spell
Of every star that heaven doth shew
And every herb that sips the dew,
Till old experience do attain
To something like prophetic strain.
These pleasures, Melancholy, give,
And I with thee will choose to live.

[1] **Hence . . . joys**
The parallel with the opening line of 'L'Allegro' is obvious, but observe the change in terms – in place of 'mirth', il Penseroso speaks of vanity, delusion and folly.

[2] **brood**
offspring; ***without father bred*** therefore, a bastard. Note that no genealogy is proposed to match that of Melancholy in the companion poem.

[3] **How little you bestead**
how little it avails you.

[4] **fixèd**
steadfast, determined; ***toys*** trifles, things of no value.

[6] **fancies**
the imagination; ***fond*** (a) foolish, silly; (b) mad, unreasonable; ***gaudy*** (a) excessively showy or ornate; (b) (perhaps) deceptive; ***shapes*** i.e. what the imagination creates; ***possess*** (a) preoccupy; (b) dominate or control, like an evil spirit. 'Joys' is the subject of 'possess', 'fancies' the object.

[7–8] **thick and numberless . . . sunbeams**
a common simile, at least as old as Chaucer; the larger comparison, however, between possession – demonic or otherwise – and floating dust in the light is original; ***gay*** (a) showy; (b) specious; ***motes*** specks of dust.

[9–10] **likest . . . train**
This alternative simile introduces yet another dimension into the comparison, which moves from images of vain occupation to figures of parasitic hangers-on; ***likest*** most like; ***hovering*** (a) poised above; (b) wavering, uncertain; ***fickle*** inconstant, unstable; ***pensioners*** (a) paid or hired soldiers; (b) hirelings, people who take pay for base motives; ***Morpheus*** classical god of dreams; ***train*** group of attendants.

[11] **But hail**
Note that the welcome to Melancholy matches its counterpart in 'L'Allegro', line 11; ***sage*** Melancholy is not only wise but encourages wisdom; ***holy*** she is not only a goddess (and therefore holy) but also disposes one to holiness. Nevertheless, just as there is no classical goddess called 'Melancholy', so also there is no traditional Christian sacred personage by that name.

[12] **divinest**
Burton called the ecstatic union with God a 'divine melancholy'; the notion is common among religious mystics.
[13] **saintly visage ... bright**
Note the paradox: dark melancholy is praised for its brilliance; the heavenly associations in these lines are a direct contradiction to their corresponding section in 'L'Allegro'.
[14] **hit**
(a) strike (as a beam of light does); (b) to fit, suit; (c) affect.
[15] **O'erlaid with black**
darkened, blackened; ***staid*** sober, free from extravagance or caprice.
[17] **Black, but such**
Perhaps an echo of the Song of Solomon 1: 5 ('I am black but beautiful, O daughters of Jerusalem').
[18] **Prince Memnon**
mythological king of Ethiopia, son of Eos (dawn) and Tithonus, an ally of the Trojans who was killed in battle by Achilles; he was considered an ideal of masculine beauty; ***sister*** only in very late Greek literature is Memnon said to have a sister, named Himera (or Hemera – Greek for 'day'). Presumably she was, like him, black and beautiful; ***beseem*** suit, fit in appearance.
[19] **starred**
(a) set among the stars; (b) outlined in stars; ***Ethiop Queen*** Cassiopeia, wife of Cepheus, king of Ethiopia, mother of Andromeda. In Greek myth she was later placed in the heavens in the form of a constellation bearing her name.
[19–21] **that strove ... powers offended**
The story of Cassiopeia's boast that she was more beautiful than the Nereids (in some versions, that her daughter Andromeda was more beautiful than they) is told in Ovid's ***Metamorphoses***, 4.687.
[22] **higher far descended**
i.e. of even more impressive ancestry.
[23–5] **Thee ... she**
Milton invents an ancestry for Melancholy as daughter of Vesta (Roman goddess of the hearth) and Saturn (father of Jupiter), the latter father of the former; both are associated with earlier, purer times.
[23] **long of yore**
of very distant times.
[24] **solitary**
Saturn ruled alone; the epithet is also appropriate for a parent of Melancholy, which is associated with solitude.
[25–6] **(in Saturn's ... stain)**
The Age of Saturn was thought of as the Golden Age, when mortals consorted freely with gods and no laws, including those proscribing incest, were necessary.
[27] **glimmering bowers and glades**
clearings in the forest, overarched with tree branches, that admit intermittent flashes of light through the rustling leaves.
[28] **woody Ida**
a forested mountain in Crete where Saturn was said to reign, and where his son Jove was supposed to have been born.
[29] **no fear of Jove**
i.e. no 'fear of god'; since Jove was not yet born, he could not be feared, but the main implication is that men had no reason to fear the gods in the Golden Age.
[30] **pensive**
filled with thought, often in a melancholy way; ***nun*** (a) a pagan priestess; (b) a woman devoted to religious life and vowed to virginity, chastity and obedience to superiors.
[32] **demure**
sober, grave, serious (and not, as in modern English, unnaturally or affectedly reserved).
[33] **grain**
colour.
[34] **train**
an elongated part of a robe that is allowed to trail on the ground behind; the train is ***majestic*** because it was worn only by women of high fashion and prestige, or by monarchs.
[35] **sable**
black; ***stole*** (a) robe; (b) mantle;

(c) veil; ***cypress lawn*** a thick, black linen, originally imported from the region of Cyprus.

[36] **decent**
(a) well-shaped; (b) not exposed.

[37] **wonted**
usual; ***state*** (a) condition; (b) dignity.

[38] **musing gait**
slow steps taken while deep in thought.

[39] **commercing**
conversing, communicating with.

[40] **rapt**
enraptured; ***sitting*** evident.

[41] **passion**
an overpowering emotion affecting the mind.

[42] **Forget thyself to marble**
meditate so steadily that you hardly seem to move, like a statue of marble.

[43] **sad**
serious or grave; ***leaden*** dark and heavy, but note also that lead was a metal associated with Saturn; ***downward*** (a) looking to the ground (as adjective); (b) a direction towards the ground (as a noun); ***cast*** (a) thrown (as a verb); (b) as a noun, shade of colour. 'Leaden' can modify either 'downward' or 'cast', depending upon which is taken as noun.

[44] **fix**
direct (the eyes) steadily at something; ***fast*** unmoveably.

[45] **Peace and Quiet**
These and the following personifications of the qualities associated with melancholy are also depicted as companions of this goddess of contemplation.

[46] **Spare**
thin, not fat; ***Fast*** fasting, abstinence from food; the personified figure of fasting looks appropriately undernourished; ***diet*** dine on simple fare.

[47–8] **hears . . . sing**
A picture of the Muses derived from Hesiod's *Theogony*, 2–4.

[49] **retired Leisure . . . gardens**
an image of the pastoral ideal of *otium* or creative leisure; ***trim*** neat, well-ordered.

[52] **Him**
the cherub of line 54; ***yon*** over there.

[53] **fiery-wheelèd throne**
an image based on the vision of Ezekiel 10: 1–2, 9–19, where there appears a throne of sapphire over a wheelwork, guided by cherubim, with burning coals within it.

[54] **Cherub Contemplation**
The figure is a complex one, based on the passage from Ezekiel but also on the analysis of the angelic orders (i.e. categories of angels) and their symbolism by pseudo-Dionysus, a Christian writer on the hierarchies of heaven. In the work of later Renaissance writers, such as Pico della Mirandola, the three orders of Seraph, Cherub and Throne stand for the fire of love, the brilliance of intelligence, and the steadfastness of justice, respectively. See also 'On the Morning of Christ's Nativity', line 28. The Cherub, as contemplation, prepared the mind for love of the Creator, and for judgement. 'Throne' may be a pun, combining the two meanings of seat of a ruler and order of angels. In any case, the sense of the passage is that melancholy is conducive to the contemplation that leads to divine things. ***Contemplation*** The '-tion' ending was pronounced as two syllables.

[55] **hist**
There is uncertainty about the meaning of this word, and even about its syntactical relationship to the passage. The *OED* lists two meanings, transitive and intransitive: (a) To summon in silence or without noise; (b) To be silent. In the first instance the verb would be parallel with the imperative 'bring' in line 51, and 'silence' would be its object; in the second, it would be the subject of 'silence' and in the subjunctive mood ('may the mute silence hist along'). A third possibility is to interpret the word as the past participle of 'hiss', to drive or send away with a hissing sound enjoining silence ('And the mute silence *shushed* along').

[56] **'Less**
unless; ***Philomel*** Philomela, the

nightingale (Greek for 'lover of song'). The sad story of Philomela, raped by her brother-in-law Tereus and deprived of her tongue by him, is told in Ovid's *Metamorphoses*, 6.412–674; she and her sister, Procne, sought revenge by cooking and serving up his son to the wicked Tereus. When he began to pursue them, all three were changed into birds – he into a hawk, Procne into a swallow, Philomela into a nightingale. Note that the corresponding bird in 'L'Allegro' is the more joyous lark.

[57] **plight**
(a) dilemma; (b) state of mind; (c) plait, something interwoven or entwined, such as her destiny. Note the oxymoronic combination of sweetness and sadness, very characteristic of melancholy.

[58] **rugged brow of night**
i.e. the nightingale's song makes the night seem less forbidding.

[59] **Cynthia**
the moon or the goddess of the moon; ***dragon-yoke*** a team of dragons pulling Cynthia's chariot; in classical mythology, the dragon-drawn chariot is usually associated with the goddess Demeter (Roman Ceres), but here Milton seems to follow the tradition (in Ovid's *Metamorphoses*, 7.218–19 and repeated by a number of Renaissance poets) that attributed this particular chariot to Hecate, another moon goddess.

[60] **accustomed oak**
apparently a familiar tree through which the speaker observes the moon.

[61] **noise**
(a) random or unorganised sound ('noise' in the modern sense); (b) gay music.

[63] **chantress**
(a) singer; (b) enchantress, sorceress; ***of the woods among*** i.e. singer or enchantress of and among the woods.

[64] **woo**
invite, entice; note the paradox – it is the speaker who attempts to attract the singing bird, though it is the bird who enchants and charms him; ***evensong*** the service (also called 'vespers') in the Church of England sung just before sunset.

[65] **unseen**
In 'L'Allegro' the speaker walked 'not unseen' (line 57).

[66] **smooth-shaven**
recently mown.

[68] **Riding**
rising, moving up; ***noon*** the sun's highest point in the sky.

[72] **Stooping through... cloud**
Of course it is the moon that is still and the cloud that moves, but Milton is describing a common sensation that is readily observable on a partly cloudy night.

[73] **plat**
plot, small area of ground.

[74] **curfew**
the bell, rung at a certain hour of the evening, that originally warned dwellers in the area to 'cover' their 'fire' for the night.

[75] **shore**
bank or land bordering a lake or river.

[76] **sullen**
solemn (as well as 'sullen' in the modern sense); ***roar*** loud sound, like the vibrations that continue to issue after a bell has been struck.

[77] **air**
weather.

[78] **still**
(a) tranquil (as an adjective modifying 'place'); (b) yet (as an adverb modifying 'removèd'); ***removèd*** secluded; ***fit*** be suitable.

[80] **Teach light**
cause the light; ***counterfeit*** give the illusion of.

[81] **resort**
company.

[82] **cricket ... bellman's drowsy charm**
two of the rare concessions in the poem to cheerful companionship.

[83] **bellman**
a nightwatchman who sounds the night hours with his bell; ***drowsy charm*** The sound of the bell was soothing (***charm*** enchantment, magical incantation) and prompted sleep

because it reassured the neighbourhood that no thieves were about.

[84] **bless**
defend against evil agencies.

[85–6] **lamp . . . tower**
i.e. Il Penseroso is burning the midnight oil (contemplatives tend to study all night).

[87] **outwatch**
stay awake until dawn; ***the Bear*** *Ursa major*, the Great Bear, a constellation that never sets; the constellation was also a symbol of perfection, since it revolves in a circle around the Pole Star.

[88] **thrice-great Hermes**
the Egyptian philosopher king Thoth, supposed author of a series of philosophical writings of the second and third centuries AD, identified with the god Hermes and called Hermes Trismegistos (three-times-great) by the Greeks. The Hermetic books were particularly influential during the Renaissance, and a central source of mystical or occult doctrines; ***unsphere*** make return to earth; according to Neoplatonic philosophy, the soul resided among the spheres of the heavens, in a star, before and after death.

[89] **Plato**
the great Greek philosopher (*c*.428–348 BC) who wrote of the existence of the soul after death and whose dialogues, particularly the *Phaedo* and the *Timaeus*, were a major source of speculation about the nature of spirits and of the afterlife during the Renaissance; ***unfold*** reveal.

[90–2] **What worlds . . . nook**
See Plato, *Phaedo*, 114 B–C, where Socrates speaks of the soul after death as 'freed from these regions within the earth and released as if from prisons; they rise upward into their pure dwelling-place and live upon the True Earth above our earth'.

[91] **forsook**
forsaken, departed from.

[92] **mansion**
dwelling-place (i.e. the body); ***fleshly*** (a) characterised by or belonging to the body; (b) of the flesh (as opposed to the spirit); ***nook*** (a) remote part of the world; (b) one of the corners of the earth.

[93] **dæmons**
spirit-beings that inhabit or associate with the various elements or regions of the universe. In the Hermetic writings, however, they are more specifically named; and certain Neoplatonic writers, such as Marsilio Ficino, offered elaborate accounts of their positions in the various realms. In heaven, for instance, they appear as angels or good spirits that guide the stars and planets, but in the elements as dæmons or evil spirits that control physical matter.

[94] **fire, air, flood, or underground**
i.e. the four classical elements of fire, air, water and earth, given in descending order of physical density.

[95] **consent**
harmony, correspondence.

[96] **With planet or with element**
i.e. the higher dæmons or angels are associated with the planets, the lower with the elements.

[97] **gorgeous**
magnificent; ***tragedy*** said by Aristotle in the *Poetics* to be the greatest of the genres – not only does it treat of the most serious matters of existence, but it also takes its protagonists from the highest ranks of society. Note the parallel with comedy, embraced by l'Allegro.

[98] **sceptred**
bearing a sceptre or royal staff; ***pall*** the mantle or cloak worn by tragic actors; ***sweeping*** passing with stately movement.

[99] **Thebes**
a famous city in Greek mythology, where the tragedies of Oedipus and his family take place; ***Pelops' line*** Pelops' descendants were Agamemnon and his children, also tragic figures in myth and drama.

[100] **Troy divine**
the site of the Trojan War, told in the *Iliad*; as a city built by the gods, it had a special status in Greek myth.

[101] **(though rare)**
With the exception of Shakespeare, Milton did not think much of the tragedies of the sixteenth and early seventeenth centuries.

[102] **Ennobled hath**
has given a higher, more serious character; ***buskined stage*** i.e. tragic theatre; the buskin was a kind of elevated shoe worn by tragic actors to give them greater physical height and render them more dramatically impressive.

[103] **sad**
serious (as elsewhere in both poems); ***virgin*** Melancholy, here addressed as though one of the Muses.

[104] **raise**
(a) awaken from sleep; (b) cause to return from the underworld; ***Musæus*** son of Orpheus and mythical author of lyric poetry; ***bower*** the laurel grove in which, according to Virgil (*Aeneid*, 6.639), he sang.

[105] **bid**
ask; ***soul*** (a) genius, gift of song; (b) the ghost or spirit of the dead singer; ***Orpheus*** the same figure in Greek myth evoked in 'L'Allegro', line 145, but with a suggestion of the Orphic mysteries and hymns, which were often placed alongside the Hermetic writings alluded to earlier in the poem (lines 88 f.).

[106] **warbled**
sung melodiously, like a bird; ***to the string*** to the lyre, a harplike stringed instrument played by Orpheus and Apollo.

[107] **drew iron tears**
i.e. brought forth tears as hot as molten iron; ***Pluto*** Hades, the classical god of the underworld.

[108] **made hell grant . . . seek**
an allusion, matching that of 'L'Allegro' (lines 145 f.), to Orpheus' attempt to lead his dead wife Eurydice from the underworld back to earth.

[109] **call up**
evoke or cause to rise from the dead; ***him*** Geoffrey Chaucer, author of the *Canterbury Tales*; ***half-told*** Chaucer's 'Squire's Tale', considered incomplete, was given an ending by Edmund Spenser in his *Faerie Queene* (iv, ii, 30–33).

[110] **Cambuscan bold**
the Tartar hero of the 'Squire's Tale'.

[111] **Camball . . . Algarsife**
children of Cambuscan.

[112] **who**
he who, i.e. Triamond, lover of Canace ***Canace*** daughter of Cambuscan.

[113] **virtuous**
powerful; ***ring and glass*** Triamond wooed Canace by offering her a mirror and a ring that endowed its wearer with magical powers.

[114] **horse of brass**
yet another marvellous present given to Canace by Triamond.

[115] **Tartar king**
Cambuscan.

[116–17] **if aught . . . have sung**
i.e. if there is anything else besides that great bards (i.e. poets) have sung of in sage (i.e. wise) and solemn tunes.

[118] **tourneys**
tournaments; ***trophies*** prizes or memorials of victory.

[119] **forests and enchantments**
typical settings of medieval and Renaissance romances; ***drear*** dreary, full of sadness or melancholy.

[120] **Where more . . . the ear**
a reference to the allegorical method, a device as ancient as the Homeric epics and particularly popular among Renaissance epic and romance authors such as Ariosto, Tasso and Spenser. The phrase may be a paraphrase of Seneca, *Epistles*, 114: 'in which more is to be understood than is heard'.

[121] **Thus night oft see me**
may night often see me thus; ***me in*** in accordance with Italian practice, when a word ending in a vowel is followed by one beginning with a vowel, these two words are probably elided metrically into one syllable; ***pale career*** dim course or path (of night, illuminated only by the moon).

[122] **civil-suited**
soberly dressed; though dawn is not

usually described as 'sober' in appearance, what Milton seems to have in mind here is the resumption of those sober *activities* that begin in the morning.

[123] **tricked**
adorned; frequently linked with ***frounced*** pleated (of cloth) or curled (of hair) and, in any case, unnecessarily ornamented or displayed; ***wont*** accustomed to do or be.

[124] **With the Attic boy to hunt**
an allusion to the story, told in Ovid's *Metamorphoses*, 7.690–865, of the love of Aurora (or Dawn, in Latin) for Cephalus ('head', in Greek), a hunter and prince of Athens, a love that ended tragically in the young man's death; Milton may be implying the dangers inherent in fancy appearances that mislead the mind. ***Attic*** of or belonging to the region of Athens.

[125] **kerchiefed in a comely cloud**
i.e. the sun is wrapped in a cloud like a head covered by a kerchief or scarf; ***comely*** attractive, appealing.

[126] **rocking**
causing treetops and bushes to move; ***piping*** whistling.

[127] **ushered**
introduced or led in; ***still*** gentle, referring to 'shower'.

[128] **gust**
the violent winds of line 126; ***blown his fill*** (a) has finished blowing; (b) has satisfied its appetite for blowing; ***his*** its, referring to 'gust'.

[129] **Ending on the rustling leaves**
i.e. the last signs of the wind are evident in the reduced movement of the leaves on the trees or, possibly, those fallen on the ground.

[130] **minute drops**
(a) drops that fall minute by minute; or (b) very small drops, a spray blown by the weakening wind.

[131–2] **fling/His flaring beams**
cast beams of light like a flare; ***His*** its.

[132] **me, Goddess, bring**
i.e. bring me, goddess (Melancholy).

[133] **archèd walks**
paths through groves whose tree branches form a canopy above.

[134] **brown**
dark; ***Sylvan*** Sylvanus, Roman god of groves, forests and fields, later assimilated to the Greek god Pan; see Virgil, *Aeneid*, 8.597–9.

[135] **monumental**
(a) colossal, like a monument in size; (b) long-enduring; (c) used for building monuments and large constructions.

[136] **rude**
(a) violent, ungentle; (b) without proper knowledge or understanding (i.e. those wielding the axe have no awareness of what they are destroying); ***heavèd stroke*** a blow delivered with great exertion.

[137] **nymphs**
dryads (female half-deities of forests and woodlands in Greek myth); ***daunt*** (a) overcome, vanquish; (b) subdue; (c) intimidate.

[138] **fright**
frighten; ***hallowed haunt*** holy dwelling-place (because the dryads are sacred presences).

[139] **close covert**
dense thicket, forest shelter or hiding-place.

[140] **profaner**
somewhat profane; i.e. contemptuous or unaware of sacred things.

[141] **day's garish eye**
The sun was often described as the 'eye' of heaven or of the world; compare with Donne's 'The Sun Rising' (p. 45), where its appearance is like the intrusion of unwanted outsiders into a private world; ***garish*** (a) excessively bright; (b) vulgarly dressed or adorned; (c) lacking in self-restraint.

[142] **with honied thigh**
The bee carries pollen rather than honey on its legs back to the hive; here, therefore, its thigh is potentially honey-laden.

[143] **flowery work**
The bee's labour in gathering from flowers suggests pleasant, enjoyable work. Note, however, that the labour of bees is an ancient symbol of toil (see Virgil, *Aeneid*, 1.430 f. and *Georgics*, 4); ***sing*** buzz or hum.

[144] **waters murmuring**
a reference to the muted sounds of a distant brook or river.

[145] **consort**
(a) fellowship, company; (b) accord, concurrence; (c) harmony, concert, singing or playing music together.

[146] **dewy-feathered**
(a) with wings of dew-soaked feathers; (b) with a touch as light as dew or a feather. The wings of the bees and the waters of the brook are both echoed in this epithet, which expresses the delicate 'enticement' to sleep of their lulling sounds.

[147–50] **And let . . . eyelids laid**
These two couplets are difficult to paraphrase, and commentators have offered differing interpretations of them. However, they seem close to a passage addressed to 'Fancy' (i.e. imagination) from Ben Jonson's *Vision of Delight*, 44–54: 'spread thy purple wings . . . ,/ Create of airy forms a stream / . . . And . . . let it . . . fall like sleep upon their eyes'. The syntax is ambiguous; 'wave' and 'his wings' may refer to either 'sleep' or 'dream'. The probable sense is that the dream, strange and mysterious, is waved (caused to hover about in the air) by the action of sleep's 'wings', and descends on to the eyelids in a stream of 'lively' images ('portraiture displayed'). All of this is perhaps clarified by medieval and Renaissance theories of visual perception, which interpreted images as propagated through air waves from the object to the eye.

[151] **sweet music breathe**
It is Melancholy who is asked to 'breathe sweet music' rather than sleep or dream.

[153] **Sent by some spirit**
One is reminded of the music Ferdinand hears, sent by Ariel, in Shakespeare's *The Tempest*, I, ii, 387; ***to mortals good*** The syntax is ambiguous: 'good' may be taken as an adjective qualifying 'mortals' (i.e. to good mortals) or as a noun (i.e. bringing good to mortals).

[154] **unseen**
invisible; ***Genius of the Wood*** a protecting deity of the forest in Roman myth; in Milton's *Arcades*, a series of pastoral dialogues written at about this time, one of the speakers is the Genius of the Wood (26–83), and he speaks of listening to the music of the spheres (61–73).

[155] **due**
properly employed.

[156] **studious**
set aside for studying; ***cloister*** space formed by the covered colonnade surrounding college buildings (presumably those of Cambridge University); ***pale*** enclosure.

[157] **high embowèd roof**
The speaker has moved from the cloister to the college chapel, with its arched Gothic ceiling; ***embowèd*** vaulted.

[158] **antic**
(a) antique, ancient; (b) carved with quaint or fantastic figures; ***massy proof*** (a) massive strength; (b) capability of holding up the great weight of the roof.

[159] **storied windows**
stained-glass windows, painted with images depicting stories from the Bible or lives of saints; ***dight*** adorned, decorated.

[160] **dim religious light**
subdued light, especially when filtered through stained glass, is frequently associated with the solemn atmosphere of religious services; ***religious*** inspiring with a sense of the sacred.

[161] **pealing**
resounding; ***blow*** play or sound (usually used of trumpets or other wind instruments).

[162] **full-voiced choir below**
the singing congregation of worshippers in the church or chapel nave, as opposed to the organ in the loft above.

[163] **service high**
solemn religious ritual; ***anthem*** (a) a sacred musical composition sung by two voices or choirs in response to one another; (b) a passage from Scripture

or other religious text set to music; ***clear*** brilliant in sound; note the contrast between the bright sound of the music and the dim light of the church interior.

[164] **with sweetness**
Compare with 'L'Allegro', lines 135–50, which speak of a different, more secular kind of sweetness.

[165–6] **Dissolve me . . . eyes**
A Neoplatonic notion of the separation of the soul from the body in the contemplation of and partial return to the divine Oneness from which all things have emanated. ***Dissolve*** loosen the bonds that hold soul and body together; ***ecstasies*** state of mystical rapture in which the body is rendered incapable of sensation while the soul, in a meditative trance, contemplates divine things (from Greek *ekstasis*, a putting out of place). This theme of mystical vision is particularly prevalent in the poetry of Richard Crashaw, who shared with his contemporary the imagery and themes of the Baroque tradition, despite the doctrinal differences that separated the two poets.

[167] **weary age**
old age.

[168] **peaceful hermitage**
a place of quiet, contemplative repose far removed from bustling life, such as a hermit might experience in his remote dwelling-place.

[169] **hairy gown and mossy cell**
These are the typical trappings of the religious hermit, living in rough, scratchy clothes in a cave in the wilderness in order to discipline his soul and learn to avoid worldly temptations; ***hairy gown*** hair shirt, a tunic made of haircloth, worn by ascetics and penitents; ***cell*** a small apartment, room, or dwelling ('mossy', however, implies that the cell is either a cave or some very primitive place with fungi and moss on its walls).

[170] **rightly spell**
(a) correctly identify or make out; (b) contemplate or scan intently.

[171] **shew**
display (show forth).

[172] **sips**
absorbs.

[173] **Till old experience do attain**
Milton has in mind the traditional Platonic scheme or 'ladder of vision', which consisted of an education of the intellect beginning with common knowledge of the sensible world, moving on to the study of nature and through the various stages of human experience to the pure contemplation of the One; ***old experience*** extensive and long acquaintance with the things of nature and of humanity.

[174] **something like prophetic strain**
Note that the exalted vision to which experience leads on the way to a perfection of human knowledge is not precisely a 'prophetic' one but 'something like' it. While 'L'Allegro' is set entirely in the present, 'Il Penseroso' aspires to a future understanding that goes beyond the enjoyment of the moment; ***strain*** kind, class, or feature.

[175–6] **These pleasures . . . live**
The conclusion echoes Marlowe's 'Passionate Shepherd to His Love'; note, in addition, that the poet has a choice between two kinds of *delight*, as well as two ways of life.

95 / *How Soon Hath Time*

How soon hath Time, the subtle thief of youth,
Stol'n on his wing my three and twentieth year!
My hasting days fly on with full career,
But my late spring no bud or blossom show'th.
Perhaps my semblance might deceive the truth,
That I to manhood am arrived so near,
And inward ripeness doth much less appear,
That some more timely-happy spirits endu'th.
Yet be it less or more, or soon or slow,
It shall be still in strictest measure even
To that same lot, however mean or high,
Toward which Time leads me, and the will of Heaven.
All is, if I have grace to use it so,
As ever in my great task-Master's eye.

An Italian sonnet rhyming *a b b a / a b b a / c d e / d c e*, the poem is rather more a defence of the poet's seeming lack of palpable achievement than an examination of the nature of time, the subject of another poem ('On Time'). Though the poet speaks of his twenty-third birthday (which fell on 9 December 1631), the poem was probably composed twelve months later, in 1632, when it was 'stolen' from him.

[1] **subtle**
(a) elusive, not easily perceived; (b) pervasive; (c) clever, crafty, cunning; (d) insidious; ***thief of youth*** i.e. time seems to rob us of our youth without our noticing.
[2] **on his wing**
in its flight. Time is traditionally personified as an old man, often with great wings, in illustration, doubtless, of the idiom 'time flies'.
[3] **hasting**
accelerating; ***full career*** a gallop at full speed (usually applied to horses).
[4] **late spring**
i.e. the time in his life when he should begin to show signs of having achieved something or, as poet, written an important poem; ***bud or blossom*** products of his intellectual labours; note the unusual rhyme, possible with the seventeenth-century pronunciation of 'showeth'.
[5] **semblance**
appearance.
[5–6] **deceive . . . so near**
i.e. 'my youthful appearance may belie the truth that I am actually much older than I seem'; ***manhood*** maturity.
[7] **inward ripeness**
spiritual or intellectual maturity; ***doth much less appear*** is much less evident.
[8] **That . . . endu'th**
i.e. that ripeness which comes to persons whose achievements suit their age; Milton was apparently of a fair and delicate appearance, so that his Cambridge friends dubbed him 'the lady'; ***That*** ripeness in line 7. The phrase ***timely-happy*** is rather striking; it may be taken to mean 'fortunate in achieving things at a suitable time'; ***endu'th*** endow, provide, enrich with. This second unusual rhyme uses a variant form of the more common 'endoweth'; however, Milton may

have also meant the verb 'endues', i.e. (a) brings in, introduces; (b) brings up, educates; (c) digests. Both words were frequently confused during the period.

[9] **Yet**
Note the 'turn' of the sonnet, the transition from the first eight lines (or octave) to the last six (or sestet), a traditional feature of the form that marks an opposition between the two sections or a development of the later from the earlier; ***it*** time.

[10] **still**
always, eternally; ***strictest measure*** (a) precisely measured in the same units; (b) regular, as in musical mensuration.

[10–11] **even/To that same lot**
'even' is to be read with the following line (cf. Shakespeare's Sonnet 116, line 12: 'even to the edge of doom'); alternatively, 'even' may be read with the preceding phrase, in which case it would mean 'equal or adequate' (i.e. Milton's ripeness will be equal to whatever his destiny provides him).

[11] **lot**
destiny; ***mean*** lowly.

[12] **Time leads . . . will of Heaven**
'Time' and 'the will of Heaven' are taken as a single complex subject of the verb 'leads'; this is a rhetorical device known as hendiadys.

[13–14] **All is . . . eye**
(a) all will be what God intends it to be if he provides me with the means ('grace') to use my time properly; (b) God sees all from an understanding perspective that I may come to share if I try ('use it so'); (c) if I learn to use my time well, it will appear of eternal value ('as ever' = eternity) in God's sight. The closing phrase is rich in ambiguities; 'all' may be taken as referring to either 'Time' or to 'ripeness'; 'grace' may be taken in a strictly theological sense (spiritual strength provided by God, divine favour) or as meaning 'creditable appearance' (echoing line 5) or 'gratitude'.

[14] **As ever**
(a) as always; (b) as is eternity; ***great task-Master's eye*** the eye of God, who designates the proper task or kind of labour for each individual.

96 / *Lycidas*

IN THIS MONODY THE AUTHOR BEWAILS A LEARNED FRIEND, UNFORTUNATELY DROWNED IN HIS PASSAGE FROM CHESTER ON THE IRISH SEAS, 1637. AND BY OCCASION FORETELLS THE RUIN OF OUR CORRUPTED CLERGY, THEN IN THEIR HEIGHT.

Yet once more, O ye laurels, and once more
Ye myrtles brown, with ivy never sere,
I come to pluck your berries harsh and crude,
And with forced fingers rude,
Shatter your leaves before the mellowing year.
Bitter constraint, and sad occasion dear,
Compels me to disturb your season due;

For Lycidas is dead, dead ere his prime,
Young Lycidas, and hath not left his peer.
Who would not sing for Lycidas? He knew
Himself to sing and build the lofty rhyme.
He must not float upon his watery bier
Unwept, and welter to the parching wind
Without the meed of some melodious tear.
Begin then, sisters of the sacred well
That from beneath the seat of Jove doth spring;
Begin, and somewhat loudly sweep the string.
Hence with denial vain, and coy excuse;
So many some gentle Muse
With lucky words favour my destined urn,
And as he passes turn,
And bid fair peace be to my sable shroud,
For we were nursed upon the selfsame hill,
Fed the same flock, by fountain, shade, and rill.
Together both, ere the high lawns appeared
Under the opening eyelids of the morn,
We drove afield, and both together heard
What time the grayfly winds her sultry horn,
Battening our flocks with the fresh dews of night,
Oft till the star that rose at evening bright
Toward heaven's descent had sloped his westering wheel.
Meanwhile the rural ditties were not mute;
Tempered to th'oaten flute,
Rough satyrs danced, and fauns with cloven heel
From the glad sound would not be absent long,
And old Damætas loved to hear our song.
But O, the heavy change, now thou art gone,
Now thou art gone, and never must return!
Thee, shepherd, thee the woods and desert caves,
With wild thyme and the gadding vine o'ergrown,
And all their echoes mourn.
The willows and the hazel copses green
Shall now no more be seen
Fanning their joyous leaves to thy soft lays.
As killing as the canker to the rose,
Or taint-worm to the weanling herds that graze,
Or frost to flowers that their gay wardrobe wear
When first the white-thorn blows,

Such, Lycidas, thy loss to shepherd's ear.
Where were ye, nymphs, when the remorseless deep
Closed o'er the head of your loved Lycidas?
For neither were ye playing on the steep
Where your old bards, the famous Druids, lie,
Nor on the shaggy top of Mona high,
Nor yet where Deva spreads her wizard stream:
Ay me! I fondly dream –
Had ye been there – for what could that have done?
What could the Muse herself that Orpheus bore,
The Muse herself, for her inchanting son
Whom universal Nature did lament,
When by the rout that made the hideous roar
His gory visage down the stream was sent,
Down the swift Hebrus to the Lesbian shore?
Alas! What boots it with uncessant care
To tend the homely slighted shepherd's trade
And strictly meditate the thankless Muse?
Were it not better done, as others use,
To sport with Amaryllis in the shade
Or with the tangles of Neæra's hair?
Fame is the spur that the clear spirit doth raise
(That last infirmity of noble mind)
To scorn delights and live laborious days,
But the fair guerdon, when we hope to find
And think to burst out into sudden blaze,
Comes the blind Fury with th'abhorred shears
And slits the thin-spun life. 'But not the praise',
Phoebus replied, and touched my trembling ears:
'Fame is no plant that grows on mortal soil,
Nor in the glistering foil
Set off to th'world, nor in broad rumour lies,
But lives and spreads aloft by those pure eyes
And perfect witness of all-judging Jove;
As he pronounces lastly on each deed,
Of so much fame in heaven expect thy meed'.
O fountain Arethuse and thou, honoured flood,
Smooth-sliding Mincius, crowned with vocal reeds,
That strain I heard was of a higher mood.
But now my oat proceeds,
And listens to the herald of the sea

That came in Neptune's plea.
He asked the waves, and asked the felon winds,
'What hard mishap hath doomed this gentle swain?'
And questioned every gust of rugged wings
That blows from off each beakèd promontory;
They knew not of his story,
And sage Hippotades their answer brings:
That not a blast was from his dungeon strayed;
The air was calm, and on the level brine,
Sleek Panope with all her sisters played.
It was that fatal and perfidious bark,
Built in th'eclipse, and rigged with curses dark,
That sunk so low that sacred head of thine.
   Next Camus, reverend sire, went footing slow,
His mantle hairy, and his bonnet sedge,
Inwrought with figures dim, and on the edge
Like to that sanguine flower inscribed with woe.
'Ah! who hath reft', quoth he, 'my dearest pledge?'
Last came and last did go
The pilot of the Galilean lake;
Two massy keys he bore of metals twain
(The golden opes, the iron shuts amain).
He shook his mitred locks and stern bespake:
'How well could I have spared for thee, young swain,
Enow of such as for their bellies' sake
Creep and intrude and climb into the fold!
Of other care they little reckoning make,
Than how to scramble at the shearers' feast,
And shove away the worthy bidden guest.
Blind mouths! that scarce themselves know how to hold
A sheep-hook, or have learned aught else the least
That to the faithful herdsman's art belongs!
What recks it them? What need they? They are sped,
And when they list, their lean and flashy songs
Grate on their scrannel pipes of wretched straw.
The hungry sheep look up, and are not fed,
But swoln with wind and the rank mist, they draw,
Rot inwardly, and foul contagion spread,
Besides what the grim wolf with privy paw
Daily devours apace, and nothing said.
But that two-handed engine at the door

Stands ready to smite once and smite no more.'
  Return, Alpheus, the dread voice is past,
That shrunk thy streams; return, Sicilian Muse,
And call the vales, and bid them hither cast
Their bells and flowers of a thousand hues.
Ye valleys low where the mild whispers use
Of shades and wanton winds and gushing brooks,
On whose fresh lap the swart star sparely looks,
Throw hither all your quaint enamelled eyes,
That on the green turf suck the honeyed showers,
And purple all the ground with vernal flowers.
Bring the rathe primrose that forsaken dies,
The tufted crow-toe, and pale jessamine,
The white pink, and the pansy freaked with jet,
The glowing violet,
The musk-rose, and the well-attired woodbine,
With cowslips wan that hang the pensive head,
And every flower that sad embroidery wears.
Bid amaranthus all his beauty shed,
And daffadillies fill their cups with tears,
To strew the laureate hearse where Lycid lies.
For so to interpose a little ease,
Let our frail thoughts dally with false surmise.
Ay me! whilst thee the shores and sounding seas
Wash far away, where'er thy bones are hurled,
Whether beyond the stormy Hebrides,
Where thou perhaps under the whelming tide
Visit'st the bottom of the monstrous world;
Or whether thou, to our moist vows denied,
Sleep'st by the fable of Bellerus old,
Where the great vision of the guarded mount
Looks toward Namancos and Bayona's hold;
Look homeward angel now, and melt with ruth;
And, O ye dolphins, waft the hapless youth.
  Weep no more, woeful shepherds, weep no more,
For Lycidas your sorrow is not dead,
Sunk though he be beneath the wat'ry floor –
So sinks the day-star in the ocean bed
And yet anon repairs his drooping head
And tricks his beams, and with new-spangled ore
Flames in the forehead of the morning sky;

So Lycidas sunk low, but mounted high,
Through the dear might of him that walked the waves,
Where, other groves and other streams along,
With nectar pure his oozy locks he laves
And hears the unexpressive nuptial song,
In the blest kingdoms meek of joy and love.
There entertain him all the saints above,
In solemn troops and sweet societies
That sing, and singing in their glory move,
And wipe the tears for ever from his eyes.
Now, Lycidas, the shepherds weep no more;
Henceforth thou art the Genius of the shore,
In thy large recompense, and shalt be good
To all that wander in that perilous flood.
   Thus sang the uncouth swain to th'oaks and rills,
While the still morn went out with sandals gray;
He touched the tender stops of various quills,
With eager thought warbling his Doric lay:
And now the sun had stretched out all the hills,
And now was dropped into the western bay.
At last he rose and twitched his mantle blue;
Tomorrow to fresh woods and pastures new.

Long considered one of the greatest poems in the English language, this pastoral elegy marks the beginning of Milton's mature work. It was written to honour the life and lament the sudden death of a young colleague at Cambridge, Edward King, who drowned during a voyage from Cambridge to Dublin in August 1637. The members of Christ's College decided to publish a commemorative volume and asked Milton to join them by contributing some verses.

The pastoral elegy belongs to a tradition reaching back to the Greek poet Theocritus (*c*.310–250 BC), who originated pastoral poetry in imitation of Sicilian shepherd songs. In his first 'Idyll' (as he called his songs) he laments the death of a song shepherd called Daphnis, who has died for love. The Idylls unite tragic and rural motifs, and their themes were extended by a later Greek poet, Moschus, who composed an elegy for a fellow poet in his 'Lament for Bion', setting the stage for a long line of poetic successors. The essential features of Moschus's elegy include not only the mourning of a fellow author but also the incorporation of a kind of nature myth in which the renewal and destruction of life in the changing seasons is compared with the dead man's fate. The form continued to be popular in Roman times; however, the greatest pastoral poet in Latin, Virgil, lamented a public figure rather than a fellow poet in his *Eclogues*. During the medieval period, the tradition was kept alive by a few allegorical poems, but it was during the Italian Renaissance that it was most fully revived. Milton not only drew on the Italian models for his passage concerning abuses in the Church but was also inspired by the formal experiments of such continental predecessors as Petrarch, Boccaccio, Mantuan, Sannazaro and Castiglione. From them he learned to liberate poetry from the stanza form and employ an effective sequence of irregularly rhyming lines for dramatic effect, combining control with liberty in a way that echoes the main theme of his elegy. In addition, there had already been a number of important examples of eclogue and pastoral elegy among Milton's English precursors, especially in the work of Edmund Spenser.

The main theme of 'Lycidas' has often been identified not as the lament for Edward King but as a long meditation on the meaning of life and the poet's vocation. The poem is noted for its contrasting passages and abrupt transitions, its irregular rhyming patterns and its startling paradoxes, the climax of which is the Christian notion that 'he who loses his life will find it' (Luke 9: 24). After an introductory section (lines 1–24), which concludes with the poet's awakened consciousness of his own mortality, the poet introduces his lament for Lycidas and weighs the value of fidelity to an ideal, of labouring to achieve it, and of the glory that is promised in heaven, if not on earth (lines 25–84). The pastoral theme is restored in the following section (lines 85–131), which follows a pattern typical of the pastoral elegy by presenting a procession of mourners, beginning with allegorical personages representing nature, continuing with Camus (who stands for the university and education in general), and ending with St Peter, the spokesman for religion, who offers a fierce denunciation of corruption in the Church. The next section (lines 132–64) returns to a vision of natural loveliness that ultimately points to the sacred Mount St Michael's, a feature of the landscape linked with the drowning of King in the Irish Sea, and reaches its climax in a triumphant conclusion to the 'monody' portion of the poem. Finally, the closing lines (186–93) provide an epilogue in which the poet, freed from the inward struggle to accept not only Edward King's death but the inevitability of his own, now has the courage to pursue his vocation with fresh resolve and hopes for the future. These final lines form a stanza of *ottava rima* and suggest a return to order after the irregular sequence of rhymes that composes the main body of the poem.

Title

Lycidas The name Milton uses for Edward King comes from *Idyll* 7 of the Greek poet Theocritus, a song uttered by a goatherd called Lycidas; a significant part of the idyll is a discussion of poetry, so Milton probably chose this Greek name to indicate that poetry would be a central theme in his elegy as well.

Subtitle

Monody (a) an ode sung by a single voice (for example, in a Greek tragedy); (b) a mournful song or dirge; (c) a funeral oration; (d) a poem bewailing someone's death; ***learned Friend*** Edward King was a fellow student at Christ's College Cambridge, a good scholar, a poet, and a promising clergyman, though his relationship with Milton does not seem to have been particularly intimate.

[1] **Yet once more**

The poem opens in a somewhat abrupt fashion with the poet's seeming uncertainty about his readiness for the task that lies ahead; though he has already written a number of substantial poems, none has posed the challenge that a traditional pastoral elegy represents; ***laurels*** the bay tree and its leaves, woven into a crown for honouring great poetic achievements and placed on the head of the poet 'laureate' in imitation of the ceremonial that dates back to Roman times; the laurel tree was sacred to Apollo, Greek god of poetry.

[2] **myrtles**

The myrtle tree was sacred to Venus,

and therefore appropriately associated with love poetry; ***brown*** dark in colour; ***ivy*** a third evergreen associated with poetry and, like the other two, used for poets' crowns; the conventional association of ivy with death and mourning is suggested by the elegiac theme of the poem; ***sere*** dry.

[3] **berries harsh and crude**
i.e. their fruit (inspiration), even though it is not yet fully ready to be plucked (***harsh*** bitter; ***crude*** unripe, raw).

[4] **forced fingers rude**
i.e. he has been obliged by the misfortune of King's death to take on a public task, though he is still immature as an artist; ***rude*** (a) without skill; (b) intrusive, out of order; (c) rough, violent.

[5] **Shatter . . . year**
Note the suggestion of violence on the poet's part in attacking this subject so early; ***Shatter*** (a) disturb; (b) cause to fall and scatter.

[6] **Bitter constraint**
(a) King's sudden death; (b) the circumstances of his having to write a poem despite his distress for his friend; ***constraint*** compulsion; ***dear*** (a) costly; (b) precious, because it offers a rare opportunity to write on a profound subject; (c) heartfelt, grievous. Observe the complex relationship between ***sad*** and ***dear***.

[7] **Compels**
catches up one of the senses of ***constraint*** in the preceding line; note the hendiadys (two substantives – ***constraint*** and ***occasion*** – express a single, complex idea), signalled by the singular form of the verb, which suggests the complexity of the poet's reaction; ***disturb*** note the echo of ***shatter***; ***season due*** (a) the period of a plant's maturity; (b) the proper time for a poet to write poetry; (c) the time when an owed debt should be paid.

[8] **ere his prime**
before reaching his fullest abilities.

[9] **young**
King was barely twenty-five when he died; implied in the adjective is the poet's expression of concern that he might perish before creating any work of lasting significance, so the elegy is as much about the speaker's fears for himself as it is a lament for a dead colleague; ***peer*** (a) equal; (b) anyone as capable as he of fulfilling both roles as clergyman and as man of letters.

[10] **Who . . . Lycidas?**
An echo of Virgil's *Eclogues*, 10.3 ('Who would refuse songs for Gallus?').

[10–11] **he knew/Himself to sing**
he himself knew how to sing (i.e. was a poet; King had published a small volume of Latin verses).

[11] **build the lofty rhyme**
i.e. construct verses in an elevated style, such as would be suitable for an epic, an elegy, or some other kind of poem on a serious and important subject.

[12] **watery bier**
King is imagined as being borne to his grave by the waters, since his body was not recovered from the shipwreck.

[13] **unwept**
without proper mourning ceremonies; ***welter*** to roll or twist the body; ***parching*** drying, withering; note that the ***tear*** of the next line suggests an antidote to the winds that would wither the body.

[14] **meed**
reward; ***melodious tear*** i.e. elegiac verses, the tearful melody of a mourning song.

[15] **sisters . . . well**
The nine Muses, daughters of Zeus and Mnemosyne (Memory), lived on Mount Helicon near the inspiring waters of the sacred well of Aganippe, which sprang up beside the altar of Zeus or Jove.

[17] **somewhat . . . string**
i.e. pluck the string of the lyre, a harp-like instrument associated with *lyric* poetry; note that the poet is slightly reticent – the lyre is to be plucked with some restraint; ***sweep*** brush the hand lightly over the string.

[18] **Hence**
Away with; ***denial vain*** pointless objections; ***coy excuse*** an excuse not truly meant or intended only for self-justification; ***coy*** (a) modest; (b) disdainful; (c) insincere; i.e. the poet will proceed boldly, not allowing himself the excuse that he is unprepared or too immature to compose an important poem.
[19] **gentle Muse**
(a) beneficent goddess of poetry; (b) thoughtful poet.
[20] **lucky words**
words that the poet would be fortunate in having addressed to him after his own death; the phrase suggests that the poet can hope for a similar honour after he dies only if he is willing to exert his best effort now for the dead Edward King; ***favour*** (a) draw attention to; (b) write a poem commemorating; ***destined urn*** i.e. his own death (in classical times, as occasionally later, bodies or their ashes were buried in urns); the basic idea seems to come from Virgil, *Eclogues*, 10.4–5.
[21] **he**
i.e. the conjectural poet of line 18.
[22] **sable shroud**
Normally a shroud is white, not ***sable*** (black), but the poet probably has in mind the earth as his shroud.
[23] **nursed . . . hill**
i.e. both were students at Cambridge University; the convention of the pastoral elegy requires the implied equation of student and shepherd in the following line.
[24] **fountain, shade, and rill**
All elements of the traditional pastoral landscape, consisting of hills, spring (***fountain***), groves (***shade***), or small streams (***rill***).
[25] **Together**
Milton does not seem to have been very close to King while they were both students at Cambridge; the following lines are meant to suggest no more than that they were both engaged in a common enterprise as scholars; ***ere*** before; ***high lawns*** pastures, downs.
[26] **opening eyelids of the morn**
(a) the rising sun; (b) the opening eyes of people waking.
[28] **grayfly**
Some kind of winged insect, possibly a beetle; ***winds*** blows, sounds; ***sullen horn*** the chirping or buzzing sound made by an insect; the shepherd's horn, used to call sheep, is suggested by this 'natural' music of the morning.
[29] **battening**
(a) feeding; (b) enclosing; the meaning is either that the flocks were fed on the dewy evening grass or that they were herded together and brought home at evening.
[30] **the star**
This would be Hesperus, the evening star that sets early in the west; it is actually the planet Venus, which also rises as the morning star, Lucifer.
[31] **sloped his westering wheel**
i.e. had descended in a curve to the west.
[32] **rural ditties**
shepherds' songs.
[33] **tempered**
tuned; ***oaten flute*** musical pipes made of oat or reed stalks.
[34] **rough satyrs**
woodland deities in Greek mythology with goat-like legs; ***fauns*** another kind of minor rural deity with goat-like characteristics, such as cloven feet; satyrs and fauns and their simple entertainments are emblematic of an uncivilised and unspoilt country environment.
[36] **old Damaetas**
a conventional pastoral figure or shepherd whose name comes from Virgil, *Eclogues*, 2.
[37] **heavy**
sad, difficult to bear.
[38] **must**
may, can.
[39–41] **Thee . . . mourn**
The woods and caves 'mourn' the dead shepherd's absence with their sounds and echoes; the first on the list of mourners in the conventions of pastoral elegy is the natural world.

[39] **desert**
(a) uninhabited; (b) empty; (c) deserted.
[40] **gadding**
wandering, straggling.
[41] **echoes**
The echoes suggest the memory of Lycidas's presence in the countryside.
[44] **Fanning . . . lays**
The trees are imagined as responding pleasurably to the songs of Lycidas; ***lays*** songs accompanied by an instrument.
[45] **canker**
an insect that devours rose buds.
[46] **taint-worm**
a parasitic worm that infects (taints) recently weaned (***weanling***) sheep.
[47] **white-thorn**
hawthorn; ***blows*** blooms, blossoms.
[48] **thy loss**
the loss of you; ***to shepherd's ear*** the loss of Lycidas's music and the companionship it provided both to nature and to fellow shepherds.
[50] **nymphs**
minor female deities in Greek mythology, often associated with bodies of fresh water (Naiades), sea (Nereides), mountains (Oreads) or groves and woodlands (Dryads); they may be used here as another name for the Muses, but they were also thought of as guardians of their natural habitats; ***remorseless*** (a) without conscience; (b) inevitable and cruel.
[50–1] **deep . . . Lycidas**
An allusion to King's death by drowning; it was reported that he had knelt and prayed as the ship was sinking.
[52] **steep**
mountainside.
[53] **bards**
traditional oral poets, with a hint of magical powers; ***Druids*** prophetic magician-priests of Celtic times; there were druidic sepulchres on Kerig y Druidion in Denbighshire, but Milton is perhaps alluding to the notion that the mountain groves were once consecrated by the Druids; note the mixture of Celtic and classical figures and the association with ancient poets, none of whom was able to save Lycidas.
[54] **shaggy top of Mona**
The mountain to which Milton alludes, Anglesey (or Mona), was then thickly forested (***shaggy***).
[55] **Deva**
the winding river Dee, which passes through Chester, from which King sailed to Ireland, and was reputed to have powers of prophecy (note the connection with the Druids).
[56] **fondly**
foolishly.
[57] **Had ye . . . done?**
i.e. even if all those named above had been present, they would have been powerless to save King.
[58] **the Muse**
Calliope, mother of Orpheus; ***for*** do for.
[59] **enchanting**
(a) charming, attractive; (b) magical, capable of casting a spell.
[60] **universal nature did lament**
According to Greek mythology, the death of Orpheus was mourned by all the natural world, including the nymphs and dryads who safeguard it.
[61] **rout that made the hideous roar**
the women who tore Orpheus limb from limb.
[58–63] **Orpheus . . . shore**
Orpheus was the archetypal singer-poet who could enchant all of nature with his song and tame the monsters of the underworld, but he was torn to pieces and devoured by the wild women of Thrace, the Ciconians; his head, which they threw into the river Hebrus, continued to sing, nevertheless, and floated as far as the island of Lesbos, where the great poetess Sappho lived; if Calliope, a Muse, could not save her own son, a poet, how could anyone expect the nymphs to have preserved Lycidas? See Ovid, *Metamorphoses*, 10.162–219.
[64] **What boots it**
What's the good (***boots*** avails); ***unceasant*** incessant, never-ending; ***care*** (a) devotion; (b) attention; (c) worry.

[65] **tend**
(a) attend to; (b) engage in; ***homely*** lowly, unimpressive; ***slighted*** little regarded; ***shepherd's trade*** here, poet's craft.
[66] **strictly**
(a) exclusively; (b) in a disciplined fashion; ***meditate*** (a) study; (b) contemplate; (c) exercise; ***thankless*** unrewarding; ***muse*** the art of poetry.
[67–9] **Were it . . . in the shade**
i.e. would it not be better to be like others and enjoy the company of girls instead of practising the difficult discipline of poetry?
[68] **sport with**
play with amorously; ***Amaryllis*** a conventional name for a shepherd girl or, in Roman poetry generally, for any pretty girl; ***in the shade*** (a) under a tree; (b) hidden away.
[69] **Neæra**
another conventional shepherdess's name; ***tangles*** locks (but with a suggestion of entrapment).
[70] **Fame**
i.e. renown gained from the writing of poetry; ***clear spirit*** a pure soul, one that is not tempted by worldly attractions; ***doth raise*** (a) that drives the spirit of dedicated poets; (b) that poets present to themselves as their incentive – note the tone of elevation and nobility attached to poetic fame as opposed to the sensual and erotic pleasures.
[71] **last infirmity of noble mind**
(a) the final temptation of an aspiring mind; (b) the ultimate desire of an aspiring mind (***infirmity*** weakness).
[72] **scorn**
reject; ***laborious*** work-filled.
[73] **But the fair . . . find**
i.e. 'But when we hope to receive the lovely reward for our labour'; ***guerdon*** reward.
[74] **burst . . . blaze**
i.e. become famous.
[75–6] **blind Fury . . . life**
a reference to Atropos, the third of the three classical Fates (not Furies – an altogether different trio) – after Clotho and Lachesis, who spun and measured, respectively, the thread of life for each person, Atropos, with her shears, cut it at the appropriate moment (that is, death); she is not traditionally described as blind, but Fortune often is; as a death-figure Atropos has been given characteristics appropriate to the arbitrary violence of both Fury and Fortune.
[76] **'But not the praise'**
The reply is in answer to the despairing statement preceding it; the praise the poet receives is not destroyed along with his life but lives on after him.
[77] **Phoebus**
Apollo, god of poetry, intelligence and the sun; touching the ears was a way to remind someone or gain attention in Ancient Rome; however, in Virgil's *Eclogues*, 6.3–5, Apollo touches the poet's ears as a sign of disapproval; ***trembling ears*** the poet's ears are agitated by fear of the god's rebuke.
[78] **'Fame is no plant'**
The metaphor suggests that fame is not fragile or subject to withering, like an ordinary plant – note that it recalls the laurel, myrtle, and ivy from the beginning of the poem.
[79–80] **glistering foil . . . world**
Precious stones were placed on a sheet of gold foil to display their sparkle; this second metaphor suggests that fame, though gem-like, requires no augmentation of its brilliance.
[80] **broad rumour**
(a) mere hearsay and gossip; (b) widespread reputation.
[82] **perfect witness of . . . Jove**
Fame endures not in the world but in heaven, and is part of God's judgement of humankind's deeds; it depends not on human but on divine witness.
[83–4] **As he . . . expect thy meed**
Phoebus transforms fame from an earthly to a heavenly reward for poetic endeavour; ***meed*** reward.
[85] **Arethuse**
A spring at Syracuse in Sicily, near

Theocritus' birthplace; here it is evoked as a symbol of Greek bucolic poetry; ***honoured*** famous; ***flood*** river.
[86] **Mincius**
A river in the Lombardy region of Italy, near Virgil's birthplace, evoked as a symbol of Roman pastoral poetry; ***crowned with vocal reeds*** the reeds growing in the river make music as the wind blows through them; a reminiscence of Virgil's *Georgics*, 3.14.
[87] **strain**
melody; ***mood*** (a) feeling; (b) style (***higher*** more serious); (c) one of the scale patterns used in Greek music.
[88] **my oat**
my flute, i.e. my pastoral poem.
[89] **herald of the sea**
Triton, a demigod of the sea, son of Poseidon and Amphitrite, who usually appears blowing a horn.
[90] **Neptune's plea**
Triton comes to speak in defence of Neptune against accusations that as god of the sea he was responsible for the death of Lycidas.
[91] **felon**
(a) savage, wild; (b) guilty of causing Lycidas's death.
[92] **hard mishap**
terrible accident; ***swain*** shepherd.
[93] **gust of rugged wings**
every wind that blows as though it had powerful wings; winds were often depicted, particularly on maps, with wings.
[94] **beaked promontory**
jutting cliff.
[96] **Hippotades**
Aeolus, a god, son of Hippotes and custodian of the winds; ***their answer*** the winds'.
[97] **dungeon**
Aeolus kept the winds in a cavern; ***strayed*** escaped.
[98] **brine**
the sea.
[99] **Sleek Panope**
a sea-nymph (one of the fifty daughters of Nereus, attendants of Neptune); she is sleek because she is always wet from the sea.
[100] **bark**
a poetic word for 'ship'.
[101] **Built in the eclipse**
i.e. at a bad time from an astrological point of view; ***rigged with curses dark*** (a) made ready for sailing while dark curses were being uttered; (b) fitted with dark curses instead of ropes, tackle and sails.
[102] **that sacred head**
Suggests both the 'sacred head' of Christ and the severed head of Orpheus as well as the pious head of Edward King.
[103] **Camus**
the river Cam, which flows through Cambridge, in Latin form and personified as though a classical river-god; ***reverend sire*** The river is given this honorific title because of its age and dignity; ***footing*** stepping, moving (like an elderly person).
[104] **mantle hairy**
The vegetation along the river is imagined as a cloak or the furry hood of a Cambridge BA; ***bonnet*** (a) hat; (b) academic headgear; ***sedge*** river-gods were often represented in Renaissance art as crowned with reeds and aquatic vegetation.
[105] **Inwrought**
(Apparently the word was introduced by Milton) (a) the reeds formed obscure or dark figures; (b) the vegetation was streaked with dark colours.
[106] **that sanguine flower . . . woe**
the hyacinth; the flower has a pattern that resembles the Greek word AIAI ('alas'). In Greek mythology, Hyacinth was a beautiful boy, beloved of Apollo, who was accidentally killed by a discus thrown by the god; the allusion recalls the death of Lycidas, blamed on natural forces that are represented here by classical gods; ***sanguine*** bloody.
[107] **reft**
taken away, bereft; ***pledge*** child (a sign of the parents' love or one to whom parents pledge their love).
[108] **Last . . . did go**
The most dignified and important of all these figures is given prominence by being placed last in the procession.

[109] **pilot . . . lake**
St Peter, who fished on the Lake of Galilee; he is called a 'pilot' here not only because he commanded his own boat but because he was also 'a fisher of men', and therefore a 'pilot' or guide of human souls; see Matthew 4: 19; Mark 1: 17 ('I will make you fishers of men'). As the first Bishop of Rome and Pope of the whole Church, Peter was given the keys to open and close the gates of heaven (Matthew 16: 19: 'And I will give you the keys of the kingdom of heaven: and whatever you bind on earth shall be bound in heaven: and whatever you release on earth shall be released in heaven.')
[112] **mitred locks**
The mitre is a ceremonial hat worn by a bishop; ***locks*** hair (not the sort of lock that a key opens); ***stern bespake*** spoke sternly.
[113–15] **'How well . . . fold!'**
i.e. 'I could have well done without many of those who, unlike you, young shepherd, creep, intrude, and climb into the sheepfold merely to satisfy their bellies'; the reference is to self-serving men who become priests in order to satisfy their own greed for wealth or power, not out of a desire to serve their parishioners (i.e. ***fold***); St Peter's speech, in these lines and those that follow, echoes numerous passages from the Bible, for instance Jeremiah 23: 1 ('Woe be unto the pastors that destroy and scatter the sheep of my pasture! saith the Lord'); John 10: 1 ('He that does not enter the sheepfold by the door but creeps in some other way is a thief and robber'); and I Peter 5: 2–4 ('Feed God's flock, which is among you, and take care of it, not because you are forced but because you want to, not for filthy money, but with a ready mind. . . . And when the chief Shepherd [Christ] appears, you will receive a crown of glory that will not fade away').
[116] **they little reckoning make**
they pay little attention to.
[117] **scramble**
fight for food or a prominent place; ***the shearer's feast*** Continuing the equation between shepherds and priests, Milton suggests a parallel between the festival held after the sheep are sheared and the Communion rites of the Church.
[118] **above . . . guest**
Echoes a number of New Testament passages; see Matthew 22: 10 ('So those servants went out into the highways, and gathered together all as many as they found, both bad and good: and the wedding was furnished with guests'); Matthew 22: 11 ('And when the king came in to see the guests, he saw there a man who did not have on a wedding garment').
[119] **Blind mouths!**
A famous image which has provoked much commentary and some controversy; the simplest interpretation of this complex double metaphor would see the ***mouths*** as a reference to the greediness of the false shepherd/priests and the blindness to their ignorance and selfishness. Note that the Greek word for bishop, *episkopos*, means 'one who watches over'. Since shepherds are supposed to watch over their flocks and be concerned with feeding them rather than gorge themselves, the image is a doubly appropriate one, though daring and unusual.
[120] **sheep-hook**
Refers both to the tool of the shepherd's trade and to the ceremonial crozier carried by a bishop; ***aught*** anything; ***the least*** in the least.
[121] **art**
trade, occupation.
[122] **What recks it them?**
What do they care?; ***they are sped*** they do well, prosper.
[123] **when they list**
when they wish or desire; ***lean*** thin, slight, poor in quality; ***flashy*** (a) insipid; (b) frothy; (c) lacking in substance, trashy; (d) void of meaning; (e) glittery; (f) transitory.
[124] **grate**
(a) produce discordant or irritating sound; (b) rub or scratch; (c) repeat

often and annoyingly; ***scrannel*** a dialect word meaning 'thin', 'reedy' or 'weak'; note that these false shepherd-clergymen's pipes are made of straw rather than the more substantial oaten reeds mentioned earlier.

[125] **sheep . . . fed**
Recalls Christ's injunction to Peter to take care of his followers (John 21: 16): 'He said to him again the second time, "Simon, son of Jonas, do you love me?" He said to him, "Yes, Lord, you know that I love you". He said to him, "Feed my sheep".'

[126–7] **swollen with wind . . . spread**
The reference is to a specific ailment that afflicts sheep, the sheep-rot or fluke, a digestive disorder that causes an intestinal swelling and infection; but it is also an attack on false preaching, which the Puritans felt was furthered by the remote and haughty attitude of the higher clergy, more committed to empty ceremonies and elaborate music than to the spread of piety and the word of God; ***rank mist*** foul and unhealthy air; ***draw*** breathe.

[128] **the grim wolf**
Not merely the traditional enemy of shepherds but an animal emblematically associated with the city of Rome, hence with Roman Catholicism, and especially with the missionary work of the Jesuits in England, who sought to convert Protestants back to allegiance to the Pope; the coat of arms of St Ignatius Loyola, who founded the Jesuits, depicts two grey wolves, and Milton may also be alluding to this iconographic feature; ***privy paw*** (a) characteristic; (b) secret, hidden; (c) involved in or knowing of a crime or plot.

[129] **apace**
(a) immediately; (b) quickly; ***nothing said*** i.e. no one complains.

[130] **two-handed engine at the door**
One of the most difficult passages in the poem. Many interpretations of this image have been advanced, though none seems altogether convincing. Some scholars interpret the image as referring to the two Houses of Parliament, to the secular and religious authority of the Court of High Commission, to the destructive forces unleashed in the Civil War, to the zeal of the Puritans, to England and Scotland or to their enemies France and Spain, to the Roman Catholic Church, to the bishops of the Church of England, to the sword of St Peter or to various other weapons mentioned in the Bible. Nor is the exact nature of the 'engine' agreed upon; some see an axe, others the scythe wielded by Father Time, and so on; ***engine*** (a) a sword or any other kind of weapon (cf. 'engine of war'); (b) any machine or device.

[131] **smite**
strike a heavy blow.

[132] **Alpheus**
a major river of Arcadia in southern Greece; it flows underground at several points and was supposed to emerge in Syracusa as part of the fountain Arethusa; the mythological story of Alpheus and Arethusa, the nymph this river-god pursued amorously, is told in Ovid, *Metamorphoses*, 5.865–978 and in the historian Pausanias' *Description of Greece*, 5.2.2; here the river is invited to return as a signal that a new phase of the poem, one inspired by a more positive outlook, is about to begin; ***dread*** fearsome, terrifying; ***voice*** (a) the speech of St Peter; (b) the tone and mood of the poem or poet.

[133] **shrunk thy streams**
i.e. that interrupted the gentler pastoral manner of the earlier part of the poem; ***Sicilian Muse*** Theocritus or the bucolic or pastoral mode.

[136] **mild whispers . . . brooks**
i.e. where live the mild whispers of shades, etc.; ***use*** live, are active.

[137] **shades**
shaded regions; ***wanton*** free.

[138] **lap**
a hollow among hills; ***swart*** dark or black; ***star*** Sirius, sometimes called the Dog Star because it is to be seen during the hot 'dog days' of late summer; ***looks*** shines; presumably

these valleys are spared the baking heat that has darkened Sirius itself, and is radiated from it to earth.

[139] **Throw hither**
turn your gaze towards the place where Lycidas lies; ***quaint*** elaborately drawn or made; ***enamelled*** glossy with bright colours, like enamel, popular during this time for its brilliant decorative qualities; ***eyes*** the centres of flowers or the flowers themselves (cf. 'daisy' = day's eye).

[140] **suck**
Note the complexity of the image; the 'eyes' are like bees that receive the 'nectar' of dew and rainfall.

[141] **purple**
to colour scarlet; here, used as a verb, it implies that the ground is made brilliant by the hues of the flowers, perhaps as an appropriate response to the 'sacrifice' of Lycidas's death ('purple' usually implies a staining with wine or blood).

[142] **rathe**
early; a dialect word; ***primrose*** a pale yellow flower that blooms a short time and grows wild in places where it is difficult to see or gather.

[143] **tufted crow-toe**
crowfoot, a plant of the genus ***Ranunculus*** that grows in clusters and is predominantly found in meadows; ***jessamine*** jasmine, an ornamental plant with fragrant flowers, usually white.

[144] **freaked**
streaked with black (***jet***).

[145] **glowing**
rich in colour.

[146] **musk-rose**
a rambling rose with clusters of large, fragrant white flowers; ***well-attired*** well-adorned or well-arrayed; ***woodbine*** honeysuckle, a climbing shrub with fragrant pale yellow flowers.

[147] **cowslips wan**
a fragrant pale yellow wild flower with a drooping, bell-shaped blossom.

[148] **sad**
(a) sorrowful; (b) grave or serious; (c) dark or neutral-tinted in colour; ***embroidery*** a technical term in seventeenth-century gardening referring to the adornment of the ground with flowers; here, however, it describes the pattern or colours of the flowers themselves.

[149] **amaranthus**
(a) an imaginary flower that is said never to fade or die; (b) an ornamental plant with coloured foliage, sometimes called 'love-lies-bleeding', an appropriate allusion in either case to the death of Lycidas.

[150] **daffadillies**
daffodils or narcissus flowers, which bloom for only a short while and are associated in mythology with the death of a young man.

[151] **laureate hearse**
His hearse is imagined as strewn with laurel because, as a poet, he deserved it as his crown.

[152] **For so**
For in such a way; ***to interpose*** (a) to inject; (b) put forward; (c) introduce.

[152–3] **For so to interpose . . . false surmise**
The poet is saying that he has introduced this passage describing the mourning of all nature in order to lessen his grief, but that he doesn't really believe in this poetic rather than real sympathy of all things for Lycidas's death.

[153] **frail thoughts**
They are frail because they are not very convincing; ***false surmise*** refers to the 'poetic' description of the imaginary response of nature.

[154] **whilst thee . . . away**
whilst the shores and sounding seas wash thee far away.

[155] **thy bones**
Lycidas's corpse.

[156] **beyond the stormy Hebrides**
i.e. into the depths of the Atlantic Ocean.

[157] **whelming tide**
the powerful ocean waves (***whelm*** to turn over or crush violently).

[158] **visit'st**
(a) travel to a place for the purpose of inspecting it; (b) dwell in a place temporarily; ***monstrous world*** the

realm where sea-monsters dwell, perhaps with a suggestion of the story of Jonah and the whale (Jonah 1: 17), traditionally interpreted as symbolising the Resurrection of the body.

[159] **thou . . . denied**
i.e. Lycidas's body could not be recovered for a funeral ceremony; ***moist vows*** the tear-filled prayers of the mourners.

[160] **sleep'st**
lie dead (but with overtones of the Christian notion that death is but a temporary sleep until the Resurrection of the body occurs); ***fable of Bellerus old*** Bellerus is not a classical figure but a local English one; Milton alludes to the legend which held that Bellerium (the south-western tip of Cornwall) was named after a fabulous giant of this name.

[161] **vision of**
(a) sight or view of; (b) apparition seen on; ***guarded Mount*** St Michael's Mount, off Penzance on the Cornish coast; a vision of Michael the archangel was said to have been seen there by medieval monks (St Michael was the militant head of the angelic host).

[162] **Looks toward**
(a) has a view of; (b) anticipates; ***Namancos*** mountains of north-west Spain; ***Bayona*** a Spanish coastal fortress about fifty miles south of Cape Finisterre, near the Namancos and part of the perceived threat to England from Roman Catholicism.

[163] **homeward**
(a) landward, towards the land; (b) towards Cambridge; ***angel*** St Michael; ***melt with ruth*** shed tears of pity and sorrow.

[164] **dolphins**
Stories of humans rescued from the sea by porpoises are frequent in Greek mythology (e.g. the story of Palaemon, a boy whose body was brought home by a dolphin); ***waft*** convey, as if by magic, on the winds; ***hapless*** unlucky.

[165] **shepherds**
other Cambridge students.

[166] **Lycidas your sorrow**
Lycidas, the object of your sorrow; ***is not dead*** a paradox, like so many of those that characterise Christian doctrine, since King has indeed died, yet he lives in another sense, as the possessor of an immortal soul.

[167] **sunk . . . floor**
Normally, one would speak of the ocean floor, the bottom or solid base of a body of water, but here ***floor*** an extended surface, thus the surface of the water. The implications of the phrase, understood in this fashion (sunk beneath the water's surface), are important, since they make sense of what follows in the next lines.

[168] **day-star**
(a) the sun; (b) the Son of God (i.e. Christ); ***ocean bed*** the sun appears to sink into the ocean itself at its setting. The death of Lycidas is compared with a natural event, the setting of the sun each day, and a supernatural one, the death and Resurrection of Christ.

[169] **anon**
right away; ***repairs*** (a) restores from damage or decay; (b) recovers, revives, restores; (c) renews, returns; ***drooping head*** i.e. like the limp head of a drowned man, the limp blossom of a wilting flower, or the fading 'head' of the setting sun.

[170] **tricks**
(a) cheats, deceives; (b) arrays, adorns; (c) draws in outline. In other words, the setting sun may be said to 'trick' its beams by rising again the next morning, thus showing that the appearance of death was an illusion or a deception (death is 'cheated' by the reborn sun), that the sun after fading into darkness is newly 'adorned' the next morning, and that both at setting and rising the sun appears for a time outlined against the sky; ***new-spangled ore*** the sun rises in a new brilliance. However, note that a 'spangle', a small, glittering metal disc, can also refer to star, so that the golden light (***ore*** gold) could be understood as coming from the night stars that are still visible at dawn. Here 'spangled'

refers to the effect of brilliance that comes from a great multitude of small individual sources of light.

[171] **flames**
shines suddenly and brilliantly; ***forehead of the morning sky*** (a) the part of the sky that first appears; (b) the sun itself, its rays imagined as hair and the upper disc as the 'forehead' (note, in preceding lines, how the references to the sun as 'head' in various senses are brought to a climax in this image).

[172] **mounted**
(a) risen; (b) placed.

[173] **dear might**
(a) precious help; (b) loving strength; (c) brave or bold power; ***of him . . . waves*** Christ, who, in a famous biblical episode, walked on the stormy waters of the Sea of Galilee. When Peter attempted to join him, he began to sink until Jesus held him up (Matthew 14: 25–31).

[174] **Where . . . along**
where, along other groves and streams . . . ; i.e. in the other world of the afterlife.

[175] **nectar pure**
(a) the drink of the gods (in Greek mythology); (b) any delicious sweet or fragrant drink; (c) here, a fragrant, cleansing oil; ***oozy locks*** Lycidas's hair is imagined as brine-soaked and seaweed-covered (***oozy*** full of moisture; also, muddy and slimy, as describing the sea bottom); ***laves*** washes. Christ washes Lycidas's hair with nectar as a gesture of comforting and nurturing, but Milton doubtless has in mind two biblical passages – John 12: 3 ('Then Mary [Magdalene] took a pound of ointment of spikenard, very costly, anointed the feet of Jesus, and wiped his feet with her hair; the house was filled with the odour of the ointment' – see also Luke 7: 38) and John 13: 5–9 ('After that he poured water into a basin and began to wash the disciples' feet and wipe them with the towel he had around his waist. When he came to Simon Peter, Peter said to him, "Lord, how can you wash my feet? You should never stoop to washing my feet". Jesus answered him, "If I don't wash them, you can have nothing to do with me". So Peter said to him, "Lord, don't just wash my feet but also my hands and my head"'). This ritual washing thus places Lycidas among Christ's apostles and disciples, further acknowledging the promise he had shown before his death as a minister of God.

[176] **unexpressive**
(a) incapable of being expressed, inexpressible; (b) not audible to those still dwelling on earth. The adjective implies that Lycidas knows a joy that his mourners cannot experience; ***nuptial song*** the image of a wedding between God (or Christ, the Lamb of God) and his Church or between God and the soul is a well-known Christian motif (see Revelation 19 and the Song of Solomon, especially as interpreted by medieval exegetes); observe that Lycidas does not hear the mourning songs or elegies uttered by those on earth but the wedding music of his union with God.

[177] **blest kingdoms meek . . . love**
i.e. either (a) the blessed and undisturbed realms where joy and love prevail; or (b) joy and love as the two kingdoms in which Lycidas dwells (metaphorically); ***meek*** (a) merciful, compassionate; (b) mild, gentle.

[178] **There . . . above**
All the saints above entertain him there (***saints*** those who, like Lycidas, have been rewarded for earthly piety with heavenly dwelling); ***entertain*** (a) find a place for, receive or welcome as guest or resident; (b) provide pleasant activities.

[179] **solemn troops**
(a) sacred company, including human and angelic members (not, as one might suppose, 'sober-faced armies'); (b) famous people in great numbers; ***sweet societies*** (a) pleasant associations, relationships, (b) the angelic choirs.

[180] **move**
(a) dance, sway in time with their

singing; (b) affect the hearer deeply; (c) demonstrate the gloriousness of their heavenly existence.

[181] **wipe . . . eyes**
i.e. unlike those who remain in mourning on earth, Lycidas will never again have cause to weep.

[182] **Now . . . no more**
Now the shepherds (i.e. poets and students of Cambridge) need no longer mourn for Lycidas.

[183] **Henceforth**
(a) from the moment of your death; (b) from the moment that we have understood the meaning of your death; ***Genius*** (a) a local deity who guards a place and the people associated with it, in Greek and Roman religion; (b) a guardian angel who does the same, in Christian belief. Note that St Michael the archangel (see note to line 161) has perhaps been replaced by Edward King as the spiritual guardian of this dangerous region, thus supplanting a Catholic tradition with a Protestant one.

[184] **large recompense**
(a) generous compensation (for his early death); heavenly (and thus more extensive) reward; ***good*** (a) efficacious as guardian; (b) helpful as guide.

[185] **all that wander . . . flood**
The line suggests multiple interpretations, beginning with the literal sense of protecting those who sail in the same waters and extending to more metaphorical senses of ***flood*** (i.e. seas) as the sea of life, spiritual dangers of life on earth, and so on. The notion of man as a seafarer in this life is a very old one (and present in some of the most ancient English poetry). Here it is brilliantly used as the climax for a passage in which the death of Lycidas must be accounted for in some positive way; ***wander***, as opposed to ***welter***, earlier in the poem, suggests the confused search of the living for the right path or goal of existence.

[186] **sang**
The poet concludes the fiction which casts his printed elegy in the guise of a song sung by an unlearned rustic; ***uncouth*** (a) unknown or unheard (since no human audience is around to hear his lament); (b) unsophisticated, unpolished; ***swain*** simple country person; shepherd; ***oaks and rills*** his only audience.

[187] **sandals gray**
The quiet and pensive morning is personified (cf. Homer's 'rosy-fingered dawn') as a goddess whose sober departure has been barely perceptible; in other words, it is now almost noon, but thanks to the poet's utterances, the passage of time has gone unnoticed.

[188] **tender**
(a) delicate; (b) affecting; ***stops*** the notes on a musical instrument, obtained by pressing down a string or covering a hole; ***various quills*** (a) the different sizes of reed that make up a panpipe or set of flutes; (b) the variety of styles that are deployed in the course of the poem.

[189] **warbling**
singing or reciting; ***Doric*** the Greek dialect in which Theocritus wrote his pastoral songs; it was supposed to indicate a rustic peasant's language rather than a learned or sophisticated literary diction; ***lay*** song.

[190] **stretched out**
(a) illuminated or made visible; (b) moved over as the afternoon wore on; (c) caused long shadows of the peaks to appear in the valleys.

[191] **dropped . . . bay**
i.e. had set beyond the waters of the Atlantic; note that the recitation of the poem encompasses an entire morning and afternoon, thus drawing a parallel made earlier between the birth and death of the day and the life span of a human being.

[192] **twitched**
(a) shook, to flick off any clinging grass; (b) tied or fastened securely; ***mantle blue*** blue is the colour of heaven and spiritual bliss. The gesture indicates that the poet has initiated a new direction, having answered to his

own satisfaction the painful questions posed by Lycidas's death.
[193] **fresh woods . . . pastures new** A shepherd must continually move his flocks to new grazing grounds; likewise, a poet must learn to attempt new forms and subjects. The last line of the poem echoes familiar biblical imagery (Psalms 65, 79, 95, 100; Ezekiel 34; and numerous other instances), but it also implies that Milton, having now shown his mastery of a major poetic form, is prepared to move on to more ambitious literary projects or, perhaps, to political action. Following the Virgilian pattern, he would now expect to write a longer poem (such as Virgil's *Georgics*, which is about farmers rather than shepherds) in preparation for composing a great epic (as *Paradise Lost*, completed many years later, was to be) or, if his temporary setting aside of poetry is implied, leave his retreat to take part in public affairs.

97 / *When I Consider How My Light Is Spent*

When I consider how my light is spent,
 Ere half my days, in this dark world and wide,
 And that one talent which is death to hide,
 Lodged with me useless, though my soul more bent
To serve therewith my Maker, and present
 My true account, lest he returning chide,
 'Doth God exact day-labour, light denied?'
 I fondly ask; but Patience, to prevent
That murmur, soon replies, 'God doth not need
 Either man's work or his own gifts; who best
 Bear his mild yoke, they serve him best. His state
Is kingly. Thousands at his bidding speed
 And post o'er land and ocean without rest:
 They also serve who only stand and wait.'

An Italian sonnet rhyming *a b b a* / *a b b a* / *c d e* / *c d e* and drawing to some extent on the Puritan notion that work and the earning of wealth is not only good but encouraged by God. Since prosperity in worldly affairs was seen as a sign of God's favour, Milton finds his situation doubly troublesome: he can achieve very little of worth in his present condition, and seems to have done something to deserve God's neglect. The defence of the contemplative life in the last line of the poem is a traditional medieval theme, but it is not altogether consonant with the 'Puritan work ethic' of the seventeenth century. The sonnet is yet another example of the poet's unorthodoxy, even within a set of radical Protestant beliefs considered revolutionary at the time. Note the way in which phrases tend to run past rhyme-endings to form what has been called 'verse paragraphs', a style typical of Milton's later writings. Observe as well the unusual treatment of the break or turn of the sonnet between lines 8 and 9. Most scholars assume that the poem refers to Milton's blindness, but this interpretation has recently been challenged.

[1] **light**
(a) sight; (b) intelligence, mind; (c) gift of knowledge or God-given abilities; ***spent*** (a) extinguished; (b) used up, exhausted; (c) employed.

[2] **Ere half my days**
i.e. before half his working time as a poet and thinker has elapsed; ***dark world and wide*** Scholars date the sonnet sometime in the mid 1650s, after Milton had become blind; if that is the case, the world seemed literally dark and wide to the poet, but the phrase also recalls the traditional Christian description of this world as a place of darkness and emptiness compared with existence in the hereafter.

[3] **one talent . . . to hide**
An allusion to the story of the servant who was given one talent by his departing master, and failed to do anything with it, as told in Matthew 25: 24–8 ('Then the one who had received the single talent came and said, "Lord, I know that you are a demanding person, reaping where you have never planted. . . . And I was afraid, and went and hid the talent you gave me in the earth. Here it is, just as you gave it to me. . . . " [And the master, displeased, commanded] "Take the talent from him and give it to the one who received ten talents"'); ***talent*** (a) ability or skill to do something; (b) a unit of money in Greek and Roman Antiquity. The poet is concerned that he has not accomplished as much as his abilities and early endowments as an author would lead God to expect of him. Compare a similar concern in 'How Soon Hath Time', lines 3–4.

[4] **Lodged**
stuck, buried; ***useless*** i.e. (a) the talent has not been put to use; or (b) the receiver of the talent, because he has done nothing with it, is useless; ***though my soul more bent*** though my heart is even more anxious or determined.

[5] **therewith**
with the talent he has been given; ***my Maker*** God (the master in the biblical parable).

[6] **My true account**
The servant in the parable was accountable for the money given him; ***account*** (a) detailed statement of money owed or earned; (b) interest or profit; (c) answering for conduct; (d) narration of some event; ***chide*** scold or rebuke.

[7] **'Doth God exact . . . denied?'**
A complex allusion to Matthew 20: 1–16, the story of a vineyard owner who hires men at different times of the day but pays all of them for a full day's labour at sunset. The labourers who have worked all day protest but are rebuked by the owner, who explains that he has chosen to be generous. The poet's question to God is similar – he asks whether or not God expects him (***exact*** require, demand), now blind, to work as though he still had his sight; ***day-labour*** (a) work performed during daytime; (b) work performed in the light of day.

[8] **fondly**
foolishly; ***Patience*** i.e. the more thoughtful side of the poet's mind which causes him to pause and reflect before complaining; ***prevent*** anticipate, forestall.

[9] **murmur**
complaint; ***soon*** right away, immediately; note the slight paradox that it is 'Patience' which replies so readily.

[10] **his own gifts**
(a) man's own gifts; (b) God's own gifts; i.e. God has no need of giving or receiving for himself; ***gifts*** (a) abilities, talents (in the usual sense); (b) presents; (c) grace (in the theological sense).

[10–11] **who best/Bear . . . best**
i.e. 'Those best serve God who most readily bear his mild yoke' (i.e. easy burden); ***his state*** (a) his condition of existence; (b) his government (which supersedes all earthly government).
[12] **kingly**
(a) like the existence of a king, without needs; (b) God alone is king and owns everything; he is therefore without need; ***Thousands*** the innumerable hosts of angels, spirits who are higher than man and the constant, faithful messengers or servants of God; ***at his bidding speed*** rush to perform at his command.
[13] **post**
convey swiftly.
[14] **They also serve . . . wait**
A phrase cited so often as to become proverbial. It expresses a defence of (a) a properly religious attitude: cf. Christ's exhortation to his disciples following the parable of the ten sensible young women who were properly prepared to greet the bridegroom at the wedding (Matthew 24: 42–25: 13); (b) the contemplative life of the mind as superior to even the most useful physical labour. Thus waiting recalls the 'Patience' of line 8 and suggests that to question God's purposes is foolish because the readiness to obey his commands is as important as executing them; ***wait*** (a) expect the imminent occurrence of an event (here, God providing the poet with clearer instructions as to what he expects of him); (b) attend upon, like a servant (i.e. to give all one's attention to serving God).

98 / *On the Late Massacre in Piedmont*

Avenge, O Lord, thy slaughtered saints, whose bones
Lie scattered on the Alpine mountains cold;
Ev'n them who kept thy truth so pure of old
When all our fathers worshipped stocks and stones,
Forget not; in thy book record their groans
Who were thy sheep and, in their ancient fold,
Slain by the bloody Piemontese that rolled
Mother with infant down the rocks. Their moans
The vales redoubled to the hills, and they
To Heaven. Their martyred blood and ashes sow
O'er all th'Italian fields, where still doth sway
The triple Tyrant, that from these may grow
A hundredfold, who having learnt thy way
Early may fly the Babylonian woe.

This Italian sonnet, rhyming *a b b a / a b b a / c d c d c d*, was written to express Milton's outrage at the treatment of the Waldensians at the 'Piedmontese Easter', 24 April 1655. They were followers of Peter Waldo, after whom this sect was named, and their movement arose in southern France about 1170. Their beliefs included a rejection of capital punishment, a claim that the Roman Church was not the Church of Christ but the Scarlet Woman of the Book of Revelation, and an opposition to the official priesthood and the authority of the Pope. Protestant Europe was sympathetic towards their form of Christianity, which in many respects anticipated the doctrines of the Reformation. An earlier understanding with the Piedmontese authorities had allowed this sect freedom of worship; its revocation in 1655 led to their enforced expulsion. Milton was Cromwell's Latin Secretary at the time, and he wrote official correspondence to other Protestant heads of state deploring the massacre. The poem is more than simply a distillation of Milton's state papers, however; it presents a bold vision of the ultimate triumph of Protestant faith everywhere.

Title
Piedmont Piedmont (literally, 'foot of the mountain') is a region in northern Italy, ruled in Milton's time by the Duke of the House of Savoy.

[1] **slaughtered saints**
massacred followers of Peter Waldo, regarded by Milton as martyrs and a holy people.

[2] **Alpine mountains**
The Alps of Switzerland and northern Italy, where the Waldensians fled, lie just north of the valleys of Piedmont; ***cold*** can be taken as referring either to 'mountains' (which still have freezing temperatures at Easter time) or to the bones.

[3] **Ev'n them**
just those, precisely those; ***kept thy truth . . . old*** a reference to the antiquity of the sect, regarded as being, like later Protestantism, a return to the pure doctrine of the early Church.

[4] **fathers worshipped . . . stones**
i.e. in pagan times, emphasising the ancient origins of the sect (***stocks and stones*** a common phrase that is a contemptuous reference to pagan idols or objects of veneration); however, the allusion is more probably to the Roman Church viewed as a later corruption of earlier Christianity – especially in its use of religious images in worship, a practice that the Puritans opposed vehemently – and to the Waldensians as forerunners of Puritanism.

[5] **thy book**
i.e. the imagined Book of Judgment in which God records the names of the blessed.

[6] **thy sheep**
your faithful followers, a traditional Christian image. The farmlands and rich pasturage of the Po valley make the image appropriate on a more literal level – note how the conventional expression 'like lambs to the slaughter' is perhaps also implied; ***ancient fold*** alluding to their venerable religious community.

[7] **bloody**
bloodthirsty, violent.

[8] **Mother with infant**
Such details were later recounted by Sir Samuel Morland, Cromwell's envoy to the Duke of Savoy, who published a full account in 1658.

[8–10] **Their moans . . . To Heaven**
i.e. their cries so echoed throughout the Piedmontese valleys (and, indeed, Northern Europe) that they reached God himself; ***sow*** the scattered bones of the opening lines are now transformed into seeds. An allusion to a well-known passage in the New Testament (Matthew 13: 3–8, a parable about the results of sowing seeds on good ground) implies that the example of the Piedmontese martyrs will bear good fruit eventually, but note a further suggestion of the story from Greek mythology of Cadmus, who killed a guardian dragon and sowed its teeth, from which sprang up the Spartoi, a group of armed warriors. Milton seems to predict that not only the House of Savoy but all of Italy will face violent retribution; ***vales***

The valleys of Piedmont are bordered by the foothills of the Alps to the north.

[12] **sway**
command, rule.

[11–12] **all th'Italian fields . . . Tyrant**
i.e. the death of the Waldensians will cause revolt to spread to those regions of Italy ruled over by the Pope of Rome. Though the Pope was Bishop of Rome and spiritual head of the Catholic Church, he was also political ruler over a number of domains in Italy that belonged to the papacy.

[12] **triple Tyrant**
The tiara or crown of office worn by the Pope was made up of three separate crowns; ***Tyrant*** despot, in the usual sense, but in Greek also one who rules alone. The papacy is structured as a monarchy with an elaborate hierarchy whose ruler is elected by the chief Church officials, unlike the more democratically inclined congregations of Protestant sects such as Puritanism; ***these*** the Piedmontese martyrs; ***grow*** (a) inspire; (b) spread, multiply, propagate.

[13] **hundredfold**
a hundred times more 'saints'; ***thy way*** God's way (as opposed to man's or Satan's).

[14] **Early may fly**
may flee before such a massacre again occurs; ***Babylonian woe*** a complex allusion. The opposition between Jerusalem and Babylon in the Old Testament sets the people of God over against a powerful pagan empire. The kingdom of Israel fell in 586 BC to Babylonian invaders led by King Nebuchadnezzar (see 2 Kings 24–5). The subsequent exile of the Jews is referred to as the 'Babylonian captivity', and it marked a turning point in the history of Israel. The opposition is maintained symbolically in the New Testament, especially in Revelation, where Babylon is personified as a wicked woman (Revelation 17: 5: 'And upon her forehead was written "Mystery, Babylon The Great, The Mother Of Harlots And Abominations Of The Earth"'). During the fourteenth century, the Popes after Boniface VIII took up residence at Avignon, in southern France, and this political 'exile' was referred to as the Babylonian captivity of the Popes. Thus the reference to Babylon also refers to Rome (the great fourteenth-century Italian poet Petrarch had called the papal court in Avignon a Babylon and a source of woe), and the attempts of the Roman Church to eliminate various non-Catholic sects. In Protestant writings the Church of Rome was often identified with the 'Whore of Babylon' in Revelation.

99 / *Methought I Saw My Late Espousèd Saint*

Methought I saw my late espousèd saint
Brought to me like Alcestis from the grave,
Whom Jove's great son to her glad husband gave,
Rescued from death by force though pale and faint.
Mine, as whom washed from spot of childbed taint,
Purification in the old law did save,
And such, as yet once more I trust to have
Full sight of her in heaven without restraint,

Came vested all in white, pure as her mind.
  Her face was veiled, yet to my fancied sight
  Love, sweetness, goodness, in her person shined
So clear, as in no face with more delight.
  But O, as to embrace me she inclined,
  I waked, she fled, and day brought back my night.

Scholars do not agree about which wife Milton describes in this Italian sonnet (*a b b a / a b b a / c d c d c d*) with only two rhymes in its sestet. His first wife, Mary Powell, died in childbirth on 2 May 1652; his second wife, Katherine Woodcock, died on 3 February 1658, some three months after the birth of their child. At least one commentator denies that the poem is about either wife, and sees it as referring to the Virgin Mary; while yet another points to the theme of the angelic lady in Italian poetry as an alternative to a biographical interpretation.

[1] **Methought**
It seemed to me as though; ***late*** (a) deceased; (b) recently; ***saint*** a soul in heaven. 'Late' may be read as an adjective modifying 'saint' or as an adverb (***late-espoused***); furthermore, it may be understood as having yet another temporal dimension as well: the wife I married only later in life.
[2] **Alcestis**
Alcestis, by the Ancient Greek tragic poet Euripides, is the story of Alcestis's love for her husband, Admetus. Upon being told that he was fated to die, she agreed to take his place in the underworld. Admetus's grief over his wife's self-sacrifice was so great that he sought the help of Heracles (Hercules), who was able to bring Alcestis back. Milton's use of the myth suggests that he, like Admetus, was greatly indebted to his wife, though precisely how is not specified in the poem.
[3] **Jove's great son**
i.e. Hercules, who was the son of the king of the gods and a mortal woman; ***glad husband*** Admetus.
[4] **by force**
Hercules was famous for his strength, which he was able to exercise even in the realm of the dead; ***pale and faint*** descriptive of Alcestis's appearance upon returning from the grave.
[5] **Mine**
the poet's wife; ***as whom*** appeared like someone; some critics, however, interpret 'whom' as referring to the Virgin Mary, mother of Jesus, since Katherine Woodcock died on the day following the feast of the Purification of the Virgin Mary; ***washed*** cleansed, purified; ***spot . . . taint*** ritual uncleanness or pollution.
[5–6] **spot of childbed . . . save**
Jewish law (Leviticus 12: 2–5) required sixty-six days of confinement for a mother after a daughter's birth as part of a ritual of purification. (Milton had a total of three daughters.) If either wife is meant, then the lines describe the apparition of the dead wife as appearing like a woman dressed in the white robes of the purification rites.
[7] **And such**
And appearing in such a way.
[7–8] **as yet once more . . . restraint**
i.e. as completely as I expect (trust, i.e. expect or hope) to see her appear when we are both in heaven.
[9] **vested**
dressed.
[10] **veiled**
There has been a great deal of argument over this detail. Since Milton was probably blind when he married Katherine Woodcock, he would never

have seen her face; however, Alcestis is also veiled in Euripides' tragedy, and the reference may be literary rather than personal; ***fancied sight*** what I imagined seeing.

[11] **in her person shined**
shone forth from her face, were directly visible in her very being.

[13] **inclined**
bent over, attempted.

[14] **day brought back my night**
If this poem alludes, as most interpreters think, to Milton's blindness, then his awakening from his dream at dawn was a loss of vision rather than a restoration of it, and daytime, paradoxically, removed his ability to 'see', or at least dream that he was seeing. Like the allusion to *Alcestis*, nevertheless, this line also echoes a number of passages from Greek and Roman poetry, from Homer's *Iliad*, 23; and his *Odyssey*, 13; and Virgil's *Aeneid*, as well, perhaps, as Dante's *Divine Comedy*, which was influenced by the first three. There may also be an allusion to the Orpheus and Eurydice myth, since this dream, unlike the story of Alcestis, has an unhappy ending. Orpheus, who managed to gain permission to retrieve his wife Eurydice from death, was told that he must not look back at her before they had left the underworld. Unfortunately he could not resist one single glance, and had to watch her be drawn back into the depths just as they were about to be reunited.

RICHARD CRASHAW

(c. 1613–49)

1634 *Epigrammatum Sacrorum Liber*
1646 *Steps to the Temple with The Delights of the Muses*
1648 Second edition of *Steps to the Temple*
1652 *Carmen Deo Nostro* (posthumous)

It is one of the ironies of literary history that William Crashaw, the father of this ardent Catholic poet, was a zealous Puritan preacher and minister in London, where his son was born around 1613. Richard was educated at Charterhouse and Pembroke College Cambridge, where he matriculated in 1631. In 1634, the year he received his BA, he published his first book, a collection of sacred epigrams in Latin. The next year he was given a fellowship at Peterhouse, a High Church milieu far removed from his father's convictions, and ordained. He became a friend of Nicholas Ferrar, who founded a religious community at Little Gidding characterised by a quasi-monastic spirit. None of these leanings was to further Crashaw's career at Cambridge, for he was forced to relinquish his position there in 1643; a year later, the Parliamentarians served notice of his formal ejection.

He went to live in Holland, then in France, and – doubtless a logical next step – converted to Roman Catholicism. His friend and fellow poet Abraham Cowley was shocked to find him living in dire poverty in Paris, but thanks to the recommendation of the English Queen (who was of French origin and had also taken refuge there), he was sent to Rome. Some time passed before a place was found for him, but finally, in 1649, he was appointed to the cathedral of the Santa Casa at Loreto. Unfortunately, he was taken ill and died in August of the same year.

Context

Seen in relation to fellow seventeenth-century English poets Crashaw seems strikingly different and, despite his admiration of Herbert, altogether unlike him in style. He is a poet attracted by extravagant imagery and metaphors, a vivid appeal to the senses, and often outrageous comparisons, even when he is concerned with matters of deep spiritual significance. Far from worrying over the mysteries and paradoxes of his faith, Crashaw seems delighted to contemplate them over and over; nor is his intense spirituality in any way disturbed by his often startling evocation of the most sensual and bodily images. Not even the metaphysical conceits of John Donne can match some of Crashaw's daring juxtapositions.

Genre

Crashaw's poetry owes many of its characteristic traits to continental models, particularly to French, Italian and Spanish poetry. With them it shares an ecstatic lyricism, a wild disregard for the more sober proprieties demanded by the Puritans who were triumphant in England at just this time, and a love of display and grand effects that reminds one inevitably of the style of Counter-Reformation art that had taken hold all over Catholic Europe. His best poems – though they are not always structured with the tight control that some think essential to any successful art – evince a brilliant imagination and their own kind of inner coherence, governed by imagery and emotion.

Critical Reception

After his death abroad at an early age, there might seem to have been little likelihood that Crashaw's verse – inspired by models and a spirit largely alien to later seventeenth- and, especially, eighteenth-century English tastes – would stir much interest, but surprisingly enough, he seems to have been read (and even borrowed from) by a number of later poets, including Alexander Pope, who thought him 'a worse sort of Cowley' but better than

Herbert. Lorraine M. Roberts and John R. Roberts, in their 'Crashavian criticism: a brief interpretive history', note that his reputation in the seventeenth century, while modest, was, by and large, positive. Though the Metaphysical style was not in vogue in Pope's day, Crashaw was being praised by the end of the eighteenth century and was beginning to be included among the established poets of English literature, still ranked above Herbert. Coleridge was one of his most appreciative and intelligent readers. In the later nineteenth century he was repeatedly and favourably compared with Shelley, and in the second half of the century five substantial editions of his poetry appeared. By the end of the Victorian era, his peculiar style was beginning to be placed in a larger historical context. It was in the 1930s, however, that the sensitive studies of Ruth Wallerstein and, slightly later, Austin Warren (in a comprehensive approach that made full use of the newly awakened awareness of Baroque art and music), along with Mario Praz's essays on Crashaw and Italy, succeeded in giving modern readers a clearer perspective on his strengths, and more tolerance for his eccentricities. Though he was often compared unfavourably with Donne or Herbert, he was to some extent a beneficiary of the revisions in literary history effected by T.S. Eliot and others; critics continued to explore the paths opened up by Wallerstein, Warren and Praz, though for many Crashaw still remained a poet of bad taste and lack of structural coherence. Most, however, were concerned with defining his relation to the Metaphysical poets, suggesting that his work was influenced more by continental than by native models. After Louis Martz's seminal examination of the 'meditative tradition', however, it became evident that continental influence was not confined to Crashaw but pervasive, and that he was neither as eccentric nor as un-English as was once thought.

Further Reading

Editions

The Poems, English, Latin and Greek, of Richard Crashaw, ed. L.C. Martin, 2nd edn (Oxford, 1957; reprinted 1966) is the standard edition, though it is rather difficult to use; *The Complete Poetry of*

Richard Crashaw, ed. George Walton Williams (New York, 1972, 1974) is easier. However, recent textual scholarship may have rendered both out of date to some extent.

Critical Studies

Ruth Wallerstein, *Richard Crashaw* (Madison, WI, 1935, reprinted 1959, 1962; New York, 1972) and Austin Warren, *Richard Crashaw: A study in Baroque sensibility* (Baton Rouge, LA, 1939; reprinted Ann Arbor, MI, 1957, 1967) were two ground-breaking studies, and the second is still an excellent introduction to the poet and his times. Mario Praz, who was also writing on Crashaw during the same decade in both English and Italian, has had the most impact on English-speaking critics through his 'The flaming heart: Richard Crashaw and the Baroque', in *The Flaming Heart: Essays on Crashaw, Machiavelli, and other studies in the relations between Italian and English literature from Chaucer to T.S. Eliot* (Garden City, NY, 1958; reprinted New York, 1973), pp. 204–63.

The following book-length studies all explore aspects introduced by the three preceding scholars.

R.T. Petersson, *The Art of Ecstasy: Teresa, Bernini, and Crashaw* (London, 1970) continues the approach established by Warren and Praz, in which various art and literary currents are taken into account; while M.F. Bertonasco, in 'Crashaw and the emblem', *ES*, **49** (1969), 530–34 and *Crashaw and the Baroque* (University, AL, 1971), relates Crashaw to the emblem books and the meditations of Francis de Sales. R.V. Young, *Richard Crashaw and the Spanish Golden Age* (New Haven, CT, 1982) shifts the focus from Italy to Spain, and makes an important case for the presence of Spanish elements besides the writings of St Teresa in Crashaw's work. Robert M. Cooper, *An Essay on the Art of Richard Crashaw* (Salzburg, 1982) covers various topics relating Crashaw to Baroque artistic and religious themes. Louis Martz, *The Poetry of Meditation* (New Haven, CT and London, 1954; 2nd edn, 1962), a fundamental reorientation of the study of English religious poetry, places Crashaw in a meditative tradition deriving principally from Ignatius Loyola to make him seem less isolated and peculiar as an English writer. See also Walter R. Davis, 'The meditative hymnody of Richard Crashaw', *ELH*, **50** (1983), 107–29.

Paul A. Parrish, *Richard Crashaw* (Boston, MA, 1980), with an annotated select bibliography, is a convenient recent introduction to the poet. M.E. Rickey, *Rhyme and Meaning in Richard Crashaw* (Lexington, KY, 1961; New York, 1973) and G.W. Williams, *Image and Symbol in the Sacred Poetry of Richard Crashaw* (Columbia, SC, 1963) are mostly studies of metrical and symbolic patterns in the poetry. John R. Roberts, 'Richard Crashaw: the neglected poet', in Sidney Gottlieb, ed., *Approaches to Teaching the Metaphysical Poets* (New York, 1990), pp. 137–43 offers a pedogogical perspective proposing various critical strategies. Graham Hammill, 'Stepping to the Temple', *SAQ*, **88** (1989), 933–59 examines Crashaw in terms of *jouissance*, relationship to the other, and the psychoanalytic theories of Lacan; while Paul Parrish, 'The feminizing of power: Crashaw's life and art', in Claude J. Summers and Ted-Larry Pebworth, eds, *'The muses common weale': Poetry and politics in the seventeenth century* (Columbia, MO, 1988), pp. 148–62 sees a strong feminist theme throughout his work.

Two important collections of essays are Robert M. Cooper, ed., *Essays on Richard Crashaw* (Salzburg, 1979) and John R. Roberts, ed., *New Perspectives on the Life and Art of Richard Crashaw* (Columbia, MO, and London, 1990), which includes 'A brief interpretive history' by the editor and Lorraine Roberts, as well as a very helpful select bibliography, and a number of essays that bring research up to date. The same scholar has published a bibliographical survey of criticism with particularly thorough summaries of each item: *Richard Crashaw: An annotated bibliography of criticism, 1632–1980* (Columbia, MO, 1985) and an update, 'Recent studies in Richard Crashaw (1977–1989)', *ELR*, **21** (1991), 425–45.

Individual poems are also discussed in the following essays: J. Tytell) 'Sexual imagery in the secular and sacred poems of Richard Crashaw', *L&P*, **21** (1971), 21–7 ('To His Supposed Mistress' and 'Hymn to Saint Teresa', among others); James Bruce Anderson, 'Richard Crashaw, St. Teresa, and St. John of the Cross', *Discourse*, **10** (1967), 421–8; Robert G. Collmer, 'Crashaw's "Death Most Misticall and High"', *JEGP*, **55** (1956), 373–80; Anthony Farnham, 'Saint Teresa and the coy mistress', *Boston University Studies in English*, **2** (1956), 226–39; Livio Dobrez, 'The Crashaw–Teresa relationship', *Southern Review*

(Adelaide, Australia), **5** (1972), 21–37; Frank Fabry, 'Richard Crashaw and the art of allusion: pastoral in "A Hymn to... Sainte Teresa"', *ELR*, **16** (1986), 373–82; and Louis Martz, 'Richard Crashaw: love's architecture', in *The Wit of Love* (South Bend, IN, 1969), pp. 113–47 all explore the 'Hymn to Saint Teresa' or the Teresian poems in general from various points of view. Sandra K. Fischer, 'Crashaw, St. Teresa, and the Icon of Mystical Ravishment', *Journal of Evolutionary Psychology*, **4** (1983), 182–95 offers a psychological reading. Maureen Sabine, 'Crashaw and the feminine animus: patterns of self sacrifice in two of his devotional poems', *John Donne Journal*, **4** (1985), 69–94 examines the 'Nativity Hymn'; as do Michael McCanles, 'The rhetoric of the sublime in Crashaw's poetry', in T.O. Sloan and R.B. Waddington, eds, *The Rhetoric of Renaissance Poetry* (Berkeley, CA, 1974) and K. Neill, 'Structure and symbol in Crashaw's *Hymn in the Nativity*', *PMLA*, **63** (1948), 101–13.

100 / *Wishes. To His (Supposed) Mistress*

Whoe'er she be,
That not impossible she
That shall command my heart and me;

Where'er she lie,
Locked up from mortal eye
In shady leaves of destiny,

Till that ripe birth
Of studied fate stand forth
And teach her fair steps to our earth,

Till that divine
Idea take a shrine
Of crystal flesh through which to shine,

Meet you her my wishes;
Bespeak her to my blisses;
And be ye called my absent kisses.

I wish her beauty
That owes not all his duty
To gaudy 'tire or glist'ring shoe-tie,

Something more than
Taffeta or tissue can
Or rampant feather or rich fan,

More than the spoil
Of shop or silkworm toil
Or a bought blush or a set smile;

A face that's best
By its own beauty dressed
And can alone commend the rest;

A face made up
Out of no other shop
Than what nature's white hand sets ope;

A cheek where youth
And blood, with pen of truth,
Write what the reader sweetly ru'th.

A cheek where grows
More than a morning rose,
Which to no box his being owes;

Lips, where all day
A lover's kiss may play
Yet carry nothing thence away;

Looks that oppress
Their richest 'tires but dress
And clothe their simplest nakedness;

Eyes that displace
The neighbour diamond and outface
That sunshine by their own sweet grace;

Tresses that wear
Jewels but to declare
How much themselves more precious are;

Whose native ray
Can tame the wanton day
Of gems that in their bright shades play;

Each ruby there
Or pearl that dare appear,
Be its own blush, be its own tear;

A well-tamed heart
For whose more noble smart
Love may be long choosing a dart;

Eyes that bestow
Full quivers on Love's bow,
Yet pay less arrows than they owe;

Smiles that can warm
The blood yet teach a charm
That chastity shall take no harm;

Blushes that bin
The burnish of no sin
Nor flames of aught too hot within;

Joys that confess
Virtue their mistress
And have no other head to dress;

Fears, fond and flight,
As the coy brides, when night
First does the longing lover right;

Tears quickly fled
And vain as those are shed
For a dying maidenhead;

Days that need borrow
No part of their good morrow
From a forespent night of sorrow;

Days that, in spite
Of darkness, by the light
Of a clear mind are day all night;

Nights sweet as they
Made short by lovers' play,
Yet long by th'absence of the day;

Life that dares send
A challenge to his end
And when it comes, say, *Welcome Friend*;

Sydneyan showers
Of sweet discourse, whose powers
Can crown old winter's head with flowers;

Soft, silken hours,
Open suns, shady bowers;
'Bove all, nothing within that lours;

Whate'er delight
Can make day's forehead bright
Or give down to the wings of night.

In her whole frame,
Have Nature all the name,
Art and ornament the shame;

Her flattery,
Picture and poesy;
Her counsel, her own virtue be.

I wish her store
Of worth may leave her poor
Of wishes; and I wish – no more.

Now if time knows
That her whose radiant brows
Weave them a garland of my vows;

Her whose just bays
My future hopes can raise,
A trophy to her present praise;

Her that dares be
What these lines wish to see,
I seek no further; it is she.

'Tis she, and here,
Lo, I unclothe and clear
My wishes' cloudy character.

May she enjoy it
Whose merit dare apply it
But modesty dares still deny it.

Such worth as this is
Shall fix my flying wishes
And determine them to kisses.

Let her full glory,
My fancies, fly before ye;
Be ye my fictions, but her story.

This unusual piece is one of Crashaw's rare secular poems. Though it is ostensibly erotic, it actually demonstrates the poet's ability to write in the Cavalier manner; in the end Crashaw's point is precisely that he has no earthly mistress and never will have one. Indeed, the poem is mostly concerned with the sort of illusionistic play of appearances that was popular among artists of the Baroque rather than with any personally felt sensuality or sexual impulse. Its delightfully artificial quality points up the playfulness of Crashaw's style, and its theme-and-variations structure and progressive metrical form (rhyming triplets of dimeter, trimeter and tetrameter verse) are quite distinct from the more complex argumentative manner of the Metaphysical poets.

Title
supposed imagined; ***Mistress*** lady whom he might love.
[1] **Whoe'er**
whosoever.
[2] **not impossible she**
lady who might conceivably exist.
[3] **command my heart and me**
i.e. who will control not only his affections but his behaviour in general.

[4] **Where'er she lie**
wherever she may reside.
[5] **Locked up . . . eye**
hidden from human sight.
[6] **shady leaves of destiny**
an allusion to the Sibylline leaves, pages that hung in the cave of the Sibyl, a prophetess and priestess of the god Apollo in Greek religion; on them was written the destiny of the world and of human beings; ***shady*** obscure, difficult to read or interpret.
[7–8] **ripe birth/Of studied fate**
i.e. her birth would be the coming to fulfilment of her long-anticipated or premeditated (i.e. studied) existence.
[8] **stand forth**
appear, be forthcoming.
[9] **fair steps . . . earth**
The notion of a lady so beautiful that she seems to have descended from heaven is a frequent one in love poetry. Dante and Petrarch both wrote of 'heavenly ladies'; here, however, the lady is an idea that has not yet taken on human flesh and walked on earth (i.e. the poet has not seen such a person).
[10–13] **divine/*Idea* . . . shine**
Plato spoke of the things we see as mere copies of the ultimate reality, which consists of the *ideas* of those things that reside in some incorruptible realm. This concept was further developed by his later followers, the Neoplatonists, who not only interpreted the ideas as coming from the divine region but also thought of the soul as pre-existent and descending into the body at birth, where it was imprisoned until it was released at death to return to its true home in God. Here, however, Crashaw, following the conceit – introduced principally by Petrarch – makes the lady a creature of divine beauty and an object of 'worship' whose body is a holy place rather than a prison.
[12] **crystal**
(a) so fair as to seem translucent or transparent; (b) glass – thus setting up the following patterns: flesh/blood; crystal/wine; Mistress/Idea.
[11–13] **shrine/Of crystal flesh . . . shine**
Fair skin was much admired in a lady – hence crystal means very white. But the notion here also includes the common image of the body as a vestment or a place of residence for the soul which is displayed, in all its brilliance, through it.
[13] **Meet you . . . wishes**
'My wishes, go and meet her.'
[14] **Bespeak**
(a) speak about; (b) reserve (her) for; (c) tell of in advance.
[15] **ye**
wishes; ***absent kisses*** i.e. he cannot kiss her because she is not yet present; his only 'kiss', like the lady herself, is imaginary.
[16] **I wish . . . beauty**
'I wish for her to possess the kind of beauty'. Compare this and the next two stanzas with Herrick's 'Delight in Disorder' (p. 250). In the following lines the poet enumerates at length his wishes (i.e. those qualities his ideal lady would possess).
[17] **duty**
(a) responsibility; (b) attention.
[18] **gaudy**
brightly coloured, festive; ***'tire*** attire, dress; ***glist'ring*** glittering, superficially brilliant; ***shoe-tie*** bright ribbons or ornamental bows used for tying up shoe; apparently pronounced 'shooty' (see Herrick, 'Delight in Disorder').
[20] **Taffeta**
a bright, glossy, thin silk; ***tissue*** a rich cloth interwoven with gold or silver; ***can*** can offer or do.
[21] **rampant**
(a) extravagant; (b) rising in the air like an animal standing on its hind legs, its forepaws in the air (the sense of the word in heraldry); (c) waving in the air in all directions; ***rich fan*** an ornately painted or embellished fan.
[22] **spoil**
(a) plunder; thus the (cosmetics) that have been plundered from a shop, as if the shop were a battlefield after a war; (b) something obtained with great effort.

[23] **silkworm's toil**
the product of the silkworm's labour, i.e. silk.
[24] **bought blush**
rouge or cosmetics that enhance facial colour (as opposed to natural colour); ***set*** fixed, calculated, not spontaneous.
[27] **commend**
(a) adorn or grace, set off to advantage; (b) recommend, direct attention to as excellent.
[28–9] **shop . . . sets ope**
i.e. a face that is naturally beautiful, not made up to be so.
[30] **white hand**
delicate powers; ***sets ope*** opens (as one opens a shop for business).
[32] **blood**
(a) natural colour; (b) good or noble inherited traits; ***pen of truth*** i.e. the rosiness of her complexion is truly put there (i.e. written) by her youth and blood (not by the false appearance of make-up applied by a brush or puff).
[33] **sweetly ru'th**
a type of oxymoron that appears frequently in love poetry (cf. *Romeo and Juliet*, II, ii, 185: 'sweet sorrow'); anyone who sees (i.e. reads) her blushing cheek will fall in love; ***ru'th*** rueth, i.e. rues or regret (because of the pangs of love he feels).
[35] **More than a morning rose**
The rose, typical symbol of the fragility of feminine beauty, blooms in the morning and can fade by sunset. The conceit is an old one; cf. Thomas Campion's song from the early 1600s: 'There is a garden in her face/ Where roses and white lilies grow'. The point is that her beauty is more lasting than a morning (i.e. freshly blooming) rose.
[36] **to no box**
(a) a rose not grown in a flower box – not an artificially cultured blossom; (b) a colour that does not come from a box of rouge or other facial paint.
[38] **play**
(a) move about here and there; (b) enjoy recreation.
[39] **carry nothing thence away**
kissing the lips in no way diminishes or depletes them.
[40] **oppress**
overwhelm, outshine.
[41] **'tires**
attire, clothing.
[42] **nakedness**
unadorned directness.
[43–5] **Eyes . . . graces**
A beautiful woman's eyes were often compared with diamonds or the brilliant rays of the sun (cf. Shakespeare's ironic disclaimer in Sonnet 130: 'My mistress' eyes are nothing like the sun'); here they are said to be brighter (i.e. to displace or outface) than either.
[44] **neighbour**
nearby.
[45] **That sunshine**
the sparkle of a diamond.
[46] **Tresses**
hair.
[47] **but to declare**
only to declare
[48] **How much . . . are**
How much more precious they themselves are.
[49] **Whose**
i.e. the tresses'; ***native ray*** natural brilliance.
[50] **tame**
(a) make seem less brilliant; (b) subjugate.
[50–1] **wanton day/Of gems**
'wanton day' is an inversion of the usual formula (the night is 'wanton' in that it is the time most often associated with love), but here wittily continued into the day); ***wanton*** playful, sportive; 'day' refers to the light cast by the gems which 'plays' in the 'bright shades' of the mistress's hair.
[51] **bright shades**
various brilliant hues; ***play*** dart about.
[52–4] **Each ruby . . . tear**
(a) 'Any rubies or pearls that she wears in her hair must blush or weep to seem themselves so outshown'; (b) 'The only rubies and pearls that dare show themselves around her are her own blushes or tears'; ***Be . . . be*** May it be . . . must be.
[55] **well-tamed**
disciplined, protected from passion.

[56] **more noble smart**
i.e. if she falls in love, it will be the consequence of a truly noble passion.
[57] **Love . . . dart**
The usual image of Love or Cupid depicts him with a bow and arrows, which he shoots into the hearts of lovers; the implication is that this ideal lady will not easily fall in love.
[58–9] **Eyes . . . bow**
i.e. she provides Cupid with a great deal of ammunition (her eyes excite great desire in her lovers).
[60] **Yet pay . . . owe**
i.e. the charm of her eyes is never exhausted because she feels fewer pangs of love than she causes; ***pay*** (a) spend; (b) supply; ***owe*** (a) possess, own; (b) are indebted for.
[62] **charm**
(a) spell to guard against evils; (b) attractiveness that tames those who might wish to violate her purity.
[63] **That chastity . . . harm**
'so that her virginity is always safe'.
[64–6] **Blushes . . . hot within**
'Her blushes are the sign neither of guilt nor of passion.'
[64] **bin**
(i.e. 'been') be, are.
[67–8] **Joys . . . mistress**
'Her joys are disciplined by her virtue.'
[67] **confess**
acknowledge.
[69] **head to dress**
i.e. ruler or commander to address themselves to.
[70] **fond**
trivial; ***flight*** brief.
[71] **coy**
shy or pretending to be shy.
[72] **does . . . right**
(a) calms the virgin's misplaced fears; (b) gives the eager bridegroom and bride the kind of privacy they have longed for.
[73] **fled**
disappearing.
[74] **vain**
(a) inappropriate; (b) unnecessary; ***as those are*** as those (tears) that.
[75] **dying maidenhead**
the loss of a girl's virginity.
[76–8] **Days . . . sorrow**
i.e. a future that does not owe its happiness to past unhappiness.
[79–81] **Days . . . night**
i.e. peace that, because the mind is clear, is unperturbed by temporary troubles.
[82–4] **Nights . . . day**
The night is made to seem less tedious because of the pleasure the lovers enjoy, but lengthy because they can enjoy their solitude so fully. Cf. Donne's 'The Sun Rising' (p. 45).
[85–7] **Life . . . *Friend***
The image is of a duel between life and death. When one person challenges another to a duel, he agrees to meet him at a specific time and place to see who will prevail. The pious person, in his love of life, tries to keep death at bay but embraces it willingly, when the inevitable time comes, because it leads to eternity.
[86] **his**
its (life's); ***end*** death.
[89–90] ***Sydneyan*** **showers . . . discourse**
an abundance of conversation as pleasant as those described in the works of Sir Philip Sidney, especially his *Arcadia,* a long romance in which the main characters discourse endlessly upon love.
[92] **Open suns**
cloudless days.
[93] **'Bove all**
above all; ***lour*** (a) look dark and threatening (as applied to the sky); (b) frown (as applied to a person); (b) lowers, i.e. abases (in contrast with 'above all').
[94] **Whate'er**
whichever.
[95] **day's forehead**
(a) the dawn; (b) the sun.
[96] **give down**
(a) make softer, less harsh or hard; (b) add feathers to a bed in order to make it more comfortable.
[97] **frame**
(a) body; (b) person.
[98] **Nature . . . name**
i.e. have nothing that is not natural.

[99] **Art and ornament**
artificiality; i.e. her beauty is natural and needs no further enhancement.
[100] **flattery**
i.e. her only flattery.
[101] **Picture**
her own image; ***poesy*** this and other poems.
[100–1] **Her flattery . . . poesy**
i.e. 'May her only flattery be portraits painted of her and poetry (especially this poem) describing her.'
[102] **Her counsel . . . virtue be**
i.e. 'Let her be so virtuous as to need no advice from another'; ***counsel*** (a) advice; (b) prudence.
[103] **I wish**
I wish that; ***store*** abundance.
[104–5] **poor/Of wishes**
i.e. that she have nothing to wish for, since she already has everything.
[107] **That her**
that lady; ***brows*** forehead.
[108] **Weave them**
Weave for themselves (because they inspire the poet to write his verse, i.e. garland); ***vows*** (a) lines addressed to the lady; (b) wishes.
[109] **just bays**
(a) well-deserved laurel crown; (b) the poetic praise of the poet.
[110] **My . . . raise**
i.e. can raise my hopes for the future.
[114] **I seek no further**
Note the reservation expressed in this line: 'If such a perfect lady exists, she will be only in my imagination.'
[117] **My wishes' cloudy character**
the obscure or unclear aspect of this poem. The implication is that if such a woman exists, the poet's purpose in writing these verses is to encourage her to reveal herself to him.
[119] **merit dare apply it**
who deserves to take this poem for a description of herself.
[121] **Such worth as this is**
such excellence as these lines describe.
[122] **fix my flying wishes**
give my vague desires a definite object to love.
[123] **determine**
(a) fix their direction towards a terminal point; (b) define the ultimate character of his wishes.
[125] **fancies**
(a) wishes; (b) imagined picture of the lady; ***ye*** the fancies.
[126] **my fictions, but her story**
i.e. 'these descriptions may be the product of my imagination, but I hope that they correspond to some actual woman.'

101 / *In the Holy Nativity of Our Lord God: A Hymn Sung as by the Shepherds*

Come, we shepherds whose blessed sight
Hath met love's noon in nature's night;
Come, lift we up our loftier song
And wake the sun that lies too long.

To all our world of well-stol'n joy,
He slept and dreamt of no such thing,
While we found out Heav'n's fairer eye

And kissed the cradle of our King;
Tell him he rises now, too late
To show us aught worth looking at.

Tell him we now can show him more
Than he e'er showed to mortal sight,
Than he himself e'er saw before,
Which to be seen needs not his light;
Tell him, Tityrus, where th'hast been,
Tell him, Thyrsis, what th'hast seen.

Tityrus. Gloomy night embraced the place
Where the noble Infant lay;
The Babe looked up and showed his face;
In spite of darkness, it was day.
It was thy day, Sweet, and did rise
Not from the east but from Thine eyes.

Chorus. It was thy day, Sweet

Thyrsis. Winter chid aloud and sent
The angry north to wage his wars;
The north forgot his fierce intent
And left perfumes instead of scars;
By those sweet eyes' persuasive powers,
Where he meant frosts, he scattered flowers.

Chorus By those sweet eyes'

Both. We saw thee in thy balmy nest,
Bright dawn of our eternal day;
We saw thine eyes break from their east
And chase the trembling shades away;
We saw thee, and we blessed the sight;
We saw thee by thine own sweet light.

Tityrus. Poor world, said I, what wilt thou do
To entertain this starry stranger?

Is this the best thou canst bestow,
A cold, and not too cleanly manger?
Contend, ye powers of heav'n and earth,
To fit a bed for this huge birth.

Chorus. Contend, ye powers

Thyrsis. Proud world, said I, cease your contest
And let the Mighty Babe alone.
The Phoenix builds the Phoenix' nest;
Love's architecture is his own.
The Babe whose birth embraves this morn
Made his own bed e'er he was born.

Chorus. The Babe whose

Tityrus. I saw the curled drops, soft and slow,
Come hovering o'er the place's head,
Off'ring their whitest sheets of snow
To furnish the fair Infant's bed.
Forbear, said I, be not too bold;
Your fleece is white, but 'tis too cold.

Chorus. Forbear, said I

Thyrsis. I saw th'obsequious Seraphims
Their rosy fleece of fire bestow,
For well they now can spare their wings,
Since Heav'n itself lies here below.
Well done, said I, but are you sure
Your down, so warm, will pass for pure?

Chorus. Well done, said I

Tityrus. No, no, your King's not yet to seek
Where to repose his Royal Head;
See, see, how soon his new-bloomed cheek
'Twixt mother's breasts is gone to bed.
Sweet choice, said we; no way but so
Not to lie cold yet sleep in snow.

Chorus. Sweet choice, said we

Both. We saw thee in thy balmy nest,
Young dawn of our eternal day;
We saw thine eyes break from their east
And chase the trembling shades away;
We saw thee, and we blessed the sight;
We saw thee by thine own sweet light.

Chorus. We saw thee, etc.

Full Chorus. Welcome, all wonders in one sight,
Eternity shut in a span!
Summer in Winter, Day in Night,
Heaven in earth, and God in man!
Great little one, whose all-embracing birth
Lift earth to heaven, stoops heaven to earth!

Welcome, though nor to gold nor silk,
To more than Caesar's birthright is.
Two sister-seas of virgin-milk,
With many a rarely-tempered kiss
That breathes at once both maid and mother,
Warms in the one, cools in the other.

Welcome, though not to those gay flies
Gilded i'th' beams of earthly kings,
Slipp'ry souls in smiling eyes,
But to poor shepherds, homespun things,
Whose wealth's their flock; whose wit, to be
Well-read in their simplicity.

Yet when young April's husband showers
Shall bless the fruitful Maia's bed,
We'll bring the first-born of her flowers
To kiss thy feet and crown thy head;
To thee, Dread Lamb, whose love must keep
The shepherds more than they the sheep.

To thee, meek Majesty, soft King
Of simple graces and sweet loves,
Each of us his lamb will bring,
Each his pair of silver doves,
Till burnt, at last, in fire of thy fair eyes,
Ourselves become our own best sacrifice.

A poem in tetrameter lines with an introductory stanza rhyming *a a b b*, followed by stanzas rhyming *a b a b c c*, the whole presented as a dialogue of two shepherds (besides the narrator) with chorus. Crashaw follows other poets of the period in merging elements of the biblical Nativity scene with the classical pastoral tradition. Compare with Luke 2: 8–20: 'There were some shepherds in that part of the country who spent all night taking care of their sheep out in the open. An angel of the Lord appeared to them, and God's brilliance shone everywhere. They were very afraid, but the angel said, "Do not fear. I come with good news that will bring great joy to all. . . . You will find a baby wrapped in swaddling clothes and lying in a manger". [After visiting the Christ child] the shepherds returned, singing praise to God that they had seen and heard all this; it was exactly as the angel had said.'

A comparison between Crashaw's and Milton's Nativity hymns reveals some key differences in emphasis and manner. Crashaw's poem is a celebration of Christ's love, power and glory with attention to intimate detail and highly charged emotion. Milton's (see p. 348) concentrates intellectually on the larger action of the redemption, with little attention to the concrete scene of the birth in a manger. Furthermore, Milton's is a 'monody', like his 'Lycidas', while Crashaw's hymn is presented in dialogue as though it were part of a dramatic script. Though both share the theatricality of Baroque poetry, Milton is more inclined to set a scene for the divine birth, Crashaw to set a stage.

[2] **love's noon**
the Christ child (see John 8: 12: 'Jesus spoke to them again, saying, "I am the light of the world. Whoever follows me will not walk in darkness"'), understood as divine love; ***nature's night*** The scene takes place literally at night, but the phrase also suggests that Christ came to earth to redeem fallen (obscured) human nature.

[3] **lift we up our lofty song**
(a) let us sing about higher or spiritual things; (b) let us sing our song in elevated style.

[4] **To wake . . . too long**
(a) to bring an end to the long cold night during which the shepherds have stayed awake watching; (b) to bring to an end the long night of fallen human nature.

[5] **well-stol'n joy**
The shepherds have stolen time away from their flocks to view the Christ child.

[6] **He**
the sun.

[7] **found out**
discovered where he lay; ***Heav'n's fairer eye*** (a) the sun (the sun is often called the eye of heaven; cf. Shakespeare, Sonnet 18, line 5); (b) Christ, who is fairer than the sun.

[8] **cradle . . . King**
This gesture of homage is meant to suggest the coming together of the lowliest and the most exalted. Furthermore, the 'cradle' is actually not even that but a 'manger' or feeding-trough for animals, while the King is, of course, God.

[10] **aught worth looking at**
the light of day cannot reveal anything, in contrast with the vision these shepherds have seen, that can rival their experience.
[12] **e'er**
ever; ***to mortal sight*** to men.
[14] **needs not his light**
i.e. no physical light can reveal the miracle that they have witnessed; ***his light*** the sun's.
[15] **Tityrus**
a conventional name for a shepherd in Greek and Roman pastoral poetry, popularised by Virgil, Eclogues 1 and 7; ***th'hast*** you have.
[16] **Thyrsis**
another conventional shepherd's name.
[17] **night embraced the place**
i.e. the stable where the Christ child was born was deep in darkness.
[18] **noble Infant**
the Christ child (who, strictly speaking, was not at all noble, since he was the son of ordinary village parents).
[20] **it was day**
The brightness of the infant's face lit up the darkness.
[21] **thy day**
(a) his birthday; (b) the light that came from him; ***Sweet*** the child. Note that Thyrsis addresses the Christ child directly, and that these two lines are repeated in chorus.
[24] **chid**
showed displeasure, reproved (past tense of 'chide'); the cold season implies a world in need of redemption from its sins (suggested by the disapproving winter).
[25] **angry north**
the north wind, Boreas, which brings cold and violent weather.
[26] **forgot . . . intent**
i.e. the wind became calm and mild.
[27] **left perfumes**
i.e. became like the spring wind, Zephyr, which signals the blooming of flowers; ***scars*** i.e. the dark marks in the earth immediately after the winter snow has melted, before the new grass has had time to cover the ground.
[28–9] **sweet eyes' . . . flowers**
The Christ child, as God, has the power of controlling or transforming nature, even at birth. In love poetry this conceit, which attributes such power to the eyes, is usually applied to the beautiful lady, who can make winter seem spring.
[29] **he**
the north wind; ***meant*** intended to bring; ***he scattered*** (a) 'he' refers to the wind scattering; (b) 'he' refers to Christ bringing in the new season.
[31] **balmy**
(a) mild; (b) fragrant; (c) soothing; ***nest*** Despite the wintry cold and the crude trough in which the infant has been laid, his presence transforms the inhospitable environment into the comforting maternal image of the nest.
[32] **Bright dawn . . . day**
God came to earth as Christ to save man from his own sins, thus giving him 'eternal life' in the form of salvation for his immortal soul. The image of the son as 'sun' and 'life' alludes to such passages as John 1: 4: 'The Word [Christ] was the source of life, and this life brought life to mankind.'
[33] **break**
dawn (as in 'daybreak'); ***from their east*** i.e. like the sun.
[34] **trembling shades**
Presumably they tremble with awe at the divine event. See John 1: 5: 'And the light [Christ] shines in the darkness, and the darkness cannot overwhelm it.' Note the inversion of the usual image: ***shades*** darkness or ghosts, which normally would frighten the child; here the child frightens them away.
[37] **Poor world**
(a) impoverished world (and therefore incapable of offering a rich welcome); (b) unfortunate world.
[38] **starry**
Christ's birth was heralded by the appearance of an unusually bright star 'in the East' which guided the Wise Men to Bethlehem and then hovered over the inn stable where he was born.

[40] **cleanly**
neat, tidy, habitually clean.
[41] **contend**
(a) struggle in combat; (b) surpass or outdo (yourselves).
[42] **fit**
(a) outfit; (b) make big enough to accommodate.
[46] **Phoenix**
the bird in Greek mythology that is consumed in flames every century and is resuscitated from its own ashes (nest) – the point being that the phoenix, by definition, can build only a phoenix nest; it cannot do otherwise.
[47] **Love's architecture is his own**
Love creates its own dwelling-place. Since Christ is divine love come to earth, the exceedingly humble birth-place (architecture) to which he submits is a measure of his concern for humanity. However, ***architecture*** could also be understood in its meaning of 'order' or 'design'; in that sense, it is God's will that his incarnation be accomplished in just this way. Note that the phrase is preceded by an implicit 'but'; the phoenix's nest and love's architecture are contrasted.
[48] **embraves**
makes fine or impressive.
[49] **Made his own bed**
i.e. (a) God made the world in which he now resides as an infant; or (b) God has created the conditions in which he chooses to become man ('love's architecture', line 47).
[51] **curled drops**
snowflakes.
[52] **o'er**
over; ***place's head*** (a) above the roof of the stable; (b) over the head of the Christ child.
[55] **Forbear**
refrain from doing something; ***bold*** presumptuous, too eager.
[56] **fleece**
the snowflakes, as opposed to the more appropriate fleece of sheep as a lining for the crib; ***Seraphim*** plural of Seraph, an angel of the highest order; Crashaw adds a redundant 's'.
[58] **obsequious**
dutiful, attentive, ready to help.
[59] **rosy fleece of fire**
The Seraphim were described as having a fiery appearance; angels are usually depicted with large, eagle-like wings; ***fleece*** here, feathers; ***bestow*** offer as a gift.
[60] **spare**
(a) do without; (b) give away.
[61] **Heav'n**
(a) God (as the Christ child); (b) the world, made as good as heaven by virtue of God's presence. The conceit suggests that (a) the angels should reside on earth, now that God has descended there; and (b) on earth, angels no longer need their wings.
[63] **down . . . pass for pure**
The angels are imagined as plucking down from their wings to provide a soft lining for the crib. Yet even this lining, pure as it would be, would not be considered adequate for the cradle of the divine child.
[65] **No, no**
The negative implies that the Christ child has as yet no need for further embellishment of his bed (see lines 68–9), which God must have chosen. (There is, of course, also an implicit reference to subsequent events in the biblical story: Herod decreed that all children under two years of age should be killed, and Jesus's parents fled to Egypt to save him from slaughter; see Matthew 2: 13–21.)
[67] **new-bloomed**
(a) pink, like a blooming rose; (b) newly born, fresh.
[68] **'Twixt**
between; in traditional representations the Christ child was frequently depicted as being nursed by the Virgin Mary or asleep with his head on her breast.
[69] **no way but so**
there is no other way.
[70] **Not to lie . . . snow**
A conceit that depends on the usual description of a beautiful woman as having a snow-white breast; in addition, the white of the Virgin Mary's

breast is emblematic of her sinlessness and purity. Compare with the image of the 'balmy nest' in line 31.

[80] **Eternity . . . span**
A typical theological paradox; God is eternal and unlimited, but having taken human form, he becomes confined, like humans, to limit and measure – ***span*** (a) confinement or enclosure; (b) a distance of about nine inches or 23 cm.

[83] **Great little one . . . birth**
Note the effect achieved by the sudden expansion of this verse to a pentameter line, suggesting the paradoxical greatness of the child.

[84] **stoops**
(a) bring to the ground; (b) subject, humiliate.

[85] **nor to gold nor silk**
because the shepherds cannot offer the child such expensive gifts.

[86] **than Caesar's birthright**
Christ was born during the reign of Augustus Caesar, the first and most famous of the Roman emperors. As God, he would be deserving of more than an earthly ruler.

[87] **Two sister-seas**
the Virgin Mary's milk-filled breasts.

[88] **rarely-tempered kiss**
an extremely gentle kiss.

[89] **both maid and mother**
Mary conceived and bore the Christ child while remaining a virgin (i.e. maid); the alliterative formula is commonplace in English, and is of medieval origin.

[90] **Warms . . . cools**
i.e. (a) the sister-seas of milk, one warm, one cool; (b) the milk, which is warm, and the kiss, which is cool (or vice versa); (c) the kiss, which provides a comfort zone by both warming and cooling as expressing the affection of both maid and mother.

[91] **flies**
(a) any winged insects; (b) glittery but insignificant things; (c) parasites or court attendants who buzz about the king. Here the contrast is between the courtiers and other attendants of the king, who would be expected to come for such a momentous event, and the lowly shepherds, whose humble welcome is more sincere and therefore of much greater value. Cf. Hamlet's description of the courtier Osric as a 'water-fly' (V, ii, 83).

[92] **Gilded**
made to take on a golden colour by brilliant sunlight.

[93] **Slipp'ry souls in smiling eyes**
i.e. deceitful or unreliable people who present themselves amiably and hospitably. Note that 'in' means 'residing behind' or 'disguised by'.

[94] **homespun things**
coarse and honest, straightforward people, like homemade wool (appropriate for shepherds); cf. Herbert's 'Jordan (1)', 11.

[95] **wit**
(a) intellectual character; (b) understanding; ***to be*** is to be.

[96] **well-read . . . simplicity**
i.e. they are educated only in their own innocence and sincerity.

[97] **young April's husband showers**
An image of fertility that can be traced back to Chaucer's *Canterbury Tales* (see the opening lines of the 'Prologue') and earlier; spring moisture is presented as the masculine principle that awakens and inseminates the dormant feminine earth.

[98] **Maia**
(a) a minor Greek goddess, associated with spring and the seasons, and mother of Hermes; (b) a goddess of the earth; (c) the Latin name for the month of May.

[99] **first-born**
The traditional sacrificial offering to God in the Bible is the first-born of the flock or (in a dedication) of one's first-born son; cf. Exodus 13: 2.

[100] **kiss thy feet**
A gesture of honour; here, however, the flowers are laid at the infant's feet as well as being made into a wreath for his head.

[101] **Dread Lamb**
Crashaw draws on the pastoral image of Christ as the 'Lamb of God' and the 'Good Shepherd' to compose this

paradoxical image of him as awesome and powerful (i.e. dread) yet gentle (i.e. lamb). He is 'dread' because (a) the shepherds had been terrified by the angel who announced the birth of Christ to them; and (b) if the Lamb of God does not list someone in his 'roll of the living', that person will fall prey to the devouring maw of the Beast of the Apocalypse (see Revelation 13: 8).
[101–2] **whose love . . . their sheep**
i.e. Christ is shepherd to the shepherds.
[103] **meek Majesty, soft King**
a further oxymoronic description of the Christ child.
[105–6] **lamb . . . doves**
usual gift offerings brought to the altar or the temple in the Bible.
[107] **fire**
(a) brilliant light; (b) divine power; (c) all-consuming love.
[108–9] **Till . . . sacrifice**
Note the expansive effect obtained by the use of a final pentameter couplet.
[108] **sacrifice**
i.e. the shepherds present their love (burning, in love poetry, is usually associated with erotic passion) and themselves as sacrificial 'victims' in a 'burnt' offering to the Christ child.

102 / *On Mr. G. Herbert's Book Intitled the Temple of Sacred Poems, Sent to a Gentlewoman*

Know you, fair, on what you look;
Divinest love lies in this book,
Expecting fire from your eyes
To kindle this, his sacrifice.
When your hands untie these strings,
Think you have an angel by th'wings,
One that gladly will be nigh
To wait upon each morning sigh,
To flutter in the balmy air
Of your well-perfumèd prayer.
These white plumes of his he'll lend you,
Which every day to heaven will send you
To take acquaintance of the sphere
And all the smooth-faced kindred there;
And though *Herbert's* name do owe
These devotions, fairest, know
That while I lay them on the shrine
Of your white hand, they are mine.

This poem, composed in rhyming tetrameter couplets, attests to the influence of Herbert's poetry on Crashaw's. Indeed, Crashaw's 1646 volume was entitled *Steps to the Temple* (though the two poets are not actually very alike). In these presentation verses, he combines compliments to the addressee with praise of the author of *The Temple*. The book is therefore both an offering to God and an offering to a friend. Of particular interest is the suggestion that the reader is a necessary part of this offering; in that sense the poem has a particular relevance for recent theories of reading and interpretative communities.

[1] **fair**
the lady addressed in the poem; 'fair' was a traditional, complimentary way of referring to a woman.

[2] **divinest love**
(a) Herbert's poetry has God's love for humanity as its focus; (b) the poet's love for God is given supreme expression in this book. Crashaw is indicating that the book is not a collection of erotic love poems, such as might be given as a gift from one lover to another, but one on sacred subjects.

[3] **Expecting**
(a) awaiting; (b) requiring; ***eyes*** The conceit in this and the following line are based on the notion – commonplace in the language of love poetry – that the beloved lady's gaze causes lovers to burn (with desire), or that her eyes sparkle like fire or dart forth flames.

[4] **kindle . . . sacrifice**
A complex image – since Christ's death on the Cross was described as the sacrifice of God incarnate, made for the sake of humanity, this image of the immolation of the book as a sacrifice has a dual reference. On the one hand, taking the pronoun 'his' as referring to 'book', the act of reading it is an offering from the reader, as priest, to God in a fashion analogous to the sacrifice of the Mass, where the words uttered by the celebrant transform ordinary bread and wine on the altar into the body and blood of Christ. On the other hand, if it refers to 'divinest love' in line 2, the phrase could mean 'reignite the sacrifice of divine love by reading Herbert's poetry' – that is, commemorate Christ's death on the Cross. Finally, there remains yet another possibility – that 'his' refers to Herbert, the author of the book. In that case, the poems are Herbert's offering to God, but they require a reader to activate them as prayers.

[5] **these strings**
The book was either wrapped as a gift or, more probably, had strings bound into its covers so that it could be tied shut.

[6] **an angel by th'wings**
An open book, seen from the side, resembles the wings of a bird or angel (see Herbert's 'Easter Wings', p. 202), but Crashaw may also be punning on the Greek word, meaning 'messenger', from which 'angel' derives.

[7] **gladly will be nigh**
Like a 'guardian angel', an attendant spirit assigned to protect and watch over an individual.

[8] **wait upon**
(a) observe, watch over; (b) anticipate; (c) attend like a servant; (d) minister to; ***morning sigh*** i.e. the first suggestion of pain, longing or dejection.

[9] **flutter**
The pages of an open book respond readily to the slightest breeze or current of air; ***balmy*** delicately fragrant; ***air*** current or breath of air.

[10] **well-perfumèd prayer**
Her prayer is fragrant either because her breath is sweet (a compliment) or because her words are pleasing to God.

[11] **white plumes**
(a) The pens (made from goose quills) with which Herbert wrote his poetry; (b) the pages of the open book, which flutter like feathers; (c) the 'wings' of Herbert's sacred inspiration; (d) Herbert's poems.

[12] **Which every day . . . send you**
i.e. 'will inspire you to think of the

things of heaven' or 'will put you in a state of ecstatic joy such as one might experience in heaven'.

[13] **take acquaintance**
visit, experience; ***the sphere*** the higher heavens; in the Ptolemaic scheme of the universe the earth was surrounded by a series of transparent concentric spheres which turned at various speeds, and carried around the stars and planets affixed to them.

[14] **the smooth-faced kindred**
the angels, here doubtless visualised as cherubs or angels, such as they were often depicted by painters in the form of male infants with wings; they are described as kindred either because the lady has become like them or because the book itself was earlier described as an angel.

[15] **owe**
(a) own; (b) take responsibility or credit for.

[16] **devotions**
(a) prayers; (b) homage paid to a person, particularly to a lady (in poetry of love or compliment); ***fairest*** the addressee of the poem (see line 1).

[17] **while I lay them**
i.e. in so far as they are my gift to you.

[17–18] **shrine/Of your white hand**
both a compliment (fine ladies were noted for the delicacy and whiteness of their hands) and a continuation of the image of sacrifice and worship from the earlier part of the poem. The lady's hand is the altar on which the book is offered (to her and also to God).

[18] **they are mine**
Crashaw indicates his admiration both for Herbert's poems (he wishes he could have written them himself or claim them as his) and for the lady, who is also the object of his devotion and the shrine to which he has brought his gift.

103 / *A Hymn to the Name and Honour of the Admirable Saint Teresa*

Foundress of the reformation of the Discalced Carmelites, both men and women, a woman for angelical height of speculation, for masculine courage of performance, more than a woman, who, yet a child, outran maturity and durst plot a martyrdom.

Love, thou art absolute sole lord
Of life and death. To prove the word,
We'll now appeal to none of all
Those, thy old soldiers, great and tall,
Ripe men of martyrdom, that could reach down
With strong arms their triumphant crown,
Such as could, with lusty breath,
Speak loud into the face of death
Their great Lord's glorious name; to none
Of those whose spacious bosoms spread a throne
For love at large to fill; spare blood and sweat
And see him take a private seat,

Making his mansion in the mild
And milky soul of a soft child.
    Scarce has she learned to lisp the name
Of martyr, yet she thinks it shame
Life should so long play with that breath
Which, spent, can buy so brave a death.
She never undertook to know
What death with love should have to do,
Nor has she e'er yet understood
Why, to show love, she should shed blood;
Yet though she cannot tell you why,
She can love and she can die.
    Scarce has she blood enough to make
A guilty sword blush for her sake,
Yet has she a heart dares hope to prove
How much less strong is death than love.
    Be love but there, let poor six years
Be posed with the maturest fears
Man trembles at, you straight shall find
Love knows no nonage, nor the mind.
'Tis love, not years or limbs that can
Make the martyr or the man.
    Love touched her heart, and lo it beats
High and burns with such brave heats,
Such thirsts to die, as dares drink up
A thousand cold deaths in one cup.
Good reason, for she breathes all fire;
Her weak breast heaves with strong desire
Of what she may with fruitless wishes
Seek for amongst her mother's kisses.
    Since 'tis not to be had at home,
She'll travel to a martyrdom;
No home for hers confesses she
But where she may a martyr be.
    She'll to the Moors and trade with them
For this unvalued diadem.
She'll offer them her dearest breath,
With Christ's name in't, in change for death.
She'll bargain with them and will give
Them God, teach them how to live
In him, or, if they this deny,

For him she'll teach them how to die.
So shall she leave amongst them sown
Her Lord's blood or, at least, her own.
  Farewell, then, all the world, adieu!
Teresa is no more for you.
Farewell, all pleasures, sports, and joys
(Never, till now, esteemèd toys),
Farewell, whatever dear may be,
Mother's arms or father's knee;
Farewell, house, and farewell, home;
She's for the Moors and martyrdom!
  Sweet, not so fast! Lo, thy fair spouse
Whom thou seekst with so swift vows
Calls thee back and bids thee come
To embrace a milder martyrdom.
  Blest powers forbid thy tender life
Should bleed upon a barbarous knife,
Or some base hand have power to rase
Thy breast's chaste cabinet and uncase
A soul kept there so sweet. Oh, no!
Wise heaven will never have it so!
Thou art love's victim and must die
A death more mystical and high.
Into love's arms thou shalt let fall
A still surviving funeral.
His is the dart must make the death
Whose stroke shall taste thy hallowed breath,
A dart thrice dipped in that rich flame
Which writes thy spouse's radiant name
Upon the roof of heaven, where aye
It shines and with a sovereign ray
Beats bright upon the burning faces
Of souls which, in that name's sweet graces,
Find everlasting smiles. So rare,
So spiritual, pure, and fair
Must be the immortal instrument
Upon whose choice point shall be sent
A life so loved; and that there be
Fit executioners for thee,
The fairest and first-born songs of fire,
Blest seraphim, shall leave their choir

And turn love's soldiers upon thee
To exercise their archery.
Oh, how oft shalt thou complain
Of a sweet and subtle pain,
Of intolerable joys,
Of a death in which who dies
Loves his death and dies again
And would forever so be slain,
And lives and dies and knows not why
To live but that he thus may never leave to die.
How kindly will thy gentle heart
Kiss the sweetly killing dart,
And close in his embraces keep
Those delicious wounds that weep
Balsam to heal themselves with. Thus
When these thy deaths so numerous
Shall all at last die into one
And melt thy soul's sweet mansion,
Like a soft lump of incense hasted
By too hot a fire and wasted
Into perfuming clouds, so fast
Shalt thou exhale to heaven at last
In a resolving sigh; and then –
Oh what? Ask not the tongues of men.
Angels cannot tell; suffice,
Thyself shall feel thine own full joys
And hold them fast forever. There,
So soon as thou shalt first appear,
The moon of maiden stars, thy white
Mistress, attended by such bright
Souls as thy shining self, shall come
And in her first ranks make thee room,
Where 'mongst her snowy family,
Immortal welcomes wait for thee.
Oh, what delight, when revealèd Life shall stand
And teach thy lips heaven with his hand,
On which thou now mayest to thy wishes
Heap up thy consecrated kisses!
What joys shall seize thy soul, when she,
Bending her blessed eyes on thee,
Those second smiles of heaven, shall dart

Her mild rays through thy melting heart!
  Angels, thy old friends, there shall greet thee,
Glad at their own home now to meet thee.
  All thy good works, which went before
And waited for thee at the door
Shall own thee there, and all in one
Weave a constellatïon
Of crowns, with which the king thy spouse
Shall build up thy triumphant brows.
  All thy old woes shall now smile on thee,
And thy pains sit bright upon thee.
All thy sorrows here shall shine;
All thy sufferings be divine.
Tears shall take comfort and turn gems,
And wrongs repent to diadems.
Even thy deaths shall live and new
Dress the soul that erst they slew.
Thy wounds shall blush to such bright scars
As keep account of the lamb's wars.
  Those rare works where thou shalt leave writ
Love's noble history, with wit
Taught thee by none but him, while here
They feed our souls, shall clothe thine there.
Each heavenly word by whose hid flame
Our hard hearts shall strike fire, the same
Shall flourish on thy brows and be
Both fire to us and flame to thee,
Whose light shall live bright in thy face
By glory, in our hearts by grace.
  Thou shalt look round about and see
Thousands of crowned souls throng to be
Themselves thy crown. Sons of thy vows,
The virgin births with which thy sovereign spouse
Made fruitful thy fair soul, go now
And with them all about thee bow
To him. 'Put on', he'll say, 'Put on,
My rosy love, that thy rich zone,
Sparkling with the sacred flames
Of thousand souls whose happy names
Heaven keeps upon thy score. (Thy bright
Life brought them first to kiss the light

That kindled them to stars.)' And so,
Thou with the lamb, thy Lord, shalt go,
And wheresoe'er he sets his white
Steps, walk with him those ways of light
Which who, in death, would live to see,
Must learn in life to die like thee.

Crashaw celebrated the figure of Teresa of Avila in three poems, of which this is the longest and, according to some critics, the finest. Written in tetrameter couplets, broken sporadically by longer lines, it describes her life, after a brief prologue, in three main stages: her early years and precocious desire to become a martyr (lines 15–64), the mystical experiences of her mature life (lines 65–109), and her death and reception into heaven (lines 109–82). His interest in her dated some time before his conversion to the Church of Rome; indeed, St Teresa's popularity was by no means confined to Catholic countries. She was the subject of a number of paintings and sculptures, including the famous scene depicted by Bernini.

Title
Saint Teresa the Spanish mystic and reformer of the Carmelite order, Teresa de Cepeda of Avila (1515–82), declared a saint by the Roman Catholic Church in 1622 and known throughout Europe for her account of her spiritual life and other religious writings, first printed in 1587. An English version of her famous *Autobiography* was published under the title *The Flaming Heart* (also the title of another of Crashaw's St Teresa poems); it was to have a great impact on as different a personality from Crashaw's as the nineteenth-century English novelist George Eliot, who speaks of the saint as a model of womanhood in *Middlemarch*.
Subtitle
Foundress Teresa was dissatisfied with the lax observances of the Carmelite convent she entered at the age of eighteen, and after a series of visions and trances, first experienced in 1554, she began to reflect on the causes of the Protestant Reformation and the need for Church reform. Accordingly, some years later she laid plans for forming a new order, based on the original rules of the Carmelites but kept more strictly. Eight years later she secretly opened a new house and, after some initial opposition, was given permission to direct a sisterhood there. The Discalced ('shoeless') Carmelites, as they were called, wore sandals made of rope, slept on straw, abstained from meat, remained confined to their cloister, and lived exclusively on charity. Though she continued to meet opposition and was even placed under arrest for two years, she prevailed eventually and founded sixteen convents for women and fourteen monasteries for men. Though her sanctity, asceticism and mysticism earned her the honour of canonisation, she was an eminently practical and even shrewd organiser who earned the high respect of her male contemporaries for her persistence and courage; ***speculation*** contemplative, visionary and intellectual ability; ***angelical*** with the intelligence characteristic of angels; ***performance*** (a) discharge or execution of duty; (b) deed, action; (c) exploit; (d) achievement; ***durst*** dared; ***plot*** plan.
[1] **Love**
i.e. God. In the usual language of love

poetry, physical love is often spoken of as a sovereign power; here Crashaw introduces the theme of love in an ambiguous phrase so that the interweaving of physical and spiritual in Teresa's mystical experiences is underlined from the start.

[2] **prove**
test; ***word*** statement, saying.

[4] **Those thy old soldiers**
male Christian martyrs who suffered or died for their faith, and are the usual models of ultimate piety and religious fidelity.

[5] **reach down**
seize with their own hands (i.e. courageously accept).

[6] **triumphant crown**
the crown of martyrdom with which such saints are usually depicted in religious art.

[7] **lusty**
vigorous and healthy.

[9] **name**
Christ.

[10] **spacious bosoms**
i.e. great hearts; ***spread*** erected, set up.

[11] **spare**
refrain from.

[12] **private seat**
inconspicuous place; St Teresa was very reserved and reticent about her personal religious experiences, in contrast with the public testimony of the martyrs.

[13] **mansion**
dwelling-place, in addition to the usual meaning.

[14] **milky**
(a) clouded in understanding, not clear; (b) not yet weaned from its mother's breast.

[15] **lisp**
utter imperfectly or falteringly.

[16] **martyr**
The original Greek word meant 'witness'; in the Christian faith, it is a title reserved for the very highest degree of sainthood.

[17–18] **Life . . . death**
i.e. that one should have to live a long life to attain salvation when it could come so much sooner. Note the economic metaphor and the pun on ***spent*** – (a) used up, exhausted; (b) paid out; ***brave*** splendid, magnificent.

[19–20] **She never . . . do**
i.e. she had no interest in understanding the connection between death and love, a paradoxical relationship that has inspired a venerable history of meditations.

[24] **She can love . . . die**
i.e. a child is capable of love and death, like all human beings, and has no need to grasp their association in order to act or experience either.

[26] **guilty sword blush**
a typical Crashavian conceit: the sword that kills the innocent child 'blushes' (is stained with blood) out of guilt for its deed; ***for her sake*** because of what it has done to her.

[29] **Be love but there**
If love is present.

[29–30] **let poor . . . fears**
even a mere six-year-old child, faced with those dangers.

[31] **straight**
right away.

[32] **nonage**
age when one is still legally subject to parents or guardians.

[33] **limbs**
physical strength or maturity.

[37] **thirsts to die**
continuing the idea of 'heats' in the preceding line.

[37] **as dares**
The subject is 'heart' in line 35.

[38] **cold deaths**
Note the contrast with 'heats'.

[39] **Good reason**
With good reason, for a good reason.

[40] **weak breast**
weak because that of a child and a girl.

[41–2] **Of what . . . kisses**
i.e. she desires a kind of love that is not to be found in the maternal affection of her mother.

[43–64] **Since . . . martyrdom**
an allusion to the first chapter of the *Autobiography*, where Teresa tells of her early childhood infatuation, inspired by her readings in the lives of

the saints, with martyrdom and her resolve 'to go to Barbary, amongst the Moors, and beg along the way as we went, so that we might come, at length, to lose our lives there for Our Lord. And it seemed that he gave us courage enough for this purpose, even at that tender age of ours, if we could have found any means to achieve it; but even the fact of our having parents seemed to be the greatest of barriers we faced.'

[47] **Moors**
a mixed Berber and Arab people of Islamic faith who conquered Spain in the eighth century but were expelled in the late fifteenth century, so that at this time they resided principally in what is now Morocco and Algeria; ***trade*** despite the animosity between Christian Europe and Islamic Africa, trading relations were never halted. Note the resumption of the metaphor of buying and selling first used in line 18.

[48] **unvalued**
invaluable, priceless; ***diadem*** her life.

[49] **dearest**
most valuable.

[50] **With Christ's name in't**
because her plan was to proselytise and spread Christianity among the Moors; ***change*** exchange.

[54] **how to die**
i.e. by her example in remaining faithful to Christ.

[55] **sown**
Missionaries were often said to 'sow the seeds of faith'.

[56] **Her Lord's blood**
Christ's blood is a traditional symbol of Christian salvation.

[61] **Never, till now, esteemèd toys**
(a) never judged as trifles until this moment; (b) trifles prized neither in the past nor even now.

[64] **She's for**
bound for.

[65] **Lo**
behold; ***thy fair spouse*** Christ (the Church was traditionally called 'the bride of Christ').

[68] **To embrace**
To yield to; ***milder martyrdom*** (a) the privations of the convent; (b) the pangs of her mystical visions.

[69] **Blest powers forbid**
Heaven forbid! (The poet expresses his shock at the implications of St Teresa's youthful scheme); ***thy*** that thy.

[71] **base**
wicked; ***rase*** cut or slit.

[72] **chaste cabinet**
guiltless cavity.

[78] **a still-surviving funeral**
a death you will survive, referring to the mystical death described in the *Autobiography*.

[79–104] **His is the dart . . . to die**
This entire section is based on a famous passage from Chapter 29 of the *Autobiography*:

It pleased our Blessed Lord that I should occasionally have the following vision: I saw an angel very near me, on my left side, and he appeared to me in bodily form, though even now I am not accustomed to seeing anything of the sort except very rarely. For, although angels often appear to me, it is without my really seeing them except in imagination. . . . But in this vision Our Lord was pleased for me to see this angel in the other way. He was not large but fairly small, yet he was of great beauty. His face was so inflamed that he appeared to be one of those higher angels who seem to be all afire, and he may well have been one of those we call Seraphim. . . . I saw that he had a long dart of gold in his hand, and at the tip of the iron below there seemed to be a little flame; and I thought that he thrust it several times through my very heart in such a fashion that after it had gone altogether through my bowels and he withdrew it, it seemed to bring with it as much as it had pierced within me and left all that remained wholly inflamed with a great love for almighty God. The pain I felt from it was so excessive that I had no desire to be relieved of it, nor can the soul be contented with anything less than God himself. It was no bodily but rather a spiritual pain, though the body cannot fail to participate in it somewhat, and, at that, even a great deal. And it is such a dear, delightful intercourse which passes between the soul and almighty God that I pray him that from his infinite goodness he will give some touch or taste of it to whoever might believe that I am lying.

[79–80] **His is the dart . . . breath**
Crashaw employs the language of erotic love (in which 'the death' means sexual consummation) in conjunction with the earlier desire for martyrdom; this use of sexual imagery as the vehicle for describing a spiritual experience was common among the Spanish mystic writers; it may appear shocking to modern sensibilities, and in our times it is more likely to be turned round: the spiritual experience interpreted as the consequence of physical causes. But this couplet is complicated by yet other inversions; ***His*** Christ's or Love's; ***make*** cause; ***death*** (a) the martyrdom she desired as a child; (b) the renunciation of the self for unity with God; (c) sexual climax.
[80] **Whose**
(a) the dart's; (b) death's; ***stroke*** note the implied sexual meaning; ***taste*** (a) experience; (b) take away, consume. The subject of the verb is 'stroke'; one would have expected the 'hallowed breath' to have tasted death, rather than the other way round, but Crashaw is recalling the offer of 'her dearest breath' in line 49; ***hallowed*** sanctified, holy because of her sainthood; ***breath*** life or spirit (*spiritus* in Latin means 'breath').
[81] **thrice dipped**
i.e. because bearing the love of the whole Trinity (Father, Son, and Holy Spirit), not simply that of Christ alone; ***rich flame*** the empyrean or heaven of heavens, the sphere beyond that of the stars and the abode of God and the angels, was composed of the element of fire.
[82] **thy spouse**
Christ; ***radiant name*** sun (also a pun on God the *Son*). The sun is a frequent metaphor for Christ in Christian literature.
[83] **aye**
for ever, eternally.
[84] **sovereign ray**
Crashaw is drawing on the traditional description of God as light – John 1: 3–9.
[85] **Beats**
shines repeatedly or constantly; ***burning*** i.e. with love or desire.
[87] **rare**
excellent.
[89] **immortal instrument**
the divine dart of love.
[90] **choice**
(a) exquisite; (b) well-aimed; ***sent*** (a) dispatched to heaven (referring to Teresa's life or breath); (b) dispatched from heaven (referring to Christ's love).
[91] **that**
in order that.
[92] **Fit executioners**
as though she had been condemned to death.
[93–4] **sons of fire, Blest seraphim**
The Seraphim (Hebrew plural of Seraph, supposed to be derived from a root meaning 'to burn') were the highest order of angels and were distinguished by the fervour of their love.
[95–6] **love's soldiers . . . archery**
This image suggest not only the classical pagan image of Eros or Cupid, son of Venus and god of love – often depicted winged and with bow and arrows – but also the death of St Sebastian, a Christian martyr who was executed by a firing squad of archers.
[97] **subtle**
penetrating, pervasive.
[104] **leave to die**
stop dying; i.e. this 'death' is so rich an experience as to be all that is worth living for. Note the expansion of the line from tetrameter to hexameter, suggesting the prolongation of Teresa's mystical death experience.

[106] **Kiss**
Crashaw emphasises Teresa's embracing of the mystical experience to indicate that her response is not simply passive but engages her active participation.
[108] **delicious wounds**
(a) the pleasurable wounds she receives from the dart; (b) Christ's redemptive wounds resulting from his crucifixion.
[110] **Balsam**
balm or fragrant, oily ointment used for medicinal purposes to soothe or heal wounds.
[111] **die into one**
i.e. when she suffers her eventual physical death.
[112] **mansion**
the body.
[114] **incense**
The bodies of some saints were preserved miraculously intact for long periods of time or exuded a sweet fragrance instead of the stench of decay; Teresa's body remained in such a state of preservation after her death. However, Crashaw chooses not to emphasise this part of her story but to describe her death in terms of the ritual use of incense in Church ceremonies; ***hasted*** hastened.
[114] **wasted**
consumed, burnt up.
[116] **exhale to heaven**
render up her breath (spirit), i.e. die.
[117] **resolving**
(a) relaxing (the limbs), loosening (bonds); (b) softening; (c) dissolving, melting; (d) transforming, converting; (e) clarifying, freeing from doubt.
[119] **suffice**
let it suffice that.
[121] **fast**
securely.
[123–4] **moon of maiden stars, thy white/Mistress**
the Virgin Mary, mother of Jesus, often depicted in Renaissance and Baroque paintings as surrounded by a halo of stars.
[125] **Souls**
Mary, considered the greatest of the saints, was frequently shown at the centre of a company of other saints.
[127] **snowy**
white in spiritual purity.
[129] **Oh . . . stand**
The line expands a foot to become a pentameter verse; ***revealèd Life*** Christ.
[130] **teach thy lips . . . hand**
allow her the supreme pleasure of kissing Christ's hand.
[132] **Heap up thy consecrated kisses!**
the heavenly answer to the inadequacy of her mother's earthly kisses in line 42 and the fulfilment of line 106.
[133] **she**
Mary.
[134] **Bending**
turning.
[135] **second smiles**
after those of God.
[136] **mild rays**
as a human being, though a privileged one, Mary has a lesser brilliance that reflects God's.
[137] **thy old friends**
whom she had seen in her visions.
[140] **at the door**
at the gate of heaven, where one is judged.
[141] **own**
acknowledge, recognise.
[143] **king thy spouse**
Christ.
[144] **build up**
elevate; ***brows*** countenance, face.
[149] **turn gems**
turn into gems.
[150] **repent to**
turn into, in compensation for the harm they have caused; ***diadems*** crowns; a traditional Christian interpretation of suffering and wrongs against a person is that they can add to spiritual glory if they are accepted in a spirit of resignation.
[151] **new**
as an adjective modifying 'deaths' = renewed, transformed; as an adverb modifying 'dress' = newly.
[152] **Dress**
(a) place upright, bring into proper

order; (b) adorn or clothe; (c) treat properly; (d) treat or cure (a wound); *erst* earlier.

[153–4] **Thy wounds . . . account**
a typical Crashavian conceit – her wounds will leave a row of scars like notches on a stone or piece of wood that mark the number of victories.

[154] **the lamb's wars**
an allusion to Revelation 5–16, which describes the appearance of Christ in the form of a lamb with seven horns and seven eyes who breaks open a sealed scroll in which are contained visions of the battles of the evil forces of the world and their punishment, culminating in the fall of Babylon. A significant part of this section is concerned with the suffering of early Christian martyrs.

[155] **works**
St Teresa's writings; *writ* written, recorded.

[156] **wit**
understanding, knowledge, intelligence.

[158] **feed . . . clothe**
Note that Teresa's writings serve different purposes on earth and in heaven.

[159–60] **hid flame . . . fire**
i.e. her words are capable of igniting the heart as a piece of flint is made to spark when it is struck by a piece of iron; the image of the flinty heart is prominent in Vaughan's poetry.

[164] **fire . . . flame**
inspiration and glory (see lines 159–60).

[167] **Sons of thy vows**
those who have joined the Discalced Carmelites.

[168] **virgin births**
i.e. her followers, here thought of as her children, comparing her with the Virgin Mary; ***sovereign spouse*** Christ as Teresa's mystical bridegroom.

[171–2] **put on . . . love**
an echo of the style of the Song of Songs (for example, at 4:8).

[172] **rich zone**
highly embellished belt or band.

[175] **upon thy score**
(a) in your list of achievements; (b) for your sake.

[175–82] **Thy bright . . . thee**
Notice, in these closing lines, the unusual amount of enjambment that serves to accelerate the pace of the ending.

[181] **Which who**
which whosoever.

ANDREW MARVELL

(1621–78)

1681 *Miscellaneous Poems* (posthumous)

◇

Few poets are more difficult to place than Marvell. In his time, he was known both as a hot-tempered Member of Parliament for Hull and as a vehement pamphleteer and political satirist. Today, he is remembered as the author of two or three of the best-known lyric poems in the English language. They appear to be easy to understand; a closer reading reveals them to be not only unusually hard to pin down, but also inexhaustible.

The son of a clergyman with strong Calvinist leanings, Marvell attended Hull Grammar School before going on to Trinity College Cambridge. While he was there, in 1637, he contributed a Latin and a Greek poem to a congratulatory volume addressed to King Charles I by the University of Cambridge. Acquaintances later recounted that he was tempted to join the Catholic Church by some Jesuits, and that his father journeyed south to 'rescue' him from their clutches: there is insufficient evidence to confirm this story. He graduated, without distinction, in 1639. Some two years later his father was drowned in the river Humber, near Hull, and the following year he went to London. Between late 1642 and 1647 he travelled in Holland, France, Italy and Spain – whether to get away from the increasing political turmoil in England or for some more positive reason is, again, not known. While in Rome, about early 1646, he wrote some satirical verses about Richard Flecknoe, a minor but popular poet and dramatist at the time.

On his return to England, he seems to have moved in Royalist circles – he published an elegy to Lord Francis Villiers in 1648, and contributed some laudatory verses to Lovelace's *Lucasta* (1649) – but Christopher Hill (in Patrides, ed., 1978) has questioned the usual assumption that he must have had Royalist sympathies at this time. Just what his early leanings were is one of the most intriguing aspects of him.

What is certain, however, is that 'An Horatian Ode upon Cromwell's Return from Ireland' must have been conceived some time in the summer of 1650. Early the following year he was appointed tutor to Mary, daughter of Lord Fairfax, the Parliamentarian general who had resigned from office following his opposition to the king's execution in January 1649, to whom Marvell was distantly related. His new employer lived at Nun Appleton, a large country house in Yorkshire – i.e. a long way from London. It used to be thought that most of the poems featured in this anthology were written during the two years he spent there.

In 1653 he moved to Eton, where he became the tutor of William Dutton, a ward of Oliver Cromwell; in the same year, Milton, who was Latin Secretary to the Commonwealth government, asked him to become his assistant. During the next few years he wrote several so-called 'occasional poems': celebrations of 'The First Anniversary' of Cromwell's government, of Blake's victory against the Spanish fleet, of the wedding of Cromwell's daughter, and in 1658, of Cromwell's death. About 1656, he also travelled on the Continent with William Dutton. In 1659 he became Member of Parliament for Hull.

At the Restoration, he helped to obtain Milton's release from prison and was re-elected to his seat in the House of Commons, a position he retained until his death. Judging by his correspondence, he seems to have been an active MP with strong opinions. He made occasional official visits abroad – to Holland in 1662, and to Russia, Sweden and Denmark with the Earl of Carlisle from 1663 to 1665. He became something of a thorn in the government's flesh during these years, producing scathing satires on its complacency and corruption. Amongst the works he wrote in this period is *The Rehearsal Transprosed*, a very successful satire in two parts. When he died, he was remembered for both his political and satirical writings, and – perhaps above all – as an example of personal courage and integrity in the face of governmental mismanagement: a man whose 'truth, wit, and eloquence' had helped to defend his country against 'the grim monster, arbitrary power'.

Context

Marvell presents an endless puzzle. His father was a strict Calvinist, yet a poem like 'The Nymph Complaining for the Death of Her Fawn' is largely based on imagery derived from the Song of Songs, a text more widely read amongst Catholics than Puritans. There can be no doubt that during the Civil Wars many of his friends were Royalists, yet about – or very soon after – the time he wrote the 'Horatian Ode' he appears to have discovered a genuine and deep-rooted admiration for Republican government. Although he was well-known as a staunch supporter of Cromwell, he could speak with regret about the events that led to the execution of Charles I, and was able to accept the Restoration without question.

Another puzzle is the nature of his relationship with Fairfax, and the manner in which he spent his time at Nun Appleton. The assumption that he was an essentially private man best able to express himself in the seclusion of Yorkshire has come under increasing scrutiny. It is still generally thought that 'Appleton House' was written there. One of his greatest works (unfortunately too long for inclusion here), it appears to consist of a traditional – albeit elaborate – description of a country house and garden. But beneath this 'literal' level are several others. Lindy Abraham has recently shown (1990) that it is also a sustained account of the alchemical opus – a conclusion less surprising than it might seem when one remembers that Fairfax had an active interest in alchemy, but none the less one that suggests the importance of an interest of Marvell's about which relatively little had previously been known.

Renewed interest in the second half of Marvell's life has suggested that many of the works assumed to have been written at Nun Appleton could well have been written much later: Allan Pritchard, for example, has argued that 'The Garden' is a post-Restoration work, on the grounds that it shows the influence not only of some poems by Katherine Philips which were not published until 1664, but also of works by Abraham Cowley ('Marvell's "The Garden": a Restoration poem?', *SEL*, **23** [1983], 371–88). If this is so, it evidently affects some of our basic assumptions about both the man and his poetry.

Royalist and Parliamentarian, Calvinist and 'Catholic', politician and meditative poet, satirist and alchemist: the material – the *prima materia* – of Marvell's greatest works is almost always a tension of opposites. In this respect, it offers a fascinating reflection of his time.

Genre

Marvell's startling imagery is borrowed from the Metaphysical poets, while his urbane tone and sophisticated mode of allusion relate him to the Cavalier poets. Yet though he belongs to both traditions, he is unlike any other major poet in this anthology. He did not habitually circulate copies of his lyric poems amongst friends, nor did he ever collect them for publication. We are left to assume that he regarded them as expressions of private concern. They are for the most part based on a fixed idea or 'theme' with which the poet plays by means of a series of witty meditations on what he sees either before him or in his mind's eye. Their final lines usually involve a paradoxical image of a complex and ambivalent kind. For this reason, Marvell appeals strongly to a modern consciousness. Contemporary criticism looks not for certainties but for multiple possibilities, and in these the poetry of Marvell is peculiarly rich.

Marvell's lyric poems are almost all derived from established genres: the *carpe diem*, the poetic dialogue, the poem addressed to a young girl, pastoral poetry, the Horatian ode, etc. As Wilcher notes, the 'I' in his poetry 'is a rhetorical device for exploring the possibilities of literary traditions, rather than a vehicle for autobiography' (1985, p. 130). They are the product of *Homo ludens* – a man playing with words not idly, but (very probably) with the implicit purpose of discovering the precise nature of the multiplicity of possibilities by which he finds himself bombarded. They are, however, never derivative: every one of the poems in this selection represents a major landmark in the evolution of their genre.

This selection gives priority to Marvell's lyric poems – partly because these are his finest works, but also because his occasional works and satires do not contribute as much to their particular genre as do his lyrics. The one exception is, of course, the 'Horatian Ode', which is far and away the finest of the occasional poems – although it must be emphasised that it is *not* a 'typical' example of Marvell's writing in this genre.

Critical Reception

Marvell's verse satires circulated quite extensively during his lifetime, albeit sometimes anonymously, and subsequently found their way into anthologies. In contrast, the lyric poems had to wait until 1681, some three years after his death, when Mary Palmer, claiming to be his widow, published *Miscellaneous Poems by Andrew Marvell, Esq*. The truth of her claim is suspect, and today the most striking feature about the collection is the last-minute removal of the three Cromwell poems, which clearly represents political conditions at the time. The volume attracted very little attention, but interest gradually increased, and a few of the poems were included in Tonson's *Miscellany* (1716). A two-volume edition of Marvell's works followed in 1726, edited by Captain Thomas Cooke; it was reissued by Edward Thompson in 1776 in three volumes. Throughout the eighteenth century he was best known for his prose writings and his reputation as a patriot. Hence the epitaph composed by his nephew, William Popple, for the monument erected to him in the church of St Giles-in-the-Fields, Hull, in 1764, in which he is proclaimed to be a 'strenuous asserter of the constitution, laws and liberties of England'.

During the nineteenth century, his prose works sank slowly into oblivion and Marvell began to be seen as a poet of nature. Interest in the lyric poems was kindled by the Reverend William Lisle Bowles, who published an edition of the works of Alexander Pope in 1806, in which he noted 'Upon Appleton House' as an antecedent of 'Windsor Forest'. William Hazlitt, Charles Lamb, Hartley Coleridge, Ralph Waldo Emerson and Edgar Allan Poe all admired Marvell as a poet of nature and feeling. In 1872–5 A.B. Grosart published a four-volume edition of his works (which continues to be the best edition of his prose works), and as the century drew to a close, Marvell's reputation as a nature poet increased.

A very different picture of Marvell began to emerge in the twentieth century. In the wake of Grierson's 1912 edition of the works of John Donne, interest began to focus on Marvell's delight in paradox and ambiguity. Indeed, his works were replete with all the qualities most admired by the New Critics. H.M. Margoliouth's standard edition of *The Poems and Letters* was published in 1927; the following year, Pierre Legouis produced the first major study: *André Marvell: poète, puritain, patriote*. William Empson discussed him in *Some Versions of Pastoral* (1935), and his reputation has continued to grow ever since. Critics are still uncovering the extent of his poetic allusions – to earlier literature, to the Bible, to theology, to contemporary science, even to alchemy. More recently, critics have turned their attention to the ideological background and implications of his work, and consequently shown a renewed interest in his satirical writings. His reputation has changed dramatically. In the nineteenth century he was admired for his 'simplicity'; his works are now regarded as some of the most complex and enigmatic of their time.

Further Reading

Editions

The Poems and Letters of Andrew Marvell, ed. H.M. Margoliouth, 2 vols; 3rd edn rev. by Pierre Legouis and E.E. Duncan-Jones (Oxford, 1971); *Andrew Marvell*, ed. Frank Kermode and Keith Walker, 'Oxford Authors' (Oxford, 1990); *Andrew Marvell: Selected poetry and prose*, ed. Robert Wilcher, 'Methuen English Texts' (London, 1986).

Critical Studies

For an excellent introduction to Marvell, see Robert Wilcher, *Andrew Marvell* (Cambridge, 1985), which includes an invaluable bibliography listing the most influential articles on separate poems. Recent collections of essays include Arthur Pollard, ed., *Andrew Marvell: 'Poems': A casebook* (London, 1980); and Harold Bloom, ed., *Andrew Marvell* (New York, 1989). The tercentenary of the poet's death produced three works of a uniformly high quality: Kenneth Friedenreich, ed., *Tercentenary Essays in Honor of Andrew Marvell* (Hamden, CT, 1977); C.A. Patrides, ed., *Approaches to Marvell: The York tercentenary essays* (London, 1978); and R.L. Brett, ed., *Andrew Marvell: Essays on the tercentenary of his death* (Oxford, 1979). Equally invaluable is Elizabeth S. Donno, ed., *Andrew Marvell: The critical heritage* (London, 1978), which covers critical reception of the works from 1673 to 1923.

T.S. Eliot's 1921 essay 'Andrew Marvell', in *Selected Essays*, 3rd edn (London, 1951) is still well worth reading, but contemporary critical debate about Marvell really begins with William Empson's discussion of some of his poems in *Some Versions of Pastoral* (London, 1935), a theme explored more recently by Donald F. Friedman, *Marvell's Pastoral Art* (London, 1970). J.B. Leishman, *The Art of Marvell's Poetry* (London, 1966) and Rosalie Colie, *'My Echoing Song': Andrew Marvell's poetry of criticism* (Princeton, NJ, 1970) are both essential landmark studies. John M. Wallace, *Destiny His Choice: The loyalism of Andrew Marvell* (Cambridge, 1968), examines Marvell in his historical context and is especially interesting on the 'Horatian Ode'. For a very useful account of criticism at this time, see Gillian Szanto, 'Recent studies in Marvell', *ELR*, **5** (1975), 273–86. Bruce King, *Marvell's Allegorical Poetry* (New York, 1977) is especially useful on the extent of the religious implications; and R.I.V. Hodge, *Foreshortened Time: Andrew Marvell and seventeenth-century revolutions* (Cambridge, 1978) situates the poems in the context of the rapid changes taking place in politics, logic, science and art.

Amongst more recent studies, Warren L. Chernaik, *The Poet's Time: Politics and religion in the work of Andrew Marvell* (Cambridge, 1983) is a provocative account of the importance of the two subjects in the subtitle. Contributions to an understanding of Marvell's religious outlook include John Klause, *The Unfortunate Fall: Theodicy and the moral imagination of Andrew Marvell* (Hamden, CT, 1983) and Margarita Stocker, *Apocalyptic Marvell: The Second Coming in seventeenth-centry poetry* (Brighton, 1986). See also Michael Wilding, *Dragons' Teeth: Literature in the English Revolution* (Oxford, 1987).

For discussions of individual poems, see the bibliography included in Wilcher (1985). Two other recent studies of 'The

Nymph Complaining' deserve mention: Phoebe S. Spinrad, 'Death, loss, and Marvell's nymph', *PMLA*, **97** (1982), 50–59, which explores its Christian symbolism and the theme of mutability; and Lindy Abraham, *Marvell and Alchemy* (Aldershot, 1990), which offers an eye-opening account of the extent of Marvell's use of alchemical imagery, especially in 'Appleton House' and 'The Nymph'. Other reappraisals of major works include Jules Brody, 'The Resurrection of the body: a new reading of Marvell's "To His Coy Mistress"', *ELH*, **56** (1989), 53–79; and Blair Worden, 'Andrew Marvell, Oliver Cromwell, and the Horatian Ode', in Kevin Sharpe and Steven N. Zwicker, eds, *Politics of Discourse: The literature and history of seventeenth-century England* (Berkeley, CA, 1987), pp. 147–80.

The standard biography is Hilton Kelliher's *Andrew Marvell: Poet and politician* (London, 1978).

Although it is in evident need of updating, Dan S. Collins, *Andrew Marvell: A reference guide* (Boston, MA, 1981) is an invaluable bibliography of secondary material; and George R. Guffey, *A Concordance to the English Poems of Andrew Marvell* (Chapel Hill, NC, 1974) is an equally essential reference work.

104 / *The Definition of Love*

My love is of a birth as rare
As 'tis for object strange and high:
It was begotten by Despair
Upon Impossibility.

Magnanimous Despair alone
Could show me so divine a thing,
Where feeble Hope could ne'er have flown
But vainly flapped its tinsel wing.

And yet I quickly might arrive
Where my extended soul is fixed,
But Fate does iron wedges drive
And always crowds itself betwixt.

For Fate with jealous eye does see
Two perfect loves, nor lets them close:
Their union would her ruin be
And her tyrannic power depose.

And therefore her decrees of steel
Us as the distant poles have placed –
Though Love's whole world on us doth wheel –
Not by themselves to be embraced,

Unless the giddy heaven fall
And earth some new convulsion tear
And, us to join, the world should all
Be cramped into a planisphere.

As lines, so loves oblique may well
Themselves in every angle greet.
But ours so truly parallel,
Though infinite, can never meet.

Therefore the love which us doth bind,
But Fate so enviously debars,
Is the conjunction of the mind
And opposition of the stars.

An analytical meditation in eight stanzas, each of four iambic tetrameters, and rhyming *a b a b*. The poem forms a marked contrast with the amorous verse so popular from the mid sixteenth century to the Metaphysical parodies of the early seventeenth century.

The poem makes a series of paradoxical assertions that pose a riddle, inviting the reader to identify the nature of the love of which it speaks. The early stanzas suggest love for God; the second half is more obviously related to love between man and woman.

Title
The beginnings of modern science in the late sixteenth century are probably responsible for the growing use of the word 'definition' in its modern sense (a succinct description of the meaning of a word or phrase). For although in Marvell's time it had been accepted as meaning (a) a formal determination regarding an issue, it still continued to mean (b) a limitation, or *something that confines* – cf. Herbert, 'Divinity', line 10; brief definitions were often included in seventeenth-century poems, but 'definition' poems as such are rarer.

Many critics have either assumed, or argued vehemently, that the poem refers to a man's love for a woman (e.g. Margoliouth, ed., p. 259) – but it should be noted that the poem makes *no* specific mention of a woman: the ambiguity is surely a central feature of it; others have argued that it is an essentially religious allegory of 'the love of the incarnate soul for its heavenly life' (Ann E. Berthoff, *The Resolved Soul*, Princeton, NJ [1970], p. 106).

[1] **My love is of a birth**
The origin of my love is; ***rare*** unusual.

[2] **'tis**
it is; ***for*** as (an); ***object*** (a) object, In the sense of something that can be examined – i.e. a subject of attention; (b) objective – i.e. the end towards which the poet's love is directed; (c) something that excites emotion; ***high*** of exalted quality.

[3] **begotten**
fathered, sired, procreated – usually used of a *male* animal or figure; ***Despair*** without hope: but note the 'personification'.

[4] **Impossibility**
the 'upon' implies a female animal or figure.

[5] **Magnanimous Despair**
Magnanimous great-minded: despair is not usually attributed to great-mindedness; the phrase is thus an oxymoron; ***alone*** only.

[10] **Where my extended soul is fixed**
extended (a) directed towards; (b) stretched towards; ***fixed*** directed towards; (b) set, established. The line recalls Donne, 'A Valediction: Forbidding Mourning' (p. 52), lines 23–4, 'an expansion/Like gold to airy thinness beat' and the 'fixed' foot of the compass at line 27.

[11–12] **Fate**
note that 'Fate' is personified as *female;* ***iron wedges drive*** i.e. Fate drives iron wedges between the poet and the object of his love – note how Fate is thus 'symbolised by the products [= iron, wedges] of one of the industries which were transforming rural Britain' at the time (Margoliouth, p. 259); ***crowds itself*** i.e. Fate then pushes itself between the poet and the object of his love.

[13] **jealous**
(a) fiercely possessive; (b) ardently attentive.

[14] **nor lets them close**
and (for this reason) will not let them join together.

[15] **Their union . . . depose**
the union of the poet with the object of his love would cause Fate to lose her tyrannic power.

[17] **therefore**
it is for this reason that.

[19] **wheel**
turn, as on an axis or pivot.

[20] **themselves**
i.e. the two poles, north and south (but maybe also 'celestial poles'); by underlining the metaphor, the distance between the poet and the object of his love is further emphasised.

[21] **giddy**
(a) etymologically, possessed by a god; (b) constantly whirring round; (c) overexcited.

[22] **new convulsion**
a further violent natural disturbance, such as an earthquake; ***tear*** tear apart.

[23] **us to join**
in order to unite us; ***the world should all*** the whole world should.

[24] **planisphere**
a flat projection of the whole earth in which the poles have been compressed together: cf. Thomas Blundevil's description in his survey of knowledge necessary for a young gentleman, first published in 1594: 'a planisphere . . . is both flat and round, representing the Globe or Sphere, having both his poles clapped flat together' (*Exercises*, 1636 edn, vi, 598).

[25] **lines . . . oblique**
lines (oblique) (a) not going straight to the point, roundabout, indirect (perhaps a comment on the poet's own argument); (b) inclined at other than a right angle; (c) perhaps a reference to the meridian lines on a map or globe that always 'slant' towards the poles and thus bisect each other at irregular angles; ***loves oblique*** (a) the roundabout way in which lovers often

approach one another; (b) the way in which lovers *lean* against one another; (c) perhaps also the way in which lovers sometimes hide themselves in the dark corners (i.e. angles) of a room or in the streets: cf. Vindice's disgust at having been hired by the Duke 'to greet him with a lady/In some fit place, veiled from the eyes of the court,/Some darkened, blushless angle' (Tourneur, *The Revenger's Tragedy*, III, v, 15).

[26] **Themselves in every angle greet** can join together at any angle.

[29–32]
This last stanza was surely influenced by *The Mistress* (1647) by Abraham Cowley (1618–67), one of the Cavalier poets: 'Impossibilities', stanza 3:

As *stars* (not powerful else), when they *conjoin*,
 Change, as they please, the world's estate,
So thy *heart* in *conjunction* with mine
 Shall our own fortunes regulate,
And to our *stars themselves* prescribe a Fate.

Note how much more condensed Marvell's image is.

[30] **debars**
prohibits (from doing something).

[31–2] **conjunction . . . opposition**
terms used in astrology: ***conjunction*** the point of closest proximity between two stars or planets; here, complete union; ***opposition*** the point of maximum distance between two stars or planets; here, inability to unite; ***stars*** note the relation of 'stars' to 'Fate'.

105 / *To His Coy Mistress*

Had we but world enough and time
This coyness, lady, were no crime.
We would sit down and think which way
To walk and pass our long love's day.
Thou by the Indian Ganges' side
Shouldst rubies find; I by the tide
Of Humber would complain. I would
Love you ten years before the Flood,
And you should, if you please, refuse
Till the conversion of the Jews.
My vegetable love should grow
Vaster than empires, and more slow.
A hundred years should go to praise
Thine eyes and on thy forehead gaze.
Two hundred to adore each breast –
But thirty thousand to the rest:
An age at least to every part,
And the last age should show your heart.

For, lady, you deserve this state;
Nor would I love at lower rate.
  But at my back I always hear
Time's wingèd chariot hurrying near,
And yonder all before us lie
Deserts of vast eternity.
Thy beauty shall no more be found,
Nor in thy marble vault shall sound
My echoing song: then worms shall try
That long-preserved virginity,
And your quaint honour turn to dust
And into ashes all my lust.
The grave's a fine and private place,
But none, I think, do there embrace.
  Now, therefore, while the youthful glue
Sits on thy skin like morning dew,
And while thy willing soul transpires
At every pore with instant fires,
Now let us sport us while we may;
And now, like amorous birds of prey,
Rather at once our time devour
Than languish in his slow-chapped power.
Let us roll all our strength and all
Our sweetness up into one ball
And tear our pleasures with rough strife
Through the iron grates of life.
Thus, though we cannot make our sun
Stand still, yet we will make him run.

Marvell's best-known poem is based on the classical theme of *carpe diem* (seize the day – i.e. make the most of your time), a lyric poem in which (usually) a male lover urges his mistress to surrender to his amorous desires before she loses the beauty that makes her attractive to him. The tradition stems from Catullus, a Roman poet of the first century BC (see 'To Lesbia [5]'), but the phrase itself [*carpe diem*] is taken from the final line of a poem by his slightly younger contemporary, Horace – somewhat ironically, in view of the subsequent history of the genre, the poem in question ('To Leuconoë') is more about the uncertainty of the future than about fading beauty. The genre became increasingly popular in the sixteenth and seventeenth centuries, both in France (e.g. the mid-sixteenth-century French poet Ronsard, 'Sonnets pour Hélène [XLIII]', in A. Gide, *Anthologie de la poésie française* [Paris, 1949], p. 64; adapted by Yeats as 'When You are Old' from *The Rose*, 1893) and in England (e.g.

Spenser, 'Fresh Spring, the herald of love's mighty king'; the Clown's song in Shakespeare's *Twelfth Night* (II, iii); also Herrick, 'To the Virgins' [p. 257]).

'To His Coy Mistress' was probably written in the late 1640s. It consists of forty-six iambic tetrameters rhyming in couplets and, like some of Donne's work, forms a sustained argument modelled on classical rhetoric. It is divided into three separate parts, like a syllogism: (1) from line 1: 'Had we but [i.e. If only we had]'; (2) from line 21: 'But'; (3) from line 33: 'Now, therefore'.

Title
Coy shy or modest, often in an affected or irritating manner; ***Mistress*** (a) a woman who has authority or control over another, or is invested with such power by virtue of a man's willingness to subordinate himself to her – a meaning borrowed from the Petrarchan tradition; (b) a woman whom the poet loves – as the context makes clear, they are not 'lovers' in the modern sense.

[1] **Had we but**
'If we only had' – note the irony implicit in the use of the conditional tense; ***world enough*** one of Marvell's most arresting expressions – it means 'sufficient space' in which to do as both partners wanted: one wonders how much 'space' the poet thinks he needs!; ***time*** enough time.

[2] **coyness**
cf. note to title; ***crime*** (a) offence – the word comes from the Latin, meaning 'offence'; (b) offence *against* the poet; (c) an offence that is *punishable*, either by the poet (i.e. he would have no justification for chastising his mistress) or by 'death', where 'die' is slang for sexual union.

[3] **think**
to form or entertain an idea; to imagine, consider.

[4] **walk and pass**
contrasts spending a brief period of time together walking (e.g. in a garden) and a longer period suggestive of a passage (e.g. to a deeper relationship); ***love's day*** (a) loveday (i.e. a day devoted to lovemaking); (b) a day set aside for settling personal disputes – both refer to something specific, thus contrasting with the general concepts of line 1.

[5–6] **the Indian Ganges**
the great sacred river of India, on the banks of which rubies (precious stones) are imagined to lie, for anyone to pick up at will: the image exploits the exotic nature of a river which, to Marvell's readers, would have been as remote as the moon is to a reader in the late twentieth century.

[6–7] **tide/Of Humber**
tide note the use of this word in place of 'banks' – it refers to the ebb and flow of the sea: here, at the estuary of the river Humber, in Yorkshire. The earthy sound of 'Humber' contrasts with the remote and exotic Ganges – the word is, etymologically, related to 'time', and is often used to describe seasonal time; ***complain*** lament, in the sense of 'ardently desire' his mistress while she casually gathers rubies on the other side of the world!

[8] **ten years . . . the Flood**
soon after the initial Creation, God angered by the sinful ways of humankind, caused such heavy rain to fall that all the inhabitants of the earth were drowned in the resulting flood, except Noah, who was ordered to build an 'ark' (boat) in which he, his family, and a male and female of every species of animal and bird survived: see Genesis 6–9: thus, 'ten years' before an almost unimaginably remote, 'legendary' event in the past: note how the exactness of the ten years and the specific biblical event highlight the comic absurdity of the unknown number of years that separate the poet from the 'Flood': one tradition actually dates the Flood as occurring in 1656 *anno mundi* (which has been taken to suggest that the poem was written in 1646).

[9] **if you please**
'but of course, *only* if you wanted to'.

[10] **conversion of the Jews**
according to Christian belief, a remote and improbable event in the distant future, usually thought of as the end of time – note not only the extraordinary hyperbole, but also the tongue-in-cheek gallantry of lines 8–10. The reference may owe something to Cromwell allowing the Jews to come back to England after several centuries of exclusion – a topic of much debate *c*.1653.

[11] **vegetable love**
the word vegetable comes from Latin *vegetare*, meaning 'to animate'; thus, 'love that grows'; there is an implicit reference to the doctrine that the soul had three parts: vegatative, sensitive and rational.

[12] **vaster than . . . more slow**
it is impossible to know which empire Marvell might have had in mind here – most probably the Greek Empire of Alexander the Great (fourth century BC) or the Roman Empire (first century BC – fourth century AD), both of which grew fairly rapidly (in terms of the life of a people) to their maximum extent, then 'slowly' collapsed. The phrase thus carries considerable irony; it may also be an anticipation of a British Empire, for English merchants were trading widely at the time; ***more slow*** this is clearly ironic, but also – in the way it undermines both 'vast empires' and all sense of urgency in the poet's courtship – plain comic.

[13–18] **An hundred years . . . your heart**
this kind of list was called a *blason* (a catalogue of a woman's beauty or most enticing attributes – cf. Donne, 'Elegy 19' [p. 38]: Marvell's lines seem to have been modelled on another poem from Cowley's *The Mistress*: 'The Diet', stanza 3:

On a sigh of pity, I a year can live;
One tear will keep me twenty* at least,
Fifty a gentle look will give†
A hundred years on one kind word I'll feast:
A thousand more will added be,
If you an inclination have for me;
And all beyond is vast eternity.‡

[14] **thine eyes**
traditionally seen as a woman's most enticing attribute: cf. Spenser, *Amoretti*, sonnets 7–10, 12, 16, 17, etc.; ***forehead*** during the Renaissance, the forehead was considered an attribute to be commented on. High foreheads were greatly prized – merely to suggest that someone had a small forehead was an insult.

[15] **breast**
not necessarily an indiscreet anticipation of intimacy – a woman's breast, in seventeenth-century iconography, related her both to Venus, as goddess of beauty, *and* to the Virgin Mary, as an ideal image of nurturing femininity.

[16] **thirty thousand**
the hyperbole is taken to its comic extreme, largely occasioned by the precision of the 'thirty' – chosen, presumably, for its comic alliteration; ***the rest*** deliberately ambiguous: (a) all the woman's other attributes; (b) euphemism (the substitution of an inoffensive word for one which, in certain circles, could cause offence) for the woman's genitals.

[17] **age**
a long period of time, as in 'Golden Age' or 'Ice Age'; ***part*** with the same ambivalence as in the previous line – the part could be an arm, or even only the forearm, but also the woman's 'private parts'.

[18] **last age**
in Christian thought, the last age is life of the just in the heavenly Jerusalem, following the Last Judgement: cf. Revelation 21–2; ***show*** reveal (to me).

[19] **state**
royal treatment, pomp.

[20] **lower rate**
ambivalent: (a) suggests that the poet

* i.e. years
† i.e. to the poet
‡ see line 24 & n.

must meet 'royalty' with 'royal' attention or lovemaking; (b) refers back to 'more slow' in line 12, implying that the best lovemaking is unhurried.

[21–2] **But at my back . . . near**
one of Marvell's most justly celebrated images: ***at my back*** behind me; ***hear*** note the verb, referring presumably to the flapping of giant wings, but also with the suggestion of something heard, behind one, which is frightening; ***Time's wingèd chariot*** the chariot, with wings, in which Time rides: ***chariot*** a two-wheeled vehicle drawn by a horse, used by the Greeks both in warfare and in competition. In the former, the charioteer stood on a small platform and held the reins while a warrior-hero companion attacked everyone in their path with a heavy thrusting-spear; there may also be a reference to the four-horsed chariot of Helios (the Sun), whose passage across the sky each day marks the time of day; ***wingèd*** not literally but metaphorically, meaning driven at great speed, by implication 'towards' the poet, mistress (and reader): a notion borrowed (a) from the Greek, in which 'winged' is often used to mean 'travelling fast'; (b) from the Latin dictum *tempus fugit* (time flies); ***Time*** a common personification, especially popular from the Middle Ages to the eighteenth century: Time = *Chronos* (Greek for 'time') was often confused with *Kronos* (Saturn, in Roman mythology), who was represented in sixteenth-to-seventeenth-century emblem-books driving a chariot and with a scythe (e.g. a mid-sixteenth-century print by Henry Leroy, in which winged dragons are drawing the chariot (in Ripa, *Iconologia*, 1593, Saturn is shown devouring a child); Saturn/Time was usually represented either as an old man or as a skeleton carrying a scythe (an instrument used for cutting hay or dry *grass*: it had a long handle at the end of which was a long, curved and sharp-edged steel blade). Implicit in the emblematic image, as here, is Time imagined in the place of the 'warrior-hero' of classical times, cutting down (as if he were cutting grass) everyone in his path: cf. 'all flesh [i.e. humankind] is *grass*' (Isaiah 40: 6; quoted in 1 Peter 1: 24); also 'as for human beings, their life is like *grass*' (Psalm 103: 15); there is a famous parody of Marvell's lines in T.S. Eliot's *The Waste Land* (1922), lines 196–7.

[23] **yonder**
situated in the direction to which the poet is referring, at some distance; ***all before us*** before all of us.

[24] **deserts of vast eternity**
desert a dry region without vegetation: from Latin *desertus*, meaning utterly abandoned or forsaken; ***vast eternity*** the phrase was probably borrowed from Cowley (see note to lines 13–18 above): the adjective comes from the Latin *vastus*, meaning immense or empty – note how 'deserts' adds substantially to Cowley's phrase, and how the image conflicts with traditional Christian belief in Paradise as a place of leisure and plenty.

[25–6] **Thy beauty . . .**
a reminder of the *blason* in lines 13–18, suggesting: 'Think how much you will lose if you allow your beauty [with sexual innuendo on beauty] to go unappreciated'; ***found*** discovered, penetrated, known (in the biblical sense of 'to be acquainted sexually'); ***thy marbled vault marble*** a hard stone much used by sculptors and architects, partly because it can be smoothed to a fine polish; ***vault*** literally, an arched roof of a building, rounded during classical times, pointed during the Gothic period (twelfth to sixteenth centuries): here (a) the imagined underground grave of the poet's mistress – many families had their own vault or crypt beneath a church; (b) her hard, cold, and dead vagina: cf. line 28.

[25–30]
these lines may refer to an epigram by Aesclepiades: 'You grudge your virginity? What use is it? When you go to

Hades, there will be none to love you there. The joys of love belong to the land of the living, but in Acheron, dear virgin, we shall lie dust and ashes' (*The Greek Anthology*, ed. W.R. Paton, 5 vols, Loeb Classical Library, 1916, I, p. 169).

[27] **My echoing song**
another of Marvell's felicitous phrases: the 'echo' was a popular device in poetry, drama and music, influenced by Golding's translation of Ovid's *Metamorphoses* (1565–7), which includes the story of Narcissus and Echo (book 3): see also Sidney, Philisides' eclogue in *The Old Arcadia* (1580/93: ed. K. Duncan-Jones, 1985, pp. 140–42); Herbert, 'Heaven' (the penultimate poem in *The Temple*, 1633); Act V, scene iii of Webster, *The Duchess of Malfi* (1613); and also Act V of Monteverdi, *L'Orfeo* (1607). In all these a phrase or melody is *echoed* by a second 'voice' – note here how the phrase implies that the 'echo' *should* be coming from the poet's mistress; only secondarily does it apply to the 'dead' echo that might be heard in an underground vault; ***worms*** medieval and Renaissance artists often illustrated worms, especially eating into a skull: the purpose was to remind the viewers of their inevitable death, and thus a warning to turn to God: a fine example is the twelfth-to-thirteenth-century 'Doomsday' mosaic in the Basilica on the island of Torcello in the Venetian lagoon, in which, beneath a representation of the 'lustful' who are condemned to hell, there is a panel of skulls penetrated by snake-like worms; ***try*** test by experiment, i.e. penetrate.

[28] **long-preserved virginity**
note how the phrase refers readers back to 'deserts [places where nothing grows/grows erect] of vast eternity'.

[29] **quaint**
(a) wise, cunning, already an archaism by the seventeenth century; (b) overscrupulous; (c) old-fashioned: it suggests two puns: an alliterative pun on 'coy/coyness' from line 2; and a pun on the Middle English noun 'queynte', meaning a woman'g genitals; ***honour*** (a) high respect paid to someone (cf. the *blason* of lines 13–18!); (b) when used of a woman, chastity, purity, good reputation; but also *mulieris pudenda*: i.e. the woman's genitals; ***dust*** cf. the Lord's punishment of humanity, for eating of the fruit of the Tree of Knowledge of Good and Evil, 'Dust you are, and to dust you shall return' (Genesis 3: 19).

[30] **ashes**
i.e. the ashes from the fire of the poet's passion/lust: cf. 'dust' in the previous line; ***lust*** strong sexual desire or appetite, a passionate longing – *not* necessarily carrying any negative moral implications.

[31] **grave**
the trench in the ground into which a dead person's coffin is placed, but possibly with a pun referring to the 'grave' expression of the coy mistress; ***fine*** notable, excellent (i.e. ironic); ***private*** (a) belonging only to the individual; (b) secluded, secret: again, ironic.

[32] **embrace**
a good example of Marvell's strikingly apt choice of word. 'Embrace' looks like a word with an unambiguous meaning – a moment's reflection will reveal that it is meant in at least five different senses: (a) to put one's arms round another person, as a sign of affection; (b) to accept eagerly an offer or opportunity; (c) to decide upon a course of action; (d) to perceive or intellectually comprehend; (e) to receive something other into oneself: here with obvious sexual innuendo.

[33–4] **youthful glue . . . dew**
the rhyme-words of these two lines have been much debated: ***glue*** the *probable* reading, but none the less a somewhat unusual word with at least two meanings: (a) that quality which attaches an individual to the physical and material world; (b) that quality which holds soul and body together (for an exhaustive analysis of the use of the word, see A.B. Chambers,

Andrew Marvell and Edmund Waller [London, 1991], ch. 2. pp. 15–56); ***youthful*** thus suggests that when a person is young (as the 'mistress' to whom the poem is addressed seems to be), his/her 'glue' is stronger – i.e. they are (a) more attached to the 'physical' world; and (b) more 'whole', in the sense that their body and soul are in greater harmony.

[35–6] **willing soul**
note the poet's assumption that in her essential self, his mistress desires sexual union; ***transpires*** emits through the skin or lungs; e.g. perspiration; ***instant fires*** urgent or pressing fires of passion: note the etymological pun: ***instant*** = *in* + *stare* (Latin) = in + 'stand' (cf. last line of poem): there may be a suggestion that his mistress is 'blushing' with desire (as in Donne's homage to Elizabeth Drury: 'her pure and eloquent blood/Spoke in her cheeks': 'The Second Anniversary', lines 244–5), but if so, it is not explicit.

[37] **let us sport us**
let us play or exercise ourselves: 'sport' was a common euphemism for lovemaking.

[38] **amorous birds of prey**
one of the most striking images in the poem, the first of two distinct and vivid images with which it ends; ***amorous*** loving – a ***bird of prey*** is a hawk, falcon or eagle that feeds on meat, plunging from high in the sky on to small animals such as rabbits or lambs and tearing them to death not only with their long, sharp talons or claws, but also with their hooked beaks; thus lovemaking is likened to attacking an innocent creature with talons and hooked beaks. This image is frequent in alchemy – e.g. Emblem 8 from 'The Book of Lambspring' (1599) in A.E. Waite, *The Hermetic Museum* (1893/1973), I, p. 291; or J.D. Mylius, *Philosophia reformata* (1622), fig. 24; also Arnold of Villanova, *Rosarium philosophorum* (sixteenth century), in which the stage known as 'fermentation' is illustrated by the king and queen making love in a pool of water, wearing their crowns and each with large wings on their backs, signifying volatility.

[39] **our time devour**
note how the idea from the previous line is taken up and reapplied: thus 'preying on [i.e. attacking and eating] one another' = greedily eating time.

[40] **slow-chapped**
a ***chap*** the jaw, especially the lower jaw of a mammal or bird of prey; thus, the ***slow-chapped*** power of time time's slowly devouring action: the phrase may have been derived from Suetonius, *Tiberius*, 21 ('*sub . . . lentis maxillis*') or from Jonson, *Sejanus*, III, i, 485–7 ('between so slow jaws').

[41–2] **Let us roll . . . one ball**
the second of the two images (cf. line 38): the phrase has obvious sexual implications; ***sweetness*** (a) the 'perfume' of their (i) sighs of love (ii) body-odour; (b) sweat; ***ball*** (a) Iago's 'beast with two backs' (cf. Shakespeare, *Othello*, I, i, 118); (b) a pomander (a ball of mixed spices and aromatic herbs, kept in drawers and cupboards to keep clothes fresh-smelling; sometimes, spices stuck into an orange and dried, for the same effect).

[43] **tear**
note the forcefulness of this verb: cf. line 38.

[44] **grate**
(a) irritations: cf. Antony's impatient answer to the messenger in Shakespeare's *Antony and Cleopatra* (I, i, 18); (b) grinding or scraping, implying that life involves toil, with a pun on 'gates of life', an ironic reversal of the phrase 'gates of death'.

[45–6] **make our sun/Stand still**
(a) as Joshua did in the war against the Amorites: 'On that day when the Lord had delivered their enemies into the hands of the Israelites, Joshua spoke with the Lord: "Stand still, O Sun, in Gibeon; stand, Moon, in the valley of Aijalon". So the sun stood still and the moon came to a halt until the Israelites had taken vengeance on

their enemies' (Joshua 10: 12–13); (b) cf. also Lovelace, 'Dialogue: Lucasta and Alexis', lines 29–30; and Psalm 19: 4–5.

[46] **yet we will make him run** perhaps an allusion to Ecclesiastes 1: 5: 'The sun rises and the sun also sets; and then it hastens [literally, 'pants'] to the place from which it arose'; one might add that Ecclesiastes makes much play of the *carpe diem* motif.

---

106 / *The Picture of Little T.C. in a Prospect of Flowers*

See with what simplicity
This nymph begins her golden days!
In the green grass she loves to lie,
And there with her fair aspect tames
The wilder flowers, and gives them names –
But only with the roses plays:
   And them does tell
What colour best becomes them, and what smell.

Who can foretell for what high cause
This darling of the gods was born!
Yet this is she whose chaster laws
The wanton Love shall one day fear
And, under her command severe,
See his bow broke and ensigns torn.
   Happy, who can
Appease this virtuous enemy of man!

O then let me in time compound,
And parley with those conquering eyes
Ere they have tried their force to wound,
Ere, with their glancing wheels, they drive
In triumph over hearts that strive
And them that yield, but more despise.
   Let me be laid
Where I may see thy glories from some shade.

Meantime, while every verdant thing
Itself does at thy beauty charm,
Reform the errors of the spring:
Make that the tulips may have share
Of sweetness, seeing they are fair;
And roses of their thorns disarm;
   But most procure
That violets may a longer age endure.

But O, young beauty of the woods,
Whom Nature courts with fruits and flowers,
Gather the flowers, but spare the buds,
Lest Flora, angry at thy crime
To kill her infants in their prime,
Do quickly make the example yours –
   And, ere we see,
Nip in the blossom all our hopes and thee.

The tradition of poems addressed to a young girl, in which a man has to come to terms with either her future or her already burgeoning sexuality, begins with an epigram by Philodemus, a first century BC poet included in *The Greek Anthology* (see above; V, p. 124). In this six-line lyric, the poet prays not to fall victim to the conflagration that he anticipates the young beauty will cause. At about the same time, the Roman poet Horace also wrote an influential ode addressed to a young girl (II, p. 5): see Leishman (1966), pp. 165–89. The original 'Little T.C.' was very probably a girl called Theophila Cornewall.

The poem, an ambivalent pastoral, is composed of five stanzas rhyming *a b a c c b d d*, made up of eight irregular iambic lines: the first six are tetrameters; the seventh is a dimeter; the last is a pentameter. The first stanza describes a girl gathering flowers in the fields and playing with them. The second and third hypothesise how this same girl is going to behave when she becomes a young woman; the fourth is a tongue-in-cheek compliment; the fifth underlines the moral that has been implicit throughout.

Marvell's work may also be indebted to (a) *Ad Amicam*, a poem which appears in *The Old Couple* (c.1620), a comedy by Thomas May (1595–1650), but which appears to have been known before this. The poet – anticipating Marvell's 'Young Love' – urges a young girl to think herself old enough to love; (b) Thomas Carew's ironic version of the quest for the *summum bonum* (supreme happiness), 'The Second Rapture' (*Poems*, 1640), in which the poet seeks to seduce a thirteen-year-old girl; but also (c) to Benlowes, *Theophila* (1652), an epic in thirteen cantos describing the progress of the soul: see especially IV, 43.

Title

Picture an *imaginary* likeness; ***Prospect*** (a) a mental survey; (b) an extensive view across a landscape or seascape.

[2] **nymph**

literally, a semi-divine female creature

of Greek mythology (e.g. dryads = wood-nymphs); metaphorically, any beautiful young woman; here, clearly a girl rather than a woman; ***her golden days*** 'golden' as in (a) the expression 'golden age', meaning a sustained high point in a nation's development; and (b) Hesiod's myth of the five ages of man: golden or patriarchal (dominated by Saturn), silver or voluptuous (Jupiter), bronze or warlike (Neptune), heroic (Mars), and iron or present age (i.e. seventh century BC): the four later ages were regarded as representing a falling away from the qualities established in the first.

[3] **green**
(a) the colour of the year's new grass in spring, when all vegetation (i.e. life) burgeons anew after the winter months; (b) traditionally identified with Christian 'Hope': a favourite colour of Marvell's: see 'The Garden', line 48.

[4] **her fair aspect**
(a) her beauty; (b) her look or glance.

[5] **wilder**
the adjective implies that Little T.C. is also 'wild', though not necessarily any more so than most children; ***gives them names*** according to the Bible, Adam named the animals (Genesis 2: 19–20), but later tradition ascribed the naming of flowers to Eve.

[6] **But only with the roses plays**
the phrase hints at pride and concern with appearance.

[7] **them does tell**
like a child giving instructions to her dolls; the phrase hints at bossiness.

[8] **What colour . . . smell**
the line is clearly ironic – the colour and smell that best become a rose are its own, not those dictated by anyone else, perhaps least of all a child.

[9] **Who can foretell**
the gentle irony continues.

[10] **darling of the gods**
the phrase may be an indication of the identity of T.C.: Theophila is Greek for 'dear to the gods'.

[11–13] **she whose chaster laws . . . her command severe**
she whose chaster laws T.C. when she becomes nubile, or a young woman – a polite way of saying that she will begin her adulthood by repudiating love. There may also be a reference to Artemis or Diana, the *chaste but severe* virgin goddess of classical Greece and Rome; perhaps especially to (a) the myth of Actaeon, a hunter [see 'bow' in line 14] who happens to see Diana bathing naked, is transformed into a stag, and killed by his own hounds (Ovid, *Metamorphoses*, 3: 138–252); (b) the myth of Adonis, with whom Venus falls in love when an arrow protruding from Cupid's quiver chances to graze her; ignoring her warnings, he goes hunting and is gored by a boar – note that both myths end in tragedy for the male protagonist (*Metamorphoses*, 10.503–739).

[12] **The wanton Love**
Eros [Greek for love between a man and woman] or Cupid [his Latin name], whose behaviour was 'wanton' in at least three senses: (a) capricious, playful, irresponsible; (b) licentious, unchaste; (c) wild, unrestrained: cf. line 5 and note; or a playful personification of an imaginary male lover of T.C. in the future; ***fear*** playful – (a) Eros is *never* depicted as afraid of anything; (b) suggestive of the timidity that the male lover will feel upon approaching someone as special as T.C.

[14] **bow broke**
(a) the bow carried by Eros or Cupid; (b) symbolic of the male lover's attempt to court T.C.; ***ensigns torn*** the banners or flags carried by an army – here, primarily a reference to the hypothetical young man's wounded pride, but there is perhaps also a pun on 'entrails': Actaeon is torn to pieces by his hounds; Adonis is gored by a boar.

[15–16] **Happy, who can**
Happy will he be who can; ***Appease this virtuous enemy of man appease*** note how this refers back to line 4; ***virtuous*** (a) chaste, showing moral rectitude; but punning on (b) etymology

of word: *vir* (Latin) = man: i.e. little T.C. is 'more manly than a man', an 'Amazon'; ***enemy*** (a) a reference to age-old joke that woman is man's enemy (e.g. Donne, 'Elegy 19' (p. 38), lines 3–4); (b) reference to an equally old metaphor in which the process of seduction and lovemaking is depicted in military terms (*ibid.*).

[17] **in time**
before it is too late; ***compound*** come to terms, i.e. with (a) T.C.; (b) the ideas being entertained and developed by the poet.

[18] **parley**
(a) discuss terms (e.g. of ceasefire or treaty) with a hostile force; (b) flirt amorously with someone; ***conquering*** (a) a commonplace – see note on 'enemy', line 16: cf. Sidney, *Astrophil and Stella*, sonnets 40, 42; or 'See how the Tyraness doth joy to see/the huge massacres which her eyes do make' (Spenser, *Amoretti*, sonnet 10, lines 5–6); (b) there may be also a reference to the word's etymology: *con* (with) + *quaerere* (to seek, to obtain by persistence).

[19] **tried**
(a) attempted (by); (b) experimented.

[20] **glancing wheels**
a fantastic double pun: ***wheels*** (a) the orbs or eyeballs; (b) the wheels of a war-chariot; ***glancing*** (a) striking but being deflected by (e.g. an arrow that hits a metal breastplate); (b) cast a momentary look – in both senses, T.C.'s eyes briefly *see* (i.e. perceive) that they are breaking hearts, but pass on 'in triumph'; but note how the notion of 'deflection' gives the conquered man a chance to survive.

[21] **strive**
struggle to resist (her attractions).

[22] **them**
those hearts (i.e. men) who quickly or *willingly* surrender; ***but more despise*** whom (T.C.) despises even more than those who try to resist her.

[23] **Let me be laid**
i.e. like a wounded or dying soldier taken from the immediate field of conflict – note the sudden change to the second person, i.e. the poet is now directly addressing (an imaginary representation of?) T.C.

[24] **glories**
(a) military victories; (b) physical perfections – the image of the male persona watching from the ***shade*** (a) a shaded place of safety; (b) a place where the persona is concealed from the object of his admiration: a further possible reference to the myth of Actaeon and Artemis; (c) because the sunlight that T.C. casts is too bright for him to bear, the poet can 'see' her only from the shade.

[25–6] **while every . . . beauty charm**
while since; ***verdant thing*** (a) green plant or leaf; (b) unsophisticated person; thus 'since every green thing [itself] is charmed [i.e. fascinated, held spellbound] by your beauty'.

[27] **errors**
(a) mistakes; (b) wayward manifestations – e.g. that tulips have no scent, that roses have thorns, and that violets quickly wither.

[28–9] **share/Of sweetness**
may also, like other flowers, give off a sweet scent; ***fair*** beautiful (as is T.C.).

[30] **disarm**
note the return to military imagery: the implication is that T.C. is a 'rose with thorns'.

[31] **procure**
bring about, obtain by care or effort.

[32] **violets . . . endure**
bloom for longer than just a day; note that violets, because they enjoyed such a short period of bloom, were traditionally a symbol of inconstancy – the suggestion is that T.C.'s beauty will last as short a time as the violets.

[33] **beauty of the woods**
refers back to 'nymph' in line 2, likening T.C. to a dryad, i.e. a wood-nymph.

[34] **Nature courts**
an ambiguous phrase: ***courts*** (a) tries to win favour or affection of; (b) tries to attract sexually; (c) unwisely invites: thus 'Nature' refers not only to the flowers of the woods but also, indirectly, to a hypothetical persona such as the poet.

[36] **Flora**
the Roman goddess of flowers; ***crime*** picking flowers when they are still in bud.
[37] **infants**
the buds of flowers: cf. 'the infants of the spring': *Hamlet*, I, iii, 39; ***infants/ prime*** is, of course, an oxymoron, since the prime of life is usually thought to be young adulthood or maturity, but in this poem childhood innocence is celebrated as the high point of human existence because it suggests the state of Eve and Adam before their Fall.
[38] **Do quickly yours**
Do does; ***example*** cutting short the flowers' lives by picking them; ***yours*** i.e. in case Flora decides to punish T.C. in the same way as T.C. is punishing the flowers: by nipping T.C.'s *life* 'in the bud' (see line 40): the line suggests that T.C. should learn to gather what is proper to gather, but beware of nipping anything 'in the bud' – note how this could refer to either present or future carelessness/ cruelty.
[39] **ere we see**
(a) before we know it; (b) before we see T.C. become a young woman.
[40] **Nip . . . and thee**
the subject of ***Nip*** is, of course, Flora; ***in the blossom*** refers to the possibility of T.C. being punished before she blossoms into a mature and beautiful woman. This constitutes another possible clue to the identity of T.C. – the year before Theophila Cornewall was born, her elder sister, also called Theophila, died in infancy; ***our hopes and thee*** note how the poet is most worried about his own hopes – this does not necessarily suggest egocentiricty; it emphasises how highly he regards T.C.

107 / *A Dialogue between the Soul and Body*

SOUL

O, who shall from this dungeon raise
A Soul enslaved so many ways?
With bolts of bones, that fettered stands
In feet, and manacled in hands
Here blinded with an eye, and there
Deaf with the drumming of an ear;
A Soul hung up, as 'twere, in chains
Of nerves, and arteries, and veins;
Tortured, besides each other part,
In a vain head and double heart?

BODY

O, who shall me deliver whole
From bonds of this tyrannic Soul?

Which, stretched upright, impales me so
That mine own precipice I go;
And warms and moves this needless frame
(A fever could but do the same),
And, wanting where its spite to try,
Has made me live to let me die:
A Body that could never rest,
Since this ill spirit it possessed?

SOUL

What magic could me thus confine
Within another's grief to pine?
Where, whatsoever it complain,
I feel, that cannot feel, the pain,
And all my care itself employs,
That to preserve, which me destroys:
Constrained not only to endure
Diseases, but, what's worse, the cure:
And ready oft the port to gain,
Am shipwrecked into health again?

BODY

But physic yet could never reach
The maladies thou me dost teach:
Whom first the cramp of hope does tear,
And then the palsy shakes of fear;
The pestilence of love does heat,
Of hatred's hidden ulcer eat;
Joy's cheerful madness does perplex,
Or sorrow's other madness vex;
Which knowledge forces me to know,
And memory will not forgo.
What but a soul could have the wit
To build me up for sin so fit?
So architects do square and hew,
Green trees that in the forest grew.

Poetic dialogues have a long tradition, both classical and medieval, but this poem differs from most examples of the genre in that Marvell does not allow one side to 'win' the argument or even reveal any kind of superiority over the other.

The poem is in four speeches, the first three of ten lines each, in iambic tetrameters rhyming in couplets. The Body's last speech has four extra lines.

The Soul begins by seeking release from its bondage to the Body; the Body continues by requesting deliverance from the Soul that possesses it; the Soul then lists various ways in which it is made to suffer bodily misfortunes; the Body retorts that only the Soul could lead the Body into such sins as it indulges in.

For an account of the genre, see (a) Leishman (1966), who traces the possible origins of the debate to either 1 Peter 2: 11 or Galatians 5: 16–25, through a late-twelfth-century Latin poem known as *The Royal Debate* and an early-thirteenth-century poem, the first genuine 'dialogue', to Vaughan, 'The Evening Watch' (pp. 209–18); and (b) Rosalie Osmond, 'Body and soul dialogues in the seventeenth century', *ELR*, **4** (1974), 364–403.

[1–2] **dungeon**
(a) literally, a small room, usually underground, used as a prison – note the etymology of the word, which comes from *dominus* = 'lord': i.e. a dungeon, being the means by which a lord retains his power, is not only synonymous with 'lord', but also the emblem of his tyranny; (b) figuratively – the Body in which the Soul is imprisoned; and perhaps also hell, to which Christ descends for three days following his crucifixion; ***raise*** suggestive of Christ's resurrection: cf. '[Christ] was crucified, died, and buried; He descended into hell. The third day he *rose* again from the dead' (the Creed, *Book of Common Prayer*); ***enslaved*** (a) imprisoned, but also (b) subject to a superior quality, in the ways listed in the following lines.

[3] **bolts**
a kind of door-lock with a sliding bolt of metal – here, used figuratively, of 'bones': i.e. the bones of the Body keep the Soul in its prison.

[3–4] **that fettered stands/In feet**
fetters metal rings fastened round the ankles of prisoners; here, the Soul is 'fettered' in *having* feet – i.e. the fact of having feet *implies* being fettered: note the appropriateness of the verb ***stands***, meaning (a) not moving, or not being able to move; (b) attending on, implying forced into attendance on (the Body); ***manacled*** metal rings fastened round wrists; here, the fact of having hands implies being manacled.

[5] **blinded with an eye**
another paradox: the Soul is 'blinded' by the sense of sight.

[6] **Deaf with . . . an ear**
drumming here, what the ear hears – i.e. the same idea as the previous line.

[7] **hung up**
suspended; ***as 'twere*** as it were, so to speak; ***chains*** a reference to the practice of binding serious criminals in chains and suspending them above the ground, either for a set time or until they died.

[8] **Of nerves . . . veins**
the Body's vital passageways are 'chains' that keep the Soul suspended in torture – the image of the Soul 'suspended' and suffering may owe something to the late medieval practice of emphasising Christ's veins and bleeding wounds in illustrations of the crucifixion.

[9] **besides each other part**
not only in the head and heart (see the following line), but in all other parts of the Body as well.

[10] **vain**
(a) useless; (b) conceited; ***double*** (a) literally, because the heart is composed of two ventricles; (b) figuratively, duplicitous, double-dealing, hypocritical.

[11–12] **O, who shall . . .**
an ironic reversal of Romans 7: 24: 'O wretched man that I am! who shall deliver me from the body of this death?'; ***whole*** entirely healthy (i.e. both in body and in spirit: cf. John 5: 6, 14).

[13] **stretched upright**
(a) the Soul is stretched upright (towards God), because the Body stands erect; ***impales*** transfixes a body with a stake – i.e. the Soul is imagined as a stake to which a prisoner is tied, especially before execution by burning.
[14] **mine own precipice**
a man is in constant danger of falling to his death, as if over a cliff, both literally and metaphorically – cf. previous line, note; also a reference to the view that it was the soul that allowed a person to walk upright.
[15] **warms . . . frame**
the Soul 'warms' and 'moves' the Body; but if the Body had no soul, it would have no needs, i.e. want nothing (be 'needless').
[16] **fever could but**
a fever or sickness would, equally well, both 'warm' the Body and cause it to 'move' about restlessly.
[17] **wanting where its spite to try**
spite malice towards someone, grudge, ill will: thus, forever wanting to discover new ways of being malicious.
[18] **Has made me live to let me die**
a play upon a Christian commonplace that a person needs to 'die' to the world in order to 'live' in union with God: cf. Donne, 'Death, be not proud' (p. 76).
[19] **rest**
rest content: cf. Herbert's play with the word 'rest' in 'The Pulley' (p. 235).
[20] **ill spirit**
the Soul – note the irony of describing the Soul in this fashion; ***possessed*** i.e. took possession of the Body.
[21–2] **What magic . . . to pine**
referring back to the notion of possession by a demon, the Soul imagines itself suffering as a result of magic – i.e. in a manner similar to the way in which Ariel is held captive by Prospero's 'art' in *The Tempest*: the verb 'pine' is thus a play on the noun used by Shakespeare when Prospero reminds Ariel how Sycorax caused the latter to be confined 'into a cloven pine' (I, ii, 274–7); thus ***another's grief*** (a) the Body's grief (i.e. unhappiness caused by the misfortunes of life); (b) Prospero's grief.
[23–4] **whatsoever . . . the pain**
whatever the Body suffers is also, paradoxically, felt by the immaterial ('cannot feel') Soul.
[25–6] **And all my care . . . destroys**
i.e. the Soul devotes all its concerns to preserving the Body from harm, but the Body, by indulging its sensual appeties, leads the Soul into mortal (deadly or destroying) sin.
[27–8] **Constrained . . . cure**
constrained (a) irresistibly urged; (b) forcibly confined or imprisoned – thus, the Soul is compelled to suffer not only the effects of the Body's diseases, but also the cure – worse because restoration to health (a) compels the Soul to suffer further indignities as the Body continues with its worldly concerns; (b) postpones the Soul's release from the body (see the following lines).
[29–30] **ready oft . . . again**
the port (i.e. harbour) = death – i.e. the Soul welcomes sicknesses that give it a 'hope' of dying; ***shipwrecked into health*** a paradox, perhaps adapting the final lines of Agrippa d'Aubigné, 'L'Hiver' (in André Gide, ed., *Anthologie de la poésie française* [Paris, 1949], pp. 189–90): the Soul seeks death, because it finds life constricting; thus anything that keeps it alive is a calamity or (in terms of the Petrarchan metaphor of life as a sea-journey) a shipwreck: note how this reverses the implicit 'reversal' in line 18 (spoken by the Body), yet finds a new expression for a commonplace.
[31–2] **But physic . . . teach**
physic the science of medicine; ***maladies*** sicknesses – i.e. there are no names for the sicknesses for which the Soul is responsible, as described in the following lines.
[33] **cramp**
(a) painful involuntary contraction; (b) restraint; (c) a metal bar with bent ends used for holding masonry – ***hope*** is usually unbounded; i.e. what we

hope for is limitless: thus, note the paradox 'cramp of hope'; ***tear*** either tear apart or tear asunder.

[34] **palsy**
a sickness producing an utter helplessness together with involuntary tremors or trembling (understood at the time to be a kind of paralysis); ***shakes*** can function either as part of a compound substantive or an unusually placed verb (the palsy of fear shakes ... – cf. comparable word order in lines 36 and 38): i.e. the Soul causes the Body to shake with the palsy of fear.

[35] **pestilence**
plague, especially the bubonic plague that periodically spread through Europe; thus, the Body affirms that it is the Soul which causes love, defined as a kind of plague.

[36] **hatred's hidden ulcer**
the hidden ulcer of hatred: thus, the Soul feeds on the invisible ulcer of hatred.

[37] **madness**
insanity, extravagance – 'cheerful madness' is a paradox; ***perplex*** confuse or confound – thus, the Soul dispels the cheerfulness of joy, which is defined as both temporary insanity and inappropriate behaviour.

[38] **sorrow's other madness**
the other madness of sorrow; ***vex*** (a) to anger, irritate or emotionally disturb; (b) to grieve or afflict – 'sorrow/vex' is thus paradoxical.

[39–40] **Which knowledge ... forgo**
forgo let go, relinquish – i.e. knowledge leads to sorrow that can never be forgotten: cf. the Greek maxim that knowledge is suffering.

[41] **but**
if not – i.e. 'only a soul could ...'; ***wit*** intelligence, quality of mind, ability.

[42] **build me up**
create, restore; ***fit*** = well suited.

[43] **So**
in the same way; ***square*** to make a round tree trunk or 'log' into a square-ended beam, post or plank; ***hew*** to cut down (a tree): note the deliberate paradoxical inversion of 'hew' and 'square'. The final couplet suggests that the Soul destroys the Body in the same way as people destroy nature – the problem lies in deciding whether Marvell is being literal or ironic.

108 / *Bermudas*

Where the remote Bermudas ride,
In th'ocean's bosom unespied,
From a small boat that rowed along,
The listening winds received this song:

'What should we do but sing his praise
That led us through the wat'ry maze
Unto an isle so long unknown,
And yet far kinder than our own?
Where he the huge sea-monsters wracks,
That lift the deep upon their backs,
He lands us on a grassy stage,
Safe from the storms and prelate's rage.

He gave us this eternal spring
Which here enamels everything,
And sends the fowls to us in care
On daily visits through the air.
He hangs in shades the orange bright
Like golden lamps in a green night,
And does in the pomegranates close
Jewels more rich than Ormus shows.
He makes the figs our mouths to meet
And throws the melons at our feet,
But apples plants of such a price,
No tree could ever bear them twice.
With cedars, chosen by his hand,
From Lebanon, he stores the land,
And makes the hollow seas that roar
Proclaim the ambergris on shore.
He cast – of which we rather boast –
The Gospel's pearl upon our coast,
And in these rocks for us did frame
A temple, where to sound his name.
O let our voice his praise exalt
Till it arrive at heaven's vault
Which, thence (perhaps) rebounding, may
Echo beyond the Mexique Bay.'

Thus sung they in the English boat
A holy and a cheerful note,
And all the way, to guide their chime,
With falling oars they kept the time.

An allegorical poem of forty iambic tetrameters rhyming in couplets. In July 1653 Marvell became tutor to William Dutton and, while at Eton, he lived in the house of John Oxenbridge. Oxenbridge was a Puritan clergyman who, following persecution by Archbishop Laud in 1634, made two visits to the Bermudas, where he also served for some time. Marvell was very probably told about the Bermudas by Oxenbridge.

The poem is in three parts: a four-line introduction describing a small boat; a central section of thirty-two lines consisting of the song sung by the sailors on the boat, in which the Bermudas are represented as an earthly Eden; and a conclusion, again of four lines.

Bermuda is the island on which the *Sea Adventure*, together with Sir Thomas Gates and Sir George Summers, was shipwrecked in 1609.

News of this quickly reached England and stimulated the publication of several pamphlets on which Shakespeare drew for *The Tempest* (1611). When it was learned that the crew had all survived and been rescued, reports began to describe the Bermudas as an earthly paradise. Parts of this poem are modelled on a poem by Waller called 'Battle of the Summer [i.e. Summers] Islands' (1645).

[1] **Bermudas**
islands in the West Indies, now called Bermuda, 'discovered' by Juan Bermudez in 1515: they were often referred to as an earthly paradise in the early seventeenth century; ***ride*** (a) float; (b) be at anchor (like a ship).

[2] **th'ocean's bosom**
in the midst of the ocean, distant from land; ***unespied*** (a) unseen; (b) unknown.

[3–4] **From a small boat . . . song**
This image plays with two traditions: (a) in Homer's *Odyssey*, Odysseus is advised that if he wishes to sail past the Sirens safely he must plug his men's ears with wax and have himself tied to the mast so that he is not seduced by the charm of their voices; (b) in Petrarchan lyrics, a man's life is often likened to a ship sailing through 'storms' (cf. line 12), until he can reach the 'port' or harbour that the love of his mistress represents; note that a pamphlet of 1613 describes a party of men led by Richard More rowing to the Bermudan shore while singing a psalm of praise (cf. lines 39–40); ***rowed*** note the play between active (the boat rows) and passive (implicitly, was rowed by sailors on the boat); ***listening winds*** not only a personification, but a similar *reversal* of an active (i.e. the sailors who were singing) and a passive agent (the winds, who are invested with active listening).

[5–36]
The sailors' song recalls the 'song of praise' sung by Moses and the children of Israel to celebrate their delivery from the Egyptians: 'I shall sing to the Lord, for he has . . . shown himself to be my redeemer. In thy unfailing love you [= the Lord] have guided your people to your holy land' (Exodus 15: 1–18).

[5] **his**
this, paradoxical though it might seem, is the crux of the poem: (a) Christ; (b) God; (c) Moses.

[6] **maze**
this word may be intended to recall the Israelites' wanderings after leaving Egypt on their way to the Promised Land: 'But God led the people about, *through* the way of the wilderness of the Red Sea' (Exodus 13: 18).

[7] **isle**
island, here, an image of a terrestrial paradise, a new Promised Land.

[8] **kinder**
(a) more benign; (b) more natural; the phrase recalls the persecution of Puritans for their religious belief.

[9] **sea-monsters**
(a) literally whales – possibly suggested by Waller's poem; (b) figuratively, the leviathan [= lit. 'that which twists or coils round']: recent scholarship suggests that the leviathan is a crocodile; but it is also a 'serpent' (cf. Isaiah 27: 1): it represented the chaos and evil that was overcome by God; (c) life's monstrous troubles and burdens; ***(he) wracks*** Christ/God (a) destroys; (b) punishes.

[10] **lift the deep . . . backs**
the image is derived from (a) the way in which whales periodically blow water (the deep, i.e. the sea) through a spout (nose) on the upper side of their heads; (b) from illustrations of such 'sea-monsters' in the corners of seventeenth-century maps, in which they seem to 'carry' the entire world – it is difficult to be certain what lines 9–10 imply.

[11] **grassy stage**
the grass suggests peace and luxuriance; the stage could be (a) an altar; (b) a stage of life; (c) perhaps also Mount Ararat, on which Noah's ark is reputed to have finally settled (cf. Genesis 6–9).

[12] **the storms and prelate's rage**
storms (a) literal storms, which threatened the boat; (b) the storms of life – a Petrarchan conceit; ***prelate*** (a) Archbishop William Laud, the High Church Anglican who persecuted the Puritans; (b) the Pharaoh of Ancient Egypt who sought to pursue the Israelites as they endeavoured to cross the Red Sea (Exodus 14).
[13] **eternal spring**
(a) a time of constant reburgeoning of life, after the cold and harsh conditions of winter (i.e. difficulties); (b) an eternal Easter; i.e. the Resurrection of Christ.
[14] **enamels**
colours brilliantly: e.g. the springtime flowers.
[15] **fowls**
birds, cf. the biblical phrase 'the fowl of the air' (Genesis 1: 26); ***in care*** refers to Adam being given use of [and, by extension, also 'care of'] every living being and plant (Genesis 1: 24–30).
[16] **daily visits**
these visits recall the dove that Noah released in order to see whether the flood that had destroyed the whole world had abated. On its second release, the dove returned with an olive leaf in its bill (Genesis 8: 11).
[17–28]
these lines are clearly derived from Waller's poem: see I, 6–11.
[17] **in shades**
the shady places beneath the overhanging trees; ***orange*** the fruit – in Europe, in Marvell's time, still a rare and exotic delicacy.
[18] **green night**
i.e. the grove of orange trees: cf. 'The Garden' (p. 499), especially stanza 5.
[19] **pomegranates**
a fruit of an evergreen tree native to North Africa, about the size of an apple. It has a tough outer skin of a rich orange colour, but is famous for the bright-red pulp surrounding the numerous seeds which are neatly arranged, as if in a piece of jewellery; ***close*** enclose (the seeds).
[20] **Jewels**
figuratively, because of the bright ruby-red pulp and seeds; ***Ormus*** Hormuz, in the Persian Gulf, famous both for precious perfumes (e.g. myrrh and frankincense) and jewellery (e.g. rubies).
[21] **figs**
soft, purple-skinned and pear-shaped fruit native to the Middle East; they were found by the advance party sent by Moses into Canaan and thus symbolise the Promised Land, a paradise here on earth (Numbers 13: 23; cf. also 1 Kings 4: 25); ***makes . . . to meet*** cf. 'The Garden', lines 35–6 and note, where the vines crush their juice against the poet's mouth.
[22] **throws**
casts carelessly to the ground; ***melons*** the word 'melon' comes from the Greek word for 'apple' and thus involves a deliberate juxtaposition of these two fruits in lines 22–3; the melon grows on or close to the ground.
[23] **apples**
probably a 'pineapple', even though pineapples do not grow on trees; but the choice of word recalls 'the fruit of the Tree of Knowledge of Good and Evil' eaten by Eve, which is traditionally identified as an apple (largely because of the analogous translations of Latin *malum* (= both apple *and* bad or evil); cf. also the Song of Songs, where the bridegroom is likened to an 'apple tree among the trees of the wood', i.e. of outstanding beauty (2: 3). Both images suggest something unique – but note that the apple that grows in a temperate climate does not grow well either in the Middle East or in the West Indies: the biblical apple probably describes an apricot; ***plants*** a transitive verb, whose subject is still 'he' and whose object is 'apples'; ***price*** (a) value, worth; (b) something that must be given, done or sacrificed in order to obtain something else – cf. 'For you are bought with a price: therefore glorify God . . .' (1 Corinthians 6: 20).

[24] **No tree . . . twice**
the apple Eve ate was also unique.
[25] **cedars**
tall evergreen coniferous trees with hard and fragrant wood, considered to be very valuable – they grow in Lebanon; they are also traditionally associated with death: cf. the story of Osiris, whose coffin was thrown into the river; later it was washed up near Byblos and came to rest in a cedar (some accounts give heather); ***chosen*** invests the cedars with value by insisting on them having been selected.
[26] **stores**
(a) to place in a location with thought to eventual use; (b) to fill.
[27] **hollow**
fathomless.
[28] **Proclaim**
(a) to make known, announce publicly; (b) extol the virtues of; ***ambergris*** a strong-smelling waxlike emission of the sperm whale, often found floating in tropical seas; it was (and still is) used to make perfume.
[29] **cast**
to throw carefully (cf; line 22 and note).
[30] **Gospel's pearl**
the wisdom of the Gospel (i.e. message) – cf. Christ's parable of the pearl: 'Here is a picture of the kingdom of heaven. A merchant was looking for pearls. One day he came across a very special but very expensive one, so he sold everything and bought it' (Matthew 13: 45–6); cf. also the Gnostic 'Hymn of the Pearl' in Hans Jonas, *The Gnostic Religion* (Boston, MA, 1958/63); pearls grew plentifully in the Red Sea, among rocks.
[31] **in**
(a) among; (b) with; ***frame*** build.
[32] **temple**
(a) the pearl of great price; (b) a holy building used for worship; ***sound*** (a) pronounce as in prayer; (b) sing; (c) bear witness to.
[33] **our**
the sailors; ***exalt*** raise, enhance, glorify.
[34] **it**
the song or hymn of praise; ***heaven's vault*** the rounded ceiling of heaven, i.e. the endless sky.
[35] **Which**
the song or hymn of praise; ***thence*** from heaven's vault; ***perhaps*** indicates the impossibility of some ***rebounding*** (i.e. echoing back from) an endless sky/heaven.
[36] **beyond the Mexique Bay**
Bermuda is situated in the Gulf of Mexico; but figuratively the phrase suggests that the song will convert pagans and Roman Catholics on the mainland of Central Mexico.
[39–40] **to guide . . . time**
chime (a) the ringing of a bell announcing a festivity; (b) the song of the sailors; ***falling*** (a) literally falling into the water and rising again; (b) refers to musical cadence: i.e. a 'downbeat'; ***kept the time*** i.e. musical time: note how the phrase inverts one's expectations – usually one would row in time to one's singing rather than row in time to a song.

109 / *The Nymph Complaining for the Death of Her Fawn*

The wanton troopers riding by
Have shot my fawn and it will die.
Ungentle men! They cannot thrive
To kill thee: thou ne'er didst, alive,
Them any harm. Alas! Nor could
Thy death yet do them any good.
I'm sure I never wished them ill,
Nor do I for all this nor will.
But if my simple prayers may yet
Prevail with heaven to forget
Thy murder, I will join my tears
Rather than fail. But, O my fears!
It cannot die so. Heaven's king
Keeps register of everything,
And nothing may we use in vain.
Even beasts must be with justice slain,
Else men are made their deodands.
Though they should wash their guilty hands
In this warm life-blood (which doth part
From thine, and wound me to the heart!)
Yet could they not be clean: their stain
Is dyed in such a purple grain,
There is not such another in
The world to offer for their sin.
  Unconstant Sylvio, when yet
I had not found him counterfeit,
One morning (I remember well),
Tied in this silver chain and bell,
Gave it to me – nay, and I know
What he said then, I'm sure I do.
Said he, 'Look how your huntsman here
Hath taught a fawn to hunt his *dear*.'
But Sylvio soon had me beguiled:
This waxed tame, while he grew wild
And, quite regardless of my smart,
Left me his fawn, but took his heart.
  Thenceforth I set myself to play
My solitary time away
With this – and very well content

Could so mine idle life have spent.
For it was full of sport, and light
Of foot and heart, and did invite
Me to its game. It seemed to bless
Itself in me: how could I less
Than love it? Oh, I cannot be
Unkind t'a beast that loveth me.
  Had it lived long, I do not know
Whether it too might have done so
As Sylvio did: his gifts might be
Perhaps as false or more than he.
But I am sure, for aught that I
Could in so short a time espy,
Thy love was far more better than
The love of false and cruel men.
  With sweetest milk and sugar first
I it at mine own fingers nursed.
And as it grew, so every day
It waxed more sweet and white than they.
It had so sweet a breath! and oft
I blushed to see its foot more soft
And white . . . shall I say than my hand? –
Nay, any lady's of the land.
  It is a wondrous thing how fleet
'Twas on those little silver feet!
With what a pretty skipping grace
It oft would challenge me the race,
And when it had left me far away,
'Twould stay, and run again, and stay.
For it was nimbler much than hinds,
And trod, as on the four winds.
  I have a garden of my own
But so with roses overgrown
And lilies that you would it guess
To be a little wilderness,
And all the springtime of the year
It only loved to be there.
Among the beds of lilies, I
Have sought it oft where it should lie,
Yet could not, till itself would rise,
Find it, although before mine eyes.
For in the flaxen lilies' shade

It like a bank of lilies laid.
Upon the roses it would feed
Until its lips ev'n seemed to bleed,
And then to me 'twould boldly trip
And print those roses on my lip.
But all its chief delight was still
On roses thus itself to fill,
And its pure virgin limbs to fold
In whitest sheets of lilies cold.
Had it lived long, it would have been
Lilies without, roses within.
  Oh help! Oh help! I see it faint
And die as calmly as a saint!
See how it weeps: the tears do come
Sad, slowly dropping like a gum.
So weeps the wounded balsam, so
The holy frankincense doth flow.
The brotherless Heliades
Melt in such amber tears as these.
  I in a golden vial will
Keep these two crystal tears, and fill
It till it do o'erflow with mine,
Then place it in Diana's shrine.
  Now my sweet fawn is vanished to
Whither the swans and turtles go,
In fair Elysium to endure
With milk-white lambs and ermines pure.
Oh, do not run too fast, for I
Will but bespeak thy grave, and die.
  First, my unhappy statue shall
Be cut in marble, and withal,
Let it be weeping too – but there
Th'engraver sure his art may spare.
For I so truly thee bemoan
That I shall weep, though I be stone,
Until my tears, still dropping, wear
My breast, themselves engraving there.
Then at my feet shalt thou be laid,
Of purest alabaster made –
For I would have thine image be
White as I can, though not as thee.

The tradition of humorously solemn poems on the death of a favourite pet goes back to classical times (Catullus, on the death of Lesbia's sparrow, I.3; Ovid, on the death of Corinna's parrot, *Amores*, II.6). John Skelton's *Philip Sparrow*, in which Jane Scroupe, a young woman of about sixteen, mourns the death of a sparrow killed by a cat, was a more immediate influence.

Marvell's poem has an unusually high percentage of monosyllables; it really captures the language of a child – yet it reaches much deeper than is usual in the genre, which tends to be sentimental. Indeed, it is so heavily laden with religious imagery that one can only wonder at the craftsmanship that made such a sustained argument possible: it almost requires a fresh memory of the Song of Songs from the Bible to appreciate the imagery.

The poem has 122 lines of iambic tetrameters, rhyming in couplets. It is divided into eleven verse paragraphs of different length; the first announces the subject; the second introduces a parallel event, the inconstancy of the nymph's lover, who is called Sylvio; the third to seventh (line 92) recount the happy life of the fawn; the eighth to eleventh tell of the fawn's death and the nymph's sorrow.

It is more than usually difficult to be certain to what extent this poem should be read as an allegory. There can be no doubt that its imagery is consistently based on religious imagery, but this only highlights the problem.

1. The imagery (especially lines 71–92) is derived more from the Song of Songs than from any other book of the Bible – i.e. from a book regarded more highly by Roman Catholics than by Protestants, let alone Calvinists/Puritans such as Marvell: the Song of Songs (*c.*930 BC) is a dramatic poem attributed to Solomon; although it seems to describe the very passionate sexual love between a Bride and Bridegroom, in the Christian tradition the work is usually interpreted as a mystical work about (a) the love of Christ (the Bridegroom) and the Church (the Bride); or (b) the love between the individual and his soul; a great many alchemical texts from the twelfth or thirteenth century onwards borrow their imagery from it, notably the influential thirteenth-to-fifteenth-century *Aurora Consurgens* (ed. M.-L. von Franz, New York, 1966); it is probable that Marvell's references to the Song of Songs owe more to alchemical works than to the Bible.

2. Despite the consistency of the religious references, it is difficult to form any clear idea of the allegorical implications of the initial situation – i.e. of a young woman, who has been deceived by a lover and is lamenting the death of a fawn killed by passing strangers: the intensity of the poem suggests an emblem. It may owe something to the story of Cyparissus (i.e. Cypress), sung by Orpheus after his loss of Eurydice. A stag with a silver collar set with precious stones, considered sacred by the nymphs, was especially loved by a young man called Cypress. One day, practising with his javelin, he accidentally killed the stag, which was sleeping in the shade of a tree, and begged Apollo, who loved him dearly, to let him weep for ever, and so he was changed into a Cypress tree. As Orpheus sings his story, the surrounding trees, amongst which were many cypresses, begin to move closer (*Metamorphoses*, 10.86–142).

Title

Complaining lamenting, mourning.

[1] **wanton**

capricious, careless, without motive, sportive, unrestrained, even immoral; ***troopers*** this word was first used to describe the army of the Scottish Covenanters which invaded England in 1640 to support the establishment of Presbyterianism in England; it was soon applied to Parliamentarian mounted troops.

[3–4] **Ungentle**
rough, cruel, noisy, ill-mannered, immoderate, not gentlemanly, with a pun on 'un-Gentile', i.e. the Jews; ***cannot thrive/To kill*** cannot hope to prosper by killing.
[4] **alive**
the nymph is addressing her fawn: thus, 'You never did the troopers any harm when you were alive.'
[5–6] **nor could . . . any good**
good (a) bring about any 'good' for the troopers; (b) blessing, in a religious sense – thus, an oblique reference to necessary sacrifice: i.e. Iphigenia was sacrificed so that the Greek army could obtain a favourable wind and so sail for Troy, where they hoped to recover Helen; Christ died to save humankind; the death of the fawn is no such death.
[7] **ill**
harm.
[8] **for all this**
in spite of what the troppers have done; ***will*** i.e. nor will she wish the troopers harm at any time in the future.
[9–10] **But**
an emphatic 'And'; ***Prevail*** (a) persuade (heaven to forget [i.e. excuse] the troopers); (b) gain mastery or supremacy over (i) 'heaven' [note the irony implicit in this meaning]; (ii) 'the world' [in its religious sense]; (c) death, represented by the death of the fawn, a reminder of the nymph's own mortality – note also how the lines remind one of Christ's similar willingness to forgive: on the Cross he said: 'Father, forgive them, for they do not know what they are doing' (Luke 23: 34).
[11] **join**
add (tears to her prayers), to enforce her request: note how the 'tears' recall the tears of Christ's mother as *mater dolorosa* [sorrowful mother]: thus what Christ is to his mother, so the fawn is to the nymph.
[12] **fail**
i.e. fail in the endeavour of getting heaven to 'excuse' the troopers for their act; ***fears*** fears for the troopers.
[13] **It**
ambivalent: (a) the fawn; (b) the nymph's plea; ***so*** i.e. with the murder forgotten or unavenged by heaven, in accordance with the nymph's prayer; ***Heaven's king*** either God or Christ.
[14] **keeps register**
maintains a record (especially of a company's 'credits' and 'debits'), implying that no evil action can be so easily forgotten.
[15] **use in vain**
do or *kill* without good reason.
[16] **Even beasts . . . slain**
'One must have a good reason for killing even animals.'
[17] **Else men . . . deodands**
a ***deodand*** an object or animal forfeited to the crown because it has been the cause of someone's death; thus 'Otherwise men would become forfeits [i.e. something surrendered to another as a penalty for a wrong committed]'; ***their*** ambiguous: (a) refers back to 'heaven's king'; (b) refers to subject of previous clause, i.e. beasts: thus, if men kill for no reason, there is no reason why they should not be given as penalty to animals (i.e. for the animals to eat); (c) perhaps also refers to 'men': i.e. men themselves must punish those who kill, even accidentally.
[18–21] **Though they . . . be clean**
they the troopers; ***wash*** one usually washes one's hands in water; to wash them in blood is a sign of guilt. There may be a reference to Pontius Pilate who, having tried to persuade the Jews to request that he release Jesus, agreed to release the revolutionary leader Barabbas as the crowd demanded: 'so he took some water and washed his hands in full view of the people, saying, "My hands are clean of [Christ's] blood; his death is your concern". And the people shouted back, "Let his blood be on us and on our children"' (Matthew 27: 24–5); ***life-blood*** (a) the blood flowing from the fawn, but note how the previous image equates the death of the fawn with the death of Christ:

thus also (b) the blood of Christ – cf. '[Let this] blood of our Lord Jesus Christ, which was shed for you, preserve your body and soul for everlasting life' (Holy Communion, *The Book of Common Prayer*); ***doth part*** is separated and goes in a different direction – i.e. the blood flowing from a wound is 'leaving' its proper channel; ***wound me to the heart*** i.e. the parting of the 'life-blood' wounds the nymph, just as Christ's death 'wounds' every Christian.

[21] **Yet could they not...**
'But even so they could not clean their hands in this way' – the idea behind the image of washing in blood (in lines 18–21) is, of course, expiation: one would expect 'washing' (in the sense of spiritually renewing oneself) in Christ's blood to expiate any guilt – but as line 21 makes clear, the crime of killing something as 'unique' as the fawn/Christ puts one (almost?) beyond redemption; ***stain*** the stain of blood on the troopers' hands.

[22] **purple**
a royal colour, thus reinforcing the parallel with Christ; ***grain*** (a) colour; (b) a bright-red dye made from the dried bodies of either of two different insects [kermes or cochineal]; (c) nature, fashion, kind.

[23] **such another**
another fawn like mine; the uniqueness of the fawn is one of its defining characteristics – Christ, too, was the 'only Son of God'.

[24] **their sin**
(a) the murder of the fawn by the troopers; (b) the sins of humankind expiated by Christ's death: thus, the troopers have killed the only thing that could have redeemed the sin they committed by killing the fawn.

[25–6] **Sylvio**
a common name in pastoral poetry – it comes from Latin *sylva* (a wood, forest). In terms of the poem's religious meaning, he may represent the Jews; ***when yet/I had not*** before I had; ***counterfeit*** (a) referring to money or a written document, not genuine, a fraudulent imitation; (b) referring to a person, someone whose aspirations for something are based on falsity: thus, 'discovered that Sylvio was not faithful or sincere in his professions of love'.

[28] **Tied in**
Attached together with; ***chain... bell*** a chain fastened around the fawn's neck, with a bell fastened to it so that the 'nymph' could know where it was by the tinkling noise made whenever the fawn moved.

[29–30] **nay, and... I do**
the negative suggests the humility of the 'nymph', even regarding a matter about which she is absolutely certain.

[31] **huntsman**
cf. the Lord's promise: 'I will send for many huntsmen, and they shall hunt the Israelites out from every mountain and hill and crevice in the rocks... I will first make them pay in full for the wrong they have done [i.e. in 'falling away' from worship of the Lord]' (Jeremiah 16: 16–18): note also the story of a Roman soldier called Eustace, who was addicted to hunting – one day, the stag he was chasing turned, 'and when he looked upon it carefully, he saw between its antlers a holy cross... and on it the image of Jesus Christ'; the Italian artist Pisanello painted this scene about 1440 (in the National Gallery, London), and Dürer made an engraving of it (*c.*1501: in the British Museum, London); a similar story is told about St Hubert (illustrated by the 'Master of the Life of the Virgin', a late-fifteenth-century German artist; also in the National Gallery, London); one of the medieval stories of the 'Grail Legend' tells us that Christ would occasionally appear to his disciples as a stag (cf. *Le Saint Graal*, ed. Hucher, 1874–8, III, 219, 224): the origin of such legends may lie in the association of the stag's antlers with the 'Tree of Life'.

[32] **fawn**
(a) literal; (b) Christ: both Origen, an early 'Father' of the Christian Church (early third century) and St Bernard

(an eleventh-century Frenchman) describe Christ as a 'fawn'; ***dear*** (a) darling [i.e. the nymph]; (b) deer, the female of a stag: a common pun in pastoral poetry (cf. line 36); (c) Christ.

[33] **beguiled**
(a) charmed; (b) deluded, cheated.

[34] **This**
the fawn; ***waxed*** grew; Sylvio grows ***wild*** in the sense that he deserts not only the nymph, but also the fawn: this may refer to the Jews turning their back on Christ who was, of course, born a Jew.

[35] **smart**
the nymph's pain.

[36] **heart**
(a) love; (b) hart: i.e. his masculine attention – another common pun; cf. lines 32, 37; ***Thenceforth*** from then on.

[38] **solitary time**
the young nymph is likened to a nun – there may be an implied pun, given that the poem most probably belongs to the period Marvell spent in relative isolation at Nun Appleton.

[39] **this**
the fawn, as an image of Christ: cf. 'Then I [i.e. Wisdom] was at [the Lord's] side each day, his darling and delight, playing in his presence continually, playing on the earth, when he had finished it, while my delight was in humankind' (Proverbs 8: 30).

[41] **sport**
fun, i.e. amusing actions.

[43–4] **It seemed . . . in me**
bless (a) attribute good fortune to; (b) sanctify: thus, the fawn seemed to (a) find joy in the nymph's company; and (b) become more holy as it became more precious to the nymph.

[46] **Unkind**
According to Genesis, human beings are made in God's image – thus, the phrase refers not only to the kindness with which one treats an animal, but also to moving away from one's own essential nature (i.e. kind).

[48–9] **. . . done so/As Sylvio did**
left the nymph, in the same way as Sylvio did.

[49–50] **his gifts**
the joy and contentment which the fawn gave to the nymph; ***he*** Sylvio – note how the hypothesis is entertained, but only to be rejected.

[51–2] **sure**
note how the nymph's reluctance to be overcertain serves to strengthen the impression of her conviction; ***for aught . . . espy aught*** anything; ***short a time*** i.e. between the fawn being given to the nymph and the troopers killing it; ***espy*** see; thus, 'if I can judge by all that I was able to observe in so short a time'.

[53] **Thy**
the fawn's; ***better*** cf. 'Your love is better than wine' (Song of Songs 1: 2), where, according to Christian tradition, 'your' is the bridegroom, i.e. Christ.

[54] **false and cruel men**
(a) the troopers who were 'false' to themselves in killing the fawn; (b) the Jews who were 'false' to the truth of the Gospel in calling for the death of Christ; (c) all lukewarm Christians at the time when Marvell was writing.

[55–6] **With sweetest milk . . . nursed**
the nymph nurses the fawn with her own fingers – the image suggests the Virgin feeding the Christ child; ***sugar*** (a) synonymous with human kindness; (b) implies the 'sweetness' (i.e. agreeableness) of the Gospel message.

[58] **waxed**
grew; ***white*** the fawn in its whiteness resembles the white unicorn – cf. the story of the unicorn which goes back to the Spanish writer Isidore of Seville (died 636) and probably earlier:

There is an animal called . . . a unicorn. It is a small animal, like a kid, but exceedingly fierce, with one horn in the middle of its head. No huntsman is able to capture him, and yet he may be captured in this way: men should lead a virgin to where he has been seen and leave her in the forest alone. As soon as the unicorn sees her, he will spring into her lap and embrace her. In this way he can be taken captive and shown to kings. Thus Our Lord Jesus Christ, the spiritual unicorn, descended into the womb of the Virgin . . . he was captured by the Jews, etc. (a ninth-century work called *Physiologus*)

See the two series of late-fifteenth-century tapestries which illustrate this theme: (a) *The Lady and the Unicorn* (Cluny Museum, Paris); (b) *Hunt of the Unicorn* (Metropolitan Museum, New York); ***they*** the nymph's fingers.

[59] **sweet a breath**
i.e. such a comforting spiritual message.

[60] **foot**
this emphasis on the *softness* of the foot may be a way of *contrasting* the meekness of the fawn/Christ with two biblical passages: (a) 'Think how severe a penalty that man will deserve who has trampled under foot the Son of God' (Hebrews 10: 29: cf. the troopers' action); (b) the Lord, as a blood-covered warrior: 'I have trampled my enemies down in my rage' (Isaiah 63: 3 – cf. the meekness of the fawn, i.e. Christ, the Son of the Lord).

[61] **white . . . hand**
signal the gentleness and innocence of the nymph/Virgin.

[62] **Nay, any**
Nay, than any.

[63] **fleet**
fast and sure-footed.

[64] **'Twas**
It [the fawn] was.

[65] **skipping grace**
cf. the Bride's words: 'See! here comes my beloved, bounding over the mountains, leaping over the hills. My beloved is like a gazelle or a young wild goat' (Song of Songs 2: 8–9).

[66] **race**
cf. 'we too, then, should cast off everything that weighs us down including the sin that clings to us closely, and start on the race that stretches ahead of us with our eyes fixed firmly on our goal, Jesus, who directs our faith and will bring it to perfection' (Hebrews 12: 1–2).

[67] **far away**
far behind.

[68] **'Twould stay . . . stay**
It would stop [allowing the nymph to catch up], then run on again, and stop again: illustrative of the way in which the Christian can never, so to speak, 'catch up with' Christ.

[69] **much**
far; ***hinds*** fully grown female deer.

[70] **trod**
ran; ***as on the four winds*** foúr two syllables (cf. Marvell, 'Upon Appleton House', line 323) – i.e. ran as if carried upon the four winds, or very swiftly; there may be an oblique reference to the four evangelists (Matthew, Mark, Luke and John), who transmitted the 'word' (i.e. life-giving spirit) of God.

[71] **a garden of my own**
a reference to the *hortus conclusus* of the Bridegroom's words: 'My sister, my bride, is an enclosed garden [*hortus conclusus*] with a fountain sealed' (Song of Songs 4: 12); i.e. the Bride's charms are 'closed' to all except the Bridegroom (i.e. Christ). In medieval Christian iconography, the Bride was equated with the Virgin Mary – thus, here, the nymph.

[72] **roses . . . lilies**
roses and lilies were a frequent way of describing a young woman's beauty: e.g. 'The rose and lily in each cheek' (quoted in Leishman [1966], p. 171); but here: ***roses*** (a) a traditional emblem of the Virgin Mary, e.g. as the *rosa mystica* (mystical rose): cf. the Bride's claim: 'I am the rose of Sharon, and the lily of the valley' (Song of Songs 2: 1); but also (b) sinners, in the sense that Christ is continually assuming humankind's sins in himself; ***lilies*** innocence associated with (a) the Virgin Mary; (b) Christ; (c) primordial innocence: cf. 'Consider the lilies in the fields: they neither have to work [as Adam had to] nor spin [as Eve had to]' (Matthew 6: 28).

[73] **it**
the garden.

[74] **wilderness**
a Garden of Eden – i.e. a place in

which Adam and Eve still did not have to work, and therefore 'not cultivated': cf. 'Sharon has become like a wilderness' and 'Let the wilderness and the solitary places be glad; let the desert rejoice and blossom like the rose' (Isaiah 33: 9; 35: 1).

[75] **springtime**
the time of regeneration, of Easter.

[76] **It**
the fawn; ***there*** the garden; the peculiar syntax of this line emphasises the 'only'.

[77] **lilies**
cf. the Bride's words: 'My love [the bridegroom, i.e. Christ] is mine and I am his. He pastures his flocks among the lilies' (Song of Songs 2: 16): lilies are white, a colour traditionally associated with (a) the (spiritual) whiteness of Christ's body; (b) Christian 'Faith'.

[78] **sought . . . lie**
looked for the fawn, in order to see where the fawn might be lying: cf. 'Seek, and you will find . . .' (Matthew 7: 7; Luke 11: 9).

[79] **could not**
because the fawn is as white as the lilies.

[80] **before mine eyes**
right in front of me.

[81] **flaxen**
the pale yellow shadow cast by the white lilies.

[82] **It like . . . laid**
It lay like a bank of lilies.

[83] **roses . . . feed**
difficult – possibly (a) feeding on the virtues associated with the Virgin Mary: constancy, fidelity, chastity, etc.; (b) feeding on the 'sins of the world' (cf. John 1: 29).

[84] **Until . . . bleed**
Until its lips almost seemed to bleed – the literalness of the image makes it difficult to grasp its metaphorical meaning: it might refer (a) to the blood that is often shown as dripping from the corner of Christ's mouth in some Baroque paintings and painted crucifixes; (b) the wine left on the lips of anyone partaking in the Mass or Holy Communion.

[85] **then to . . . trip**
then it would come (step) nimbly or lightly towards me.

[86] **print . . . lip**
i.e. get the nymph to share the burden of the fawn's passion: red represents charity as *caritas*, passionate love between an individual and God/humankind.

[87] **But all its chief delight**
And yet the thing it enjoyed the most: Duncan-Jones (ed., 1971) has noted that fawns really do like to eat rose petals: this suggests that Marvell might have based his poem on a scene he had witnessed.

[88] **On roses . . . fill**
emphasises that Christ's task was to take humankind's burden on his shoulders; only secondarily did he endeavour to get humanity to share it with him.

[89] **virgin limbs**
limbs the fawn's legs, but treated as if they were *arms* with which to embrace a female fawn; ***virgin*** unacquainted with love between the male and female of its species; ***fold*** envelop, enfold.

[90] **whitest sheets of lilies**
cf. 'The reign of the Lord, our God Almighty, has begun. Let us rejoice! His bride [i.e. the Church] is ready, and she has dressed herself in dazzling white linen, because her linen is made of the good deeds of the saints [i.e. believers]' (Revelation 19: 8); the phrase may also be an allusion to white as the colour of Faith – i.e. instead of embracing a young female, the fawn delighted to wrap itself in its own Faith.

[92] **Lilies without, roses within**
cf. the Bride's description: 'My beloved is fair [i.e. white] and ruddy [i.e. healthily red-cheeked, etc.].' (Song of Songs 5: 10); ***Lilies***, here the body; ***roses*** blood (i.e. the blood of Christ's Passion).

[93] **faint**
breathe its last gasp.

[94] **die . . . saint**
cf. Donne, 'A Valediction: Forbidding Mourning' (p. 52), lines 1–2.

[95] **weeps**
cf. 'Then, being in an agony, he prayed more earnestly, until his sweat turned to drops of blood that fell on the dry ground' (Luke 22: 44 – cf. also Matthew 26 and Herbert, 'The Agony' [p. 197]); also: 'During his life on earth, Christ prayed loudly and with tears to the one who had the power to save him from death' (Hebrews 5: 7).
[96] **Sad, . . . a gum**
sad here, in an unusually forceful sense, suggestive of Christ's agony rather than just a downcast expression; ***gum*** (a) sap or resin that drips from a tree (e.g. a balsam tree); (b) frankincense (see line 98) or myrrh (a gum from a tree found in the Near East, used in incense and perfumes).
[97] **so**
just as, in the same way; ***balsam*** a tree which, when 'wounded' by a knife, exudes a fragrant resin.
[98] **frankincense**
an aromatic gum or resin that comes from various East African trees and is used for its fragrance or for medicinal purposes.
[99–100] **The brotherless Heliades . . . amber tears**
Heliades daughters of Helios (the sun): after the death of Phaëthon, his sisters were turned into poplar trees and their tears into amber (see Ovid, *Metamorphoses*, 2.340–66).
[101] **vial**
a cylindrical glass bottle used (a) for collecting precious liquids or, (b) in Roman times, for collecting tears so that one can give or send them to another person as a sign of one's feelings – cf. the praise of the Lamb the Redeemer: '. . . the four living creatures and the twenty-four elders fell down before the Lamb [i.e. Christ]. Each of the elders had a harp, and they held golden vials [i.e. bowls] full of incense, the prayers of God's people, and they were singing . . .' (Revelation 5: 8); cf. also the prayer of lament: 'Record my lament in your book, O Lord, and store every one of my tears in your vial' (Psalm 56: 8).
[104] **Then place it in Diana's shrine**
Diana (Roman equivalent of Greek Artemis) – the goddess of chastity, as well as being a huntress, and thus also goddess of hunting; she was also the goddess of childbirth, and there may be a further reference to the desired 'new birth' as a spiritual being sought by the offering.
[106] **Whither**
to the place where [i.e. death in Elysium]; ***swans*** because the swan is reputed to sing only once in its life, when it is on the point of death (hence 'swan song'), it signifies the complete satisfaction of a desire equivalent to Simeon's prayer after seeing the Christ child: 'Lord, now let your servant die in peace, as you promised, for I have seen your salvation' (Luke 2: 25–35); ***turtles*** turtledoves – because turtledoves are always seen in pairs, they are age-old symbols of fidelity in love (cf. 'the time of the singing of birds is come and the voice of the turtle is heard in our land': Song of Songs 2: 12); turtledoves were used in sacrifice – e.g. the sacrifice offered to the Lord for the Virgin Mary's 'purification' following the birth of Christ (Luke 2: 24); note the closeness of the two biblical references.
[107] **Elysium**
In Greek mythology, almost all souls went to Hades, an underworld, after death; the only exceptions were those who were fortunate enough to be allowed to go to the Elysian Fields, the classical equivalent of heaven; perhaps more specifically, the heaven of shepherds and shepherdesses in Renaissance pastoral poetry – the word 'elysium' means 'happy, delightful'.
[108] **milk-white lambs**
a traditional symbol of innocence and purity: e.g. (a) Christ, as 'Lamb of God, who takes away the sins of the world' (John 1: 29); (b) the opening of Spenser's *Faerie Queene*, I, i, where Una leads a white lamb as an emblem of her purity; ***ermines*** a weasel whose

winter coat is white; its fur is used in Europe for decorating official robes. Ermine fur on a judge's robe stands for the 'purity' of judicial office.

[109] **run too fast**
hurry so fast to Elysium/heaven.

[110] **bespeak**
(a) arrange for; (b) announce the need for; ***grave*** suggestive of the tomb in which Christ's body was laid for three days, during which time he 'descended into hell'; ***die*** (a) literal death; (b) the 'death to the world' of ecstasy produced by contemplation of the divine.

[111] **unhappy statue**
a statue of the nymph weeping – i.e. of a young *mater dolorosa*; cf. Michelangelo's *Pietà* (a statue of a *young* woman holding in her arms the dead Christ [who was about thirty-three years old at the time] stretched across her knee), in St Peter's, Rome.

[112] **withal**
in addition.

[113] **Let it be weeping too**
(a) recalls the fate of Niobe, who was slain by the arrows of Diana and Apollo for her excessive pride in her children; but also (b) recalls Mary Magdalene, after Christ's entombment – cf. 'and Mary stood outside the tomb, weeping' (John 20: 11).

[114] **Th'engraver . . . spare**
i.e. there is no need for any stonemason to engrave my name on the pedestal of the statue.

[115] **so truly thee bemoan**
mourn so deeply and sincerely for the fawn.

[116] **stone**
i.e. even though the nymph will be a stone statue, she so deeply laments the fawn that the stone itself will weep – note the important pun: 'stone' = (Latin) *petra*: i.e. 'Peter', the 'Rock' on which the Church was built (Matthew 16: 18), where the Church is also Christ's 'Bride' (e.g. in Christian interpretation of The Song of Songs).

[117–18] **wear/My breast**
wear down or make furrows in my breast, as the drops of water erode the stone; ***themselves engraving there*** the tears will leave a permanent record of themselves on her breast, i.e. in her heart (the breast is the seat of the heart and affections) – a further suggestion of the *mater dolorosa*.

[119] **at my feet**
suggestive of the imagery of the tapestries of the *Lady and the Unicorn*, in which the Lady sits with a white unicorn at her feet.

[120] **alabaster**
a very white marble – i.e. the nymph will erect a statue of the dead fawn.

[121] **would have**
(a) would like; (b) will insist that.

[122] **White as I can**
(a) as white as I can get the stonemasons to find; (b) as white [innocent, morally spotless] as I am able to be; ***though not as thee*** (a) cf. 'Can a mortal man be more righteous than God, or the creature purer than his Maker?' (Job 4: 17) – the answer, clearly, is no: i.e. the nymph remains humble to the end; (b) though she is not sufficiently deluded to think that the image could be whiter than the fawn itself.

110 / *The Mower Against Gardens*

Luxurious man, to bring his vice in use,
  Did, after him, the world seduce
And from the fields the flowers and plants allure,
  Where Nature was most plain and pure.
He first enclosed within the garden's square
  A dead and standing pool of air,
And a more luscious earth for them did knead,
  Which stupefied them while it fed.
The pink grew then as double as his mind:
  The nutriment did change the kind.
With strange perfumes he did the roses taint,
  And flowers themselves were taught to paint.
The tulip, white, did for complexion seek
  And learned to interline its cheek.
Its onion root they then so high did hold
  That one was for a meadow sold.
Another world was searched, through oceans new,
  To find the *Marvel of Peru*.
And yet these rarities might be allowed
  To man, that sovereign thing and proud,
Had he not dealt between the bark and tree,
  Forbidden mixtures there to see.
No plant now knew the stock from which it came:
  He grafts upon the wild the tame,
That the uncertain and adult'rate fruit
  Might put the palace in dispute.
His green seraglio has its eunuchs too,
  Lest any tyrant him outdo,
And in the cherry he does Nature vex,
  To procreate without a sex.
'Tis all enforced, the fountain and the grot –
  While the sweet fields do lie forgot:
Where willing Nature does to all dispense
  A wild and fragrant innocence,
And fauns and fairies do the meadows till,
  More by their presence than their skill.
Their statues, polished by some ancient hand,
  May to adorn the gardens stand:
But howsoe'er the figures do excel,
  The gods themselves with us do dwell.

In the posthumous first edition of Marvell's poems, there is a series of four consecutive poems about a 'mower'. Although they seem to read as a sequence, whether they were designed as such and whether the sequence of four is complete is not known. This is the first: it has forty iambic lines of alternating pentameters and tetrameters, rhyming in couplets. Although it belongs generally to the pastoral tradition, in which praise of moderation, modelled on Horace, is the standard theme, here the poet urges a complete abandonment of ornamentation and a reversion to simple country life, and meditates on the ways in which cultivation has destroyed the characteristics of plants and trees in their natural state.

At a literal level, this is a poem about a garden; but it can also be seen as a reflection of Marvell's Puritan sympathies. The Puritans sought simplicity not only in religion, but also in 'manners' – i.e. in everyday behaviour: the irony of this is that it was the severity of their so-called 'work ethic' that led to England's economic growth during the seventeenth century – i.e. to a materialist society in which 'ornament' is highly prized.

Marvell's pastoral and lyric poems often borrow from Pliny's *Natural History*. Pliny 'The Elder' (AD 23–79) was a soldier and administrator of the Roman empire who wrote a great many works, but only his long *Natural History* (finished 77 AD) has survived: it is an encyclopaedia of knowledge of the time, describing customs, attitudes and beliefs under some 20,000 headings. Despite its evident confusion of fact and mythology, it was regarded as an 'authority' throughout the Renaissance. Marvell seems to have known it well; his references often come from either books 12–19, which cover botany, or books 20–27, which discuss the medical attributes of plants. Pliny was often regarded as 'a martyr to Nature and the study of Nature' as he died while trying to discover the reason for the cloud of ashes that was followed, a few days later, by the eruption of Vesuvius which buried Pompeii and Herculaneum (near present-day Naples, in southern Italy). The *Natural History* was translated by Philemon Holland (1601/1635): references here are to the more standard text.

Title
Mower someone who cuts grass; in temperate climates such as that of England, the grass grows very fast in the spring and early summer. During the months of May, June and perhaps early July, farmers periodically cut the grass in their meadows and let it dry as 'hay', which can then be kept and used as fodder for cows, etc., during the long winter months; thus a ***mower*** is a farm labourer who cuts the grass in a meadow with a scythe – one of the simplest of farm duties; but note the biblical implications: cf. 'all humankind is grass' (Isaiah 40: 6); remember also that 'Time' is usually personified as an old man or skeleton holding a scythe (see 'To His Coy Mistress', lines 21–2 and note); ***Against*** a diatribe or forceful verbal attack on; ***Gardens*** the kind of highly 'artificial' garden common in the seventeenth century – typically a blend of formal walkways decorated with plants as exotic as the owner could afford and a 'kitchen garden' in which the gardener would endeavour to grow as many different kinds of fruit and vegetables as the local climate allowed; cf. Francis Bacon's essay on 'Gardens' in *Essays* [1597/1625] ('World's Classics', 1937/66, pp. 187–95), which mentions an astonishing number of trees, plants and flowers; also John Dixon Hunt's article on gardens in Marvell, in Patrides, ed. (1978), pp. 331–51.

[1] **Luxurious**
lecherous, voluptuous: probably occasioned by Pliny: 'The invention to have gardens within a city came up

first with Epicurus, the doctor and master of all voluptuous idleness' (19, iv); note that grass, in May, grows almost too quickly – cf. Hamlet's rising indignation as he watches Claudius at prayer: 'He took my father grossly, full of bread,/With all his crimes full blown, as flush as May' (the irony of this phrase, which suggests that Hamlet's father had an overabundance of crimes on his conscience, is not noted as often as it should be: *see Hamlet*, III, iii, 81); ***man*** Adam (see following line); ***bring his vice in use*** (a) cause his vice to be practised by others; (b) establish his vice as a custom.

[2] **Did, after... seduce**
seduce corrupt, cause to 'fall' in the biblical sense; ***after him*** is syntactically ambivalent – thus, (a) Adam, having been seduced into temptation by Eve, corrupted the world and caused others to fall likewise; (b) Adam corrupted those who came after him.

[3] **allure**
i.e. did *allure* (a) tempt or entice; (b) attract by means of personal charm; note the pun: Eve both 'tempted' Adam *and* attracted him by her personal charm – Marvell suggests that Adam 'tempted' or 'attracted by means of his charm' the fields to deck themselves with flowers and plants.

[4] **Where Nature... pure**
Where Nature, hitherto, had been both plain and pure – i.e. without the kinds of flowers and plants grown in gardens at the time of Marvell, breeds which were the result of considerable cultivation.

[5] **garden's square**
the area enclosed as a garden, with a possible suggestion that such geometric shapes are unnatural; some editors argue that garden is plural (gardens' square), but this would not greatly alter the sense.

[6] **dead... air**
the suggestion is that air enclosed by the walls of a garden will grow stale in the same way as a pool or pond will stagnate.

[7] **luscious**
(a) rich; (b) cloying, voluptuous – i.e. as Eve appeared to Adam after he had eaten the fruit of the forbidden tree; ***knead*** work clay or moist flour with the fingers to a desired consistency: in the second of the Genesis creation myths, Adam was made from clay or 'the dust of the ground' (Hebrew *adam* = man; *adamah* = ground or soil – Genesis 2: 7).

[8] **which... it fed**
stupefied made stupid, deprived of sensation; ***them*** refers to 'flowers and plants' in line 3; ***it*** refers to the earth; thus: 'which caused the flowers to lose their [natural] properties while the earth became yet more "luscious" [and lascivious] as a result of feeding on their waste'.

[9] **The pink... his mind**
pink pink blooms or flowers; ***grew double*** prospered in outward appearance – where a flower or plant originally had only one flower per stem, cultivation had given it two; ***as his mind*** duplicity, no longer 'at one' with nature and God – note how this undermines the previous clause.

[10] **nutriment**
(a) the earth; (b) the 'double-headed' pink flowers; ***kind*** (a) the nature of the flowers – i.e. creating new species, etc.; (b) the nature of the soil – i.e. enriching/denaturalising it.

[11] **strange**
(a) alien, i.e. not naturally pertaining to the roses; (b) peculiar or eccentric; ***taint*** (a) to dye or tinge with colour; (b) slightly affect or alter; (c) to introduce corruption.

[12] **paint**
i.e. to wear cosmetic 'make-up', with the implication that make-up is not only unnatural, but also cheapens – i.e. whores wear make-up.

[13–14] **The tulip... its cheek**
in the 1630s there was a fashion for tulips, so gardeners sought to produce tulips of ever more exotic colours; ***white*** originally white; ***for complexion seek*** seek to have its cheeks 'interlined' with, or painted with 'lines'

of different colours (cf. line 12 and note).

[15–16] **onion root . . . sold**
onion root a tulip grows from a 'bulb' (i.e. a round root shaped rather like an onion, which also grows from a bulb) in the spring, and withdraws into it again after its period of blooming; ***so high did hold*** during the 1630s, enormous sums were paid for tulip bulbs; ***meadow*** i.e. a whole meadow was paid for a single bulb – remember that a mower works in a meadow.

[17–18] **Another world . . .** *Marvel of Peru*
Another world i.e. the 'New World', the American continent, from which merchants were introducing into Europe previously unknown species of plants and flowers – e.g. the potato, a tubular root, was brought back from America in the late sixteenth century; ***oceans new*** oceans hitherto little known by European navigators and merchants – in this context, the Atlantic, but given that the specific instance cited in line 19 is only an example, also the Pacific and Indian oceans; ***Marvel of Peru*** a brightly coloured plant [*Mirabilis Jalapa*] found in the West Indies: i.e. the New World.

[19] **rarities**
plants and flowers hitherto little known to Europeans; ***allowed*** given to man for him to enjoy.

[20] **that sovereign thing and proud**
God gave Adam *dominion* over all animals and 'living things', i.e. also plants (Genesis 1: 28) – but note ***thing***, applied to man, which undermines 'sovereign', and ***proud*** points also to 'vain' i.e. 'empty'.

[21] **dealt between**
performed the office of go-between or pander between a man and woman; here, introduced illicitly; ***between the bark and tree*** (a) where one places the stem of a plant which one wants to graft on to another; and (b) a proverbial expression often used in the seventeenth century to refer to interference between a man and his wife – i.e. two entities which should remain inseparable.

[23] **Forbidden mixtures**
i.e. bringing two different species of plants together by means of grafting – possibly based on Pliny's disapproval of interfering with nature by overuse of grafting (15, xv); it may also refer to Mosaic law ('You shall not allow two different kinds of beast to mate together. You shall not plant your field with two kinds of seed': Leviticus 19: 19; cf. Deuteronomy 22: 9).

[23] **stock**
a felicitous choice of word: (a) a plant into which a graft is inserted; (b) line of ancestry; (c) the trunk of a tree.

[24] **He**
the gardener; ***wild*** a wild plant; ***tame*** a cultivated plant – cf. 'All trees that are tame . . . may well be grafted into stocks of the wild' (Pliny, 17, xv).

[25] **uncertain and adult'rate fruit**
the product of such grafting – ***uncertain*** because it is a 'new' species, hence its qualities – e.g. of endurance, etc. – cannot be known; ***adult'rate*** because it is the fruit of 'wild' and 'tame' flowers.

[26] **palace**
(a) the residence of a king or queen; (b) the whole court; ***dispute*** i.e. everyone would be arguing about the merits of a 'new' species.

[27] **seraglio**
(a) enclosure, i.e. walled garden; (b) harem, i.e. the (green) plants and flowers are the gardener's wives; ***eunuchs*** Turkish sultans employed eunuchs to look after their wives, for obvious reasons; here, the 'eunuchs' are presumably the gardener's assistants.

[28] **tyrant**
i.e. another gardener; ***outdo*** by producing an even more amazing bloom.

[29–30] **And in . . . a sex**
vex puzzle in a disturbing or embarrassing manner; ***procreate*** produce offspring; ***without a sex*** possibly a reference to a ***stoneless*** cherry, as 'stone' = testicle; thus, 'by producing

a cherry tree the fruit of which has no stones, man threatens the reign of Nature'.
[31] **enforced**
(a) the product of art, not natural – i.e. the fountains are artificial, so too are the grottos or caves created by landscape gardeners; (b) ravished, raped.
[32] **sweet**
(a) pleasant-smelling; (b) pleasant to be in; ***forgot*** ignored by man.
[33] **Where...**
i.e. in the natural fields, or wild meadows; ***willing*** always ready to help, foster or encourage; ***all*** all plants.
[34] **wild... innocence**
'wild' flowers; 'innocent' (a) etymologically, *unharmed (by man)*; (b) uncontaminated by any wrong – note the paradox wild/innocent.
[35] **fauns... till**
fauns rural deities worshipped by country people in Roman times – they had a human face and chest, and a goat's body, legs and horns on top of an otherwise human head; ***fairies*** tradition maintained that fairies were natural gardeners; ***till*** to prepare land for cultivation – cf. *before* the Fall: 'The Lord God having made earth and heaven, there were initially neither shrubs nor plants growing wild upon the earth, for God had not sent any rain, and nor was there a man to *till* the ground' (Genesis 2: 5); *after* the Fall: 'the Lord God drove Adam out of the garden of Eden to *till* the ground from which he had been taken' (Genesis 3: 23): cf. line 7, note.
[36] **presence... skill**
i.e. where fauns and fairies 'are', the ground is ready for cultivation; where they are not, humankind has to work.
[37] **Their statues**
the statues of fauns and fairies in the Mower's garden: it was common to have such statues in a garden in the seventeenth century; ***ancient hand*** (a) a Roman sculptor – i.e. many such statues had been brought back from Rome by young noblemen returning from the so-called Grand Tour round Europe, a normal part of a young man's education at the time; (b) the hand of God (i.e. the rain).
[38] **May to... stand**
(a) may serve to adorn gardens; (b) may embellish gardens so that they look superior.
[39] **howsoe'er... excel**
no matter how much the natural fauns and fairies do excel the statues.
[40] **gods... dwell**
ambivalent: (a) fauns/fairies, i.e. gods in the sense of beneficent powers; (b) fauns/fairies, i.e. gods in the sense of jealous or malevolent powers that will punish man if he does not pay them due respect; perhaps also (c) the gods of classical Greece and Rome.

111 / *The Mower to the Glow-Worms*

Ye living lamps, by whose dear light
The nightingale does sit so late
And, studying all the summer night,
Her matchless songs does meditate!

Ye country comets, that portend
No war nor prince's funeral,

Shining unto no higher end
Than to presage the grass's fall!

Ye glow-worms, whose officious flame
To wand'ring mowers shows the way,
That in the night have lost their aim
And after foolish fires do stray,

Your courteous fires in vain you waste,
Since Juliana here is come:
For she my mind hath so displaced
That I shall never find my home!

This is the third of the 'mower poems'. The second, 'Damon the Mower', consists of the mower's song about how Juliana has wounded him – a theme referred to in the last stanza of this, the following poem, which is the shortest in the sequence.

The poem has five stanzas, each of which is composed of four iambic tetrameters and rhymes *a b a b*. Note the double incongruity: the disparity between the rustic mower and the sophistication of his thoughts, and the contrast between the theme and its undermining in the final stanza.

Title
Glow-Worms small flying insects, the rear part of whose bodies emits a surprisingly bright light.
[1] **living lamps**
glow-worms.
[2] **nightingale**
a small reddish-brown bird of the thrush family, celebrated in European literature because, during the spring and early summer, the male sings its richly melodious song at night.
[3] **studying**
devoting time and attention – Holland's translation of Pliny uses the verbs 'study and meditate' about the young nightingale learning to sing.
[4] **matchless**
exceptional, without equal; ***meditate*** think upon, plan, execute.
[5] **country comets**
the glow-worms, likened to 'comets' because of their tail; the phrase wittily joins the local and familiar with the otherworldly; many country people at the time believed that comets were a sign of an imminent disaster; ***portend*** foreshadow, anticipate, give warning of.
[6] **Nor . . . funeral**
Neither a war, nor (even) a prince's funeral.
[7] **unto**
for; ***end*** purpose.
[8] **to presage the grass's fall**
presage foreshadow, anticipate, give warning of; Pliny, in the *Natural History*, notes that the time when glow-worms shine coincides with the time of year when grass is mown or cut.
[9] **officious**
(a) efficacious, zealous, attentive; (b) serving a necessary 'office' or function; ***flame*** the light of the glow-worm is seen as the 'fire' of a torch.
[10] **wand'ring**
(a) walking idly; (b) crazy, lunatic – i.e. the light of the glow-worms provides a 'torch' which the poet uses to see where he is going.
[11] **night**
the night was a traditional image for

(a) ignorance; (b) having 'lost one's way' in life – cf. 'If a man chooses to walk at night, he will stumble, because he has no light to see by' (John 11: 10); ***lost their aim*** (a) lost their way; (b) forgotten what their purpose was in being out at night.

[12] **foolish fires**
a loose translation of the Latin phrase *ignis fatuus* used to describe the phosphorescent light that hangs over a marsh: i.e. something responsible for deluding or misleading – thus also 'foolish fires' of love; ***stray*** (a) wander, chase; (b) deviate in moral purpose.

[13] **courteous**
considerate, in that they provide the mower with light; ***in vain*** to no purpose.

[14] **Juliana**
the name of the mower's beloved; ***here is come*** has moved to the neighbourhood in which the mower lives.

[15] **displaced**
removed something (here, the mower's mind) from its proper place or function – i.e. driven the mower crazy.

[16] **home**
(a) literal 'home'; (b) figuratively, peace of mind, sanity.

112 / *The Garden*

How vainly men themselves amaze
To win the palm, the oak, or bays,
And their uncessant labours see
Crowned from some single herb or tree
Whose short and narrow vergèd shade
Does prudently their toils upbraid,
While all flowers and all trees do close
To weave the garlands of repose!

Fair Quiet! Have I found thee here?
And Innocence? – thy sister dear!
Mistaken long, I sought you then
In busy companies of men.
Your sacred plants, if here below,
Only among the plants will grow:
Society is all but rude
To this delicious solitude!

No white nor red was ever seen
So am'rous as this lovely green!
Fond lovers, cruel as their flame,
Cut in these trees their mistress' name:
Little, alas, they know, or heed,

How far these beauties *hers* exceed!
Fair trees! Wheres'e'er your barks I wound,
No name shall but your own be found!

When we have run our passion's heat,
Love hither makes his best retreat.
The gods, that mortal beauty chase,
Still in a tree did end their race:
Apollo hunted Daphne so,
Only that *she* might laurel grow,
And Pan did after Syrinx speed,
Not as a nymph, but for a reed!

What wondrous life is this I lead!
Ripe apples drop about my head;
The luscious clusters of the vine
Upon my mouth do crush their wine;
The nectarine and curious peach
Into my hands themselves do reach;
Stumbling on melons as I pass,
Ensnared with flowers, I fall on grass!

Meanwhile the mind, from pleasure less,
Withdraws into its happiness:
The mind, that ocean where each kind
Does straight its own resemblance find;
Yet it creates, transcending these,
Far other worlds and other seas,
Annihilating all that's made
To a green thought in a green shade.

Here at the fountain's sliding foot,
Or at some fruit-tree's mossy root,
Casting the body's vest aside,
My soul into the boughs does glide.
There like a bird it sits, and sings,
Then whets, and combs its silver wings;
And, till prepared for longer flight,
Waves in its plumes the various light.

Such was that happy garden-state,
While man there walked without a mate:
After a place so pure and sweet,
What other help could yet be meet!
But 'twas beyond a mortal's share
To wander solitary there:
Two paradises 'twere in one
To live in paradise alone!

How well the skilful gardener drew
Of flowers and herbs this dial new,
Where from above the milder sun
Does through a fragrant zodiac run
And, as it works, the industrious bee
Computes its time as well as we.
How could such sweet and wholesome hours
Be reckoned but with herbs and flowers!

Besides Francis Bacon's essay on 'Gardens', contemplative poems on rural peace and solitude were popular in the seventeenth century – e.g. those by James Shirley and Abraham Cowley, both of which extol the virtue of withdrawal from the world. M.-S. Røstvig has convincingly argued that Marvell's poem also belongs to the tradition of the *beatus ille*, in which a sophisticated, educated man seeks the peace of rural obscurity (see *The Happy Man*, Oslo, 1962).

This poem in nine stanzas of eight iambic tetrameters each, which rhymes in couplets, has usually been assigned to about 1650, while Marvell was working for General Fairfax; but Allan Pritchard has recently argued that it was written after the Restoration. Marvell also wrote a Latin version of it which omits (or now lacks) stanzas 5–8: it is not known which he composed first.

The first two stanzas contrast the busy world with the quiet and solitude found in a garden; the third reflects on the poet's love of trees; the fourth and fifth reveal the charms of a garden for a life of retirement; the sixth and seventh, the heart of the poem, reveal the effect of the garden on a contemplative mind; the eighth compares this state with that enjoyed by Adam; the last reflects on the perfection of the garden worked by God.

An example of a sophisticated man seeking rural activity is provided by the king's soliloquy during the battle on which his monarchy depends, and in which he maintains that he would rather be a shepherd than a king (Shakespeare, *Henry VI: Part 3* [c.1591], II, v, 1–54). In the seventeenth century, rural solitude replaced the yearning for rural activity: e.g. Katherine Philips, 'A Country Life', or the conclusion of Benlowes, *Theophila* (1652, though circulating in manuscript about 1650), in which the last two cantos are entitled 'The Sweetness of Retirement'.

[1] **vainly**
(a) uselessly, to no avail; (b) conceitedly: cf. 'A Dialogue between the Soul

and Body', line 10; ***amaze*** (a) confuse, perplex; (b) send mad.

[2] **the palm, the oak, or bays**
a palm-leaf garland was awarded as recognition for *military*; an oak-leaf garland, for *civic*; and a laurel-garland (bays = laurels), for *poetic* achievement.

[3] **uncessant**
never ceasing, tireless, constant.

[4] **Crowned**
cf. the garlands won for achievement; ***herb or tree*** the bay leaf (from a bay tree) was used as a herb; the palm, oak and bay are trees.

[5] **short and narrow verged**
the short (and short-lasting) and narrow-bordered (or relatively confining) shade of a *single* tree (i.e. a palm, oak or laurel tree); i.e. the shade of a single tree invites repose, but will offer only a limited respite from the exertions of the ambitious seeker after glory.

[6] **prudently . . . upbraid**
prudently (a) wisely; (b) rightly; ***toils*** efforts; ***upbraid*** a felicitous pun (a) censure; (b) wind into pleats (i.e. transform into a 'garland').

[7] **all**
contrast with 'single'; ***close*** unite, come together (cf. 'The Definition of Love', line 14).

[8] **garlands**
here, the meaning is clearly figurative – i.e. why seek after military, civic or poetic glory, which is only one kind of achievement and will be crowned by only one kind of garland, when you could seek after a multidimensional repose represented by a garland composed of *every* different kind of flower or leaf.

[9–10] **Fair Quiet**
an unusual personification of the silence that the poet finds in the garden – a necessary prerequisite for meditation; the word [*Alma*] used in the Latin version suggests that 'fair' is not only beautiful, but also 'favourable'; ***And*** together with; ***Innocence*** is often personified, but note the ambivalence of the word: (a) free from moral guilt; (b) not guilty of hurting or harming anything or anyone – implicitly, one can achieve military glory only by killing others; civic glory by elbowing someone else aside; or poetic distinction (often) by satirising someone else.

[11] **Mistaken long . . .**
'For a long time I made the mistake of seeking you . . .'

[12] **busy**
bustling, active; ***companies of men*** (a) human company; (b) military companies.

[13–14] **Your sacred plants . . . will grow**
If the plants sacred to Quiet and Innocence do grow here on earth, it can only be among plants (i.e. not in 'companies of men').

[15–16] **Society . . .**
'For society . . .'; ***all but rude/To*** (a) almost rudely dismissive of; (b) uncivilised, in the sense of ill-formed for, not sufficiently sophisticated to enjoy 'solitude'; (c) ignorant of.

[17–18] **white nor red . . . green**
red and ***white*** are colours associated with a woman's beauty; ***am'rous*** (a) lovely (in a now obsolete 'passive' sense); but perhaps also (b) amorous, loving; ***green*** refers to the garden. There is also a play on the religious symbolism of these colours: ***red*** charity; ***white*** faith; ***green*** hope.

[19] **Fond**
doting, foolish; ***cruel*** to the trees; ***flame*** passion.

[21] **Little . . . they know, or heed**
'Little do they know or take notice of, acknowledge'.

[22] **these beauties**
the beauty of the trees; ***hers*** the mistress of any of the 'fond lovers' – note how the emphasis (in the 1681 text, capitalised) increases the poet's scorn of their 'idealisation' of a mere woman, as opposed to the 'real' beauty of a tree!

[23–4] **wheres'e'er**
wheresoever – i.e. in whatever part of the trunk the poet might 'wound' the tree (by cutting the bark), it would at least be with the name of the tree on which he was writing.

[25] **run our passion's heat**
(a) hurried (because 'time flies', i.e. moves very fast) to a time beyond that when we are 'heated' by thoughts of love; also (b) run, in the sense of run away from (i.e. escaped from the confusion into which love throws one): cf. the following line; possibly also (c) a deliberate pun, as the word 'heat' is recorded as having been used in 1663 to mean 'a single course in a race' (*OED*): this need not constitute evidence that the poem is post-Restoration (1660), as the word may have been in use in this sense before.

[26] **Love hither . . . retreat**
Love (a) a personification of the 'passion' referred to in the previous line; and (b) a higher form of love than simply carnal love, as suggested by line 25; ***hither*** to here; ***(make a) retreat*** withdraw (a) from the world (like a hermit: this is further suggested by the corresponding word in the Latin version: *hortus*, which suggests the *hortus conclusus*, the 'enclosed garden' in Song of Songs 4: 12); and (b) from a battle (implying that to experience 'passion' is to be at war with both oneself and the other); ***best*** most meritorious – i.e. to 'retreat' deserves praise!

[27–32] **The gods . . . mortal beauty**
gods Apollo and Pan; ***mortal beauty*** Daphne and Syrinx; ***still*** always; ***race*** (a) running competition; (b) hereditary line (ironic); ***hunted*** chased, as if Daphne were an animal, his 'prey'; ***so*** in this way, for this reason; ***Only that*** for the sole purpose; ***she*** the emphasis underlines the suggestion of a feminine being desiring to become a plant; ***grow*** grow into, become a 'laurel tree' – note the irony: the ***laurel*** is awarded to poets, who are condemned in the first stanza; ***speed*** hurry, as if he were an arrow about to bring down or kill an animal at which it was shot.

The reference is to two myths: (a) Apollo and Daphne: Apollo, struck by one of Cupid's arrows, fell in love with Daphne (*daphne* is Greek for 'laurel'); she fled and he pursued her; just as he was about to catch her, she begged her father, a river-god, to transform her, and he obliged by changing her into a laurel tree (Ovid, *Metamorphoses*, 1.452–567); (b) Pan and Syrinx: Pan fell in love with a nymph called Syrinx (*syrinx* [a] reed; [b] pipe), whom he pursued until she begged to be transformed, and she was – into a reed, out of which Pan fashioned a panpipe, a kind of flute (*Metamorphoses*, 1.689–712). Marvell wittily adapts the usual stories by having Apollo chase Daphne *in order that* she transform herself into a laurel (a plant), and Pan chase Syrinx *because he wants* a reed – i.e. another plant!

[33] **wondrous**
to be wondered at, in the sense of 'filled with mystery' or even 'arousing awe'.

[34–40] **drop**
fall deliberately; in this catalogue of fantastic delights Marvell invests the fruit with volition (the ability to want or desire something; see line 37) – probably derived from Holland's embellishment of Pliny, in which Pomona, the 'nymph and goddess' who presides over gardens and fruit trees (cf. Ovid, *Metamorphoses*, 14. 623–771), describes how her abundant fruits offer themselves to man of their own accord: 'lo, they are ready to drop down and fall into your mouth, or else to lie under your feet' – this sentence is not in the Latin original ('Proem' to Book 23); ***luscious*** richly and deliciously sweet; ***clusters of the vine*** bunches of grapes; ***do crush*** note that the subject of the verb is the 'clusters of the vine' – i.e. the grapes push themselves against the poet's mouth so hard that their juice bursts from them as 'wine'; cf. the 'luscious wine' whose 'bunches . . . did themselves into [the hands of the passers-by] incline', Spenser, *Faerie Queene*, II, xii, 54; for the rhyme, cf. Jonson, 'To Penshurst' (p. 120), lines 43–4; ***nectarine*** a variety of peach with a smooth and shiny skin; ***curious*** strange, exquisite; ***Stumbling*** . . . Marvell wittily exaggerates the profusion of the

garden's pleasures – cf. the biblical story of the Creation, where Adam and Eve live in Eden without having to work; i.e. food comes to them without effort; the ***melons*** and the ***flowers*** are so plentiful that he trips over them; to a Puritan, 'stumbling', 'ensnared', and 'fall' would all suggest 'sin': in an Edenesque garden, one's only 'fall' could be to fall on ***grass*** – which is soft and, like all vegetation, symbolic of growth; also, being green, suggestive of (Christian) hope.

[41] **from pleasure less**
from lesser pleasure – i.e. although the poet enjoyed the profusion of different fruits and even falling on the grass, this represented only a sensual pleasure of less significance than the cerebral pleasure which he describes in stanza 6.

[42] **Withdraws into...**
note how this represents another 'retreat' (cf. line 26).

[43–4] **The mind...find**
the word ***ocean*** cf. 'Whatsoever is engendered and bred in any part of the world beside is found in the sea' (Pliny) – i.e. every creature on earth has its counterpart in the sea: e.g. sea-horse, sea-lion, sea-anemone, etc.); but the sea is also a traditional symbol of the totality of the mind, especially the creative unconscious; the image may also be suggestive of Platonic 'ideas' in which what is found in the ocean/mind is the 'original' of what is seen on earth; ***kind*** species; ***straight*** immediately; ***resemblance*** its mirror-image.

[45–6] **Yet it creates...other seas**
The mind does not only find a mirror-image of everything in it, but it also *creates* very different worlds that greatly 'surpass' (in the number and kind of beings found there) either the real world or the immediate mental image that one has of it; ***other... seas*** other 'worlds-within-worlds', like those found by the mind/ocean in line 43.

[47] **Annihilating all that's made**
(a) reducing the whole created world; (b) considering the whole world as of no value compared to (a green thought).

[48] **a green thought...shade**
green (a) a thought promoting growth; (b) unripe, naive – note the whimsical irony; (c) innocent, in the sense of not causing any harm to anyone; ***shade*** the shadow cast by the tree beneath which the poet is sitting – the double use of 'green' emphasises the colour's associations with (a) new and vigorous growth; (b) freshness, and hence both unripeness and innocence; the phrase 'green shade' goes back to Virgil, *Bucolics*, 9.20, although here the 'shade' refers to the colour of the leaves above the shadow.

[49] **sliding foot**
(a) the base of the fountain is slippery because it is wet; (b) the water that spills over the base of the fountain is in constant motion: translated from Virgil, *Culex*, line 17.

[50] **mossy root**
i.e. the base of the tree trunk which is covered with moss.

[51] **the body's vest**
the garment of the body.

[52–3] **soul**
The likening of the soul to a bird is implicit in both *The Epic of Gilgamesh* and Egyptian mythology, where *Ba* (the soul) is represented by a bird with a human head; in Christian iconology, the Holy Spirit is represented by a white dove (Matthew 3: 16); Marvell's use of the image is probably derived from alchemy and Hermetic philosophy: e.g. J.D. Mylius, *Philosophia reformata* (1622); ***boughs*** branches of a tree; ***glide*** fly; ***sits*** i.e. on the branches.

[54] **whets**
preens, smooths (the feathers of its wings); ***combs*** i.e. tidies its feathers by the use of its bill.

[55] **longer flight**
i.e. the flight the soul will make at the moment of the poet's death; perhaps also the necessary imagination to compose a long poem.

[56] **Waves . . . various light**
the soul is likened to a bird whose wings, as it preens its feathers (plumes), reflect (wave) the multi-coloured light of eternity for the poet, thereby giving him a taste of eternity while in his garden.

[57] **that happy garden-state**
state a country inhabited by people; thus, the happiness enjoyed by Adam when he lived in the Garden of Eden and 'walked with God'.

[58] **mate**
i.e. before the creation of man's partner, Eve.

[59] **a place**
Eden; ***sweet*** highly agreeable and sweet-smelling (because of the flowers there!).

[60] **What other help . . . meet**
Eve was created as an 'an help *meet*' (i.e. a necessary and appropriate companion) for Adam: see Genesis 2: 18, 20; Marvell is being ironic: the sense is: 'given that Eden was Paradise, man did not need a companion'.

[61–2] **'twas**
(a) it was; (b) it must have been: clearly ironic; ***a mortal's share . . . there share*** lot, destiny; thus, even in Paradise, man was mortal, and no mortal can expect the perfect happiness of being able to enjoy his solitude.

[63–4] **'twere**
it were, i.e. it would be – 'It would be a double Paradise if only man could live alone in Paradise.'

[65] **the skilful gardener**
(a) the man who laid out the garden in which the poet is sitting; (b) God.

[66] **this dial new**
a sundial, the 'bed' of which was composed of flowers and herbs, at the centre of which was a gnomon (the pin, pillar or plate of a sundial), the position of whose shadow on the flower bed indicated the time of day; the seasons would have been indicated by the variety of flower displayed – a gardener would periodically have changed these, according to the 'season' (spring, summer, etc.); the ***new*** suggests that the flower-bed sundial had only recently been laid out.

[67–8] **Where from above . . . fragrant zodiac run**
the sun is ***milder*** because its rays pass through the fragrance that rises from the flowers of the dial, likened to a ***zodiac*** because they represent the entire seasonal cycle; note the verb ***run***, which refers back to line 25.

[69–70]
These lines involve an elaborate bilingual pun based on *carpe diem* ('seize the day'). Suggested by a phrase from a poem by the first century BC Roman poet Horace, in which he speaks of a bee 'seizing [i.e. pollinating] the pleasant thyme' (Latin *carpere thyma*: see Horace, 'Carmina (IV)', lines 2, 27–9). Thyme is a garden herb, used in cooking; the pun concerns 'thyme/time'. While *carpe diem* poems are invariably love poetry, Marvell here employs a pun on the tradition in an essentially meditative poem. The pun is *not* obvious in English, and requires either knowledge of the Latin version of the poem or a very good memory of Horace – it is a 'private joke' (Legouis, 1928), further evidence that Marvell's lyric poems were written for his own pleasure rather than public circulation; note also that a bee can 'seize its thyme/time' – or rather, the pollen – only when the flowers are open, i.e. during daylight, while the poet meditates in his garden; ***computes*** calculates, reckons, takes into consideration, appraises.

[70–2] **sweet and wholesome hours**
wholesome whole-making, thus 'holy'; ***hours*** the hours spent in the garden; ***Be reckoned*** (a) be appraised or appreciated; (b) be given its proper and considerable importance; ***but with*** except by means of, unless one reflects on.

113 / *An Horatian Ode upon Cromwell's Return from Ireland*

The forward youth that would appear
Must now forsake his muses dear,
  Nor in the shadows sing
  His numbers languishing.
'Tis time to leave the books in dust
And oil the unused armour's rust,
  Removing from the wall
  The corslet of the hall.
So restless Cromwell could not cease
In the inglorious arts of peace,
  But through adventurous war
  Urgèd his active star
And, like the three-forked lightning, first
Breaking the clouds where it was nursed,
  Díd through hís own side
  His fiery way divide.
For 'tis all one to courage high,
The emulous or enemy,
  And with such to inclose
  Is more than to oppose.
Then burning through the air he went
And palaces and temples rent –
  And Caesar's head at last
  Did through his laurels blast.
'Tis madness to resist or blame
The force of angry heaven's flame
  And, if we would speak true,
  Much to the man is due,
Who, from his private gardens where
He lived reservèd and austere –
  As if his highest plot
  To plant the bergamot –
Could by industrious valour climb
To ruin the great work of time
  And cast the kingdoms old
  Into another mould.
Though justice against fear complain
And plead the ancient rights in vain:

But those do hold or break
As men are strong or weak.
Nature, that hateth emptiness,
Allows of penetration less:
And therefore must make room
Where greater spirits come.
What field of all the Civil Wars,
Where his were not the deepest scars?
And Hampton shows what part
He had of wiser art,
Where, twining subtle fears with hope,
He wove a net of such a scope
That Charles himself might chase
To Carisbrooke's narrow case,
That thence the royal actor born
The tragic scaffold might adorn.
While round the armèd bands
Did clap their bloody hands,
He nothing common did or mean
Upon that memorable scene:
But with his keener eye
The axe's edge did try,
Nor called the gods with vulgar spite
To vindicate his helpless right,
But bowed his comely head
Down, as upon a bed.
This was that memorable hour
Which first assured the forcèd power.
So when they did design
The Capitol's first line,
A bleeding head where they begun
Did fright the architects to run:
And yet, in that, the State
Foresaw its happy fate.
And now the Irish are ashamed
To see themselves in one year tamed:
So much one man can do,
That does both act and know.
They can affirm his praises best
And have, though overcome, confessed
How good he is, how just

And fit for highest trust:
Nor yet grown stiffer with command,
But still in the Republic's hand;
How fit he is to sway
That can so well obey.
He to the Commons' feet presents
A kingdom, for his first year's rents
And, what he may, forbears
His fame, to make it theirs:
And has his sword and spoils ungirt,
To lay them at the public's skirt.
So when the falcon high
Falls heavy from the sky,
She, having killed, no more does search
But on the next green bough to perch,
Where, when he first does lure,
The falc'ner has her sure.
What may not then our isle presume
While Victory his crest does plume?
What may not others fear
If thus he crowns each year?
A Caesar, he, ere long to Gaul,
To Italy, a Hannibal,
And to all states not free
Shall climacteric be.
The Pict no shelter now shall find
Within his parti-coloured mind,
But from this valour sad
Shrink underneath the plaid,
Happy, if in the tufted brake
The English hunter him mistake,
Nor lay his hounds in near
The Caledonian deer.
But thou, the Wars' and Fortune's son,
March indefatigably on
And for the last effect
Still keep thy sword erect –
Besides the force it has to fright
The spirits of the shady night:
The same arts that did gain
A power, must it maintain.

The title of this 120-line ode, composed of alternating tetrameter and trimeter couplets, announces its influence by the odes of the Roman poet Horace (65–8 BC); it also borrows considerably from the *Pharsalia* (or *Civil Wars*) by a slightly later Roman poet, Lucan (AD 39–65) and Tom May's translation (2nd edn 1631).

Ostensibly, it is a poem praising Cromwell, but its central *tableau* undermines such a view. Few poems manipulate ambiguity so well and so consistently, and it has even been suggested that the very *form* of the poem, which never allows the reader to 'settle', contributes to this ambivalence. Lines 1–8 offer a strangely ambivalent introduction; lines 9–44 reflect on how Cromwell came to power; lines 45–72 contrast his achievement with the behaviour of Charles I on the day of the latter's execution; lines 73–90 offer ambiguous praise of Cromwell; lines 91–120, based on two images of hunting, speak of the ambivalence of Cromwell's achievement.

A new wave of Irish problems began in 1632, when Charles I made his favourite, Thomas Wentworth, Lord Deputy of Ireland. Wentworth had begun his political life as an MP closely associated with opposition to royal high-handedness. In 1628, however, he accepted a peerage and became a favourite of the king. He criticised the corruption of others, but was not himself averse to reaping the benefits of office. He governed Ireland efficiently, totally dominating the Irish Parliament: as late as 1640, they agreed to contribute £180,000 to the king. But his ruthlessness earned him the epithet 'Black Tom Tyrant', and as soon as the Irish found themselves freed of him (Wentworth, made Earl of Strafford in 1640, was tried by the Commons and executed in May 1642), they rebelled. Several thousand Englishmen lost their lives in the ensuing years. The king tried to appoint an army leader to subdue Ireland again, but the Long Parliament was wary of entrusting any royal favourite with such power. Irish resistance to English presence in the country continued throughout the Civil Wars.

In 1649, Oliver Cromwell was sent to subdue the ongoing insurrection. He landed on 15 August and began a devastatingly effective nine-month campaign. He captured Drogheda after a bloody battle, brutally crushed the rebellion elsewhere, and returned in triumph to England in May 1650. He launched his invasion of Scotland on 22 July.

Thus Marvell most probably conceived his 'Horatian Ode' in early July 1650 – i.e. shortly before he took up his position as tutor in Lord Fairfax's household. It is often assumed that it must have been 'written' at this time: there is no evidence to confirm this. Marvell might have written it in retrospect, or returned to the poem he had conceived in 1650 and either added to or otherwise revised it. It cannot constitute 'evidence' of what Marvell felt in 1650. Ever since Cleanth Brooks and Douglas Bush crossed their historico-critical swords over it in the mid 1940s, its compelling poetic structure and its biographical and ideological implications have aroused considerable debate. A reader coming to it for the first time is strongly urged to 'read it well' before entering the fray.

[1–16]
These opening lines, and several other passages, seem to borrow from May's translation of *Pharsalia*, I, 144 ff. – e.g. 'restless', 'forward', 'lightning... from a cloud/Breaks through', etc. But what is awkward in May is transformed into powerful poetry by Marvell.

[1] **forward youth... appear**
forward (a) presumptuous; (b) keen to make his mark; ***appear*** emerge from obscurity on to the world's stage.

[2] **now**
although not at the beginning of the

sentence, the word is used in imitation of classical Greek, in which 'now' very often introduces a fresh 'turn' in the events; a device still widespread in seventeenth-century English: the poem thus begins *in medias res*; ***forsake*** abandon; ***muses dear*** the 'Muses' addressed by such an ambitious young man, who is imagined as a poet: lines 1–4 constitute an ironic reversal of the invocation of the epic Muse: cf. the opening of Homer's *Iliad* or Virgil's *Aeneid*, in which the poet begins by seeking the help of the Muse(s) to tell his story; thus the lines refer primarily to Marvell rousing himself to tackle his theme rather than to his subject, Cromwell – but note that the entire poem has to do with Cromwell's 'forwardness' and desire to 'appear'.

[3–4] **Nor in the . . . languishing**
and not languish in the 'shadows' or darkness, singing his (languishing) poems: moralists often denounced the *vita umbratilis*, a life lived in the shadows, i.e. lacking in honour and glory; ***languishing*** (a) refers to the poet – growing more and more dispirited because the love he feels for the young woman to whom he is addressing his amorous verses is unrequited; (b) refers to the poet's ***numbers***, his feeble, lifeless, love-sick poems/songs; ***sing*** love poems of the sixteenth and early seventeenth centuries were often set to music and sung, usually to the accompaniment of a lute; ***in the shadows*** (a) the dark corners where the poet would pine and concoct his poems; (b) the darkness (of night) from which the poet would sing his poems to the mistress of his imagination.

[5–8] **'Tis time . . . the hall**
It is high time the young man abandoned his study and became a soldier; ***books in dust*** suggests that the proper place for a book is on a shelf, gathering dust; ***corslet*** metal armour used to protect the body – in peacetime it was often hung as decoration on the walls of large rooms such as the hallway of a family home; if it became rusty, ***oil*** was used to clean it – an ironic description of what must have been happening in a great many homes in 1642.

[9–10] **So restless Cromwell . . . peace**
So in this way, thus, for; ***restless*** cf. Herbert, 'The Pulley' (p. 235); ***cease*** (a) stop, rest, be content or satisfied with; (b) remain inactive; ***inglorious arts of peace*** (a) poetry, as already mentioned – note the irony!; (b) farming, see lines 29–32.

[11–12] **But through . . . star**
through (a) by means of; (b) in the course of; ***adventurous*** (a) impossible to predict; (b) rash; (c) challenging, in the sense that war favours those who show resolution; ***Urgèd*** drove forcefully; ***active star*** suggests that the (astrological) 'star' (perhaps Mars) beneath which he was born, and thus by which he was guided, made him *inherently* 'active'.

[13] **three-forked lightning**
an arresting image borrowing from both classical and Christian tradition – the 'thunderbolt' (i.e. lightning) was an attribute of Zeus; the 'three-forked' suggests that it has the power of the Christian trinity.

[14] **Breaking . . . nursed**
(a) Bursting through, but also (b) breaking up, the clouds (i.e. military and political faction) where the lightning (i.e. Cromwell) originated.

[15–16] **through his own side . . . divide**
i.e. Cromwell appeared suddenly among (burst through) and divided (broke up) the ranks of the Parliamentarian supporters. Cromwell began to emerge as a leader among anti-Royalist forces only in the late 1640s, some two years before the poem was written; ***fiery way*** (a) divided the party to which he adhered like fire – cf. 'For remember that the Lord will come in fire, his chariots like a whirlwind, to unleash his blazing anger and punish the wicked with fire. For the Lord will test people both by his

sword and by his fire' (Isaiah 66: 15–16); (b) divided it by means of his 'fiery' temper.

[17–20] **For 'tis all one . . . to oppose** ***courage high*** a personification of someone who shows great courage; ***emulous*** people who are determined to imitate, equal or excel – here, the sequel tells us that the word refers to other Parliamentarians (i.e. members of Cromwell's own political faction); ***inclose*** to shut in on all sides (i.e. prevent from effective action); note how although the verb is active, the sense is passive (to be inclosed: cf. line 51 and note); ***more*** more galling, or 'worse'; ***oppose*** to be opposed; thus: 'To someone of great courage, rivals in his own party who hold him back (because they are more timorous than he is) are more irksome than opponents.'

[21] **Then**
For this reason, thus, and so, with the sense of inevitability; ***burning through the air*** i.e. like lightning; ***air*** there may be a pun on 'air' as the way Cromwell regarded the nature of the Parliamentary debate – i.e. as just hot air or wasted breath.

[22] **palaces and temples rent**
rent split or divided; i.e. Cromwell divided not only the country's powerful families (who lived in large houses) but also the Church (temples); ***palaces***, of course, also refers to the king's home and his function as head of state.

[23–4] **And Caesar's head . . . blast**
Caesar's head is ambiguous – it is usually taken to mean (a) Charles I, who was executed on 30 January 1649: Pliny mentions a belief that lightning will not strike a laurel tree (*Natural History* 2, 56); but note also (b) Cromwell – i.e. Cromwell had already won so many laurels (victories) that he was threatening to become another Caesar – a self-made king (in Greek, *tyrannos* means both king and tyrant).

[25–6] **'Tis madness . . . flame**
note how the strength of this assertion draws attention to itself, and how the literal meaning is undermined by the metaphorical application: (a) the statement is literally true, for a practising Christian; but (b) it is ironic, given that the 'heaven' refers not to heaven, but to Cromwell.

[27] **And**
ambiguous: (a) a *continuation* of the idea mentioned in the previous line; (b) a contrast with it (i.e. = 'but'); ***if we would speak true*** again, ambivalent: (a) literal; (b) ironic.

[28] **Much**
(a) great achievements; (b) great confusion; ***due*** (a) owed to Cromwell for his achievement; (b) has been caused by.

[29–32] **private gardens . . . bergamot**
before the 1640s Cromwell was a wheat farmer in Huntingdon, and subsequently a grazier near St Ives: the phrase probably refers (a) to him being a 'private', as opposed to public, person; and (b) someone whose first concern was with his relation to the *land*, as opposed to political ideology – but note how 'land' implies ideology; ***reserved*** ambivalent = (a) reticent, reluctant to reveal personal feelings; (b) kept distinct, set apart for future use, purpose, or even fate; ***austere*** (a) harsh, stern, severely simple; (b) strict in moral behaviour: used ironically; ***plot*** (a) ambition; (b) a small area of land used for cultivating fruit and vegetables; ***plant*** were to plant; ***bergamot*** a kind of pear.

[33–6] **Could . . . mould**
these lines refer back to 'the man . . . who' in lines 28–9, and thus contrast the 'gardener' with a man of valour; ***industrious*** not only (a) hard-working, but also (b) carefully calculated; ***valour*** personal courage; ***climb*** refers back to 'plot' and thus contrasts the natural growth of a pear tree with political aspiration; ***the great work of time*** (a) the slow-growing pear tree; (b) the political institutions associated with the monarchy; ***kingdoms*** plural, primarily England and Wales, but

also Scotland and Ireland; ***old*** long-established; ***another mould*** i.e. a Commonwealth or republic, as opposed to a monarchy – note that this poem is usually thought to have been written long before Cromwell established such a republic.

[37–8] **Though justice . . . in vain**
These lines continue to refer to Cromwell, but they are deliberately ambiguous: ***justice*** (a) Cromwell's (i.e. Parliament's) 'just' or legitimate grievances against the king; (b) the king's 'divine right' to govern; ***fear*** (a) fear of reproval by a monarch who rules by divine right; (b) fear of popular insurrection; ***complain*** (a) express dissatisfaction; (b) state a grievance; (c) utter a moan or groan because oppressed by a heavy burden; similarly, ***ancient rights*** (a) the rights of the people, as enshrined in Magna Carta (1215) and Parliamentary tradition; (b) the king's right to govern: thus, either (a) Although Cromwell/Parliament has/have a right to object to the king's tyrannies, any appeal to the rights gradually accorded them since Magna Carta will be useless; (b) Although the king has a right to object to the threat against him, there is no point in him looking to his divine right to rule.

[39–40] **But those do hold . . . weak**
Given the ambiguity inherent in the previous lines, their conclusion is a key concept in the poem – ***those*** refers to 'ancient rights'; ***do hold*** stand as valid; ***as*** depending on whether: note how the next four lines illustrate this claim.

[41–2] **Nature . . . less**
penetration the entering of a space already occupied: thus, 'Although Nature hates a vacuum, it is even more averse to one space being occupied by two bodies simultaneously.'

[43–4] **And therefore . . . come**
note the ellipsis: 'therefore *even a king who rules by divine right* must give way' to a 'greater spirit' (i.e. Cromwell).

[45–6] **What field . . . scars**
implicit in these lines is the classical code of 'virtue' – he is bravest who has won the most scars. Cromwell was wounded at the Battle of Marston Moor, but the reference is rhetorical: i.e. 'At every battle, it was Cromwell who fought most bravely'; ***What*** In what, or 'which is the'; ***field*** battlefield; ***scars*** both literal and figurative wounds: the latter suggests that every victory Cromwell won cost him a great deal – i.e. he was 'wounded' both *in* and *by* every encounter.

[47–8] **And Hampton**
after the capture of Charles I by Parliament in June 1647, he was held at Hampton Court, a large royal palace to the west of London (there may be an ironic reference to the fact that it was built by Cardinal Wolsey, a onetime commoner, who gave it to Henry VIII in 1526); on 11 November he managed to escape to Carisbrooke Castle on the Isle of Wight, where he was betrayed into the hands of Parliament. Marvell appears to subscribe to a rumour which held that Cromwell had prompted the king's flight in order to advance his own ambitions – no evidence exists to corroborate this story; note the ironic switch from 'battlefield' to 'palace'; ***what part/He had of wiser art*** the degree of his political astuteness: ***part*** suggests not entirely honest, i.e. deceitful.

[49–52] **Where, twining . . . narrow case**
twining forming string or rope by twisting several separate strands together; ***subtle*** finely woven, like a net – i.e. Cromwell played upon the king's hopes and fears; ***scope*** (a) encompassing kind, extent; (b) purpose: note the irony of (a), given that (b) is to hem Charles in even more tightly; ***chase*** hurry or flee, with a pun on 'the chase' = hunting, Charles's favourite sport (although the verb is active, the sense is passive: i.e. 'be chased' [cf. line 19 and note]); ***narrow case*** small container – (a) a prison cell; (b) a casement = window: i.e. effectively, an even more cramped prison than Hampton, with smaller

windows from which to look out on the world.

[53–4] **That hence . . . adorn**
note the ellipsis – the second capture of Charles I and his trial are not mentioned: the implication is that Cromwell engineered the king's would-be flight in such a way that it led directly to the latter's execution; ***thence*** from there (i.e. Carisbrooke); ***royal actor*** suggests (a) being a king implies playing a part: cf. 'part' in line 47; (b) Cromwell manipulated the king, as if he were a theatre director and the king only a *good* actor; and (c) the raised platform in the following line is a 'stage'; ***born*** (a) 'born actor'; (b) borne, i.e. carried, taken; ***scaffold*** a raised wooden platform specifically used for executions; ***adorn*** decorate, or provide the decoration.

[55–6] **While round the armed bands**
While the armed soldiers watching . . . their 'bloody' hands inculpate them as much as Cromwell, and remind one of Pontius Pilate washing his hands, i.e. declaring his innocence of any responsibility for crucifying Christ (cf. Matthew 27: 24–5).

[57–8] **He nothing common did or mean**
He Charles I; the contrast is primarily with the common and mean-minded behaviour of the soldiers who clapped, but by ellipsis it includes Cromwell, who (it is suggested) trapped the king; ***that memorable scene*** the king's execution on 30 January 1649.

[59–60] **But with . . . did try**
keener sharper, i.e. than either his executioners or the 'axe's edge'; ***edge*** there is a pun on the Latin (*acies* = sharpness of [a] sight and [b] the blade of a knife or axe); this has the effect of personifying the 'axe', which thus stands for the king's executioners – note the implicit parallel with the 'trial' of Christ; ***try*** test.

[61] **Nor called**
Nor did Charles I call upon/implore/swear at; ***the gods*** use of the 'pagan' plural underlines how futile and 'vulgar' (i.e. common or base) such a request would have been; ***spite*** implies that such a request would only have demonstrated an ill-will towards the divine which the king clearly did not feel.

[62] **vindicate . . . helpless right**
vindicate to establish the existence of; ***helpless*** (a) because no one came to his aid; (b) his 'right' to rule is ineffective without help from others.

[63] **comely**
handsome.

[64] **Down**
'bow . . . down' is a tautology: the placing of 'down' at the beginning of the line emphasises the finality of the action, and anticipates the sequel; ***as upon a bed*** just as resting one's head on a pillow is the last action of the day, so this is the last action of the king's life – perhaps borrowed from Browne's meditation, in which he says that he takes his farewell to the world in 'a colloquy with God':

> . . . O make me try,*
> By sleeping, what it is to die;
> And as gently lay my head
> On my grave, as now my bed.
> Howe'er I rest, great God, let me
> Awake again at last with Thee,
> And thus assured, behold I lie
> Securely, or to 'wake or die.
> (Thomas Browne, *Religio Medici*, 1643, II, 12 [London, 1965], pp. 85–6)

[65–6] **This was . . . forced power**
Given the dignity accorded to Charles I in the preceding lines, the emphatic 'this' and repetition of 'memorable' make these lines heavily ironic; ***assured*** ensured, which raises the question: how could anything good come of a government which established itself in this way?; ***forced power*** (a) government that has established itself by force; (b) *un*natural government – cf. lines 119–20.

* = learn

[67–70] **So when . . . to run**
So Just as, or In the same way; ***they*** the Ancient Romans; ***design*** plan, intend to build; ***Capitol*** a hill in Rome. Livy tells how the excavators, digging the foundations for a temple to Jupiter on the hill, came across 'a man's head, face and all, [preserved in perfect condition]: which sight . . . plainly foretold that [Rome] should be . . . the capital . . . of the whole world' (*Annals*, I. 55. 6; also told by Pliny, 28, 4): Marvell contributed the ideas of 'bleeding' and the 'fright' of the architects; ***first line*** (a) the foundations for the temple; and, by inference, (b) the 'line' of Caesars that ruled Rome, beginning with Julius Caesar; ***bleeding head*** refers back to that of Charles I; ***where they begun*** where they began digging; ***architects*** (a) those who were physically involved in digging; but also (b) those who planned the building – i.e. the 'architects of state' such as Cromwell was in 1649; ***to run*** the head so frightened the builders that they ran away – this contrasts with the 'clapping' that followed upon the execution of Charles I: the architects who were frightened could refer to the moderates, like Fairfax, who had taken fright at the thought of killing the king.

[71] **And yet**
ironic, but none the less suggests a possibility that good might come of the execution of Charles I; ***that*** that sign (i.e. the head); ***State*** i.e. Rome.

[72] **happy fate**
the prosperity reserved for it by Destiny – but note that 'fate' very often means *un*fortunate destiny: thus an oxymoron.

[73–4] **And now . . . tamed**
now note how reflection on past events is suddenly displaced by a realisation of a present problem: Cromwell had landed in August 1649 in Dublin, from where his army quickly and brutally forced the country to surrender (i.e. tamed it): the entire campaign lasted barely nine months, by the end of which Ireland had been almost entirely brought to heel, even though pockets of resistance continued for a further two years.

[75–6] **So much . . . act and know**
So much . . . ambivalent (cf. line 65): Marvell clearly admires Cromwell's achievement, yet by insisting that it is built upon a 'bleeding head' he makes his admiration ironic; ***know*** know how to act, i.e. brutally.

[77–80] **They can . . . trust**
They the Irish; ***affirm*** state strongly, corroborate: ***and have*** i.e. have affirmed. There is little or no historical evidence for this claim: it may not, however, be ironic, as Marvell was no great admirer of the Irish: note (a) the deliberate and ironic juxtaposition of 'overcome' and 'confessed'; (b) the etymology of ***trust***, from an Old Norse word meaning 'strong', thus implying that one has no choice but to put one's trust in someone as strong as Cromwell – again, deeply ironic; ***highest trust*** divine right, as of Charles I, who was executed for acting as if he had it.

[81–90]
These lines are probably borrowed from Lucan's *Pharsalia*, 9.192–200.

[81–2] **Nor yet grown . . . hand**
refers to Cromwell; ***yet*** (a) not yet; (b) not at all – note the ambiguity; cf. 'still'; ***stiffer*** more rigid, hard to work with; ***still*** (a) for the moment, implying that Cromwell is not always going to act for the public good; (b) always, thereby implying that everything Cromwell did was for the common or public good.

[83–4] **fit**
note how repetition of 'fit' underlines the irony – cf. 'memorable' (lines 58, 65); ***sway*** to rule or control affairs of state: these lines represent a reformulation of a commonplace attributed to Solon, a Greek lawmaker of the sixth century BC.

[85] **Commons' feet**
ambivalent: (a) the Folio has 'Common', i.e. the feet of the 'common man' or ordinary citizen; (b) the probable reading is 'Commons',

i.e. the feet of the House of Commons: the 'lower' House (the 'upper' being the House of Lords). Note the irony of feet/Commons (=lower House): the image is borrowed from the idea of a chivalric hero laying his 'prize' (i.e. what he has won by his strength) at the feet of his sovereign.

[86] **kingdom**
i.e. Ireland; ***first year*** i.e. Cromwell's 'first year' as Commander-in-Chief; ***rents*** the word implies that Cromwell owed the House of Commons 'rent' for his appointment – note what an unsettling idea this is: i.e. for every year he is in office, a Commander-in-Chief is under an obligation to defeat a new kingdom: clearly ironic.

[87–8] **And, what he may . . . it theirs**
what he may in so far as he is able: again, clearly ironic; ***forbears*** abstains, renounces or makes little of – ironic, as Marvell's poem not only makes much of Cromwell's 'fame', but almost apotheosises him (i.e. makes a god of him); ***theirs*** i.e. Parliament's (the House of Commons).

[89–90] **spoils**
plunder – again, ironic, as it undermines the claim made in line 79; ***ungirt*** taken off, as a sword from a belt – this, of course, implies that the 'spoils' are something Cromwell carried on him as if they were his own clothing; ***skirt*** i.e. at the feet of Parliament – note how the 'skirt' makes Parliament into a woman, a queen whom Cromwell is happy to serve, but in a deeply ironic fashion, as the following lines make clear.

[91–6] **So when the falcon . . . has her sure**
falcon a bird of prey that hovers high in the sky waiting for a smaller bird or fieldmouse to pass beneath it, on to which it dives with lightning speed to kill and subsequently devour; ***no more does search*** i.e. search *for food*, as she has already eaten her fill – hence the bird goes to rest on the branch (bough) of a tree – the ***green*** in line 94 may refer to the 'inexperience' or 'naivety' of those who gave Cromwell his command: but note how lines 91–4 describe the action of a *wild* falcon; in line 95 we are made suddenly aware that this falcon has been trained by a falconer (someone who engages in the ancient sport of training a bird of prey to kill and then return to the owner, who holds out a 'lure' or a piece of meat to attract its attention). The parallel with Cromwell (the falcon) and Parliament (the falconer) is disturbing.

[97–100] **What may not . . . each year**
our isle the British Isles; ***presume*** impudently take for granted or expect; ***While*** as long as; ***his crest does plume*** Victory is seen as a 'plume' (feather) on the crest of Cromwell's helmet – the image may be ironic, but the following two lines are clearly not; ***others*** (a) other countries, i.e. other than Ireland; (b) other people; ***thus he crowns*** this is what he achieves.

[101–2] **A Caesar . . . Hannibal**
Marvell hypothesises that Cromwell may proceed to invade Gaul (i.e. France), as Julius Caesar did, from Italy, in 58 BC, or Italy, as Hannibal, the Carthaginian general, did in 218 BC in a famous example of taking the enemy by surprise. After subduing Spain, Hannibal led his army, which included elephants, over the Alps (a mountain range) and entered Italy from the *north* (Carthage is modern-day Tunis – i.e. he marched through Spain and the south of France). At the time Caesar was only a general; he later accepted the equivalent of sovereignty – cf. line 23; Hannibal was the *enemy* of Rome – the first suggests ambition, the other the possibility of conquest by an 'illegitimate' claimant.

[103–4] **And to all states . . . climacteric be**
climacteric an adjective meaning fatal, critical or marking an epoch – i.e. Cromwell's attack upon such states would prove a decisive moment in their history; ***free*** a good example of Marvell's dry irony – i.e. before

Cromwell's imagined arrival, such people in other countries will be living under the yoke of an oppressor, just as the England of Charles I was an 'Eleven Years' Tyranny'; but given the worry Marvell expresses in line 99 ('What may not others fear . . . ?'), the reference to freedom is heavily ironic, and the nature of the new freedom is open to question.

[105–8] **The Pict . . . the plaid**
Pict Scot – the word comes from the Latin *picti*, meaning 'painted' (i.e. tattooed): it becomes the basis for a three-way pun (painted/particoloured/plaid); ***his parti-coloured mind*** the Scots had long been torn by clan and factional rivalry (i.e. political 'parties'), but Marvell says this would afford them no protection against a man of Cromwell's resolution; ***this valour sad*** poor showing of strength or resolution, not steadfast – i.e. the instinct to seek refuge in a faction or clan, in the hope that this would ensure protection; ***plaid*** the tartan garment worn by the Scots, resembling the later kilt – each clan wore a different tartan or design composed of crossed stripes.

[109–12] **Happy . . . deer**
Happy refers to the Scot/Pict; ***tufted brake*** thickets of small trees, bushes, etc., that would provide concealment for him; ***mistake*** i.e. if he were not noticed by the English army (hunter), because of his tattoos/plaid (i.e. camouflage); ***Nor lay his hounds . . .*** i.e. if the Englishman did not let loose his hounds to chase (a) a Caledonian (i.e. Highland) deer near enough to where a Scot was hiding for him to become his prey; (b) a Scot, as if he were a Caledonian deer.

[113–14] **But thou . . . indefatigably on**
thou Cromwell; ***the Wars'*** (a) the Civil Wars between Royalists and Parliament (1642–6, 1648–69); and the war with Ireland (1649–50); (b) Ares/Mars, the Greek/Roman god of war; ***Fortune*** a personification, i.e. the goddess – classical precedents suggest that the phrase is used ironically. An equivalent phrase in Sophocles is ironic (*Oedipus Tyrannos*, 1080); in Horace, a literal Latin equivalent is humorous (*Sermones*, 2.6, 49); ***indefatigably*** without tiring, relentlessly: cf. line 9; ***on*** i.e. to Scotland.

[115–18] **And for the last effect . . . shady night**
The closing lines make plain Marvell's doubts about Cromwell; ***for the last effect*** (a) in order to put further fear into the Scots (with the suggestion that this might not have been necessary); (b) in an attempt to ward off any disaster; ***keep thy sword erect*** cf. Book 11 of *The Odyssey*: Odysseus wards off the spirits from the underworld (shady night) with his drawn sword – an ironic reference, as here the image refers to the threat that Cromwell poses for the Scots.

[117] **Besides the force**
'for or because, apart from the Scots'; ***it*** the sword, both literal and metonymic (cf. lines 15–16 and note); ***has to*** *also* has to – note the implication: i.e. the sword is *under an obligation* to frighten into submission (a) the Scots; (b) ***the spirits of the shady night*** – cf. note to line 116; but also the spirits of the dead whom Cromwell has slain, including – the poem implies – Charles I, against whom he will have to defend himself, as did Odysseus. For the notion of obligation, cf. line 86 and note.

[119–20] **The same arts . . . maintain**
the final couplet is ominous, as it implies that what was won by the sword will now have to be defended by the sword: ***arts*** arts of (a) duplicity, stratagem; (b) war; ***A power*** the 'right' to rule a kingdom; ***must it maintain*** must now (see if it can) maintain the power it has won: cf. Anthony Ascham, in a pamphlet about the political confusion just before the king's execution: 'the Usurper . . . will find himself obliged to secure his conquest by the same means he obtained it' (*A Discourse: Wherein is Examined What is Particularly Lawful during the Confusions and Revolutions of Government*, July 1648).

HENRY VAUGHAN

(1622–95)

1650 *Silex Scintillans*
1655 *Silex Scintillans*, 2nd edition, with new 'part II'

Henry Vaughan and his twin brother Thomas were born in Newton, Wales. During the turbulent years that led up to the Civil War, they both studied at the staunchly Royalist university of Oxford where, in the late 1630s, Henry began writing poetry modelled on that of Jonson and Donne. When the Civil War broke out in 1642, Henry returned to Wales, where he became secretary to a judge: it is possible that he actually fought for the king at some time in 1645. In 1646 he married Catherine Wise and shortly after began to practise as a medical doctor, a profession in which he remained all his life – it is not known what training he received for this. He lived all his life by the river Usk, near the region once inhabited, according to Tacitus (a Roman writer, contemporary with Christ), by the Silures, which explains why he described himself as 'Silurist' on the title-pages of his books and on his tombstone. He had four children by his first wife, who died in 1653/54; about two years later he married her sister Elizabeth, by whom he had four further children.

His twin brother Thomas took holy orders and became a vicar in Llansantffread in the early 1640s; he held this post until the Puritans deprived him of his living [i.e. his job as vicar] in 1650. He had a keen interest in Hermetic philosophy, and published several works on this subject, including *Anima Magica Abscondita: or a Discourse on the Universal Spirit of Nature* (1650). Throughout the seventeenth century these works, which now hold little interest except for the scholar, enjoyed much greater success than Henry's poetry. Henry and Thomas also had a younger brother, William, who died in 1648.

Henry's first published work was *Poems, with the Tenth Satire of Juvenal* (1646), the short poems of which are witty, lightweight verses very much in the style of Jonson or Herrick. Juvenal's tenth Satire is, of course, 'The Vanity of Human Wishes', now better known in Johnson's version, which appeared almost exactly a century later (1749). Most of the poems eventually published as *Olor Iscanus* (The Swan of Usk) had probably been written by the end of 1647, although they were not published until 1651. It is a richly varied collection, with poems in both English and Latin about politics, war and manners, including prose translations of some of Plutarch's moral essays as well as verse translations of parts of Ovid's *Tristia*, Boethius's *Consolations of Philosophy* (*c*.520), and some Latin odes written by his near-contemporary, Casimir Sarbiewski (1595–1640), a Polish Jesuit whose works, mingling stoicism modelled on the Latin poet Horace with Christianity, celebrate a life of retirement.

The poems published as *Silex Scintillans* (The Flint Sparking) in March 1650 are not only more emphatically religious in tone, they are also qualitatively better than any of his previous work. Vaughan acknowledged that his poems were much indebted to 'the blessed man, Mr. George Herbert, whose holy life and verse gained so many pious converts (of whom I am the least)'. The second edition of 1655 includes an extensive series of new poems as Part II. All the poems in this anthology are from *Silex Scintillans*.

Vaughan also wrote several prose works. The most important of these, *The Mount of Olives: Or Solitary Devotions* (1652), was designed to encourage the Episcopalian traditions of devotion and meditation that had been banned by the Puritans. It ends with two 'discourses' – the first is called 'Man in Darkness'; the second is a translation of Anselm's 'Man in Glory'. He translated four essays as *Flores Solitudinis* (The Flowers of Solitude, 1654) and two medical works by Heinrich Nolle (*Hermetical Physick*, 1655, and *The Chymist's Key*, 1657). *Thalia Rediviva* (The Muse Revived) is a collection of miscellaneous verse, including works by his brother Thomas: although it was published only in 1678, most of Vaughan's pieces date from the late 1650s.

Context

Vaughan was deeply indebted to Herbert, but his best work none the less reveals a truly original poetic voice. Herbert wrote during a personal retirement at a time of peace: his style is firmly rooted in the tradition of wit that marks English verse between 1590 and 1640, and shows little – if any – sign of the political agitation that was to lead to the execution of Charles I in 1649; even references to the religious agitation occasioned by the Puritans are few. Vaughan, in contrast, grew up during a period when the restlessness was increasingly difficult to ignore. He was twenty-one when the Civil Wars broke out – a staunch Royalist, strongly averse to the objectives of both Puritans and extremist views in Parliament. In this sense, his poetry is more obviously a personal reaction to the changes in religious practice brought about by the Puritan Revolution. Note that although he was a Royalist, his works were published in 1650 without difficulty, as the second edition five years later confirms.

Genre

Vaughan's work is usually considered as part of the Metaphysical school of poetry. It used to be thought that he experienced a mystical conversion in the late 1640s: there is no evidence for this. Reading his complete works, one is more inclined to believe that the change from the young Cavalier poet to the mystical poet of *Silex Scintillans* was a gradual one, occasioned by a combination of the Civil Wars, his reading of Herbert, his interest in the Hermetic philosophy espoused by his brother Thomas and, of course, most of all by his own temperament.

Judging by his poetry, he spoke English with a markedly Welsh accent. Rhymes that look today like half-rhymes were almost certainly full rhymes to his ear (e.g. abroad/shade, falls/scales, in 'Regeneration', lines 2, 4 and 18, 20). A feature of Welsh verse is the accumulation of descriptive phrases (e.g. 'The Night', stanza four); another is the heavy use of alliteration (e.g. the same stanza, especially lines 23–4). As in Herbert's poems, there are numerous echoes of biblical passages, but in Vaughan's best works there is a much more marked emphasis on the poet's personal experience of God, whether by analogy or vision.

A distinguishing feature of his verse is the vividness with which he describes the world of nature – mountain scenery, waterfalls, flowers and, perhaps especially, the feeling of the omnipresence of vegetative growth.

Critical Reception

Vaughan seems to have been very little read during his own lifetime and in the eighteenth century, but during the course of the nineteenth century he attracted increasing attention, largely because of his interest in nature. He has often been compared to Wordsworth, and he is still described by some as a proto-Romantic.

Twentieth-century readers have been inclined to look with equal interest on his Hermeticism, his Neoplatonism, and his echoes of George Herbert. His current reputation stands at a kind of watershed. Some argue that his works only rarely sustain the excellence of their opening statements; others argue that the fuller dimensions of his poetry have yet to be properly understood and appreciated. Critics who work on Vaughan tend to be deeply committed to his merits and, perhaps for this reason, their studies of his verse and thought often reveal a high degree of personal enthusiasm. The extensive annotations provided here are designed to illustrate the strength and coherence of his best works, and the claim that he is a poet of intense lyricism and mysticism whose verse offers surprisingly dense intellectual and literary textures.

Further Reading

Editions

Although *The Works of Henry Vaughan*, ed. L.C. Martin, 2nd edn (Oxford, 1957) is still recognised as a standard edition, both *Henry Vaughan: The complete poems*, ed. Alan Rudrum, 'Penguin English Poets' (Harmondsworth, 1976) and *The Complete Poetry of Henry Vaughan*, ed. French Fogle (New York, 1964) provide better texts. For a good introductory selection, with three useful essays, see *George Herbert and the Seventeenth-Century Religious*

Poets, ed. Mario Di Cesare, 'Norton Critical Edition' (New York, 1978).

Critical Studies

The best introduction is Alan Rudrum, *Henry Vaughan*, 'Writers of Wales' (University of Wales, 1981), although Kenneth Friedenreich, *Henry Vaughan*, 'Twayne' (Boston, MA, 1978) will be easier to come by.

For a good overview of recent criticism, see the 'Special Issue on Henry Vaughan', ed. Jonathan F.S. Post, in the *George Herbert Journal*, **7**, nos 1 and 2 (1983–4).

Important studies of continuing interest include Ross Garner, *Henry Vaughan: Experience and the tradition* (Cambridge, 1959); E.C. Pettet, *Of Paradise and Light: A study of Vaughan's 'Silex Scintillans'* (Cambridge, 1960); Elizabeth Holmes, *Henry Vaughan and the Hermetic Philosophy* (Oxford, 1962); Louis L. Martz, *The Paradise Within: Studies in Vaughan, Traherne, and Milton* (New Haven, CT, 1964); Cleanth Brooks, 'Henry Vaughan: quietism and mysticism', in *Essays in Honor of Esmond Linworth Marilla*, ed. Thomas A. Kirby and William J. Olive (Baton Rouge, LA, 1970), pp. 3–26; James D. Simmonds, *Masques of God: Form and theme in the poetry of Henry Vaughan* (Pittsburgh, PA, 1972); and A.J. Smith, 'Henry Vaughan's ceremony of innocence', *Essays and Studies*, **26** (1973), 35–52, most of which are discussed in Robert E. Bourdette, Jr, 'Recent studies in Henry Vaughan', *ELR*, **4** (1974), 299–310.

More recent major studies are Thomas O. Calhoun, *Henry Vaughan: The achievement of 'Silex Scintillans'* (Newark, DE, 1981); Rachel Trickett, 'Henry Vaughan and the poetry of vision', *Essays and Studies*, **34** (1981), 88–104; and Jonathan F.S. Post's especially useful reappraisal, *Henry Vaughan: The unfolding vision* (Princeton, NJ, 1982). Gerald Hammond has taken a linguistic approach in 'Henry Vaughan's verbal subtlety: wordplay in *Silex Scintillans*', *MLR*, **79** (1984), 526–40.

Some landmark articles on individual poems include Melvin E.A. Bradford, 'Henry Vaughan's "The Night": a consideration of metaphor and meditation', *Arlington Quarterly*, **1** (1968), 209–22, Leland H. Chambers, 'Henry Vaughan's allusive technique: biblical allusions in "The Night"', *Modern Language*

Quarterly, **27** (1966), 371–87; and Leland H. Chambers, 'Vaughan's "The World": the limits of extrinsic criticism', *SEL*, **8** (1968), 137–50. Michael Kirkham explores the influence of 'They are all gone into the world' on 'This lime tree bower my prison' in 'Metaphor and the unitary world: Coleridge and Henry Vaughan', *EIC*, **37** (1987), 121–34.

The standard biography is still F.E. Hutchinson, *Henry Vaughan: A life and interpretation*, revised edn (Oxford, 1971).

Imilda Tuttle has provided a *Concordance to Vaughan's 'Silex Scintillans'* (University Park, PA, 1969).

114 / *Regeneration*

Arise O north, and come thou south-wind, and blow upon my garden, that the spices thereof may flow out. (Song of Songs 4: 16)

A ward! And still in bonds! one day
I stole abroad:
It was high Spring, and all the way
Primrosed and hung with shade.
Yet was it frost within,
And surly winds
Blasted my infant buds, and sin,
Like clouds, eclipsed my mind.

Stormed thus, I straight perceived my Spring
Mere stage and show;
My walk a monstrous, mountained thing
Rough-cast with rocks and snow!
And as a pilgrim's eye,
Far from relief,
Measures the melancholy sky
Then drops, and rains for grief,

So sighed I upwards still. At last
'Twixt steps and falls
I reached the pinnacle where placed
I found a pair of scales.

I took them up and laid
In th'one late pains;
The other, smoke – and pleasures weighed
But proved the heavier grains.

With that, some cried '*Away!*' Straight I
Obeyed and, led
Full East, a fair, fresh field could spy.
Some called it '*Jacob's bed*':
A virgin soil which no
Rude feet e'er trod,
Where (since he stepped there) only go
Prophets and friends of God.

Here I reposed but, scarce well set,
A grove descried
Of stately height, whose branches met
And mixed on every side.
I entered, and once in –
Amazed to see't! –
Found all was changed, and a new Spring
Did all my senses greet.

The unthrift Sun shot vital gold
A thousand pieces,
And heaven its azure did unfold
Chequered with snowy fleeces.
The air was all in spice
And every bush
A garland wore. Thus fed my eyes –
But all the ear lay hush.

Only a little fountain lent
Some use for ears,
And on the dumb shade's language spent
The music of her tears.
I drew her near and found
The cistern full
Of divers stones, some bright and round
Others ill-shaped and dull.

The first (pray mark!) as quick as light
Danced through the flood,
But the last, more heavy than the night,
Nailed to the Centre stood.
I wondered much but, tired
At last with thought,
My restless eye that still desired
As strange an object brought.

It was a bank of flowers, where I descried
(Though 'twas mid-day)
Some fast asleep, others broad-eyed
And taking in the ray.
Here, musing long, I heard
A rushing wind
Which still increased, but whence it stirred
Nowhere I could not find.

I turned me round, and to each shade
Dispatched an eye
To see if any leaf had made
Least motion or reply.
But while I listening sought
My mind to ease
By knowing where 'twas, or where not,
It whispered '*Where I please*'.

'Lord', then said I, '*On me one breath,*
And let me die before my death!'

This, the first poem in *Silex Scintillans*, is an allegorical account of regeneration through personal experience of God. It consists of a succession of emblematic scenes: whilst no specific source has been identified, close parallel may be found in emblem-books, especially those by Francis Quarles and George Withers, both of whom published works entitled *Emblems* in 1635.

It is in ten stanzas of eight iambic lines which scan: tetrameter/dimeter/tetrameter/trimeter/ trimeter/dimeter/tetrameter/trimeter, and rhyme *a b a b c d c d*.

The poet is seeking escape from sins by which he feels imprisoned. Quickly realising that this desire is not entirely appropriate, he has a vision of a pair of scales that confirms his intuition. He is thereupon led away to the East where, at the same spot where Jacob rested, he has a further vision of a shaded grove with a fountain in it. Still unable to understand his own experience, he finally hears a 'rushing wind' that convinces him that regeneration is possible anywhere: it depends only on one's spiritual attitude.

The title may refer to Christ's reply to Peter, when the latter asked what the disciples would get for having abandoned everything to follow him: 'In the coming *regeneration*, when the Son of Man will sit in heavenly splendour, you shall sit beside me. Anyone who has left brother or sister, father or mother, or children or property in order to follow me will be repaid many times over and given eternal life. Then many who now are first will be last, and those who are last, first' (Matthew 19: 28–30). The biblical verse of the motto combines two translations of the Song of Songs (i.e. 'the best of songs'; also called 'The Song of Solomon') – that of the so-called Geneva Bible of 1560 and that of King James's 'Authorised Version' of 1611. The Song of Songs is a poem that describes the love between a bridegroom (identified in Christian tradition as Christ) and his bride (identified by St Bernard in the twelfth century as the individual soul). In the fourth chapter, the bridegroom praises his beloved's attributes. Vaughan has adapted the verse so as to identify the wind with Christ, and the garden with his own soul: he has it as an end-motto; modern convention places mottos at the head of a poem or essay.

[1] **A ward . . . in bonds**
ward (a) a person, usually a minor, who is under the legal protection of a guardian, in lieu of a parent; (b) a prisoner; ***in bonds*** (a) in chains, imprisoned; (b) under obligation; the phrase should be read in the light of St Paul's definition of what relation to God implies: 'For all who are moved by the Spirit of God are the sons of God. For the spirit you have received is not a spirit of bondage [= slavery] retaining you in a state of fear, but a spirit that makes you children of God, and enables you to call upon "Abba, your Father"' (Romans 8: 14–15).

[2] **stole abroad**
moved away secretly, escaped elsewhere by furtive means.

[3] **high Spring**
the middle of spring, the season when plants burst again into leaf and flower after the winter, and animals give birth to their young.

[4] **(was) *Primrosed***
a ***primrose*** is a small yellow flower that appears in the spring, associated with the pursuit of pleasure: cf. Shakespeare's variations of the biblical metaphor of the broad way 'that leadeth to destruction' (Matthew 7: 13): (a) Ophelia's retort to her brother Laertes: 'Do not, as some ungracious pastors do,/Show me the steep and thorny way to heaven,/Whiles like a puffed and reckless libertine,/Himself the *primrose path of dalliance* treads' (*Hamlet*, I, iii, 47–50); (b) the porter's reference to those that go 'the *primrose* way to the everlasting bonfire' (*Macbeth*, II, iii, 18–19).

[6] **surly winds**
cf. a definition by the poet's brother: 'an irreligious spirit, one that hath more of the hurricane, than of Christ Jesus' ('To the Reader', Thomas Vaughan, *Lumen de Lumine*, 1651).

[7] **my infant buds**
buds closed flowers before they burst into bloom; here, suggestive of the poet's burgeoning soul (see Thomas Vaughan, *Lumen de Lumine*, p. 84): the phrase recalls Laertes' advice to Ophelia: 'The canker galls the infants of the spring, /Too oft before their buttons be disclosed' (*Hamlet*, I, iii, 39–40); because the 'buds' refer back to 'primrose', the phrase emphasises that the entire process is a mental or spiritual one.

[8] **eclipsed**
cast (my mind) in darkness, just as the moon, when it comes between the sun and the earth, casts the latter in darkness.

[9] **Stormed thus**
While beset by such 'storms' of thought; ***my Spring*** emphasises that the persona is describing a 'Spring' (or regeneration) of the mind/spirit.
[10] **Mere stage and show**
'to be' mere stage and show: the likening of the world to a stage was a commonplace: e.g. Shakespeare: 'All the world's a stage' (*As You Like It*, II, vii, 139): the metaphor has biblical authority: e.g. 'Surely every man walketh in a vain show' (Psalm 39: 6); in Vaughan's translation of Psalm 104, he writes: 'Thine eyes behold the earth, and the whole stage/Is moved and trembles' (*Silex*, 2nd edn, 1655).
[11] **My walk**
my attitude (to be); ***a monstrous, mountained thing*** unnatural, inflated.
[12] **Rough-cast**
roughly or unevenly covered.
[14] **relief**
(any) help.
[15] **Measures**
looks across, as if for help; ***melancholy*** note this example of the pathetic fallacy (the tendency of writers to ascribe to nature the emotions of human beings).
[16] **drops**
(the pilgrim) falls to his knees; ***rains*** weeps.
[17] **sighed**
(a) longed for (in which case the ensuing lines are figurative); (b) struggled, as if he were now a pilgrim literally climbing.
[18] **'Twixt**
Between, in the sense: 'after a long climb during which I frequently stumbled'.
[19] **pinnacle**
the summit; ***where placed*** upon which was placed, at which place.
[20] **scales**
cf. 'Scales and balances are the Lord's concern' (Proverbs 16: 11), or Daniel's interpretation of the writing on the wall: 'TEKEL: You have been weighed in the scales and found unworthy' (Daniel 5: 27). This biblical image was much used by artists, especially painters, in illustrations of the Last Judgement: e.g. the altarpiece by Rogier van der Weyden, painted 1443–6, now in the Hôtel-Dieu, Beaune, France: note that it is usually St Michael who holds the scales.
[21] **took them up**
lifted the scales; ***laid*** placed.
[22] **In the one**
on one side of the scales; ***late pains*** (his) recent troubles.
[23] **The other smoke**
In the other (he placed) smoke (i.e. worldly ***pleasures***).
[24] **But**
an emphatic 'And', suggesting surprise; ***heavier*** the 'smoke' of worldly pleasures is heavier, signalling that the pilgrim was on a course for damnation; ***grains*** scales were used to measure wheat – note that the word 'grains', although it describes something that is intrinsically small, also implies something else, much larger (e.g. a sack of wheat).
[25] **With that**
whereupon; ***some*** it is not clear who: perhaps angels representing the voices of the pilgrim's conscience; ***Straight*** immediately.
[26–7] **led/Full East**
led directly towards the East, i.e. (a) from where the sun is 'reborn' each day; (b) the direction taken by Jacob when he set out to visit his brother Laban in Haran (Genesis 29: 1); (c) the direction in which Jerusalem lies: cf. Donne, 'Good Friday, 1613: Riding Westward' (p. 79), line 10 and note.
[28] ***Jacob's bed***
Jacob, on his way from Beersheba to Haran, stopped for the night. Using a stone for a pillow, he fell asleep and dreamed of a ladder that reached from earth to heaven. In the dream, God promised the surrounding land to Jacob and his descendants. When Jacob awoke, he referred to the place where he had slept as the 'house of God, the gate of heaven' (Genesis 28: 10–22).
[29] **virgin soil**
(a) soil never touched by human feet;

(b) a state never contaminated by original sin.

[30] **rude**
rough, naked: cf. the words spoken to Moses by God, from the burning bush at Horeb, when Moses was instructed to lead his people out of Egypt: 'Remove your sandals, for the place where you stand is holy ground' (Exodus 3: 5).

[32] **Prophets and friends of God**
cf. 'Although [Wisdom] is only one, she can do everything; although unchanging, she renews everything; century after century she enters into holy souls, and makes them the friends of God and Prophets' (Wisdom of Solomon 7: 27); Abraham was called 'the Friend of God' (James 2: 23).

[33] **scarce well set**
scarcely had I settled down to sleep – note how it is ambiguous whether the following lines refer to a dream that the pilgrim had as soon as he fell asleep, or whether no sooner has he settled down to sleep than he notices something which causes him to get up again.

[34] **grove**
a word frequently used in pastoral poetry; used here to indicate a cluster of tall trees whose intermingling branches made it resemble a church or cathedral – cf. 'I found myself in a grove of bay [trees]... it was not a wood, but a building. I conceived it indeed to be a Temple of Nature' (*Lumen de Lumine*, pp. 3–4).

[41] **unthrift**
prodigal, spendthrift; ***shot*** aimed, sent speeding; ***vital*** life-giving.

[42] **A thousand pieces**
in a thousand separate rays: cf. line 68.

[43] **azure**
a serenely blue sky; ***unfold*** reveal.

[44] **Chequered**
cf. 'a chequer of mixed clouds and light' (*Lumen de Lumine*, p. 1); ***snowy fleeces*** clouds, with perhaps an oblique reference to Christ as 'lamb of God'.

[45] **The air was all in spice**
cf. the poem's motto from the Song of Songs.

[49–50] **Only a little... for ears**
The only sound that could be heard; ***fountain*** a symbol of Christ's grace: cf. the story of the Samaritan woman, whom Jesus met by Jacob's well (i.e. a cistern). She was taken aback when he reprimanded her for not asking him for a drink of living water, for he did not even have a bucket with which to bring it up from the well. Jesus replied: 'Whoever drinks from this well will become thirsty again, but whoever drinks the water that I shall give him, shall never thirst again; it will [give] him eternal life' (John 4: 3–14).

[51] **the dumb shade's language**
the rich visual and olfactory 'message' produced by the quiet of the well-shaded grove; ***spent (on)*** let flow, disturbed.

[52] **The music of her tears**
her tears the tears of the fountain – the phrase, borrowed from William Habington's 'To the Earl of Shrewsbury', involves a double pun: (a) on 'spheres' ('the music of the spheres'); (b) the tears of the *mater dolorosa* (the figure of Christ's mother weeping at the foot of the Cross).

[53] **I drew her near**
I drew near to her.

[54] **cistern**
the pool of water formed by the fountain (cf. the well in the story of the Samaritan woman).

[55] **divers stones**
divers various; ***stones*** souls: cf. 'So come to him, our living Stone – the stone rejected by men but choice and precious in the sight of God. Come and let yourselves be built, as living stones, into a spiritual temple...' (1 Peter 2: 4–5 & ff.); an image much used in Hermetic philosophy: 'Transform yourselves from dead stones into living philosophical stones' (Thomas Vaughan, *Anima Magica Abscondita*, p. 35); also: on the Day of Judgement 'the cursed shall like stones and lead

be thrown downward: but the blessed shall like eagles fly on high' (Paracelsus, *Of the Nature of Things*, transl. J.F. [1650], p. 98).

[57] **The first**
i.e. the 'bright' and 'round' souls of the saved; ***quick*** not only fast, but living.

[58] **flood**
the water.

[59] **the last**
the 'ill-shaped' and 'dull' stones of the damned; ***more heavy*** passing more slowly, more despondently – note the deliberately mixed metaphor.

[60] **Nailed to the Centre**
this image is deeply ambivalent. ***Centre*** (a) earth; (b) hell, which was located in the centre of the earth; in both cases, the meaning is that the souls of the damned are 'fixed' for ever – cf. Vaughan's description in 'The World Contemned': 'The flesh . . . draws us back to the Earth, as to its proper centre and original; but the soul being descended from the Father of Lights is like the sparks of fire still flying upwards' (from *Flores Solitudinis*); the last phrase of this passage suggests a third meaning of 'centre': by virtue of the verb ***Nailed***, the ***Centre*** is also (c) Christ's Cross, a reminder that Christ came into the world in order to save sinners: cf. 'If we say that we have no sin, we deceive ourselves, and the truth is not in us. If we confess our sins, he is faithful and just to forgive us our sins, and to cleanse us from all unrighteousness . . . . he is the propitiation for our sins: and not for ours only, but also for the sins of the whole world' (1 John 1: 8–9; 2: 2). It is because the pilgrim is still unable to confess *his* sins that he cannot decipher this image: cf. line 48.

[63–4] **My restless eye . . . brought**
restless because the pilgrim has still not understood what he has experienced; ***As strange an object*** the regeneration for which the poet yearns; ***brought*** discovered, fell upon (i.e. a vision almost equivalent to that for which the poet is longing as described in the following stanza).

[65] **described**
caught sight of, succeeded in discerning.

[67] **Some fast asleep**
the spiritually slothful: cf. 'The Night', lines 23–4; ***broad-eyed*** awake.

[68] **taking in**
basking in, enjoying (Christ's blessing/the sun); ***ray*** God and Christ were both symbolised by the sun.

[69] **musing long**
after pondering for a long time.

[70] **A rushing wind**
a conflation of two biblical passages: (a) 'On the day of Pentecost, the apostles were all together, when suddenly there came from the sky a sound like *a mighty rushing wind* which filled the entire house in which they were sitting. And there appeared to them tongues as of fire, dispersed among them and resting on each one. And they were all filled with the Holy Spirit . . . ' (Acts 2: 1–4); (b) 'The wind blows *where it wills*; you hear the sound of it, but you do not know where it comes from, *nor where* it is going. So with everyone who is born of spirit' (John 3: 8).

[71] **whence it stirred**
from where it came.

[72] **No where**
It has been suggested that Vaughan intended 'nor where', which would have echoed the phrase from John 3: 8.

[73] **each shade**
each part of the shade described in line 51: cf. also line 4.

[74] **Dispatched an eye**
dispatch to send something; thus, 'sent my eye' or 'looked'.

[76] **Least**
any, the least; ***reply*** i.e. the poet wanted to see whether the wind caused any leaf to move.

[79] **where 'twas, or where not**
from where the rushing wind did or did not come.

[80] **It**
the wind; ***where I please*** cf. the spirit

which blows 'where it wills' in John 3: 8.
[81] **On me one breath**
Breathe on me (but) once.

[82] **let me die before my death!**
let me discover you (and so 'die to the world') before I die.

115 / *The Retreat*

Happy those early days! When I
Shined in my Angel-infancy.
Before I understood this place
Appointed for my second race,
Or taught my soul to fancy aught
But a white, celestial thought;
When yet I had not walked above
A mile or two from my first love,
And looking back (at that short space)
Could see a glimpse of his bright face;
When on some *gilded cloud or flower*
My gazing soul would dwell an hour,
And in those weaker glories spy
Some shadows of eternity;
Before I taught my tongue to wound
My conscience with a sinful sound,
Or had the black art to dispense
A several sin to every sense,
But felt through all this fleshly dress
Bright *shoots* of everlastingness.
O how I long to travel back
And tread again that ancient track!
That I might once more reach that plain
Where first I left my glorious train,
From whence the enlightened spirit sees
That shady city of palm trees.
But (ah!) my soul with too much stay
Is drunk, and staggers in the way.
Some men a forward motion love,
But I by backward steps would move
And, when this dust falls to the urn,
In that state I came, return.

A meditation on the desire to return to the innocence of childhood based on the text: 'I tell you, whoever does not accept the kingdom of God like a child will never enter it' (Mark 10: 15). The poem is composed of thirty-two iambic tetrameters, rhyming in couplets. The title plays upon two meanings of the word: ***retreat*** can mean (a) backward movement; (b) withdrawal from the world to a secluded place for the purpose of religious meditation or devotion. Note how the first verse paragraph (lines 1–20) deals predominantly with time; the second (lines 21–32) predominantly with space.

[1–2]
note how the first two lines govern the whole of the first verse paragraph.

[3] **this place**
the world in which Vaughan lived: England during the Commonwealth.

[4] **my second race**
'second' because the pre-existence of the soul is assumed (see last line): cf. also 'We are surrounded by a great cloud of witnesses [to faith in Christ], for which reason we must throw off every encumbrance, every sin to which we cling, and resolutely run the race for which we are entered, our eyes fixed on Jesus, on whom faith depends from start to finish' (Hebrews 12: 1).

[5] **aught**
anything.

[6] **white, celestial thought**
white the colour of faith and purity; ***celestial*** heavenly.

[7] **yet**
still.

[8] **mile or two**
a relatively short distance; ***my first love*** the love of Christ that the poet had as a child: cf. Christ's message to Ephesus: 'But I have this against you: you have left your first love' (i.e. 'you do not love me now as you did at first': Revelation 2: 4): human inability to sustain a love of God is a major theme of both the Old and the New Testament.

[9] **that short space**
the time of his childhood.

[10] **his**
Christ's, whose presence is implicit in line 8.

[11] **gilded cloud**
it was out of a thick cloud that God spoke to Moses and gave him the Ten Commandments (Exodus 19–20) and, at the moment of Christ's baptism by John the Baptist, that a voice spoke from a cloud, announcing: 'This is my own son' (Luke 9: 35); also, perhaps more specifically, Jesus's promise of his second coming: 'Then men will see "The Son of Man coming on the clouds with great power and glory"' (Mark 13: 26, quoting Daniel 7: 13); ***flower*** cf. 'Man born of a woman has a short and troubled life. He blossoms like a flower and then he withers' (Job 14: 1–2) and 'Consider how the lilies grow in the fields, ... Even Solomon in all his splendour was not dressed as well as them. If that is how God clothes the grass in the fields, which is here today and tomorrow is thrown onto the fire, will he not take even greater care in clothing you?' (Matthew 6: 28, 30).

[13] **weaker glories**
i.e. the cloud and the flower.

[15–16] **Before ... sound**
conscience conscience, but also 'soul' – note how the poet's words first reveal his sin: cf. 'Do not be bitter, or over-passionate, or angry. Do not shout or insult anyone, or even say anything that could cause hurt' (Ephesians 4: 31); thus, 'Before the poet had become accustomed to saying hurtful things that offended his own conscience'.

[17–18] **black art**
witchcraft, evil design; ***dispense*** distribute; ***several*** separate, different; thus, 'or been sufficiently wicked to allow each of his senses to indulge in a separate sin' (e.g. listening to evil-minded gossip or seeking sensual pleasure).

[19] **fleshly dress**
the poet's physical body: ***dress*** because 'covering' the soul.

[20] **Bright *shoots* of everlastingness**
intimations of the soul: cf. 'The conscience, the character of a God stamped in it, and the apprehension of eternity, do all prove it a shoot of everlastingness' (Owen Felltham, *Resolves* [1634], p. 197), possibly based on God's promise to Ezekiel: 'O mountains of Israel, you will shoot forth your branches, and yield your fruit to my people of Israel' (Ezekiel 36: 8); also Christ's reminder to his disciples to be ready to recognise the signs of his second coming: 'Behold the fig-tree, and other trees. When they shoot forth [i.e. burst into leaf and flower], you know that summer is at hand. In the same way, when you see these things [the signs: wars, earthquake, famine, etc.] come to pass, you shall know that the kingdom of God is at hand' (Luke 21: 29–31).

[21] **O how I long to travel back**
see Mark 10: 15, quoted above in the introduction to this poem.

[22] **tread**
this verb is used in the Bible to describe physical treading or trampling (e.g. the Lord trod or trampled on his enemies or those of his people who forsook him, as upon a winepress: Isaiah 63: 3–6); it is contrasted with 'walk', which is used to signify submission to God (e.g. 'Let us walk in the light of the Lord', Isaiah 2: 3–5).

[24] **glorious train**
succession of glorious experiences.

[25] **From whence**
From where: i.e. from the innocence of/pertinent to childhood; ***enlightened spirit*** not the enlightened child, but the spirit of a person who can 'travel back' to a time pertinent to that of childhood.

[26] **palm tree**
cf. 'And Moses went up from the plains . . . and the Lord showed him . . . the plain of the valley of Jericho, the city of palm-trees . . . and the Lord said unto him, "This is the land which I promised to Abraham, to Isaac, and to Jacob, saying I will give it to your children"' (Deuteronomy 34: 1–4): here, an image of the heavenly Jerusalem, as described in Revelation 21: 2 ('And I, John, saw the holy city, the new Jerusalem, coming down from God out of heaven, dressed like a bride for her husband').

[27–8] **stay**
delay; ***soul . . . is drunk and staggers*** cf. Plato:

Socrates: 'Did we not agree . . . that when the soul enquires into things by way of the physical senses – whether sight or hearing or any other sense . . . – such contact with the physical world will draw it into the realm of things that change, thereby causing it to lose its way and become confused and *dizzy, as though it were drunk?'*

'We did.'

'But when the soul enquires into something after its own fashion, it passes into the realm of the pure and everlasting and immortal and changeless . . . and this condition of the soul we call wisdom.' (*Phaedo*, 79 c, d)

[29] **a forward motion love**
love to move forwards.

[31] **dust**
the dust of his own mortal body, after death and cremation; ***urn*** the urn used for his own ashes, after death.

[32] **that state I came**
implies a pre-existent state: see line 4.

116 / *The Morning Watch*

O joys! Infinite sweetness! With what flowers
And shoots of glory my soul breaks and buds!
All the long hours
Of night and rest,
Through the still shrouds
Of sleep and clouds,
This dew fell on my breast.
O how it bloods
And spirits all my Earth! hark! In what rings
And *Hymning Circulations* the quick world
Awakes and sings!
The rising winds
And falling springs,
Birds, beasts, all things
Adore him in their kinds.
Thus all is hurled
In sacred *Hymns* and *Order*: the great Chime
And Symphony of nature! Prayer is
The world in tune,
A spirit-voice
And vocal joys
Whose *echo* is heav'n's bliss.
O let me climb
When I lie down! The pious soul by night
Is like a clouded star whose beams, though said
To shed their light
Under some cloud,
Yet *are* above
And shine and move
Beyond that misty shroud.
So in my bed,
That curtained grave, though sleep (like ashes) hide
My lamp and life, both shall in thee abide.

The **Morning Watch** is the first watch of the day, during the very early dawn (3.00–6.00 a.m.); the time of morning prayer. This is therefore a morning prayer of thanks to God in thirty-three iambic lines: generally, two pentameters, followed by four dimeters, a trimeter, a further dimeter, with an interestingly varied rhyme-scheme. The poet is drawing a parallel between the new day and the reawakening of his soul. Note the importance of two rhyme-words that appear both at the beginning and the end (shroud/cloud).

[1] **infinite sweetness**
cf. 'O book! Infinite sweetness' (Herbert, 'The Holy Scriptures (1)', line 1): by implication, Vaughan is contrasting Herbert's delight in the Bible with his own delight in nature.
[2] **shoots**
see 'The Retreat', line 20 and note; ***breaks*** as in the expression 'dawn breaks', signifying a sudden change from one state to another, suggesting here that the poet's soul was 'asleep' before its 'breaking' (cf. 'The Dawning', lines 6, 48); ***buds*** the branches on a plant or tree that appear dead all winter suddenly burst into buds in the spring.
[5] **shrouds**
sheets which conceal, especially those which cover a corpse.
[6] **clouds**
the uncertain forms encountered in dreams.
[7] **dew**
in the Bible, frequently used to describe God's grace: e.g. Isaac's blessing of Jacob: 'May God give you the dew of heaven' (Genesis 27: 28).
[8] **bloods**
awakes, cause to become infused with vital or life-giving spirit.
[9] **spirits**
gives spirit to; also, highly rarefied substances linking the soul and the body; ***earth*** body; ***rings*** concentric circles, each of which encloses a different level of creation: e.g. stones, plants, animals and birds, man and woman, angels: see 'The World', line 2 and note.
[10] ***Hymning Circulations***
rotations, singing songs of praise; perhaps also a reference to the recent discovery of the circulation of the blood by William Harvey (1578–1657): cf. lines 8–9; ***quick*** living.
[13] **falling springs**
the fountains of streams, the water from which gathers in a pool before overflowing and descending a slope.
[14] **things**
creatures.
[15] **him**
Christ; ***in their kinds*** in a fashion appropriate to each different species.
[16–17] **hurled**
thrown violently: note the paradox of hurling in *Hymns* and *Order* (it is possible that Vaughan intended 'whirled'); ***Chime*** the sound of a bell, especially one announcing the time of day or a festivity.
[18] **Symphony**
harmony of sound produced by different instruments; the modern use of the word 'symphony' dates only from the mid eighteenth century, about the time of Haydn.
[19] **in tune**
where everything exists in harmony: cf. 'Prayer . . . a kind of tune, which all things hear and fear' (Herbert, 'Prayer (1)', line 8).
[20] **spirit-voice**
voice of the spirit, as opposed to talk about material concerns.
[22] ***echo***
i.e. the sound of the prayer heard in heaven – because prayer is a God-given grace, it originates in heaven, and is reflected back to heaven by humanity.
[23] **climb**
ascend, i.e. in or by way of [the poet's] prayers.
[24–30] **The pious soul . . . misty shroud**
one of Vaughan's most startling conceits, as it hinges on likening a star, which lies 'above' the clouds, to the soul, which lies 'below' them.
[25–7] **though said**
though popularly believed; ***shed their light*** cast their light diffusely; ***Under*** on the underside of; thus, 'although it is commonly thought that clouds prevent the light of a star reaching earth, diffusing it so that all that can be seen of it is the shimmering light on the underside of a cloud'.

[28–30] **Yet *are*... shroud**
move act, animate; thus, 'None the less, its light really belongs in heaven, where it shines and animates, far above the shimmering light that can be seen on the underside of the cloud.'

[31] **So in my bed**
'In the same way, when I lie in bed, asleep' (see line 6).

[32] **curtained grave**
a common kind of bed in the seventeenth century was the four-poster, in which posts at each corner supported a canopy from which curtains hung, entirely enclosing the bed; the likening of a bed to a grave was a commonplace of Renaissance poetry, and an image much used in alchemy (cf. Donne, 'The Sun Rising' [p. 45], lines 19–20); ***sleep*** note the relation of sleep and 'clouds' in line 6; ***ashes*** embers, which appear to have lost their heat, whereas closer inspection will reveal that they still retain it; indeed, in the seventeenth century the embers of the previous evening's fire were very often used to relight the fire in the morning; ***hide*** appear to hide.

[33] **lamp**
the light and heat of his soul: cf. the parable of the ten young women told to his disciples by Jesus:

'The kingdom of Heaven will be like this. Once there were ten young women who took their oil lamps and went out to meet the bridegroom. Five of them were foolish, and the other five were wise. The foolish ones took their lamps but did not take any extra oil with them, while the wise ones also took containers full of oil for their lamps. The bridegroom was late in coming, so the young women grew tired and fell asleep.

'It was already midnight when the cry rang out, "Here is the bridegroom! Come and meet him!" The ten young women woke up and adjusted the flame on their lamps. Then the foolish ones said to the wise ones, "Our lamps are going out. Could you give us some of your oil?" The wise ones replied that they hadn't enough, and so it was that while the foolish young women were away looking for more oil for their lamps, the bridegroom arrived and the wise young women went in with him to the wedding feast. When the foolish young women returned, they found the door locked against them. Hearing their pleas to be let in, the bridegroom answered, "Certainly not! I do not know you."' And Jesus concluded, 'Watch therefore [be always ready], because you do not know the day or the hour when I shall return.' (Matthew 25: 1–13)

[33] **shall in thee abide**
cf. Jesus's words to his disciples: 'I am the vine and you are the branches. He that abides in me [lives in me – i.e. 'is faithful to me'] and in whom I abide [in whom I am present] will be fruitful in all his or her endeavours, but without me you can do nothing' (John 15: 5).

117 / *Peace*

My soul, there is a country
Far beyond the stars
Where stands a wingèd sentry
All skilful in the wars.

There above noise and danger
Sweet peace sits crowned with smiles
And one born in a Manger
Commands the beauteous files.

He is thy gracious friend
And (O my soul, awake!)
Did in pure love descend
To die here for thy sake.

If thou canst get but thither,
There grows the flower of peace,
The Rose that cannot wither:
Thy fortress and thy ease.

Leave then thy foolish ranges,
For none can thee secure
But one who never changes:
Thy God, thy Life, thy Cure.

A poem of twenty iambic trimeters, rhyming *a b a b*, and making considerable use of feminine endings. The poet reminds himself of the qualities of Paradise, and that the only way to get there is by way of Christ. Note the importance of the concept of 'peace'. It was made into a well-known Anglican hymn (*General Hymns: Ancient and Modern: Revised*: No. 286), sung in five verses, each of four lines.

[1] **country**
Paradise.
[3] **wingèd sentry**
an angel guarding the gates of Paradise – cf. the Cherubim, a kind of angel, that God placed at the entrance to the Garden of Eden in order to guard it (Genesis 3: 24).
[4] **All skilful in the wars**
angels were traditionally associated with the fight between Good and Evil, hence their skill in war – the image may have been suggested by Revelation 12: 7 ('And there was war in heaven: Michael and his angels fought against the dragon') or by Ezekiel's vision: see especially Ezekiel, chapter 10.
[5] **above**
beyond; ***noise*** the bustle of the material world; ***danger*** not only physical danger (war, sickness) but also, and more specifically, the danger of falling away from the love of God.
[6] **peace**
note the personification; here, a separate figure from Christ, but Christ was also identified with peace: 'For he is our peace' (Ephesians 2: 14).

[7] **one born in a Manger**
manger a box or trough in a stable from which horses and cattle eat; the *one born in a Manger* Christ: cf. the angel's message to the shepherds: 'Do not be afraid, for today, in the city of David, your saviour has been born, Christ the Lord! And this is how you will recognise him. You will find the baby wrapped in strips of cloth, lying in a manger' (Luke 2: 11–12).
[8] **beauteous files**
an army of angels: cf. the vision of John, in which he sees Christ enthroned and surrounded by four creatures (a lion, a bull, a figure with a man's head, and an eagle, representing the four evangelists: Mark, Luke, Matthew and John respectively), by twenty-four elders, and endless *files* of angels: 'Again I looked, and I heard angels, thousands and millions of them! They stood round the throne, the four living creatures, and the elders, and sang [praises] in a loud voice' (Revelation 5: 11).
[9] **friend**
used in its biblical sense: cf. the lesson Jesus gives his disciples immediately after teaching them 'the Lord's Prayer': 'Imagine that you have to go to a friend's house at midnight and say to him, "Friend, lend me three loaves of bread. A friend of mine, who is on a journey, has just arrived at my house and I haven't anything to give him to eat." Suppose your friend were to answer: "Don't bother me! My family and I are in bed and the house is shut up for the night. I can't give you anything." I assure you that even if your friend does not give you the bread because he is your friend, none the less he will give you all you ask for if you are not ashamed to keep on asking.... And so I tell you, Ask, and you will receive; seek, and you will find; knock, and the door will be opened to you... your Father in heaven will give the Holy Spirit to those who ask him' (Luke 11: 1–13).
[10–12] **And... thy sake**
According to Christian belief, Jesus Christ 'descended' from heaven to earth out of his love for humankind in order to take upon himself collective human original sin, the consequence of Adam's disobedience. The most impressive seventeenth-century version of this belief is contained in Milton's *Paradise Lost*, written only a few years later than this poem and published in 1667: see especially books 3 and 10.
[13] **thither**
there, i.e. Paradise.
[14] **There**
emphatic (it is only there that...).
[15] **The Rose that cannot wither**
cf. 'Fast [= secure] in thy Paradise, where no flower can wither' (Herbert, 'The Flower' [p. 237], line 23): from early medieval times, the *Rose* was associated with the Virgin Mary, albeit with scant biblical authority: one text commonly cited is 'Listen to me, you holy children, and bring forth fruit, as the rose that is planted by the brooks of the field' (Ecclesiasticus 39: 13); but here, *Rose* is Christ, perhaps because a rose has thorns (cf. Christ's crown of thorns, John 19: 2–5) and red is the colour of *caritas* or perfect spiritual love.
[16] **fortress**
refers to 'Rose', but note the contrast of textures and qualities.
[17] **ranges**
purposeless wanderings.
[18] **none can thee secure**
no one can protect you.
[19] **But**
except.
[20] **Cure**
(a) care, i.e. as object of the poet's attention; (b) restoration to health; (c) the being to which the poet entrusts his spiritual welfare (cf. 'curate').

118 / *The Dawning*

Ah! What time wilt thou come? When shall that cry
'The Bridegroom's Coming!' fill the sky?
Shall it in the evening run
When our words and works are done?
Or will thy all-surpassing light
Break at midnight
When either sleep or some dark pleasure
Possesseth mad man without measure?

Or shall these early, fragrant hours
Unlock thy bowers
And with their blush of light descry
Thy locks crowned with eternity?
Indeed, it is the only time
That with thy glory doth best chime!
All now are stirring, every field
Full hymns doth yield!
The whole Creation shakes off night
And for thy shadow looks the light.
Stars now vanish without number.
Sleepy planets set and slumber.
The pursy clouds disband and scatter.
All expect some sudden matter.
Not one beam triumphs, but from far
That morning star!

O at what time so ever thou
(Unknown to us) the heavens wilt bow
And, with thy Angels in the *van*,
Descend to judge poor careless man
Grant I may not, like puddle, lie
In a corrupt security
Where if a traveller water crave
He finds it dead, and in a grave.
But as this restless vocal *Spring*
All day and night doth run and sing
And, though here born, yet is acquainted
Elsewhere, and flowing keeps untainted,
So let me all my busy age
In thy free services engage,

And though (while here) of force I must
Have commerce sometimes with poor dust,
And in my flesh though vile and low
As this doth in her channel flow,
Yet let my course, my aim, my love
And chief acquaintance be above.
So when that day and hour shall come
In which thy self will be the Sun
Thou'lt find me dressed and on my way
Watching the break of thy great day.

This fusion of experience and parable is a meditation on the parable of the wise and foolish young women as told in Matthew 25: 1–13. The poet likens the dawn to the second coming of Christ. It is in forty-eight iambic lines, mostly tetrameters, with an initial pentameter, and four intermittent dimeters, rhyming in couplets.

[1] **what time wilt thou come?**
thou Christ. The reference is to the parable of the wise and foolish young women (see 'The Morning Watch', note to line 33), which was based on the Palestinian custom whereby the bridegroom went to fetch his bride from her parents' home. In this parable, Christ exhorts those who believe in him to be always prepared for his coming, as they know 'neither the day nor the hour' when he will return.
[3] **run**
be heard continuously.
[4] **our words and works**
all that we have said and done in the course of the day; ***done*** finished.
[6] **midnight**
when we might least expect or desire it.
[7] **dark**
forbidden, erotic.
[8] **without measure**
to such an extent that man is powerless to resist it.
[9] **fragrant**
sweet-smelling, because the world is fresh again after the night.
[10] **Unlock thy bowers**
bowers dwelling-places, inner rooms, private places – i.e. 'provide the key to those secret places where you live'.
[11] **their**
refers to 'hours', i.e. the very early morning; ***blush*** the faint pink of dawn; ***descry*** reveal, catch sight of, succeed in discerning.
[14] **chime**
literally, the sound of a church-bell announcing the time; figuratively, 'agree'.
[15] **All**
all things in nature.
[16] **hymns**
literally, songs of praise, usually of God; here, it refers to the sounds of the birds (and animals) awaking to a new day. During the spring and summer (i.e. while birds are raising their young), at the first sign of dawn, all birds begin chattering loudly, a phenomenon popularly called 'the dawn chorus'; ***yield*** produce, as if the hymns were a harvest.
[18] **for thy shadow looks the light**
the light seeks out (in order to lighten) the shadow of night cast by God the previous evening.
[19] **without number**
refers to 'stars', thus: 'the countless stars now fade from sight'.

[20] **Sleepy**
because diving towards the western horizon; ***set*** (a) to move below the horizon; (b) fade, like the stars; ***slumber*** go to sleep (when they are no longer visible).
[21] **pursy**
(a) puckered, like cloth; (b) swollen, heavy; ***disband*** break up.
[22] **All expect**
everything expects; ***sudden matter*** unexpected event.
[23–4] **Not one beam . . . morning star!**
the ***morning star*** Christ: cf. 'I Jesus have sent my angel to you with this testimony for the churches. I am the root and offspring of David, the bright morning star' (Revelation 22: 16) – i.e. Christ's appearance casts all other 'beams' of light in the shade.
[25–6] **at what time soever . . . (' . . . ') wilt bow**
'at whatever time you . . . decide to bow [i.e. lower] the heavens (so as to descend to earth)', cf. the psalmist's call upon God to help him in battle: 'He bowed the heavens, and came down; thick darkness was under his feet' (Psalm 18: 9; also 2 Samuel 22: 10).
[27] **van**
vanguard, the front ranks (as of an army); note the analogy between 'front ranks' and early morning.
[28] **poor**
inadequate, insignificant (if without God); ***careless*** without thought or care of God.
[29] **like puddle**
stagnant or polluted water: the image may have been inspired by the prophet Nahum's description of the Ancient Assyrian city of Nineveh, to which the Jews were once subject, as a dried-up pool (Nahum 2: 8).
[30] **corrupt security**
feel myself to be protected by false gods and idols (such as those of the Assyrians: see Nahum 1: 14).
[31] **Where if . . . a grave**
i.e. *dead* water – these lines are intended to contrast with the story of the Samaritan woman, who was taken aback when Christ reprimanded her for not asking him for a drink of 'living water' (John 4: 3–14): cf. 'Regeneration', lines 49–56 and note.
[33] **restless**
ceaselessly moving; ***vocal*** making a constant noise; ***Spring*** a fountain of living water and, thus, by analogy, Christ – cf. 'Regeneration', line 49.
[34] **run**
flow; ***sing*** the sound of the water continuously splashing up or out from the spring: note the parallel with 'hymns' in line 16 and note.
[35–6] **here born**
i.e. arising, coming into existence here; ***acquainted/Elsewhere*** i.e. knows of another existence (i.e. the invisible pool deep underground or in the mountainside, from which the spring gushes – note the analogy with Christ, and heaven); ***flowing*** by flowing; ***untainted*** pure.
[37] **busy**
a commonplace about life, but also, perhaps, because Vaughan was a practising doctor.
[38] **free services**
a paradox (being 'free' means *not* to be in 'service' to another), the purpose of which is to emphasise the freedom one wins by surrendering oneself to Christ: cf. 'O God, . . . whose service is perfect freedom' (the 2nd Collect, for Peace, at Morning Prayer, *Book of Common Prayer*).
[39] **while here**
i.e. on earth (as opposed to heaven); ***of force*** of necessity, unavoidably.
[40] **commerce**
dealings; ***poor dust*** trivial mortal concerns.
[41] **in**
accept that I live within; ***vile*** (a) morally depraved; (b) contaminated; ***low*** (a) dejected; (b) low-lying.
[42] **this doth**
this which (flows).
[43] **course**
progressive movement, as of a life, direction; ***aim*** objective.

[44] **chief acquaintance**
most important concern.
[46] **they self . . . Sun**
'you, Christ, will come in place of the sun' (which rises each day).

[47] **dressed**
ready, prepared; ***on my way*** i.e. already setting out (to meet Christ).
[48] **Watching**
(a) on guard [i.e. looking after his own soul]; (b) alert, ready; (c) admiring.

119 / *The World*

All that is in the world, the lust of the flesh, the lust of the eyes, and the pride of life, is not of the father but is of the world. And yet the world, and everything in it that people lust after, passes away, whereas he who does the will of God will live for ever. (1 John 2: 16–17)

I saw Eternity the other night
Like a great *Ring* of pure and endless light,
All calm as it was bright,
And round beneath it, Time – in hours, days, years,
Driven by the spheres –
Like a vast shadow moved, in which the world
And all her train were hurled.
The doting Lover in his quaintest strain
Did there complain:
Near him, his lute, his fancy, and his flights,
Wit's sour delights,
With gloves and knots, the silly snares of pleasure
Yet his dear treasure:
All scattered lay, while he his eyes did pour
Upon a flower.

The darksome Statesman hung with weights and woe
Like a thick midnight-fog moved there so slow
He did not stay nor go;
Condemning thoughts (like sad eclipses) scowl
Upon his soul,
And clouds of crying witnesses without
Pursued him with one shout.
Yet digged the mole, and lest his ways be found
Worked under ground

Where he did clutch his prey – but One did see
That policy:
Churches and altars fed him, perjuries
Were gnats and flies,
It rained about him blood and tears, but he
Drank them as free.

The fearful Miser on a heap of rust
Sat pining all his life there, did scarce trust
His own hands with the dust,
Yet would not place one piece above, but lives
In fear of thieves.
Thousands there were as frantic as himself
And hugged each one his pelf:
The down-right Epicure placed heaven in sense
And scorned pretence,
While others, slipped into a wide excess,
Said little less.
The weaker sort slight, trivial wares enslave
Who think them brave,
And poor, despisèd Truth sat counting by
Their victory.

Yet some, who all this while did weep and sing,
And sing, and weep, soared up into the *Ring*,
But most would use no wing.
O fools (said I), thus to prefer dark night
Before true light,
To live in grots and caves and hate the day
Because it shows the way,
The way which from this dead and dark abode
Leads up to God,
A way where you might tread the Sun and be
More bright than he.
But as I did their madness so discuss
One whispered thus,
This Ring the Bridegroom did for none provide
But for his bride.

A visionary poem in four stanzas of fifteen lines, each stanza made up of two pentameters followed by alternating trimeters or dimeters and pentameters, with a final dimeter, rhyming *a a a* and thereafter in pairs. The poet's vision of Eternity is followed by a number of cameos of different 'types' of men, each of whom is so engrossed in his worldly concerns that he shows no desire for Eternity: this leaves the poet wondering.

[1–7] **I saw... moved**
The image is probably derived from Plato: '[The father who created the world] made an image of eternity which is time... parted into months and days and years.... These are the forms of Time which imitate eternity and which move in a circle measured by number' (Plato, *Timaeus*, 37 ff.); it may also owe something to Isaiah's description of God: 'Have you not understood what the foundations of the earth are? They were made by him who sits upon the circle of the earth, and for whom the people below are as small and insignificant as ants. He stretched out the heavens like a curtain, and folded them around him like a tent in which to live' (Isaiah 40: 21–2); ***Ring*** throughout history, people have conceived totality (i.e. the world, the cosmos) as an enormous circle.

[5–6] **Driven by.../like a vast shadow.../in which**
all refer to 'Time'; ***driven*** moved, given movement or impulse: cf. Donne, 'Good Friday, 1613: Riding Westward' (p. 79), lines 1–6 and note.

[7] **all her train**
train a procession of people that follow after someone of great importance; thus, 'everything that follows (and is therefore 'subject to') Time': i.e. everything in the world; ***hurled*** brought confusedly together: see 'The Morning Watch', note to lines 16–17.

[8] **doting**
extravagantly or foolishly infatuated; ***quaintest*** most ingenious, clever, elaborate; ***strain*** manner: cf. Herbert's phrase, 'The wanton lover in a curious strain' ('Dullness', line 5).

[9] **complain**
grieve over the treatment accorded him by his mistress.

[10] **fancy**
(a) a spectral apparition, perhaps of his mistress; (b) fantasy; ***flights*** (a) pens made from the wing feather of a large bird; (b) arrows, i.e. Cupid's darts; (c) flights of fantasy: lute, fancy, and flights are all clichés associated with a lover.

[11] **Wit**
(a) the mind; (b) lively intelligence; ***Wit's... delights sour*** peevish, bitter; i.e. the pains in which doting lovers take pleasure.

[12] **knots**
ribbons, tied in a knot to signal love for someone; ***silly*** foolish, naive.

[13] **Yet... treasure**
But none the less of great value to the lover.

[14] **pour**
(a) cause to flow (i.e. tears), with a pun on 'pore', to study closely; i.e. the lover is a student who should have been studying.

[15] **flower**
a symbol of transitoriness, referring here to the lover's emotion – cf. 'the flower fades but the word of God will last for ever' (Isaiah 40: 8).

[16] **darksome**
gloomy; ***Statesman*** one who holds an office of state; ***weights*** symbols of his office, such as heavy golden chains that he might wear round his neck; ***woe*** suggesting that power does not bring happiness.

[17] **Like a thick midnight-fog**
an impenetrable night-time fog makes it impossible for one to travel; ***there*** i.e. the statesman forms part of the same vision as described in the opening lines, even though it is not clear exactly where each of the figures in the poem belongs in the 'train' (line 7).

[18] **did not stay nor go**
neither stood still nor moved anywhere (i.e. the statesman's worldly cares have brought him to an impasse, a situation in which he is stagnating).

[19–20] **Condemning . . . soul**
Condemning thoughts (a) thoughts the statesman has of condemning others; (b) thoughts by which he himself is damned; ***sad*** dark; ***eclipses*** here, refers to the way the statesman's countenance is darkened by his evil thoughts; ***scowl . . . soul*** these evil thoughts appear forbidding and threatening both *on* and *to* his soul.
[21–2] **clouds of crying witnesses**
(a) people pursuing the statesman, like a swarm of insects, to intercede on their behalf in a law-court (i.e. worldly concerns), probably offering bribes; (b) a crowd of witnesses to faith in Jesus Christ (cf. lines 46–7) and 'We are surrounded by a great cloud of witnesses [to faith in Christ] (Hebrews 12: 1); cf. 'The Retreat', note to line 4) – i.e. people figuratively calling upon the statesman's conscience.
[23–4] **mole**
(a) literally, a small rodent that burrows underground in search of worms, reputed to be blind; (b) figuratively, someone who works in darkness; someone who is devious: here, refers to the statesman who avoids the 'crying witnesses' (i.e. he is morally blind) – the image was probably derived from Herbert: 'Like *moles* within us, heave, and cast about;/ And till they foot and clutch their *prey* . . .' ('Confession', lines 14–15); ***lest*** fearing that; ***under ground*** deviously.
[25] **prey**
the word suggests that the statesman was willing to kill in order to advance himself (see 'blood' in line 29); it also recalls a well-known phrase from Isaiah's prophecy of Christ's coming: 'Woe to those who enact unjust statutes and who write oppressive decrees, depriving the needy of judgement and robbing the poor among my people of their rights, making widows their *prey*, and plundering the orphans' (Isaiah 10: 1–2); ***One*** God.
[26] **policy**
strategy.
[27] **Churches . . . fed him**
he extorted money not only from churchmen, but even from the money (the collection) given by the congregation and blessed at the altar.
[27–8] **perjuries/ . . . flies**
uttering wilfully false evidence was of as little consequence to his conscience as were gnats and flies to his body.
[29–30] **It rained . . . free**
the blood (of those whom the statesman was responsible for killing) and the tears (of those whose appeals for assistance he ignored) descended upon him profusely – cf. 'On the day Lot left Sodom, fire and sulphur *rained down* from heaven and killed the sinners. The same will happen on the day the Son of Man is revealed' (Luke 17: 29–30); ***but he . . . free*** the Israelites were forbidden to eat or drink blood (see Leviticus 7: 26), and were expected to assist all those in need: cf. Job's defence: 'If I have failed to give to the poor, or caused a widow to weep . . . let my arms be broken' (Job 31: 16, 22); more specifically, the image recalls John's vision of the Great Whore of Babylon, the original of all perversion: 'And I saw that the woman was *drunk with the blood* of God's people and the blood of those who were killed because they had been loyal to Jesus' (Revelation 17: 6); ***as free*** freely, i.e. in great quantity.
[31] **fearful**
frightened; ***rust*** see note to lines 34–5 below; the word indicates that the miser's treasure has lost any value it might have had.
[32] **there**
the miser also forms part of the original vision.
[33] **dust**
i.e. the rust.
[34–5] **Yet would not . . . thieves**
would not give one piece of his treasure towards a good action – cf. 'Do not store up for yourselves treasure on earth, where it is subject to rust and to moths and where it is coveted by thieves, but store up

treasure in heaven, where it cannot be spoiled by rust or moths, and where there are no thieves to steal it' (Matthew 6: 19–20).

[36] **frantic**
madly excited.

[37] **pelf**
money (a term of contempt).

[38] **down-right Epicure**
a person solely devoted to pleasure – hence one who believes sensual pleasure is 'heaven'.

[39] **pretence**
the tacit claim of righteous critics to having greater spiritual or moral worth than the Epicure – note how Vaughan applies a negatively loaded word to the righteous.

[40] **others, slipped into a wide excess**
gluttons, etc.

[41] **Said little less**
i.e. held the same scorn of 'pretence' as the Epicure.

[42–3] **The weaker sort . . . brave**
weaker the more (morally) feeble of those whom the poet sees in his vision, materialists; ***brave*** magnificent; thus: 'The more morally corrupt are entirely possessed by their love for small, everyday articles, which they imagine are of magnificent value.'

[44] **And**
has the value of 'meanwhile'; ***despisèd*** early Christians identified Christ with the suffering 'Servant of the Lord' who would rescue his people, but was 'despised and rejected by men' (Isaiah 53: 3); cf. also St Paul's warning: 'Whoever despises this advice [that men should live in holiness] is not only despising his fellow men, but also God who gave us his Holy Spirit' (1 Thessalonians 4: 8); ***Truth*** (a) a personification of truth, recalling Jesus's teaching about freedom: 'know the truth, and the truth will make you free' (John 8: 32), suggesting that those who despise 'Truth' are figuratively imprisoned; also (b) Christ: cf. 'I am the way, I am the truth, and I am life' (John 14: 6) – the image is derived from Herbert: 'While Truth sat by, counting his victories' ('The Church Militant', line 190); ***counting*** reckoning, assessing; perhaps with an ironic reference to the psalm about Zion (Jerusalem): 'When the Lord calls the names of his people, he will count [take into account] that these people were born there' (Psalm 87: 6); ***by*** nearby.

[45] **Their victory**
the 'victory' of the lover, statesman/mole, miser, epicure, gluttons, and materialists – clearly ironic.

[46–7] **Yet some . . . weep and sing**
this line may have been suggested by John's vision, after the breaking of the sixth seal, of a great multiracial and international crowd praising and giving thanks to God (Revelation 7: 9–17); also, later in the same work, those 'who had won victory over the beast' (Revelation 15: 2–4).

[47] **the *Ring***
as in line 2; but here, also heaven, the New Jerusalem.

[48] **would use no wing**
had no wish to soar up, i.e. take flight.

[49] **to prefer dark night**
cf. the mole (line 23).

[50] **Before**
in preference to.

[51] **in grots and caves**
grots grottos; the phrase may be adapted from God's promise to Ezekiel after the fall of Jerusalem: 'As surely as I am God, those that live in the ruins shall be killed, those that live in the country I shall give to the wild animals for them to eat, and those that hide themselves in the forts [= mountains] and caves shall die of disease' (Ezekiel 33: 27); it would seem to imply that the inhabitants belong to the baser aspect of nature – cf. also Plato's parable of the cave, as told in *The Republic*, book 7.

[52] **the way**
a reference to Christ as the 'way': 'I am the way, I am the truth, and I am life: no one comes to the Father except by me' (John 14: 6).

[55] **tread the Sun**
walk *above* the sun (because one

would be in a higher sphere) – the image recalls the angel whom John sees in his vision, standing on the sun and shouting 'Come and present yourselves at God's great feast!'; the feast in question is a feast in which all those who rejected God (i.e. the lover, statesman, etc.) are eaten (Revelation 19: 17).

[56] **than he**
than the sun – i.e. a soul in Paradise is brighter than the sun.

[57] **discuss**
reflect upon (in words).

[58] **One**
God; ***whispered*** cf. the 'still, small voice' with which God spoke to Elijah (1 Kings 19: 12).

[59–60] **ring**
this word is seldom used in the Bible, and its occurrence here may be an oblique reference to the parable of the prodigal son who returns home and admits to his father that he is no longer fit to be called his son: 'But the father called his servants, "Hurry! Bring him the best robe, and a *ring* for his finger and shoes for his feet"' (Luke 15: 22); ***bridegroom . . . bride*** the bridegroom is Christ (see 'The Dawning', line 2 and note); the ***bride*** the Church, here, more specifically, those whom Christ 'chooses', presumably including the poet (who was *male*); for the image, cf. Hosea 2: 16–19; the entire Song of Songs; and Revelation 19: 7–9; 21: 9–10.

120 / *'I walked the other day'*
[The Flower]

I walked the other day, to spend my hour,
    Into a field
Where I sometimes had seen the soil to yield
    A gallant flower.
But winter now had ruffled all the bower
    And curious store
  I knew there heretofore.

Yet I whose search loved not to peep and peer
    I'th'face of things
Thought with myself, 'There might be other Springs
    Besides this here
Which, like cold friends, sees us but once a year,
    And so the flower
  Might have some other bower.'

Then taking up what I could nearest spy
I digged about
That place where I had seen him to grow out,
And by and by
I saw the warm Recluse alone to lie
Where fresh and green
He lived of us unseen.

Many a question intricate and rare
Did I there strow,
But all I could extort was that he now
Did there repair
Such losses as befell him in this air
And would ere long
Come forth most fair and young.

This past, I threw the clothes quite o'er his head
And, stung with fear
Of my own frailty, dropped down many a tear
Upon his bed,
Then sighing, whispered: '*Happy are the dead!*
What peace doth now
Rock him asleep below!'

And yet, how few believe such doctrine springs
From a poor root
Which all the winter sleeps here under foot
And hath no wings
To raise it to the truth and light of things,
But is still trod
By every wandering clod.

O Thou! – whose Spirit did at first inflame
And warm the dead,
And by a sacred incubation fed
With life this frame
Which once had neither being, form, nor name, –
Grant I may so
Thy steps track here below,

That in these masques and shadows I may see
        Thy sacred way,
And by those hid ascents climb to that day
        Which breaks from thee
Who art in all things, though invisibly!
        Show me thy peace,
    Thy mercy, love, and ease!

And from this care, where dreams and sorrows reign,
        Lead me above
Where light, joy, leisure, and true comforts move
        Without all pain.
There, hid in thee, show me his life again,
        At whom dumb urn
    Thus all the year I mourn.

A parabolic poem in nine stanzas, each of seven iambic lines of alternating pentameters and dimeters and with a final trimeter, rhyming *a b b a a c c*. The poet is mourning for someone close to him: it is generally thought that the poem was occasioned by the death of his brother William. While walking in a field one winter's day, he remembers where, earlier in the year, he had seen a flower, and wonders whether there might be other kinds of regeneration besides seasonal regeneration. Uncovering the root of the flower, he meditates on the analogy it presents for him.

[1] **my hour**
an hour which the poet reserves each day for meditation.
[3] **sometimes**
some time before, or previously.
[4] **A gallant flower**
cf. 'Then went I to a garden and did spy/A gallant flower/The Crown Imperial' (Herbert, 'Peace', lines 13–15).
[5] **ruffled**
shaken, disturbed, i.e. caused (the bower) to lose the kind of tranquillity it enjoyed in the summer; ***bower*** an arbour or quiet place sheltered by trees or climbing plants.
[6] **curious store**
strange things.
[7] **I knew there heretofore**
I had seen there previously.
[8–9] **search . . . of things**
note how 'search' is the subject of this clause: cf. 'I applied my heart to know, to *search,* and to seek out wisdom and to understand the reason of things' (Ecclesiastes 7: 25); ***peep*** the word may be derived from Isaiah's warning: 'But when they tell you to seek out fortune tellers and other mediums that *peep* into things and mutter, "Should not everyone seek out their God, and consult the dead on behalf of the living?" then measure their words against what is here written and you will see that there is no light in them' (Isaiah 8: 19–20); ***I'th'face of things*** In the face of things, directly, with desire to find out everything about the subject.
[10] **Thought with**
thought to, reasoned with; ***other Springs*** other kinds of spring (i.e. regeneration) than seasonal: spring is the season when flowers bloom.

[11] **Besides this here**
apart from the spring, which comes only once a year.

[12] **cold friends**
unemotional friends, friends who keep their distance.

[13] **And so the flower**
And, in the same way, the flower.

[14] **Might have . . . bower**
might live in another, secret place (different from the garden 'bower' in line 5).

[15] **what I could nearest spy**
the nearest object that could serve the poet as a spade.

[17] **him**
it, the flower.

[18] **by and by**
after some time.

[19–21] **I saw . . . of us unseen**
cf. Herbert, 'The Flower' [p. 237], stanza 2; ***Recluse*** literally hermit, one who lives apart from society; here (a) the root or 'bulb' from which the flower grows and into which it shrinks again after blooming; and, by analogy, (b) Christ, whose life is cyclical (birth, crucifixion, Resurrection) and, by virtue of the times when Christians celebrate these moments, also seasonal (Christmas = winter; Good Friday and Easter Sunday = spring); ***fresh and green*** as a root or bulb, which lies underground, is neither 'fresh' nor 'green'; this signals that the analogical meaning takes precedence over the literal: ***fresh*** this word may have been suggested by Elihu's words to Job, speculating that an angel might appear to a sick man to release him from his sufferings, 'Then his body will become once again *fresher* than a child's: he will return again to the days of his youth' (Job 33: 25); ***green*** this word echoes a phrase attributed to God when he is telling Jeremiah of his dismay at what his chosen people have become: 'I used to call them a green olive tree that bore beautiful fruit' (Jeremiah 11: 16); 'green' is also traditionally associated with 'hope', and hope is Christ: cf. 'May God, the source of hope, fill you with joy and peace because you have believed in Jesus Christ, and may the Holy Ghost continue to make your hope grow' (Romans 15: 13); ***He*** (a) the root, (b) Christ; ***unseen*** Christ is 'unseen' because it is so difficult to 'live in Christ'.

[22] **intricate**
perplexingly difficult to answer; ***rare*** an unusually ambivalent word: (a) unusual; (b) vague, not well conceived; but (c) remarkably sharp.

[23] **strow**
strew, i.e. scatter like seeds in a flower bed, or flowers over a grave.

[24] **extort**
obtain in answer to persistent questioning or demand.

[25] **repair**
make good again, with a possible pun on 'repair', to retreat to.

[26] **Such losses as befell him in this air**
(a) such damage to the flower's intrinsic beauty as was received while it grew to bloom; (b) the wounds to Christ's nature that he received while in the world.

[27] **ere long**
before long, soon.

[28] **Come forth most fair and young**
the insistence on 'fair' (beauty) and 'young' is a reminder of the parallel between the Near-Eastern 'dying God' called Adonis, who was eternally young and beautiful, and Jesus. The cult of Adonis involved women planting flower seeds in trays with very little earth in them. When the flowers bloomed, the women rejoiced. Within a day or two, because they lacked moisture, the flowers withered and died, whereupon the women mourned the death of Adonis. But note also the difference: the Easter celebrations in the Christian tradition begin with the remembrance of Christ being crucified while his mother and Mary Magdalene weep for him. Three days later he *rises from the dead* to take his place in heaven beside God, his father (Mark 16: 19).

[29] **This past**
as soon as the poet had obtained this 'answer'; ***I threw . . . o'er his head*** he replaced the soil over the root/Christ.
[30–1] **stung**
affected with sharp mental pain; ***fear/Of my own frailty*** (a) fear of his unworthiness; (b) fear of his unwillingness to assume responsibility for Christ's death; ***tear*** note how the 'tear' waters the bed in which the root lies, thereby inviting the flower to grow and bloom again.
[33] ***Happy are the dead***
note the paradox contained in the word 'dead' – on the one hand, indicating a profound disillusion with the world; on the other, an envy of those who have died, or can die, to the world – cf. 'Blessed are the dead which die in the Lord . . . that they may rest from their labours' (Revelation 14: 13).
[35] **Rock him asleep**
suggestive not of Paradise (where Christ sits at the right hand of God the Father), but of the Christ child in a manger. Note that Christmas, which immediately follows the shortest day of the year, heralds the New Year: the ***peace*** (line 34) is thus the 'peace' of those who watched over Christ at this time (Mary, Joseph, the shepherds), the 'peace' of love and belief. This same fusing together of Easter and Christmas can be seen in lines 38–9.
[36] **And yet**
in spite of the closeness of the analogy; ***such doctrine springs*** that such a divine message or lesson can be learned.
[38] **all the winter**
the root lies underground all winter; the period from Good Friday to Easter Sunday is three days.
[39] **no wings**
figuratively, i.e. that would enable the root to rise above the earth in which it is bedded, as Christ rose at the Resurrection.
[41–2] **But is still trod/By every . . . clod**
trod see 'The Retreat', line 22 and note; it is an important part of the Christian tradition that Christ was 'despised' – cf. the identification of the stone which the builders rejected with Christ (Luke 20: 17); but also 'What then will happen to the person who despises the Son of God? . . . It is a terrifying thing to fall into the hands of the living God' (Hebrews 10: 29, 31); also the parable from the Sermon on the Mount: 'You are like salt for all mankind. But if salt loses its saltiness, there is no way to make it salty again. It is worthless, and so it is thrown out and people trample on it' (Matthew 5: 13).
[43–4] **O Thou! . . . the dead**
Thou Christ; ***whose Spirit . . . this frame inflame*** light with holy fire; ***warm*** quicken, give life to; ***the dead*** (a) the literally dead: in the course of his ministry, Christ raised several people from death to life: e.g. Jairus's daughter (Mark 5: 21–42) and Lazarus (John 11: 1–44); (b) the spiritually dead: cf. 'the new covenant consists not of a written law but of Spirit: the written law brings about death; the Spirit gives life' (2 Corinthians 3: 6); cf. also the phrase from the Apostles' Creed: 'The third day [after his crucifixion, Jesus Christ] rose again from the dead. He ascended into Heaven, where he sits at the right hand of God the Father Almighty, and from where he will judge both the quick [living] and the dead' (*Book of Common Prayer*).
[45–6] **And by . . . this frame**
incubation a reference to the 'Spirit of God that brooded or moved over the face of the waters' at the Creation (Genesis 1: 2): cf. 'the Holy Spirit, moving upon the chaos – which action some divines [i.e. churchmen] compare to the incubation of a hen upon her eggs, did . . .' (Thomas Vaughan); ***fed*** cf. Jesus's assurance: 'I am the bread of life . . . whoever eats it will never die' (John 6: 48, 50); also: 'The Scriptures tell us that "Man cannot live on bread alone, but by every word that God speaks"'

(Matthew 4: 4, quoting Deuteronomy 8: 3); ***life*** eternal life, granted through Christ's sacrifice: 'For God so loved the world that he allowed his only son to be sacrificed, so that everyone who believes in him will not die but have eternal life' (John 3: 16); ***this frame*** (a) the body of the poet; (b) the world.

[47] **Which one . . . name**
refers both to (a) the poet, and (b) the world (i.e. chaos).

[48–9] **so/Thy steps track here below**
track follow, i.e. in Christ's footsteps; thus, 'here on earth follow so closely in your footsteps'.

[50] **masques and shadows**
masque a kind of stylised play popular in the early seventeenth century, partly set to music and including both songs and dances, usually drawing on neoclassical situations and designed to exploit elaborate sets and stage machinery. Ben Jonson wrote many; the Ceres scene in Shakespeare's *The Tempest* is a masque; the phrase implies that the outer world is a 'theatre' or 'show' peopled by 'shadows' (i.e. players, actors): a Renaissance commonplace derived from Plato's theory of ideal forms: e.g. Shakespeare, *A Midsummer Night's Dream*, Puck's closing speech: 'If we shadows have offended'; cf. 'Regeneration', line 10 and note; Vaughan's suggestion is that Christ's 'doctrine' resides in every action and every creature, as it does in the flower/root, and is only waiting to be understood (see line 54).

[51] **Thy sacred way**
cf. Jesus's words: 'I am the way, I am the truth, and I am life: no one comes to the Father except by me' (John 14: 6); and: 'As it is written in the Book of Isaiah: "Someone is shouting in the desert, 'Get ready the way of the Lord, make a straight path for him! Every valley must be filled in, and every mountain levelled out. . . . Everyone will see God's salvation!'"' (Luke 3: 4–6, quoting Isaiah 40: 3–5).

[52] **those hid ascents**
(a) a reference to the 'mountains' referred to in Luke 3: 5 (see previous line); (b) those concealed 'meanings' which, when understood, allow the soul to take wing in order to ascend to Christ – cf. 'the Great Chain of Being', moving upward from the stones to God (see E.M.W. Tillyard, *The Elizabethan World Picture* [1943], ch. 4).

[52–3] **that day/Which breaks from thee**
the final Day of Judgement; ***breaks*** suggesting here that the world was 'night' prior to the day 'breaking' (cf. 'The Morning Watch', line 2 and note, and 'The Dawning', lines 6, 48); ***from thee*** as a result of you, as your doing.

[55–6] **thy peace**
'God's peace, which is far beyond any human understanding' (Philippians 4: 7): cf. line 34; ***mercy*** cf. St Paul's greeting: 'May God the Father and our Lord Jesus Christ give you grace, mercy, and peace' (1 Timothy 1: 2); ***ease*** cure, restoration to (spiritual) health: cf. the Hebraic assumption that all who honour the Lord 'will live at ease' (Psalm 25: 13).

[57] **this care**
(a) grief – biographically, this grief may have been occasioned by the death of Vaughan's younger brother William in 1648; also (b) a life of material cares – cf. Christ's exhortation to his disciples: 'Be on your guard! Do not let yourselves become occupied with . . . the cares of this world, or the day of [Christ's] second coming will catch you unawares, like a trap' (Luke 21: 34); ***dreams*** false dreams, fancies, wishful thinking, concern with material things, etc.

[58] **Lead**
cf. Jesus's exhortation to his first disciples: 'Follow me!' (e.g. Matthew 4: 19).

[59] **move**
exist, coexist, give meaning to life.

[60] **all**
any.

[61] **hid in . . . again**
thee Christ; ***his*** probably refers to

William; ***hid*** cf. 'For you have died, and your life is hidden with Christ in God' (Colossians 3: 3); ***show me his life again*** let me see him again in heaven, i.e. in eternal life.

[62] **dumb urn**
the urn of (William's) ashes, 'dumb' because it cannot speak – note how, in this penultimate line, the 'urn' is seen both as the 'opposite' of the flower of the poem (the urn is not in a field) and also as 'equivalent' to it (in the sense that meditation upon death brings the poet to reflect on Christ's death/Resurrection) and thus the promise of eternal life.

[63] **Thus all the year I mourn**
(a) mourns (for William); and (b) yearns (to find Christ).

121 / *'They are all gone into the world of light'*

They are all gone into the world of light
   And I alone sit ling'ring here:
Their very memory is fair and bright
      And my sad thoughts doth clear.

It glows and glitters in my cloudy breast
   Like stars upon some gloomy grove,
Or those faint beams in which this hill is dressed
      After the sun's remove.

I see them walking in an air of glory
   Whose light doth trample on my days:
My days which are, at best, but dull and hoary,
      Mere glimmering and decays.

O holy hope! and high humility!
   High as the Heavens above!
These are your walks, and you have showed them me
      To kindle my cold love.

Dear, beauteous Death! The jewel of the just,
   Shining nowhere but in the dark.
What mysteries do lie beyond thy dust
      Could man outlook that mark!

He that hath found some fledged bird's nest may know
At first sight if the bird be flown;
But what fair well or grove he sings in now,
That is to him unknown.

And yet, as Angels in some brighter dreams
Call to the soul when man doth sleep,
So some strange thoughts transcend our wonted themes
And into glory peep.

If a star were confined into a tomb
Her captive flames must needs burn there,
But when the hand that locked her up gives room,
She'll shine through all the sphere.

O father of eternal life and all
Created glories under thee!
Resume thy spirit from this world of thrall
Into true liberty.

Either disperse these mists, which blot and fill
My pérspectíve still as they pass,
Or else remove me hence unto that hill
Where I shall need no glass.

In this justly celebrated work, the poet recalls friends or relatives who have died and, he assumes, ascended to heaven. This stirs a meditation on the power of his thoughts about *their* situation to reawaken his own yearning for union with God. It is in ten stanzas, each stanza of four lines rhyming *a b a b*.

[1] **They**
Although it is not clear who 'they' refers to, it is possible that the reference is to the deaths of his younger brother William (died 1648) and his first wife Catherine (died *c.*1653–4); ***the world of light*** heaven, the New Jerusalem.
[2] **sit ling'ring**
'lingering' (a) literally sitting and thinking about those he has lost; (b) slow to make his own departure, i.e. showing no signs of dying.
[4] **And my . . . doth clear**
thinking of where they are clears or lifts the sad thoughts occasioned by their death.
[5] **It**
the world of light – note how the heaven of line 1 has been *internalised*; ***my cloudy breast*** cf. 'Regeneration', line 8; 'The Morning Watch', lines 6–7.
[6] **stars . . . gloomy grove**
stars the dead: each star is seen as the soul of someone who has died and been saved by Christ; ***gloomy grove*** (a) dark clearing in a small wood; (b) the poet's melancholic thoughts.

[7–8] **Or those faint beams... remove**
this hill a phrase that contrasts with 'that hill' in line 39 – (a) literally, the image is of a hillside still illumined by the sun after the sun has set: one would expect such a hill to be one the poet is facing, rather than the hillside on which he is; (a) by analogy with 'cloudy breast' and 'gloomy grove', also *the poet;* ***sun*** (a) the sun; (b) Christ; ***remove*** departure, disappearance from sight or experience.

[9] **air of glory**
the radiance of heaven – cf. Peter's promise: 'And the God of all grace, who called you into his eternal glory in Christ, will himself, after your brief suffering, restore, establish and strengthen you on a firm foundation' (1 Peter 5: 10).

[10] **trample**
walk or weigh heavily: the word was probably borrowed from Herbert: see 'Jordan (2)' (p. 230), lines 11–12: cf. 'The Retreat', line 22 and note; ***my days*** my life.

[11] **hoary**
grey or white with age.

[12] **Mere glimmering and decays**
only (a succession of) intimations of Christ, which always weaken.

[13] **holy hope**
the poet's hope of joining in heaven the people referred to in the first stanza; ***high humility*** an oxymoron.

[15] **These**
(a) the places the poet sees in his vision, where his friends are walking; (b) refers to 'holy hope' and 'high humility'; ***your*** refers to the people mentioned in stanza 1; ***walks*** favourite places for walking: 'walking with God', having complete faith in God (see Genesis 3: 8, also 5: 22, 24); cf. also John's epistle: 'But if we walk in the light, as [God] is in the light, we have fellowship one with another, and the blood of Jesus Christ his Son cleanses us from all our sins' (1 John 1: 7); ***you*** (a) the poet's departed friends or relatives, in heaven; (b) Christ.

[16] **To kindle my cold love**
the poet's memory of his departed friends/relatives reawakens his lapsed yearning for union with God – cf. 'The Retreat', line 8 and note; ***kindle*** to set fire to, stir, cause to glow with passion; ***cold love*** cf. 'I walked the other day', line 12 and note.

[17] **the jewel of the just**
Death is the 'jewel' of good men because they can hope for Resurrection (see Luke 14: 14).

[18] **Shining nowhere but in the dark**
but except; thus, (a) a paradox, as nothing 'shines' in the dark; (b) a daring equation with Christ – cf. 'The light shines in the darkness, so brightly that the darkness cannot extinguish it' (John 1: 5): daring because Christ is usually identified not with Death, but with Life (see John 14: 6: 'I am the way, the truth, the [eternal] life').

[19] **thy dust**
(a) the dust to which all people return after death: cf. 'for you are dust and will return to dust' (Genesis 3: 19); (b) the 'dust' that surrounds the story of Christ, making it difficult to penetrate to the heart of its significance.

[20] **Could**
If only; ***outlook that mark*** man could (a) see beyond death; (b) outstare (i.e. outface) death.

[21] **fledged bird**
a young bird which has only just acquired the feathers that will allow it to fly: the bird is a common symbol for the soul.

[22] **be flown**
has flown away.

[23] **But what fair well... grove**
but which beautiful spring (i.e. fountain) or small wood.

[25] **brighter dreams**
biblical tradition is rich in dreams sent by God, e.g. Jacob (Genesis 28: 12); Joseph (Genesis 37: 5); Solomon (1 Kings 3: 5): angels appear frequently as messengers (e.g. Genesis 22: 15; Exodus 3: 2; Judges 2: 4): indeed, the word comes from the Greek *angelos* = messenger.

[27] **wonted themes**
the subject of (our) usual thoughts.
[29] **If a star . . . tomb**
star (a) the soul; (b) Christ; ***into*** inside; ***tomb*** (a) the body: an image derived from Hermetic philosophy – cf. 'the garment you wear . . . the living death, the sensible carcass, the sepulchre, carried about with us' (Everard, *Divine Pymander of Hermes Trismegistus*, 7: 7); (b) the tomb in which Joseph of Arimathaea laid Christ (Matthew 27: 57–60).
[30] **Her**
the star's; ***must needs*** would necessarily continue to.
[31] **when**
if, as soon as; ***the hand*** the hand of God; ***gives room*** (a) allows (the star) to shine as far as it is able to shine; (b) releases (the star).
[32] **She'll**
She (the star) will; ***sphere*** the world.
[33–4] **all/Created glories under thee**
refers to the biblical 'Chain of Being' implicit in God's words to the first Adam: 'I am putting you in charge of the fish, the birds, and all the wild animals' (Genesis 1: 28).
[35] **resume**
take back; ***thy spirit*** (a) God's spirit, i.e. (b) my soul – God always filled his chosen servants with his 'spirit': e.g. 'And [God] has filled Bezaleel with the spirit of God, in wisdom, in understanding, and in knowledge' (Exodus 35: 31); ***thrall*** slavery (to worldly concerns).
[37] **these mists**
(a) the poet's 'sad thoughts' (see line 4); (b) the poet's desire for union with God (i.e. his yearning is so ardent that it 'mists up' the telescope).
[38–9] **which blot . . . as they pass**
which continue to obscure and render useless the poet's telescope as they occur.
[38] **perspective**
(a) a telescope, i.e. an instrument that allows the poet to see distant things clearly; (b) meditation: cf. 'Meditation is the soul's perspective glass: whereby, in her long remove, she discerneth God, as if he were near [at] hand' (Felltham, *Resolves* [1634], I, xiv).
[39] **that hill**
the hill of Sion or Jerusalem (see Isaiah 10: 32), but here, referring to the Jerusalem established in heaven at the Last Judgement.
[40] **no glass**
cf. 'Now we see only puzzling reflections in a glass, but then [i.e. when we come into God's love] we shall see things face to face' (i.e. clearly: 1 Corinthians 13: 12).

122 / *The Night*

One night Nicodemus went to Jesus and said to him: 'Rabbi, we know you are a teacher sent by God, for no one could have done what you have done unless God were with him.' (John 3:2)

Through that pure *virgin-shrine*,
That sacred veil drawn o'er thy glorious noon
That men might look and live, as glow-worms shine
And face the moon:
Wise Nicodemus saw such light
As made him know his God by night.

Most blest believer he!
Who in that land of darkness and blind eyes
Thy long expected healing wings could see
When thou didst rise,
And what can never more be done,
Did at mid-night speak with the Sun!

O who will tell me where
He found thee at that dead and silent hour?
What hallowed solitary ground did bear
So rare a flower?
Within whose sacred leaves did lie
The fullness of the Deity!

No mercy-seat of gold,
No dead and dusty *cherub*, nor carved stone,
But his own living works did my Lord hold
And lodge alone;
Where *trees* and *herbs* did watch and peep
And wonder, while the Jews did sleep.

Dear night! This world's defeat.
The stop to busy fools. Care's check and curb.
The day of spirits. My soul's calm retreat
Which none disturb!
Christ's progress – and his prayer time!
The hours to which high Heaven doth chime.

God's silent, searching flight:
When my Lord's head is filled with dew and all
His locks are wet with the clear drops of night!
His still, soft call.
His knocking time. The soul's dumb watch,
When spirits their fair kindred catch.

Were all my loud, evil days
Calm and unhaunted as is thy dark tent,
Whose peace but by some *angel's* wing or voice
Is seldom rent,
Then I in Heaven all the long year
Would keep, and never wander here.

But living where the sun
Doth all things wake, and where all mix and tire
Themselves and others, I consent and run
To every mire,
And by this world's ill-guiding light,
Err more than I could do by night.

There *is* in God (some say)
A deep but dazzling darkness, as men here
Say 'It is late and dusky', because they
See not all clear –
O for that Night! where I in him
Might live invisible and dim.

This, perhaps Vaughan's greatest work, is a meditation on the story of Jesus and the Jewish leader Nicodemus, as told in John 3: 1–21. It is in nine stanzas of six iambic lines, rhyming *a b a b c c*.

In the first four stanzas, the poet asks how he could have an experience similar to that of Nicodemus, in which his image of Christ as a flower is contrasted with the stone laws given to Moses; in the next two stanzas, the poet describes what night means to him; in the last three, he develops his wish to live not in the purposeless world but in God's night, which he identifies with heaven.

motto
The story of Nicodemus, a leader of the Pharisees (a fundamentalist sect that observed Hebraic law to the letter, but whose zeal brought them into conflict with many Jews), is found early in the Gospel of St John. It begins with the Pharisee coming to Jesus by cover of night to find out more about his teaching. Jesus tells him that no one can see the kingdom of God unless he is born again – i.e. born of the spirit. He also forecasts his own crucifixion, which will occur 'so that everyone who believes in him will have eternal life', and continues: 'the Light has come into the world, but people prefer darkness to the Light'. Nicodemus thus represents the Old Law being converted to the New. Note especially how Vaughan makes darkness into something positive. The 'night' may also owe something to Psalm 18: 11: 'He made a hiding place of the darkness around him'.

[1] ***virgin-shrine***
an extraordinary image, 'virgin' indicating a space untouched by man, 'shrine', a space sacred to God – thus, (a) the night; (b) Christ, who, being both 'pure' and a son of God, is himself a 'virgin-shrine'; it is very unlikely, as some commentators have held, that there is any reference to Artemis (Diana), the virgin goddess of the moon.

[2] **sacred veil**
(a) the night: cf. the psalmist's description of God, 'who stretches out the heavens like a veil or curtain' (Psalm 104: 2); (b) the flesh of Christ: cf. 'So now, my friends, the blood of Jesus makes us free to enter boldly into the sanctuary by the new, living way which he has opened for us through the veil [curtain], the way of his flesh' (Hebrews 10: 19–20); ***noon***
(a) the sun, at midday; (b) the Son, i.e. Christ, in all his glory: cf. 'We saw his glory, the glory he had because he

was the only Son of God' (John 1: 14); thus, the dark covers (veils) the sun/Son (i.e. Christ), because Christ is so bright that people cannot look at him directly in all his glory.

[3–4] **look and live**
cf. God's words to Moses: 'There shall no man see me and live' (Exodus 33: 20); ***as glow-worms shine glow-worm*** (a) worm, a seventeenth-century term of contempt – cf. 'I am a worm and no man' (Psalm 22: 6; cf. Job 25: 6); (b) glow-worm, a kind of beetle, the wingless female of which emits light from the tip of its abdomen. Thus, the poet desires that, just as glow-worms can shine by the light of the moon but are invisible in the brighter light of day, so people can approach Christ by night, when his diffused light will enable them to 'glow' just a little, rather than by day, when Christ's dazzling light would blast them. Although there is a clear parallel here between Christ and Apollo, the brightest of all the Greek gods, a God of distance whom none could approach except his parents, it is unlikely that Vaughan intended this to add anything to the meaning of the image.

[5] **such light**
cf. Christ's words 'I am the Light of the world' (John 9: 5).

[6] **made him know**
allowed him to recognise.

[7] **Most blest believer he!**
Nicodemus; ***blest*** blessed.

[8] **that land of darkness**
(a) Israel, the land that rejected Christ – cf. 'people prefer darkness to the Light, because their deeds are evil' (John 3: 19); also (b) Egypt which, in the Old Testament, symbolises a land of darkness that threatens to hold Israel prisoner; cf. also the darkness that God cast over the Egyptians for three days, during which he allowed the Israelites to continue enjoying their light during their first Passover (Exodus 10: 21–3); ***blind eyes*** (a) the literally blind – cf. the story of how Jesus healed the man born blind, in which appears the phrase 'I am the Light of the world' (John 9: 1–12); (b) those who failed to recognise Christ as the true son of God: 'He was in the world, and although the world was made by him, yet the world knew him not' (John 1: 10).

[9–10] **long expected healing wings**
cf. Malachi's prophecy that the day of the Lord was approaching, and the Lord's promise: 'But for you who fear my name, the sun of righteousness shall *rise* with healing in his wings' (Malachi 4: 2).

[12] **mid-night**
cf. 'there is a wonderful time coming, but because it will begin in the night, there are many who will not see it, by reason of their sleep and drunkenness: yet the Sun will shine on the Children [of 'Hermetic' wisdom] at Midnight' (Jacob Behmen, Preface, *Three Principles of the Divine Essence*, transl. 1648); ***the Sun*** (a) the sun, punning on (b) 'son', i.e. Christ, as 'the true Light' (John 1: 9).

[13–14] **O who . . . hour?**
where the poet would like to know 'where' Nicodemus found Christ, with the implication that he would go to the same place; ***dead and silent hour*** standard epithets for the night, used here to highlight Vaughan's more original argument that the night is a time of salvation.

[16] **rare**
(a) unusual; (b) of uncommon excellence; ***flower*** in the sense of 'finest part or essence' – a daring paradox, as flowers symbolise transitoriness (e.g. 'the grass withers and the flowers wilt, but the word of the Lord is everlasting': Isaiah 40: 8) – note how the poet uses an image from nature where one does not expect it.

[17] **sacred leaves**
leaves are another symbol of transitoriness – cf. when God punishes his enemies, 'the stars will fall like leaves from a vine or a fig-tree' (Isaiah 34: 4); but also a reference to the man who delights in the way of the Lord: 'He is like a tree . . . whose leaves

never fade' (Psalm 1: 3); ***lie*** cf. the parable of the mustard seed which, although it is the smallest of seeds, grows to become a tree, 'in which birds make their nests in its branches' (Matthew 13: 32).

[18] **The fullness**
all the attributes.

[19–20] **No mercy-seat . . . stone**
God instructed Moses to construct an 'Ark' (box) to contain the Covenant he had made with the Israelites (the two stone tablets on which were written the Ten Commandments): the ***mercy-seat*** was the lid; at each end there was to be a ***cherub*** (i.e. winged creature); the ***carved stone*** the stone tablets (Exodus 25: 17–20). All these belong to the Old Covenant (hence 'dead and dusty'), to which Nicodemus also or previously adhered, which is contrasted in the following lines with the New, living, spiritual Covenant with Christ.

[21–2] **living works**
the works done by Christ during his ministry; ***my Lord*** Christ; ***hold/And lodge*** (a) were contained by the flower of line 16; (b) appeared as attributes of Christ; ***alone*** only.

[23–4] **Where . . . sleep**
Where where the flower lies; ***trees and herbs*** (a) aspects of the natural, living world; (b) symbols of growth and spiritual value; ***watch . . . wonder*** cf. the shepherds who were watching their flocks when instructed by an angel to go and admire their newly born Saviour (Luke 2: 8–20); ***while the Jews did sleep*** (a) the Jews who slept through Christ's birth; (b) the Jews who 'slept' through his ministry (cf. St Paul's exhortation: 'the time has come for you to wake from your sleep' (Romans 13: 11): the story of Lazarus, whom Christ raises from the dead, is a more emphatic version of this (John 11: 1–44); and (c) the parable of the seed told by Jesus to his disciples: 'The Kingdom of God is like this: a man scatters seed in his field, and while he sleeps at night and works during the day the seeds will be growing. And yet he does not know how this happens' (Mark 4: 26–9).

[25] **defeat**
annulment – i.e. night cancels or undoes the day's work, and thus the ambitions of the day or the world.

[26] **stop to busy fools**
busy fools not necessarily literal 'fools'; probably foolish busybodies who waste their time in worldly concerns – tradesmen, perhaps even Vaughan's acquaintances; ***stop*** because even busybodies need to rest, and thus at night the poet is free from interruption; ***Care's*** see 'I walked the other day', line 57 and note; ***check and curb*** the temporary end to our everyday worries and concerns.

[27] **the day of spirits**
cf. 'night is the working-time of Spirits' (Vaughan, in 'Of Life and Death', in *Flores Solitudinis*); ***my soul's calm retreat*** the state into which my soul withdraws.

[29] **Christ's progress**
Vaughan added a note to his poem referring to two passages: 'Very early next morning he got up and went out. He went away to a lonely spot and prayed' (Mark 1: 35); and 'His days were given to teaching in the temple; and then he would leave the city and spend the night on the hill called Olivet' (Luke 21: 37) – these suggest that just as Christ prays at night, so night is the time when Christ 'enters' and 'advances' in the poet's soul; ***his prayer time*** the time when Christ prayed.

[30] **chime**
literally, the sound of a church-bell announcing the time; figuratively, 'best agree' – night and heaven agree, because night is the time of perfect peace.

[31] **God's silent, searching flight**
searching making distinctions between qualities – the phrase recalls the Lord's 'flight' through the land of Egypt on the night of the first Passover, when he killed the first-born of every Egyptian family, but spared the Israelites who had obeyed him

(Exodus 11–12: 1–36); here, as the following line indicates, the image is of Christ/God urgently seeking for one who will hear this knocking.

[32–3] **When my Lord's head is filled with dew...**
cf. the Bride's so-called 'dream-song' in which she hears the Bridegroom knocking: 'I sleep but my heart is awake. Listen! my beloved is knocking: "Open to me, my sister, my dearest, my dove, my perfect one; for my head is drenched with dew, my locks with the moisture of the night"' (Song of Songs 5: 2); also an alchemical image: 'In that skull distilleth the dew from the White Head, which is ever filled therewith; and from that dew are the dead raised to life' (from *The Greater Holy Assembly*, an alchemical or Hermetic work: see B.T. Stewart, *PQ*, **29** [1950], pp. 417–21).

[34] **his still, soft call**
God spoke to Elijah in a 'still, small voice' (1 Kings 19: 12).

[35] **His knocking time**
cf. the quotation from The Song of Songs 5: 12, above; but also – and perhaps more specifically here: 'Behold I stand at the door and knock: if any man hear my voice, and open the door, I will come in to him, and will sup with him, and he with me' (Revelation 3: 20): cf. Donne, 'Holy Sonnet 14: "Batter my heart"' (p. 77), line 2 and note; ***dumb*** because the *soul* does not speak.

[36] **When spirits... catch**
fair kindred finer relatives; i.e. when the spirit of the soul 'catches' (i.e. responds to) the call of the finer Holy Spirit, sent by Christ.

[37] **loud, evil days**
(a) the poet's youth, spent in noisy revelry; (b) used figuratively, to contrast with the quiet and 'sacred' peace of the night.

[38] **unhaunted**
unfrequented, little used; ***thy dark tent*** (a) the night: cf. 'He stretched out the heavens like a curtain, and folded them around him like a tent in which to live' (Isaiah 40: 22); (b) the tabernacle – i.e. that used by the Israelites as they wandered in the desert.

[39] **but**
except.

[40] **rent**
(a) disturbed; (b) torn.

[42] **keep**
stay, remain, be – i.e. night, in the poet's view, *is* heaven; ***here*** here on earth.

[43–4] **But living... wake**
these lines are more ambiguous than they might seem: (a) living in the world, where the sun always puts an end to night, but also (b) the Son (Christ), who 'wakes' all things from their spiritual sleep: cf. Romans 13: 11, quoted above, note to lines 23–4.

[44] **all mix and tire**
where all things waste themselves in needless commerce; ***mix*** may be a specific reference to the Hermetic belief that we are mortal because we are impurely mixed (cf. Donne, 'The Good-Morrow' [p. 43], line 19 and note); ***tire*** refers to the Hermetic belief that all things are slowly being worn down until they reach their final destruction: cf. 'The Good-Morrow', line 21 and note.

[45] **consent**
give way to temptation.

[46] **every mire**
cf. the call for God's help: 'I am sinking in deep mire [i.e. mud], where there is no solid ground; I am about to drown' (Psalm 69: 2).

[47] **this world's ill-guiding light**
the sun.

[48] **Err**
stray from Christ's way – cf. Christ's injunction: 'Always choose to go through the small gateway in life, for whilst the gate to hell is large and the road that leads there is well-surfaced and used by many, the gate to eternal life is small and the road to it is hard to find: there are few prepared to travel by it' (Matthew 7: 14); note that if one wants to be at a given place at sunrise (i.e. Christ's manifestation),

one has to start one's journey while it is still dark.

[49] **There *is* in God (some say)**
note that the poet does not claim to have experienced this himself; ***some say*** a few, wise people maintain.

[50] **A deep but dazzling darkness**
a paradox, but also a commonplace of Renaissance and Hermetic thought, largely derived from Dionysius the Areopagite (*c.* AD 400–500), author of a *Mystical Theology* in which he develops ideas about divine darkness, divine unknowing: e.g. the 'Darkness where truly dwells . . . the One who is beyond all', 'the super-essential Darkness which is hidden by all the light that is in existing things', etc. Vaughan may have read Dionysius himself, or he may merely be referring to his brother's paraphrase: 'That which is above all degree of intelligence is a certain infinite, inaccessible fire or light. Dionysius calls it Divine Darkness, because it is invisible and incomprehensible' (Thomas Vaughan, *Lumen de Lumine*); ***dazzling*** (a) for men such as the poet, so bright as to be blinding, in the sense of turning them completely away from the world; and (b) for most other men (i.e. the 'men here'), confusing, because they cannot understand God's mysterious ways.

[50–2] **as men here say . . . not all clear**
whereas men, here on earth, say that it is late and dark because they do not see things truly – the poet is contrasting reality (*is*, in line 49) with erroneous belief (*men/Here say*); i.e. men do not usually understand that light/experience of God resides in darkness.

[53] **where**
the night as a *place*.

[54] **O for that Night! . . . dim**
the poet yearns for the reality of God's night (i.e. experience of dazzling light); ***him*** (a) the night; (b) Christ/God; ***dim*** inconspicuous – note how the desire inverts the relation between reality and erroneous belief posited in lines 49–52. The poet, in contrast to most other men, believes in the reality and surrenders himself to it, accepting that he is 'dim' in comparison with the 'dazzling darkness', whereas 'dusky' reveals the limited understanding of most men here on earth.

123 / *The Waterfall*

With what deep murmurs through time's silent stealth
Doth thy transparent, cool, and wat'ry wealth
    Here flowing fall
    And chide and call,
As if his liquid, loose Retínue stayed
Ling'ring, and were of this steep place afraid:
    The common pass
    Where, clear as glass,
    All must descend
    Not to an end,
But, quickened by this deep and rocky grave,
Rise to a longer course more bright and brave.

Dear stream! Dear bank, where often I
Have sat and pleased my pensive eye,
Why, since each drop of thy quick store
Runs thither whence it flowed before,
Should poor souls fear a shade or night,
Who came (sure) from a sea of light?
Or since those drops are all sent back
So sure to thee, that none doth lack,
Why should frail flesh doubt any more
That what God takes, he'll not restore?

O useful element and clear!
My sacred wash and cleanser here,
My first consigner unto those
Fountains of life, where the Lamb goes!
What sublime truths and wholesome themes
Lodge in thy mystical, deep streams!
Such as dull man can never find,
Unless that Spirit lead his mind
Which first upon thy face did move,
And hatched all with his quick'ning Love.

As this loud brook's incessant fall
In streaming rings restagnates all
Which reach by course the bank and then
Are no more seen, just so pass men.
O my invisible estate,
My glorious liberty, still late!
Thou art the Channel my soul seeks
Not this with cataracts and creeks.

An emblem-poem of forty iambic lines, rhyming in couplets and divided into four stanzas. The first is of twelve lines, with alternating pentameters and dimeters, with the last pair being inverted; the remainder of the poem is in tetrameters – the second and third stanzas are of ten lines; the last is of eight.

The poet, meditating on an emblem of a waterfall, draws a number of parallels between the action of the waterfall and the life of the spirit, causing him to realise that most people just disappear without hope of coming into Christ's kingdom. The poem ends with his assertion that he earnestly seeks to follow the way of Christ.

[1–6]
In spite of the vivid impression made by these lines, and the clear reference to place ('Here', 'this steep place' – see also lines 13–14), it is very unlikely that this poem was composed, or even

conceived, while Vaughan was sitting near any real waterfall; rather, the waterfall is a vividly imagined *emblem* on which he is meditating.

An 'emblem' was a characteristic mode of representation in the seventeenth century – it usually consisted of a woodcut or engraving, of a highly symbolic nature, whose meaning – usually didactic – was explained in a short poem (called an *explicatio*) printed beneath it. Several books of 'emblems' were published in the seventeenth century: e.g. Francis Quarles, *Emblemes* (1635).

[1] **stealth**
secret, devious or surreptitious progress – the poet is, of course, addressing the (imaginary) waterfall.

[2] **thy**
your (the waterfall's); ***wealth*** abundance, profusion, luxurious plenty: i.e. the water of life ('living water', John 4: 10; see 'The Dawning', line 31 and note).

[4] **chide**
scold, rebuke: cf. 'The Lord is merciful and loving; he is not easily roused to anger, but patient in his love; he does not constantly chide us, nor does his anger ever last' (Psalm 103: 8–9); ***call*** summon, demand presence of: cf. 'For God made his promise to you and your children, and to all who are in distant lands – indeed, to all whom the Lord our God calls to himself' (Acts 2: 39); and God's promise: 'For it is written in the Scriptures, that "all who call upon the lord will be saved"' (Romans 10: 13, quoting Joel 2: 32).

[5–6] **As if**
(which was necessary) because; ***his*** refers to the water; ***loose*** (a) not densely packed, i.e. straggling; (b) morally lax, wanton in behaviour; ***stayed*/*Ling'ring*** (lingering) showed a reluctance to proceed; ***this steep place*** (a) the steep sides that surround the waterfall; (b) an image of the imagined edges of the known world (conceived as a flat earth), in which the water of the oceans overflows; thus, anyone approaching such limits would be approaching their 'final judgement'; thus (c) an entrance to an afterlife – especially (as the water falls downwards) hell.

[7] **common pass**
pass a passage used by fish in order to pass over a weir or waterfall; here, the passage or channel through which all people must proceed (i.e. be judged) – i.e. the common human lot.

[8] **clear**
transparent: i.e. on the Day of Judgement, the soul of every person is transparent, in the sense that God can see all their sins.

[9] **descend**
if Christ spent three days in hell, then so must everyone 'descend' to spend some time there.

[10] **an end**
i.e. not to stay there, as if 'hell' were a final destination.

[11] **quickened**
(a) made to flow more quickly; (b) given or restored to life; ***this deep and rocky grave*** combines water and stone – i.e. living water (or spirit, cf. John 4: 10) plus living stone (cf. 'So come to him, our living Stone', 1 Peter 2: 4, see 'Regeneration', line 55 and note); ***grave*** it was one of Christ's qualities that he could raise the dead to life: e.g. Jairus's daughter (Mark 5: 21–42); and Lazarus (John 11: 1–44): see also 'I walked the other day', lines 43–4 and note; the entire phrase in line 11 is, of course, a paradox that refers explicitly to the 'tomb carved out of solid rock' in which Christ was laid after the crucifixion, which was sealed by a stone, and from which he rose on the third day (Matthew 27: 57–28: 7) – i.e. just as Christ descended and rose again, so does the water fall into the pool at the base of the waterfall, descend below the surface, and rise again as spray.

[12] **longer**
(a) more difficult to achieve; (b) longer-lasting; ***course*** cf. St Paul's premonition of martyrdom: 'But I do not account my life of any value nor as precious to myself, if only I

may accomplish my course and the ministry which I received from the Lord Jesus, to testify to the gospel of the grace of God' (Acts 20: 24): here, ***longer course*** eternity, i.e. heaven; ***brave*** beautiful, resplendent.

[13–14]
these lines are often likened to the opening lines of William Wordsworth's 'Tintern Abbey': but note that ***dear*** in Vaughan's poem is 'spiritually dear', as in St Paul's phrase 'dearly beloved', i.e. dear friends (e.g. 2 Corinthians 12: 19); ***pleased*** given spiritual satisfaction to; ***pensive*** thoughtful, with (eyes opened to) spiritual understanding: cf. Jesus's claim: 'I came into this world to judge, so that those who were spiritually blind could gain spiritual insight, whereas those who want only to see with their natural eyes should become spiritually blind' (John 10: 39): cf. Jesus's explanation: 'The reason I use parables is because people look, but do not see, they listen, but neither hear nor understand' (Matthew 13: 13).

[15] **thy**
(a) the water's; (b) Christ's; ***quick store*** living or life-giving abundance.

[16] **thither whence it flowed before**
flows to that place from where it previously came – i.e. (a) the water that rises in spray falls again as rain, then seeps into the underground pool, from which it rises again from a spring (cf. 'The Dawning', lines 35–6 and note); (b) Christ's spirit brings a person to heaven, where the spirit originates.

[17] **poor**
even the spiritually poor; ***a shade*** a shadowy place, such as hell; ***night*** hell is usually envisaged as dark.

[18] **Who came (sure)**
Since they (certainly) came; ***sea*** note that the second day of creation was given to forming the ocean (by separating the ocean from the sky) and the third to forming dry land (by separating land from the sea): thus ***sea*** original state or origin of things; ***sea of light*** heaven: cf. (a) the myth of the Fall – i.e. were it not for original sin, we should all 'walk with God' in Paradise (Genesis 2–3); (b) 'The World', lines 1–2, and 'They are all gone into the world of light', line 1.

[19] **sent back**
i.e. the water/spirit returns to its origin.

[20] **So sure**
so certainly, i.e. there can be no doubt about this; ***thee*** (a) the origin of the stream to which the waterfall belongs; (b) Christ; ***that none doth lack*** (a) not one of the drops is diminished; (b) none of the souls goes without Christ's blessing.

[21–2] **Why should . . . restore?**
frail flesh man who so easily succumbs to worldly temptations; thus: 'Why should poor mortals suspect that God will not restore what he takes?' (i.e. although he dies, he will be given eternal life).

[23] **useful**
because it has many uses; ***element*** a substance that defies reductive analysis – e.g. earth, water, air, fire.

[24] **sacred wash**
baptism; ***cleanser*** (a) used for cleaning the body; (b) holy water (water blessed by a priest) is used to signify cleaning the soul.

[25–6] **consigner**
someone who (a) hands something or someone over; or (b) delivers something/someone to a second or third party: ***first consigner*** (a) the water of baptism; (b) Christ; ***unto those/Fountains of life/ . . . goes*** cf. 'For the Lamb which is in the middle of the throne shall feed [those dressed in white robes who are saved], and shall lead them to living fountains of waters: and God shall wipe away all tears from their eyes' (Revelation 7: 17).

[27] **wholesome themes**
lessons that make (the attentive person) 'whole' or healthy.

[28] **Lodge**
reside, inhabit; ***mystical*** containing a 'hidden' spiritual meaning; ***deep*** profound.

[28] **Such as**
the kind which; ***dull*** slow of (spiritual) understanding.
[30–1] **Unless that Spirit . . . Love**
Spirit the spirit of God; ***thy face*** the face of the water – cf. 'And the spirit of God moved upon the face of the waters' (Genesis 1: 2); ***hatched*** in Hermetic philosophy, refers to the act of creation out of primeval darkness; see 'I walked the other day', lines 45–6 and note; ***all*** everything; ***quick'ning Love*** quickening, i.e. God's life-giving Love, which refers not only to God who saw that his Creation was 'good', but to his ultimate gift to humanity – cf. 'For God so loved the world that he gave to the world his only Son, so that everyone who believes in him will not die but have eternal life' (John 3: 16).
[33] **brook**
the stream of which the waterfall is part; ***incessant*** continual, ceaseless, never-ending.
[34] **streaming rings**
the expanding 'rings' of water that continually form around the base of the waterfall; ***restagnates*** makes stagnant again; ***all*** everything, all those rings of water.
[35] **which reach by course**
by course (a) in succession; (b) by their flowing; thus, 'which are driven repeatedly, as a result of their flowing, against'.
[36] **Are no more seen**
i.e. the rings, upon reaching the bank, are broken up and disappear; ***just so pass men*** (most) people live and die in exactly the same manner – i.e. their lives are *not* moved by the Spirit referred to in line 30.
[37] **O my invisible estate**
represents the poet's desire to be different from the 'men' referred to in the previous line; ***estate*** condition – cf. God's promise to restore even Sodom and Samaria to prosperity because Jerusalem had fallen lower than them: 'They will be returned to their former estate, just as you and your daughters will also return to your former estate' (Ezekiel 16: 55); ***invisible estate*** the poet's 'inheritance' in heaven.
[38] **My glorious liberty**
cf. St Paul's vision of what the future holds for the faithful: 'although God planned that the whole material world will decay, he gave us hope of a new world in which we shall free from slavery to evil and be allowed to enjoy the *glorious liberty* of the children of God' (Romans 8: 21); ***still late*** still valid, no matter how long I have taken to discover this.
[39] **Channel**
the watercourse, or 'way' of Christ: cf. 'I am the way . . .' (John 14: 6).
[40] **cataracts**
waterfalls; ***creeks*** i.e. the steep banks against which the rings of water perish.

KATHERINE PHILIPS

(1632–64)

1664 *Poems. By the Incomparable, Mrs. K.P.* (unauthorised)

1667 *Poems. By the most deservedly Admired Mrs. Katharine Philips*

The most admired woman poet of the seventeenth century, 'Orinda' (as Katherine Philips called herself in poems and letters) was born, possibly on New Year's Day, in 1632 in London, daughter of James and Katherine Fowler. She was taught to read by a cousin and educated at Mrs Salmon's Presbyterian School for Girls. In 1648, at the age of sixteen, she was married to James Philips, a distant relative, thirty-eight years her senior and MP for Cardiganshire, in Wales. Despite this difference in age, theirs seems to have been an affectionate relationship. Although her background was Puritan, Philips developed Royalist sympathies and friendships; when her husband was threatened with prosecution and ejection from his parliamentary seat, her friend Sir Charles Cotterell used his court connections to save him. Indeed, so much of a Royalist did she become that later she could count the queen among her readers.

Philips divided her time between London and her home at the Priory in Cardiganshire, but though she had a devoted circle of appreciative friends in Wales, she longed to become more widely known. Unfortunately, she died of smallpox on a visit to London, at the height of her fame. During the last sixteen years of her life, 'Orinda' became well known as a writer; she translated two plays by the French dramatist Corneille, the first of which was successfully produced in her lifetime. Two of her poems were set to music by the composer Henry Lawes, who also set texts by Milton and Waller. She had two children – a boy, who died shortly after his birth, and a daughter, who lived to marry and have children of her own. Katherine Philips died before she could publish her collected works, but an unauthorised volume appeared shortly before her death and spurred her to prepare an official edition. The book that appeared three years later was due to the labours of her friend Sir Charles.

Context

The work of Katherine Philips contrasts with that of other women poets of the later seventeenth century: her contemporary, the somewhat eccentric Margaret Cavendish (1624–74), Duchess of Newcastle; the brash Mrs Aphra Behn (1640–89), the first successful professional woman writer; and Anne, Countess of Winchelsea (1661–1720), born after the Restoration and therefore of an altogether different generation. Behn's wide-ranging literary production includes plays and novels as well as poetry, and her Restoration libertinism contrasts with the much more sedate character of 'Orinda'. Philips is a much more careful craftsman than Newcastle, if less daring in pursuing adventurous new themes. 'Orinda's' poetry reflects both Cavalier and Metaphysical currents, whereas the Countess of Winchelsea is obviously a neoclassical poet in the mould of the Augustan poets of the late seventeenth and early eighteenth centuries. Certainly in the eyes of her contemporaries and later generations, Philips was the outstanding woman poet of the century.

Genre

Philips's poetry illustrates many of the popular genres of the mid-century; she wrote pastoral poems and dialogues, epithalamions, political poems, epitaphs, elegies and love lyrics, along with various occasional types – verse commemorating departures or celebrating important events. Her two most prominent themes, however, are retirement and friendship. Contemporaries considered her poems on this last subject her best. She made use of the conventions of Metaphysical love poetry to write on the motif of Platonic friendship between women; the attraction of her verses was that they asserted a philosophy of friendship somewhat at variance with the accepted notions of relationships between men and women. She assumes that women can be friends with other women, and not simply objects of worship or people too weak in intellect to contribute fruitfully to intelligent conversation. Her wit and skill, along with a certain scepticism about love goddesses and ardent young men, give her language an air of amused detachment that seventeenth-century readers appreciated and, judging by the popularity of her writings, approved of.

Critical Reception

The reputation of 'The Matchless Orinda' among her literary friends was considerable. Henry Vaughan praised her as early as 1651, and Andrew Marvell apparently alludes to one of her poems in 'The Garden' (p. 499). John Dryden did not hesitate to claim the honour of having met her, and even of being related by marriage. Her style belongs to that last flowering of elegant poetry that includes the contemporary verse of her rival, Edmund Waller, and her admirer, Andrew Marvell. Succeeding generations were equally laudatory. Her fame began to fade in the later eighteenth century, but John Keats was aware of her work and praised one of her lyrics, and Edmund Gosse published an essay on her in 1881. Recently, however, there has been a growing interest in her poetry precisely because it offers a woman's point of view that was, even in her own time, of equal interest to educated people of both sexes.

Further Reading

There is no readily available edition of Philips's writings, but George Saintsbury included her in his *Minor Poets of the Caroline Period* (London, 1905; reprinted Oxford, 1968), pp. 485–612. A facsimile edition of *Poems* (1667), with an introduction by Travis Depriest, has been published by Scholars' Facsimiles and Reprints (New York, 1992). For selections with brief introductions, see Moira Ferguson, ed., 'Katherine Fowler Philips', in *First Feminists: British women writers 1578–1799* (Bloomington,

IN, 1985), pp. 102–13; Mary R. Mahl and Helene Koon, eds, 'Katherine Philips', in *The Female Spectator: English women writers before 1800* (Bloomington, IN, 1977), pp. 154–64 (includes an unpublished poem); and Elizabeth H. Hageman, 'Katherine Philips: the Matchless Orinda', in Katharina M. Wilson, ed., *Women Writers of the Renaissance and Reformation* (Athens, GA, 1987). Hageman's introduction is highly recommended, and the selections are accompanied by a useful bibliography.

The canon of Philips's poetry is not yet established; Paul Elmen, 'Some manuscript poems by the Matchless Orinda', *PQ*, **30** (1951), 53–7, first pointed out the need for a complete re-examination. Claudia A. Limbert, 'The poetry of Katherine Philips: holographs, manuscripts, and early printed texts', *PQ*, **70** (1991), 181–98, gives an account of the problems still facing an editor forty years later. Claudia Limbert has published 'Two poems and a prose receipt: the unpublished juvenilia of Katherine Philips', *ELR*, **16** (1986), 383–90. Patrick Hungerford Thomas's unpublished PhD dissertation at University College Wales in 1982 ('An edition of the poems and letters of Katherine Philips, 1624–1664') is the closest to a 'complete works' yet produced.

The best monograph on the poet is Patrick Thomas, *Katherine Philips (Orinda)* (Cardiff, 1988). An older account, Philip Webster Souers, *The Matchless Orinda* (Cambridge, MA, 1931), contains useful information but judges the poetry harshly. See also Lucy Brashear, 'The forgotten legacy of the "Matchless Orinda"', *Anglo–Welsh Review*, **65** (1979), 68–79; and Maren-Sofie Røstvig, *The Happy Man: Studies in the metamorphoses of a classical ideal, 1600–1700* (Oxford, 1954), pp. 348–59 for her relationship with the literary tradition in general.

A number of essays concern Philips's 'circle' and her theme of friendship: W.G. Hiscock, 'Friendship: Francis Finch's discourse and the circle of the Matchless Orinda', *RES*, **15** (1939), 466–68; Earl Miner, *The Cavalier Mode from Jonson to Cotton* (Princeton, NJ, 1975), pp. 300–02; Patrick Thomas, 'Orinda, Vaughan and Watkyns: Anglo–Welsh literary relationships during the Interregnum', *Anglo–Welsh Review*, **62** (1976), 96–102; Lillian Faderman, *Surpassing the Love of Men: Romantic friendship and love between women from the Renaissance to the present* (1981), pp. 68–71; Mary Libertin, 'Female friendship in women's verse: toward a new theory of female poetics', *WS*, **9** (1982), 291–308; Harriette Andreadis, 'The Sapphic Platonics of Katherine Philips, 1632–1664' *Signs: Journal of Women in Culture and Society*, **15** (1989), 34–60; Celia A. Easton, 'Excusing the breach of nature's laws: the discourse of denial and disguise in Katherine Philips' friendship poetry', *Restoration: Studies in English Literary Culture, 1660–1700*, **14** (1990), 1–14; Mary Ann Radzinowicz, 'Reading paired poems nowadays', *Lit: Literature Interpretation Theory*, **1** (1990), 275–90. Allan Pritchard, 'Marvell's "The Garden": A restoration poem?', *SEL*, **23** (1983), 371–88, points out Philips's influence on Marvell's poem.

Some recent critics have looked at Philips in terms of the specific problems faced by a woman poet: Jennifer Waller, '"My hand a Needle Better Fits": Anne Bradstreet and women poets in the Renaissance', *Dalhousie Review*, **54** (1974), 436–50; Dorothy Mermin, 'Women becoming poets: Katherine Philips, Aphra Behn, Anne Finch', *ELH*, **57** (1990), 335–55; Claudia A. Limbert, 'Katherine Philips: controlling a life and reputation', *South Atlantic Review*, **56** (1991), 27–42.

124 / *Friendship's Mystery. To My Dearest Lucasia*

Come, my Lucasia, since we see
  That miracles men's faith do move
By wonder and by prodigy,
  To the dull angry world let's prove
  There's a religion in our love.

For though we were designed t'agree,
  That fate no liberty destroys,
But our election is as free
  As angels, who, with greedy choice,
  Are yet determined to their joys.

Our hearts are doubled by the loss,
 Here mixture is addition grown;
We both diffuse, and both ingross;
 And we whose minds are so much one,
 Never, yet ever are alone.

We court our own captivity
 Than thrones more great and innocent:
'Twere banishment to be set free,
 Since we wear fetters whose intent
 Not bondage is, but ornament.

Divided joys are tedious found,
 And griefs united easier grow:
We are ourselves but by rebound,
 And all our titles shuffled so,
 Both princes and both subjects too.

Our hearts are mutual victims laid,
 While they (such power in friendship lies)
Are altars, priests, and offerings made,
 And each heart which thus kindly dies
 Grows deathless by the sacrifice.

A poem in the style of John Donne, addressed to a close friend, in six stanzas of five tetrameter lines each, rhyming *a b a b b* . It was set to music by Henry Lawes. The poem explores the paradoxical relationship between freedom and captivity that is also the subject of Lovelace's 'To Althea, from Prison' (p. 325). Here, however, the central question is the nature of predestination and freedom, a topic that was particularly relevant in the 1640s and 1650s, after control of the government had fallen to the Calvinist Parliamentarians. Philips was brought up as a Presbyterian and understood the implications of the doctrine of predestination well; as an adult, she seems to have rejected her earlier religious schooling in favour of the wider notion of freedom taught in High Church circles.

Title
Mystery (a) a religious truth; (b) a Christian religious rite or sacrament.
[1] **Lucasia**
Philips's literary name for her close friend Anne Owen, addressee of a number of poems and letters.
[2] **miracles men's faith do move**
The New Testament contains many instances in which miracles cause men to have faith (cf. John 4: 48: 'Unless you see signs and wonders, you will not believe'). Donne often speaks of mysteries, and of the 'miracles' performed by lovers he celebrates in his poetry. Note the double meaning of 'men' – (a) males sceptical of feminine friendship; (b) human beings in general.

[3] **wonder**
amazing deed; ***prodigy*** extraordinary accomplishment.
[4] **dull angry world**
Compare with Donne's 'dull sublunary lovers' ('A Valediction: Forbidding Mourning' [p. 52]).
[5] **religion in our love**
Though religious metaphors and the language of worship were commonplace in the poetry of love between man and woman (e.g. in Donne's poetry), Philips intends to demonstrate, in the style of Metaphysical wit, that the same exaltation can apply to Platonic friendship between women.
[6] **designed t'agree**
destined to be brought together.
[7] **fate**
i.e. that they were designed to agree; ***no liberty destroys*** Their deep agreement does not destroy their individual free wills.
[8] **election**
(a) free choice; (b) in Christian doctrine, especially in Calvinism, the condition of being chosen by God to be saved.
[9] **greedy**
(a) marked by intense desire; (b) rich, extensive.
[10] **determined to their joys**
i.e. angels choose their joys freely, despite the fact that they are destined to be happy.
[11] **doubled by the loss**
the loss of one's heart in love of another leads to a doubling, since the two hearts are united.
[12] **mixture**
i.e. of the two hearts or souls of the lovers.
[13] **diffuse**
to spread out; ***ingross*** gather together. Both these terms come from alchemical terminology and indicate the transformation of lower or baser elements into higher or purer ones by the combination of different metals or substances.
[14–15] **one . . . alone**
a motif also inspired by Donne; note the implied pun: 'alone' i.e. all one.
[16] **court**
encourage, seek; ***captivity*** i.e. imprisonment in one another's souls.
[17] **Than thrones more great and innocent**
which is more exalted and less harmful [***innocent*** (a) harmless; (b) without sin or wrong] than supreme political power over another.
[18] **banishment to be set free**
a paradox, insisting that were they to be free from one another, they would also be exiled from one another as well.
[19] **fetters**
(a) external tokens of their friendship; (b) ties of love that bind them; ***intent*** purpose.
[20] **ornament**
enhancement, i.e. of their love.
[21] **Divided joys**
(a) mixed pleasures; (b) incomplete joys; (c) solitary joys, joys not experienced in one another's company.
[22] **griefs united**
i.e. 'misery loves company'; one can overcome sorrows by sharing them with another.
[23] **We are ourselves but by rebound**
(a) one is aware of oneself only in relation to another; (b) one can understand oneself only by the reflection provided through another person; ***rebound*** reflection of light or image.
[24] **titles**
(a) names; (b) social rank – in other words, we are who and what we are only because of our relationship to others; ***shuffled so*** because the two friends are so spiritually intimate, their names or titles as individuals can no longer be distinguished.
[25] **Both princes . . . subjects too**
perhaps inspired by Donne's 'The Sun Rising' (p. 45), lines 21–2 ('She's all states, and all princes, I'). In true friendship, neither person can dominate the other.
[28] **altars, priests, and off'rings made**
The opening argument – 'There's a

religion in our love' – is brought to its climax in these lines, which evoke the image of a sacred sacrifice in which a victim is offered up on an altar, except that here each person is altar, priest and offering to the other, hence all three at once.

[29] **kindly**
(a) according to its kind or nature, naturally; (b) benevolently, without hesitation; ***dies*** The popular pun on 'to die' (i.e. to consummate physical love) is used in a spiritual sense here. Each heart dies to (becomes like) the other, losing its own identity.

[30] **deathless**
In a literal sacrifice, the victim is put to death. The immortality promised in the poem is to be understood in several senses: (a) the love of friendship (as Plato describes it in his *Symposium*) is higher than mere sexual or physical love, and can lead one to a love of the divine; (b) the friendship between the two women, celebrated in Orinda's verse, will be given poetic immortality. Note that both are transformations of themes in Donne's poetry (e.g. 'The Canonisation' [p. 48]).

125 / *An Answer to Another Persuading a Lady to Marriage*

Forbear bold youth, all's heaven here,
And what you do aver,
To others courtship may appear,
'Tis sacrilege to her.

She is a public deity,
And were't not very odd
She should dispose herself to be
A petty household god?

First make the sun in private shine,
And bid the World adieu,
That so he may his beams confine
In complement to you.

But if of that you do despair,
Think how you did amiss
To strive to fix her beams which are
More bright and large than this.

Philips's own version of the Cavalier style introduces a down-to-earth scepticism which – in this poem of four quatrains, each containing alternating tetrameter and trimeter lines rhyming *a b a b* – shows her witty impatience with both the self-deceived lover and the ridiculously haughty lady he adores.

Title
Answer response; *Another* a preceding poem is also addressed to a young man in love; *Persuading* It is the addressee who is attempting to persuade the lady to marry him.

[1] **Forbear**
give up; *bold* (a) courageous, daring; (b) presumptuous, too impetuous; *youth* the infatuated young man; *all's . . . here* It was a commonplace of lovers to speak of the lady as a 'heaven' – note how this notion is continued ironically in the third and fourth stanzas.

[2] **what**
whatever; *do aver* may claim to be true.

[4] **sacrilege**
(a) an outrage against a person or thing consecrated to God; (b) the profanation of something held sacred (in this instance, the haughty lady, who considered herself too divine to stoop to his attentions).

[5] **public deity**
i.e. she is famous for her beauty and desired by a great number of men; Philips makes ironic use of the convention, at least as old as Petrarch's sonnets, of the beautiful lady as a goddess.

[6] **were't not**
would it not be.

[7] **dispose herself**
(a) prepare itself; (b) put herself in a settled state; (c) put herself in a favourable mood; and, possibly, (d) dispose of herself.

[8] **petty household god**
The household gods of the Romans were humble guardian spirits of the home; the poet asks the love-struck young man how he can expect his goddess to agree to become what most seventeenth-century women actually were – custodians of the household and little more.

[9] **sun . . . shine**
An impossibility, since the sun is the most public of all heavenly bodies; the idea perhaps echoes Donne's conceit, in 'The Sun Rising' (p. 45), of having the sun shine on the lovers alone (Philips seems to allude to this very poem elsewhere).

[11] **confine**
(a) imprison or keep indoors; (b) banish; (c) retain within limits; (d) restrict someone's actions or attentions – note that all these meanings can be applied to the lover's attempts to confine the lady as well.

[12] **complement**
(a) that which completes or makes perfect; (b) a personal accomplishment or quality; (c) politeness or courtesy (i.e. compliment); by retracting its beams, the sun will seem as dull and lacking in brilliance as the lover does, and will no longer rival him.

[13] **of that**
of persuading the sun.

[14] **did amiss**
acted erroneously.

[15] **fix her beams**
make her eyes look on you alone.

[16] **More . . . this**
It is a commonplace of love poetry from Petrarch on that the lady's eyes are brighter than the sun; cf. Shakespeare's reaction in Sonnet 130 ('My Mistress' eyes are nothing like the sun'). The poet manages to belittle the lover's efforts at the same time as she ridicules the lady's pride and absurd self-esteem.

126 / *Epitaph: On Her Son H.P. at St Syth's Church, Where Her Body Also Lies Interred*

What on earth deserves our trust?
Youth and beauty both are dust;
Long we gathering are with pain
What one moment calls again.
Seven years' childless marriage past,
A son, a son is born at last,
So exactly limned and fair,
Full of good spirits, mien, and air
As a long life promisèd,
Yet, in less than six weeks, dead.
Too promising, too great a mind
In so small room to be confined;
Therefore, as fit in heaven to dwell,
He quickly broke the prison shell.
So the subtle alchemist
Can't with Hermes-seal resist
The powerful spirit's subtler flight,
But 'twill bid him long good night.
And so the sun, if it arise
Half so glorious as his eyes,
Like this infant, takes a shroud,
Buried in a morning cloud.

Philips, like her contemporary, Marvell, wrote in a number of styles. This elegy in tetrameter couplets is reminiscent of Jonson's poems on the deaths of his two children (pp. 101, 104).

Title
H.P. Hector Philips died a few weeks after his birth in April 1655.
[3] **Long we gathering are**
We spend a long time gathering; ***with pain*** (a) with hardships; (b) with great care.
[4] **calls again**
recalls, takes back. One is tempted to see in this image something of a household conceit describing a person carefully sweeping up dust, only to have it blown away by a sudden breeze.
[7] **limned**
depicted, portrayed.
[8] **mien**
(a) bearing; (b) face.
[11] **Too promising**
compare with Jonson's 'too much hope' in 'On My First Son' (p. 104). Did Philips, perhaps, hope that her son would inherit her talent?
[12] **so small room**
such a small space.
[13] **as fit**
just as worthy.
[14] **prison shell**
the body.
[15] **subtle**
ingenious, skilled; ***alchemist*** a student

of alchemy, the science of converting base metals such as copper into silver or gold. However, the discipline also had spiritual dimensions, and the attempts to transform metals through a process of heating in a sealed retort that 'killed' and then 'revived' them in successively more perfect forms were meant to parallel a change in the soul of the alchemist. Another aspect of the operation was the search for a universal solvent (which could transform any material) and a universal remedy (panacea).

[16] **Hermes-seal**
hermetic seal, airtight closure or covering.

[17] **powerful spirit**
(a) liquid under pressure, obtained by distillation; (b) one of the alchemical substances or elements heated in a retort; (c) one of the fluids, vital, nature, or animal, that pervades the human body; (c) the soul; ***subtler*** more rarefied, finer; ***flight*** escape.

[20] **his eyes**
the deceased infant's. The usual comparison would be with a beautiful woman's.

[21] **shroud**
(a) burial cloth; (b) veil.

[22] **morning**
doubtless a pun on 'mourning', in which case *cloud* is mist or cloud of grief.

127 / *On the Welsh Language*

If honour to an ancient name be due
Or riches challenge it for one that's new,
The British language claims in either sense,
Both for its age and for its opulence.
But all great things must be from us removed
To be with higher reverence beloved.
So landscapes which in prospects distant lie
With greater wonder draw the pleasèd eye.
Is not great Troy to one dark ruin hurled,
Once the famed scene of all the fighting world?
Where's Athens now, to whom Rome learning owes,
And the safe laurels that adorned her brows?
A strange reverse of fate she did endure,
Never once greater than she's now obscure.
Even Rome herself can but some footsteps show
Of Scipio's times or those of Cicero.
And, as the Roman and the Grecian state,
The British fell, the spoil of time and fate.
But though the language hath the beauty lost,
Yet she has still some great remains to boast;
For 'twas in that the sacred bards of old

In deathless numbers did their thoughts unfold.
In groves, by rivers, and on fertile plains,
They civilised and taught the listening swains,
Whilst with high raptures and as great success,
Virtue they clothed in music's charming dress.
This Merlin spoke, who in his gloomy cave
Even destiny herself seemed to enslave,
For to his sight the future time was known
Much better than to others is their own;
And with such state predictions from him fell,
As if he did decree and not foretell.
This spoke King Arthur, who, if fame be true,
Could have compelled mankind to speak it too.
In this once Boadicca valour taught,
And spoke more nobly than her soldiers fought.
Tell me what hero could do more than she,
Who fell at once for fame and liberty?
Nor could a greater sacrifice belong
Or to her children's or her country's wrong.
This spoke Caractacus, who was so brave
That to the Roman fortune check he gave,
And when their yoke he could decline no more,
He it so decently and nobly wore
That Rome herself with blushes did believe
A Briton would the law of honour give
And hastily his chains away she threw,
Lest her own captive else should her subdue.

Philips shows an unusual sensitivity to the Welsh environment she encountered after her marriage, and in this poem in pentameter couplets she opposes the point of view of her poetic rival, Edmund Waller, by arguing that the British languages are as capable as Greek or Latin of sustaining a lasting memory of great deeds and events. She anticipates by a century the enthusiasm for the Celtic past that was celebrated by Thomas Gray and his contemporaries.

[1–2] **honour . . . new**
The opening lines suggest an old family of distinguished name whose prestige is challenged by one that has recently come into prosperity.

[3] **British language . . . in either sense**
i.e. the Celtic language (Welsh) spoken by the native Britons before and during the Roman conquest, or the Germanic language (English) introduced afterwards by the invading Anglo-Saxons; ***claims*** puts forward a claim.

[5] **removed**
made distant or remote.

[9] **Troy**
the ancient city in Asia Minor whose

war with the Greek forces and eventual fall was the subject of Homer's *Iliad* and *Odyssey*; ***hurled*** violently cast down.

[12] **safe**
secure; ***laurels*** crown of leaves awarded for victory or distinction in poetry.

[13] **reverse**
reversal.

[14] **Never once greater . . . obscure**
'Never as great in the past as she (Athens) has become in our present memory'; ***obscure*** remote from observation.

[15] **footsteps**
traces.

[16] **Scipio**
either Scipio Africanus the Elder (237–183 BC), the Roman general who defeated Hannibal of Carthage in 202 BC, or his descendant, Scipio Africanus the Younger (185–129 BC), the general who burned Carthage at the end of the Third Punic War; ***Cicero*** Marcus Tullius Cicero (106–43 BC), Roman politician and author, renowned for his oratorical eloquence and literary style.

[18] **British fell**
The Roman conquest of Britain, planned as early as the Emperor Augustus, was complete by AD 79. Names of two prominent rulers who resisted are given in lines 35 and 41; ***spoil*** prey.

[19] **language**
Welsh.

[21] **that**
Welsh; ***sacred bards of old*** poets were highly regarded, even revered, by the Ancient Celts.

[22] **deathless numbers**
immortal verse.

[24] **swains**
(a) followers; (b) men, youths or boys.

[25] **raptures**
inspired state.

[26] **Virtue they clothed . . . dress**
Clothed their moral truths in music.

[27] **This**
Welsh; ***Merlin*** the magician and prophet of Arthurian and other medieval legends.

[28] **destiny . . . enslave**
i.e. by being able to predict the future.

[30] **their own**
their own times.

[31] **state**
greatness, power.

[34] **it**
Welsh. In the Arthurian legends, the Celtic king is sometimes depicted as the emperor of the known world.

[35] **Boadicca**
Boudicca (or Boadicea), a British queen over what is now Norfolk, who revolted against Roman rule in AD 60 after the death of her husband, Prasutagus, led to the seizure of their wealth, the humiliation of their family, and an attack on their tribe. Joined by the rest of East Anglia, she and her tribe burned several towns and military posts and slaughtered – according to Tacitus – 70,000 Romans and Britons allied with them. The Roman governor Suetonius Paulinus defeated her forces only with great difficulty, and she either took poison or died of shock, avoiding capture; ***valour taught*** by persuading her countrymen to revolt.

[36] **than her soldiers fought**
because they were eventually defeated.

[37] **Tell me . . . liberty**
Philips clearly takes pride, as a woman poet who had herself achieved success in the public eye, in Boudicca's daring.

[40] **Or . . . or**
either . . . or.

[41] **Caractacus**
the Celtic King Caradoc (first century AD), ruler of the British tribe of Trinovantes. His realm lay in the west, and he led the resistance against the Romans in AD 43–7. He retreated to south Wales, but he was defeated on the Welsh Marches in AD 50. Claudius displayed him and his family in a triumphal procession through Rome, then granted them pardon and life.

THOMAS TRAHERNE

(1637–74)

◇

Little is known of Traherne's early life, but it is said that he was the son of a shoemaker from Hereford who benefited from having rich relatives who assumed responsibility for his education. He went to Brasenose College Oxford, and was ordained into the Church in 1660, the year of the Restoration. From 1657 he held a clerical post at Credenhill, a village near Hereford. In 1667 he became chaplain to Sir Orlando Bridgeman, Lord Keeper of the Great Seal; he stayed with him until 1672. Much of his best poetry dates from this time.

The only work he published during his lifetime was an anti-Catholic prose tract, *Roman Forgeries* (1673); a year after his death, *Christian Ethics* appeared.

Further manuscripts not only of some poems but also of *Centuries of Meditation*, a fascinating prose work written while the poet lived at Credenhill which is considerably indebted to Marsilio Ficino and other Neoplatonists, were discovered in the winter of 1896–7. The poems were published in 1903 by a London bookseller called Bertram Dobell, in the order in which they were found – an order which many critics have seen as representing a sequence. Dobell published the *Centuries of Meditation* five years later.

The so-called Burney manuscript, *Poems of Felicity* – the same poems but in the sequence arranged by the poet's brother Philip, who had clearly edited many of them – were discovered in the British Museum in 1910. The title is probably Traherne's own. The *Selected Meditations* were discovered in 1964, and the most recent find (1982) is of manuscript entries covering the first two letters of the alphabet for an extraordinary encyclopaedia-like project in both prose and verse called *Commentaries of Heaven*.

Context

Although it is difficult to be absolutely certain about dates, Traherne's best poetry most probably belongs to the post-Restoration period – in other words, long after Donne, King, Herbert, Marvell and Vaughan. With the return of Charles II, the entire mood of the country changed: the public was tired of Puritanism; having been deprived of theatre during the Interregnum, it wanted entertainment and received it in the so-called Restoration Comedies (Etherege, *Love in a Tub*, 1664; Wycherley, *The Country Wife*, 1675). None the less, although this period is better known for its lax morals, a keen interest in religion continued, as the very different works of Milton (*Paradise Lost*, 1667) and Bunyan (*Grace Abounding*, 1666; *The Pilgrim's Progress*, 1678) show.

Genre

Although Traherne's poetry is not of the same quality as that of his predecessors, two examples are included here to illustrate how the tradition that had begun with Donne came to its natural end. Traherne's work is of interest for at least two reasons. First, his poems represent the final phase of the seventeenth-century religious lyric, and reveal an important facet of the religious mind of Restoration England. Secondly, his work has a unique, almost childlike innocence which gives it considerable charm. Among his poems are a number that could be called pre-Romantic; like Vaughan, whose poetry is often said to resemble Wordsworth's, his themes of innocence and visionary wonder sometimes seem to anticipate the work of William Blake.

Traherne is one of the few poets still writing so-called 'Metaphysical' poetry after the publication of Milton's epic in 1667. It is curious to see in the work of a poet who bears so little resemblance to Milton, and in a poem ('On Leaping Over the Moon') belonging to such a radically different genre, several marked allusions to *Paradise Lost*.

Critical Reception

Traherne's poetry, totally unknown to the literary public before the twentieth century, has emerged as several manuscript copies of his work have come to light, including one discovered as recently as the 1980s. His *Poetical Works* (1903) gradually attracted considerable interest – initially, doubtless, as a result of the renewed appeal of the Metaphysical poets. His place, however, is rather among the poets of the 'meditative tradition's as Louis Martz (1964) has defined it. Some critics feel that his prose meditations are of greater interest than his poetry. His reputation reached a peak in the 1970s, and whilst his place on the fringes of the canon is certainly assured, it is widely argued that his unique innocence is of more interest than his poetic excellence. Close reading of the two examples included here, however, may suggest otherwise.

Further Reading

Editions

The standard editions are still *Centuries, Poems and Thanksgivings*, ed. H.M. Margoliouth, 2 vols (Oxford, 1958) and *Poems, Centuries and Three Thanksgivings*, ed. A. Ridler (Oxford, 1966). See also the *Commentaries of Heaven: The Poems*, ed. D.D.C. Chambers (Salzburg, Austria, 1989).

Critical Studies

For a good introduction, see Malcolm M. Day, *Thomas Traherne*, 'Twayne' (Boston, MA, 1982).

The best of the early studies are James Blair Leishman, *The Metaphysical Poets: Donne, Herbert, Vaughan, Traherne* (Oxford, 1934); Louis L. Martz, *The Paradise Within: Studies in Vaughan, Traherne, and Milton* (New Haven, CT, 1964), K.W. Salter, *Thomas Traherne: Mystic and poet* (London, 1964), Harold G. Ridlon, 'The function of the "Infant-Ey" in Traherne's poetry', *SP*, **61** (1964), 627–39, which explores the importance of the theme of infancy and childhood; and Carol L. Marks, 'Thomas Traherne and Cambridge Platonism', *PMLA*, **81** (1966), 521–34.

A.L. Clements, *The Mystical Poetry of Thomas Traherne* (Cambridge, MA, 1969); Stanley Stewart, *The Expanded Voice: The art of Thomas Traherne* (San Marino, CA, 1970); and Alison J. Sherrington, *Mystical Symbolism in the Poetry of Thomas Traherne* (London, 1970) are all discussed in Jerome S. Dees, 'Recent studies in Traherne', *ELR*, **4** (1974), 189–96. See also Patrick Grant, *The Transformation of Sin: Studies in Donne, Herbert, Vaughan, and Traherne* (Montreal and London, 1974).

More recently, Sharon Cadman Seelig, *The Shadow of Eternity: Belief and structure in Herbert, Vaughan, and Traherne* (Lexington, KY, 1981) offers a good comparative study. For a Marxist approach, see John Hoyles, 'Beyond the sex-economy of mysticism: some observations on the Communism of the imagination with reference to Winstanley and Traherne', in Francis Barker, Jay Bernstein, John Coombes, Peter Hulme, Jennifer Stone and Jon Stratton, eds, *Literature and Power in the Seventeenth Century* (Colchester, Essex, 1981), pp. 238–57. Allan Pritchard has examined the latest manuscript to be discovered in 'Traherne's "Commentaries of Heaven" (with selections from the manuscript)', *University of Toronto Quarterly*, **53** (1983), 1–35. Richard Douglas Jordan, 'Thomas Traherne and the art of meditation', *Journal of the History of Ideas*, **46** (1985), 381–403; N.I. Matar, '*The Temple* and Thomas Traherne', *English Language Notes*, **25** (1987), 25–33 (which explores Traherne's indebtedness to Herbert); and James J. Balakier, 'Thomas Traherne's Dobell Series and the Baconian model of experience', *ES* (Nijmegen, The Netherlands), **70** (1989), 233–47 are all useful.

Further research could begin with A.L. Clements, 'Thomas Traherne: a chronological bibliography', *Library Chronicle*, **35** (1969), 36–51; and its sequel, A.L. Clements, 'Addenda to "Thomas Traherne: a chronological bibliography"', *Library Chronicle*, **42** (1978), 138–45. See also William McCarron and Robert Shenk, *Lesser Metaphysical Poets: A bibliography, 1961–1980*, 'Checklists in the Humanities and Education', no. 7 (San Antonio, TX, 1983); and George Robert Guffey, *A Concordance to the Poetry of Thomas Traherne* (Berkeley, CA, 1974).

128 / *The Return*

To infancy, O Lord, again I come,
That I my manhood may improve!
My early tutor is the womb:
I still my cradle love.
'Tis strange that I should wisest be
When least I could an error see.

Till I gain strength against temptation, I
Perceive it safest to abide
An infant still, and therefore fly
(A lowly state may hide
A man from danger!) to the womb,
That I may yet new-born become.

My God, thy bounty then did ravish me!
Before I learnèd to be poor
I always did thy riches see
And thankfully adore:
Thy glory and thy goodness were
My sweet companions all the year.

This short poem takes the form of a prayer of firm intent, presenting life as cyclical (infancy → manhood → infancy), in which the final stage is of course modelled on Christ's words to Nicodemus, 'Unless a man is born again, he will not see the Kingdom of God' (John 3: 3). Few poets have so well captured the spirit of these words.

It is in three stanzas, each of six iambic lines, rhyming in couplets; generally tetrameters, except the first line of each verse, which is a pentameter, and the fourth line, which is a trimeter.

Title
the word 'return' is often used in the Bible to indicate humanity's need to 'return' to God – e.g. 'Let us return to the Lord' (Hosea 6: 1); for the theme of 'infancy', cf. Vaughan, 'The Retreat' (p. 529).

[1] **infancy**
babyhood or very early childhood, from the Latin 'unable to speak' – i.e. a stage in human development before speech, which sees distinctions and definitions rather than wholeness and unity. Contrast the importance speech has for Donne with its apparent absence of significance for Traherne.

[2] **improve**
to make better, with a pun on 'prove' in the sense of 'demonstrate or make manifest'.

[3] **tutor**
(a) personal instructor; (b) someone or something that 'watches' over – usually, a minor; i.e. the poet's first 'tutor' was the womb. Figuratively, the womb is that out of which the whole being emerges, rather than just

that part of a person which is represented by (e.g.) speech.

[4] **cradle**
bed or cot for an infant.

[5] **wisest**
(a) have most knowledge, be most sagacious; (b) have most understanding of things beyond verbal comprehension, such as the mysteries of religion.

[6] **error see**
(a) see a fault in others; (b) see a fault in oneself – note the etymology from 'err', to wander away from (e.g.) orthodox opinion or behaviour; i.e. before one learns to recognise orthodoxies, one cannot err. There is an implicit reference here to original sin – i.e. to Adam and Eve, whose 'eyes' were opened by the temptations of the serpent, and 'they knew that they were naked' (Genesis 3: 7) – that is, they could 'discriminate' and see 'difference' (error); ***see*** (a) to experience by way of the sense of sight, which implies selection of one sense, rather than all five; (b) to understand, mentally discern.

[7] **against temptation**
to resist temptation.

[8] **Perceive**
apprehend, here with the entirety of the mind: contrast with 'see' in line 6; ***abide*** remain, in the sense to 'stay', as if infancy were a home.

[9] **still**
(a) yet; (b) calm; ***fly*** (a) hurry, as on wings; (b) flee, escape – note the ambiguity of progressive and regressive movement.

[10] **A lowly state . . . danger!**
'Just as a man's humble status is proof against danger, or a man can avoid danger by assuming a more humble status, so a "retreat" into the womb preserves a man from the snares of the world' – note the proverb 'Shame creeps in with pride, but Wisdom belongs to the lowly [i.e. those who are humble in their wisdom]' (Proverbs 11: 2); also Christ's exhortation: 'Come to me, all of you whose work is hard and who are heavy laden, and I shall give you rest. Learn to bear my yoke and to learn from my example: for I am gentle and lowly [i.e. humble-hearted]. Then will your souls find rest' (Matthew 11: 28–9).

[11–12] **to the womb . . . new-born become**
cf. Christ's words to Nicodemus: 'In truth, in truth, I say to you, unless a man is born again, he cannot see the kingdom of God' (John 3: 3) – note that the Greek for (born) 'over again' can also mean 'from above'; i.e. born of heavenly spirit.

[13] **bounty**
(a) a very generous gift; here it refers specifically to the poet perceiving the possibility that he can be 'new-born' – note the etymology from French *bonté* = goodness; (b) a gift offered by a sovereign to the mother of triplets – note the run of three qualities: riches, glory, goodness in lines 15–17; ***then*** in babyhood; ***ravish*** (a) seize a person with delight, enrapture; (b) transport a person forcefully.

[14] **Before I . . . to be poor**
Before ambiguous – either (a) before the poet as an *adult* learned that he could be new-born, he could none the less 'see' God's riches, etc.; (b) before the poet as a *child* learned to discriminate, to understand distinctions (e.g. between rich and poor): cf. Christ's Sermon on the Mount: 'Blessed are the poor in spirit, for they shall inherit eternal life' (Matthew 5: 3) and Christ's answer to the man who asked how he could gain eternal life: 'If you wish to go the whole way, sell all that you have and give it to the poor: in this way you will gain riches in heaven' (Matthew 19: 21).

[16] **adore**
and (did) adore thy riches (i.e. 'bounty'); ***thankfully*** gratefully – cf. 'Thanks be to God for his unspeakable gift' (2 Corinthians 9: 15): note 'unspeakable' (cf. for which words learned past infancy are not adequate); also St Paul's advice: 'Let the peace of God govern your hearts, for you have been called to this peace as

the separate members of a single body. Be always thankful for this' (Colossians 3: 15).
[17]
there is no ambiguity in the last lines: they refer only to the period of infancy; ***goodness*** French *bonté,* bounty; the Lord is described as 'abundant in goodness' (Exodus 34: 6), and one of the most famous psalms ends with the reminder that 'goodness and mercy' shall accompany those who live 'in the house of the Lord' (Psalm 23: 6); ***companions*** note the etymology of the word from Latin *panis* (= bread): cf. Christ's description of himself as 'the bread of life' (John 6: 35, 48), remembered at Holy Communion/Mass, when the faithful partake of the 'bread of life': 'Whoever comes to me will never hunger, and whoever believes in me will never thirst' (John 6: 35).

129 / *On Leaping Over the Moon*

I saw new worlds beneath the water lie,
New people – yea, another sky
And sun which, seen by day,
Might things more clear display –
Just such another
Of late my brother
Did in his travel see – and saw by night
A much more strange and wondrous sight!
Nor could the world exhibit such another,
So great a sight, but in a brother.

Adventure strange! No such in story we
New or old, true or feigned, see.
On earth he seemed to move
Yet Heaven went above!
Up in the skies
His body flies
In open, visible, yet magic, sort.
As he along the way did sport
Over the flood he takes his nimble course
Without the help of feignèd horse.

As he went tripping o'er the King's high-way,
A little pearly river lay
O'er which, without a wing
Or oar, he dared to swim –

Swim through the air
On body fair!
He would not use nor trust *Icarian* wings
Lest they should prove deceitful things,
For had he fall'n, it had been wondrous high –
Not from, but from above, the sky.

He might have dropped through that thin element
Into a fathomless descent
Unto the nether sky
That did beneath him lie,
And there might tell
What wonders dwell
In earth above. Yet doth he briskly run
And bold the danger overcome –
Who, as he leapt, with joy related soon
How *happy he* o'er-leapt the moon.

What wondrous things upon the earth are done
Beneath, and yet above, the sun?
Deeds all appear again
In higher spheres, remain
In clouds as yet.
But there they get
Another light, and in another way
Themselves, to us *above*, display
The skies, themselves this earthly globe surround:
We are even here within them found.

On heav'nly ground within the skies we walk
And in this middle centre talk.
Did we but wisely move,
On earth in Heav'n above,
Then soon should we
Exalted be
Above the sky, from whence whoever falls
Through a long dismal precipice,
Sinks to the deep abyss where Satan crawls
Where horrid Death and Déspair lies.

As much as others thought themselves to lie
  Beneath the moon, so much more high
    Himself he thought to fly
    Above the starry sky,
      As *that* he spied
      Below the tide.
Thus did he yield me in the shady night
  A wondrous and instructive light,
Which taught me that under our feet there is,
  As o'er our heads, a place of bliss.

In this parable, the poet meditates on a night-time vision or dream in which he sees his brother walking over a puddle of water, reflected in which he sees a day-time world – i.e. his brother is walking not only on water, but also 'on' the reflected sky: heaven. The moral is drawn that earth itself is a heaven, if humankind could only open their eyes to it.

It is in seven stanzas, each of ten iambic lines of different length (pentameter, tetrameter, trimeter, trimeter, dimeter, dimeter, pentameter, tetrameter, pentameter, tetrameter), rhyming in couplets.

The poem requires one to remember the story of Christ who, one day, sent his disciples out in a boat while he prayed. When he had finished, he went to join them, walking on the water. The disciples were terrified. Peter then wanted to see if he also could walk on the water. He started out well enough, but when the waves got rough he lost faith and began to sink. He called out to Jesus for help. Jesus caught hold of him; they both got back into the boat and crossed the lake safely (Matthew 14: 22–33).

[1–3] **I saw . . . and sun**
It is difficult to be certain quite what these lines refer to – they could have been instigated by a 'vision' or waking fantasy, or they might be an imaginative amplification of a scene reflected in the water of a pool or lake; they might even be just a rhetorical opening to a deliberately formulated poetic 'emblem'; ***saw*** note this verb, the first of many uses, and how emphatically 'visual' the poem is.

[3] **seen by day**
had it been seen by day.

[4] **Might . . . display**
was able to reveal the world just as clearly as the sun of the solar system.

[5–7] **Just . . . another**
A similar sight; ***Of late*** recently; ***travel*** from 1660 to 1676, the poet's brother Philip was in Smyrna (now Izmir, on the west coast of modern Turkey). It may be that Philip wrote Thomas a letter in which he described a dream or vision; another possibility is that Smyrna lay in what was then usually called the Levant, from French *levant* (= rising) i.e. Smyrna lies where the sun rises (here, spiritual awakening).

[7] **and saw by night**
note how this continues, syntactically, from line 3; this lends weight to the argument that the poem refers to a dream, but the 'night' could equally refer to a spiritual night – i.e. a state of ignorance before spiritual insight.

[8] **much more strange . . .**
either (a) a dream-vision even stranger than Philip's experience; or (b) more strange because it revealed 'day' (cf. 'sun' in line 3) by night; ***wondrous*** wonderful, inspiring wonder.

[9] **exhibit**
refers back to 'display' in line 4; ***such another*** (a) an equally striking sight, dream or experience.
[10] **great**
momentous, significant, awe-inspiring; ***in a brother*** (a) a brother (i.e. the poet, Thomas) of the person dreamed about (Philip); (b) a brother in the sense that the poet recognises his 'other self' in his own dream or vision.
[11] **Adventure**
an unusual or exciting experience; ***No such...*** 'We do not encounter stories as exciting as this in either ancient or modern tales, whether true or fiction.'
[13–16] **On earth...**
one must assume that this refers to what the poet sees in *his* vision; ***Yet Heaven... above!*** and yet heaven spread above him – i.e. although his brother seemed to be walking on earth, he was really moving in heaven, the heaven reflected in the water.
[17] **open**
candid, not secret or mysterious; ***yet magic*** yet outside the norms of ordinary behaviour, supernatural.
[18] **did sport**
wandered, went.
[19] **Over the flood**
refers (a) to the 'water' of line 1; (b) a stretch of water encountered by the brother; (c) the 'over' or 'above' haven – cf. the Creation story, in which God makes a firmament (or 'vault') ***between*** the waters. He calls the firmament 'heaven' (Genesis 1: 6–8) – thus the waters 'above' heaven are the skies of line 15, and heaven is envisaged as occupying a 'middle space' between the stars and the 'waters' on earth; ***takes... nimble course*** moved or advanced deftfootedly, in an agile manner.
[20] **feignèd horse**
imagined horse.
[21] **tripping**
walking lightly, easily, nimbly; ***King's high-way*** i.e. the poet dreams of the event happening in England, even though Philip had a similar dream in Smyrna.
[22] **little pearly river**
a small river as bright as pearl.
[24] **swim**
not literally, but in the sense of 'cross a body of water'.
[26] **On body fair!**
not necessarily 'riding' anything; the 'body' is probably that of the brother.
[27] **Icarian wings**
i.e. the wings of Icarus. In Greek mythology, Daedalus, a great craftsman, equipped his son Icarus with wings of wax. When Icarus flew too close to the sun, the wax melted and he was plunged to his death: cf. Ovid, *Metamorphoses*, 8.183–235.
[20–30] **Had he fallen... sky**
from 'above the sky' because the brother was 'walking' on the sky reflected in the water.
[31] **thin element**
the air.
[32] **fathomless**
measureless, impossible to measure – here specifically because pertaining only to a 'vision'.
[33] **nether sky**
a clever oxymoron: 'nether' means 'lower' – i.e. the sky reflected in the water.
[35] **there**
(in) the reflected sky.
[36] **wonders dwell**
the verb suggests that 'wonders' refers to human beings.
[37] **Yet doth he... run**
In spite of such calamitous possibilities, the brother advances hurriedly to confront them.
[38] **bold**
boldly; ***the danger*** i.e. the danger of falling into an immeasurable abyss (i.e. hell) – but note the sequel, which tells us how 'little' the danger was!; ***overcome*** i.e. merely by *jumping* over the puddle of water in which the poet is seeing the reflected heaven/hell.
[39–40] **with joy related soon**
as he was soon to relate; ***o'er-leapt the moon*** i.e. the moon reflected in the water.
[41] **wondrous**
wonderful, mysterious, inexplicable.

[42] **Beneath . . . above**
i.e. 'beneath' the sun of the world; 'above' the reflected sun.
[43–4] **Deeds all . . . spheres**
'Every one of our actions will appear – is mirrored – in a higher world or sphere' – i.e. whatever we do here on earth is taken account of in heaven.
[44–5] **remain/In clouds as yet**
i.e. our deeds are still obscure to us while we live on earth – cf. St Paul's consolation: 'For now we see through a glass, darkly [Here on earth we see only puzzling reflections in a mirror], but [when we attain eternal life in Christ] we shall see things clearly' (1 Corinthians 13: 12).
[46] **there**
(in) heaven; ***get*** assume, take on.
[47] **light**
significance, appearance.
[48] **us *above***
'above' because the sky is imagined as being 'below' – thus 'reveal their nature to us who are above them' (i.e. in 'heaven' here on earth).
[49] **The skies**
the plural suggests both heaven and the 'heaven here on earth'; ***themselves*** (which) themselves, emphasising the 'worlds within worlds' nature of the image.
[50] **even here**
even on earth; ***within*** if the two heavens are both above and below us at all times, then we are contained in them.
[51] **heav'nly ground**
specifically, the 'heaven here on earth' implicit in the last line of the previous stanza; ***walk*** the word reminds one of the biblical sense in Genesis 5: 24: 'And Enoch walked with God' – i.e. walked in God's way or followed his commands (cf. also Genesis 17: 1; 24: 40).
[52] **this middle centre**
(a) the world, which lies between the two 'heavens': note that one of them is 'heaven here on earth'; (b) heaven, i.e. the 'firmament' – cf. note to line 19; ***talk*** in the sense of waste time in idle chatter.
[53] **move**
act.
[54] **On earth in Heav'n**
on earth which is 'within' heaven.
[56] **Exalted**
cf. 'God has exalted [Jesus] with his own right hand to be a leader and saviour' (Acts 5: 31) – Traherne implies that we should be similarly exalted, if only we could act wisely.
[57] **Above the sky**
i.e. to an as yet unspecified degree of heaven; ***falls*** (a) a reference to Satan's 'fall' from heaven, as described in *Paradise Lost*; also (b) an echo of Adam's 'Fall' from Paradise – see Genesis 3; also (c) a 'fall from grace' (Galatians 5: 4).
[58] **precipice**
cf. 'the verge of Heaven' over which Christ drives Satan in *Paradise Lost*, 6, 853–66; ***long dismal*** because in Milton's epic, Satan and the rebel angels fell for nine days (6, 867–79) to land on a 'dreary plain, forlorn and wild,/The seat of desolation' (1, 180–81).
[59–60] **the deep abyss**
cf. in Milton's *Paradise Lost* the space between hell and earth is referred to as 'the nethermost abyss' (2, 969), on the edge of which Milton's Satan meets his own daughter, Sin, and their son, Death; ***crawls*** when Satan arrives in hell, he is transformed into a serpent (10, 229–584); it is also as a serpent that he tempts Eve (9, 48–191, 412–838).
[60] **Déspair**
Despair is not personified in Milton's epic *Paradise Lost*; also an echo of the lines written above the Gateway to Hell in Dante's *Divine Comedy*: 'Abandon all hope, ye who enter' (*Inferno*, III, 9).
[61] **As much as**
in the same way as; ***thought . . . lie*** thought that they lay.
[62–3] **so much more . . . to fly**
so he aspired as much higher (i.e. into true heaven).
[65] **As that . . . tide**
As lay that world which he saw

beneath him [in the reflected water]' – note how 'tide' is associated with changeableness, and thus contrasts with the unchanging state of heaven.

[67] **Thus**

In this way; ***he*** Traherne's brother Philip, who is also (in the context implicit in the vision) the poet's 'other self'; ***yield me*** give up to me, tell me, impart to me; ***shady night*** a night filled with 'shadows', i.e. the forms encountered in the dream or vision.

[68] **wondrous**

inspiring wonder; ***light*** moral (story).

[70] **bliss**

(a) perfect joy or happiness; (b) the state of being in heaven.

INDEX OF TITLES AND FIRST LINES

◇